GREAT GARDENS
OF BRITAIN

1 A gateway in the orchard at Cotehele.

2 FRONTISPIECE *Primula* 'Rowallane Rose', of vivid flame-rose tint, a chance seedling found at Rowallane many years ago.

ENDPAPERS Kip's view from an imaginary static balloon of Dyrham house and garden, published in 1712. The levelled ground between gate and house is still there, likewise the terraces, the ponds and waterfall, and also some of the lime trees in the bottom left corner, with the graded banks. The garden beyond the house has vanished and was turned into parkland later.

GREAT GARDENS OF BRITAIN

Graham Stuart Thomas
OBE, VMH, DHM, VMM
Gardens Consultant to the National Trust

Including 16 water-colors of plants raised in the Trust's gardens, and pencil drawings, by the author

Foreword by the Earl of Rosse KBE, VMH

MAYFLOWER BOOKS

ISBN 0 8317 3974 6

Manufactured in Great Britain

First American edition

A note about the photographs

BECAUSE IT WOULD BE IMPOSSIBLE to take all the photographs, both coloured and monochrome, in one year for a book like this, I have been at pains to give the date of photography wherever possible. This will I hope placate those who detect old pictures, interest historians now and in the future, and prove that the Trust does indeed care for its gardens through the years.

G. S. THOMAS

IN THE TEXT properties belonging to the National Trust are set in capital letters, except within their own entry in Part III

To the

HEAD GARDENERS OF THE NATIONAL TRUST,

and all members of the Garden Staffs,
whose unstinted efforts have resulted in a general standard
of maintenance of which all may be proud, and whose co-operation
over the years has been a constant satisfaction,
this book is dedicated by
the Author

Gratitude

IT IS NOT UNTIL one starts to write such a detailed book as this that one realises how inadequate one's knowledge is, but the Trust being what it is – a freemasonry of expertise – donors, tenants and colleagues have all been helpful when I have turned to them. To all of them I tender my best thanks for their ever-ready interest and assistance. Especially have I appreciated the readiness with which so many of them have perused chapters or garden entries which particularly concerned them, and their invaluable comments, advice and corrections. In this category I must include John Sales, Ivan Hills, my long-suffering friend James Russell, and some members of the Garden History Society.

My special thanks are due to Ray Desmond and Peter Hunt who freely made available to me their invaluable records of essays on specific gardens published in periodicals over the last hundred years or more. I feel that the quotations I have used from these old writings have enriched the book considerably.

Since it was impossible in one year to be able to draw and paint all the flowers *in situ*, I have been favoured with certain blooms from Wisley and the Savill Gardens. This has been a great convenience and advantage.

Figures in any sort of order turn my brain into a kind of cotton-wool, but fortunately they do not have this effect on my brother Geoffrey; accordingly the translation into the metric system of the statistics was passed, thankfully and with great relief, to him. Rosemary Verey has kindly helped with some photography from old books and once again Margaret Neal has produced order from my scribbled papers and has made the book intelligible to the staff of Weidenfeld and Nicolson, who, needless to add, have been co-operative throughout.

Acknowledgments

The majority of the photographs in this book were taken by the author. For permission to use the others the author and publishers would like to thank the following (numbers are the illustration and plate numbers):

C. H. D. Acland: XX; Aerofilms Ltd: 13, 27, 98; T. P. Burr: 79, 179; Peter Coats: XXVIII; Lady Elton: 59, 60; D. J. Evans: 42; A. J. Hancock: 121; A. F. Kersting: 28; A. H. Lealand: 82, 85; P. R. Miles: 10, 44, 50, XXXVIII; A. G. Murdoch: XXXVII; The National Trust: endpapers, 5, 8, 9, 15, 16, 20, 21, 22, 25, 40, 45, 51, 53, 56, 57, 58, 77, 78, 88, 100, 104, 109, 120, 139, 150, 158, 163, 166, 194, 196, 198, XXVII; Sheila Orme: 41, 116, 195; The Royal Horticultural Society: 136; D. J. Sales: 94; R. van Hoey Smith: 154; Rosemary Verey: 18, 32, 62, 63, 145; Jeremy Whitaker: 102

CONTENTS

A note about the pictures *4*

Gratitude *6*

Acknowledgments *6*

FOREWORD BY THE EARL OF ROSSE *9*

PART I
Introduction 11

1 ON VISITING GARDENS *13*

2 THE NATIONAL TRUST *19*
Looking after the gardens 23

PART II
The Garden in History 29

3 EARLY GARDENING UP TO THE COMMONWEALTH *31*

4 THE LATER STUARTS *41*

5 THE GEORGIAN PERIOD *61*
The Inspiration 62
The Classical Influence 64
Chinese Influence 66
Gothick Taste 66
The English Landscape Garden 68
The Picturesque 72
Trees and Shrubs 74

6 THE VICTORIAN ERA ONWARDS *76*
Formal Gardening 78
Garden Buildings 79
The Gardenesque 81
Hardy Exotic Plants 82
Arboreta 84
The Interpreters 86

PART III
Impressions of the Gardens 91

Map 90

Notes 92

The Gardens 93

PART IV
Features of Garden Design 263

7 AVENUES AND TREES *264*

8 BOUNDARIES AND BARRIERS *268*

9 STONE IN GARDENS *272*

Table of Garden Specialities *276*

List of plants raised at, or first grown in, or distributed from, the Gardens now owned by the National Trust *280*

Bibliography *281*

Plant Index *280*

General Index *290*

FOREWORD

THIS IS A BOOK which needed to be written and for which a keen demand can safely be predicted. It is always a privilege to be invited to contribute a Foreword, and a specially pleasurable one when the subject is dear to one's heart and the author is a friend of long standing. It must be more than thirty years since he and I first met at Nymans with my parents-in-law; Mrs. Messel and he shared a particular love of old-fashioned roses, of which her collection was at the time unrivalled. We were consequently already well acquainted when he first joined the Staff of the National Trust as Gardens Adviser in 1956, as he relates in the book. We have worked together in close partnership throughout the subsequent years and I have learned to appreciate increasingly his expertise in all horticultural matters; above all, his consuming love of all plants, from forest trees to modest herbs, for their own sakes.

Few people realize today that the properties of the National Trust remained on a very small scale, despite its name, for almost fifty years from its foundation in 1895. It was only in the mid-1930s that the first inhabited great country house, Blickling, came into its possession on the generous initiative of the late Lord Lothian; the real flood of offers, due to the ever heavier burden of taxation, did not begin to take effect till after the end of the War in 1945. Gardens more often than not were automatically included and accepted almost incidentally. Some were of outstanding importance and, difficult and varied as were the problems arising from the necessity to ensure for the future care of the houses and their contents, it soon became apparent to those responsible for running the Trust that the problems presented by the gardens could be even harder to resolve. In particular most houses, however ancient or grand, lend themselves to management on a Committee basis in a way that few gardens do, a point rightly emphasized in the book. Also they usually call in the long term, because of their labour-intensive nature, for an even greater expenditure on maintenance, if standards are to be adhered to. The Royal Horticultural Society proved to be similarly concerned about the need to ensure the future of the country's historic gardens and agreed to take joint action. At the invitation of the late Lord Aberconway, I gave a lecture on the Trust's existing gardens at the Horticultural Hall in 1953; the Joint Committee, to which Graham Thomas refers, was formed immediately afterwards.

In the course of the subsequent twenty five years a number of Gardens have come into the Trust's possession on the strength of their own intrinsic quality, irrespective of the merits of an accompanying house; or even when, as in the case of Sheffield Park, the equally desirable house was unfortunately excluded from the offer. A point has now been reached when those in its care comprise perhaps half of all those of Grade I quality in the country; certainly, as is stated in the book, their aggregate contents amount to "the biggest horticultural collection" in one ownership there, and possibly anywhere in the world. Their acceptance has not been achieved without considerable misgiving in some cases, because of the degree of financial risk involved. Gardens disintegrate under neglect even more quickly than old buildings; some that otherwise could certainly not have survived were adjudged of sufficient importance to be accepted with what have since proved to be inadequate endowments. I must here add my voice in paying tribute to the Queen's Institute of District Nursing, without whose generosity the funds to meet the resulting annual deficits could not have been found.

Graham Thomas very properly calls attention to the danger, as a result of so many gardens being in one ownership, of their "having the stamp of the Trust"; it is a danger which can apply equally to the interior decoration of period houses. In both instances such an accusation has indeed been made on occasion, and the main safeguard lies in the superintendents' being aware of the danger, and therefore continually on the watch against it. Not only does he enlarge on the subject here, but he holds strongly to the belief, as I do, that each garden should, as far as possible, retain its own special flavour and also the personality bestowed on it by its creators. The ultimate sanction rests with visitors (especially Trust members) and occasional callings to order about any apparent failing can do nothing but good.

In general constructive criticisms are healthy for any organization that caters for the public. Every garden suffers from one disability as compared with a house, where all necessary annual maintenance can be carried out during the winter months. Lawns and weeds only start into growth in April; consequently a garden labour force should ideally be half as large again from then until July as during the rest of the year, if the standard of upkeep is not to suffer at what is the peak period for visitors. Some gardens are by their nature more vulnerable than others in this respect and occasional liability to criticism must be accepted.

Just as visitors are entitled to expect good maintenance, they should be able to count on finding flowers at all seasons. Many country house gardens were only designed, when in private ownership, to be at their best in spring and again in late summer, with an awkward gap in June and July, just when most private gardens of today are at their most glorious. The concentrated wealth of colour that can be totally appropriate in a confined space would be quite out of place at, for instance, Petworth or Tatton. Nevertheless, a wide choice of midsummer flowering shrubs exists, which merge happily in large scale plantings; they include such families as *Buddleia*, *Deutzia*, *Genista*, *Hypericum*, *Kolkwitzia*, *Philadelphus*, *Spiraca* and above all Shrub and Climbing Roses.

There are, however, exceptional gardens where the Trust can, for historical reasons, teach as well as give pleasure, and where bright colour can be an intrusion. Fashions come and go and it can afford, with the vast number in its possession, sometimes to present what is not now fashionable as sort of open-air museums. Stourhead is not only as fine a classical landscape garden as exists, but it is fully documented. Later introduction of bright rhododendron hybrids into the main vistas had brought in a jarring note of garishness when in flower. The decision to move them to the shadows of the higher slopes, where incidentally they grow better, was unquestionably right; the original conception is once more intact. Equally well documented period gardens have more recently been restored at Westbury and Ham and work is almost complete at Erddig.

In the Foreword to a book which contains a mass of fascinating information, it is only possible to pick out and comment on a few salient points. Graham Thomas has uniquely wide knowledge of the Trust's Gardens as well as lifelong experience of horticultural practice. Nevertheless, the compilation of this book must have called for wide and intensive research. As a result it is a work of real scholarship which all the same is never dry, because it is written with a genuine love of the subject and of each garden as an individual entity. It deserves to be read by all devotees of gardens, as I am confident they will enjoy it and profit from it as I have.

The Earl of Rosse KBE

PART I

Introduction

3 The summerhouse of knapped flints at Mottisfont.

4 Part of the 3-mile long double avenue of lime trees, planted at Clumber Park *c.*1845. Photo 1960.

1

ON VISITING GARDENS

A garden may be said to be the aura of a home. Without it a country house or cottage lacks its right and proper atmosphere, and is left as bald as a small child's drawing. A garden is also a paradise in its own right, in the strictest sense of the term; and its claim to be paradisal springs from an engaging episode in the history of words. When Xenophon, somewhere about the year 400 BC, was in Asia Minor, more as a traveller than warrior, he visited the garden of King Cyrus, still famous in legends, and brought back to Greece one of the Persian words for a garden, which he hellenised as *paradeisos*. Garden and paradise are therefore synonymous. It was at a later date that Paradise came to mean a celestial abode having no particular reference to its horticultural charms. What greater compliment to the garden could history have paid?

Sir William Beach Thomas, from *Gardens*, 1952

GARDENING BEGAN BY GROWING PLANTS in a given area and was, as Horace Walpole wrote in 1770, "probably one of the first arts that succeeded to that of building houses, and naturally attended property and individual possession. Culinary, and afterwards medicinal, herbs were the objects of every head of a family: it became convenient to have them within reach, without seeking them at random in woods, in meadows and on mountains, as often as they were wanted".

Today gardening is an activity involving emotions and the exercising of choice, but in early days – when many of the race went hungry – the idea of abundance was seen as part of paradise. For this reason the cultivation of fruits, herbs and vegetables was considered an approach to the ideal and there was no urge for artistry in the arrangement of the plants in gardens. But in countries of the highest civilisation the beauty and form of plants gradually led to their artistic use: on the one hand was the area given to their cultivation for food, trade or study and on the other the realms of artistry were measureless. In considering the different styles of gardening this is the first major division; as extremes today we have the market garden with its regimented produce contrasted with a Koraku-en, a Versailles, a STOURHEAD or a HIDCOTE.

As a general rule the productive kind of garden, from the market garden to the splendid kitchen gardens with their additional flower borders, is of formal design. Otherwise gardens can be formal, or informal, whether they be areas devoted to collections of plants regardless of their placing, or areas of studied design where plants are chosen for their special contribution to the scheme.

Though today's methods of cultivation have caused many an old rule of nature to be abandoned, kitchen gardens have remained virtually the same in the western world through the centuries; moreover they have been the repository where plants have been treasured, nearly lost and brought forth again as tastes and interests change. From the tiniest cottage garden with its rows of cabbages and carrots growing side by side with roses and gooseberries, or apple trees under which are found snowdrops and violets, to the vast Edwardian kitchen gardens with their flower borders, fruit trees on walls and wires, plots of onions and herbs, marrows on heaps, nutteries, melon and grape houses, even conservatories, there is one long and abiding standard of good husbandry, thrift and neatness which is a delight to see. These are gardens in the truest sense of the word, and they have remained since the beginning of gardening, regardless of changing fashion.

There are few great produce gardens left today. They require too much labour and their small plots are unsuitable for machinery. The required crops are much more cheaply produced in the open field. And yet I feel sure that if there were some splendid examples in our great estates and they could be open to visitors together with the rest of the house and grounds, people would flock to see them. The enthusiasm – and the temptation on a warm peach-ripening afternoon – would be enormous.

Instead it is the greater creations in the realm of gardening art which attract the visitors. In each garden, whether formal or informal, the choice of design and plants is limitless, indeed very seldom do we find one garden resembling another, in spite of the same animate and inanimate materials contributing to their whole.

Garden visiting has become a popular pastime and owes its compulsion to a variety of motives: perhaps we might see a new plant which we should like to acquire for our own garden, a plant association we might try to copy, a design which could be adapted to our own plot. This is the positive, acquisitive approach. There is also the joy of seeing beautiful things and being in the open air; beauty is a panacea for the hurrying day. Small or large, old or new, no garden that we visit can fail to stir our senses. So long as we take home with us a new joy, a new peace and a new experience our visit has been worthwhile, whether we have a garden of our own or not. As Joseph Addison wrote in 1712, in *The Spectator*: "A garden ... is naturally apt to fill the Mind with Calmness and Tranquillity, and to lay all its turbulent Passions at Rest."

This book has been planned with two main ideas in mind. One is to try to record many facts about the National Trust's gardens and to add some of the many thoughts and experiences which have occurred to me during more than twenty years' association with the Trust. The other is to try to present these facts and thoughts so that they may perhaps help the visitor to see the reason for so great a diversity of gardening styles, to say nothing of the plants.

As likely as not one gains some conception of a great and famous garden before actually visiting it; usually photographs of it have been seen but, though they give a little preparation, the reality is beyond one's grasp until one passes through the garden door. A really great garden wedded to a great house, seen for the first time on a beautiful day, can be a transcendent experience. I would go further: if we can add to this the prerequisite that the garden *must* be approached from the house or proper entrance, that we can be unharassed and alone and the light, the day, the time and the year can be chosen, then the experience may equal or surpass the contemplation of any other work of art. There are so many things which contribute to the whole: the state of upkeep, the care in planting, the transition from formality by the house to the distant landscape, the angle of the light, bird song, the blended colours and fragrance of plants, the smell of the earth after a shower, the combined age and youth of plants – an endless progression of mingled beauty, which will last in our senses through the years, and may never be recaptured again in the same garden.

In later chapters I shall attempt to show why and how garden artistry changed over the centuries; let us here consider it as a whole in relation to other arts.

5 Perched on its cliff, Dunster Castle faces south, and the sunny slopes provide homes for many tender plants. Lombardy Poplars below the Castle give a sense of scale.

The masterpiece of architecture, sculpture or painting is done once and for all; apart from its setting and lighting it remains more or less constant, but it gradually deteriorates. Poetry is perhaps the most lasting of all arts because words can be so easily reprinted and their sense conveyed through the practised voice. The evanescent art of music can be recreated by musical artists whenever they so desire, from the thoughts of musicians hundreds of years before. But all these arts are in a way finite; garden art is infinite and far more involved. Unlike poetry and music it can never be repeated exactly even by skilled gardeners; it is multi-dimensional, like sculpture – it must be enjoyed and experienced from the front, from side to side, and perhaps from the back. It often embodies architectural principles, as it has to have some relationship, usually, with a house: nobody in his right mind, for instance, would lay a concrete terrace in front of an old brick dwelling. Planting a garden has been likened to painting a landscape, which is a good simile so long as only one view is contemplated, but this is seldom possible or desirable; the planting must run smoothly in, shall we say, a musical or poetical progression. Many of the rules which govern traditional forms of art come into the art of gardening.

In addition, the art of garden planting is never static. It varies through each year and from year to year. The effect can never be guaranteed, whatever skill or experience is brought forth to achieve it. Even with constant skill the garden one year may be less beautiful than in another – hence the owner's wish that one had seen it last week; or the jealous neighbour's intimation that one should have seen it five years ago, or that "it will, of course, improve with time" – perhaps the most futile of all comments because without "time" one cannot make a garden.

To our art, therefore, the climate, the soil, the plants and *time* are important. Not just the time of day or of season, but the passing years so that trees and shrubs may become graceful with age, and the ground be mellowed by nature's growth; time too for cutting back, replacement and rearrangement. Perhaps for one hour in one day in a year, when maturity has been reached and decay has not set in, all things are perfect. That, then, is the perfection of garden art.

Later chapters will shew where examples of different styles of gardening can be seen, and explain why one kind of formal design is quite different from another, how one kind of landscape may have little relation to the next. But it is very seldom one comes across an untouched, period picture. The succeeding generation may have had different tastes. Thus in one garden we may find an ancient formal avenue and formal walls of the 16th century, over which has been laid a Victorian design; an 18th-century landscape "enriched" with recently-introduced conifers and rhododendrons; a garden of classical formality distracted by flowers of all kinds. Sometimes a mixture of all styles pervades.

In surveying and visiting so many gardens as has been my lot, I think it natural to value most those gardens which shew, unadulterated, the style in which they were created – as at HAM HOUSE, at FARNBOROUGH HALL, WADDESDON or SISSINGHURST CASTLE. However, if one can forget the puristic approach, one's senses can glory nonetheless in later additions and accept them as the taste of successive generations.

Fashion comes and goes, taste remains. In our garden visiting we should bear this in mind, and be charitable. After all who can define taste? It can vary in two individuals, even though

6 Architecture blends into the garden through loggia, hedges and topiary at The Courts, Holt, while trees and plants approach to the very walls of the house. Photo 1977.

7 In the Edwardian Rose Garden at Polesden Lacey. Photo 1964.

both are influenced by the same environment. It is an intangible trait and the only important point about it is to be honest in one's affections. So long as we educate ourselves so that we can determine when some taste is well below the accepted level – which is only another way of saying that we must know more about bad taste than good – we shall be able to assess the taste which governs the fashion in gardening. And there is nothing so helpful in this education than looking at gardens, and trying to absorb their history and the stresses that have made them what they are.

These two elements, fashion and taste, have been the prerogative of the wealthy throughout all history. They sought to interest themselves and to impress their visitors with the "latest" fashion, expressed by their own, or the prevailing, taste. These fashions and tastes were in part governed by international and national happenings, religious perhaps, or economic, and were swayed by complexities in thought and tradition.

Stresses have occurred repeatedly. A severe form of stress was provided by Elizabeth I's progresses, when the Queen, accompanied by the entire court, would favour one of her unfortunate subjects with a lengthy visit; ruination might result from repeated visits. Wars and national tantrums upset what should be the steady development of a garden. Gambling, or backing the wrong power, has been the end of many a great home and family. Taxes and forced economies have always been with us. And yet in the intervening periods gardens have been restored, altered or recreated, an ever-changing pattern. With such past adversities in mind, the need for charity in assessing a garden is again apparent and it would be as well to add here that, though I stated garden art could well stand comparison with other arts, it must be admitted that very seldom is the artist's intention ever realised. Time is important, but time does not stand still awaiting the consummation of the scheme. Few of us spend half a century tending one garden; few of us today have enough faith in the future to plant for two hundred years hence, yet this is what the 18th-century landscape school did, to our lasting benefit. Only the National Trust can seek to look forward in this way.

It is a joy in plants which is the great prepossession of the modern British gardener. Hugh Armytage Moore at ROWALLANE used to say that a collection of plants did not make a good garden; his garden was a great collection of plants, but he had the touch and taste to place them so that they did not appear as individuals, but were subservient to the whole scheme. Collections of plants form however a reservoir from which we all benefit, so once again charitableness must come into our assessment of gardens; there is so much beauty in a plant that their possession can be everything to some poetic spirits, regardless of their placing.

I am sometimes asked which I like best of all the various gardens I have visited. I find the question impossible to answer. I could name six favourites one minute and change to six others the next. One cannot compare a MOUNT STEWART with a SNOWSHILL, or the reverse, yet both have their place and admirers, and both have lessons for us to learn.

Charitableness, the pursuit of beauty in design, and the reverence for beautiful plants must go hand in hand when we visit gardens. The strength of masonry and the majesty of trees act as the backdrop to the tranquil lawns and the colourful foreground. In our governing of gardens we admire all that nature gives us, while at the same time holding her at bay. Is not this the essence of gardening? It is art allied to work. Directly we relax the picture fades, the lines become blurred and nature proceeds to "surge softly back". Man's noblest efforts of wood or stone or iron, if left unattended, will one day succumb to the forces of nature, forces which are gentle and soft in their remorseless creeping.

2

THE NATIONAL TRUST

As to my garden, the walk, and the houses adjacent to the garden, I give them in perpetuity to those of my friends mentioned below, who desire to devote themselves in common to study and philosophy therein, for everyone cannot always travel: provided that they shall not be able to alienate this property; it shall not belong to any of them individually, but they shall own it in common as a sacred possession, and shall enjoy it peaceably and amicably as it is just and fitting.

From the Will of Theophrastus, 4th century BC

The gardens were open to the visits of every stranger; and the country flocked round to walk, to criticize, to admire, and to do mischief. . . . All the windows of his temple and the walls of his retreats were impressed with the characters of profaneness, ignorance and obscenity; his hedges were broken, his statues and urns defaced, and his lawns worn bare. It was now, therefore, necessary to shut up the gardens once more, and to deprive the public of that happiness which had before ceased to be his own.

Oliver Goldsmith, 1728–74, essay *On the Tenants of Leasowes*

"I THINK YOU WILL FIND they do things very slowly; there is so little progress. They seem to stand still." These scarcely comforting words were levelled at me when I started working for the Trust. I knew nothing about the Trust; I was not a member. An old friend had become one of their Area Agents some fifteen years before, but the act had awakened no curiosity in me, until I began to realise that some of the most renowned gardens in the land were owned by the Trust. So I applied to fill the vacancy caused by the early death of the Trust's first Gardens Adviser, Miss Ellen Field. I was asked to report and advise on a few famous gardens, and to attend the meetings of the Gardens Committee. It was soon after SHEFFIELD PARK, the wonderful East Sussex garden, had been purchased – partly with money from various funds and partly by public appeal. It seemed incredible to me that anyone who had even heard of such an act of faith and courage should at that time, in a review of a book, use such a phrase as "the dead hand of the National Trust". I resolved then and there that I would do all I could to make nonsense of such a statement.

The Trust was founded in 1895 by Miss Octavia Hill, Sir Robert Hunter and Canon H.D.Rawnsley. Each had realised that the growth of population, the spread of industrialisation and a lack of planning were rapidly spoiling much of the beauty of England. To halt this uncontrolled destruction, to educate public opinion and to give people access to the countryside they agreed to set up a body of responsible private citizens who would act as trustees for the nation in the acquisition and ownership of land and buildings worthy of permanent preservation.

8 The garden at Moseley Old Hall when the Trust accepted it in 1962.

The variety of its properties today might surprise its early supporters. These include mountains and moorland, coastland and woods, commons and pastures, lakes, waterfalls, bridges and canals. Many of its open spaces are designated as nature reserves. Its buildings include prehistoric and Roman antiquities, mediaeval chapels and castles, villages, cottages, mills, inns, barns and dovecotes. Its parks and gardens illustrate many different types and periods. Its country houses large and small – some of them houses in which famous people lived or worked – contain important collections of pictures, furniture, tapestry, books, sculpture, silver, china and musical instruments.

Before the Second World War, several great houses, surrounded by gardens of quality, had come into the Trust's care. The war caused great havoc in gardens. Furthermore, after the war the owners of large gardens were faced with an impossible situation when, in perhaps their declining years, they were to be called upon to refurbish their gardens with probably only half the staff that they were able to afford in 1939. It became obvious that many gardens would disappear, particularly those which, though of national importance, had not in their midst a house of like value which might be offered to the Trust.

The Trust, therefore, after consulting with the Royal Horticultural Society, evolved a plan for the acceptance of such works of art and botanical importance. An appeal was launched by a Gardens Committee, newly formed between the two bodies, for a Gardens

9 The site in illus. 8 transformed. An aerial view of the garden at Moseley Old Hall, in 1977, with the knot garden (laid out by the Trust in 1963), copied from a design of 1640. The beds are edged with box; beyond is a portion of the arbour.

Fund to be established. The new committee, formed of equal numbers of representatives of the Society and the Trust, had as its terms of reference: to recommend to the Trust gardens worthy of acceptance under the new scheme; to recommend expenditure from the Gardens Fund on the maintenance of the gardens so accepted; to manage these gardens on behalf of the Trust.

There is no doubt that this was a popular move with the gardening public and as a result certain legacies were left to the Trust to provide an annual income for the maintenance of its gardens. Every year the well-known yellow-covered catalogue of the National Gardens Scheme is launched, and yearly the multitudes pay their pence for admission. It was a wonderful and encouraging gesture when the Queen's Institute of District Nursing decided to hand to the Trust a share of its profits. A representative of the Institute was invited to join the Gardens Committee. The annual sum, amounting to several thousand pounds, has been of inestimable benefit in bolstering the slender means of the Gardens Fund; without it, some gardens which were accepted without adequate endowments would have fared ill.

I soon learnt that there were no half-measures in the Trust; the standard set was high and I found that everyone concerned, from the Executive Committee, through the London and various Area Offices to the staff on the ground were all filled with a desire, an eagerness, to do their very best. The Trust engenders enthusiasm and goodwill. I cannot do better than cite the remarkable series of work groups which have been organised throughout the country annually since 1967. Called Acorn Camps very appropriately, they are manned by young folk of both sexes, who are willing to come and work on almost any project, as an annual holiday, just for the good of the cause and the satisfaction of doing it. Is not this a very remarkable thing these days? Does it not refute wholeheartedly the "dead hand of the National Trust"?

The Trust is managed by a voluntary Council and Committees with a Head Office staff in London, and voluntary Committees and Regional staff through the country. Its affairs have always been run very economically and it is remarkable that the paid staff, including those at the properties, which comprise almost 400,000 acres, number less than 1,200. There are sixteen Regions and the staff are able to call on the expert help of specialists in various fields, such as its Gardens, Forestry, Furniture, and Paintings Advisers.

Having held my post of Gardens Adviser for eighteen years, while the gardens needing attention increased from seven to over one hundred, a Horticulturist was added to the staff. On my partial retirement in 1974 he, John Sales, assumed the post of Adviser; we seldom disagree over points, and I feel very happy at the continuity that has been established. Of all the Trust's possessions, gardens would suffer most from neglect, misunderstanding, or confused advice, since they are constantly developing. And though the Gardens Committee ceased to officiate as a separate body, having been merged in 1970 with the newly-formed Properties Committee, its work is continued by this Committee and particularly by its Garden Panel.

The first gardens to be accepted by the Trust after the last war were HIDCOTE and BODNANT, followed soon by NYMANS, SHEFFIELD PARK, TRENGWAINTON and others. The Committee also had a special charge to look after great gardens attached to its fine houses, such as STOURHEAD, BLICKLING HALL, CLIVEDEN, HARDWICK HALL, MONTACUTE, PACKWOOD HOUSE, POLESDEN LACEY, POWIS CASTLE, TINTINHULL and UPTON HOUSE. This was no small undertaking for me to visit annually, to advise and report on. There were many other important gardens where the local staff wanted help, some large and some small.

By this time I was working *with* the Trust, not *for* it. All my colleagues were anxious to improve our gardens. Many had suffered from neglect during the war from which they had not and would not recover. Without the advantage of the inspired drive of our Regional Agents and all the other benefits accruing from our team of experts the problem would have been insurmountable. There were of course exceptions, but in many gardens there were untidy corners, neglected masonry, and a general lack of good husbandry. Some of the pictures in this book prove these to be no idle self-satisfied words. The team-work of the Trust overcomes all obstacles so long as it is given the means and the time; the desire and expertise is there. There is no doubt that over the years the general upkeep of the Trust's gardens has improved. Everyone has contributed; and not least our many Head Gardeners and their staffs, and although I may mention them again I feel that this is the place where I should record the complete loyalty I have had from them all. In fact almost all of them seem to have welcomed my visits, though nearly always I have left them with a long list of work to do, and major projects to be discussed with Regional staff and Committees. I certainly derive pleasure from seeing jobs well done, the gardens gradually assuming a well-cared for appearance – and all this has not been achieved through employing extra labour, but by the good husbandry and forethought of Agents and Head Gardeners.

LOOKING AFTER THE GARDENS

I LIKE TO THINK that in the words "look after" we can read a combination of all the things the Trust seeks to do: to preserve static and historic features, to improve derelict areas, to maintain in the best condition possible all its gardens, including any replanting or reorganisation that may be necessary from time to time, and all of this goes hand in hand with aesthetics and good husbandry.

This brings me to a difficult subject but I am determined to write about it because I feel it is one of the least understood aspects of gardening and something whereby the Trust stands in perpetual danger. It is in deciding what plants to use for each given area. Voluntary committees do sterling work for the Trust but we have learnt that committees are unsatisfactory for running gardens; all great gardens have been made by an individual or a succession of individuals. The mere fact that a committee is formed so that there shall be majority agreement carries with it obvious dangers. One is that each time it meets one or more members may be absent and so there is not proper continuity of thought, and as a consequence there is often a shuffling of ideas from time to time. But Regional Committees are responsible for the gardens in their regions, and it is important that they shall be involved in establishing and reviewing policy. On the other hand the interpretation and implementation of policy can only be resolved by expert staff, subject to the Regional Committee being happy with the progress.

There is danger with a body such as the Trust, which owns so many gardens, that through this corporate or individual thought its gardens might tend to become alike, or bear the stamp of the Trust. It could happen in several ways; for instance, in areas such as Cornwall – where already the gardens are somewhat similar and are within easy reach of each other – if the several head gardeners were to give each other their favourite plants, each garden would display the same plants in the same week. We ask our staff not to indulge in this very natural practice, but rather, if they have the desire, to seek out something different.

But is not the same danger likely to accrue from the attentions of one gardens adviser? This is something that over the years I have fought against, and, I hope, have conquered. The last thing I want to hear filtering through the daisy roots will be "that's the sort of thing that man Thomas always did in the Trust's gardens"! Apart from any other consideration I learnt long ago that one's favourite plants are not necessarily favourites with other people, and that every colour and every plant are beautiful in their own right but sometimes offend when used in the wrong place. Flowers and plants are best appreciated when in harmony, or in harmonious contrast with their neighbours, and it is not until one has seen many a garden and learnt about the multitudes of plants that can be grown in this country, that one is qualified to advise on this vast yet delicate subject. This does not mean the gardens adviser is always right; one of the great things about the Trust is the whole-hearted co-operation and pooling of ideas.

The design of a garden can bring a delightful interplay of ideas and we all benefit from such exchanges. When it comes to selecting a plant or plants for a given area or project, it is sometimes quite difficult to make a choice, in spite of there being many thousands of different kinds in cultivation out-of-doors today. The actual flowers must not be allowed to bulk too largely in making our choice; they are with us, generally, for less than one month's duration. There are many more things to be considered: first, the climatic conditions, the soil and the site. Next, how high and wide the plant will grow, whether it is to be bulky or delicate in habit, drooping or upright; whether it is to be sympathetic to its neighbours or a contrast to them; what quality of foliage is required, dull or glossy, green or other colour, large or small, and also of course the quality, poise, colour and duration of the blooms. I

10 Yew hedges line the approach to Blickling Hall. They were planted in the 17th century and trestles and ladders are necessary for their annual clipping. Photo 1976.

have not mentioned the lasting quality of the leaves, evergreen or deciduous, whether the main joy is to be obtained from flower, leaf, berry, autumn colour or winter twig, nor fragrance. Some plants have a delicious fragrance, others are objectionable, notably some species of *Cotoneaster* and *Sorbus*, and several viburnums.

After all these major considerations we are left with the intangible criterion of suitability or taste; what we might choose for one garden might be quite out of place in another, apart from the fact that in true "period" gardens we like sometimes to use only "period" plants.

Just as gardens fall into certain categories in one's mind, due to their design and content, so also plants have a way of being stored in separate compartments in our memories. Apart from the obvious separate categories of soil likes and dislikes, height and spread and season, there is an indefinable something which keeps certain plants apart and rules them out of certain projects. I cannot explain it, but it is something that comes by degrees, by study and thought, to all of us.

Fortunately our many colleagues on the staff of the Trust seem to sense this even if with their wider preoccupations they may not completely understand it. We try not to sweep away plants and effects gathered or loved by previous generations, nor to alter without good reason, but rather to let the Trust's wise tolerance play its part.

Sometimes I think we humans are too greedy in our gardens. We want colour from flower or foliage throughout the year and are sometimes pulled up abruptly by a gentle thought about green being the most important colour of all. Green from evergreen shrubs satisfied the Restoration gardeners; Capability Brown needed greensward and beeches for his major effects; laurels and lawns formed the basis of most Victorian gardens. Enthralled as were the first Elizabethans by all that was new and rich and delightful, we moderns are bemused by the incredible variety spread before us, and perhaps our greedy appetites should be calmed, assuaged; our good fortune at having ransacked the world's open spaces to enrich our gardens should result in gratitude.

It is a fact that the Trust's gardens amount to the biggest horticultural collection ever cared for by one organisation. Their vast diversity in size and geographical distribution alone poses a heavy responsibility; their huge collection of plants, their priceless assembly of garden architecture, their history and design add further dimensions which it is difficult for the casual visitor to grasp. The Trust's success depends not only on the care and forethought of a few gardens advisers, but also on many other experts in different walks of life, in which the Trust is so rich.

The Trust also owns some quite small gardens, interesting because the estates were lived in by noted figures. Because I shall not be including them again in this book, I will mention a few by way of example: HARDY'S COTTAGE (Thomas Hardy), SHAW'S CORNER (Bernard Shaw), HILLTOP (Beatrix Potter), QUEBEC HOUSE (General Wolfe), WASHINGTON OLD HALL (George Washington).

Until the formation of the joint Committee described in an earlier paragraph, the Trust's gardens were looked upon as mere extras to the great – or small – houses; they were simply the curtilages of whatever house was accepted. The Gardens Committee's recommendations changed all this, and after a period of some twenty years, during which so many famous gardens reached the Trust's sheltering arms, gardens have become an integral part of the Trust's general scheme, and also have revealed their great popularity with visitors.

It is pleasant for a visitor to enter a garden and to find it in a good state of upkeep. Visitors expect tidiness and also respect it; nothing engenders visitors' sometimes careless habits more than an untidy garden. But few of those visiting gardeners – or of the hordes of sightseers who are not gardeners – have any inkling of the ceaseless battle which goes on. This battle is against nature, a formidable adversary with arms of incalculable diversity and resource, on the one hand, and against the wear and tear of people on the other. To counter this double-pronged attack we have hard work and knowledge supported by money and enthusiasm. On a glorious June day it is easy to be persuaded that we are holding the fort well, even winning; at other times we feel unnerved by the never-ending combat. Apart from the many small failures which are part of the lot of every gardener's life there are the major disasters – a shrub in a key position suddenly dying, a tree falling, a drain becoming blocked and causing floods.

For the maintenance of life on this planet nature provides an incredibly intricate balance, which we upset the moment we start farming or gardening. Both operations are founded on an endeavour to grow what we want and to exclude what nature wants. Nature is intent on growth and the breaking down of growth in order to sustain future growth. We want growth to be sustained continually. To achieve her ends she produces microscopic bacteria, fungi and low forms of life and insects all of which – though they may have a beautiful life of their own – are preparing suitable conditions for the higher forms of life, for their own evolution and demise. Thus iron rusts and wood rots, stone disintegrates; the spores of mildew and black spot carried by the wind alight on our roses; honey fungus rambles through the soil and attacks the roots of plants, the necks of shrubs and trees are vulnerable to collar-rots; wilt attacks clematises and Michaelmas daisies, eelworm stunts phloxes, caterpillars and a host of insects large and small devour or maim every kind of growth. Even some of the birds are aligned against us: blackbirds take the berries regardless of approaching

Christmas or a "hard winter", sparrows spoil crocuses and primroses, and bullfinches disbud many of our trees and shrubs which should be gay with flowers in spring. Even in Chaucer's day other birds were troublesome:

Therein a goldfinch leaping pretilie
Fro bough to bough; and as him list, he eet
Here and there of buds and floures sweet.

Then there are the mice which find their way up tall stems to devour seeds before they are ripe, moles which play havoc with lawns, rabbits and hares so troublesome when snow is on the ground, neighbours' dogs and cats which have unmentionable habits, and deer, cattle and horses whose long legs and necks and weighty bulk often defeat seemingly impenetrable guards and fences.

Gardeners have always had to cope with all these things, but never in the past – except on the occasion of a garden fête or party – with the numbers of human visitors that are our lot today. A kind and interested visitor can be an encouragement and a delight; in the mass visitors can be like locusts, destroying what they enjoy. These are perhaps unkind words, yet they are truthful. Great or small gardens were designed for the enjoyment of the few; today our great gardens suffer from the many. This is not usually realised: what harm can be done to a garden by just walking round it? Numerous feet not only wear away grass paths but cause eventual compaction of the soil to the detriment even of shrubs and trees. Numerous feet tread down grass verges, break wooden steps and carry stones onto the lawns in wet weather. In their delight at the beauty of plants visitors misplace labels, pick seed pods, and steal cuttings and plants. Small plants in trough gardens such as at HIDCOTE disappear as fast as we plant them. There are other visitors who persist in holding long conversations with the garden staff who are usually hard pressed to find enough working hours in the day. Children like testing the resilience of hedges and topiary by bouncing off them and love to scatter handfuls of shingle on to immaculate lawns. Children *of all ages* find it irresistible to peel bark off trees grown specially for this effect, such as *Acer griseum*. Somewhere I came across the following quotation which may perhaps help the amorous to resist temptation:

Fond lovers
Cut in these trees their mistress' name.
Little alas! they know or heed
How far these beauties hers exceed.

It is all part of a vicious spiral. To help pay for the maintenance of a garden its gates are opened to visitors; costly car parks have to be made, still more costly lavatories may have to be added. The bigger the car parks and lavatories, the more people; if refreshments are provided more people still will come, very often *not* principally to see and absorb the beauties of the garden; the more people the bigger the car parks, more attendants and more wear and tear. But the National Trust is a body for the preservation and enjoyment of its holdings by its members and the public.

This is not just an author's tale of woe; it is a statement of facts. What can the Trust do about it?

It has first and foremost a devoted staff on the spot. It is on the head gardeners and their assistants that the bulk of these troubles fall, from nature or from visitors. And they cope remarkably well. They are of widely different outlook. Some may have been brought up in the old methods which are never quite out of date; in fact one always wears a cabbage leaf in his hat in very hot weather to keep his head cool; another may be able to discuss the intricacies of the inside of a machine as well as he can prescribe for the successful cultivation

of meconopses. The most experienced among them have very widespread knowledge; not only how to nourish and cultivate the garden, but an understanding of machines and their maintenance, weedkillers and their values and uses (though we seldom use these except in initial clearance of persistent weeds and for path cleanliness), fungicides and insecticides and their application. Other things are of equal or greater importance: how or when and where and in what way to plant things – combining the practical and the artistic – and the skill of pruning as opposed to "cutting back".

11 Considered to be about 350 years old: the Sweet or Spanish Chestnut avenue at Croft Castle. Photo 1959.

A training longer than that required for a surgeon or lawyer is needed to produce a first-class head gardener. Apart from all the knowledge that has to be acquired there are other skills required of them, tact for instance in personal relationships, and an understanding that there is a right – in fact a best – time for doing every job for the fullest results and advantage. Gone are the days when the head gardener would keep his peach houses locked against the master of the house, or would not permit anything but the barest of necessities to be attended to on the Sabbath. I once heard of a gardener, a strict Sabbatarian, who used to put his one and only cockerel into solitary confinement over the weekend.

We should not make gardens were it not for the beauty of plants and this needs to be drummed into the young who are seeking a career in horticulture. The most valuable among our garden staff are those who know what every plant in their garden is, and its manifold idiosyncracies. The practical matters concerned with machinery, chemicals and the like can all be found in text books, and in any case are constantly changing with changed methods and expediencies. Plant lore has to be acquired and stored in the memory. It cannot be acquired in just a few years and the student has to be dedicated throughout his life. Every few years the Trust likes to organise, when funds permit, a Head Gardeners' Tour. The days are spent in visits and the evenings in discussions and lectures resulting in the pooling of knowledge.

There is no doubt that the improvement registered in the upkeep of so many of our gardens is due to the drive and dedication of our devoted staffs. It is not due to increasing the staff, but rather to simplifying over-elaborated designs, the use of advanced machinery and other aids, and the general good husbandry engendered by the experienced Agents.

And so in this great family of gardens we not only have all sorts of garden styles, plants and history, but some great workers, and splendid personalities. Though my visits are usually over well before the gardens close of an evening I am sure this is not the end of the day for the staff. After shutting the gates and doing the other necessities I visualise their quiet stroll round the garden, able at last to admire their beautiful plants and shrubs in peace. "What a wonderful life you must have looking after this beautiful garden," say the visitors; of course they have, if not they would not stay. But life is never unadulterated bliss, and they, garden philosophers, know it.

PART II

The Garden in History

12 Steps lead to the Octagon, overshadowed by Chusan Palms, at Clevedon Court.

13 The 15th-century tower and moat at Oxburgh Hall. The parterre is of 19th-century conception, directly derived from a French design of the very early 18th century. Photo 1960.

3

EARLY GARDENING UP TO THE COMMONWEALTH

. . . I have a Garden plot,
Wherein there wants nor hearbs, nor roots nor flowers;
(Flowers to smell, roots to eate, hearbs for the pot),
And dainty Shelters when the welkin lowers:
Sweet smelling Buds of Lillies and of Roses
Which Rosemary banks and Lavender incloses.

And all without were walkes and alleys dight
With divers trees enrang'd in even rankes;
And here and there were pleasant arbours pight,
And shadie seats, and sundry flow'ring bankes,
To sit and rest the walkers wearie shanks:
And therein thousand payres of lovers walkt,
Praysing their god, and yeelding him great thankes.

Edmund Spenser, ?1552–99

IN EARLY DAYS THE TERM GARDENING embraced many things including the growing and studying of plants. In the 17th century in this country it gradually became divided into separate pursuits, such as observing and describing plants which developed into the science of botany, the uses of plants which developed medically and culinarily, the cultivation of plants, eventually to become a profession or hobby, and the design of gardens which developed into an art. We are mainly concerned with the last two pursuits.

Without attempting to turn this book into a major treatise on the history of gardening we must recall that our own gardening is of comparatively recent development. Ancient civilizations all practised it, from the Sumerians and Babylonians – the Hanging Gardens of Babylon are often quoted – and the Egyptians, who first portrayed the transplanting of trees, to the Romans; Virgil, in his *Georgics or the Art of Husbandry*, written in 30 BC, described the grafting of fruit trees onto different root-stocks. The Romans had forcing-houses with windows of mica to produce flowers for winter feasts; they also knew about fumigation. It may be well to recall here also that they grew the Autumn Damask Rose, which was the only garden rose in Europe which flowered a second time, after the summer display. This grows at MOTTISFONT.

Much has been inherited through the centuries from these various countries and also from China, where plants were cultivated for their own interest. Through the Romans this accumulation of knowledge from the Old World flowered in Italy and later in Spain; the Moors adjusted old Roman gardens and made new ones in Spain and Portugal while we were in the "Dark Ages".

Gardening, which in those days was mainly concerned with the *need* for plants, grew gradually from small beginnings. There was always an orchard – or wort yard – for the growing of plants and fruit trees of many kinds, and in Saxon times no less than 500 useful plants were enumerated. Chaucer describes how roses of "swete savour" were grown on or near castle walls and towers. Apart from what filtered in through the religious houses, the Crusaders, and indeed traders, brought about the first real acquaintance with eastern tastes in gardens.

In hotter countries water and shade were not only essential but also desirable; indeed water has been a principal factor in gardening in every country. Since water and ablutions were always necessary parts of life, what more natural than that the water should be used in an ornamental way in the seclusion of the garden? Plots were divided by canals and a different level provided the excuse for a waterfall. The art of conveying water from higher ground had been exploited since Roman days, and fountains followed as a matter of course.

Shade was provided by trees and arbours. It is a strange fact that the word "arbour" derives from "herber", a place for growing plants; it also was used to describe a covered alley while today it usually means a nook or covering for a secluded seat.

But before growing your plants, using the water or giving shade, it was necessary to enclose a plot against the depredations of animals. Plaited or woven branches, palisades – perhaps like the traditional, clumsy, split fencing as used around CHARLECOTE PARK to this day – and hedges as well as walls were used to keep out intruders, as of course were ditches and canals of water. The garden at ST JOHN'S JERUSALEM is surrounded by a moat dug out in mediaeval days.

From the above few remarks about the fundamentals of gardening and garden design, it will be seen that nothing in our gardens can be called really new; everything derives from much older schemes and traditions. It is equally true to say that the practice of gardening changed little until machinery and chemicals became widely used, but the art of garden design and taste changed greatly in this country through the centuries.

Most of the gardening in times after the Norman conquest was done by the two great types of landowner, the clerical and the secular, around the religious houses and castles. Not only was the organised labour available, but the privileged inmates of the castles would have needed an area away from the noisy communal castle life. In the 1420s James I of Scotland wrote about his period of captivity at Windsor, and described a garden which he daily saw:

Now was there made, fast by the Towris wall
A garden fair; and in the corners set
An arbour green, with wandis long and small
Railed about and so with trees set
Was the place, and Hawthorne hedges knet,
That lyf was none walking there forebye
That might within scarce any wight espy.

This is probably how our garden art started in this country.

Little remains to us of the gardens of the long mediaeval period, through the Wars of the Roses and other troublous times when the foundations of such old dwellings as COTEHELE and SCOTNEY CASTLE were being laid, and the great tower of OXBURGH HALL was being built. But we know that gardens in the days of Henry I embraced an astonishing array of diversions and spectacles; there were fenced areas for menageries, others for plants and trees, areas for archery and warlike pursuits, fountains, pavilions and fish pools.

While England was troubled with civil wars, Italy was beginning to develop her superlative formal gardens, which were to set such a precedent in Europe and to have so much influence through succeeding centuries.

We can then perhaps visualise England after the Wars of the Roses returning to more peaceful times under the Tudors. Much of the countryside would have been in its natural forest state with castles occupying commanding positions, settlements straddling fords, but all habitations at least in touch with water.

In the enclosing of gardens and orchards there were two conflicting ideals, the natural and the formal. The formal scheme of garden design follows fairly readily from the enclosure of plots of ground. The division of the ground was usually into four, associated with the points of the compass or the seasons, or quarters of the day. Sometimes the Cross inspired the division into four. Such is Sir Thomas Tresham's NEW BIELD (Building) at LYVEDEN.

The informal method is probably older. Before the days of enclosed plots the needed plants would be grown by inserting them in the uncultivated ground. A level or sloping sward might then be fenced for an orchard and in the mixture of plants growing naturally in the grass much pleasure was taken, though this cannot be connected with conscious formal design. The flowery meadows, or Mary gardens, depicted in old tapestries give us an idea of this early division between the formal and informal in gardens. Chaucer in his version of *The Romaunt of the Rose* gives a delightful picture of the beauty of a flowery meadow:

14 A corner of the Tournai tapestry, between 1477 and 1479, at Montacute House, depicting Jean de Daillon, Governor of Dauphiné. The *millefleurs* design has connections with Chaucer's flowery mead, Bacon's wild heath and the naturalising of bulbs and flowers in grass in our modern gardens.

There sprang the violete al newe,
And fresshe pervinke riche of hewe,
And floures yelowe, whyte and rede:
Swich plentee grew ther never in mede,
Ful gay was al the ground and queynt
And poudred, as men had it peynt,
With many a fresh and sondry flour
That casten up a ful good savour.

Wild strawberries, daisies, cowslips, primroses, Lent Lilies, harebells and many others are seen in old pictures and tapestries.

From these humble beginnings sprang Bacon's "wild heaths", and our own naturalising of bulbous plants today. Nearest to the "flowery meads" of ancient times are the areas of rough grass or woodland where all sorts of plants are encouraged to grow wild. Certain areas at ASCOTT, and the little orchard at ACORN BANK, the slope above the lake at SIZERGH CASTLE, the lawn surrounds at ARLINGTON COURT, the dell slopes at GLENDURGAN, and Cowslips at CLANDON PARK come to mind. At DERRYMORE is an unusual mixture of white Bluebells and double Cuckoo Flower which follow Lent Lilies, while Ladies' Tresses Orchids grow in the sward at UPPARK, BERRINGTON HALL, and STANDEN.

Besides the conventional crocuses, daffodils and bluebells, anemones, tulips, wild strawberries, primroses, fritillaries, Mourning Widow, Cranesbill, Marguerites, Sorrel and a hundred other wildings each in their season turn a rough patch into something of delight. The scythe comes in July and hay is made, in the same way as in the earliest of orchards. This establishment of plants, native or foreign, is an absorbing pursuit and something to be treasured, fostered and increased in these days of pure grass farming, in areas where cowslips and other flowers and orchids at one time grew together.

We can now look more closely at the development of cultivated gardens. With the

Tudors firmly on the throne and as England moved towards the magnificence of Elizabeth I's long reign and more peaceful times, the discomfort of great castles as dwellings became apparent. This caused the rich – deriving much of their wealth from the Dissolution of the Monasteries and of course assuming the income from disinherited or beheaded neighbours – to build themselves great dwelling houses, set with large glass windows, such as splendid HARDWICK HALL. LACOCK ABBEY, ST JOHN'S JERUSALEM, MORVILLE HALL and MOTTISFONT ABBEY are examples of religious foundations which were turned into dwellings. The profession of architect was first recognised in the reign of Elizabeth I and this in due course affected gardens considerably. The curtilage of a house was given a design and became a place of beauty and not merely an enclosure for outdoor interests and the growing of plants.

Meanwhile some garden schemes had developed. As like as not a garden would have a surrounding wall and an arbour on a raised terrace, perhaps with corner "towers", often with seats ensconced in the wall and carpeted with camomile or another fragrant herb. Corner arbours are to be found at WESTBURY COURT and turfed seats at SISSINGHURST, but these are modern creations. This privy garden would have beds which, originally plain and rectangular, became elaborately divided and partly aligned. This style possibly originated in Italy and reached us through Holland, deriving from earlier skills in plasterwork, embroidery and in the decoration of furniture. Similarly, from raised originals, the beds became lower and were edged with some dwarf plant like Thrift or Marjoram, and later Dwarf Box, after its introduction from Holland in the 16th century. (It is amazing that this dwarf box edging, *Buxus sempervirens* 'Suffruticosa', and the Yellow Dutch Crocus should have been propagated ever since, vegetatively, with so little variation. Neither produces seeds but they have remained healthy and virus-free.) The beds became more elaborate,

15 A Flemish tapestry of the 17th century at Dyrham Park, shewing many delightful features, including corner arbours.

earning the name of "knot garden": the designs represented lovers' and other knots and patterns. The beds and borders would have included the Marigold, *Aster amellus*, Christmas Rose, Hollyhock, Sweet William, Madonna Lily, Crown Imperial, daffodils, hyacinths, Globe Artichoke, *Acanthus mollis*, the German Iris and *Iris pallida*, tulips, auriculas, *Paeonia officinalis*, Love-in-the-Mist, *Saxifraga cotyledon*, most from Europe or the countries bordering the Mediterranean. To them would be added rhubarb, gooseberry, currant, raspberry, the castor oil plant, the ancestral roses, *R. gallica*, *R. damascena*, *R. alba*, lavender and rosemary, together with Liquorice, root vegetables and others of many kinds.

For all that Nature, by her mother wit
Could frame in earth and form of substance base
Was there; and all that Nature did omit,
Art, (Playing Nature's second part) supplied it.

Edmund Spenser, *The Faerie Queen*

To appreciate a knot garden, which reached its highest development during the late 16th and early 17th centuries, one should be able to look down upon it. For this the windows – now ample and filled with glass – provided an excellent view, but the mount was also useful. The recently-constructed knot garden at LITTLE MORETON HALL (hall and moat were completed in 1590) has the advantage of one mount within the moat, and one outside it, but there is no proof that either mount was part of the original conception. There is also a notable mount at DUNHAM MASSEY in Greater Manchester. These mounts were also used as vantage points for scanning the country and probably had a much earlier, possibly religious, origin, likewise the raised walks which assumed such great proportions in the ensuing century.

16 Early 18th-century painting of the entire garden and landscape at Dunham Massey, Greater Manchester, shewing house, mount, moat, and formal waters.

Garden hedges provided shelter and privacy, and added to the design of the garden by dividing it into sections; they also acted as a clothes-line on sunny days! *Pyracantha* was used as well as quickthorn, common box and privet, and they must have been a cheering sight in winter. Bladder Senna, Jerusalem Sage, *Philadelphus coronarius*, Lilac, and the Laurustinus and roses may have joined them for this purpose. The clippings from hedges of rosemary, and edges of hyssop, thyme, lavender, and santolina would have been useful for strewing the floors. Climbing plants for the arbours were the Virgin's Bower, sweet white Jasmine, the yellow *Jasminum fruticans*, honeysuckles and Sweet Brier or Eglantine and the Musk Rose, *Rosa moschata*. All of the above are to be found at WESTBURY COURT, MOSELEY OLD HALL and HAM HOUSE.

There were vineyards and orchards in great number. Practically all the types of fruits we grow today were cultivated long before the Tudors. The inmates of dovecotes not only provided sound and movement for the garden but flesh for the pot. Bees in their straw hives – before wooden ones were made – needed protection from the wet and for this there were covered places, known as bee-boles, in the garden wall, as at PACKWOOD, near to what was at that time an orchard.

Flowers, herbs, vegetables and fruits were often cultivated all together, as much delight being obtained from their growth and attraction as from their uses. Spenser's butterfly – and no doubt the busie bee – enjoyed

Coole violets and Orpine growing still,
Embathed Balme, and cheerfull Galingale,
Fresh Costmarie, and breathfull Camomile,
Dull Poppie, and drink quickening Setuale,
Veyne, healing Vervein, and head purging Dill,
Sound Savourie, and Basil hartie-hale,
Fat Coleworts, and comforting Perseline,
Cold Lettuce and refreshing Rosmarine.

Lawns were mown for games and archery. Bowls, ninepins and tennis have ancient beginnings and a levelled bowling alley may be seen at MELFORD HALL. Gradually all grass came under the scythe and lawns became spacious and decorative as well as useful. It requires great skill to mow a lawn with a long-handled traditional scythe. I knew an old and expert head gardener whose finished product was a wonderful sight, the curved swaths divided by the opposite curves of the return cuts.

There is no doubt the Elizabethans wanted novelty. They were becoming fledged and prosperous, were seeing the world, and above all, I believe, the British hybrid race was coming to one of its peaks. The architects decorated their houses and garden walls with obelisks and other ornaments, such as may be seen on the Gatehouse at CHARLECOTE, on the walls at MONTACUTE and HARDWICK HALL. Places were found for statues, a taste obtained from Italy by way of France – a taste which spread from indoors to the garden, underlining the fact that in many ways a garden was considered an outdoor room. While the great houses that sprang up were partly for living in, they were also for entertainment, as like as not to be invaded by the Queen and all her retinue. They had to impress, outside as well as inside. Thus the Queen would have entered LYME HALL by the imposing front doorway; have seen the original house at OSTERLEY PARK, the noble front of WAKEHURST PLACE, gentle BARRINGTON COURT, dignified MONTACUTE and KNOLE. What images these wonderful old buildings conjure up!

Amusement was not neglected and in the gardens were ingeniously designed fountains which spouted water on the unwary visitor. Fruits were produced out of season by forcing

17 The Elizabethan garden house at Melford Hall. The raised bowling green is to the right of the building. Photo 1961.

or retarding, and shelter houses originated somewhere between the time of these new pavilions and the orangeries of the next century.

There was a love of garden arrangement, a love of flowers and growing things, a great awakening in architecture and the arts. Owners became proud of their success in gardening and they welcomed their visitors in peace and plenty. Over the garden gate at MONTACUTE is this delightful invitation: "Through this wide opening gate, none comes too early, none returns too late." However sour, wine was provided whenever possible from the grapes in the owners' vineyards. The remains of vineyard terracing may be seen at DUNSTER CASTLE.

The fact that books were published on plants and flowers proves that there was an established gardening public. Henry Lyte's *A New Herbal or Historie of Plants*, a translation of Dodoens' Flemish work of 1569, was produced while he was living at LYTES CARY, in 1578. Another astonishing list of plants is that of John Gerard; his *Herball* of 1596, also derived from Dodoens' industry, catalogued over a thousand different plants.

William Turner and Thomas Tusser were other famous authors of the period; their work is also mainly concerned with plants and cultivation rather than garden design. Botanical science was in its early stages but it had arrived.

The Dutch were the great European plant enthusiasts at the time, both for flowers and fruit; vegetables were coming into their own again after having been neglected for hundreds of years. Herbs and fruits were of course essential, vegetables tolerated and flowers appreciated. Rare bulbs began to arrive from the Middle East, partly because they were suitable for packing and conveying in a dry state and, unlike seeds, there was little delay in the production of their flowers. Besides being devoured raw or cooked, apples were used for cider and for drying for the winter; pears likewise for the making of perry. *Cornus mas*, the Cornelian cherry, was liked for preserving, and rosemary was so much needed for strewing and seasoning that even sunny walls were spared for it, thus helping to minimise possible loss in very cold winters; fragrance in those insanitary days was as much valued from the floors as from the seasoning which disguised the flavour of stale meats. The new great houses had

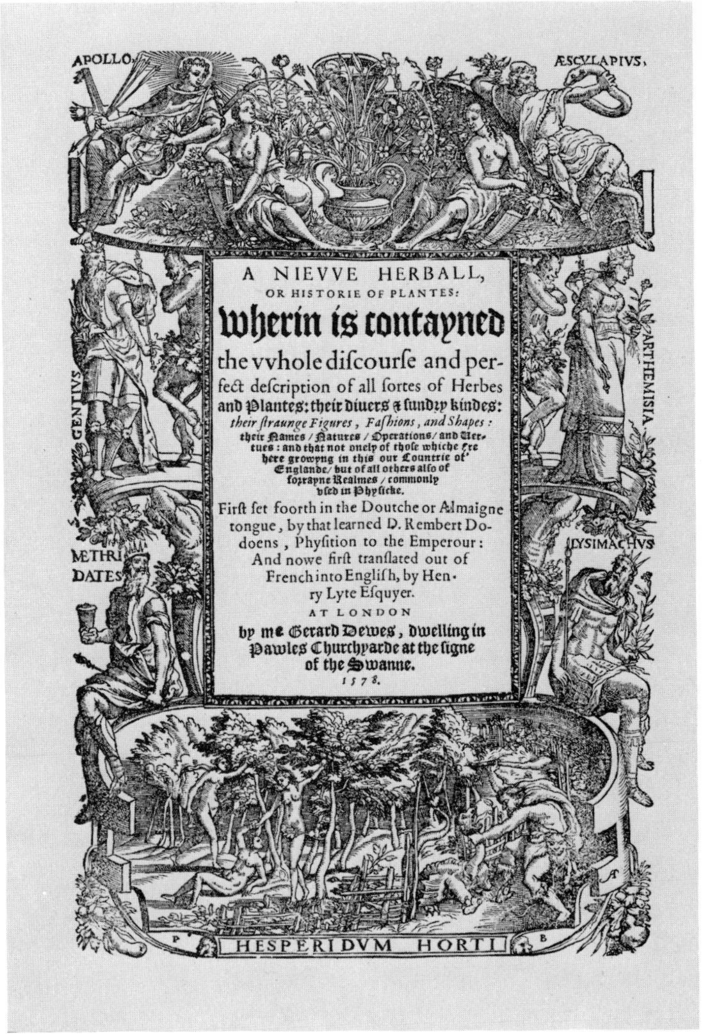

A NIEVVE HERBALL,
OR HISTORIE OF PLANTES:
wherin is contayned
the vvhole diſcourſe and perfect deſcription of all ſortes of Herbes and Plantes: their diuers & ſundry kindes: *their ſtraunge Figures, Faſhions, and Shapes:* their Names / Natures / Operations / and Vertues: and that not onely of thoſe whiche are here growyng in this our Countrie of Englande / but of all others alſo of forrayne Realmes / commonly vſed in Phyſicke.
Firſt ſet foorth in the Doutche or Almaigne tongue, by that learned D. Rembert Dodoens, Phyſition to the Emperour: And nowe firſt tranſlated out of French into Engliſh, by Henry Lyte Eſquyer.
AT LONDON
by me Gerard Dewes, dwelling in Pawles Churchyarde at the ſigne of the Swanne.
1578.

18 Henry Lyte lived at Lytes Cary and produced his book in 1578. The title page shews Apollo and his son Aesculapius at the top with a vase between them containing peonies, lilies, irises and daffodils. Below, Pan leers at Gentius and Artemisia, while yet again he is turned into a caryatid on either side, over Mithridates and Lysimachus. At the bottom the Hesperides guard the golden apples in the garden, but the dragon which assisted them in their task is being killed by Hercules. The interwoven garden fence is typical of mediaeval and later times.

still-rooms for the distilling, drying and preserving of garden produce, and the vivid orange petals of Marigolds were grown to decorate the dishes, the humble Violet for adding sweetness. It is a poignant thought that among such multitudes of garden flowers and plants the Violet is one of the few which is still grown by us in its original state. Not for nothing was it supposed to stand for constancy.

Gerard's book gives us an excellent insight to the numerous plants which had reached our shores from countries far afield. He catalogues the following: Love-lies-bleeding (*Amaranthus caudatus*), from the tropics; Indian Shot (*Canna indica*), from South America and the West Indies; the Date-Plum (*Diospyros lotus*), from the Far East; the Sunflower (*Helianthus annuus*), from the western United States; the red Day Lily (*Hemerocallis fulva*), from Asia; the Yellow Day Lily (*Hemerocallis flava*), perhaps from China; the Tree Mallow (*Hibiscus syriacus*), from India and China; and the potato (*Solanum tuberosum*), from South America.

Various evergreens were treasured such as the Myrtle, Western Arborvitae, *Yucca gloriosa*, *Phillyrea latifolia*, the Bay Laurel, the Holm Oak, the Maritime and Stone Pines; the Laburnum and the Judas Tree would also have been found.

Apples, pears and plums; red, white and black currants; cherries, medlars, quinces and filberts were grown in quantity. Melons, pumpkins, gourds, cucumbers, peas and beans and many salads joined the root vegetables.

There was no abrupt change in English gardening after the accession of James I. Gardening in Scotland was not as advanced. The one thing which James set in motion was the cultivation of mulberries in order to start silk factories. The White Mulberry (*Morus alba*) is the best food for silk worms and thousands were sent to different towns for planting. The Black Mulberry was also planted and it is probable that some of the oldest trees in English gardens are originals or derived from layers raised from them. In my experience, while seeds of White Mulberry germinate freely, those of the Black do not; in fact it may well be that the Black as we know it is an ancient – very ancient – cultivar of derivation before history, like the Olive, and its seeds are seldom borne in this country. We have old mulberries at CHARLECOTE PARK, CLEVEDON COURT and CLIVEDEN, while at Hatfield House there is a tree reputed to have been planted by Elizabeth I. A Black Mulberry, owing to its rough bark, its mode of growth and the incapability of healing its wounds, often looks older than it is.

The art of the garden critic – so prevalent today, when everybody thinks they know how a garden should be arranged and run – may be said to have been started by Francis Bacon, Lord Verulam, who wrote a book of essays on diverse matters and included one *On Gardens*. This is regarded more as the outcome of his thoughts on the matter, inspired by visiting many gardens, than as a description of any particular garden. It seems to usher in a new dimension, that of taste, and it behoves all of us gardeners to read it once a year to bring us back to the essentials of gardening. Through his essay shines his love of the beauty of plants, and particularly those whose fragrance is free on the air, and an orderly mind tells us how to arrange a garden of some 30 acres. We hear of grass "finely shorn", and gravel paths; shady alleys, a mount with a banqueting house on top, fountains and moving water; fruit trees and flowers for beauty, interest and use *throughout the year*. Knots and topiary were to be avoided as "but toys for children", and statues he considered did not add to the true pleasure of a garden. Great stress was laid upon shady alleys and arched hedges, the alleys to be wide enough for four to walk abreast. Beyond all this formality was to be a heath or natural wilderness, without trees, but with thickets of Sweet Brier, Woodbine, with pinks and Periwinkle, Lily-of-the-Valley and other flowers, together with gooseberries and currants trained into standards.

One who eventually profited from some of Bacon's advice was Sir Ralph Verney at the old CLAYDON HOUSE, Buckinghamshire. He was a noteworthy gardener and in 1655 desired to purchase 2,000 Sweet Briers; he imported tulips, ranunculuses and melons from Persia, and later on made a gift of 200 rowans to Charles II. By 1621 Oxford Botanic Garden had been started, and shortly contained, as it does today, a vast number of plants; the stress in gardens was still on the grand mixture and delight in all growing things, but discrimination was creeping in. There was time and encouragement to indulge in country house visiting; Henry Wotton records in 1624 a visit to Ware Park, Hertfordshire; the owner had troubled to arrange his flowers in a sequence of colours in the garden, surely the earliest reference to this art. After the Restoration we find the influence of Continental taste, especially Italian, increasing in architecture; classical design was replacing the uncontrolled ostentation of the heyday of Elizabeth.

It is interesting that Bacon desired some "wild" gardening as well as the formal. The two styles play Cox and Box throughout our garden history. His admonishments about knots and such like were not heeded: from simple designs of the previous century they became more elaborate and intriguing. Some designs by the Reverend Walter Stonehouse in 1640 are extant, and one was copied by the Trust in 1963–4 at MOSELEY OLD HALL. Stone, wood and lead as well as dwarf plants were used for edgings, and thorn, rosemary and box for hedges. The yew was little used and not recommended, possibly because it had for so long been fostered for the production of bows and pike staffs.

The best defence for a garden was a prickly hedge, sometimes reinforced by an earth-wall or a moat; from the moat the idea of developing fishponds, or stew-ponds (i.e. enclosed as in a stew), had grown in earlier times. There is a noble fish-pool or stew-pond at LACOCK ABBEY, and another at GUNBY HALL.

Gardening was still a term for gathering all outdoor delights into one scheme: herbs, vegetables, fruits, flowers, pheasantries, fish and its accompaniment of water, and the time to enjoy such things. It was to benefit the owner in all ways, and this enjoyment is echoed in the old Dutch Flower Pieces of the 17th century, where with the flowers are mingled insects, animals, birds' nests and fruits, to say nothing of dead game birds.

With the publication of John Parkinson's *Paradisi in Sole Paradisus Terrestris* in 1629, the myths and suppositions of earlier writers fled, and we are given a vast tome filled with precise details about plants; in addition he gives full rein to his appreciation of the beauty of plants and devotes a later, smaller part of his book to vegetables and fruit.

Even though the country, from prosperity and peace, was moving gradually towards religious dispute and eventually civil war, gardens and gardening continued to progress during the reign of Charles I. Apart from the Italian architectural influence, the desire for evergreens from Southern Europe and elsewhere grew, and with all the exotic plants being introduced new and special ways of coping with the tenderness of some of them were devised. During the Commonwealth we read of hotbeds and plant houses, and concave walls to trap the sun. By 1659 the Cedar of Lebanon had arrived and it, together with the Holm Oak (Evergreen Oak or Ilex), was to prove a notable addition to English gardens; no other broad-leafed evergreen grows so large in our climate, and it has become very much part of the great estates and parks. Also recorded by Sir Thomas Hanmer in his *Garden Book* of 1659 are other "greens" such as Laurustinus, *Pyracantha*, *Arbutus* (whether introduced from Southern Ireland or the Continent) and such tender things as myrtles, oranges and lemons. Some other notable additions from abroad in the early 17th century were the Horse Chestnut, the European Larch, the False Locust or Acacia, and the Virginian Creeper; the last two hail from North America.

But we are at a dividing point in garden history. Though they may overlap in many ways and forever, the gardeners and garden lovers were separating from the close observers of plants, and a new science was being born – botany. But this was not all; the gardeners themselves were separating still further into those who grew plants for their own merits, either formally or informally in the area to be known as the flower or kitchen garden, leaving others who were almost to eschew plants and gain their refreshment from design superimposed upon nature. Their ideas and tendencies were fostered by the earliest writers on gardens such as Thomas Hill in his *The Profitable Art of Gardening*, 1579.

Suffice it to say here that the constancy of the violet has remained with those who cultivate it and all the many plants that go to make up the cottage gardens and the great walled kitchen gardens of later ages. Regardless of the storms that were about to rage, gardening continued and plants were grown, but for nearly two hundred years English garden design was to become the plaything of fashion. Perhaps it has been ever since, and always will be.

4

THE LATER STUARTS

Shall we never more
That sweet militia restore,
When gardens only had their towers,
And all the garrisons were flowers;
When roses only arms might bear,
And men did rosy garlands wear?

Andrew Marvell, 1621–78

AS EARLY AS THE RESTORATION IN 1660 we can begin to detect a segregation of different types of gardens or garden areas. This was in great part due to the need for special cultures for the wide variety of plants being grown.

Thus flowers and bulbs would be in one area, usually with fruit trees and vegetables elsewhere, exotics handy to shelters, and there would be an arrangement of architectural design carried out with hedges and trees ready for the relaxation of the owner and his guests. The Elizabethan and early Jacobean gardens with their mixed plantings were giving way to two types, as mentioned earlier, that of the plantsman and that of the artist. The dividing of the ways was in progress, but there was still that other division of the formal and the informal. We hear of fountains being allied to rock-work decorated with shells. Though nothing remains to us of this evanescent nature, we know that at PACKWOOD in 1664 there was already the Roman Bath *in situ* in the garden west of the house, known as the Fountain Court. There is also a sundial dated 1667. It is strange that these garden baths were sometimes made the more chilly by facing north; there is one in this position at POWIS CASTLE, though this is likely to be much later. It is possible that the Mount at PACKWOOD was also created around this time, likewise the box hedges surrounding the late 19th-century yew garden, which was then an orchard. At PACKWOOD we have one of the first examples of the separation of the productive area from the ornamental area. There was not only the Fountain Court with the orchard to the south but the present position of the kitchen garden – across the road – is recorded by 1723. Yews had already been taken to heart by gardeners, witness the topiary garden at Levens Hall, Cumbria, and the age of straight lines had dawned.

The Restoration brought with it not only a new liberality but also much more influence from Europe. The Italian examples of architecture were joined by French garden design (derived from Italian sources) and also a reinforcement of the same ideas by the Dutch. King Charles II and his exiled followers had seen many a splendid garden in the new mode, whereby gardening as it had been known was given up as a pastime by the wealthy, and a new fashion was ushered in. This was, briefly, the imposing of man's ideas upon nature in the extreme, governing and restraining her from her natural exuberance, and confining the enjoyment of the gardened areas by long vistas of hedges and avenues; though extensive, the general effect was controlled, with formal water or elaborate parterres accompanied by much clipping and training of trees and bushes.

The trend towards this style had been getting ever stronger since Henry VIII's use of topiary at Hampton Court; indeed it is usually claimed that the Romans were expert in the art, and from their term *topiarius*, a person who laid out or looked after the ornamental garden, descends our word for the clipping of bushes into fancy shapes. One of the great basic contrasts in gardening artistry was soon appreciated – the contrast seen in Italian paintings of the tall tapering cypress with the rounded outline of the Stone Pine. Possibly some of the clipping was instinctively aimed at such contrast in this country, where the Italian Cypress was not proving reliably hardy, and the Stone Pine in any case would take over fifty years to achieve its globose head. The box bush, apart from thorn and other shrubs, remained a favourite for clipping but after the Restoration it began to give way to the English Yew, which has remained the best and favourite evergreen for the purpose ever since. The Dwarf Box was used more frequently for knot gardens which had become much more elaborate and were now known as parterres.

The Trust laid out a similar period box knot garden at MOSELEY OLD HALL; King Charles stayed here, among other places, after the disastrous battle of Worcester in 1651.

Another garden conceit of the time was the maze or labyrinth. Probably no example is extant of an Elizabethan or even Stuart-period design. The origin of the labyrinth is lost in the mists of time; it can be traced in one form or another through Roman and earlier civilisations. The motives seem to be religious or recreational – the searching for the supreme centre of things, the capture of the heart of civilisation, and all possible variations on these themes. "Labyrinth" derives from Greece and Crete; "maze" from a Scandinavian word. Both were created by cutting a pattern in turf, outlining the pattern with stone, dwarf plants or shrubs, and eventually the hedged maze evolved, becoming secular as opposed to the pavement designs in churches. Fruit bushes were sometimes used to create the hedges. Our best maze is at GLENDURGAN, Cornwall, laid out by the Fox family in 1833, with hedges of Cherry Laurel. It is completely informal in design, and bears some resemblance to an ancient one which was at Poitiers in France. There is a formal maze of beech hedges at TATTON PARK, Cheshire, but this again is of recent origin. Perhaps the best kept and most impressive maze in the country is one of yew at Hatfield House. This was planted in 1841.

For the next fifty years or so after the Restoration we are concerned with a formal style of gardening, derived from the Continent. It is fascinating to recall that this formal style was carried out with the same materials as the 18th-century English landscape style, i.e. trees, grass and water, but with what different results!

The most grandiose schemes were being produced in France by Le Nôtre for the Sun King, Louis XIV, who throughout his long reign had an immense influence on the trends of art in all its forms. Flowers were used in France more as a colourful adjunct to the masterly parterre "cutwork" designs, whereas in Holland the Dutch clung closely to what has remained their principal contribution to gardening, the care and production of flowers and plants. These they added to their formal designs but enjoyed to the full the plants' interest and diverse beauties. True to their age-old traditions, the English made the best of both worlds; their gardens were less vast and impersonal than the French, and their enthusiasm for plants did not rise above the sober appraisal of their beauty and uses, and did not make and break fortunes as in Holland, where tulip mania was rife in the 1630s. An echo from this period is found in the flower vases at DYRHAM PARK.

The principal reason for these new extensive gardens was for somewhere for both owner and guests to walk and dally. Their increased prosperity and leisure gave rise to the newly-discovered pleasure of walking – and there was nowhere else to do it. There were no well-metalled roads and footpaths, and the rough countryside was not yet looked upon with approbation. Horrific things like mountains and crags were shut out with tree screens.

And if one goes for a walk one needs the occasional seat, flights of steps, sheets of water, fountains, hedged alleys and shady nooks, avenues and vistas to tempt one ever onwards, along gravel paths and close greensward. Samuel Pepys noted that English gravel and lawns were the best in Europe, and that borders of flowers spoilt the walks. As in earlier times the level greens were used for bowls and other games; in fact The Mall and Pall Mall record that the French game of *paille-maille*, an early type of croquet, was played in those areas by Charles II. The best grass seed was obtained from Syria.

Several of the Trust's great houses were built during the long Stuart dynasty: FELBRIGG HALL, 1620; BLICKLING HALL, 1628 (on the site of a much older moated house and hence the dry moat today); LANHYDROCK, 1640. Abraham Hill was busy from 1645 rebuilding the house and planting his trees at ST JOHN'S JERUSALEM, and it is possible that some of the old limes and the cedar date from the years soon following. At EAST RIDDLESDEN HALL, perhaps mid-17th century, whose formal 17th century style garden was laid out by the Trust in 1973–4, may be seen mews for keeping hawks, a popular pursuit through many centuries. THE VYNE – a site for grape-growing – was altered to its present form *c.*1650, at which time the Garden Pavilion to the east of the house was built. ASHDOWN HOUSE was built by a Dutch architect in 1665. The Parterre of box and gravel, laid out here by the Trust in the early 1950s, illustrates the more flowing pattern as opposed to the knot gardens of LITTLE MORETON HALL and MOSELEY OLD HALL.

19 To be in keeping with the house, the 17th-century style box parterre at Ashdown House was laid out by the Trust *c.*1955, as a foreground to the old lime avenue. Photo 1969.

At HAM HOUSE we have one of the oldest garden designs still more or less intact, dating from 1673. From paintings in the house it has been possible to reinstate the square plats of grass, and to restore its Wilderness. "Wilderness" is a revealing appellation for a scheme which is, to us, of considerable formality; it reveals however that when almost all lines in a garden were straight, anything departing from this, with free-grown trees, hedges, and curving paths, might deserve the title of a wilderness.

The garden at CHARLECOTE PARK was developed in severe style as can be seen in plate XXVII, dated 1696; it brings out particularly well the avenue stretching relentlessly across the fields, and also what must be one of the first areas set aside for vegetables and fruits in the right-hand corner. Plum trees still grow on the site, though little remains of the rest of the original garden layout altered later by Capability Brown.

The creation of avenues posed some problems, for example what to do with the intervening spaces and also the actual planting. In wooded country there was no problem, and the opening of vistas and reinforcing them with rows of trees was a fairly simple matter. But the dislocation of farming land by the planting of an avenue must have been considerable. One of this period remains at LYME PARK opposite the south front portico, across the pond which was altered in Charles II's reign. Some other famous avenues of the period are that of Sweet Chestnuts at CROFT CASTLE planted early in the 17th century, the Sycamore Avenue at LANHYDROCK, dating from about 1650, and the avenue of oaks and beeches at CASTLECOOLE, about 1700.

In areas near to the house the intervening spaces were often filled in with trees, not in a scattered natural fashion, but in solid design, with further radiating alleys leading off in all directions, sometimes in later years threaded by meandering walks. In miniature this can be seen in the Wilderness at HAM HOUSE; the radial lines from the given centre are hedged alleys connected first by an elliptical path uniting them all, and serpentine paths in the greater areas. Very often the whole scheme was a sort of giant quincunx, both of trees and vistas. The quincunx was a pattern of tree planting in "staggered" rows so that vistas were not only four-square but diagonal as well. In small scale it has been reproduced at WESTBURY COURT around the new parterre, at TRERICE, and at SUDBURY HALL.

The original garden of BLICKLING HALL dates from 1629, where a similar wilderness design was made. It was at the far end of the present garden spinneys with their radial walks; although on similar lines as at present, it was much smaller. It was enlarged and simplified in the mid-18th century and elaborated later. Its present design owes much to 17th-century influence.

The trees in themselves are a study. In the actual gardens fruit and nut trees of all kinds were enjoyed, but not the greater native trees, which were part of the unkempt and still frightening wild countryside. These natives would be chosen for the big avenues and the bigger woodlands; the whole idea of re-afforestation was encouraged by John Evelyn.

Dramatic use was made of water in Italian gardens, noted for their frequently steep slopes, and the noise and splash and cooling effect were important contributions to enjoyment. In France and Holland, on flatter terrain, more value was placed on stillness – though there were indeed great fountains – and reflection. In England the ponds and lakes were given rectangular or other geometric shapes. The great formal water at CASTLE WARD dates from the first half of the 17th century at which time also several rectangular lakes were laid out at UPTON HOUSE. These lie below what was undoubtedly at one time a formal sloping garden, set with clipped yews on the slopes. The large rectangular ponds at ERDDIG date from about 1720, which was when the surrounding walls were built. It was not until about 1650 that the skill was developed of pumping water uphill, and UPPARK (1685–90) is generally looked upon as being one of the first houses where this skill was utilised. Pipes were made of elm tree trunks and pumping rams and windmills were employed. Informal water (in other words the River Thames) was used as an eye-catcher in the splendid view from the south front of CLIVEDEN.

One of the greatest aids in studying these historic places is the extensive series of engravings of country houses and their gardens by Johannes Kip, from drawings by Leonard Knyff, all seemingly drawn from a static balloon. Undoubtedly some exaggeration occurred, some artistic licence was taken, and sometimes gross imagination or wishful thinking was called upon, but, to take just two examples, those of DYRHAM PARK and WESTBURY COURT, much has been found authentic and has indeed been substantiated by remains of paths, walls and written records. At DYRHAM, laid out in 1692–1702, much of the garden to the west of the house is at least still indicated though somewhat obliterated by subsequent alterations. The Dutch style of design is perpetuated at WESTBURY COURT on a more intimate scale, and the Kip engraving shows many details of the canals and their plantings.

One of the most dramatic gardens of the time was created at POWIS CASTLE by the Earl of Rochford, a friend of King William, *c.*1722, though it is probable that he elaborated earlier terraces. Here is an Italianate treatment of a steep rocky escarpment, using successive terraces for marble busts in niches, an aviary and an orangery, all connected by flights of steps and

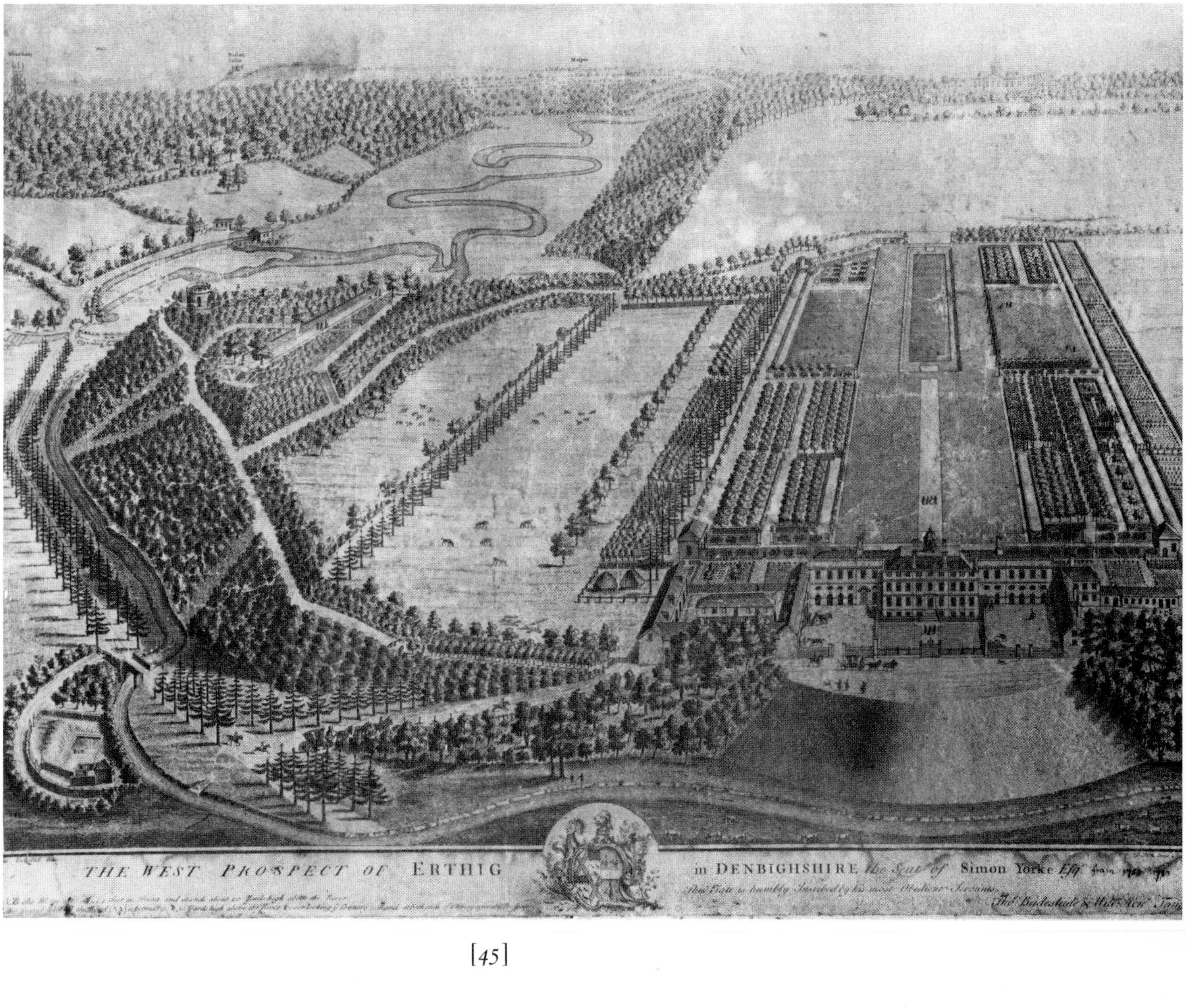

20 The house at Erddig, from an engraving by Thomas Badeslade, in 1738.

guarded by balustrading. It also had a strangely asymetrical water garden below – of which only a trace remains.

In 1709 A.J. Dezalliers d'Argenville published in France a book on garden design called *La Théorie et la Pratique du Jardinage*. It is important for two reasons: one, because it is about the only work setting forth the precepts of Le Nôtre, and the other because being translated into English first by John James (*The Theory and Practice of Gardening*, 1712), and later by Philip Miller in his *Gardener's Dictionary* of 1731, it had a profound effect on English garden design for many years, even after fashion had decreed that straight lines were "out". D'Argenville included designs of parterres which he recommended, and one of these, called by him a *Parterre de Compartiment*, was copied at OXBURGH HALL in 1840 by Sir Henry Paston-Bedingfeld, the 6th Baronet. This parterre, though somewhat modified, remains substantially the same and is, I believe, unique in British gardens.

It seems from what one reads of the Stuart period and earlier that the summers must have been hot. The stress is so often on shade – not from great trees, but from alleys and arbours; arbours of greenery or of woodwork where meals could be taken and small orchestras could play. In short, the garden was at last a great and worthy adjunct to the house, which had not yet reached the spaciousness of the 18th century and still savoured of confinement, giving rise to the need of more ambulating space to escape from the army of servants and the visitors.

O blessed shade! O gentle cool retreat
From all th'immoderate heat
In which the frantic world does burn and sweat;

Who that has reason, and his smell,
Would not 'mong roses and jasmin dwell
Rather than all his spirits choke
With exhalations of dirt and smoke,
And all th' uncleanness which does drown
In pestilential clouds a pop'lous town?

Abraham Cowley, 1618–67

The garden provided peace and quiet, and great variety not only of plants and views, but of games and in fact of everything that was not found indoors. Garden buildings were becoming more elaborate, and in particular those designed to house plants from warmer countries, the oranges and lemons, myrtles and pomegranates and various "Indian" exotics which were reaching the country in ever-increasing numbers, either directly or via the Jardin des Plantes in Paris and Dutch growers. It was no doubt partly to attract some of the trade that went to Holland that George London started his famous nursery at Brompton Park in 1681; joined later by Henry Wise, the firm of London & Wise carried on until 1713 and was the principal source of trees and plants in this country. London designed a garden at HANBURY HALL during the early years of the new century; the Orangery was completed after 1732 and is a delightful example of garden architecture. Apart from the excitement of being able to pick one's own oranges, the pursuit was perhaps partly political, in compliment to the House of Orange.

By degrees primitive methods of heating had been improved and John Evelyn describes an ingenious device for pumping hot air into the buildings. Otherwise pans of charcoal or the old Roman techniques of furnace and hot-air flues in floor and walls were used. The orangeries were the precursors of the greenhouse. There was indeed so much enjoyment to be had from the garden that during William and Mary's reign, and also Queen Anne's, even the owners of the new small country houses were indulging in large gardens and orangeries.

In large gardens variety was sought not only from surprises in design but also in contrast of foliage. King William was keenly interested in gardening and particularly favoured evergreens for shelter and privacy. He made great alterations and improvements at Hampton Court. In his reign and that of Queen Anne the box parterres, evergreen hedges and clipped specimens reached their apogee. Flowers were completely banished to the kitchen gardens, and coloured stones, sands and gravels, brick dust, glittering spars and coal took their place in the parterre beds. In the quincuncial plantings and wooded groves variegated shrubs – the new hollies such as the variegated Hedgehog Holly, and the now extinct variegated *Phillyrea* – were used for contrast. Portuguese laurels were trained into standards, being the nearest suitable hardy substitute to represent the formal shapes of pruned orange trees, and have remained a principal formal feature of our gardens ever since. Topiary reached an absurd height of fashion and was ridiculed by Alexander Pope in *The Guardian* in 1712. Besides being clipped into the form of animals and persons, it was formed into other patterns including sundials. A Victorian example of such an extravagance is fashioned in box and yew at ASCOTT. Topiary of later date is found in many of our gardens. At CLIVEDEN in the Long Garden are some excellent specimens, and the Edwardian box-edged beds, originally containing herbaceous plants, are filled with variegated *Euonymus* to foster a parterre-style of planting.

In spite of its excesses, the art of gardening had reached its greatest formal style. The actual design and proportion of its different parts was carefully studied for the best effect: the width of path and grass, the juxtaposition of ornamental parterres and bare plats of greensward, the severe clipping contrasting against distant trees, the length and breadth of water and the height of fountains. Hotbeds in frames and the orangeries gave another dimension to culture which had reached the high level at which it was to remain, apart from the addition of pure glasshouse culture, until the present day, and in these productive areas an ever-increasing number of plants was grown. There were no weedkillers – except boiling water and precious salt – and no machines for cultivating. All work was done by hand, aided by the spade and shovel, the scythe and the wheelbarrow, with the horse and cart for bigger jobs. The initial outlay was enormous and even at the low level of pay for gardeners the upkeep of the elaborate parterres and shaped shrubs was costly. Armies of "weederwomen" were employed. The weederwoman of today is usually the busy housewife herself. Small wonder was it that a new and less expensive type of gardening was to be welcomed later in the century by the trendsetters.

Several of the Trust's great houses took shape in the early 18th century. UPTON HOUSE, PECKOVER HOUSE, BENINGBROUGH HALL and ANTONY come to mind and in all of them the walled kitchen garden was placed away from the dwelling.

Though flowers were mainly banished from fashionable gardening they had not lost their place in the nation's affections, as numerous poems tell. In art they were to the fore as well, in drawings and paintings, in gardening and other books and in the exquisite wood carvings of Grinling Gibbons. They were probably accorded as much approbation as were furniture and pictures inside the dwellings, and perhaps for this reason, apart from Gibbons' unequalled inspiration and skill, they grace the rooms at PETWORTH HOUSE and SUDBURY HALL.

Just as furniture and all indoor decoration in the house became more elaborate, so I think grew up the idea of "improving" flowers. Through the ages there is continuing evidence that mankind treasured the bigger and better flowers which cropped up by chance, and kept them in cultivation by vegetative propagation. We have an early inkling of the desire for improvement from Andrew Marvell, though he could not have visualised the lengths to which hybridisation and improvers of nature's beauties could carry their debasing art – if indeed it may be called an art:

Meantime, whilst every verdant thing
Itself does at thy beauty charm,
Reform the errors of the Spring;
Make that the tulips may have share
Of sweetness, seeing they are fair,
And roses of their thorns disarm;
But most procure
That violets may a longer age endure.

During this long period, though the style of design moved away from ornamental planting, all the Elizabethan traditions continued in regard to fruits, vegetables, herbs and flowers, though relegated to separate areas and culture on walls. Meanwhile a continual stream of plants was being brought to this country, many of which were to remain favourite embellishments of our parks and gardens through to the present day.

I have already mentioned the Lebanon Cedar and Holm Oak; these were joined by the following: (I am not claiming that any of the examples in our gardens were planted as original introductions, but call attention to some fine specimens.) Horse Chestnut (*Aesculus hippocastanum*), from Greece and Albania in the early 17th century; Larch (*Larix decidua*), from the European Alps and Carpathians, *c.*1620 (WALLINGTON); Acacia (*Robinia pseudacacia*), from the eastern United States in the early 17th century (ATTINGHAM PARK); Swamp Cypress (*Taxodium distichum*), from the southern United States, *c.*1640 (GLENDURGAN); Black Walnut (*Juglans nigra*), from the United States in 1686 (LACOCK ABBEY, SALTRAM); Pencil Cedar (*Juniperus virginiana*), from east and central North America, *c.*1664 (KILLERTON, HAM HOUSE); Cork Oak (*Quercus suber*), from Southern Europe and North Africa in 1699 (KILLERTON); Sweet Gum (*Liquidambar styraciflua*), from the eastern United States in the 17th century (OSTERLEY PARK); Tulip Tree (*Liriodendron tulipifera*), from North America, *c.*1688 (STOURHEAD, KILLERTON, GLENDURGAN, LEITH HILL); Cockspur Thorn (*Crataegus crus-galli*), from east and central North America in 1691 (WESTBURY COURT); Honey Locust (*Gleditsia triacanthos*), from the eastern and central United States in 1700 (ANGLESEY ABBEY); Flowering or Manna Ash (*Fraxinus ornus*), from Southern Europe and Asia Minor in the 17th century (STOURHEAD).

From South Africa arrived the two garden "geraniums" (*Pelargonium zonale* and *P. peltatum*); the Nasturtium (*Tropaeolum majus*), the Tomato, and the Passion Flower from South America. New hardy plants were represented by *Alyssum saxatile*, *Aquilegia alpina*, *Dianthus caryophyllus* and *D. plumarius* (Carnation and Pink), and the Oriental Poppy. From our new colonies across the Atlantic appeared the following plants and their progeny are still popular today: *Lobelia cardinalis*, 1626, *Solidago canadensis*, 1648 (Golden Rod), *Aster novi-belgii*, 1710 (Michaelmas Daisy), *Heuchera americana*, 1656, and *Sprekelia formosissima*, 1658, the Jacobean Lily from Mexico, so popular with embroiderers of fire screens and the like in the 19th century.

The Red Hot Poker (*Kniphofia uvaria*) had arrived in 1705 from South Africa, and our old friend and ground-cover the Rose of Sharon, *Hypericum calycinum* had been introduced in 1656.

The hybrid London Plane had occurred by about 1700, probably in Italy. The Cabbage Rose, or "Rose of a Hundred Leaves" (*Rosa centifolia*), a hybrid, had originated prior to 1625, probably in Holland, and the Polyanthus, a hybrid between the Primrose and the Cowslip, was recorded by 1665.

I *Rhododendron* 'Conroy' (*R. cinnabarinum* var. *roylei* × *R. concatenans*) raised at Bodnant in 1937, and *Chaenomeles superba* 'Rowallane' raised at Rowallane.

The flowers in plates I–XVI are reduced to four-fifths of their actual size.

II *Magnolia loebneri* 'Leonard Messel', a seedling from *M. stellata rosea*, raised at Nymans, with *Forsythia suspensa atrocaulis* 'Nymans Variety', noted for its large pale flowers and dark brown wood.

III The Flower of the Snow (*Chionodoxa luciliae* of gardens) which was introduced to cultivation from Western Turkey by George Maw, and first flowered at Benthall Hall in 1877.

IV ABOVE *Rhododendron* 'Vanessa Pastel' raised at Bodnant in 1930, a hybrid between *R. griersonianum* and 'Soulbut'.

V RIGHT Two shrubs remarkable for the colour of their young foliage: *Pieris formosa forrestii* 'Wakehurst' is brilliant scarlet in spring gradually fading to yellowish green and later to dark green; 'Rowallane' is a self-sown seedling at Rowallane whose clear yellow leaves retain their pale colouring until well into July.

VI OPPOSITE *Meconopsis sheldonii* 'Slieve Donard'. A plant given to the Donard Nursery in the late 1930s from Mount Stewart, where it had been known as 'Prain's Variety', having come from a Miss Prain in Northern Ireland. A sound perennial, a hybrid between *M. grandis* and *M. betonicifolia*.

VII ABOVE A fragrant rhododendron raised at Trengwainton, 'Laerdal', a hybrid between *R. dalhousiae* and *R. johnstonianum*, with *Kennedya rubicunda*, which grows in an open glass shelter on the house.

VIII ABOVE *Campanula latiloba* 'Hidcote Amethyst', which originated as a sport from *C. latiloba* at Hidcote during the 1960s. *C. latiloba*, *C.l.* 'Highcliffe' (*left*) and *C.l.* 'Alba' are shewn for comparison.

IX OPPOSITE *Hypericum* 'Hidcote' and *Penstemon* 'Hidcote'. The origin of the former is unknown, the latter and *Fuchsia* 'Hidcote' were raised from seed at Hidcote in the early 1950s.

x 'Rubicunda', a penstemon grown at Lyme Park since it was raised there in 1906. It is one of the rather tender bedding hybrids usually called *P. gloxinioides* in gardens.

xi Lord Anson's Blue Pea, a perennial plant introduced in 1744 by Admiral Lord Anson: *Lathyrus nervosus*, a native of the Magellan Straits of South America.

XII ABOVE *Hypericum* 'Rowallane', which originated as a self-sown seedling at Rowallane many years ago. It is considered to be a hybrid between *H. hookeranum* 'Rogersii' and *H. leschenaultii*. It is only suitable for sheltered gardens.

XIII RIGHT *Camellia × williamsii* 'Citation', raised at Bodnant prior to 1960.

XIV *Crocosmia masonorum* 'Rowallane Yellow' which occurred as a sport among plants of *C. masonorum* at Rowallane in the early 1970s; the flowers often have a tinge of orange around the throat.
Dianthus 'Hidcote' originated at Hidcote prior to 1950.

XV Two beautiful plants for late summer: *Eucryphia × nymansensis* 'Nymansay' and *Fuchsia* 'Mount Stewart'. The latter has been grown for many years at Mount Stewart; the former was raised in 1914 at Nymans, a chance hybrid between *E. glutinosa* and *E. cordifolia*.

XVI *Gentiana asclepiadea* 'Knightshayes' raised at Knightshayes
in the 1960s from seeds from Miss Nellie Britton.
A pale blue form, which grows freely at Sizergh Castle and at Wallington,
as well as the normal dark blue, are shewn for comparison.

5

THE GEORGIAN PERIOD

And he will refit the old library in the most exquisite Gothic taste, and garnish its shelves with the most valuable volumes; – and he will draw plans and landscapes, and write verses, and rear temples, and dig grottoes; – and he will stand in a clear summer night in the colonnade before the hall, and gaze on deer as they stray in the moonlight, or lie shadowed by the boughs of the huge old fantastic oaks . . .

Sir Walter Scott, *Waverley*, 1814

SO FAR GARDENING IN ENGLAND had been one continued progression on increasingly formal lines, while the increasing diversity of plants introduced to the country took less and less part in design. It is interesting to note that the most comprehensive books on the then passing fashion of formality did not appear until the early 1700s, culminating in Philip Miller's *The Gardeners' Dictionary* in 1731. The whole tradition of English gardening had come via France and Holland from Italy and perhaps Spain and Portugal; its evolution can well be called horticulture, the cultivating of the garden in its greatest developments. Its materials had been trees, evergreen bushes, grass, gravel and water, strictly governed and controlled. In spite of its lengthy vistas, the eye was controlled and the whole was prescribed. The imposing of man's will upon the landscape was autocratic: everything was bent to that will. But the transformation that came about was due to a more democratic and liberal outlook, not the less favoured because of its contrast to the autocracy of France.

The change in taste that took place in the 18th century still owed its beauties to the same materials but evergreens were in the main exchanged for buildings of various kinds and the views, though still controlled, and still to be apparently limitless, were wide and embraced as much of the landscape as possible. This transformation was due to a number of factors. Travellers, painters, writers, all had their influence and once again the impact came from Italy. In spite of the perfection attained with the formal style, within a quarter of a century estate owners were happy to contemplate obliteration of the avenues and alleys, straight paths and formal waters, and the adoption of sinuous walks and meandering streams. One can picture the dismay of the garden staff at exchanging the carefully-kept parterres for a stretch of rough grass and a few clumps of native trees which would not create the desired effect during their lifetime.

Garden design had its say. An invention of the French in the previous century, the ditch used as an invisible boundary (impassable by animals), was described by Dezalliers d'Argenville in his book *La Théorie et la Pratique du Jardinage*, written in 1709. This was used by Bridgeman and others to provide a boundary, and the surprised "Ah, ha" of the visitor became the ha-ha of later times. This one feature made possible the whole idea of expansive 18th-century gardening. In early days in walled gardens a vista along a great gravel walk would terminate in a metal grille or *clairvoyée* – as at HAM HOUSE – but sometimes a ditch just beyond the wall would take the place of a grille. An example, probably early, is at BLICKLING HALL; it is a wide ditch with sloping sides and a hedge at the bottom; a later example of the same shape, but with a wall at the bottom is at MELFORD HALL. Both of these are however the result of making a raised walk and are not true ha-has. Another is at MONTACUTE. The real 18th-century ha-has consist of a ditch, walled on the garden side, as at CROFT CASTLE, BERRINGTON HALL, HARDWICK HALL, BENINGBROUGH HALL, CHARLECOTE PARK and CLAYDON; some of recent construction by the Trust are those at SALTRAM, KILLERTON, TRELISSICK and LACOCK ABBEY.

Forestry, or perhaps we should call it in this instance the growing of trees, also had its say. It is difficult to visualise the primeval state of England, so little of it remains. Even such comparatively unaltered areas such as DANBURY COMMON, HATFIELD FOREST and CHARNWOOD FOREST are not entirely in nature's care, although the Trust looks after them with a light rein. Even WICKEN FEN, that delight of the naturalists, has to be cropped and maintained and the water kept at a high level artificially. Elsewhere we have been felling trees since the first Briton cut down a bush to burn.

From those early days man took the easy way of procuring timber, i.e. by using the smaller trees. It required very great expertise to fell a really large tree, to say nothing of reducing it by manual process into sawn lengths. Fortunately oak, ash, sweet chestnut, elm and lime all grow again from the stumps and over the centuries a programme of coppicing produced the bulk of the timber needed for building, furniture, firewood, posts, gates and fences, and carts and wagons. Only great houses, churches, cathedrals and ships demanded the use of big timber. John Evelyn was the first to write about the gradual depletion of big timber and he sought to get people to plant more trees. Even so, the country produced practically all its own timber, apart from fir stems for the masts of ships, until the great expansion of shipping in the 19th century. The clearing of woodland for food production was gradual and went hand in hand with the coppicing of woods. Large areas had long been set aside for the chase, and it was these which formed the royal forests and later gave rise to the parks – sometimes quite small – surrounding country houses. Since animals would have prevented re-growth of tree stumps, in these areas pollarding instead of coppicing was resorted to, so that the new growth would be out of their reach. Old beech pollards are to be seen in Savernake Forest, while pollarded willows are a common sight along streams.

Be it remembered, that English *gardening* is the purposed perfectioning of niggard *Nature* and that without it England is but a hedge-and-ditch, double-post-and-rail, Hounslow-heath and Clapham-common sort of a country, since the principal forests have been felled.

Thomas Moore, 1830

THE INSPIRATION

IN THE 17TH CENTURY the houses of the great were usually placed near to a town or village; later, and particularly during the 18th century, positions were chosen well away from the common herd, on an eminence in beautiful surroundings. There was a need therefore to embellish "parks" with trees, and for the means to exclude animals without spoiling an extensive view with the line of a hedge or fence. So the stage was set for the transformation scene.

Once again the inspiration came from the Continent. The intelligentsia took journeys – the Grand Tour – mostly to Rome and Greece, and were followed by many a scion of noble

21 At Anglesey Abbey hangs this picture by Claude Lorraine, painted in 1663, of the Father of Psyche sacrificing at the Temple of Apollo. It was this kind of idyllic landscape that inspired English garden landscape designers a hundred years later.

family. The beauty of the countryside impressed them; though their first glimpses of the Alps may have overawed them, on their return journey they perhaps drank in their beauty. Thereafter the horrors of untamed countryside were no longer avoided. A hundred years earlier the French artists Claude and Gaspar Poussin had immortalised the soft beauties of the Roman Campagna, with its interesting classical ruins, while Salvator Rosa had depicted nature in all her ferocity. Their paintings impressed the English travellers who purchased them eagerly and brought them home.

Having inherited a great house and formal garden, or having built a new house on a beautiful site, one had to do something with it; something which would impress one's visitors. And if this new scheme should take less labour in upkeep than a great formal garden and so release cash for the indulgence of one's whims, so much the better. Having already, perhaps, indulged one's whims on the architecture of the house, there would be fresh opportunities in erecting fancy garden buildings.

The above outlines a few of the more practical matters, but the heart of the matter was not practical but aesthetic in every way. In previous decades the writers about gardening had been practical in approach, recording what they had seen. Now for the first time the art of gardening was to be swayed by literary experts. Joseph Addison and Richard Steele were the first noted agitators, followed by Alexander Pope and William Shenstone, both of whom practised what they preached in their own gardens, the former at Twickenham and the latter at The Leasowes, near Birmingham. Shenstone is said to have invented the term "landscape gardener"; it is interesting to note that it derived directly from landscape painting. Bacon, in his essay *On Gardens*, a hundred or more years earlier had expressed a preference for a more naturalistic outlook. He had been scarcely heeded. William Mason in his *The English Garden* wrote: "I had before called Bacon the prophet, and Milton the herald, of true taste in Gardening (on account of their introducing 'natural wildness'). I here call Addison, Pope, Kent, etc., the champions of this free taste, because they absolutely brought it into execution." Spenser as well as Milton among poets had stressed the beauties of nature; now Addison ("We see the marks of the Scissars upon every Plant and Bush"), and particularly Steele, poured ridicule on the stiff formality of gardening.

Taste did not change at once. Long straight walks were still laid out, though they were mostly in arbitrary, not geometric, patterns. In the early part of the 18th century Charles Bridgeman was designing garden landscapes, and the intervening areas between his long rides were filled with spinneys with meandering walks through them. These were closely related to the wildernesses of formal outline of the previous century.

THE CLASSICAL INFLUENCE

THOUGH THERE WERE many imitators, the Georgian period was spanned almost completely by three famous designers, William Kent, Lancelot – "Capability" – Brown and Humphry Repton. Lord Burlington did much to lead the new fashion.

Kent's most famous work extant is at Rousham, Oxfordshire. Anything farther removed from Jacobean formality could hardly be conceived; in addition to being almost totally informal it carries with it classical overtones. In fact all these early gardens were meant to appeal to those well-versed in classical learning. They took as much understanding as their counterparts in Japan.

It is a simple matter to plant trees in straight lines for avenues or in quincunxes, but informal grouping will test the sensitivities of the most experienced planter, and the smaller the groups the more difficult they are to place.

At CLAREMONT, Vanbrugh built a great house (later demolished) and the Belvedere, *c.*1715, which dominates the hill above the present house and the garden landscape. The Belvedere represents the first essay in mock-mediaeval building and thus links with follies both Gothick and otherwise. To Bridgeman is attributed the remarkable Amphitheatre, a vast complex of turf slopes, and the original formal, circular lake. This was transformed into a natural-looking sheet of water by Kent, who also built the Island Pavilion. Bridgeman and Kent were still using something of the gardeners' art, as opposed to that of the poet, but Pope's well-known lines express the spirit of the *avant garde* at the time:

To build, to plant, whatever you intend,
To rear the column, or to arch the bend,
To well the terrase, or to sink the Grot;
In all let nature *never be forgot . . .*

He gains all points who pleasingly confounds,
Surprizes, varies, and conceals the Bounds.
Consult the genius of the place in all;
That tells the waters, or to rise, or fall;
Or helps th' ambitious hill the heav'n to scale,
Or scoops in circling Theatres the vale,

Calls in the country, catches open glades,
Joins willing woods, and varies shades with shades,
Now breaks, or now directs, th' intending Lines,
Paints as you plant, and as you work, designs.

Kent's and Pope's aims were to create a classical paradise and I think we may say that nobody arrived nearer to their ideals than Henry Hoare.

It is a very wonderful thing that, in that century of great landscape designers, the creator of the Virgilian landscape at STOURHEAD relied very greatly on his own ability. Hoare dammed a stream joining some small pools to make a chain of lakes, four of which, and one in particular, form the central feature of the artificial landscape. From 1741–65, he built the bridge, three classical temples, the Grotto and the Rock Arch, all of which were to be seen in progressing round the lake, one at a time, as one walked from light to shade, from gloom to shine. Classical allusions were at every turn. The Rock Arch, like the Grotto at CLAREMONT, is seen against the prevailing light in true Claudian tradition.

Classical buildings were also being erected in another great layout of the period, WEST WYCOMBE PARK. The various temples, including the Temple of Music which is so beautifully reflected in the lake, are in a setting of wooded or open landscape by Thomas Cook, a pupil of Brown's. Other great houses being built were NOSTELL PRIORY, 1733, and its bridge and lake, 1759; CLANDON, 1735, and FLORENCE COURT, *c.*1758.

22 F. Nicholson's watercolour of the prospect from the present entrance at Stourhead, 1813–14. It shews the stone bridge, the Pantheon and the Temple of Apollo (left).

The kitchen garden had become very much parted from the landscape and, to provide shelter for crops and fruit trees, great walled enclosures were being built, although it is worth noting that as long ago as Henry VIII's reign, the walls surrounding the productive area of the garden at Nonsuch had been up to 4.2 m (14 ft) high. Sir Walter Blackett built the great portico wall at WALLINGTON HALL, *c.*1735, of a similar height, to keep the cold winds out of his garden which later became woodland. Walled gardens are in many of the Trust's properties including TRENGWAINTON, where, even in Cornwall's mild climate, special sloping beds were constructed to catch all the sun's warmth.

Running concurrently with the classical taste in buildings but developing rather later were the Chinese (chinoiserie) and the Gothick – not to be confused with the original European Gothic.

CHINESE INFLUENCE

THE TASTE FOR the Chinese had as its protagonist Sir William Chambers, the architect who built the Pagoda at Kew, then the estate of the Duke of Kent. This eastern influence was inevitable. Though plants from Far Cathay had been reaching our gardens via merchants' devious inland routes through the Middle East, European travellers were now astonished to observe for themselves the buildings and gardens perfected by two thousand years of culture in China. The Chinese loved flowers and the quiet required for their contemplation. Their use of tufa rock influenced the construction of grottoes, and this same stone was used in gardens over here. Their use of soft colours, sympathetic shapes and the gradation of both was noted and had its effect in the development of our younger art. In the late 17th century Sir William Temple, in his essay on gardens, called attention to the fact that the Chinese did not favour the planting of trees in straight lines, but preferred groupings on more natural or artful lines. This is a general way of observing how Chinese thought affected ours. Lord Macartney, in his *Journal*, recording his ambassadorial visit to China in 1793, mentions that the summer residence of the Chinese Emperor at Jehol was "a charming place" which might have given Capability Brown happy ideas; the buildings, he claimed, did much to "aid, improve and enliven the prospect".

The Chinese taste in gardening and art was popular for a brief period in the middle of the century and is superbly exemplified by Luke Lightfoot's fantastic carving in CLAYDON HOUSE. It is echoed in old wallpapers, notably at SALTRAM HOUSE and POWIS CASTLE, and also in some garden furniture such as the Chippendale-style garden seat at WALLINGTON which stands by the China Pond. This traditional Chinese pattern of woodwork was no doubt fostered in a country where the bamboo – which does not lend itself to carving – was the main structural timber. In the Trust's gardens it is mainly found in the Chinese House at SHUGBOROUGH; it was built about 1747. The interior is beautifully decorated. The little building – standing on a mound as was recommended for such pavilions – has as a complement a lacquer-red bridge. The present one is however a Victorian cast-iron effort which replaced the original. (The noted English example of a Chinese-style garden is at Biddulph Grange, Staffordshire, but this was not laid out till 1850.)

GOTHICK TASTE

BY CONTRAST, THE GOTHICK had come to stay. One of its earliest appearances (1720) is at Shotover Park, Oxfordshire, in the final and delightful building at the end of a long canal. Later Gothick within the Trust's gardens is found in the Octagon and the Summerhouse (1788) on the terrace at CLEVEDON COURT. At SALTRAM HOUSE a long terrace and ha-ha,

23 The Temple of Flora built at Stourhead *c.*1745 framed by one of the many fine Tulip Trees, in 1955.

24 The Gothick curtain wall, *c.*1790, at Croft Castle is decorated by *Rosa brunonii* 'La Mortola' and *R. filipes* 'Kiftsgate'. Photo 1964.

extending almost from the house directly westwards a few feet away from the present avenue of limes, led to the little Gothick "Castle" built in 1772; across the lawn is the Gothick Chapel of 1776 and a classical Orangery, 1775. There is a small Gothick summer house of split flints at MOTTISFONT, and a small pretty building covered with shells in HATFIELD FOREST. Reflected magically in the lake, the house at SHEFFIELD PARK – originally called Sheffield Place – was assuming its craggy array of architectural delights in 1775, by which date the Gothicisms of Sanderson Miller at LACOCK ABBEY and WIMPOLE HALL were complete. At CASTLE WARD we have an interesting example of a difference of opinion between husband and wife, and as a consequence one side of the house is classical and the other the new-fangled Gothick, both inside and out.

THE ENGLISH LANDSCAPE GARDEN

THE ENGLISH LANDSCAPE GARDEN may be said to have arrived in its broadest sense after 1750. In the following year Capability Brown started on his lucrative, busy, and influential career as a designer of landscapes and houses. In spite of the fact that he had had early training as a gardener, by degrees he left gardening severely alone, banishing the flowers, fruits and other plants to separate walled gardens, often far away from the house.

Possibly Kent erased a few of the great formal gardens but his follower, Brown, was a philistine if one looks at it in that way. He had no respect for – even an abhorrence of – the straight line, and far from exaggerating nature to educe the most from her various moods and topographical aberrations, he converted her to a suave and repetitious formula of gently undulating grass, lakes and widened rivers of serpentine outline, and played mightily on Kent's theme of trees in clumps. Indeed, compared with what was to follow, his landscaped parks might even merit the word "formal". Further, by seeking to set the house in limitless parkland, with apparently no garden, he had little use for the ha-ha, and rough-grazing by cattle, sheep or deer ranged up to the windows. The clumps of trees had to be fenced; otherwise the "gardening" was done by animals. What a saving in labour! – and how economical and productive! Yet the separate walled gardens filled with fruit, vegetables and flowers, the most extravagant of all styles of gardening as far as labour is concerned, were now coming into their own.

A small neat Garden claims to be preferrd
To those of larger Size with Shabby Mien,
Where nothing but disorder can be seen.

But every Beauty ceases when compard
With what we in the fragrant Orchard find.

The Garden Plots can never fail to please
Which most abound with sweet and fragrant flowers,
Where all the Fountains are with Torrents fed,
And all the Walls with painted Fruits are clad.

Sir John Clerk of Penicuik, 1731

With the transformation of the fashionable garden into a controlled landscape, the flower, vegetable and fruit garden became a necessary adjunct. It was pleasant, even in less favourable weather, to walk in a kitchen garden, or a great parterre, but for the landscape garden good weather was essential.

Brown at least turned many infertile areas into profitable parkland. Everything was overcome by this plausible, twinkly-eyed expert. Most of his clients were content to see vast transformations and apparently had so much faith in his powers that he could persuade them to alter rivers, pipe ditches, move roads and villages, all in order to plant many hundreds of thousands of trees – in many more than a hundred estates – which would not give the effect desired for well over fifty years. What faith they had, and how safe seemed their world!

In his own way Brown was a great "planner" and operating as he did while that other great planning operation was going on – the Enclosures – his work was fortuitously made the easier by the amalgamation of the farming areas into greater units, while his desire for grass, more and more grass, was linked with improved farming. Some of the most beautiful stretches of parkland in the country are of his contrivance, for instance at PETWORTH HOUSE. His clumps of trees, and those of Repton's and later developers of the landscape, were not only the outcome of artistry, but fostered fox-hunting by providing cover in areas enclosed and under cultivation.

Brown was not allowed his own way everywhere, however; although he did not fell the old avenues at CHARLECOTE, his treatment of the park at that property in 1760 is highly successful. He adjusted Kent's CLAREMONT, but fortunately left Bridgeman's Amphitheatre intact. He laid out at least the two lowest lakes at SHEFFIELD PARK, where already were growing ancient Sweet Chestnuts and English Oaks which still astonish by their mighty girth. The fact that the terrain at POWIS CASTLE was so steep and "incapable" may have saved these noble terraces from Brown and the other designers of his time.

The beech was Brown's favourite tree. He must have been instrumental in planting many tens of thousands, interspersed on some soils with oak. It is an interesting thought that the most recent geologically of our native trees, the beech, has only been common in Britain for some three thousand years. Brown's choice increased its standing. The rounded graceful outline of the beech, merging so well into small clumps or vast woodlands, presented just the outline needed for Brown's new England. In a guide to Burghley House in 1797 it was stated that "Brown's efforts are indistinguishable from Nature"!

Rather later in reaching these shores were the Spanish or Sweet Chestnut and the Sycamore. The former was popular in creating artificial woodland; the latter was probably not chosen for planting but, being so prolific of seed, infiltrated into most woodlands and uncultivated ground. Owing to its hardiness and capability of withstanding gales of all sorts it has established itself all over these islands, though it is scarce in Northern Ireland. A superb tree when well grown, it has proved most useful in giving shelter to dwellings in windswept uplands like HARDWICK HALL, or near the coast, like FELBRIGG, and in this way has undoubtedly been of great consequence in enriching the landscape.

And so, having spent a thousand or more years gradually denuding the countryside, trees by the many thousands were planted by land-owners, partly for ornament, but also for the good husbandry advocated by John Evelyn a hundred years previously. His trees came in most usefully for building the great ships of the Navy in the wars with Napoleon. The meandering hedgerows of the older, cropped countryside grew firewood for the peasants; with the Enclosures Act a great planting of hedgerow trees, including elm, took place. Thus have ash, elm and oak been preserved in our farming land until recently.

There is no doubt that Brown created much of what we know and admire today as typical English landscape. Those rather neat clumps have opened out and their edges have softened; the old trees lean and look like original patriarchs of the countryside. The sloping land leads from the dwelling to the placid lake; he so placed BERRINGTON HALL in 1780, its splendid portico looking away over the contrived natural landscape to the hills of the CROFT CASTLE estate.

While STOURHEAD and SHEFFIELD PARK have been given a fresh coat of paint, so to speak, from time to time, in the shape of exotic trees and rhododendrons, the landscape design at FARNBOROUGH HALL remains almost as it was intended; it was probably designed by Sanderson Miller in the third quarter of the 18th century. It is a particularly interesting landscape in that it largely consists of what is in effect a terrace walk, harking back to the days of formality – except that it is an informal walk. From the house it leads gently upwards in a great and gentle curve, with temples at halting points and an obelisk at the top. The terrace commands views over a chain of lakes and away to Edgehill. A somewhat similar terrace of grass was started much earlier at POLESDEN LACEY, and extended and improved by Sheridan in 1797. Both terraces are protected from the north by belts of beeches. Another great terrace-garden was laid out in Yorkshire, on the escarpment above RIEVAULX ABBEY.

Brown's influence was extensive and continuing. Humphry Repton, after studying gardening, botany and drawing, first set himself up as an architect but later as a landscape gardener – the first who adopted this term – in 1788. Living at Aylsham, Norfolk, he had already met William Windham of FELBRIGG, and had access to his library. It seems to me that while Brown had mainly looked out from the house to his landscapes, Repton thought more of the setting of the house. His famous Red Books, in which he displayed sketches of properties with superimposed flaps shewing his suggested improvements, reveal him as an artist-gardener. Nowhere is this better demonstrated than at PLAS NEWYDD. He realised the fundamental difference of looking at a picture and creating a landscape garden, beautiful from many view-points. He continued the idea of consulting the "genius of the place" and hiding boundaries, and thought that the various offices, walled gardens and the like should be concealed, but not placed at inconvenient distances from the house. He also liked the house to have a terrace or formal area in front of it, and had no use for rough grass extending to the very walls; he planted some avenues and thought that certain parts of the garden should take specialised planting – such as roses, alpines, American plants and the like.

Particularly he had a feeling for the use of plants, and a knowledge of their appropriateness to complement different architectural styles and the sense of light and shade; for example, avoiding the use of conical trees near Gothick buildings. Perhaps he had read and appreciated John Dyer's words:

Below me trees unnumber'd rise,
Beautiful in various Dies:
The gloomy Pine, the Poplar blue,
The yellow Beech, the sable Yew,
The slender Firr, that taper grows,
The sturdy Oak with broad-spread Boughes . . .

Repton brought with his artist's eye the use and fitness of contrast of texture, and used oaks, hollies, thorns, sycamores and other trees as a relief from Brown's preference for beech and oak trees. Though sympathetic to the protagonists of the Picturesque, derived from the application of the landscape painters' art to the art of garden and landscape design, he remained an individual with individual tastes. He also had a care for the modest flowers. He was thus the originator of the style of gardening which was to extend with modifications to the present day.

Sir Uvedale Price, one of Repton's critics, was one of the first to advocate the planting of rhododendrons together with other evergreens in the landscape. This was a turning point and from it stem the hundreds of acres of Cherry Laurel and Pontic Rhododendron in so many of our great landscape gardens – STOURHEAD, CLUMBER PARK, CLAREMONT and TATTON PARK among them. Evergreens were much prized – as they were in the previous century. Gradually new kinds were introduced and distributed. In *The Spectator*, in 1717, Addison posed the desirability and possibility of having a garden devoted entirely to native and exotic evergreens. We can well understand such a desire, when we remember that our only native evergreens were yew, holly, box and ivy, and the juniper and pine.

Many of the clumps of trees in the drive from the Knutsford entrance at TATTON PARK are of Repton's placing. This splendid approach to the house took the place of the straight avenue of beeches within the garden, which he asked to be varied by felling certain trees. He probably planted the splendid double avenue from the Rostherne gate.

At ATTINGHAM in 1797 he made alterations to the line of the river and enlarged it, incorporating the old bridge over the Tern into his scheme, and designing woodlands and great clumps of trees to accentuate the gently undulating land. Similar work was started at ANTONY in 1804, while at UPPARK, with its commanding view away to the distant sea from the top of the chalk downs, he left his mark on house and garden. The terraces to the south were largely obliterated but were in part brought back into the scheme of things by the Trust in 1973–4; the Gothick summerhouse, the mount and the dairy may well be of his design or placing. An intriguing underground passage with ventilation shafts and grilles connects his game-larder to the kitchen allowing the servants access out of sight from the front portico. Something of the same sort occurs at GAWTHORPE HALL and CLIVEDEN.

As if there were not enough architectural styles already in use – the mediaeval and Gothic, the classic, Chinese and Gothick – Repton sought to bring in the Indian, inspired by Sir Charles Cockerell and his son. The Indian-style mosque-like building of Sezincote stands above the meadows which slope down to a lake and woods, and with the Thornery – a water garden of intriguing beauty whose great rocks remain as placed in 1805 – is one of the highlights of English gardening. It may have been devised by Repton.

Beautiful garden buildings were rising all over the country. The temples and the bridge at CLUMBER PARK, the orangery and other delights in the garden at TATTON; the Temple of the Winds at MOUNT STEWART; the bow-fronted garden house at OSTERLEY PARK, the orangeries at Heveningham and at LYME PARK; the CLANDON PARK grotto and, later, the orangery at BLICKLING and also the mile-long lake in the park.

THE PICTURESQUE

MEN OF LETTERS who had swayed taste in the early part of the century had their counterparts towards the end of it when Richard Payne Knight and Sir Uvedale Price tried to lead the trend still more towards the Picturesque style. They were somewhat thwarted by the non-compliance of Repton's own more horticultural thoughts. Nevertheless the Picturesque did exert a considerable sway. It is here that we may more legitimately recall Bacon's "heath" and the later wilderness for they are connected by the desire to emulate nature, and her excesses in particular. The terrors of the wild landscape, far from being inhibiting, were now being enjoyed by travellers who had a safe home to return to, and artists and poets were extolling the "awfulness" of crags and precipices, stupendous waterfalls, immense crooked old trees, and noble ruins.

There the Scottish fir
In murky file lifts his inglorious head,
And blots the fair horizon. So should art
Improve thy pencil's savage dignity
SALVATOR! *if where, far as eye can pierce,*
Rock pil'd on rock . . .

William Mason, from *The English Garden*, 1782

To the Picturesque is owed the splendid waterfall and grotto at Bowood, Wiltshire; the grotto and rock arch at STOURHEAD; the Grotto at CLAREMONT, and the Sanderson Miller ruin at WIMPOLE HALL. The grass terrace at RIEVAULX, with its two classical temples, had been made on the high escarpment so that one could look down on the ruins of the Abbey below, and away to a wonderful stretch of country. The layout at CRAGSIDE may be considered as a late example. Grottoes had an influence later on rock gardens. Repton was an advocate of rustic woodwork, and in this vein we can recall the Bear House near the quarry garden at KILLERTON and the rustic summerhouse at MOTTISFONT, and many more immortalised in print and photographs but which could not stand the ravages of the weather. One of Repton's most noted landscapes is at Endsleigh, Devon, complete with shell house and grotto, but also a formal terrace, which was laid out in the early 19th century.

One notable exponent of the true Picturesque took up landscape advice in 1820 after Repton's death. He was William Sawrey Gilpin, an artist by nature and training. Though in date he extends into the Victorian era his taste was of the 18th century and so I include him here. To him we owe an important feature of the landscape at CLUMBER PARK, which was laid out by Brown with later touches by Repton. Gilpin added the Lincoln Terrace extending eastwards from the house, for he subscribed to the idea of a firm architectural foreground to a dwelling. He also put this idea into practice at SUDBURY HALL where his terraces remain, while at SCOTNEY CASTLE his recommendations by letter caused the owner to develop the garden along Picturesque lines. The view from the upper garden includes the old castle and dwelling surrounded by a moat. It is one of the earliest examples of a nearly-ruined building being restored somewhat in order to retain it as an eye-catcher; so many others were deliberately built to represent ruins. One hears little of this sort of thing before 1760. The composition of the picture at SCOTNEY contains all that the most ardent devotee

25 Sanderson Miller executed this sketch of his proposed Gothic Folly for Wimpole Hall in the early 18th century; it was built later in the century and looks much the same today.

of the Picturesque could desire, including the sombre contrast of dark pines against deciduous trees, and the horizontal line of an old cedar in the distance. By this date cedars and Holm Oaks had been taken to heart by the great landowners, until today we accept them as typically English. By contrast the two other foreign trees with an equal influence, the Lombardy Poplar and the Wellingtonia, are often upsetting in the landscape. Gilpin, however, saw in the hardy Lombardy Poplar and Scots Pine the nearest substitutes for the tender Claudian cypress and Stone Pine. Until the arrival in the middle of the 19th century of the columnar cypresses and the like from North America, the Lombardy Poplar was the only fastigiate tree which could be relied upon to create the vertical line of the tender Italian Cypress.

These 18th-century exponents of the Picturesque had their opposite number in John Sutherland in Northern Ireland. He laid out the park at DERRYMORE HOUSE, where he made play with light and shade in the Reptonian tradition. "The very fine improvements of Derrymore show the correct and elegant taste of Mr. Sutherland, who planned them and supervised their execution. The young plantations already display a fine appearance of wood; the approaches are extremely well planned, and the cottage, which is as yet the only residence, is without exception the most elegant summer lodge I have ever seen." This impression of Sutherland's taste and skill is in Sir Charles Coote's survey of Co. Armagh written in 1804, some twenty-five years after planting.

Even by 1770, Thomas Whateley had realised what had happened: "Gardening, in the perfection to which it has been lately brought in England, is entitled to a place of considerable rank among the liberal arts. It is as superior to landskip-painting as a reality to a representation. . . . Nature, always simple, employs but four materials in the composition of her scenes, *ground*, *wood*, *water* and *rocks*. The cultivation of nature has introduced a fifth species, the *buildings* requisite for the accommodation of men."

ALTHOUGH GREAT DESIGNERS continued to lay out gardens in the grand scale, the English Landscape Garden may be said to finish, very conveniently, with the coronation of Queen Victoria, and tradition gave place to change in all things. But for the first time the steady advancement of landscape gardening had become something for the artist-gardener to marvel at; moreover, though we had for so long been importing ideas from the Continent, for the first time the waves surged back and the Jardin Anglais engulfed the gardens of Europe. France, Germany and Russia in particular accepted this new style and many imitations were made. Most of them were fashionable copies, without the overtones which they were originally intended to convey. English taste in garden art had made itself felt for the first time; in my opinion it was to recur again later. Meanwhile the compass and set square were brought into use again, and plants – that great collection of delights which had been preserved in cottage gardens and in the great walled kitchen gardens for nearly two hundred years – were brought into the open once more, for the embellishment of the immediate surrounds of the home, much augmented by numerous arrivals from far countries.

TREES AND SHRUBS

THE TREES INTRODUCED in the previous century were by now more plentiful and were being planted freely. Numerous nurserymen started in business and the trade was considerable, both among native trees and some of the conifers and other exotics from Europe and North America. From 1747 dates the Ilex Grove at CLIVEDEN, and perhaps some Lebanon cedars through the country. In addition to planting, use was made of existing woods, as at CLIVEDEN, where rides were cut through them to chalk escarpments and viewpoints.

Under cover, in the orangeries and frames, what to us are old favourites were beginning to become known, such as the florists' cyclamen (1731); the arum (*Zantedeschia aethiopica*) from South Africa (1731); the *Gloxinia* (1731) and the *Dahlia* (1789) both from South America, and the *Cineraria* (*Senecio cruentus*) from the Canary Isles (1777). A number of plants subsequently used for bedding had arrived but I will leave these until the next chapter. Early in the 18th century the large-fruited strawberry arrived from South America and in time gave rise to our modern strains.

Our garden rhododendrons and roses stem mainly from species introduced during the 18th and early 19th centuries. For instance the ubiquitous *Rhododendron ponticum* had arrived by 1763; it was joined by *R. luteum* (*Azalea pontica*) in 1793 and thereafter a constant stream of species important in later hybrids was introduced: *R. caucasicum*, 1803, *R. calendulaceum*, 1806, *R. catawbiense*, 1809 and *R. arboreum*, 1815. These and their hybrids form the backbone of many a shrub garden today. The genuine *R. arboreum* may be seen at NYMANS, KILLERTON, WAKEHURST, TRELISSICK, TRENGWAINTON, MOUNT STEWART and ROWALLANE, raised from seeds collected in the wild. They form rather narrow dense trees with one or a few erect trunks and achieve 7.6–12.1 m (25–40 ft) in height. Hybrids are more common, and these, variously ascribed to "Russellianum" or "Altaclarense", are very often of great size, much broader than high, forming luxuriant mounds. It is these hybrids which are so dominant in the garden landscape at FLORENCE COURT, and also at KILLERTON, STOURHEAD and LANHYDROCK. They are the largest of evergreen shrubs for the warmer parts of Britain and have become naturalised.

The original four hybrids of the China Rose arrived around 1800 and became absorbed during the next seventy years into the European strain. *Rosa chinensis*, one of the parents, has never been introduced to cultivation; the other, *R. gigantea*, is tender but grows at MOUNT STEWART. The hybrids were: "Slater's Crimson China" (1792) which provided true dark crimson colouring; "Parson's Pink China" (1793) which we now call "Old Blush"; "Hume's Blush Tea-scented China" (1809) and "Parks's Yellow Tea-scented China" (1824) both of which seem to be extinct in these islands; the last two provided, from *R. gigantea*, the long petals of modern roses, and also the delicate tea-scent. These roses have had more influence on garden design than any other foreign flowering plants. Likewise, *Magnolia denudata*, 1789, *Camellia japonica*, 1739, and the *Hydrangea*, late 18th century, have become mainstays of our gardens.

Some important trees were brought in too, such as the Weeping Willow (*Salix babylonica*), *c.*1730, the Tree of Heaven (*Ailanthus altissima*) 1751, the Purple or Copper Beech (*Fagus sylvatica* "Purpurea"), known on the Continent since 1680, and *Quercus coccinea*, 1691, and *Q. rubra*, 1724, the two splendid autumn-colouring American species. Also from America came *Magnolia grandiflora* in 1734, so often grown against the walls of our great houses.

Turning to herbaceous plants, the foundations for future popularity, selection and hybridising were laid in some North American species: *Helenium autumnale*, 1729, *Phlox paniculata*, 1730, *Monarda didyma*, 1744, and *Gypsophila paniculata*, 1759.

Those interested in plants must have been thrilled to see all these new arrivals and to hear accounts of them from their discoverers. Contrary to what might be thought, Richard Colt Hoare at STOURHEAD was "taken" by them and started planting exotics, including species of birch, maple, thorn, ash and oak from North America; he added variegated hollies, junipers, and phillyreas, almonds and cherries, without respect for the planting of his uncle. His additions at the end of the 18th century have today mostly disappeared, but his taste indicated what was to follow all over the country in the next century.

This wealth of new plants was welcomed by many of the influential writers and planters, Shenstone, Uvedale Price and Colt Hoare among them. It was criticised by others and in particular Chevalier Charles Sckell of Bavaria, who wrote in 1833 that "the palette of the landscape-painter . . . is now loaded with such a mass of colours and tints, that his means are super-abundant". He found some English gardens "a real chaos of unconnected beauties". There is no doubt he was right; this collecting spirit has been the downfall of the British garden, as much as, botanically, it has made them famous.

Paradise, and groves
Elysian, Fortunate Fields – like those of old
Sought in the Atlantic Main – why should they be
A history only of departed things,
Or a mere fiction of what never was?
For the discerning intellect of Man,
When wedded to this goodly universe
In love and holy passion, shall find these
A simple produce of the common day.

William Wordsworth, from *The Recluse*

6

THE VICTORIAN ERA ONWARDS

> Geometrical gardens of a deplorable type are things of our own time . . . Moreover, on top of all this formality of design . . . were grafted the most formal and inartistic ways of arranging flowers that ever came into the head of man . . . "bedding out" and "carpet" gardening is simply a further remove in ugliness. The painted gravel gardens of Nesfield and Barry . . . were an attempt to get rid of the flowers and get rigid patterns instead.
>
> William Robinson, from *The English Flower Garden*, 1883

MANY THINGS CONTRIBUTED TO THE COMPLETE CHANGE in gardening fashions after the death of Repton and Gilpin. What we might call the absolutism of Brown had given way to Repton's more enlightened appreciation of gardening as a whole, the most important fundamental being the return to some formality around the house. This is the one thing which has remained with us ever since and is the basis on which most modern garden design rests. From the grand landscape the informal part of the garden gave way to an introduction of specimen trees and shrubs on the lawns extending from the formal terrace and borders. Throughout English gardens much of this has been swept away, partly because of the difficulty of upkeep, but traces of it remain at KILLERTON, ARLINGTON COURT, BLICKLING HALL, LANHYDROCK, PENRHYN CASTLE, ASCOTT, WADDESDON, TATTON PARK and DUNHAM MASSEY.

The main reason for this style of planting was because of the huge influx of new trees and shrubs from the temperate parts of the world, but I will leave this matter until later.

Other changes in fashion and taste were due to the greater number of wealthy people about, many of them industrialists who wanted a place in the country where they could impress their friends. The rich were very rich and were able to employ numerous gardeners, who worked long hours. The lawn mower was invented in 1832 and gradually replaced the scythe, and other factory machinery encouraged speedy reproduction of cast-iron seats, vases, greenhouses – in fact almost everything; coal was still cheap and glass plentiful, and as a result greenhouses increased in size and number beyond belief. Every great walled kitchen garden had its range of houses for grapes and peaches, its conservatory and frames, and from them came forth hosts of tender foreign plants for putting in beds on the lawns in summer. The love of plants, well grown and separated from each other, was the desire. From 1836 until the 1914 war the head gardeners dominated their staff – and very often their employers – completely. One likes to think that those powerful head gardeners, with their numerous minions, were able to have jobs done correctly at the correct time – something that we find difficult to achieve today in the garden. For traditional crafts there is always an exactly right time.

26 Begonias and sweet smelling Heliotrope alternate with spring bedding plants in the formal garden at Ascott, backed by variegated shrubs. Photo 1959.

The head gardeners now had much to draw upon. What we call "geraniums" – both the Ivy-leaf and the usual scarlet ones (*Pelargonium peltatum* and *P. zonale* respectively) – had been introduced in the early 18th century; the dwarf blue *Lobelia erinus* in 1752, the yellow *Calceolaria* in 1830, the scarlet *Salvia coccinea* in 1772 and the Dahlia in 1789. Important summer flowers were already in cultivation: the China Aster (*Callistephus hortensis*), *Zinnia elegans*, Mignonette (*Reseda odorata*), the *Gladiolus* and *Verbena*. From California came *Clarkia* and *Godetia*, from the Southern States *Phlox drummondii*. Not only were flowers used to excess in the great bedding schemes; by using tender plants with impressive foliage, a new style originated known as subtropical bedding. Large-leafed cannas or Indian Shot, greenhouse palms and cycads, *Cordyline australis, Eucalyptus globulus, Fatsia japonica* – which is perfectly hardy – were used. This style of gardening is still carried on by municipal authorities in their public parks but very little is seen today in the gardens of the Trust. It is splendidly done at LYME PARK by the Metropolitan Borough of Stockport, and good flower-beds are also found at ASCOTT, NYMANS, LANHYDROCK and a few other gardens. In the main, where beds are still allowed, colour is now provided by roses and other permanencies, for the sake of economy in labour.

It was opportune for the gardeners of the period that the Pampas Grass (*Cortaderia selloana*) was introduced in 1848; it became a favourite for planting – isolated from everything – on lawns both large and tiny. Today one of its most impressive displays is at SHEFFIELD PARK, where it accentuates the autumn colour of trees and shrubs and the dark green of conifers.

FORMAL GARDENING

AFTER THE LONG PERIOD of the English Landscape Garden and the banishment of flowers from the surrounds of the house, garden owners were very ready to welcome them back. Some of the new formality was eclectic, but some of it was nostalgic, a longing for the knot gardens and parterres of earlier centuries. There were many imitations, some truly traditional such as the pretty *Parterre de Compartiment* at OXBURGH HALL (see Chapter 4). Less elaborate but more impressive is the terrace design at WADDESDON, laid out in the late 19th century. These are both designs of beds on gravelled areas, whereas most Victorian designs were of beds arranged in a setting of grass lawn, as at LYME PARK.

Having already built two houses, and the MUSSENDEN TEMPLE in Northern Ireland, the Earl of Bristol, Bishop of Derry, employed Francis Sandys to build ICKWORTH for him. Started in 1790 it was scarcely finished in thirty years. In spite of the date of starting it is

27 In this aerial snow scene, at Cliveden, taken in 1952, looking north, the curving Thames is on the left; the great parterre in the foreground.

appropriate to mention it here, because its garden, presumably laid out at the same time, is an early example of formality after the long period of informal landscapes. Like much of the edifice, the garden has few straight lines, but the compass was freely used.

There were now many architect-designers of gardens and, almost before ICKWORTH was finished, Joseph Paxton had started his schemes at Chatsworth, Derbyshire; the terraces at TATTON PARK are also his, laid out in the mid-19th century.

Sir Charles Barry, the designer of the Shrubland Park and GAWTHORPE HALL gardens, worked for the Duke of Sutherland at CLIVEDEN and it is believed laid out the parterre on the south front, with the aid of the head gardener. The vast scale of the formal parterre (for want of a better word) at CLIVEDEN must make it one of the largest, if not in fact *the* largest, in England today. It is reminiscent of a 17th-century design at HAM HOUSE, which was small and intimate, but to be of any consequence in so extensive a landscape and in front of so huge a terrace and house, the scale had to be vast. ERDDIG received 19th-century embellishments in 1850 and again about 1905; these added considerably to the interest of the garden.

The magnificent formal terraces at KNIGHTHAYES COURT are the work of the architect who designed the house, William Burges; and no doubt in the early days they were the subject of much "in-and-out" gardening, while today their broad simplicity acts as a platform for the house and accentuates the beauty of the landscape sloping away from them. The terraces date from 1863; the yew-hedged bowling green from the 1880s. The terraces at SHUGBOROUGH are post-1850, and a Victorian-style rose garden was laid out by the Staffordshire County Council to the Trust's design in 1966. The terraces at HUGHENDEN date from 1882, while the Walled Garden at PENRHYN CASTLE with its terraces and loggia are somewhat earlier. LANHYDROCK was altered once again; its Jacobean formality was swept away – except the old avenue – in the 18th century, and soon after 1850 the gatehouse was joined by new walls to the house and fresh terraces were designed by Sir George Gilbert Scott. A small formal garden with yew hedges, pool and topiary is at WESTWOOD MANOR, designed by E. G. Lister, and substantial topiary is at GREAT CHALFIELD MANOR.

Unless we look at old pictures we can get little idea of the extravagance and extent of the ornamental gardens of Victoria's reign. At CHARLECOTE, in the forecourt, at WESTBURY COURT, SPEKE HALL and elsewhere there were great formal plantings, beds and borders filled with brilliant flowers for the summer. At BLICKLING HALL only the shaped yews and the big herbaceous squares remain of the much dissected design; the whole area was adjusted in the 1930s by Norah Lindsay. The little formal hedged parterre at LANHYDROCK, with its narrow paths and box edging, remains to us as a charming small example of this style of gardening, while on a larger scale the Dutch garden at LYME PARK – a nice reminder in 1900 of a past fashion – is still in good fettle.

GARDEN BUILDINGS

GARDEN BUILDINGS also underwent a change. Apart from the new greenhouses and conservatories, orangeries in the grand manner were built at LYME PARK, *c.*1820, and at CHARLECOTE PARK, 1858. The DYRHAM orangery, built in 1717, was given a glass roof in the 19th century. One of the saddest things in gardening is that the ancient sunk garden to the north of the house at MONTACUTE, dating from the 17th century, was altered around 1890; it had a mount in its centre but this was taken away and the balustraded pool placed there instead. Though beautiful in itself it is sad to think that, within a garden of that period possessing a raised walk, the mount has not been preserved.

What we may term summerhouses were of very varied styles. Stone and bricks were still used, but wood, either painted or "rustic", with the bark left on, was also in demand.

PECKOVER HOUSE has one of each. The rustic garden house called the Bear's Hut at KILLERTON and the Maori Hut at CLANDON PARK come to mind; thatched shelters at COTEHELE and TATTON PARK – and indeed the graceful Gothick Lady Charlotte's Bower in this last garden. Metalwork is found in the pretty rose pergola at WADDESDON, and also in its splendid and extensive aviary. A long walk at PENRHYN is covered with metal arches of Victorian fashioning, and likewise the rose garden at NYMANS has metal arches; here there is also a raised bed on a lawn, fashioned like a basket, with an arched handle, covered with Winter Jasmine.

Owners have loved through the centuries to alter their houses and gardens. Two interesting examples are the imposing entrance to the orangery at POWIS CASTLE, brought from the front of the castle in 1900, and the peristyle at the end of Sheridan's walk at POLESDEN LACEY which was likewise once at the entrance to the house.

We have little to shew from the craze for ferns which reached such proportions from roughly 1840 to 1860. Special glasshouses complete with rockeries for ferns were made. The orangery at MONTACUTE was added to the 16th-century raised walk in the 19th century, but in Jacobean style; it contains a fern-rockery of tufa moistened by dripping water, and the Maidenhair fern has thrived there for many years. Our only hardy fern collection is at SIZERGH CASTLE, but this did not start until 1926. At TATTON PARK there is a fern-house dating from 1859 which contains Tree Ferns (*Dicksonia antarctica*) specially imported from New Zealand, with various other kinds. A small fernhouse is at PECKOVER HOUSE and a rocky dell is filled with Royal Fern at STANDEN.

Many great walled gardens were brought to a high state of cultivation at this time. These contained all the old well-loved flowers, vegetables and fruits, systematically cropped without the aid of modern contrivances and sprays. This is where the young "improvers" learnt the crafts of digging, hoeing, pruning and tying the hard way.

But it does not do to think only of the great gardens and the gardens of the great. Horticulture was kept alive also by owners of smaller houses and by humble cottage dwellers. The 19th century was to see a remarkable awakening to the beauties of flowers and numerous books were written, specialist societies formed and flower shows organised, particularly in the industrial Midlands and the north. Deprived during the day of light and air, and also deprived of creative and interesting work, miners and factory workers turned to flowers for relief during what little spare time they had. Pinks and auriculas, ranunculuses, gooseberries and other fancies were cultivated to a high degree, ready for their recognition towards the end of the century by William Robinson and Gertrude Jekyll. Many old favourites have been preserved in the gardens now owned by the Trust, such as *Penstemon* 'Rubicunda', raised at LYME PARK in 1906.

Soon will the high Midsummer pomps come on,
Soon will the musk carnations break and swell,
Soon shall we have gold dusted snapdragon,
Sweet William with its homely cottage-smell,
And stocks in fragrant blow;
Roses that down the alleys shine afar,
And open, jasmine-muffled lattices,
And groups under the dreaming garden-trees,
And the full moon, and the white evening-star.

Matthew Arnold, from *Thyrsis*

All the main garden styles – topiary, formal and informal water, grottoes and rockeries,

statuary and garden ornaments – were given free rein; only the vineyards declined and were practically non-existent for a hundred years, thanks to the wines obtainable by cheap transport from the warmer parts of Europe.

28 The aviary at Waddesdon. Late 19th-century construction, restored in recent years by the Trust.

THE GARDENESQUE

J. C. LOUDON INVENTED this term for yet another style of gardening, but it also owes something to Humphry Repton. It is an effort to design a garden to shew off the plants. Something of this style of design exists at ASCOTT and STANDEN. The idea also owes much of its popularity to the genus *Rosa.* When Napoleon's Empress Joséphine started the ever-growing cult of the Rose at her château at Malmaison the design of the garden was entirely new. It had nothing of the knot garden or parterre, nothing of hedged formality, nothing of the great landscape garden. Its paths were straight or curved and threaded through the area so that one passed group after group of plants. At Malmaison the plants were mostly roses. The Rose therefore breaks ground not only as the first genus to have a garden made for it, but also because its climbing varieties created the need for pergolas, arches, pillars and swags. Through the century it ushered in the need for all manner of embellishments, reaching their height of fashion around 1914. Little of this remains in our gardens today, but is echoed in the pergola at POLESDEN LACEY, the treillage on the BODNANT terraces and in the rose garden at SHUGBOROUGH. To the roses were added early in the 19th century the well-known *Clematis montana* and wistarias; these, no less than Veitch's *Ampelopsis*, have transformed many an ugly building or graceful arch into a thing of great beauty.

HARDY EXOTIC PLANTS

FROM THE VERY BEGINNING of our gardening we have hankered after evergreens to enliven gardens in winter. The yew, holly, juniper and box, apart from the Scots Pine, were our only native evergreen shrubs. Many others were imported from warmer countries; some like the Cherry Laurel, *Rhododendron ponticum* and *Phillyrea latifolia* proved to be hardy; others like the Sweet Bay and Myrtle did not. During the 19th century a great transformation was to take place. Innumerable hardy evergreens, both conifers and broad-leafed shrubs, were to be introduced mainly from North America and the Far East. The Douglas Fir, named after its discoverer, was to prove a useful timber tree; a magnificent stand of it is at KNIGHTSHAYES COURT, over one hundred years old, to say nothing of the finest stand in England, at CRAGSIDE. The Monterey Pine and the Monterey Cypress are the mainstays for shelter in coastal gardens; *Abies grandis*, *A. procera*, the Sitka Spruce and *Thuja plicata* are now all common trees of great size. STOURHEAD has fine specimens of the last three. Later the Lawson's Cypress arrived and now, in its many forms, is the commonest conifer in our gardens. As one goes about the country the whereabouts of a great house can often be detected by the conical top of a Wellingtonia, or the flat top of a Redwood. The Wellingtonia, like the Lombardy Poplar, has left its mark in our landscape; particularly good specimens are at SHEFFIELD PARK.

However, most of these tall conical evergreen trees are best while young and perfect. It is not a pleasant sight to see evergreens poking above the skyline of native trees in the English landscape and we do not yet know to what height the Wellingtonias will grow. So long as they remain shapely all is well but another high-growing tree, lauded by John Evelyn, the Silver Fir (*Abies alba* or *A. pectinata*), makes many a great estate unsightly today, for the ugly, scraggy, flattened heads of these trees have reared well above the beeches and oaks. I think these and other coniferous giants are better placed in valleys, as at BODNANT, where they not only grow better, but will not be so likely to upset the skyline in the future.

Evergreens also came from Chile – *Berberis darwinii* and *Escallonia macrantha* for instance, two very popular plants today; from China and Japan *Mahonia japonica* and *Cryptomeria japonica* joined the *Camellia* and bamboos in our gardens. Ever greater numbers of hardy deciduous trees and shrubs arrived too, completely to change the sort of planting as at historic WADDESDON, where every other shrub is a Cherry Laurel and every other tree is a Horse Chestnut. *Buddleia davidii*, *Cornus nuttallii* and *C. kousa*, cotoneasters, viburnums, berberises, *Malus floribunda*, species of *Rosa*, *Parrotia* and hundreds more were propagated by leading nurserymen. A garden of little character at RUFFORD OLD HALL has been improved and given interest simply by the addition of exotic shrubs and plants; the same may be said about ARDRESS, BENINGBROUGH HALL, FENTON HOUSE and PLAS-YN-RHIW. French nurserymen were to the fore in hybridising and selecting new flowering shrubs and were the greatest raisers of garden roses as will be seen by the names in our garden of old roses at MOTTISFONT. The 19th century saw a great increase in new varieties. True to gardening tradition, the Victorians treasured any abnormality in plants; trees and shrubs with foliage other than green became popular, particularly evergreens. ASCOTT is a noted example and at BENINGBROUGH HALL grows a fine Variegated Oak, planted by the Duke of Cambridge in 1898.

As for rhododendrons, both hemispheres contributed, particularly the Far East, and a constant stream of species, deciduous and evergreen, dwarf and tall, arrived mostly as seed collected in the wild over a period of about a hundred years. Some of the fruits of these plant-hunting expeditions by hard-working commissioned botanists and gardeners are to be found at KILLERTON, NYMANS, WAKEHURST and TRENGWAINTON.

Since many of these trees and shrubs came from North America, and preferred lime-free soil – such as rhododendrons, kalmias, andromedas (*Pieris*), species of *Vaccinium*, *Enkianthus* and many lesser genera – they were frequently planted in an area known as the American Garden, and this title remains to this day at BENINGBROUGH HALL, though poorly represented, and indeed in a few nurserymen's catalogues of the less up-to-date class.

The cult of the rhododendron brought about numerous woodland gardens, particularly in the west from Cornwall to the north of Scotland, and on Anglesey, where PLAS NEWYDD is a noted example. Rhododendrons are impressive in flower, easy to grow if the conditions are right and in particular gave the master of the house an outlet for gardening in a big way, completely apart from the garden proper. In general the influence of the rhododendron was bad upon garden design; they were usually planted to excess and without due regard to their eventual size. Examples are at TRELISSICK and TRENGWAINTON, though much combing out has been done. At LANHYDROCK, in the upper part of the garden, they are well spaced, and were it not for the deciduous trees and shrubs the same might be said of SHEFFIELD PARK. At ROWALLANE they are used in great masses, well separated, but for an example of rhododendron planting where they are in scale with the vast landscape one must go to Lochinch, Wigtownshire.

Some of the plants brought from abroad have settled down like natives in England. How many of us have thought of the American snowberry (*Symphoricarpos albus*) other than as a native? It looks like one and behaves like one. For behaviour we might class with it the running bamboos from the Far East, *Arundinaria anceps* and *A. vagans*, but they do not look like natives. They are all dense-growing weed-suppressors, and *Arundinaria anceps* is one of the best of wind-resisters for Cornwall. Some of our ditches are becoming choked with the great bog arum or *Lysichitum*. *Griselinia littoralis* and *Pittosporum tenuifolium*, both from New Zealand, are commonly seeding themselves in moist western gardens. And where should we be without the Oval Leaf Privet? While *Ligustrum vulgare*, the Common Privet with its handsome jet berries, is a well-known plant on our chalk downs, it is not a good hedging plant and not reliably evergreen; *Ligustrum ovalifolium* was not introduced from Japan until *c.*1885, and has since become by far the most common evergreen hedging plant, and as useful in our climate as the Common or Cherry Laurel. Many of our gardens have collections of *Camellia* species and varieties from the Far East. One special spot comes to mind at COMPTON CASTLE, in a high-walled court; here very old and quite young specimens grow, as well as a splendid Loquat.

Besides trees and shrubs, and the annuals and tender plants I have already mentioned, many hardy perennials were being brought in: Aquilegias, *Cardiocrinum* or *Lilium giganteum*, *Alchemilla mollis*, *Thalictrum delavayi* (*T. dipterocarpum*); alpine plants such as haberleas, *Aethionema grandiflorum*, *Armeria caespitosa*; bulbs like *Nerine bowdenii* and *Colchicum speciosum*, and for indoors the African Violet and the Poinsettia.

The age of speciality had arrived, not only among the industrial cottagers, but among owners of small and large gardens. Of rose devotees there were many, while numerous other genera had their enthusiasts. One such was George Maw, the author of *The Genus Crocus* in 1886. He lived at BENTHALL HALL, and the remains of his rock garden and the area occupied by his frames can still be seen, though the design of the garden is of a later date by a subsequent owner.

ARBORETA

ONE SEES FEW LAKES and greater water gardens today without the huge leaves of *Gunnera manicata* and the crimson spikes of *Primula japonica* and other species; few winter gardens without *Hamamelis mollis*, few gardens of any sort without the Winter Jasmine. In short apart from the aspects of garden design already noted, a new fashion arose in the early 19th century; its only echo in the past being in the collections of plants amassed by the Elizabethan gardeners. The arboretum was born. It was the revival of the interest in watching plants grow and forming collections of exciting new plants from abroad: it was something that undoubtedly appealed more to the owner of a great garden than to his head gardener, who was so occupied with his fruits, vegetables and flowers, his mowing and clipping. Here was a hobby which could be indulged in by the owner with a minimum of labour, and it was no doubt quite as much an excitement as was a delicious peach, a new lake or a topiary triumph.

. . . a vision
Seen by rare travellers on Tibetan hills . . .
Forrest and Farrer, Fortune, Kingdon Ward,
Men that adventured in the lost old valleys,
Difficult, dangerous, or up the heights,
Tired and fevered, blistered, hungry, thin,
But drunk enough to set a house on fire
When the last moment of their worthless quest
Startled them with reward . . .

V. Sackville West, from *The Garden*, 1946

One of the first arboreta started was at KILLERTON. Here the owner had the advantage of advice from John Veitch of the later famous nursery firm, and by 1808 the Beech Avenue and the sweet chestnuts had been planted, the walks laid out, and the ice-house built. From about 1832 great conifers, magnolias and many rhododendrons were planted on the hill and the result today, seen from neighbouring approach roads, gives perhaps the most impressive skyline of any arboretum in the country: healthy Wellingtonias, Hemlocks and other conifers standing high above the native trees, while rhododendrons of massive proportions spill on to the lawn below. In spring many magnolias contribute their floral beauty.

GLENDURGAN was started a few years later and lies in a beautiful valley. Once again the skyline – this time contrasted by the water of the Helford River – is impressive, with Swamp Cypress, *Cunninghamia lanceolata* and other trees. One can well imagine the delight garden folk must have had in watching the new trees growing higher every year; and what rivalry there must have been. The Deodar Cedar, for instance, is so very beautiful when young – something which we are apt to forget today since it has become so familiar to us.

Most big gardens have their arboretum, however small it may be. The above properties are particularly devoted to rhododendrons, but other trees and shrubs are also to be found in them. A good assortment is at OSTERLEY PARK; a small arboretum is at EMMETTS, and there are two collections of trees at ANGLESEY ABBEY. The most recently-planted arboretum, from 1935 onwards, is WINKWORTH; this and SHEFFIELD PARK were two of the first to be planted specially to display the glory of autumn colour – a comparatively new departure in gardening. Our native trees and shrubs give their best colour mainly in November, but the exotics are brilliant from early October onwards, contributing the main colour to St Luke's "Little Summer".

29 OPPOSITE
Looking down from the top of the arboretum at Killerton in 1965. The Californian Wellingtonia (*Sequoidadendron giganteum*) towers above Himalayan tree rhododendrons (*R. arboreum*).

IN THE LAST CHAPTER I mentioned the influence, mainly architectural, of China. Eastern influence has always been with us. Indian influence is found in the renowned garden at Sezincote, in the pavilions and walls of the forecourt at HANBURY HALL – so strangely joined to the house – and in patterns of beds and paths at CASTLE DROGO. From ancient civilisations the scroll work known as arabesque derives, a tribute to the Moors, which gave rise to the flowing parterre patterns of the French gardens and others of much later design. These could be looked upon as a last ripple from the 18th century, but perhaps are more rightly considered as Victorian eclecticism. Yet another wave of eastern influence was about to break upon our shores, this time from Japan. Having been closed to travellers and traders for over two hundred years, in 1860 Japan's ports were again opened, and a longing for Japanese plants and more especially Japanese goods and garden design quickly grew. The enthusiasm happened to coincide with, and influenced, the aesthetic movement of the pre-Raphaelites and their *art nouveau*. Though their gardens were derived from those in China, the Japanese had elaborated and added to the mystique of their tradition. The ceremonial and overtones of the Japanese garden are beyond western comprehension, but stone lanterns, bronze storks, bridges of various design over serpentine waters, stepping stones and the like, together with dwarfed trees, rocks, raked sand and bamboo screens became the vogue. Many of these ideas underlie certain modern garden design: the stone slab bridge in the water garden at CLIVEDEN is in direct Japanese tradition. Our only example of a Japanese garden is at TATTON PARK; like all such copies it lacks the true touch both in construction and maintenance, but is a very fair representation or interpretation of the style.

Gardens embodying something of the architectural features of the *art nouveau* movement are at WIGHTWICK MANOR and STANDEN, both created during the early years of this century. But *art nouveau* did not really influence garden planting apart from the use of bamboos.

It will be seen that every possible taste and every possible plant, in gardens large and small, both formal and informal, embellished with a wide variety of manufactured ornaments, seats, balustrades and also garden buildings of classic, Gothick or rustic persuasion formed the groundwork to houses old or new. The remarkable thing is that in a hundred years or so no typical Victorian garden evolved. There was no national style. All was mixed, involved, eclectic. There was nothing lasting, all-pervading or distinctive as in previous centuries. Perhaps it was just as well. Today we are experimenting with all the new materials in building and no really distinctive style has evolved. Buildings were certainly more uniform, or at least in several styles, during Victorian times, while they were experimenting with their gardens and plants. The extravaganzas have for the most part been simplified to suit today's conditions but enough is left to give us an idea of what was enjoyed. It remained for some interpreter to arrive who could try to unify the numerous collections of every sort and point the way to the better use of all the old plants and also the new.

THE INTERPRETERS

A MAN WITH pronounced taste, erratic but mainly traditional, was William Robinson, author of *The Wild Garden*, *The Garden Beautiful*, and *Home Woods and Home Landscape*, and editor of the gardening paper, *The Garden*. Through his examples and writing he did much to arrest the muddle into which gardening was drifting. He sought to popularise all the old garden plants of the cottager and also those which had been cared for in the great kitchen gardens. He had decided opinions on the CLIVEDEN Parterre and, though contrary to his love of natural gardening, he designed a knot garden for himself and the terrace at KILLERTON. There is no doubt we owe much today to his *The English Flower Garden*, first published in 1883, and frequently reprinted. Garish bedding schemes were anathema to him and as a rule he preached gardening with nature. To the contrary, Sir Reginald Blomfield, an architect, sought to re-establish classical architecture in gardens, and was an antagonist worthy of his pen. A small addition to the house at HATCHLANDS was designed by Sir Reginald and the whole garden design there, the work of the owner, owes much to his influence. Another ardent lover of the classical and formal in garden design was Harold A. Peto; to him we owe the water garden at BUSCOT PARK. As an effort to retain interest in an exceptionally long and narrow site it is remarkable for its inventiveness and is one of the last great essays in formal water gardening.

The whole thing might have dragged on with neither faction achieving anything much had it not been for Gertrude Jekyll. After an early life devoted to the practice of art in many forms she took to gardening, and, having met William Robinson, contributed to *The Garden* and eventually became its editor. In addition, she wrote several garden books and practised what she preached at her home, first at Munstead House and later at Munstead Wood, Surrey. Her garden art was founded on a great appreciation of colour, proportion and suitability and was tempered by the English cottage-garden style of her county, although at times she could have been influenced by the general *mélange* of plants such as we find at GUNBY HALL in the walled gardens, and at PAYCOCKES. It has been said that whereas in the 18th century the landscape had been adapted to painting, she "translated painting into terms of gardening". At BARRINGTON COURT is a garden originally planted, and perhaps laid out by her, and her style of planting is still faithfully fostered. Her influence is found also in the Sunk Garden at MOUNT STEWART, and in the Walled Garden on the dunes at LINDISFARNE CASTLE. This has been replanted with many of the plants of her original choice. The arch-exponent of the herbaceous border during the Edwardian period and later, her gradations of colour have been copied ever since. From her examples spring the pair of borders recently planted at CLIVEDEN; other herbaceous and colour borders are at BLICKLING HALL, BODNANT, ICKWORTH, KILLERTON, LYME PARK, LYTES CARY, POWIS CASTLE, WAKEHURST and WALLINGTON.

Another traditionalist who, though much younger, co-operated with her was Sir Edwin Lutyens, the architect. Together they provided characteristic houses and gardens of a wholeness that had scarcely appeared before, by marrying formal structures with informal planting. Our best example of Lutyens' work is at CASTLE DROGO, where the garden is laid out with great aplomb up a hillside. With these protagonists gardening may be said to have reached a new height of beauty, interest and appropriateness, fostered in no small way by the founding of *Country Life* in 1897, not only the weekly magazine but also the vast tomes devoted to houses and gardens, so freely illustrated.

The general trend since William Robinson first stirred in print has been towards two distinct styles – once again the formal and the informal. Some smaller gardens echoing the revised formal style are BATEMANS, where Rudyard Kipling laid out a rose garden and rectangular pool in the early years of this century, CHARTWELL, and the terraces and grand stairway at UPTON HOUSE designed between 1927 and 1930. This, like the water garden at BUSCOT, is full of imagination.

BODNANT, in many respects embodying all that is best of the English garden tradition, received its first plants just over a hundred years ago. In 1876 many of the great conifers were planted which spring from the depths of the Dell to an immense height. Likewise the two splendid cedars were planted below the house ready for the inspiration that gave rise to the series of terraces designed by the second Lord Aberconway and developed and embellished by him for fifty years. Here are small formal beds for roses, balustraded walls and mural fountains, reminiscent of Italian gardens; patterned brick paths as favoured by Gertrude

30 The main vista at Hidcote in 1937, with Rouen Lilacs in flower.

Jekyll; treillage of French derivation; a long formal pool; an open-air theatre; a garden house built in 1740 and transported to its present position in 1939. The whole is planted with a great assortment of many of the best plants introduced to British gardens. The result is a splendid setting for the house and a prelude to the view towards Snowdon, miles away.

A little later, on ground with only a gentle gradient, the Marchioness of Londonderry laid out MOUNT STEWART in Northern Ireland. Here again are terraces, a pattern of beds leading to a sunken garden with Spanish-tiled house, another sunken garden with corner beds surrounded by a raised walk and pergola. In addition to its sentimental overtones, its design and catholic collection of plants, colour is handled in accordance with the original planting.

It is but a step in history and aesthetics from these big designs to quintessential HIDCOTE; Lawrence Johnston designed this from 1905 onwards, but it did not make its full impact until after the First World War. With its firm architectural design – but including also a stream garden of informal treatment – it brings us right into modern gardening. It is a series of enclosures, each one devoted to a colour scheme of different plants and each one in beauty through the season. Its design and planting has had more influence on modern gardening than any other and GREY'S COURT, TINTINHULL, SISSINGHURST and THE COURTS, Holt, are built upon its ideals. Gertrude Jekyll would have been pleased with all five; they embody much of her delight in the mixed style of planting.

If this selection of formal gardens with their rich informal planting may be derived from earlier formal styles we must turn elsewhere for the inspiration which eventually combined the arboreta with artistry. In this category we can I think place SALTRAM HOUSE, a beautiful assortment of choice shrubs and trees planted by the 3rd and 4th Earls of Morley. They were relatives of Sir George Holford who laid out Westonbirt Arboretum in Gloucestershire. TRELISSICK adds to this little group of beautiful gardens of trees and shrubs, but has the advantages of a varied terrain, while the late Victorian and Edwardian – and later – planting of exotic trees and shrubs at STOURHEAD and SHEFFIELD PARK adds interest to those two historic landscape gardens for the botanically minded. As mentioned in the last chapter, Richard Colt Hoare started the taste for exotics in the late 18th century at STOURHEAD. It was turned into a pleasaunce of rhododendrons during this century. Captain A. Soames at the same time was busy adding huge clumps of rhododendrons and placing countless trees and shrubs which would turn the lake landscapes at SHEFFIELD PARK into a varied fire of autumn colour, punctuated by dark conifers.

During the same years that MOUNT STEWART was being made, a neighbouring garden, ROWALLANE, was being planted by Hugh Armytage Moore. It is very much part of the rocky landscape and I usually liken it to an 18th-century landscape garden planted with all the new shrubs and trees. It is therefore also an arboretum. Out of all these spring two further great modern gardens. One, KNIGHTSHAYES COURT, we have already glanced at for the sake of its substantial Victorian terraces; Sir John and Lady Heathcoat Amory created the garden in the wood from 1950 onwards. Here is beauty and rarity happily combined. This I think can be claimed to represent in excellent manner the mid 20th-century idea of a woodland garden, with low maintenance and "natural" or "ecological" planting – all an outcome of the economy of the time. A garden on National Trust land, displaying a great variety of rhododendrons and other shrubs and trees to advantage in a natural woodland setting, has been developed during the last twenty years at STAGSHAW, Ambleside, by Cuthbert Acland. Gardening is in his blood, as he was born at Killerton. Finally we have ANGLESEY ABBEY, developed by Lord Fairhaven from 1930; it is so spacious that it easily embraces all the traditional garden styles; arboretum, avenues, rose garden, herbaceous borders, patterned beds, vistas with statuary and vast lawns, the whole in gentle transition one from another; a large area but economical to maintain.

IT WOULD BE TOO MUCH to expect that the last half century would provide a uniform new type of garden, considering the limitless riches of tradition, design and plants that were available. But I think that out of it all arise two highly successful styles, the woodland garden and the Hidcote ideal. There is no doubt that these garden types are spreading as far and wide as the *Jardin Anglais* did.

The great influx of trees and shrubs during the late 19th century was at least equalled in variety if not in the ultimate size of the new arrivals in the early years of this century. During the first twenty-five years the following were introduced from the Far East, all to become much desired and as popular in our gardens as their propagation and cultural requirements allow: *Acer griseum*, *Berberis wilsoniae*, *Sorbus sargentiana* and many other species of all three genera; several birches; *Prunus yedoensis*, *Juniperus recurva coxii*, *Magnolia campbellii mollicomata* and *M. sinensis*; numerous rhododendrons, *Clematis armandii* and *C. macropetala*. But it was not only trees and shrubs; there was the blue poppy, *Meconopsis betonicifolia (M. baileyi)* and *Gentiana sino-ornata* and others of both genera; numerous primulas including *P. florindae*, nomocharises and lilies. Such a galaxy of new plants for our gardens can never occur again.

The last great excitement was the discovery, in 1945, in the hinterland of China, of a legendary tree, which had only been known as a fossil – *Metasequoia glyptostroboides*. Today it arouses as much interest as the "Big Trees" of California did a hundred years ago; good specimens are at KILLERTON and STOURHEAD.

Northern Ireland
Belfast
SPRINGHILL
Newtownwards
ARDRESS HOUSE
MOUNT STEWART
Enniskillen
ROWALLANE
CASTLE WARD
CASTLECOOLE
FLORENCE COURT
Downpatrick
DERRYMORE
ASCOTT
Leighton Buzzard
WADDESDON MANOR
Aylesbury
PRINCES RISBOROUGH MANOR HOUSE
High Wycombe
HUGHENDEN MANOR
GREYS COURT
DORNEYWOOD
CLIVEDEN
FENTON HOUSE
Reading
London
ST JOHN'S JERUSALEM
OSTERLEY PARK
HAM HOUSE
Esher
OWLETTS
WEST GREEN HOUSE
CLAREMONT
POLESDEN LACEY
QUEBEC HOUSE
KNOLE
HATCHLANDS
Sevenoaks
CLANDON PARK
Westerham
EMMETTS
Guildford
Dorking
CHARTWELL
Tunbridge Wells
Godalming
LEITH HILL
East Grinstead
WINKWORTH ARBORETUM
STANDEN
WAKEHURST PLACE
SCOTNEY CASTLE GARDEN
NYMANS
Cuckfield
Midhurst
PETWORTH HOUSE
SHEFFIELD PARK
UPPARK
BATEMANS
LINDISFARNE CASTLE
Alnwick
CRAGSIDE HOUSE
WALLINGTON
Morpeth
Newcastle-upon-Tyne
R. Tyne
GIBSIDE CHAPEL
Carlisle
Durham
Penrith
ACORN BANK
Middlesbrough
ORMESBY HALL
Kendal
SIZERGH CASTLE
RIEVAULX TERRACE AND TEMPLES
Lancaster
BENINGBROUGH HALL
TREASURER'S HOUSE
York
Keighley
EAST RIDDLESDEN HALL
Padiham
Preston
Bradford
Leeds
Wakefield
GAWTHORPE HALL
RUFFORD OLD HALL
NOSTELL PRIORY
R. Trent
Manchester
Liverpool
SPEKE HALL
Stockport
Worksop
Llandudno
LYME PARK
CLUMBER PARK
TATTON PARK
HARDWICK HALL
Lincoln
GUNBY HALL
Skegness
BODNANT GARDEN
LITTE MORETON HALL
PLAS NEWYDD
Bangor
PENRHYN CASTLE
Wrexham
Stoke on Trent
Llangollen
ERDDIG
SUDBURY HALL
Cromer
Pwllheli
CHIRK CASTLE
Stafford
Nottingham
FELBRIGG HALL
SHUGBOROUGH
Derby
BLICKLING HALL
PLAS-YN-RHIW
Shrewsbury
King's Lynn
Norwich
BENTHALL HALL
ATTINGHAM PARK
MOSELEY OLD HALL
Leicester
Wisbech
PECKOVER HOUSE
Welshpool
Swaffham
Telford
WIGHTWICK MANOR
Peterborough
POWIS CASTLE
MORVILLE HALL
OXBURGH HALL
Bridgnorth
DUDMASTON
Birmingham
LYVEDEN NEW BIELD
Oundle
PACKWOOD HOUSE
Coventry
Northampton
R. Gt Ouse
Bury St Edmunds
CROFT CASTLE
BERRINGTON HALL
Stratford-upon-Avon
Cambridge
ICKWORTH
Leominster
HANBURY HALL
CHARLECOTE PARK
ANGLESEY ABBEY
Worcester
HIDCOTE MANOR
FARNBOROUGH HALL
WIMPOLE HALL
MELFORD HALL
THE WEIR
Broadway
Banbury
Sudbury
Hereford
SNOWSHILL MANOR
Cheltenham
UPTON HOUSE
Aylesbury
See detail
WESTBURY COURT GARDEN
Gloucester
Oxford
Faringdon
BUSCOT PARK
WEST WYCOMBE PARK
High Wycombe
Swindon
ASHDOWN HOUSE
Bristol
DYRHAM PARK
Reading
London
Cardiff
CLEVEDON COURT
LACOCK ABBEY
GREAT CHALFIELD MANOR
Croydon
Bath
THE COURTS, HOLT
THE VYNE
Maidstone
Canterbury
Minehead
WESTWOOD MANOR
Trowbridge
Basingstoke
Guildford
SISSINGHURST CASTLE
Dover
STOURHEAD
Crawley
Tunbridge Wells
ARLINGTON COURT
TINTINHULL HOUSE
Salisbury
Winchester
SMALLHYTHE PLACE
Barnstaple
DUNSTER CASTLE
LYTES CARY
Romsey
Midhurst
Rye
MOTTISFONT ABBEY
LAMB HOUSE
KNIGHTSHAYES COURT
Ilminster
Yeovil
Lewes
KILLERTON
Southampton
Chichester
Hastings
BARRINGTON COURT
Okehampton
Exeter
Brighton
Eastbourne
ALFRISTON CLERGY HOUSE
CASTLE DROGO
COTEHELE
Tavistock
Bodmin
BUCKLAND ABBEY
LANHYDROCK
Newquay
Plymouth
TRERICE
SALTRAM
TRELISSICK
Penzance
Truro
Salcombe
ANTONY HOUSE
Falmouth
SHARPITOR
GLENDURGAN
TRENGWAINTON
ST MICHAEL'S MOUNT

PART III

Impressions of the Gardens

31 The Herb Garden at Scotney Castle.

Notes

Statistics

IN THE FOLLOWING PAGES I have not given detailed descriptions of the gardens, but rather have I tried to give some of my impressions as well as those of other writers, some of long ago. Full particulars of the histories of the families who created the gardens and architectural and other details are given in the Guides for each property, published by the National Trust.

Some smaller gardens, which did not merit a page to themselves, are mentioned in the foregoing chapters where their special features have relevance.

Under the name of each garden I have given an indication of its geographical position and briefly the donor's name and date of acceptance, and have included certain statistics. I hope these may help visitors to assess the type of gardening that is needed in each property, and to know roughly the size of the garden in advance of visiting. All the statistics given are only *approximate*.

The AREA is that portion of the property tended by the garden staff.

The SOIL has only a note about whether it is limy or acid.

The ALTITUDE may vary within the garden.

The RAINFALL is the annual average.

The TEMPERATURE is the average for January.

The last is, as will be understood, highly variable, but gives some indication of the resistance of the plants to the usual winters.

Plant names

THE BOTANICALLY MINDED will perhaps be bored by my use of vernacular or popular names for some plants, but I ask them to bear in mind that this book is written for those who are novices at gardening as well as the experienced. I felt that to interlard the Impressions of the gardens with too many Latin names would make reading difficult for the uninitiated. The relevant Latin terms are to be found in the Plant Index.

The Table of Garden Specialities on p. 276 will act as an additional index for use with the Impressions.

Future research

ONE NEVER COMES to the end of gardens in the Trust; new ones arrive from time to time, but my list is complete up to the spring of 1978. The information given is in accordance with what has been discovered to date as well, but archival research is constantly proceeding; accordingly I offer my thanks in advance to anyone who will notify me of any inaccuracies or omissions.

The Gardens

ACORN BANK
Temple Sowerby, *Cumbria*

Given in 1950 by Mrs McGrigor Phillips

AREA 1 ha ($2\frac{1}{2}$ acres)	Just north of
SOIL Limy	Temple Sowerby,
ALTITUDE 75 m (250 ft)	6 miles east of
RAINFALL 1143 mm (45 in.)	Penrith on A66
TEMPERATURE 3°C (37°F)	

AT ONE TIME this house was known as Temple Sowerby Manor, but the Trust reverted to its original name in 1969. It is a happy re-naming. There are fine oaks along the drive, but on walking round the walls to the north of the garden in spring time there is a delightful surprise. A steep escarpment, well-peopled with oaks, slants down to a rushing brook and the sound of the water rises over hosts of daffodils. In the Walled Garden, in the little orchard areas, are more daffodils interspersed with other bulbs; at one moment it is enriched with the yellow of the native tulip, *Tulipa sylvestris*, and double *Anemone nemorosa* 'Vestal', at another with sheaves of the late Pheasant Eye Narcissus.

The warm brown stone of the house seems to exude a spirit of welcome. Around the walls are broad borders of flowers and shrubs continuing in beauty until the autumn. *Lilium pardalinum* flourishes against a shady wall with *Primula florindae* at its feet, while the yellow bells of *Clematis tangutica* on the wall itself contribute to the colour scheme. Elsewhere there are numerous older roses including Rugosas, *R. alba* 'Céleste' and Burnet Roses.

In 1969, plans were made to convert the old kitchen garden into a garden for herbs and medicinal plants, trees and shrubs. In the borders there are over 180 different kinds. There you may go to take notes for the improvement of your cuisine and to study cures for all the ills that ever beset mankind. Or so it seems!

32 "The root of Solomon's Seale ... taketh away ... any bruise, black or blew spots gotten by fals or women's wilfullnesse, in stumbling upon their hasty husbands fists." An engraving from Henry Lyte's *Herball* of 1578 (see under Lytes Cary, and illus. 18).

ANGLESEY ABBEY
Lode, *Cambridgeshire*

Acquired in 1966 under the will of the 1st Baron Fairhaven

AREA 36 ha (90 acres)	In Lode village,
SOIL Limy	6 miles north-east of
ALTITUDE 30 m (100 ft)	Cambridge on the B1102
RAINFALL 584 mm (23 in.)	Cambridge–Mildenhall
TEMPERATURE 3.5°C (38°F)	road

HALF A CENTURY is not long in the life of a great garden, although some gardens have virtually disappeared during such a period. The garden at Anglesey Abbey, one of the very few gardens of large size to have been created in recent years, has matured since its inception in 1930. During this time all the spinneys and garden woodlands were planted to enhance with their

33 In commemoration of the Coronation of Queen Elizabeth II in 1953 these columns, weighing 2 tons each, were erected in the midst of a great lawn at Anglesey Abbey, surrounding a statue of David by Bernini. Photo 1969.

sculptured greenery the views and separate areas of the terrain, which is, with a few small undulations and excavations, undeniably flat. In some directions there was a scattering of fine, large native trees. Under or around these cowslips, primroses and violets still grow.

Great dates have left their mark at Anglesey. The Silver Jubilee of our Queen in 1977 prompted the replanting of the trees bordering what was the Daffodil Walk. Her accession was marked by the erection of a group of pillars on Temple Lawn in 1953. An immense avenue 1,400 feet long was planted to commemorate the Coronation of King George VI and Queen Elizabeth in 1937. There is a row of Lombardy Poplars marking the Silver Jubilee of King George V and Queen Mary in 1935. A "commemoration urn" was placed at the end of the Daffodil Walk in 1930 by Lord Fairhaven and his brother, to record the 800th anniversary of the founding of the abbey. Yet earlier, Queen Victoria's Jubilee in 1887 is marked by the Lombardy Poplars planted on the millstream bank. Just prior to this, in the 1860s, some cedars, pines and a Weeping Silver Lime were planted near to the house. This was built in the early 17th century from the ruins of the abbey, which suffered so much, like others, in the Dissolution. For four hundred years it had existed, for some time as a priory and then as an abbey, and the undulations of the lawn in front of the house indicate where foundations lie. Before this, we are told, the quarry in the garden furnished coprolite, a valued fossilised dung.

There stands this venerable house, then, in its setting of lawns. Its abbey stone furnishes the quoins, and maybe the clunch, or hard chalk, of its walls. It is a very English setting, with its greensward, paths, cedars and tall trees around it. The design of the garden is firm, decisive, but leans as much towards the traditional English landscape garden as it does to earlier formality. Perhaps it is foolish to try to "date" it. (See illus. 21.)

It is unwise to hurry round the garden in an hour or so. This will not do justice to its spaciousness. In the first place there is too much of it to see comfortably in less than half a day, and secondly the whole spirit of the place spells peace and gentleness, so that hurrying is out of context. There is also the light. East Anglia, a comparatively flat region, depends much upon the immense arc of sky that is always visible. The light can alter so much the enjoyment of a great vista, a piece of statuary, an embowered nook or a colourful planting of flowers, that one wants to go again and again before venturing to take a friend round the best way. I find myself wandering off in different directions at different times of the year.

In spring one instinctively goes to the spread of early bulbs in the Monks' Garden, a small area of rough grass with old fruit trees. And then there is that moment in April when 4,000 blue and white hyacinths in formal beds in grass flood the hedged enclosure with scent. An English spring, April and May, is particularly kind to Anglesey, for the burgeoning spinneys have an infinite variety of greens, and the annual spread of forget-me-not in the big curved walk enhances the prevailing greenery. By the end of May the large D-shaped herbaceous garden begins to enthrall us, broad clumps of colour being grouped against a background of beech hedges, heightened later with towering spikes of delphiniums. By August dahlias have taken over from the forget-me-nots and hyacinths, and particularly in the latter garden the contrast of flower and foliage colour is remarkable (see plate XIX). There is a

34 The Hyacinth Garden at Anglesey Abbey where 4,000 bulbs, blue and white, are annually planted when the dahlias have been lifted in autumn. Photo 1967.

35 The Porphyry Vase (1.9 m [6 ft 4 ins] in diameter) at Anglesey Abbey.

moment in early autumn when one longs for the leaves to fall, to reveal the value of the evergreens, while knowing full well that some weeks of interest yet remain to us in the tinted leaves.

Lawns are great beguilers. They lead one from garden to arboretum, from pond to avenue, from tree to tree – and there are many good trees to be seen. The Hungarian and the Algerian Oaks, the Japanese Hop Hornbeam, Honey Locust, Black Walnut, and Indian Chestnut, are all of good size, and numerous unusual species have more recently been planted by the Trust.

Lawns, trees and hedges are nature's "bones" of the garden. They are accentuated by a great variety of urns, vases and statuary. They surprise us by their range of material – metal, marble, stone or composition – their range of size, from the intimate Huntsman and his Hounds in a green glade to the majesty of The Wrestlers, towering yards above our heads on a sweep of grass for which immense is the only word. The porphyry vase, under its canopy of Chinese influence, leads us to the most recent portion of the garden where a long green walk is punctuated by a series of busts of the twelve emperors, and again by The Warriors. There is no end to their richness and variety, and their sources are documented. In a garden even of a hundred acres on dramatic terrain they could scarcely have been accommodated; here, on the flat, they add a needed enrichment to the garden scene.

No garden is without its disasters. Elm disease has ruined many of the plantations but replanting progresses. The Daffodil Walk is now to be called the Jubilee Avenue – the ribbons of yellow are a thing of the past owing to a virus infection. This has not fortunately had any effect on the succeeding misty white of Cow Parsley which gives such joy in May. Sometimes disasters come in the nick of time. I am recalling the debates that went on in the late 1960s concerning the needed thinning of the Coronation Avenue. This was planted with four rows of trees on either side – a truly majestic conception – of alternating specimens of Horse Chestnut and London Plane. The idea was that one or the other would have to be felled in due course. We had decided on the removal of the Chestnuts, being the tree of shorter life, when the terrible summer storm of 1968 occurred. Many of the planes were halved, split and broken, and just in time; the result was that all were removed and for the next fifty years and more we hope the chestnuts will lend their splendour to the scene. The same mixture of trees was planted in the Long Ride in Windsor Great Park, but so far, I gather, there has been no unanimity on which species shall be selected for the future.

ANTONY HOUSE
Torpoint, *Cornwall*

Given in 1961 by Sir John Carew Pole

AREA 10 ha (25 acres)	5 miles west of
SOIL Lime-free	Plymouth via
ALTITUDE 30 m (100 ft)	the Torpoint car ferry,
RAINFALL 1016 mm (40 in.)	2 miles north-west
TEMPERATURE 6°C (43°F)	of Torpoint

IT IS NOT SURPRISING that this great house, which is still lived in by the family that built it in 1721, should have many historical points of interest, especially since the different generations have travelled widely. During the last hundred years or so the strongest influences have come from the Far East and the far west. There is an ancient wide-spreading hickory below the house, and also many *Magnolia grandiflora*, both natives of the United States. But the eastern influence predominates. There are stone carvings from the north west-frontier of India, a Burmese temple bell and two Japanese stone lanterns, a Loquat from eastern Asia, and a fine specimen of the Maidenhair Tree from China. Very much in the English tradition are the long hedges and topiary specimens, one of tall pointed shape like a wigwam, and a Lebanon Cedar.

The plants mentioned may perhaps be more than one hundred years old. Nobody knows exactly, but the trees and the ornaments are later embellishments to a layout which we owe in great part to Humphry Repton, who made several visits to Mr Pole Carew around 1800. From what one can gather the owner listened to advice and proposals and then made up his mind eventually to manage without Repton. Repton's advice was always written, and usually lengthy, though carefully phrased so that there could be no ambiguity. Here is a sample from his Red Book on the property.

The shape of the ground at Antony is naturally beautiful, but the attention to the farmer's interest has almost obliterated all traces of its original form; since the line of fence which the farmer deems necessary to divide the arable land from the pasture is unfortunately that, which of all others, tends to destroy the union of hill and valley: it is generally placed exactly at that point where the undulating surface changes from convex to concave and of course does the greatest mischief which can be produced by any intersecting line, for it will be found, that a line of fence following the shape of the ground, or falling in any direction from the hill to the valley, tho' it may offend the eye as a boundary, yet it does not injure the beautiful form of the surface, and may in some instances even improve it. I must therefore give it as my opinion, that no great improvement can be expected at Antony, till almost all the present fences be removed, altho' others may be placed in more suitable directions.

This is the age-old war between the practical farmer and the artist. I could cite many examples in the properties of the Trust where, of late years, we have had to reduce or remove fences erected in our parks which, though of some practical importance, completely spoiled the view. In every case a happy solution has been found, as it probably was in Repton's day.

Repton's influence was considerable at Antony. He arranged extensive tree planting to the east and north of the house, particularly around and over Jupiter Hill (but not so that it "resembles a Bonnet upon the Top of the Hill") from which the loveliest view of the house is obtained. Jupiter Hill is so named because at one time there was placed upon it a figurehead from a ship called *Jupiter*. The groves of Holm Oaks which frame the views are believed to have been planted about 1760, before Repton's visit; he desired to remove various small trees and shrubs in the foreground to reveal them. "These limes removed, a large mass of evergreen oaks should be suffered to present themselves unencumbered by any other trees, and when the plantation at the back of Jupiter's hill will warrant the measure, a glade of lawn should be introduced to shew the turn in the shape of the ground."

This whole northern front is based not only on the house itself but on the long, terraced, gravel walk which runs due west – though partly grassed over – between yew hedges to the Burmese bell, and then, in parallel, back to the west front of the house. This second walk is lined with *Magnolia grandiflora*, free grown as bushes, and takes you past the wigwam. In Repton's words: "The magnificence and convenience of an ample terrace is that part of ancient gardening which I have frequently dared to preserve".

36 The Burmese temple bell and Japanese stone lanterns at Antony.

He desired to build a pavilion at the east end of the terrace, to finish it, but this idea was not accepted. Today a yew hedge terminates it and the old flat-topped Lebanon Cedar has grown up and started to decay since Repton's time. It was not shewn in his drawings.

Apart from its history, Antony is noted for a collection of over 500 Day Lilies, many of them new hybrids from the United States, gathered together by the late Lady Carew Pole. They include a few species, and some hybrids raised at Antony.

ARLINGTON COURT
Barnstaple, *North Devon*

Given in 1946–7 by Miss Rosalie Chichester whose family had owned the estate since the 14th century

AREA 10 ha (25 acres)	7 miles north-east
SOIL Lime-free	of Barnstaple,
ALTITUDE 243 m (800 ft)	on east side of A39
RAINFALL 1143 mm (45 in.)	
TEMPERATURE 6°C (43°F)	

ONE OF THE NUMEROUS WAYS of appreciating the beauty and interest here is to go first into the house, to see the accumulation of personal trivia – though much of it does not really deserve this belittling adjective – in which Miss Chichester took so much delight. From our point of view her paintings of flowers are of the greatest interest, but in every room her love of growing things is mirrored: not only flowers, but birds and animals, and also shells and stones. She valued so much these things of nature that by erecting a high iron fence around her eight miles of boundaries she enclosed the whole area as a preserve. And so it has remained.

If you go there on a brilliant spring day it will strike you as a home of infinite beauty and variety. Primroses, violets, anemones, Siberian *Claytonia* and Japanese primulas grow naturally in the grass. Many native trees, shrubs and plants are to be found in the Nature Trail which threads its way through woodland to the lake shore. In the damp climate lichens abound and no less than twelve species have been counted hanging in streamers from the splendid specimen of variegated sycamore. Large rhododendrons guard the lawns, and several species of ash have been planted. In August the Hortensia hydrangeas are of a brighter and more intense blue than any I know.

37 *Hydrangea paniculata* 'Floribunda' has reached tree-like proportions at Arlington Court. Photo 1970.

The house in its setting of lawns and trees is well placed and looks towards an obelisk commemorating the 1887 Jubilee of Queen Victoria. The hoary stone tower of the Church looks down upon it all.

The actual garden is some distance away. It is small, with three terraces and a fountain pool, guarded by a pair of metal herons; these occur repeatedly on the estate, being part of the family crest. This formal garden is believed to have been laid out in 1865 and perhaps the two old Monkey Puzzle trees were planted at the same time; these were felled in 1976, being unhealthy, and a pair of young trees have been put in to continue the tradition. In the rock banks are dwarf azaleas and many small plants including the rare Queen Anne's Double Daffodil, and there are colchicums for autumn. Two herbaceous borders are on the top level together with a conservatory, and places for seats have been made against the back wall of what was a long range of glasshouses. A young Maidenhair Tree and an old plant of the variegated form of *Fatsia japonica* are to be seen, together with a good Victorian touch: a group of brilliantly-variegated yellow shrubs and trees.

On the west side of the house are more hydrangeas, including some very large old specimens of *H. paniculata* 'Floribunda', some 3 m (10 ft) in height.

In 1838 Loudon, in his *Gardener's Magazine*, mentions that many trees were moved into important landscape positions from the outer grounds here, and he describes the method of transporting and planting. Oaks, Portuguese Laurels and others were moved when twenty or more feet high, and apparently successfully. No doubt some of the old specimens we see today were planted at this time. May they continue to give shelter to this high, exposed garden in the future, and benefit from the saplings planted in recent years.

ASCOTT
Leighton Buzzard, *Buckinghamshire*

Given in 1950 by Mr and Mrs Anthony de Rothschild

AREA 15.5 ha (39 acres)	½ mile east of Wing,
SOIL Limy	2 miles south-west of
ALTITUDE 75 m (250 ft)	Leighton Buzzard,
RAINFALL 635 mm (25 in.)	on south side of A418
TEMPERATURE 3.5°C (38°F)	

ONE OF THE FUNDAMENTALS OF today's gardening – and with perhaps equal truth it may be applied to all gardens other than the earliest ones which were devoted to produce – is that both garden and house are one thing, indivisible. They unite in being specially created for the greater enjoyment of life. The Rothschilds, with their resources, talents and enthusiasm, certainly enjoyed life and when Leopold de Rothschild came to live at Ascott in 1874 he laid out the garden, closely linked with the outline of the house. Both are very much products of the late 19th century.

He was fortunate in having as a helper a director of one of the most famous nurseries of all time, James Veitch & Sons of Chelsea; the name Veitch is commemorated in many plants and also in one of the Royal Horticultural Society's most coveted awards, the Veitch Memorial Medal. Mr de Rothschild could have had no better adviser, and it is a wonderful thought that today we can go to Ascott and see a garden mirroring the taste and planting of the period.

A house of 1606 is lost in the Victorian buildings. Traces of the moat and fish ponds of that early date remain. As long ago as 1891 *The Gardeners' Chronicle* commented upon the variety and ingenuity of the topiary "clipped into fantastic shapes". Topiary is still much in evidence and includes the big sundial laid out on the ground in clipped golden box, with a yew gnomon and a quotation "Light and shade by turn but love always" in golden yew. (How true this is of a garden; no garden prospers unless it is taken to heart.)

In 1896 *The Gardeners' Chronicle* again commented on the delights of the garden, adding that "we need less of the formal and stiff style of gardening so prevalent in the earlier part of this century. The entire design ... is unique in its way ... the owner himself acted as landscape gardener."

Wherever you go at Ascott, you are conscious of the two major characteristics of the garden: the wide lawns sloping away to extensive views, and the assembly of trees and shrubs, many of them evergreen. But whether evergreen or deciduous, they often have tints other than plain green: coppery, silvery, variegated and tinted in great variety. In winter time the whole place glows with a sunlit effect from the yellow variegated yews and hollies.

While such plants were much to the fore at the time, perhaps their popularity at Ascott depends partly upon

38 The summerhouse at the end of the sunken, sheltered Madeira Walk at Ascott.

the fact that the house was for many years used as a hunting lodge from autumn to spring. And this is again perhaps echoed in a formal walk – sheltered under the lee of lawns and trees – known as the Madeira Walk. Many tender shrubs as well as roses and honeysuckles grow on its wall.

The Madeira Walk is one of several formal features that develop well away from the house on the lower lawns. In formal settings are two fountains, one a huge spread of figures in a circular pool surrounded by golden yew hedges, and the other a slender composition in a scalloped pool. This is in the Dutch Garden, guarded by mounds of golden yews, the scene of displays of bedding plants, renewed twice yearly. Heliotrope and begonias alternate with polyanthus and forget-me-not – the compositions are endless (see illus. 26). Above it tufa was used to create a small cavern dripping with water; the rockery bank, partly of the same stone, and partly of Cheddar limestone, was one of the earliest of its kind, completed in 1896.

But to return to the trees. There are so many that I can only mention a few and leave it to you to explore, but do not miss the two Swamp Cypresses on the lawn, which mark the site of an earlier pond. Nearby is a mound of junipers, *J. media* 'Pfitzerana' surrounding a large plant of *J. chinensis* 'Japonica Aurea'. You cannot miss the Blue Cedars, the Golden Cedar, American Oaks so splendidly red in autumn, Beeches Weeping, Cut-leafed, Copper and Weeping Copper; *Liquidambar, Cercis, Catalpa, Magnolia, Acer*, Paper Birch and Tulip Tree, and many more. It has been a laudable tradition to mark royal occasions by planting groups of trees.

Near the house where the ground slopes away to the south-west is a ravishing sight in spring, for bulbs of innumerable kinds are naturalised in the turfy banks, daffodils, tulips, fritillaries (the "Guinea Hen Flower"), anemones, scillas and crocuses, while in the flat ground of the area devoted entirely to trees, more consciously an arboretum, is a great display of naturalised daffodils. Different kinds line the walks in their thousands, yellow and white, white and yellow, interchanged with freedom. Here are also some noted trees, the white-flowered *Aesculus chinensis, Acer griseum*, the evergreen *Quercus canariensis* and *Tilia petiolaris* among them.

Ascott is a garden for all seasons. The herbaceous border and roses contribute largely to the interest in summer, while the ponds and lake are spread with waterlilies of many sizes and colours. Yet with all this delight my mind goes back specially to one very clear spring day. I was standing to the south-west of the house; my eyes instinctively turned towards the half-timbered building, against which it seemed a thousand magnolia blooms, pinky-white, had burst open to greet me. The 'Golden Milkmaid' Holly added its decisive tint and the foreground was spread with bulbs overhung with apple blossom. (See plate XVII.)

ASHDOWN HOUSE
Lambourn, *Oxfordshire*

Given in 1956 by Cornelia, Countess of Craven

AREA 2.4 ha (6 acres)	2½ miles south of
SOIL Limy	Ashbury, 3½ miles north
ALTITUDE 152 m (500 ft)	of Lambourn,
RAINFALL 762 mm (30 in.)	on west side of B4000
TEMPERATURE 4°C (39°F)	

MANY OF OUR GARDENS are sited in well chosen spots and Ashdown is no exception. The road winds along the foot of a dramatic steep arm of the downs, and suddenly the house with its two pavilions comes into view, across a sloping meadow littered with sarsen stones. It has the proportions and charm of a doll's house, and, like ANGLESEY ABBEY, is built of hard chalk or clunch with stone quoins; the high-pitched roof is surmounted by a golden ball, as at SUDBURY HALL. It was built for Elizabeth of Bohemia, mother of Prince Rupert, in 1665. It is likely that the layout of the then fashionable avenues originates from that date or soon after.

In 1724 the Kip engraving shows the house in the middle of a forest cut by four rides. The western vista is marked by a short avenue of limes; to the north a new avenue of limes was planted in 1970. There is also a short avenue to the south. It is interesting to find old lime trees arranged in two arcs, partially encircling the house on the east side, leading into straight rows.

The Trust inherited no garden here but a box parterre was laid out on gravel about 1955 to a design by Mr A. H. Brookholding Jones (see illus. 19). The design was adapted from 17th-century engravings. An experience not to be missed is to look from the windows across the swirls of clipped box towards the old lime avenue, once pollarded or clipped, and to lean backwards to a time when such a display would have been *à la mode*.

ATTINGHAM PARK
Shrewsbury, *Salop*

Acquired in 1953 under the will of the 8th Lord Berwick

AREA 8 ha (20 acres)	4 miles south-east
SOIL Lime-free	of Shrewsbury,
ALTITUDE 30 m (100 ft)	on north side of A5
RAINFALL 686 mm (27 in.)	
TEMPERATURE 3°C (37°F)	

ATTINGHAM HAS a long history. Before the present house was built in 1785 there was a busy mill on the site, worked by the long straight race of the River Tern. Hammers went on all through the night until 1760, milling and sharpening implements for domestic use, the chase and war. The weir was there to harness the waters near the mill, and another weir was made below the great stone bridge on the A5 road from which such a splendid view of the "new" house is obtained. By 1785 the mill had gone but its foundations are still visible below the upper weir.

To this scene came Humphry Repton in 1797, producing a lengthy Red Book with his usual sketches; he called attention to defects in the views to and from the house and explained how he would remedy them. In few of his Red Books does he so continually decry the opinions of the writers on gardening of the time, Richard Payne Knight and Uvedale Price; nor for that matter does he spare the efforts of Capability Brown. "I trust that time only will be wanting to ripen them [his plans] into effect and that in spite of the wild theories of *picture gardeners*, Attingham will be a lasting monument of Lord Berwick's taste, in having committed its improvement to the rational plans of a Landscape Gardener." He signed the book as "Your Lordship's most obedient and very humble servant", but the essay is scarcely humble; he puts forth his taste in no uncertain way. But one feels in reading the essay that he took an almost modern standpoint in trying to make the flat terrain worthy of the great house. He did not consider the remains of the old mill suitable near the new house. He saw no reason to extend the park in the manner of Mr Brown and considered that "provided the boundary can be properly disguised the largest park in the kingdom need not exceed two or three hundred acres", unless by bringing in more land dramatic scenery accompanied it. There was no point in enlarging a park and then having to put large areas under the plough. In other words he was prepared to "make do" with the land visible from the house. He sought to add to its beauty by creating a sheet of water between the two bridges – instead of a network of brooks meandering through marshy ground – and by an extensive park-planting scheme. He united scattered clumps of trees and generally disposed of spinneys and woods so that the house and immediate "lawns" appeared to be set in a limitless park.

There is no doubt that his rational ideas were thoroughly effective and the beauty envisaged lasted a hundred years or more. Now the Trust's task is to reinforce his tree planting, some of which has decayed, and, one day, to recreate his sheet of water towards the great bridge by widening and dredging the marshy banks of the River Tern. Much has been achieved, but much remains to be done.

Meanwhile under the great portico of the house yew hedges and knot gardens had been made in this century. These were removed in 1976 by the Trust so that the house once more stands proudly on its slight eminence, unencumbered by small features. It is protected from the north-east by a grove of large Lebanon Cedars, some dating from Repton's time. Red Oaks, Dogwoods, Sumach and American Thorns contribute autumn colour near the water, while beyond the cedars is a walk, developed during the last one hundred years or so, following the river and thence curving back towards the house; it is known as the Mile Walk. Where it leaves the river and turns to the west a particularly large cedar stands, with Grey Poplars in a naturalised thicket across the water. Rhododendrons are freely planted. At one point, at a junction of rides, a circle of Honey Locusts has been set and a number of shrubs for summer effect have been added. Approaching the walled garden is a nut walk and an avenue of False Locusts. In it there is an interesting apicultural feature – a bee-house probably of the 18th century, around which an orchard is being created. In addition there are numerous shrubs, fine oaks and beeches.

It has been the work of many years to get rid of unsightly fences; to achieve planting which embellishes the park and yet will allow distant low hills to be seen across the flat land; and to tidy the immediate surrounds of the house. Attingham is not a garden; its garden was a productive one, hidden by protective high walls. I think the Trust would agree with Repton's quotation of Mr Burke's dictum: "Where disposition, where decorum, where congruity are concerned; in short wherever the best taste differs from the worst, I am convinced that the understanding operates and nothing else." Further on he makes his Parthian shot: "I shall never be brought to believe, as Mr Price asserts, that the best Landscape-painter would make the best Landscape-gardener, any more than that the best dancing master should be the most perfect Gentleman, because the Art of dancing is one of the parts of a Gentleman's education." Humphry Repton was indeed the first noted landscape designer who could see the rationality required to bring together the needs of a garden and the flights of fancy in the landscape.

BARRINGTON COURT
Ilminster, *Somerset*

Acquired in 1907 largely through the generosity of Miss J. L. Woodward

AREA 3.6 ha (9 acres) SOIL Limy ALTITUDE 22 m (72 ft) RAINFALL 762 mm (30 in.) TEMPERATURE 4°C (39°F)	At the east end of Barrington village, ½ mile east of B3168, 3 miles north-east of Ilminster

THE HOUSE has stood as it is, almost untouched outside, for four hundred and seventy years. It has been claimed that Lord Daubeney pulled down an older house, which had been built soon after the Conquest and possibly the five-sided piece of land on which it stands was even then surrounded by its moat. Today one keeps coming on the moat as one goes round the garden. The house dreams away, rich in its vertical lines and spiral finials and chimneys, an even dreamier house than MONTACUTE. Strangely, at one time the Phelips of MONTACUTE owned Barrington Court; it changed hands several times after Lord Daubeney's death and was eventually bought by William Strode of Shepton Mallet. It was probably his son, another William, who built a stable quadrangle in 1666. And so we have the best 16th-century architecture, and also the best of the 17th-century style – the traditional Gothic and the Renaissance style of Wren.

The old house was in a poor state when it was first offered to the Trust early in this century. Subsequent work by the architects Messrs Forbes and Tate resulted in the building's being restored for the Trust's tenant, Colonel A. A. Lyle, and at the same time the stable building was turned into a dwelling house. While the main lines of the garden and walls and also the subsidiary buildings were the work of Forbes and Tate, Gertrude Jekyll provided planting plans for all the borders, beds and paths – Lutyens was not the only architect she worked with. Her original plans are at Berkeley, California, together with many other Jekyll papers.

39 A small wooden bridge at Barrington Court.

Surrounded by meadows and by its moat the old house has become the key piece in the whole majestic design. There are impressive avenues of Horse Chestnuts which form a cross, one focussed on the house, one on a low, distant range of thatched cottages with standard Portuguese Laurels in front of them. The crossing lengths of drive each focus on to a separate dwelling. Farm buildings, cottages and the two dwellings are all in traditional style, and thus the old house dominates and blends with everything.

The 17th-century stable block on the other hand dominates the garden, walled and in sections though not necessarily rectangular. The sections fit into old buildings – 17th-century ox-pens for instance – and what walls were originally there. One of the most colourful parts of the garden lies outside the walled enclosures; it consists of a wide border filled with traditional flowers. Another border has for contrast bold clumps of acanthuses and, behind, shrubs including *Ceanothus arboreus*.

The Lily Garden lies directly to the west of the Strode building; its broad flagged terrace is above the main area which contains a lily pool in its midst surrounded by raised beds, then a path of beautiful brickwork, and large borders of flowers backed by shrubs on the walls (see plate XXI). The design, if not by Miss Jekyll, is very much of her style. She could not have indulged her fancies into making a sunk garden for the simple reason that the water in the moat is so little below the level of the ground. The skilful use of shallow steps and raised beds gives the impression of a much greater divergence in levels than really exists. She intended the four square corners of the raised beds to be filled with yuccas, while between them the connecting beds were to be filled with crinum lilies and hydrangeas. Today we find the corner beds contain the crinums while the connecting beds have been given lime-free soil and contain azaleas. The tall traditional herbaceous plants with some annual flowers solidified by clumps of bergenias and the contrasting foliage of crinums brings us very much into the Jekyll gardening style.

Apart from the original plans there are few records about the garden. The late Christopher Hussey, writing in *Country Life* in March 1928, gave us his impressions of this garden and suggested that the main part was envisaged as being 610 mm (2 ft) lower and criticises the high "Surreyish" parapet of the terrace. In fact, on his suggestion, the parapet was lowered and this was considered an improvement.

We cannot be sure whether Miss Jekyll designed the other areas though she made planting plans for them. There is a rose garden of circular array in a square, walled enclosure with a statue in the centre. Another enclosure she gave to irises and roses; the irises remain, but the roses have been replaced by purple clematises and lavenders. When the irises are trimmed over in July this garden comes into its summer display of purplish colouring: the several *Clematis jackmanii* on supports are surrounded with lavenders, the irises interspersed with pink and purple Horminum, petunias and Heliotrope. Solidity is given by a bold, stepped central sundial and some spiral box bushes; the whole is in a setting of grass paths, surrounded by wall shrubs on three sides and a billowy box hedge on the fourth.

This box hedge keeps the eye from taking in at the same time a long colour border beyond it, stretched all along the north side of another Jekyll-patterned brick path. Originally this border was used for cut flowers, for vegetables during the last war, and in 1960 the present scheme of colour was devised by Mrs Lyle. At one end, bolstered by a group of good greenery – *Euphorbia*, *Piptanthus* and *Helleborus* – yellow starts the colouring, including a Weeping Laburnum. The colour gathers way in rich orange reds, dark reds and purples and tails off with cool lavenders and blues at the far end, where the flowers are augmented by the Rugosa rose 'Roseraie de l'Haÿ' in flaming purple, with lilacs for accompaniment for its early crop of bloom. The box hedge, path and border are enormously enhanced by a large overhanging Common Ash tree. It will often be found that this tree, though greedy at the root and providing no spring or autumn colour nor flowers of any garden merit, still manages to be graceful and imposing; it gives the impression that it was here in the days when the ox-pens were built, behind the border.

Yet another walled enclosure contains a four-square layout of a kitchen garden, complete with espalier fruit trees. The productive part of the garden has no lack of admirers today but the labour needed to keep such a garden trim by hand-work is heavy.

Thanks to Sir Ian Lyle, who kindly allows these gardens, as well as the house, to be often open, one is able to go and spend a few hours in the peace of a traditional English garden. It seems that the 1930s are still with us. Many of Miss Jekyll's shrubs and plants are still in the garden; her design and her beautiful paths endure; the architects' walls and handsome gates embellish the whole; many shrubs and trees have been planted of late years. Barrington Court is not just a period piece, it is a continuing effort: effort that has been made ever since this swift flowing moat first flowed round the old house, protecting it and bringing it moisture.

BATEMAN'S
Burwash, *East Sussex*

Acquired in 1940 under the will of Mrs Rudyard Kipling

AREA 4 ha (10 acres)	½ mile south of
SOIL Lime-free	Burwash on the A265
ALTITUDE 75 m (250 ft)	Hawkhurst–Heathfield
RAINFALL 762 mm (30 in.)	road
TEMPERATURE 4.5°C (40°F)	

TO US, TODAY, because we know little of its early history, Bateman's conjures up Kipling and the many facets of his writing. But it is a pleasant old house, part Jacobean, with later additions, and sits comfortably in its meadows surrounded by low hills and great oaks. The stone for the house came from the nearby quarry, water was supplied by well and by the Dudwell River at the end of the garden; of timber there was no shortage. The ironmaster who built it about 1620 built well, but it later became a farmhouse when the coal and iron of the Midlands created a partnership which ousted the Sussex industry. Who knows but that the 'Maiden's Blush' rose under the front windows has not seen the shifting fortunes of it all? Somebody with an eye to gardening lived there before Kipling, because when he purchased it in 1902, he found the two rows of pleached limes which cross the lawn already growing.

40 Rudyard Kipling's design for the rose garden at Bateman's, dated 1906.

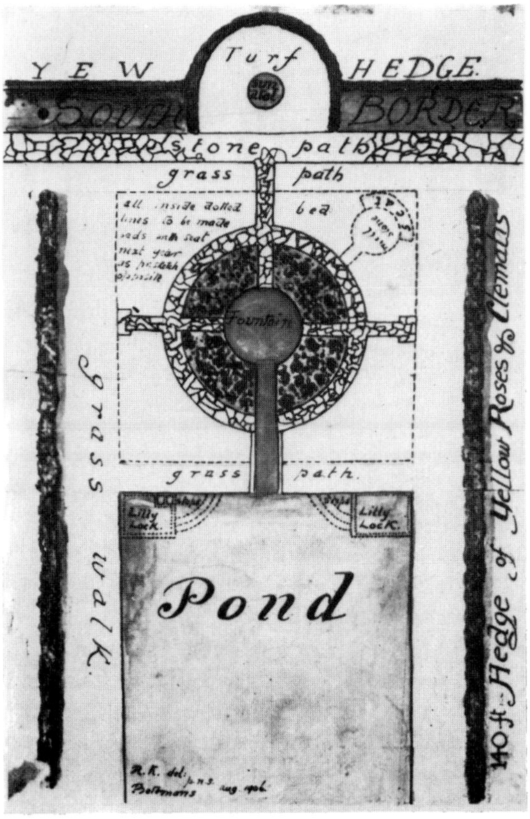

41 TOP Bateman's house and pleached limes from the rose garden. Photo 1977.
42 ABOVE The pear alley at Bateman's designed by Rudyard Kipling. Photo 1977.

It is a peaceful place, both inside and out. The Kiplings had the right touch. They planted all the yew hedges and presumably established the paths, which are flagged with rough Purbeck stone found in the neighbourhood. The hedges give us an intriguing garden divided quite simply into a series of rectangles. The main area is to the south of the house with Kipling's pool and rose garden alongside the pleached limes. The roses are all early types of Floribundas: 'Betty Prior', 'Mrs Inge Poulsen', with 'Frensham' added later. Two little lead figures and a small fountain give point to the scheme. Beyond is an area, reaching towards the river and mill, containing a number of beautiful trees and shrubs, sheeted in spring with daffodils, fritillaries, anemones and other bulbs, while, anchored by its massive taproots, *Lysichitum americanum* grows at the sides of the river. It has handsome yellow arums in spring followed by immense paddle-shaped leaves. The giant leaves of *Gunnera manicata* or Chilean Rhubarb are equally solidly anchored. And well they need be, for in times of flood the river can sweep everything before it. In fact on one visit I was confronted by a lake in place of the lawn and rose garden. Though the waters soon subsided they took with them all the goldfish who no doubt enjoyed their freedom.

On the other side of the drive is the mulberry garden; a young tree has been planted to replace the original. Here is also *Acer davidii*, one of the Chinese Snake-Bark species, beautiful at all seasons. The borders are filled with flowers and through the gate, which bears "RK" in its scroll-work, is a pear-alley under-planted with spring flowers and decorated with clematises outside for summer colour. The kitchen garden is now mostly lawn, but a long border contains an interesting collection of herbs. After Mrs Kipling died, Mr C. Woodbine Parish became the Trust's tenant, and developed the garden considerably. The walls around the Kitchen Garden are his.

The year's delights recur without fail – the bursting buds, the flowers, the fruits, particularly Kipling's

This season's Daffodil
She never hears
What change, what chance, what chill
Cut down last year's;
But with bold countenance,
And knowledge small,
Esteems her seven days' continuance
To be perpetual.

Beyond to the west gently rears the age-old hill, affectionately known as Pook's for some sixty years and likely to retain this title into the future. In spite of all this quietness and timelessness, "It is later than you think" says the sundial, and so "Take the flower and turn the hour, and kiss your love again".

BENTHALL HALL
Broseley, *Salop*

Given in 1958 by Mrs J. Floyer Benthall and endowed by Sir Edward Benthall

AREA 1.2 ha (3 acres)
SOIL Limy
ALTITUDE 189 m (620 ft)
RAINFALL 686 mm (27 in.)
TEMPERATURE 3°C (37°F)

4 miles north-east of Much Wenlock via B4376 and B4375, 6 miles south of Wellington, 1 mile north of Broseley

IT IS MANY YEARS since I first glimpsed the Hall in the November sunshine, as I went up the long, curving lane. Like so many English country houses, it later disappears from view, hidden by trees and the little church, to reappear when once the garden is reached. Then it was apparent that what had flaunted like yellow flags in the distance were the leaves of the Japanese Angelica Tree, *Aralia elata*. It grows freely on the substantial rock gardens in front of the house which is the second to stand on this site, the late 16th-century stone building having replaced a much earlier one.

Looking out from this vantage spot the pottery works on the rising ground beyond the marsh are much in evidence. A mile or so away are the clay deposits which provided the means whereby a tile manufacturer in the late 19th century made horticultural history at Benthall. There are several trees in rough grass to the east of the house and it is in this spot that some crocuses are naturalised, planted about a hundred years ago. In the spring appear hybrids between *Crocus tomasinianus* and *C. vernus*, and in the autumn *C. speciosus*, *C. pulchellus* and *C. nudiflorus* are to be seen, while in June the Martagon Lily flowers from old established groups. The originals were planted by George Maw, one of two brothers who owned the tile works. George became a keen botanist and gardener and grew choice alpine and bulbous plants, many of his own, collecting in Europe, Turkey and North America. Every gardener knows the 'Flower of the Snow', *Chionodoxa luciliae* (see plate III); it flowered in this country for the first time at Benthall in 1877, receiving the Royal Horticultural Society's First Class Certificate two years later. Much of George Maw's cultivation was done in the kitchen garden, but his rockery can still be seen, rather obscured by bushes in the tree-covered area, together with a depression made for a set of frame lights. His great triumph, after years of study, was the publication of *The Genus Crocus*, completed in 1886, and now a priceless rarity.

This is all very interesting as gardening history, but most of the garden that we know today round the house – the rockeries, retaining walls, pools and shrub banks – were made by the next owners, Mr Robert Bateman and his wife. Having built the place, the Benthall family moved away, but repurchased it in 1934, after a lapse of two hundred years or so in ownership. The whole of the garden is peopled by unusual plants and shrubs, and fortunately Sir Paul Benthall carries on the tradition.

Tree peonies and old roses thrive against the dovecote, which is partly covered by a Silk Vine, so called from the silky hairs in the seed pods. At the top of the Bateman's terraced Pixie Garden is a shrub grown for its autumn beauty, *Dipteronia sinensis*. Large clumps of *Veratrum viride*, the Indian Poke of North America, and the Balkan *Acanthus* grow on the main rock gardens. Nearby is a variegated Cornelian Cherry, and a brilliant blue-grey form of the Colorado Spruce. In spring, here and there through the garden may be seen the little triangular rich green leaves of *Arisarum proboscideum*, the 'Mouse Plant', so intriguing to all. Under dense trees by the church the naturalised alien *Geranium nodosum* thrives and is always in flower from spring to autumn to greet the visitor. Sir Paul tells me that *G. phaeum*, the Mourning Widow Cranesbill, grows freely and most appropriately in churchyards in the district.

43 Mr Bateman's terraced Pixie Garden at Benthall Hall.

BERRINGTON HALL
Leominster, *Hereford and Worcester*

Accepted by the Treasury on the death of the 2nd Lord Cawley and transferred to the Trust in 1957. Endowed by Vivienne, Lady Cawley

AREA 4 ha (10 acres)
SOIL Lime-free
ALTITUDE 106 m (350 ft)
RAINFALL 635 mm (25 in.)
TEMPERATURE 4.5°C (40°F)

3 miles north of Leominster, on west side of A49

CAPABILITY BROWN and others of his time destroyed many of the earlier formal gardens. But here at Berrington he started from the beginning, chose the position for the house, which was designed by his one-time assistant and son-in-law, and landscaped the parkland to the south and west. Thus this is one of the few 18th-century gardens in the Trust which has remained untouched, at least on one side of the house.

The soft warm tint of the rosy brown sandstone and the similarly coloured gravel is a delightful local touch, and is to some minds a perfect background to growing plants. Certainly it creates a friendly atmosphere though some may prefer the grey gravel and stone of other districts. Brown's austerity permitted no gardening on the sunny fronts, where the great portico oversees the tranquil landscape. As likely as not during your visit herons, shy inhabitants of the tree tops, will flap slowly across the sky from the heronry beyond

44 *Thladiantha oliveri*, a native of China, is a climbing perennial plant related to gourds and marrows. Flowers rich yellow. It thrives on a sunny wall at Barrington Court.

Brown's "pool". The lawns in late summer – or perhaps at the first sign of autumn – are sprigged all over with the delicate spires of the Ladies' Tresses orchids. Later the Neapolitan hardy cyclamens cluster in pink and white under the trees and shrubs near the house, and no sooner are their dark green leaves, so prettily and variously marbled with silver-grey, copiously bunched on the ground than one can look for the spearing shoots of snowdrops. In January these herald a long succession of blossom from bulbs, plants, shrubs and trees. But the botanical gardener must walk to the garden proper on the other side of the house.

Here along sunny walls will be found the rare perennial relative of the vegetable marrow, *Thladiantha oliveri*, a herbaceous climber very free with its rich deep yellow flowers. Species and varieties of *Clematis*, from the evergreen winter-flowering *C. cirrhosa balearica*, spring-flowering *C. armandii*, and onwards to summer and autumn hybrids are well represented; a striking combination being found in the lavender-blue 'William Kennett' and the orange-flowered *Eccremocarpus scaber* from Chile. Roses include 'Phyllis Bide' – constantly in flower – the spring-flowering 'Mme Grégoire Staechelin' and autumnal *R. bracteata*. The pink of 'Mme Grégoire' overlaps with the flowering of four immense old wistarias.

The climate at Berrington is fairly mild and it is not surprising that Lord Cawley's family have for long tried and found rewarding several rare and tender shrubs. *Buddleia colvilei* – the Kew form with such surprisingly large flowers held in a huge drooping spray amongst handsome large leaves – and the white-flowered *Crinodendron patagua*, *Phygelius aequalis*, a figwort in coral-red, the variegated *Daphne cneorum* and a *Carpenteria californica* claim attention, to say nothing of an ancient Chinese Juniper and the great column of the Oriental Spruce. New plantings of rhododendrons and camellias are nearby.

In spite of the busy road so near to the park, this is essentially a quiet place with views to the wooded hills of CROFT CASTLE and its ambrey, and, even though it can only be seen from points of vantage, one is always conscious of the "high reared head of Clee" not far away, the proud dominant hill beloved by Housman.

BLICKLING HALL
Aylsham, *Norfolk*

Acquired in 1942, under the will of the 11th Marquess of Lothian

AREA 18.9 ha ($46\frac{1}{2}$ acres) SOIL Lime-free ALTITUDE 30 m (100 ft) RAINFALL 635 mm (25 in.) TEMPERATURE 3.5°C (38°F)	$1\frac{1}{2}$ miles north-west of Aylsham, on north side of B1354, 15 miles north of Norwich

ONE OF THE EARLIEST garden plans owned by the Trust is at Blickling. Hanging in the house is a design dated 1729 clearly shewing something of the present arrangement of radial paths within the confines of the raised walk. The present house was started in 1611, on the site of an older one, which may or may not have been the same as that owned by Harold Godwinsson in pre-Conquest days but which was given a moat about 1390. This was fed from the nearby water courses, which drain into the lake, and which fed a fishpond just north of the house. The moat was drained before 1611, and has been dry ever since; there are records of summer bedding plants being used in it in 1676–7.

There is nothing retiring about Blickling Hall. It stands four-square to the main road – a style adopted in our early history – not at the end of a winding drive in an extensive park. Flanked first by hedges of yew planted in the 17th century, and then by gabled outhouses, the eye absorbs it without hindrance, spellbound by the prospect of lawn and hedge, brick and stone, corner towers and Dutch gables: an indelible impression. The yew hedges, 94.4 m (310 ft) long, are still 5.1 m (17 ft) high as they were in 1873, but are, at 4.2 m (14 ft), 1.2 m (4 ft) wider; they were stated to be two hundred years old in the *Journal of Horticulture* of that date (see illus. 10). And in the forecourt of the house on one of the gabled wings is a young plant of the Blickling Pear which received an Award of Merit from the Royal Horticultural Society in 1907, raised long before in this garden by a Mr W. Allen.

On walking round the house we get our second impression, that of a splendid Jacobean house surrounded by a gentle 18th-century landscape. There is the lake which stretches away to the north for a mile before curving out of sight – just such a stretch of water as Brown or Repton might have contrived. It is not definitely attributable to either of these famous designers, but was in existence by 1770, when Arthur Young, in his *Tour of the Eastern Counties*, commented upon the way that some "woods of majestic oaks and beech dip in the very water, while others gently retire from it and only shade the distant hills. . . . It is strikingly beautiful." I think you will dwell on it, as he did, "with uncommon pleasure".

We will not be waylaid by the beauty of flowers, but will walk straight up the central path of the garden, more or less to the east, pausing for a moment if it is early morning, for at that time the east front may be beautifully sunlit, framed by big trees. Just beyond the Temple is the great surprise. What seemed like a garden surrounded by limitless parkland ceases abruptly with a raised walk of gravel, broad and satisfying. To build up this lengthy terrace a wide ditch was dug out; this has a hedge in the bottom of it and is not a true ha-ha. The walk turns a right angle at the north end and returns towards the house. We can imagine the same thing happening at the other end, but possibly alterations took place here later. At all events if the design in the house be examined it will be apparent that the two squares of woodland thus enclosed on either side of the main walk to the Temple constitute a rectangular garden of even greater antiquity (*c.* 1629) than the

45 Detail from a Blickling estate map of 1729 shewing crossing and diagonal paths within shrubbery or "wilderness" in the bottom right corner. The "New Pond" at top, centre.

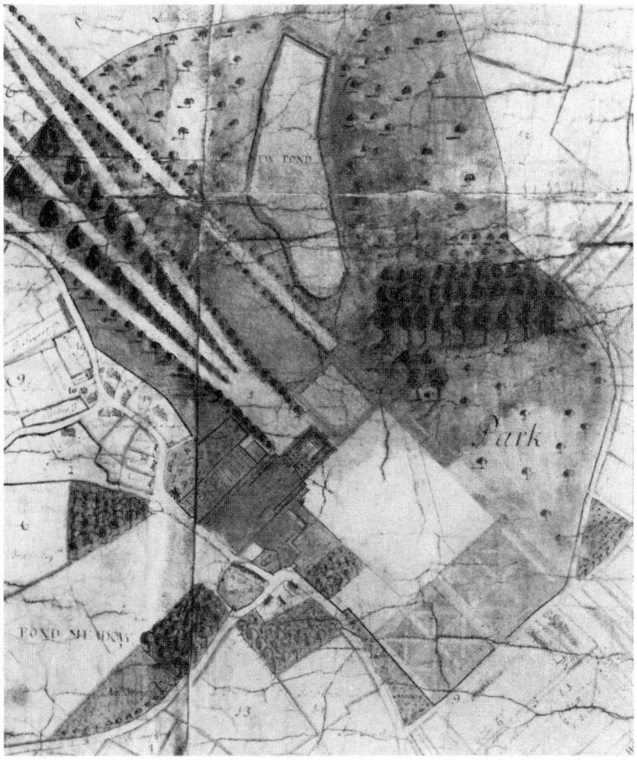

similar design of the Wilderness at Ham House. The raised walk is certainly in the style of the time.

Today the two sets of radial paths, which meet at circular clearings, are lined with trees, some planted in avenue fashion, others cut through oak woodland (see illus. 180). The 19th century probably saw the scheme re-drawn and the trees planted; the woodland areas enclosed are underplanted with yews. The rides are lined with rhododendrons in many places. Besides large groups of Pontic Rhododendrons there are earlier flowering varieties, and of recent years some late flowering kinds have been put in to prolong the display, including 'Romany Chal', fragrant 'Albatross' and 'Inamorata', 'Azor' and *R. discolor*; another sweetly-scented plant is the *Azaleodendron* 'Fragrans'.

The Temple was not built until 1760. It is interesting how the drip from the copper-clad roof has destroyed the foliage of the yews beneath, in a vertical line.

It is very easy at Blickling to envisage a great 17th-century parterre on the lawn east of the house. In all probability there was one, because this was the only site available apart from the entrance front. What we look at today is an adaptation of the expansive array of beds laid out for the Marchioness of Lothian in 1872. The scheme included the four big corner beds, the sentinel yews (though only a few feet high) and the strangely-shaped lengths of isolated yew hedge towards the steps which are always spoken of – with some pride and imagination – as the "grand pianos". It is recorded that the design of this garden is by W. A. Nesfield, with terrace steps and walls by Sir Digby Wyatt. During this building and levelling the surplus soil was used to fill in the near end of the lake, thus enlarging the lawn.

The impression from the windows of the Long Gallery is all that can be desired: the grand view terminated by the Temple, framed by its trees and spring-flowering shrubs; the two-acre formal layout, the broad stone steps, the clipped yews and the summer galaxy of colour (see plate XVIII). It is not as Lady Lothian had it, nor do we have the army of old pensioners whom she kept out of the kindness of her heart to tend the numerous little beds. In the 1930s Mrs Norah Lindsay rearranged it all. Beyond the steps the beds were removed so that the gravel walk is now flanked by quiet greensward, with shrubs linking this to the taller trees: Mount Etna Broom, *Acer nikoense* and *A. griseum* from Japan and China respectively, *Parrotia persica, Elaeagnus augustifolia, Malus sieboldii* and others. In the formal garden she swept away the many fussy beds but kept the four big corner ones, filling them with herbaceous plants of graded height, the two near beds being given the quiet tones of pink and blue, mauve and white, while the pair beyond are decked with yellow and orange flowers. The Nankeen Lily grows and flowers well, also *Yucca filamentosa*, Tree Mallows, tall blue *Lactuca plumieri*, and many another summer stalwart. To each square she gave an embroidered border of

46 Looking across the formal garden at Blickling. The yew 'grand pianos' and Sir Digby Wyatt's walls and steps are to the left. Photo 1956.

catmint spiced by roses; still of her planting are 'Else Poulsen' and 'Kirsten Poulsen' in pink and crimson, and 'Locarno' and 'Gloria Mundi' in red and orange, to tone with their respective beds. In spite of the many hundreds of roses that have been raised since, no pairs of varieties match so well nor give such continuous colour.

Looking again from the Long Gallery window, the eye catches the fountain and herms. These, together with the urns and other ornaments in the garden, were bought at the sale of Oxnead, the home of the Earl of Yarmouth, before 1872. At Oxnead the fountain graced a lawn with flower-beds, and the herms stood unguarded in the grass; they were placed likewise near the Grand Pianos until the Trust moved them to their niches by the wall about 1960. Lady Lothian had the bank around the fountain thickly planted with *Hosta plantaginea.*

If you descend into the moat you will have a very different impression. Here is a narrow alley where sun or shade contrive homes for fastidious plants. In the shade are camellias and Japanese anemones, hostas and ferns, with the Climbing Hydrangea and its close relative *Schizophragma hydrangeoides* ascending the north wall, where the great hairy leaves of *Hydrangea sargentiana* find shelter from wind. Considering how the north-west wind from the lake buffets the hall it is surprising to find some rather tender roses and other plants on the sunny east wall. Here are *Trachelospermum jasminoides*, the autumn-flowering *Buddleia auriculata* and *B. crispa* which produces its flowers in June and autumn, giant yellow honeysuckle *Lonicera tragophylla*, the Claret Vine and roses 'Cramoisi Supérieur Grimpante' (1885), 'William Allen Richardson' (1878), 'Paul's Carmine Pillar' (1895), 'Paul's Single White' (1883), 'Gloire de Dijon' (1853), *R. laevigata* and *R. cooperi* (of gardens).

Maybe it is September and if so you will be entranced by the Neapolitan cyclamens by the steps above the moat. These have all been established of late years in the dry rooty soil under the big trees, from seeds raised from the older colonies on the other side of the hall. This upper walk is shrouded by Japanese Cherries, but early colour is given by Bearded Irises of many colours, and later by dahlias and *Aster frikartii* 'Mönch'. Along the back border are shrub roses, *R. virginiana*, hybrid sweet briers, 'Sir Thomas Lipton' and 'Mrs Anthony Waterer', the Japanese Moss Rose, and the ancient 'Duchess of Portland'. This was well established when I first went to Blickling in 1955, and may well have been there for a hundred years or more. It is a most historic rose, resembling somewhat the Red Rose of Lancaster, but producing its flowers repeatedly until the autumn. It was found by the Duchess of Portland in Italy about 1800, a hybrid between the Autumn Damask of Roman antiquity and the Crimson China rose, which had been introduced in 1792. This historic plant is in the parentage of all modern roses.

From the seat on the grass slope at the end of these upper borders one of the fairest prospects in English horticulture is obtained. From this vantage point the summer colour schemes of borders and beds can be fully enjoyed, with the backcloth of the house and the immensely long view down the lake. It has the same sort of corridor-view so beloved by Flemish painters, the distance enhanced by bold foreground work. To balance the house is a huge dome of light green, a tree of wide proportions. It is an Oriental Plane, enhanced by the dark green of Turkey Oaks beyond. As long ago as 1894 its branches were stated to be 14.5–18 m (16–20 yds) long and to have rooted in the turf; today the old central trunk still stands, surrounded by these self-made layers, covering an area of about 836 m^2 (1000 sq yds); primroses and lilies grow in its shade.

Terminating the broad walk are steps up to a large seat, given to the Trust by Messrs R. G. Carter Ltd, who carried out extensive restoration to the house from 1960–70. It is from a design by William Kent and was copied from one in the theatre at BODNANT.

There is another point to be considered and that is the border above the terrace wall and steps. Whatever time is your visit, the impression will be of a filled border giving colourful interest for a minimum of attention. First are the red-brown stems and leaves of peonies; later they flower profusely. Frothing over their backs and the coping of the wall in July is a mass of starry cream flowers of Virgin's Bower, or *Clematis flammula*; by the time these flowers have changed to a cloud of silky seed heads, the peony leaves are assuming their autumn tints. And for the whole of the season the irregular fringe of Lambs' Ears has provided a *piano* accompaniment of silvery grey.

Let us next visit the Orangery, considered to have been built about 1820, perhaps by John Adey Repton,

Humphry's son. (Humphry, by the way, lies buried in Aylsham churchyard and his tomb has been recently restored.) I had always been of the opinion that terracotta was an easy colour to deal with; this is so indoors as a rule. Like human flesh it can be assorted successfully with a wide variety of tones. But when the orangery interior was redecorated it was at once apparent that colours had to be chosen carefully. There was the attendant difficulty that light only came in horizontally, that there was no heat and very little soil. Flowers were obviously not going to be the main foil, but foliage which would last in beauty for the whole of the "open" season. Eventually the choice was narrowed to plants with blue-green leaves and those with cream variegation. Rhododendrons like *R. cinnabarinum* and *concatenans* did not approve, and made their exit, despairing. *Hosta sieboldiana elegans* is an unparalleled success, also the cream-variegated privet, *Ligustrum ovalifolium* 'Argenteum'. In both of the ante-rooms stands a large tub holding *Cupressus cashmiriana*; though by no means hardy these have so far appreciated the slight shelter of the building, and contribute their quota of blue-green from the weeping, lacy branches.

There is one further little touch of Mrs Lindsay's, for in 1936 she redesigned the Secret Garden in the wooded area to the north of the main vista to the Temple. Here she found a wall and summerhouse with seat, and set out the paths and surrounding hedges. The sundial bears the date 1697. To one side lies a little shrub garden devoted to fragrant shrubs and lilies, with vermilion-red lily flowers in May of the Chilean *Hippeastrum pratense*, brought from the kitchen garden where thousands of bulbs have thriven for many years, without protection, against an east-facing wall.

BODNANT GARDEN
Talycafn, Colwyn Bay, *Gwynedd*

Given by the 2nd Lord Aberconway, with further gifts by the 3rd Lord Aberconway

AREA 32 ha (80 acres)	8 miles south
SOIL Lime-free	of Llandudno and
ALTITUDE 30 m (100 ft)	Colwyn Bay, on A496
RAINFALL 1016 mm (40 in.)	
TEMPERATURE 6°C (43°F)	

THE PRESENT Lord Aberconway's great-grandfather purchased the house and estate in 1875, refacing the house with blue granite, with yellow mullions. Many of the great native trees derive from a hundred or more years earlier, but the big conifers date from the end of the 19th century. Much of the very early garden, including a sloping lawn, shrubberies and the Laburnum Arch (see plate XX), dates from the 1880s.

Prior to the First World War the series of broad Italianate terraces was constructed, preserving the two large cedars on the third terrace. At the top of these is the Rose Terrace, lovely through the summer, and gay in the spring with various small edging plants. If you are there at tulip time, and it is a clear sunny day, you will just have passed a vast carpet of vivid blue, from *Gentiana acaulis* – a breathtaking sight by the house. The terraces take their cue from the line of the gentian walk and march grandly downhill, with first the Rose Terrace whence there is a wonderful view towards Snowdonia, seen through the red-brown stems of an ancient *Arbutus andrachnoides* planted in 1906.

Then there is the Croquet Terrace with wall-fountain shrouded in white Japanese Wistarias, *W. floribunda* 'Alba' whose racemes may exceed 610 mm (2 ft) in length, and the large-flowered *W. venusta*. *Magnolia campbellii* grows well; it was 4.5 m (15 ft) in 1915, had doubled its height in 1928, and is now about 16.7 m (55 ft). Its hybrid 'Charles Raffill' is nearby. They flower very early, even before *Camellia reticulata* 'Captain Rawes' appears, followed by the white flowers and scarlet leaves of Forrest's *Pieris*; later the dwarf Korean Lilac opens, fragrant rhododendrons, and the white *Carpenteria californica*, and late display is given by hoherias from New Zealand, *Buddleia crispa*, *Lespedeza bicolor*, hydrangeas, and eucryphias from South America. There is not a dull moment.

Next the Lily Pool, its crimson and pink waterlilies so perfect a contrast for the blue cedar, while blues and pinks of hydrangeas add their quota from shady borders. Then the descending flights of steps, curved beneath the pergola on which grow many roses, including 'Easlea's Golden Rambler', 'Climbing Lady Hillingdon' and 'Gardenia' interspersed with the lavender-blue flowers of the climbing *Solanum*. Arriving at the Lower Rose Terrace we can take in its Jekyllian patterned brick paths; the roses flower and grow well, a great variety of moderns being grown, while, behind, the 'Goliath' *Magnolia* covers the wall with its large glossy leaves and huge fragrant white flowers in late summer. A different line altogether is provided by the weeping Mount Etna Broom, a shower of tiny yellow flowers in August.

We have now arrived on the Canal Terrace. At one end is an open-air stage, hedged with yews, at the other a small building – brought from Gloucestershire in 1938. I remember seeing it in 1939 and was immensely impressed to think that the operations of reduction, transport and erection could have been carried out so quickly. It was originally a summerhouse, *c.* 1740, but later was used as a pin mill. Its reflection in the still water of the canal is one of the much-sought views in the garden; the borders along either side of the extensive plats of grass contain summer flowers of blue, mauve and pink enhanced by silvery foliage.

One of my favourite spots in the spring is the North Garden, just beyond the Lily Terrace. There is much contrast of growth here, from tall background trees, the

47 Majestic trees in the Dell at Bodnant. Photo 1937.

spire of an Italian cypress, and the varied rounded hummocks of rhododendrons, including those early, dainty-flowered species of the Azalea Series, *R. schlippenbachii* and *R. albrechtii*. Their flowers, pale pink and deep rose respectively, are wide open and develop before the leaves. In this they are very different from the flower shape of their neighbours, species and hybrids of the Cinnabarinum Series, whose flowers are tubular and waxy, from darkest port-wine tint through coppery pinks to flame and the yellow of 'Bodnant Yellow'. These all overlap with the lavender-blue of *R. augustinii*, which grows so freely here.

As if this were not enough, Bodnant has to offer a garden of a different type altogether. Apart from a little formal touch here and there, uniting the numerous informal delights, the rest is, shall we say, in the Welsh vernacular. There is the *raison d'être* to start with, the little River Hiraethlyn which, leaving placid pools above, thunders over a waterfall and thence is a rushing brook, chattering and splashing its way down to the Conway River. In the Dell it passes lofty conifers, firs, hemlocks, redwoods, *Abies grandis*, 53 m (175 ft) high, and cypresses of immense height; white- and coppery-barked birches (*Betula ermanii*, *B. albo-sinensis septentionalis* and *B. utilis prattii*), a weeping Wellingtonia and many another tree of note. Though many exceed 30 m (100 ft) in height they are not visible from the upper terraces, being deep down in the valley. Here and there little streams gush out of the sides of the rocky gorge,

contributing to the general sound of water passing over rocks, and making habitats for small plants, while sprinkled through the trees are rhododendrons of impressive size, port and leafage – *R. calophytum* and *R. falconeri* among them.

If you can go to Bodnant first in summer, when most, apart from the terrace gardens, is a poem in greens, or in autumn when every other bush and tree is aflame in yellow, red, russet or coral, you will not be distracted by too many flowers and can enjoy the design and immense contrasts between terrace and dell, still pool and rushing stream, the majesty of trees, the inviting winding walks and the distant views. And keep to your promise to go again in spring.

Words cannot convey a tithe of the colour and beauty that makes up the spring fairyland of Bodnant. To start with there are rhododendrons everywhere of every colour, yellow, orange, red, pink, white, lilac and purple, flowering from earliest spring to midsummer. They have long been a speciality at Bodnant, and many were raised from seeds direct from the Himalayas; hybrids have been raised, in fact between the wars the late Lord Aberconway, with his head gardener F. C. Puddle, was one of the pioneers among hybridists. With them, but mainly earlier, are camellias of every tint, and scattered throughout the garden lowly azaleas of the Japanese sort add their cool tints to the scene after the camellias. Magnolias abound, white and blush and rosy, small bushes or great trees, many sweetly scented. There is for example a large specimen of *M. sargentiana robusta*, and one of *M. sprengeri* 'Claret Cup' raised at Bodnant, also *M. denudata*, *M. veitchii*, *M. watsonii* and *M. macrophylla*. Under and among this galaxy of spring star-performers are the lowly plants, the Japanese and Chinese primulas, Himalayan blue, yellow and flame poppies (*Meconopsis* species) and white New Zealand *Libertia*; Californian *Lewisia* and Chinese *Primula forrestii* grow in retaining walls. *Lunaria rediviva*, *Actaea alba*, *Euphorbia griffithii* 'Fireglow', hellebores, rodgersias are there with *Kirengeshoma* for autumn, and a generous grouping in many areas of hydrangeas.

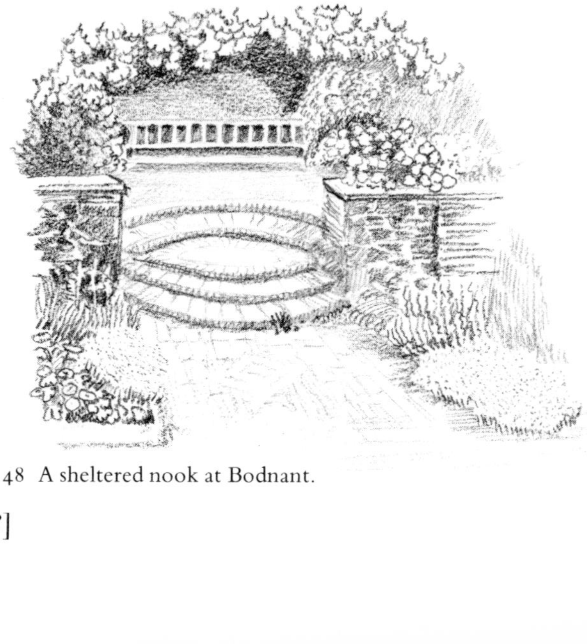

48 A sheltered nook at Bodnant.

You will need a whole long afternoon to enjoy the entire garden. The plan in the guide asks us to do as we have done, to descend the terraces, traverse the glade, then to ascend to the Mausoleum and shrub borders above the Dell. Here are some entrancing views, looking down onto great conifers and tall magnolias. Along the borders will be found many choice species, not only shrubs, but trees as well – for instance a vigorous *Nothofagus dombeyi*, *Prunus serrula*, whose coppery bark vies with the most polished cherrywood walking stick, and *Acer griseum* which is nearly as colourful. There is much spring floral beauty from *Magnolia sprengeri elongata*, *Sycopsis sinensis*, *Lomatia hirsuta*, and various other shrubs, to the later pale yellow flowers of *Magnolia cordata*, *Viburnum hillieri*, *V. erubescens* and *Styrax hemsleyana* which is usually laden with its white blooms.

Later we reach a little informal pool embowered in *Rhododendron williamsianum*, and come out on to the level sward of the top lawn where the hybrid *Rhododendron* 'Elizabeth', raised here in 1933, almost warms the air with its brilliant scarlet bell-flowers in May. If I lived at Bodnant I feel I should often bless the mind that left the uninterrupted view across the front lawn to the south where in the meadow is a natural low eminence crowned with a few native oaks. Apart from daffodils and bluebells in the spring it is devoid of colour – the perfect antidote in its greenery and gentle form to the splendours of horticulture away below. The Chilean Fire Bush, *Embothrium coccineum lanceolatum*, gives a dazzling display in this area in spring; mostly from the special form raised at Bodnant from seeds brought from the Norquinco Valley in the Andes by Harold Comber. It is called after its native valley. It is so brilliant a colour that it shames everything within sight. Sometimes it is effectively contrasted with copper beeches or hazels, but one most ravishing example at Bodnant is where it has been given a group of Blue Cedars as a background.

Next we arrive at the Round Garden. This is the home of numerous rare dwarf shrubs and plants, such as daphnes, rhododendrons, vacciniums, gaultherias and *Anemone narcissiflora*. *Rhododendron davidsonianum* in clear pink with chestnut eye is particularly in evidence nearby. There used to be four yellow cypresses here in the 1930s and the surrounding bed was annually decorated with conventional mixtures of lobelias, geraniums and the like. After the war the cypresses were removed, the sea of weeds dug up, and the present beds were made. To the surprise of all one of the most prevalent weeds was *Lobelia erinus*!

Somewhere here is a wall, on which grows *Rosa sinowilsonii*, the rose with the largest and most handsome leaf, with small white fragrant flowers in June; it commemorates E. H. Wilson, who with Forrest and Kingdon Ward contributed so much to the gardens of this century, by their indefatigable travels in the Far East. But stop – if it is late May or early June – what is that glimpse of yellow? Step aside and you will see the crowning glory – a tunnel of laburnums originally planted a hundred years ago over metal frames, the whole arc above one's head, stretching for a curving length of 54.8 m (180 ft), hung with thousands of yellow racemes, their colour and their fragrance assailing our senses. A little later *Rhododendron* 'Winsome', raised at Bodnant in 1930, gives a splash of rich, coppery, cerise-pink.

As you leave the garden you will catch glimpses of the house clothed in pyracantha, almost dominated by the bulky, towering specimens of dark green cypresses (*Chamaecyparis lawsoniana* 'Erecta Viridis'). This splendid conifer was raised at Knaphill Nursery, Woking in 1855, and has been the main vertical evergreen line in gardens ever since. In complete contrast is a small lawn, where the silver weeping pear echoes in its rounded shape the domes of white and palest lavender Yunnan rhododendrons; across the lawn stretch the long shadows.

Gone are the days when annually at the Chelsea Show there would be an exhibit of new rhododendrons from Bodnant. Well do I remember seeing the vivid tones of 'Elizabeth', 'Fabia Tangerine', and others of their style and colouring. Today they are all over the country; to follow is the exquisite 'Vanessa' and its paler 'Pastel' (see plate IV), while *R. aberconwayi*, raised from seed collected in the wilds in the Far East, carries on this distinguished name into hybrids of the future. Bodnant has been blessed by successive generations of keen horticulturists and the place goes forward under the family's guidance for the benefit of us all (see illus. 169).

In the early 1930s my old friend, A. T. Johnson, who gardened on the other side of the valley, invited me for a weekend, adding that Bodnant would be open to visitors on the Saturday and that "this would be a pleasure you mustn't forego, and a duty you mustn't neglect". I have seldom been in North Wales since without this duty and pleasure. (See also plates I and XIII.)

BUCKLAND ABBEY
Tavistock, *Devon*

Acquired in 1948 through the help of Viscount Astor, Capt. A. Rodd and the Pilgrim Trust

AREA 1.2 ha (3 acres)	6 miles south of
SOIL Lime-free	Tavistock, 1 mile south
ALTITUDE 75 m (250 ft)	of Buckland
RAINFALL 1016 mm (40 in.)	Monachorum,
TEMPERATURE 6°C (43°F)	west of the A386

SIR FRANCIS DRAKE purchased this property from the Grenville family to whom it had been given by Henry VIII in 1541. The house has important naval associations therefore, but the Plymouth Corporation, to whom the

49 Flight of steps to the Herb Garden at Buckland Abbey.

property is leased, take great care of the garden as well. Some trees date from long before 1948, particularly the rows of yews whose age cannot be accurately guessed.

As if in confirmation of Drake's famous circumnavigation, the garden is full of exotic plants of equally all-embracing provenance. By the solid old building are two magnolias of great size: the 'Bull Bay', as it is called, from the United States, and Delavay's species from South Yunnan. There is a good specimen of the West Himalayan Spruce and of the Himalayan Pine; *Mahonia lomariifolia* from China and Formosa and *Actinidia kolomikta* from Manchuria; the "Parrot's Bill" or "Lobster Claw" from New Zealand and *Eucryphia* from Chile. Europe is not left out; the lesser Periwinkle is used skilfully as ground cover under the yews.

While the general effect is of a noble old building in its setting of sloping lawns, surrounded by a rich assembly of exotic shrubs, behind the main mass of the building, a surprise awaits you. Here is a series of box-edged beds filled with herbs and medicinal plants, mostly European. Sweet Cicely, Mints, Self-Heal, Lovage, Fennel and Balm mingle with Lungwort and Hellebore, with a backcloth of the Chinese *Vitis coignetiae*, indigoferas and wistarias. No month can pass at Buckland without its display of flowers.

BUSCOT PARK
Faringdon, *Oxfordshire*

Given by Mr E. E. Cook in 1948

AREA 8 ha (20 acres)	2 miles south-east of
SOIL Limy	Lechlade on the A417
ALTITUDE 75 m (250 ft)	Lechlade-Faringdon road
RAINFALL 686 mm (27 in.)	
TEMPERATURE 3.5°C (38°F)	

THE PARK and grounds at Buscot are typical of many great houses in that the inventiveness of several owners has resulted in considerable alterations. Building the house in 1780, Edward Loveden Townsend had an eye for the landscape as well, for he presumably made the two lakes to the north-west and east of the house. His house stood proud and free on its eminence with the cupola of the stable block well below. The entrance drive approached the house from the north-east. Robert Campbell, who purchased the property in 1850, altered the entrance drive, transferring it to the north-west of the house, thus taking advantage of traversing the Little Lake as we do today. It is a very pleasant approach, through trees, rising towards the gate piers, obliquely to the house. Some years ago the whole place had a majesty derived from English Elms of great size – now unhappily dead. Fortunately, the late Lord Faringdon was an assiduous planter of trees, so that there are many young ones rapidly growing for the future. The prospect from the south front is enhanced by radiating drives and a distant grille, set in low walls centrally across the lawn. A back drive runs downhill to the south-east. His forethought here was most fruitful in results; he planted a triple avenue, the central rows being of limes, with plane trees outside; in between were poplars for quick effect. These were felled in the late 1960s, to give space for the other two avenues. Our experience at ANGLESEY ABBEY where planes suffered wind-damage seems likely to be repeated here, and so probably the limes will be retained for the future. There are several other young avenues, one of Fastigiate Oak; here the nurserymen supplied two types, one broad and one narrow, ruining the necessary uniformity of an avenue. Young plants of the better type have been purchased with a view to replacement.

If you stand on the steps of the house you can see the grounds stretching away both east and west, for great distances; each terminates in a sheet of water. Let us first go west, through the bowl-shaped kitchen garden, with great walls built probably by Loveden Townsend, past the fountain pool at its base, complete with statue, placed there in this century. Beyond, uphill, through yet another wall, is the reservoir brought into existence by Robert Campbell soon after 1860. He needed it mainly because he sought to grow superlative sugar beet on his farmland. At the side of this reservoir, banked and bordered by the trees, stands a small Temple. From the Temple, past the house and to the farthest east part of the grounds is a distance not far short of 1.6 km (1 mile).

No doubt in an effort to weld this great length into a united whole, the first Lord Faringdon engaged Harold Peto to design a water garden east of the house, probably in the first decade of this century. The vista is long, a cutting through the tree-covered area, hedged mainly with box. The water is cunningly made to flow down and through a great variety of falls and rills, into geometrical pools and under bridges; first narrow, then widening, sometimes disappearing altogether, then

50 Harold Peto's formal water garden at Buscot Park, laid out early in this century.

contracting again until it comes to rest in the lake. In all of this Peto brought his "revived Renaissance" touch to bear in the formal stonework, and I think you will find that, in spite of its length of 76.2 m (250 ft), the interest is well sustained by his inventiveness, coupled with the tinkle of water, the occasional reflections, sculpture and ancient earthenware jars, and the cooing of pigeons.

The lake to which we have come has a small temple on the far shore, and once again is bordered by trees. The whole place is well enriched by trees, both natives and a sprinkling of exotics. Here and there are dense thickets where one might picture being enacted the Briar Wood legend of which the original paintings by Burne-Jones are in the house.

The fateful slumber floats and flows
About the tangle of the rose.

Roses in beds are not far away and are reached on one of the several routes back to the house which take you past many of the recent tree plantings.

CASTLE DROGO
Drewesteignton, *Devon*

Given by Mr Anthony Drewe in 1974 with endowment, helped by bequests made by Miss St Paul and Mr C. S. Morris

AREA 4.8 ha (12 acres)
SOIL Lime-free
ALTITUDE 305 m (1000 ft)
RAINFALL 1143 mm (45 in.)
TEMPERATURE 5°C (41°F)

At Drewesteignton, 2 miles north-east of Chagford, 1 mile south of A30

ELSEWHERE I have essayed to explain how different are the properties of the National Trust. It is perfectly obvious to anybody that unless an architect or a garden designer deliberately tries to repeat a scheme, all houses and gardens do tend to be different from one another. Even so, there is something about the phrase "the Gardens of the National Trust" that tends to bracket them together, giving perhaps to the less informed visitor a feeling that they are somehow related to each other.

When you visit Castle Drogo I think you will have great difficulty in thinking of any house or garden with affinity to it. In the first place the terrain is as dramatic as it could be, the house standing starkly on the edge of an escarpment with the Teign far below. It is a stone, castellated building of some size, designed by that mastermind, Edwin Lutyens, for the Drewe family. He also designed the garden. The building was never completed but a huge solid square of clipped yews partly compensates for the uncompleted wing. Two small portions near to the castle and chapel have been given quiet plantings of dwarf evergreen plants and shrubs respectively. From the courtyard you can walk back along part of the drive or delve into the extensive planting of rhododendrons below it. Here are both species and hybrids. The former include *R.R. aberconwayi*, *albrechtii*, *neriiflorum*, *souliei*, *valentinianum*, and that charmer for buttonholes *R. carolinianum*. Hybrids will be found through a long season likewise, from *R.* 'Nobleanum' and 'Bo Peep', 'Cornish Cross', 'St Breward' and 'May Day', to the late-flowering 'Polar Bear'.

In Devon and Cornwall, where one takes for granted woodland gardens, it comes as a surprise to mount a flight of steps at Castle Drogo and alight on a big formal garden. At the first corners of the great square are architectural "boxes" of yew hedges, each containing four beds of shade-loving plants and four Weeping Camperdown Elms – at least they were there on my last visit; I hope the ravages of the elm disease will spare them. They have been there for fifty years or more, ever since the garden was planted, and make a cool dark approach to the bright, open, formal garden. An unusual array of rectangular rose beds surrounds the big lawn, sunk below the general level, while above, held

51 Garden designed by Sir Edwin Lutyens at Castle Drogo, *c.*1920. Note the huge circular lawn.

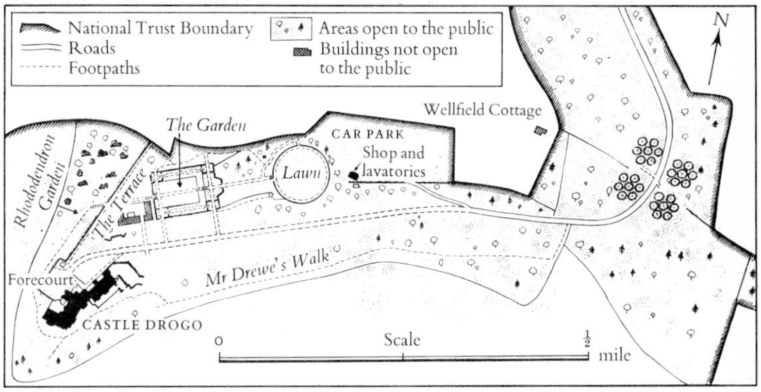

52 Path with an Indian motif at Castle Drogo, between herbaceous borders.

by low walls, a long parterre leads from one yew-hedged corner to the next. Fresh from designing the new city at Delhi, eastern thoughts seem to have gone to Lutyen's head for he used a well-known Indian motif for the arrangement of flanking flower borders on either side of the parterre ways. At first sight they appear to be sinuous; on inspection we find the motif is composed of equal lengths of straight, curve, straight, reverse curve, straight. (This design is derived from lines in one direction of a chequer-pattern; when crossed at right angles the pattern closes intriguingly.) On a brilliant day the colours of the roses and herbaceous plants furnish what is a remarkable yet quiet design on two levels.

Now let us mount the double flight of steps at the end and walk between the shrub borders, up and up the slope, wondering what is beyond the two dark green cypresses. It will have to be good and decisive after what we have seen and passed through. Instead, there is *nothing*. Nothing, that is, apart from a vast circular lawn completely encompassed by a tall yew hedge. A void so large that one quickly brushes away the initial thought that there ought to be a central something. The void is satisfying in itself, and needs no belittling of its undisputed proud possession of the site. I like to think that Lutyens visualised the terraced garden as a link with the weight of the empty lawn at one extremity balanced by the jutting bossy castle at the other.

Lutyens did his best to persuade the Drewes to employ Gertrude Jekyll on the planting of the drive and garden. Though she submitted ideas, they were not accepted, and Mr Julius Drewe employed instead George Dillistone, a garden designer and enthusiast of some note who had gardened earlier for him in Kent. For many years Dillistone had been prominent in the artistry of gardening and plants, including lilies and irises. He included both among his plants at Castle Drogo, and in replanting the long borders many of his favourite plants and lilies have been replaced. In an article in *The Garden* for March 1923 he described vividly a garden of lilies, recalling how the "gorgeous masses of Tiger Lilies . . . lifted their orange splendour at regular intervals throughout the picture . . . There are some garden pictures that one never forgets." I think you will find the same ease in recalling your impressions of Castle Drogo garden.

CASTLE WARD
Downpatrick, *Co. Down*

Given and endowed in 1953 by the Ulster Government, after the death of Lady Bangor

AREA 16 ha (40 acres)
SOIL Lime-free
ALTITUDE 24.3 m (80 ft)
RAINFALL 762 mm (30 in.)
TEMPERATURE 7.2°C (45°F)

7 miles north-east of Downpatrick, off the A25 Downpatrick–Strangford road

OUR GARDENS are full of surprises, and surprises galore await the visitor at Castle Ward. First there is the view of the house. The short drive among fine native beeches and oaks brings us to an extensive view towards that most beautiful of Northern Ireland's waters – Strangford Lough. Between us and the lough, poised on slightly rising ground, is the house, built with Georgian dignity of stone imported specially from Bath. But go round to the side which faces the lough and a transformation takes place; this side is in the Gothick taste. And so it continues inside, half the rooms being classical and half Gothick, due to the opposed whims of Bernard Ward and his wife (later Lord and Lady Bangor) in the late 18th century. All around are gentle slopes of grass and great trees, huge Irish yews and a variety of shrubs, including the lavender-blue daisy-bush from the Chatham Islands, *Olearia semidentata*, which has as companions the tabular display of white flowers of *Viburnum plicatum* 'Mariesii' and towering bushes of orange-scarlet Chilean Fire Bush.

Beyond the shrubs one comes to a screen of yews, and then to a walled, formal garden with grass terraces studded with tropical-looking, palm-like trees, the Cabbage Tree of New Zealand. In June these cast a delicious sweet scent afar on the air from their large bouquets of tiny white flowers. To echo their exotic character a series of dwarf palms has been planted both in the beds under the cordylines and also to punctuate the surrounding borders. These beds and borders, apart from the trees, are indicative of the kindly climate at Castle Ward, for many plants are thriving which we should find too tender in Surrey. *Mimulus aurantiacus* and *M. cardinalis*, cannas and calceolarias, *Verbena rigida*, Purple-leafed *Pittosporum*, the Kangaroo Apple, arums, and *Mitraria coccinea* find congenial homes, to conjure up the exotic effect, and to mirror somewhat the Victorian taste which dictated the design.

The rock garden has a number of interesting plants and shrubs, including fine specimens of *Picea glauca albertiana* 'Conica' and the brilliant yellow dwarf Chinese Arborvitae, *Thuja orientalis* 'Nana Aurea'.

These brief glimpses of the garden must serve until you are able to pay a visit. If it is in early May your cup of joy will be filled by the old avenue of limes, in tender green leaf, thickly spread with bluebells.

What with the beautiful landscape, the intriguing Georgian house, the garden enriched from the four corners of the earth and the avenue, we may feel that little more can be in store. But beyond the staff quarters, connected with the house by an underground passage, it is a short step to the great formal water of the 17th century. As an eye-catcher at the far end, stands on its hillock a romantic tiny castle, Audley's Tower, while on top of the steep bank guarding the water from the north is an 18th-century temple. It may not all be garden, but as a place of pilgrimage I know of no other with quite so varied an array of historic and beautiful features.

CHARLECOTE PARK
Stratford-upon-Avon, *Warwickshire*

Given in 1946 by Sir Montgomerie Fairfax-Lucy, Bt

AREA 1.2 ha (3 acres)	4 miles east of
SOIL Neutral	Stratford-upon-Avon,
ALTITUDE 30 m (100 ft)	6 miles south of
RAINFALL 635 mm (25 in.)	Warwick, on the B4086
TEMPERATURE 4°C (39°F)	Stratford-Banbury road

LIME TREES as a rule do not blow down in gales and they live for hundreds of years. We shall not know when the majestic avenue from the West Lodge gates at Charlecote was planted until the growth rings can be counted. But the avenue was already established by 1760 since Lancelot Brown was forbidden to fell this and the old elm avenue which used to approach the house from the east when he was looking for his usual "capabilities". He was allowed to alter the line of the River Hele to join the Avon and to remodel the portion of the park to the north of the house, which can be viewed from the promontory at the end of his North Garden, where still grow two most ancient mulberries, almost prostrate with the weight of years. In 1955 the North Garden was a bramble-infested wilderness; it was gradually cleared and the hedges patched and pruned.

Before Brown's day, as every schoolboy knows, the young Shakespeare was arraigned by Sir Thomas Lucy in 1558 for poaching. The Lucy family has lived at Charlecote ever since 1247, through varying fortunes and veering fashions in garden design. Few old pictures show a more splendid layout than that attributed to Jan Stevens of 1696 (see plate XXVII), but little is left save the exquisite gatehouse of 1550–1. This gem of architecture gives upon the garden forecourt and leads to the original porch to the house; the exterior of the house, which has assumed an immemorially settled appearance, is only a little over a hundred years old.

The garden was elaborated in Victorian times. Over 20,000 bedding plants were produced annually, many for a series of beds in the garden forecourt, the outlines of which can still be seen in the lawns in dry weather. The pretty balustrading on the garden walls and the Orangery, and no doubt much of the terracing and the planting of the cedar trees, dates from this period. The stone for the balustrading is very soft and some clever repairs were carried out by the Trust from 1970 onwards with exact replicas of the sections, made of reconstituted stone. The quaint rustic aviary and the Judas Tree beside the orangery were added during the 19th century.

There are several good shrubs and plants in the forecourt borders – broken by the steps and attendant leaden figures of a shepherd and shepherdess by John Cheere, *c.*1718 – but for me the garden is chiefly treasured for housing, years ago, a poor wizened plant of *Clematis viticella* 'Elegans Plena'. This was growing to the north of the great gates by the house; it was carefully lifted and all the plants at present in gardens have been propagated from it. Apart from the big plant at Abbotswood, Gloucestershire which died about 1965, this was the only plant I had ever seen. The wistaria on the house is of considerable age, probably a hundred years, but the surrounding borders containing shrubs were added by the Trust in 1956, when the rest of the garden was restored. On the west side of the house, which overlooks the river, is a landing stage and a sunken rose garden where the soft blue-green foliage of Jackman's blue rue and *Euphorbia myrsinites* acts as a foil to the floral colour.

An addition by the Trust is the border along the side of the North Garden, which, instead of the original assortment of played-out shrubs, now contains a collection of plants mentioned in Shakespeare's plays. Here grow Heartsease, Dog Violet and Sweet Violet, Columbine and Burnet; deadly Hemlock and Aconite; Saffron and Cuckoo Flower. Around the park, where the Royalists camped prior to the battle of Edgehill in

1642, the deer-proof palisade is annually maintained in the traditional ways of four hundred years ago (see illus. 182). And so history goes on.

CHARTWELL
Westerham, *Kent*

Bought by a group of friends of Sir Winston Churchill and given to the Trust in 1946 with an endowment

AREA 9 ha (22 acres)
SOIL Lime-free
ALTITUDE 121 m (400 ft)
RAINFALL 762 mm (30 in.)
TEMPERATURE 3.5°C (38°F)

2 miles south of Westerham, forking left off B2026 after $1\frac{1}{2}$ miles

I LIKE TO THINK that four components contributed to what is Chartwell today. First, there was the lie of the land; next, there were two great minds, and fourthly a generous gift. The lie of the land was there from the beginning, also the major portions of the house. To those came a brain and far-ranging eye which could take in the whole of the concept, as it could all the events that had contributed to its age; the building of walls and the suave full lines of a magnolia bloom were but details, the flooding and damming of the valley a major task. The prospect from the house was thus enhanced by a great sheet of water, reflecting the billowing trees which ascend the slope beyond.

An eye more concerned with smaller details created the more intimate portions of the garden proper: the idea of the Pavilion with its overtones of family history, the terraces and hedges, and the repetitive flower pattern of the borders. Here are the flowers, the soft colours which alone could act as a foreground to the landscape. The cool colours are echoed in the house so that both inside and out the scheme is united, whole.

And then for their golden jubilee the family presented Sir Winston and Lady Churchill with a collection of golden roses. The borders filled with roses, backed by a low hedge, gather into a circle in the middle on risen ground, and the flagged path is edged with silvery stachys and catmint.

I do not propose to assess Chartwell as a garden except to say that I have been enthralled by its quiet beauty on each visit. Who today, who heard those ringing tones and stirring phrases, could go to Chartwell without thinking back to the times that brought them forth, or looking at the garden through rosy spectacles?

But the beauty that is Chartwell's needs no rosy spectacles. It is a traditional garden that gives pleasure from its firm and formal lines around the house, its lavish borders of shrubs and flowers, its terraces, slopes, hedges and steps, and that rich English view beyond.

53 The broad sweep of lawn terminates in a vine-covered pergola, leading to the Marlborough Pavilion, designed by Philip Tilden in the 1920s to Lady Churchill's ideas, at Chartwell.

CHIRK CASTLE
Wrexham, *Clwyd*

Purchased from Lt. Col. Ririd Myddelton by the Welsh Office in 1978. The National Trust will be given the property in 1981, after repairs are completed, and is meanwhile managing it for the Welsh Office.

AREA 2 ha (5 acres)
SOIL Lime-free
ALTITUDE 213 m (700 ft)
RAINFALL 1000 mm (40 in.)
TEMPERATURE 4.5°C (40°F)

Off the A5, entrance $\frac{1}{2}$ mile from Chirk village

AT THE ENTRANCE to the park is a pair of splendid iron gates. In 1719 these gates stood on the north side of the castle, but were moved here in 1770, and prepare us for an impressive home. They are of magnificent workmanship and the open-work piers contain realistic flowers – a preparation for the garden side of things. But first we shall be captivated by the extensive views over the countryside as we approach ever nearer the castle. It dates from the end of the 13th century, but was adjusted in succeeding centuries, and today is a superb climax, its drum-shaped corner towers dominating the hilltop.

An engraving of 1742 shews the garden complete with terraces and balustrades, but, though some of the terraces remain, the balustrades have been replaced by yew hedges. These and the great topiary pieces are considered to have been planted in the mid-19th century; a photograph reproduced in *Country Life* in 1901 shews them quite small. Mrs Norah Lindsay had a hand in the garden here in the first part of this century

54 Chirk Castle and its impressive topiary in 1976.

and asked for them to be allowed to broaden. The result, though entailing an increased amount of clipping, is highly impressive. Their wide bases and high conical tops have been likened to Welsh hats.

The castle walls tower high above the topiary, and are covered with a rich medley of climbing plants; roses and the Climbing Hydrangea are interlaced with the largest flowered of the climbing honeysuckles, *Lonicera tragophylla* and *Solanum crispum*; Tree Peonies luxuriate at their feet. The rose garden nearby is reputed to have been laid out by Mr Algernon Myddelton Biddulph earlier in this century.

A completely different style of gardening greets us if we go across the lawn, through an opening in the hedge, and descend some steps. This whole area had become derelict during the Second World War, and has been embellished largely through the efforts of Lady Margaret Myddelton. The pre-war design by Lady Howard de Walden included a very extensive herbaceous border, but now this is replaced by a good assortment of flowering trees and shrubs, while, opposite, trees and shrubs grow in an informal way in rough grass. The scene in spring is alive with daffodils and cherries, followed by early and late flowering rhododendrons and azaleas, *Cornus nuttallii*, *Genista cinerea* (of gardens), and many other delights. A fine *Eucryphia glutinosa* reserves its flower for late summer and if you wend your way through the winding grass walks in June you may find the rare Flowering Ash, *Fraxinus spaethii*, producing its fluffy white flowers, near to a small pool providing a home for primulas. A very large European Larch grows hereabouts.

A further length of lawn takes us past the Hawk House to a terrace from which extensive views are obtained; on clear days it is said that hills in fourteen counties can be seen. Lord Howard de Walden (he and his wife were tenants from 1910 to 1946) kept hawks and hence this little building, which was unfortunately badly damaged by fire in 1977, is a feature of the garden today. Around it are many a choice shrub, plant, arranged on rocky borders. The shrub garden continues on the right of this lawn, and includes some large

Rhododendron arboreum specimens, planted in the last century. These provide shelter for some of the more tender shrubs.

Though the climate here is relatively mild, the castle stands high and the great enemy is wind. It became much open to wind damage after the last war when many sheltering oaks, dating from the 17th century, were felled. Extensive woodland planting of late years has improved matters and now the Chilean Fire Bush and Chilean Lantern Tree grow well. Some of the shelter has been rapidly achieved by Douglas Firs which cast their sweet fragrance on warm days through the garden.

CLANDON PARK
Guildford, *Surrey*

Given in 1956 by the Countess of Iveagh with an endowment

AREA 3.2 ha (8 acres)	At West Clandon on A247,
SOIL Limy	3 miles east of
ALTITUDE 75 m (250 ft)	Guildford; if using A3
RAINFALL 686 mm (27 in.)	follow signposts to
TEMPERATURE 4.5°C (40°F)	Ripley to join A247

THE RECTANGULAR red-brick house bulks large from whichever way it is approached. It replaced in about 1730 a much earlier house which had an extensive formal garden and canal. Capability Brown arrived in 1776 and decided that the formal terraces and canal were inelegant, proceeded to restore the natural contours, and to create the gently-outlined lake. He also built the two lodges on the main road and joined them with the very fine iron gates, taken from the original fore-court. During this period, or soon after, the Grotto above the house was probably built (see illus. 189). Because the house is less appealing when seen obliquely, Holm Oaks and other evergreens have been recently planted on the north side of the house, which in time will compel the eye to enjoy only a frontal approach from east, south or west.

The new gardens, around the house and beside the lakes, became splendid and famous towards the end of the 19th century. *The Gardeners' Chronicle* for 1885 extols them. By 1910 the Cranley Avenue had been planted leading from the west front of the house, a double line of trees on either side, copper and green beeches. The Maori hut had also arrived but was originally sited by the second lake where there were extensive plantings of daffodils and irises – including, surprisingly, on that limy soil, varieties of Japanese iris – Madonna Lilies, primulas, and Day Lilies. Greenhouses produced quantities of bedding plants, with tree ferns and palms for decorating beds on the lawns.

Although the park is privately owned, the Trust owns the house, the two lodges, gates and the drive to

55 The Maori hut at Clandon Park.

the house, its surrounding lawns, the grotto, the Maori hut, and the present entrance and car park, together with the sunk garden quite near to it, recently restored by voluntary help. From the house, visitors have the benefit of seeing the lake, which Lord Onslow – who owns it – has recently dredged, and the little temple standing on a knoll, surrounded by thousands of daffodils.

Spring is indeed a wonderful moment at Clandon, when the cowslips are sprinkled over the rough grass near the sunk garden. On the lawn stands *Magnolia acuminata* and a group of 'Dissectum' forms of *Acer palmatum*; *Clematis armandii* softens the strong colour of the bricks on the west side of the house; on the east side *Hydrangea petiolaris* thrives. Evergreens recently planted merge the lawns into the neighbouring woodland. In 1976 hornbeams were planted to form two matching *palissades à l'Italienne*, like those at HIDCOTE – in other words, two squares of hedges on stems – flanking the Parterre.

In the house is the fabulous selection of treasures left to the Trust by Mrs Hannah Gubbay. I have been searching for years for the special form of *Anemone nemorosa* which bears her name, without success. Will interested gardeners please note?

CLAREMONT LANDSCAPE GARDEN
Esher, *Surrey*

Accepted by the Treasury in lieu of death duties, and given to the Trust in 1949

AREA 19.5 ha (49 acres)
SOIL Lime-free
ALTITUDE 30 m (100 ft)
RAINFALL 635 mm (25 in.)
TEMPERATURE 4°C (39°F)

On south edge of Esher, on east side of A307 (no access from A3 Esher bypass)

WHEN THE LEAVES of all the deciduous native trees have fallen, making a carpet of varied brown tints, the evergreens come into their own and "the holly bears the crown". This annual transformation in earlier centuries revealed the paucity of native evergreen shrubs for our gardens. This is why, in order to make believe that summer never ended, the planters of gardens have for so long welcomed every evergreen that could be induced to grow in our equable but maligned climate. Many exotic evergreens suffer in cold winters but the common or cherry laurel, *Prunus laurocerasus*, introduced in 1576, the Portuguese Laurel, *Prunus lusitanica*, introduced in 1648 and *Rhododendron ponticum*, introduced in 1763, are perfectly hardy and have naturalised themselves in many a garden and woodland. If it was William Shenstone who first recommended the Laurel for landscape planting, his memory must have been cursed by many a generation of gardeners since, for both this and the Pontic Rhododendron are luxurious wayward spreaders, rooting and seeding as they go; they are both capable of a spread of 15.2 m (50 ft) or more, and a height nearly as great when growing amongst trees.

One of the places where one could see these evergreens luxuriating to the full in the 1960s was at Claremont. Apart from narrow winding paths, practically the *whole* of the garden landscape was covered by an impenetrable jungle of evergreens up to some 7.6 m (25 ft). Today, thanks to a generous gift from the Slater Foundation and an untold amount of work, much of it by voluntary workers and also students from Merrist Wood Agricultural College, the landscape and its principal features have been revealed. Even in 1882 *The Gardeners' Chronicle* records how great improvements had lately been effected "by cutting down laurels and rhododendrons. The eye grows weary of so much common laurel". In 1836, the *Gardener's Magazine* had a different tale to tell: "The formation of an underwood of laurels, by laying down the long straggling branches of the old plants, so that they now completely cover the surface, is one of the most masterly things of the kind that has been done anywhere." The answer is that these evergreens form an admirable weed-suppressing cover, so long as they are kept under control. Henry Hoare planted many laurels at STOURHEAD, and so we may conclude that both here and in many other estates they were used to create an evergreen under-cover to the wooded areas; so far the earliest record of their use at Claremont is 1784. Thomas Whateley in *Observations on Modern Gardening*, 1770, makes no mention of evergreens at Claremont, but extols the pleasant way in which the trees are planted, thinning out towards the verges of the wooded areas with "groupes, sometimes of no more than two trees; sometimes of four or five, and now and then in larger clusters".

Whateley would have been admiring trees planted some fifty years earlier, for our story at Claremont starts with Sir John Vanbrugh, the renowned architect

of Blenheim and Castle Howard, who built a house for himself near to these grounds, in 1708. Some seventy years later this house was pulled down and another was built nearby. On the top of the hill behind it stands Vanbrugh's imposing Belvedere, built about 1715. It was during the ownership of Thomas Holles-Pelham, Earl of Clare, who bought the property from Vanbrugh, and later became Duke of Newcastle, that Claremont as we know it today mostly took its shape.

Both the house and the belvedere are outside the land owned by the Trust, but it is from the belvedere that the succession of views was intended to be enjoyed. The building looks down a long grass slope, with hedged sides, to a bowling green of considerable size, around which stand yews at least two hundred and fifty years old. It was perhaps this "terras" that Thomas Whateley noted as being "much superior to the rest of the garden". He also gained another impression and wrote: "Immediately under the eye, the gaudy Shrub, and the ornamental though useless Exotic, may be admitted; but for more distant objects, and in less embellished situation, the Timber-tree ought to prevail." This has influenced the Trust's recent planting.

Farther down is a replanted avenue of limes, which turns left up to the view point (the site of the mausoleum, formerly the Gothick tea-house, of the Princess Charlotte) and from here you look down upon the lake, over the mighty sloping and steps of the Amphitheatre.

The Amphitheatre, recently cleared of its stunted cedars and laurels and sown with grass, was designed by Charles Bridgeman in about 1727. A similar scheme is found in D'Argenville's *La Théorie et la Pratique du Jardinage*, 1709, described as "*Escalier mesle de Rampes et de Pailliers*". (This astonishing array of earthworks is shewn in J. C. Loudon's *Encyclopaedia of Gardening*, 1827, attributed to the garden at Newliston, Linlithgowshire, but I have ascertained that no such amphitheatre ever existed there.) The Amphitheatre covers between three and four acres. Bridgeman's lake was a small circle, a formal feature, but this was altered by William Kent in the early 1730s to the present

56 TOP The lake, amphitheatre and the New House (Island Pavilion) at Claremont, depicted anonymously in 1738.
57 ABOVE The amphitheatre at Claremont was cleared of its dense covering of laurels, sycamore etc. in 1976/6. This photograph was taken in 1977, soon after the re-grading of the slopes had been completed and the sown grass had germinated.

58 The bowling green at Claremont being given a dressing of lime in 1976, prior to sowing with grass. Vanbrugh's belvedere had been totally obscured for years by a dense mass of laurels and brushwood over the whole area in the photograph.

design, with his island and its pavilion. The lake has recently been dredged and the pavilion restored.

If you go southwards round the lake from the entrance good views are obtained from the walk ascending the Mound, on what was the west side of the old London road; the new road was made so as to include the Mound in the garden, in 1771–2. Descending the wooden steps the slope of the old road carries you back to the lake walk and to the Grotto (see illus. 188).

A grot there was with hoary moss o'er grown,
Rough with rude shells, and arch'd with mould'ring stone,
Sad silence reigns within the lonesome wall
And weeping rills but whisper as they fall.

Sir Samuel Garth, *Claremont*, 1715

At first there was a cascade of rusticated stonework on this site, but this was in all probability adapted around 1770 from the rather prim design of old prints to its romantic "natural" appearance today; it has recently been mended and some fallen rocks replaced. There is a pleasant view from the clump of old Scots Pines beyond, and before long an excellent view of the island pavilion. Thence, if we go as far as the large Cedar of Lebanon by the lakeside – which was figured on the cover of W. J. Bean's *Trees and Shrubs*, 1914 – the path takes us to the curving ha-ha, and so back to the Camellia house which stands just below the belvedere. Lebanon Cedars, incidentally, have always grown well at Claremont; Loudon's *Gardener's Magazine* in 1836 cites a tree 30 m (100 ft) high and trees of all ages and sizes are there today.

The Camellia house – whose foundations remain – was built about 1825. Some of the old plants have survived neglect of fifty years or more; they are varieties of *Camellia japonica* and include 'Nobilissima'.

My somewhat confusing itinerary has been taken because all great gardens should be seen from where they were designed, progressively, i.e. from the dwelling for which they were the setting. Though the Trust does not own Vanbrugh's belvedere, the present owners of Claremont, Claremont School, have agreed in a most co-operative spirit to our opening up what was one of the most impressive views towards it, so that it can be seen once again from the Bowling Green.

Towards the lake are some exceptional trees. Besides the cedar already mentioned, there is a good Redwood, *Sequoia sempervirens*; *Cryptomeria japonica* and *Cunninghamia lanceolata*; the latter was mentioned in Loudon's *Gardener's Magazine* of 1836. Over the rest of the area beech and oak predominate, many over two hundred years old. Here and there hybrids of *Rhododendron arboreum* are to be seen lighting the walks with crimson in early spring. Hollies and yews grow to great size.

It was a wise selection of site for this garden landscape. The terrain is dramatically undulating. The soil, light and sandy and highly conducive to growth of all kinds, is naturally mounded up into considerable heights, but lies on a foundation of clay, as so often happens at about this distance from London.

Many people have passed times of happiness in the landscape at Claremont, and we hope that its restoration will be the means of proving yet again how the Trust's possessions cover every type of ornamental gardening in the British Isles, and moreover give the type of pleasure for which it was intended. It has been extolled time and again, since Samuel Garth's eulogies of 1715:

But say, who shall attempt th' adventurous part,
When Nature borrows dress from Vanbrugh's art;
If by Apollo taught, he touch the lyre,
Stones mount in columns, palaces aspire,
And rocks are animated by his fire:
'Tis he can paint in verse those rising hills,
Their gentle valleys and their silver rills;
Close groves and op'ning glades with verdure spread,
Flowers sighing sweets, and shrubs that balsam bleed;
The gay variety the prospect crown'd,
And all the bright horizon smiling round;
Whilst I attempt to tell how ancient fame
Records from whence this villa took its name.

In her comments, Her Royal Highness The Princess Charlotte did not think much of his analysis of the origin of Claremont and described it as "a motley farrago of mythological foolery, of druidical superstition, of metaphysical absurdities of natural history . . . a laboured panegyric". I leave readers to investigate this for themselves.

CLEVEDON COURT
Clevedon, *Avon*

Transferred to the Trust through the Treasury in 1961 and endowed by Sir Arthur Elton, Bt, whose family had owned the house since 1709

AREA 3.2 ha (8 acres)	$1\frac{1}{2}$ miles east of
SOIL Limy	Clevedon on the B3130
ALTITUDE 30 m (100 ft)	Bristol road
RAINFALL 813 mm (32 in.)	
TEMPERATURE 5°C (41°F)	

GERTRUDE JEKYLL wrote in 1901 in her *Wall and Water Gardens*:

The upper [top] terrace shows not unskilful management of a rather abrupt transition from the wooded slope to pure formality ... Next comes a grand retaining wall, buttressed at short intervals and planted with good wall shrubs. The weakest point in [this] the middle terrace is the poverty of scheme in the succession of small square beds that break forward in each bay between the piers ... with stiff little edgings showing an outer margin of bare earth ... the front line of the beds comes too far forward into the grass by about one-fourth of its projection ... The proportion would be much better with a greater width of grass and a lesser width of flowers ... The planting at the base of the lowest wall seems in these more horticulturally enlightened days to be quite indefensible. The foot of one of the noblest ranges of terrace walls in England is too good to be given over to the most commonplace forms of bedding, whereas it presents the best and most becoming site for some of the noblest plants; for *Magnolia* and *Bignonia*, *Yucca*, *Carpenteria*, *Choisya* and *Romneya*.

At that time, Clevedon Court was still at the height of its Victorian splendour and presented an example of what gardening was at the time. *Country Life Illustrated*, 2 December 1899, had been lavish in its praise of all that Miss Jekyll frowned upon. Whether or not her strictures were taken to heart is not recorded; the passage of time, two wars, and the present garden staff of only one have all contributed to a radical change, and might even please our critic today.

In all probability the steeply sloping site at Clevedon Court has been occupied as a dwelling since Roman times; looking out to what would in those days have been a frequently flooded marsh, Clevedon Court was built in about 1320 and has been the dwelling of the Elton family since 1709. Court Hill was more or less bare at that time, but was planted in the early 19th century so that now it is heavily wooded, predominantly with Holm Oak, which, like *Arbutus unedo* in the lower reaches, has become naturalised. The whole array of trees forms a splendid backcloth to the unique terraced gardens. An immense London Plane guards the corner of the short drive, spreading over spring bulbs with hosts of violets nearby. A Black Mulberry, recorded as ancient in 1822, is as fruitful as ever.

One of the most appealing and varied views is from the west end of the house. Those not concerned solely with gardens will note Clevedon church across the meadow. Above the lawn the mellow brick wall and steps support the Octagon, built about the middle of the 18th century (see illus. 12). But first let us amble along the sloping lawn where magnolias provide an unforgettable picture in spring, while in summer – supported on posts over the grass on the fringe of what was once a rose garden – is a large plant of the Himalayan Musk Rose, *Rosa brunonii*. Its single white flowers and far reaching fragrance compel attention in June. The variegated Cornelian Cherry grows nearby, enhanced by dark evergreens.

The Octagon – from the roof of which the accompanying photographs were taken – commands the length of what in Victorian times was given the name of the Pretty Terrace; the pleasant level sward carries you to the far end, to a Gothick summerhouse shelter. From earliest spring to late autumn shrubs and plants on the high wall and in the border give colour and interest. The whole of the garden bank is warm and sunny, with limy soil, providing good homes for a number of tender plants. The mahogany foliage of *Photinia serrulata* in spring, yellow *Jasminum primulinum* (semi-double), *Buddleia colvilei* 'Kewensis' with its immense drooping crimson trusses and others carry one on till late summer, when *Canna iridifolia*, various ceanothuses and *Abelia grandiflora* flower; great gaunt specimens of *Mahonia lomariifolia* bloom in November. Through the door at the end is a rock-bank where the yucca-relative, *Puya alpestris* from Chile, produces its astonishing sea-blue flowers in spikes above the prickly grey leaves in favourable years.

The top terrace, known as the Esmond Terrace – because Thackeray's *History of Henry Esmond* was drafted in part there – is much as Miss Jekyll would like it. The informal touch unites the long grass walk to the seeding Strawberry Trees fringing the lower woodland. We can look down on the lower garden, the house, the Octagon, the magnolias and some tall Chusan Palms. These are Chinese, whereas the dwarf bushy Palm along this walk, *Chamaerops humilis*, is the only palm native of Europe and rarely seen in gardens. A Judas Tree gives its rosy carmine flowers every spring.

There is always a charm about a garden where love and care, with the hazards of fashion and error, are visible, generation after generation.

Whose garden walks are still beset
With flowers which may have strewn the way
Of Tudor or Plantagenet,
And yet are passing sweet today . . .

59 ABOVE A photograph taken in 1901, of the Pretty Terrace at Clevedon Court which earned the disapproval of Gertrude Jekyll.
60 RIGHT The same terrace photographed in 1977.

It seemed thus to a minor poet visiting Clevedon in 1866, while a few years later Sir Arthur Elton returned from London to note plaintively in his diary that a "floral haemorrhage" had beset his quiet, seemly planting. Here at Clevedon Court the timeless walls support the plants that have delighted us all. Time stands still under the great cedar above the top terrace, and in the hundreds of winters – the gardeners' planting time – that have gone by, each decade has added something to the whole. The terraces are well endowed with plants, only a tithe of which have occurred to me as I write many miles away. But you must go and see it all for yourself. You will not be disappointed.

CLIVEDEN

Maidenhead, *Berkshire/Buckinghamshire*

Given in 1942 by the 2nd Viscount Astor

AREA 72.8 ha (180 acres)	On the left bank
SOIL Lime-free, overlying chalk	of the Thames,
ALTITUDE 75 m (250 ft)	off B476, 2 miles
RAINFALL 686 mm (27 in.)	from Taplow
TEMPERATURE 4°C (39°F)	

IT WAS VERY UNUSUAL in 1666 for a house to be built on a hill away from a village and in wild country. John Evelyn, used to straight avenues, parterres, hedged alleys and formal waters, gave his impressions in 1679 when he visited "Cliefden that stupendious natural Rock, Wood & Prospect of the Duke of Buckinghams . . . The grotts in the chalk rock are pretty . . . a romantic object . . . altogether answers the most poetical description that can be made of a solitude, precipice, prospects . . . on the platforme [of the house] is a circular view to the uttmost verge of the Horison, which with the serpenting of the Thames is admirably surpassing. The land all about barren and producing nothing but ferne." He might well have been describing a property typical of tastes a century later.

Not content with the natural cliff and vale, the top of the hill was levelled, and the house brought forward, perched to greatest advantage above William Winde's great brick terrace – John Evelyn's "platforme", 122 m (400 ft) long and 7.6 m (25 ft) wide. The ground floor on the north was and still is level with the top of the terrace on the south front. The operation involved a great deal of earth-moving but provided ample space for cellars and the central and end pavilions under the terrace.

A few years before Evelyn's visit the Duke of Buckingham had eloped with the Countess of Shrewsbury, after killing her husband in a duel at Barne Elmes; at sometime during the 19th century this was commemorated to the east of the house by the date 1668 and a rapier marked by beds cut in the turf.

In 1687 the place was bought by the Earl of Orkney, who added several architectural features. One is the Blenheim Pavilion, commemorating his signal successes in that battle. It lies at the far end of what is known as Queen Anne's Walk, so-called because legend has it that the sovereign gave Lord Orkney the handsome stone urn which terminates the walk. To the south-west of the house is another building, an octagonal temple, which was later converted to a chapel. Orkney employed Charles Bridgeman in the 1720s to design many of the walks, mostly straight, some framed with yews; probably the Green Drive is his also, an avenue which crosses the present entrance drive and extends as far as the main road to the south and the outskirts of the Water Garden to the north. The big lawn to the south was laid out also at this time, with banks on either side lined with elms and a raised circle at the far end.

Cliveden has been "in the news" throughout its long history, partly because it was at a convenient distance from London. In 1739 it was rented by Frederick, Prince of Wales; we do not know what his impressions of the place were but they must have been favourable. During his tenancy it is believed that the avenue of Common Limes, 420.6 m (460 yards) long, was planted. It is of considerable width, 45.7 m (50 yards), matching the width of the house, and leads directly to the old yew hedges which were recorded as being 2.4 m (8 ft) high in 1752. They enclose the forecourt, now lawns, but in those days fully gardened. Today the limes are elderly, to say the least, and heavy with mistletoe; in early leaf in April the gaiety of the scene is enhanced by a generous scattering of daffodils under them. It has been suggested that the Prince's surgeon was inspired to plant the numerous Holm Oaks to the west of the avenue in 1747, which today form a unique feature of the grounds, known as the Ilex Grove. The glades of level lawn thread their way through the dark cumulous masses of greenery which have more than just a silver lining at the approach of summer when their creamy-grey young foliage develops. In truth the Ilex Grove, at all times an area of unusual beauty, is then transformed. Not far away, beyond the Blenheim Pavilion, is a small amphitheatre in which "Rule Britannia" was first played in 1739, music composed by Dr Thomas Arne for Thomson's *Masque of Alfred.* Music was also played in the central pavilion of the great terrace which has the most intense and lively powers of echo; the end pavilions had been turned into aviaries.

Just prior to 1800 the house suffered disastrously from a fire, only the colonnades linking it to its two wings and the great terrace remaining. It was rebuilt and again burnt in 1849; the Duke of Sutherland, the then owner, commissioned the present house in 1850. In the early 19th century the statesman George Canning gained favourable impressions at Cliveden, lingering long under the giant oak that is associated with him, enjoying the famous view along the Thames. This tree has for years been leaning and twisting with the weight of the branches and has been propped since 1900.

It was during the Duke of Sutherland's twenty years of ownership that Cliveden became horticulturally famous. Queen Victoria was a frequent visitor and a statue in memory of Prince Albert was placed in the Ilex Grove in the 1860s, happy in its cool verdegris-green against the dusky oaks.

The Duke was served by a head gardener of considerable ability, J. Fleming. It is thought that Sir Charles Barry, the architect of the new house, may have been the designer of the huge Parterre stretching away to the south of the house, but *The Gardeners' Chronicle* of 1877, Vol. 2 states that it was laid out by Mr Fleming between 1851–3 (see illus. 27). Certainly Barry's design of 1851–2 is quite different, as also the Comte D'Orsay's of 1830; both incorporated the circle at the far end. In salutation of the Comte, the Rose 'D'Orsay' was planted in the Rose Garden recently. By 1862 *The Journal of Horticulture*, Vol. 28, calls attention to the magnificence of the parterre, a flower garden covering 1.4 ha ($3\frac{1}{2}$ acres), the triangular beds edged with clipped privet and spruce, and partly filled with azaleas and rhododendrons. Spaces were left for hollyhocks, gladioli and foxgloves and summer and spring bedding. For the spring bedding over 20,000 plants were used as well as nearly 10,000 tulips. The sentinel clipped yews which now punctuate the scheme were coaxed into substantial shape in nursery ground and moved into place in 1976 by the Trust, replacing some poor box pyramids; these had been put in after Mr Fleming's time for he had roses in their little beds.

The far circle of the parterre has a longer history than the triangular beds, and used to be planted with shrubs and plants, and its embankments date back to *c.*1720–3.

No doubt Fleming had numerous assistant gardeners; thousands of annual plants were used under the long terrace wall, a wavy line of colour. This was

61 The great marble Fountain of Love, by Ralph Waldo Story, *c.*1895, with a glimpse of the urn at the far end of Queen Anne's Walk, at Cliveden. Photo 1967. Mistletoe grows freely on the lime trees.

before the walls were covered with climbing plants. In the Ilex Grove he had further Victorian delights. Depressions in the lawn to this day shew where the Ribbon Borders were, weaving in and out, with a bow here and there, in all 610 mm (2 ft) wide and 274.3 m (300 yds) long. One of the effects was composed of white forget-me-not and the blue Cliveden Pansy – now extinct, I fear. Bedding had reached a pitch it had never before attained anywhere, some 60,000 plants being used annually. Before about 1862 it had been the custom to create summer colour by the use of tender exotic flowers, replacing them in autumn with an assortment of little evergreen bushes. Fleming, the innovator, changed all this. He it was apparently who started the fashion of putting spring flowering plants and bulbs into the beds in autumn instead of the evergreens – a practice adopted everywhere ever since. His little book *Spring and Winter Flower Gardening*, published in 1870 explains his methods and gives examples of the associations of plants which he used.

In those days old thorn trees lined the long turf banks of the levelled lawn. William Robinson, editor of *The Garden*, gave his impressions in that paper in 1872: "The great flower garden, one of the most repulsive examples of the extra formal school, thrusts itself in a rather awkward manner into the grand landscape." (Even so it has had its admirers and was in fact copied in general outline at Lees Court, Faversham, Kent, in about 1921.) However, the drive approaching from the east, laid out during the 19th century, earned Robinson's praise – "undoubtedly one of the finest things that has been done in the way of Landscape Gardening near London for many years past".

The Duke of Westminster owned Cliveden for twenty-three years after purchasing it from the Duke of Sutherland in 1870; at about this time the clock tower, the pavilion on the terrace and the forecourt walls and grilles were built. It then passed into the hands of William Waldorf Astor (later the 1st Viscount Astor) in 1893 and this is when so much of Cliveden as we know it took shape, finalising an accretion of three hundred years. Each owner has added his bit, according to the taste of the time. Lord Astor added much, but in particular the Borghese balustrade on the south front, with its fountain pools; the several marble well-heads under the terrace, and the Borghese statue at the far end of the parterre; the Roman sarcophagi in the forecourt and the urns and vases, jars and statuary distributed over the garden. His son, the 2nd Viscount, was a great tree planter, and sought to thicken woods everywhere; much of the rich beauty of Cliveden is due to his imagination. He loved Lombardy Poplars and caused many scores to be planted in the fields beyond the river which give such an extraordinary uplift to the landscape.

If you follow the lower paths along the top of the escarpment you will come to an oval garden, with high walls of tufa and a dripping well at one end; it was laid out as an Italian garden by the 1st Viscount, but altered to a memorial cemetery for the Canadian soldiers who died in the Cliveden War Hospital from 1914–8. The Long Garden, complete with statues and topiary, was begun by him in 1902 and the long sinuous beds were filled with flowers. On its wall are several unusual shrubs: the Narrow Leafed and the Californian Sweet Bays, *Buddleia auriculata*, so fragrant in autumn, *Actinidia kolomikta*, with pink foliage, *Calycanthus occidentalis* or Allspice, *Dipelta floribunda, Ribes speciosum*, a Californian gooseberry with scarlet, fuchsia-like flowers, *Drimys winteri*, *Azara microphylla* from South America, and *Staphylea colchica*. He laid out too the Water Garden, bringing to grace it in 1900 the

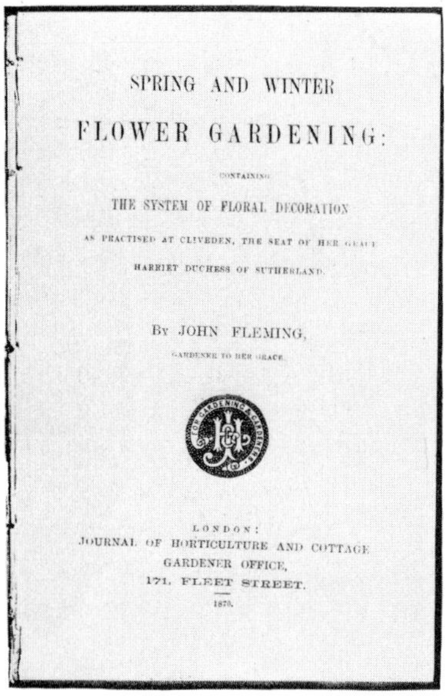
SPRING AND WINTER

FLOWER GARDENING:

CONTAINING

THE SYSTEM OF FLORAL DECORATION

AS PRACTISED AT CLIVEDEN, THE SEAT OF HER GRACE

HARRIET DUCHESS OF SUTHERLAND.

BY JOHN FLEMING,

GARDENER TO HER GRACE.

LONDON:

JOURNAL OF HORTICULTURE AND COTTAGE GARDENER OFFICE,

171, FLEET STREET.

1870.

62 LEFT The title page of John Fleming's book, written when he was head gardener at Cliveden.

63 BELOW View of the great flower garden at Cliveden from John Fleming's book of 1870.

Japanese Pagoda which had been used in the Paris Exhibition of 1867. The many springs hereabouts filled the duck pond, originally a small affair but enlarged in 1893 by Lord Astor; he made it into a serpentine piece of water around a magnolia hillock. Much of this portion was restored by the Trust in 1974. The 2nd Viscount had the larger portion made in 1905; it contains golden carp and orfe. On its banks are numerous moisture-loving plants: King Cups in spring, followed by primulas, irises, astilbes and Day Lilies, Purple Loosestrife accompanied for long by various Japanese azaleas and rhododendrons. If you are there in early autumn on a mild damp day you may be suddenly aware of the fragrance of strawberries from the fallen leaves of *Cercidiphyllum japonicum*. The flat water is contrasted by outcrops of rock, a stone bridge, waterlilies, giant leaves of *Gunnera* and the arching, rustling bamboos and weeping birches. In spring scillas and primroses grow under bush wistarias, in autumn colchicums flower under magnolias, and in one approach to the garden white daffodils are spread under Japanese Cherries to the accompaniment of lavender-blue rhododendrons.

In the days of the 3rd Viscount I paid my first visit, before appearing on the Trust's behalf, in order to help with shrub roses for the rose garden and also for the bathing-pool garden. Tucked away in a clearing of the woodland to the north-west of the forecourt was originally a bowling green, later a tennis court. Lord Astor decided to turn it into a rose garden and a design by Geoffrey Jellicoe was adopted. It is an entirely novel conception, the beds fluid and informal in shape, accompanied by pretty arches and some statuary. At midsummer both old and new roses give off a rich scent in the tree-bounded enclosure, aided by mock orange and a plant of the 'Kiftsgate' rose which has enveloped a tree.

Lord Astor's special favourite was the rhododendron. He enriched many of the rides and woodlands with species and hybrids which together give a long flowering period. Unfortunately in his eagerness to get effect he planted too closely and in subsequent years so many needed moving every winter that the garden staff was unable to tend the historic parts of the garden properly. My colleagues and I had a special meeting with Lord and Lady Astor to see what could be done about it. Before lunch we were taken on to the great terrace and, when tactfully asked what he was going to do about the neglected Parterre, Lord Astor rejoined – "Extraordinary thing, you know, we grew cabbages there during the war and have never been able to grow a thing there since!" After lunch the great opportunity for further discussion on the garden was whisked away by someone who mentioned croquet; almost at once coffee was ordered to be served on the lawn, croquet was played, and we left at about 4.15, without having achieved our object at all.

But since then, for the last decade or so after Lord Astor's death, the Trust has been responsible for the garden (see plate XXIII). The parterre hedges have been cleaned out, nursed to health, and the beds planted with cotton lavender and *Senecio*; the Long Garden hedges have been treated likewise and the beds planted with variegated dwarf *Euonymus fortunei*; the Water Garden has been tidied, the pond dredged, improvements made to the stepping stones; innumerable laurels, creeping over the lawns have been cut back throughout the drives; Queen Anne's Walk has been trimmed once again; shrubs and climbers on walls are now under control. On the south front were many overgrown climbers; *Actinidia chinensis*, *Wistaria sinensis*, *Rosa banksiae* – both double white and double yellow – *Solanum crispum* 'Glasnevin', a fig and *Celastrus orbiculatus*. Among them are less vigorous shrubs; an old Pomegranate for instance; the sweet-smelling Winter Sweet and *Viburnum* 'Fulbrook', by far the best of the hybrids of *V. carlesii*. *Magnolia grandiflora* is trained on the walls by the central flights of steps.

Though I have given you above some impressions of the garden by other people I have contributed few of my own. I have not in fact mentioned the majesty of the long approach drive, nor the huge marble fountain erected by Mr W. W. Astor where the route turns abruptly left to approach the house. Nor have I mentioned the beauty on a somewhat misty autumn day, when the views from the long woodland walks open out through the trees, yellow and brown, to the reaches of the Thames and the fields beyond. Nor the surprise after descending a steep dark slope under yew trees to the tufa stone balustrade which takes you to the river. Nor of the little grotto, believed to be Victorian, tucked away under a bank and looking down the valley, and the unique circular fruit garden with its crossing arched alleys, which needs a sponsor for its resuscitation and maintenance. I have only briefly referred to the Green Ride, a relic of the 17th century which strikes out like a corridor from the water garden area away through the woods until you turn right and come upon the statue of the Duke of Sutherland which commands such a wonderful view of lawn and house far away. Cliveden is so vast and varied that you could enjoy walking there for more than one day without using the same paths. It is at once one of the Trust's largest gardens and the most historically varied, giving interest to those bent upon architecture, garden ornaments, the history of design, horticulture and nature unadorned. For four hundred years this place has entranced owners through times turbulent or peaceful. Perhaps their lives and actions were not a little swayed by the majesty of Cliveden, embosomed in trees, floating on its platform of chalk high above the Thames.

CLUMBER PARK
Worksop, *Nottinghamshire*

Bought in 1946 by public subscription to which local authorities contributed largely

AREA 8 ha (20 acres)	5 miles south-east of
SOIL Lime-free	Worksop, east of
ALTITUDE 30 m (100 ft)	the A6009/A616 road
RAINFALL 635 mm (25 in.)	to Ollerton
TEMPERATURE 3.5°C (38°F)	

SHERWOOD FOREST, conjuring up stories of Robin Hood, was a very large area, neglected for crops in early and mediaeval times mainly because of its poor sandy wastes mingled with dark oak woods. In the early 18th century some 4,000 acres of land adjoining it were enclosed by the Duke of Newcastle, and it was his nephew who in 1770 set about building a noble house and creating the park as it is today.

The most impressive approach is from Apley Head gate, whence an avenue of lime trees leads to the site of the house and stretches indeed for some three miles towards a gate on the other side of the park (see illus. 4). The limes were planted just before the middle of the 19th century; the avenue is 18.2 m (60 ft) wide, composed of a duplicate row on either side placed at 9.1 m (30 ft) each way; in all 1,296 trees. Perhaps earlier, but noticeably during the 1960s, these trees were almost defoliated annually by caterpillars until nourishment was added to the poor and over-burdened soil, since when the trouble has been negligible.

However poor the soil may be in some parts, the Duke at least had sufficient water, and both Brown and Repton had a hand in modelling the lie of the land and planting trees. It was left to Richard Payne Knight to complete the layout in 1794. By then the house stood overlooking the lake which was made by damming the River Poulter in two places; two temples and a bridge grace its shores, designed by the architect of the house, Stephen Wright. The power and water supply for the house was for long derived from a turbine near to the bridge and the rough rocks and semblance of a grotto remain from the turbine housing and cascade. William Sawrey Gilpin provided another touch: he extended the formal gardens in front of the house downstream, creating a further formal walk known as the Lincoln Terrace, complete with vases, flower beds and landing stage. An Algerian Oak grows at the far end.

So there was the house and the buildings, the wastelands and trees, the long snaky lake set in a very shallow valley in the midst of this great area of land. The Cedars of Lebanon and the Turkey Oaks – so free of growth on some of the land that would not produce a good English Oak – were there, but it is difficult to visualise it all now. The house caught fire in 1879 and it was demolished in 1938. Meanwhile the Chapel was built in 1890. This it is which stands so proudly dominating the gentle landscape and lake today. Some of my best impressions of the park include this Chapel, whether from the far side of the lake, embowered in soft-tinted rhododendrons, or from the bridge half a mile away, its spire reflected in the water, framed by distant trees.

In a seemingly static landscape much has happened. The Lincoln Terrace was restored to something of its former glory by the Trust in the early 1970s; the outline of the house terraces have been marked out and made good; trees have been planted in quantity everywhere, including a further length of avenue. The void created by demolishing the house has in part been taken over by the stable block and the dignity of the Chapel. Today millions enjoy Clumber Park and its teeming wild life, in the air, on ground and in and on the water. Water-fowl abound and the air is lively with their cries. It is hoped that the walled kitchen garden, some distance from the site of the house, may be given a new lease of life before long.

64 The Lincoln Terrace at Clumber Park after restoration in 1974.

COTEHELE
Calstock, *Cornwall*

Given in 1947 by the Treasury, which had accepted it in lieu of death duties from the 6th Earl of Mount Edgcumbe

AREA 4.8 ha (10 acres)	On west bank of
SOIL Lime-free	the Tamar, 6 miles west
ALTITUDE 75 m (250 ft)	of Calstock, 8 miles
RAINFALL 1143 mm (45 in.)	south-west of Tavistock
TEMPERATURE 5.5°C (42°F)	

THE APPROACH to Cotehele is fascinating. From the main road the high-banked lanes twist and turn, ever descending, until at the last turn you are on a level stretch at the end of which is the entrance gate. Even so, as we shall see in a moment, sea level has by no means

65 ABOVE One of the surprises at Cotehele is to open the door to reveal this view of the terraced garden below the house. Photo 1961.
66 RIGHT Soft pinky-white blooms of *Magnolia soulangiana* 'Alexandrina' and 'Rustica Rubra' at Cotehele. Photo 1963.

been reached. The sea is well below the house and garden, down by the quay where King George III and Queen Charlotte arrived in 1789 on a visit during their stay at Saltram.

Much of the house at Cotehele dates from the 15th century, resting on older foundations. The site was chosen no doubt because of the springs of clear water; at one time the upper spring ran below the house, effectively acting as a drain. Cornish houses tend to face east, as this one does, to avoid the perennial battering of south-west gales; today one's vision of a Cornish valley garden is generally of one protected from cold winds, and one of the jobs undertaken some twenty years ago was to reinforce the tree screen in the lower reaches of this garden, and indeed all around it.

The garden is no period piece, rather has it developed over the centuries, taking advantage of the natural contours and assets, though its present design mostly dates from Victorian times, with considerable later planting. The Edgcumbe family owned Cotehele from the 14th century onwards.

The entrance drive passes a 15th-century barn of considerable size and some old sycamores. It is common in Cornwall to find trees of this species of great size and, in the air so fresh and clean from the sea, their light grey bark is noticeable particularly when mottled with mosses and lichens. Various climbing plants are on the grey granite walls, ceanothus, the evergreen filigree of *Cissus striata*, and in late summer the Trumpet Creeper producing its orange-red flowers. If you go through the inviting archway you will be in the little courtyard of the original house, beautifully cobbled and terraced. Here in shelter will be found wistarias, honeysuckles and masses of Algerian Irises.

I well remember my first visit to Cotehele; I looked in at the little court, then went through the side court – where there are several camellias – and opened the high gates. Spread over the orchard up to the distant wall was a display of delicate-tinted daffodils and narcissus, toning well with the grey stone tower. Through one of the several decorative white-painted gates (see illus. 1) I was led to the upper garden. Here is a series of lawns on different slopes and levels, their centre-piece being a rectangular pond with an island in the centre. It is fed by a chattering rill of sparkling water, and is guarded by an ancient Judas Tree, a Tree of Heaven, a Tulip Tree and a Yellow-Twigged Ash (*Fraxinus excelsior* 'Jaspidea'). Alone among ash trees, its leaves turn to bright yellow in autumn. In the summer we can enjoy the waterlilies, clumps of shrubs and fuchsias, agapanthuses and a herbaceous border, mostly given to yellow flowers. By the side of the rill, on my first visit, stood a patriarchal Cork Oak with a trunk 1.5 m (5 ft) through. This collapsed a few years later but fortunately two young trees were already established nearby.

In after years an alteration was made to the herbaceous border; it was divided into two and an opening made in the hedge. The nursery area beyond, used mainly for flowers for cutting for the house, was realigned and a central grass path was made. From the seat at the top a pleasing view is obtained, and one day another Cork Oak will shade it.

If we go through the white gate by the rill we re-enter the Orchard, pass along the top path, by roses and eucryphias and a row of white thorns, a medlar and a quince, and eventually come to a dark grove of rhododendrons. The Weeping Silver Lime was planted in 1956. Through the grove is a door in a wall. It is always a pleasant surprise to open this – especially if the white wistaria is in flower – and to be met by the east front of the house. It was rebuilt in 1862, at which time the terraces were no doubt made. Thirty years later they were described in *The Garden* as "quaint old terraces filled with hardy flowers". The whole thing – the grey stone of the house, ancient portal, beds, strips of grass and retaining walls, was delightfully outshone on my first visit by the two magnolias (*M. soulangiana* 'Alexandrina' and *M.s.* 'Rustica Rubra') which arise from the Lower Lawn. The crimson-purple of *Primula* 'Wanda', dark and pale wallflowers and the glint of red from a 'Japonica' enlivened the terraces. Later there are pink and crimson roses over silvery foliage, and on the walls of the house are the Macartney Rose, a Passion Flower whose orange fruits in early autumn are as conspicuous as its intriguing summer flowers, *Magnolia grandiflora*, and two old hybrid roses, 'Zéphirine Drouhin' and the climbing form of 'Souvenir de la Malmaison'.

The next surprise is to enter a short tunnel whose arched exit frames the whole of the valley garden, with its pool, summerhouse, well-spring, mediaeval dovecote (re-roofed in the early 1960s by the Trust) and away to the arches of a distant viaduct. Here are great clumps of early rhododendrons, the crimson of *R. arboreum* hybrids being most conspicuous, while deeper down in the valley coppery-purple domes of Japanese Maples contrast with white rhododendrons. Later on there are other rhododendrons, azaleas, enkianthuses, hydrangeas, hoherias, and a large *Davidia involucrata*. The pond overflows down a central rill in the cleft of the steep-sided valley, spread with King Cups, primulas and mimulus, and the large leaves of *Peltiphyllum peltatum* and hostas; at the bottom the giant Gunnera reigns supreme. And everywhere are ferns, particularly the Lady Fern. They spread along the banks and germinate in every crevice, and unify the whole valley and its shrubs into a soft green dell. If you are fortunate and are able to go to Cotehele at about the end of May you may be able to stand among the ferns, with the clear green of a lime tree above you, and look up into the white, glistening, nodding chalices of *Magnolia wilsonii* or *M. sinensis*, each with its central boss of crimson stamens. They add an entrancing fresh fragrance, and are one of the year's highlights.

The meadow above the garden was released a few years ago from being a nursery garden for cutting daffodils for market, and some trees were planted, including an English Oak in memory of Sir Winston Churchill. Was it a coincidence that this young tree burst into growth with widespread branches thrusting outwards manfully?

From the terraces may be seen a tower on the field above. This, the Prospect Tower, is triangular with concave walls. It is possibly a look-out tower, but may be a folly, perhaps built to mark the visit of King George III.

THE COURTS, HOLT
Trowbridge, *Wiltshire*

Presented by Major T. C. E. Goff in 1943, with an endowment

AREA 2.8 ha (7 acres)	3 miles north of
SOIL Limy	Trowbridge,
ALTITUDE 60.9 m (200 ft)	2½ miles east of
RAINFALL 762 mm (30 in.)	Bradford-on-Avon,
TEMPERATURE 4.5°C (40°F)	on south side of A3053

WHILE THE HOUSE – only turned into a habitation by the last mill owner in *c.*1840 – may intrigue the architecturally minded, the garden is of considerable interest and beauty. Its features can only be discovered by crossing one of the lawns, as if to reserve its surprises until an actual tour of the garden is made. This was the intention of the late Lady Cecilie Goff, when Major Goff and she came to live at The Courts in 1920. She was an admirer of Gertrude Jekyll and believed that a garden should bring surprises at every turn; her achievement here was to create a mainly formal garden, divided into areas by yew and holly hedges, and lavishly planted (see illus. 6). We have come to recognise this style of gardening as particularly of this century, and it cropped up inevitably owing to the persuasive traditional influences that were at work. Lady Cecilie had to hand with the property a number of pieces of stone statuary left by Sir George Hastings, who occupied The Courts from 1900–11. They are replicas of those with which he embellished Ranelagh House, Barnes.

There are many ways of exploring the garden and every part owes much to the beauty of variegated shrubs and plants which are used to accentuate the colours of the flowers. A lasting impression I have is of the enticing walk marked by sentinel Irish Yews. Between the yews are glimpses of a wide flower border, colourful from early spring onwards until autumn. Another memory is the surprise one gets from walking under the Deodar cedar, which dominates the lawns, indeed the whole garden, to where a long mown path leads between borders of shrubs and plants to a small stone temple built by Sir George. Here again beautiful flowers and leaves accompany you at whatever season you call.

The garden used to be watered by the stream from GREAT CHALFIELD MANOR, but this has dried up and so today the next surprise, the formal Lily Pool, has to be kept filled by a pump. At the height of summer the

67 Though seldom seen in gardens *Xanthoceras sorbifolium* was introduced from China in 1866. White flowers with carmine eye. It flowers well at The Courts, Holt.

billows of the Smoke Bush flowers screen the pool, so fully set with waterlilies of all colours. Marsh plants grow around it, including the pale yellow form of our native Flag Iris, the Citron Day Lily, *Rudbeckia maxima* and the Red-Ink Plant whose pink flowers are followed by tall spikes of maroon-black fruits, with heavy staining power. At the side of the pool are bays of Floribunda roses; I have been surprised to find 'Salmon Spray', raised in 1923, still giving a good account of itself. In the background are a *Xanthoceras* and a *Koelreuteria*, rare small trees which flower in spring and summer respectively. By the stream is a fine *Cornus macrophylla*, planted in 1926, a Swamp Cypress, *Chaenomeles* 'Knaphill Scarlet' and *Escallonia* 'Iveyi'.

These specimens lead you through to a meadow, planted by Miss Moyra Goff in 1952 as an arboretum, and eventually you can return to the main lawn through the yew hedges.

These form the background to further portions of garden with wide niches provided with paving, seats and ornaments. Everywhere are good plants with coppery foliage adding variety when flowers are scarce. In the various beds and borders are Vilmorin's *Potentilla* in silver and cream, pink lilies from the South African crinums, buff lilies from Henry's Chinese lily, purple bells from the herbaceous *Clematis integrifolia*, and autumn floral and seed colour from *Polygonum* 'Reynoutria'. In contrast are the conical shape of the dwarf Alberta White Spruce, a rare pendulous form of the Italian Cypress, and the Nikko Maple. In autumn the dark green of the cypress enhances the pink of the maple, while on the pergola the huge leaves of Coignet's Vine turn to scarlet and the Teinturier or Dyer's grape to dark crimson.

In the pretty conservatory – attributed to Sir George Hastings – among other things, is a Maréchal Niel Rose; from its doors one sees the angle of the house and loggia contrasted by the topiary and the cedar.

The Courts is so called because it was where the weavers of the 16th century brought their disputes for arbitration, though no tangible proof of this now exists. They were subject to error and trial – and may we not say that in making a garden we are also subject to trial and error, the result here being a garland of beauty round the level lawns?

CRAGSIDE HOUSE
Rothbury, *Northumberland*

Transferred by the Treasury to the Trust in 1977, the endowment contributed partly by the second Lord Armstrong

AREA In all 380 ha (940 acres)	At Rothbury, 13 miles
SOIL Lime-free	south-west of
ALTITUDE 152 m (500 ft)	Alnwick (B6341) and
RAINFALL 1524 mm (60 in.)	15 miles north-west
TEMPERATURE 4°C (39°F)	of Morpeth (B6334)

"VERY LARGE", "vast", "gigantic" and eventually "stupendous" are the adjectives that come readily to mind in trying to convey on paper some of the impressions gained on traversing this unique estate. The first Lord Armstrong – as Sir William Armstrong – became impressed with this craggy hillside and built a small house here in 1863, but employed the celebrated architect Richard Norman Shaw to add to it to the extent that it contained over a hundred rooms by 1884. It has remained a Victorian masterpiece both inside and out ever since.

In choosing the site Sir William must have been captivated by the peace and quietness, broken only by birdsong, the sound of water falling and the soughing of the wind through the few trees on the high moorland and in the valleys; it must have been a delightful change from his busy factories and works. But without an inventive mind his efforts to establish a house here would have been stultified. The steep hillside came to his aid; the water from above was harnessed to generate electricity and gushed forth over a cascade into one of the garden lakes. Today the cascade unfortunately no longer works, but the lakes – placid sheets of water, all connected with the Debdon Burn – form part of the scenic interest of the place.

But before enticing you to visit Cragside I had better explain that it has no real garden. Rather is it a natural rock garden of grey weatherworn carboniferous limestone of almost unbelievable extent. The house itself stands on a platform surrounded by a stone terrace and immense rocks, some of which have been rearranged to form rough paths and stepping stones, now happily more visible than they were a few years ago, thanks to Acorn Campers and other voluntary workers, since when the rapidly encroaching jungles of Pontic Rhododendron and the North American Shallon have been partially cleared. Together with pernettyas and *Holodiscus discolor*, azaleas, *Berberis stenophylla*, *Rubus spectabilis* and Dogwood and birches they form the connection between the rocky hillside and the towering conifers. Here and there are variegated yews and hollies – including a fine Weeping Silver Holly – Mountain Pine and *Picea abies* 'Nana Compacta' of great size.

None other – and no less – than Alan Mitchell, the renowned tree expert, recorded his impressions of the conifers in the *Quarterly Journal of the Royal Forestry Society* for April 1975, claiming the reasons for a "notable superiority in continued growth of the species involved seem to be cool, damp growing seasons combined with the long daylight hours". Such is the variation in altitude of the estate that in many places one looks down upon trees well over a hundred feet high. Many of the most majestic conifers from western North America have reached record heights for England here. Many surpass 45 m (150 ft). Western Hemlock, Douglas Fir, Nootka Cypress, Californian Red Fir, Noble Fir, Giant Fir are joined by the Oriental and Tiger-Tail Spruces, Caucasian, Spanish and Grecian Firs. Much less in height but also remarkable for the species are specimens of the Swiss Arolla Pine, another Hemlock, *Tsuga mertensiana* in blue-green, and the Blue Colorado Spruce. But they do not constitute an indigestible mass. Views between them are maintained; man's touch is added to the natural scenery where first a graceful suspension bridge spans the burn, and farther along a stone bridge. At about this spot the water begins to race, swelling here and there into pools, and is eventually confined in a deep gorge and tumbles tempestuously over a fall of 4.5 m (15 ft). Ferns add soft light greenery everywhere, and certain spots suggest that special holes were made for ferns in the rocky banks and escarpments.

All this is within a short walking distance from the house. For longer exploration, the rest of the estate, to be opened in due course as a country park in conjunction with the Northumberland County Council, offers the extensive beauty of woods and moorland, rocks and lakes. I wish one could have access to King Edward VII's diaries to find his impressions of Cragside when as Prince of Wales he and Princess Alexandra stayed there in 1884. Another hope for the future is that we shall find perhaps *Rhododendron* 'Norman Shaw' growing there; a fitting way to commemorate him who thought out the design of the house, creating those craggy gables over the craggy hillside.

CROFT CASTLE
Leominster, *Hereford and Worcester*

Bought from Mrs Owen Croft in 1957 with a grant from the Ministry of Works, and endowed by Lord Croft with the help of members of the family and friends. The Croft family has lived here since the Domesday Book except between 1746 and 1923

AREA 2 ha (5 acres)	5 miles north-west
SOIL Lime-free	of Leominster,
ALTITUDE 167 m (550 ft)	9 miles south-west of
RAINFALL 635 mm (25 in.)	Ludlow; on the B4362
TEMPERATURE 4.5°C (40°F)	Presteigne road

WE WILL NOT PRETEND that there is a great, or even a noted garden at Croft, but certain features of the grounds of this five-hundred-year-old castle make a visit well worthwhile. There is for instance the assembly of oaks of good size along the approach drive, making an irregular avenue. Next the short Gothick curtain-wall at the entrance, over which those very vigorous roses *R. filipes* 'Kiftsgate' and *R. brunonii* 'La Mortola' are trained, making festoons of white, sweet-scented blooms at midsummer (see illus. 24). There is a border of shrubs and plants between the drive and wall, giving way to rough turf under the big trees, Holm Oaks and others, where Neapolitan cyclamens had settled down well. They were raised at BLICKLING HALL and established here during the 1960s.

Opposite, the wide lawn follows the line of the ha-ha to the Church; on it are large trees including a Wellingtonia and an old lime tree which has spread into a small grove, its low branches having rooted in the ground. Around the castle are various good shrubs and climbing plants, clematises and roses, camellias, aralias, lavenders. Climbing rose 'Lady Hillingdon' in warm apricot and *Clematis viticella* 'Royal Velours' are particularly pleasing against the soft grey walls. The wine-red 'Guinée' rose and the double yellow Banksian rose also thrive, near to the glittering dark green of *Viburnum utile*. Richard Payne Knight, whose uncle resided at Croft, would have appreciated this mixture of plants; in *The Landscape*, 1794, he wanted gardens to be decked in "all the variegated flow'ring race", a new concept at the time followed by Richard Colt Hoare at STOURHEAD. In the little Secret Garden, to the west of the castle, grow a number of small fragrant plants. Among them will be found *Helianthemum* 'Mrs Croft' raised at Croft in 1925.

In the park is an Incense Cedar, a Wellingtonia and a Redwood, the Indian Cedar, and some large Geans or Common Cherries.

But, full of interest as all these are, they may be found in many gardens, and are not what takes me to Croft. First, there is the wonderful silence; a silence which is green, not golden, from the wide sloping acres and miles of woodland where oaks excel. The silence comes upon us as we walk down the drive. The old castle of the Croft family broods over the view to the south. Apart from a ditch and some terracing in the rough grass there is nothing indicating a garden other than the small pool, probably added in the 18th century. The planners of that age did not tamper with Croft; the old Oak Avenue remains and also the still more wonderful one of Sweet Chestnuts lining an earlier approach from the west. One of the rows is over three hundred years old and the trees are of a majestic size (see illus. 11). Like CHARLECOTE and LANHYDROCK, therefore, Croft did not lose its straight avenues in the 18th century, though the theories of Richard Payne Knight and Uvedale Price – who lived not far away – are echoed in the Fish Pool Valley.

Many of the plants grown in the 18th century are to be found in the walled garden which has been laid out in recent years by members of the Croft family.

An avenue of limes leading out from the west side of the castle, across the field, has recently been established, also a new avenue of beeches approaching the curtain-wall, replacing old trees which, for safety's sake, had to be felled. History goes marching on at Croft.

DORNEYWOOD
Burnham Beeches, *Buckinghamshire*

Given in 1942 with an endowment by Lord Courtauld-Thompson, as an official residence for a Secretary of State or Minister of the Crown

AREA 2.8 ha ($6\frac{3}{4}$ acres)	South-west of
SOIL Lime-free	Burnham Beeches,
ALTITUDE 75 m (250 ft)	1 mile east of
RAINFALL 762 mm (30 in.)	Cliveden
TEMPERATURE 4°C (39°F)	

THE SHORT DRIVE leads us to a collection of buildings of traditional charm. The house itself is naturally the major piece in the setting, but many other buildings, barns and cottages are grouped together. The garden is of varied attractions, divided into compartments by hedges, with borders of roses, flowers and shrubs. There is a small, deep bowl-shaped area, possibly an earlier gravel pit, which has considerable horticultural attractions and, all in all, the garden is beautiful the whole year, first with spring bulbs, then various flowering shrubs, many roses and herbaceous plants and finally autumn colour. In the bowl are ground-covering shrubs and prostrate roses, shrubs of arching habit and, to add height to the slopes, sentinal junipers and cypresses and weeping trees.

Since it is the official residence of the Foreign Secretary, the Trust decided to give point to the necessary planting of trees by including species from as many countries as possible. There are young specimens of the following among others: *Acer campestre*, from Europe, *A. opalus*, from Italy, *A. platanoides*, from Norway, and *A. rubrum*, from Canada; *Aesculus indica*, from the north-west Himalayas; *Arbutus menziesii*, from California, and *A. unedo*, from Ireland and Spain; *Betula papyrifera humilis*, from Alaska, and *B. pendula* 'Dalecarlica', from Sweden; *Castanea sativa*, from Italy; *Fraxinus angustifolia*, from southern Europe and North Africa, and *F. oxycarpa*, from Persia; *Liriodendron tulipifera*, from eastern North America; *Mespilus germanica*, from south-east Europe and Asia Minor; *Nothofagus procera*, from Chile; *Prunus sargentii*, from Japan; *Quercus canariensis*, from Algiers, *Q. frainetto*, from Hungary, and *Q. rubra*, from eastern North America; *Sorbus latifolia*, from France; and *Tilia oliveri*, from China.

The Foreign Secretary of the day can be imagined strolling around the garden, pondering on the tractability of trees compared with people.

DUDMASTON
Bridgnorth, *Salop*

Given by Lady Labouchere in 1977

AREA 3.2 ha (8 acres)	$3\frac{1}{2}$ miles south-east
SOIL Lime-free	of Bridgnorth on west
ALTITUDE 75 m (250 ft)	side of A442
RAINFALL 889 mm (35 in.)	
TEMPERATURE 4.5°C (40°F)	

THE OLD DEVONIAN red sandstone is much in evidence at historic Bridgnorth, and the rock crops up here and there around Dudmaston, providing the eminence on which the house stands and also noteworthy features in the garden. We are prepared for richness by the approach drive, passing great oaks and cedars, and are not disappointed by the prospect on the garden front. This is enhanced by the ground which falls away to the Big Pool; this attractive sheet of water acts as a sort of stage for Brown Clee and other distant hills, and the whole prospect is framed by trees – great ones around and dainty birches, willows and maples towards the water. Captain Wolryche-Whitmore, Lady Labouchere's uncle, was a great forester and tree planter, and to him we owe much of the beauty of the landscape. The pool was made during the last century, by adjustment to the dams of smaller pools; the water flows from ground on the other side of the main road and eventually joins the Severn. By the water grows a giant Cuckoo Flower or Ladies' Smock, *Cardamine raphanifolia*, reputedly brought from Norway by Alice Mary Wolryche-Whitmore in the early part of this century.

Besides the creation of the pool, the second quarter of the 19th century was noted for the terracing of the grass slope on this garden front; the steps remain, leading us down to the pool, with the 18th-century Ladies' Bath tucked away under the steep rock-bank on the left. Owing probably to the tapping of the supply for the needs of Birmingham, water no longer flows from the stone spout. On the other side of this grass slope the sandstone crops out nobly and has led to the construction of steps and steep sunny ledges where Rock Roses, heaths, thymes, lavenders and escallonias thrive. Here we should pause for a moment; the position is marked by a sundial whereon the Golden Weddings of former Wolryche-Whitmores are recorded. I was last there in spring; the words carved on the sundial reminded me that the heavy rain on that April day would soon pass:

Shadow and Sun
So too our lives are made
Yet think how great the sun
How small the shade.

Brilliant sun soon lit up the sweeps of cool-tinted daffodils in the valley of grass and great oaks to the south; the chiff-chaff and the willow warbler sang their care-free songs.

Through spring and summer, and finally with autumn colour, this garden area to the south is colourful with shrubs and plants. Magnolias, rhododendrons and azaleas, mespilus, Japanese cherries, a Snowdrop Tree, *Kalmia latifolia* and *K. angustifolia* 'Rubra', are accompanied by cowslips and primroses in the grass, besides daffodils. Many of these shrubs are of ancient planting, dating back to the last century, when the assembly became known as the American Border. On a sunny wall the Spanish rose 'Gava' thrives; this, with 'Lorenzo Pahissa', was brought from Madrid by Lady Labouchere; many shrub roses, old and new, are well established and on a sheltered border are *Acanthus*, sedums, yuccas and buddleias. Later flowers come from eucryphias, Allspice, and hydrangeas. An old garden like this with contributions from many generations, is not complete without the quince, mulberry and medlar, and the comparatively new Dawn Redwood, all of which are represented. Mrs Dorothy Hadoke contributed much of the later planting while Captain Wolryche-Whitmore was alive, and since 1966 when his niece, Lady Labouchere came to live here.

DUNSTER CASTLE
Minehead, *Somerset*

Given by Lt-Colonel Walter Luttrell, MC, *in 1975*

AREA 6 ha (15 acres)
SOIL Lime-free
ALTITUDE 15 m (50 ft)
RAINFALL 1016 mm (40 in.)
TEMPERATURE 5.5°C (42°F)

In Dunster,
3 miles south-east of
Minehead on A396

DURING A HOLIDAY in north Somerset in 1938 I paid a visit to Dunster Castle; it was open in aid of charity and the village street, castle, folly and the garden all made an indelible impression on me. Horticulturally it was a remarkable visit: I had never seen the Arum 'Lily' of our greenhouses growing in the open air before, nor 'Mimosa' (*Acacia dealbata*) doing likewise. Moreover apart from growing well, the latter was sending up a forest of suckers. And, of course there was the remarkable lemon.

In those days one struggled up the steep drive from the main street, and realised, on passing under the mediaeval gateway; how difficult it would have been for invaders to win this first approach: Dunster Castle is perched on a high conical hill, the site occupied for a thousand years, serving in Saxon times as a frontier fortress against Celts and roving Norsemen (see illus. 5).

Apart from the way the castle emerges from its bower of trees and dominates the village, the fairest impression, I think, is the present entry route across the park with its fine native trees. During the centuries a succession of routes spirally ascending the hill have been made. The reward when you get to the top is one of the finest panoramic views anywhere in the country.

There is very little gardening on the hill itself. In an engraving of the early 18th century the western slopes of the hill are shewn covered with a series of terraces. Vestiges of these still remain and I believe they constituted a fairly extensive vineyard. There are some fine trees among the natives, including a Cork Oak and its hybrid the Lucombe Oak. Ferns abound but are notably limited to the Hart's Tongue and the Soft Shield Fern, a rare combination, at least in the gardens of the Trust. One of the earliest foreign evergreens to be introduced to British gardens, the Laurustinus, which arrived in the late 16th century, has become naturalised. In this warm climate it produces abundant indigo-coloured berries and any branch touching the soil takes root. The Spurge Laurel is also found in quantity.

The sunny terrace at the top, immediately under the castle, grows some remarkable plants. First there is the old Lemon plant, which was mentioned as being old and well established in Loudon's *Gardener's Magazine*, Vol. 18, 1842. This grows against the wall of the castle, and is protected in winter, but fruits regularly. Is there another plant outside on our mainland? It is surely the ultimate in examples of the devotion of gardeners to the plants under their care. Below it is a border of hundreds of *Echeveria glauca* with *Beloperone guttata* nearby, *Beschorneria*, *Mandevillea suaveolens*, the Carob or true Locust, an Olive, camellias, Tree Peonies, the European dwarf Palm and the Chusan Palm. 'Mimosa' and *Colletia armata* grow on this sunny terrace and there, in the Swan Pool (the swan is a metal fountain), grows the same clump of Arums I photographed in 1938.

The site of the keep, made into a bowling green in the early 18th century, is being replanted and from here some of the most remarkable views are obtained. Several good shrubs already grow here, *Feijoa*, *Rosa anemonoides*, a Judas Tree, magnolias and roses, and a large specimen of *Cotoneaster serotina*.

At the foot of the hill flows the River Avill, which some hundreds of years ago contributed to the defence of the castle. In fact the sea has receded and the rich pastures are a result. The Avill flows from an old mill, under an intriguing narrow pack-horse bridge (rebuilt in the 18th century) and then through an area developed as a water garden during the last one hundred years or so. Here are the giant leaves of gunneras, the New Zealand flax and watsonias, besides *Cornus kousa*, a tall twisted Pekin Willow; *Arundinaria fastuosa*, a Sweet Bay of some 12 m (40 ft), tall conifers and other trees. A *Celastrus* ascends one tree to about 18 m (60 ft). There is thus a very wide disparity in the types of gardening here, and variety of impressions.

DYRHAM PARK
Chippenham, *Avon*

Bought by the Ministry of Works from Mr J. W. R. Blathwayt in 1956 and transferred to the Trust in 1961

AREA 2.4 ha (6 acres)
SOIL Limy
ALTITUDE 136 m (450 ft)
RAINFALL 762 mm (30 in.)
TEMPERATURE 4°C (39°F)

7 miles north of Bath, west of the A46 Bath–Stroud road, 2 miles south of M4

FOR ABOUT two and three-quarter centuries the present house at Dyrham has sat comfortably across the valley of the park; little remains of the earlier manor house which was transformed. At first the entrance was below, from the village, approaching the west front, church and stable block. Today this is the garden front.

For about one hundred years the formal terraced garden shown in the Kip engraving was a *tour de force*, and had little to compare with it in England. This, William Blathwayt's great formal layout, was created late in the 17th century, just when people were beginning to tire of clipped and circumscribed formality and were welcoming the open views and changed style of gardening which matured during the 18th century (see illus. 15). Little remains of the formal layout, but the line of limes parallel to the church seems to be the original, and the two ponds, though less formal than they were, are certainly authentic. The wall below them, with niches, is thought to have been rebuilt by Repton or in his period, although I have always thought it oddly placed for a landscape composition, lying as it does across the ground exactly where the most distant view is obtained from the terrace of the house.

Originally the drive approached directly to the house from the west and John Povey, William Blathwayt's nephew, writing from Whitehall in 1700, describes the two ponds as fishponds, fed by "A Cataract of about 15 ft and another of about 6 ft". The water reaches the ponds from the upper park, under the stable block, and in those days on going through the house to the east front one was confronted by what was described as "a triumph of symmetry over geography" covering the entire rising ground of the park. Povey continued with his impressions: "Before you are on top of the Hill a Cataract abt. 50 foot High another throwing a good Body of Water abt. 20 foot high and under is a large Cataract of water descending the whole hill and coming underground to the Parterre" with further fountains and basins, walks and terraces. Stephen Switzer in 1718 claimed that "very considerable Sums have been expended to bring these Gardens to that Perfection which I some Years since saw them in."

Subsequently when the Bath road became an important highway, the entrance was made from it and the formality was swept away, and from the twin lodges a new drive swept gracefully down to the east front. C. Harcourt-Masters, the Bath surveyor, was responsible for much of this, before Repton's visit. The park has recently been handed to the Trust and replanting has started. A few trees including some cedars and a pair of plane trees, like the Holm Oaks on the other front, remain from earlier planting.

The water supply for the ponds accumulates on the hill to the east side of the house, and has occasioned much work from time to time. Soon after construction of the ponds, the gardeners took two weeks to wheel away the mud after a storm. More recently the Trust has dredged the ponds, but silt continues to accumulate.

The orangery, so much a part of old gardens, was built about 1701 and is a very early example of this sort of building. The Latin on the frieze may be translated: "Observe moderation, hold the end in view, and follow nature's law." This injunction would be more applicable to the general style of gardening of the 18th century than to the severities of the 17th century. The making of artificial shelters for plants can scarcely be described as following nature's law, but, when *Jasminum polyanthum* is in flower, close your eyes and you might imagine the whole building to be full of its oranges, lemons and myrtles, their flowers exhaling sweet scent.

EAST RIDDLESDEN HALL
Keighley, *West Yorkshire*

Given by Mr J. J. and Mr W. A. Brigg in 1934

AREA 8 ha (20 acres)
SOIL Lime-free
ALTITUDE 75 m (250 ft)
RAINFALL 889 mm (35 in.)
TEMPERATURE 3.5°C (38°F)

West Riding.
1½ miles north-east of Keighley on the A650 Keighley–Bradford road

WHILE THE HALL has been well cared for ever since it came to the Trust in 1933, cash was not available for any attempt at tidying up the surrounding land. The first view of the mid 17th-century house across the old fishpond was obscured by natural growth of willows and other trees. The peculiar layout of walls behind the house precluded any semblance or possibility of privacy. But a great effort was made and in the early 1970s, thanks to the generosity of two benefactors, a wall which projected at right angles from the porch at the back of the house was taken down and re-erected so that it now encloses the garden on the vulnerable side. It joins another old wall in which are niches, reputedly mews for falcons, though Sir Reginald Blomfield in *The Formal Garden in England* ascribes them to perches for peacocks.

With the wall removed it was decided to make a formal garden – not a slavish period piece, but a neat and orderly design. The difficulty was that all the walls ran away at varying angles. However, the unwanted corners and angles were taken up by varying the width of the surrounding borders, and a rectangular plan was evolved. It has a short avenue of pyramid apples and pears, a small, sunken, paved rose garden with box hedges, and a chequered planting of Mophead Acacias on a small side lawn. The borders are filled with a modern scheme of shrubs and plants designed to provide beauty and interest throughout the season.

EMMETTS
Ide Hill, *Kent*

Acquired in 1965 with an endowment under the will of Mr C. W. Boise

AREA 1.6 ha (4 acres)
SOIL Lime-free
ALTITUDE 182 m (600 ft)
RAINFALL 889 mm (35 in.)
TEMPERATURE 3.5°C (38°F)

1½ miles south of A25 on Sundridge to Ide Hill road

THIS IS AN ARBORETUM of four acres of well-drained soil, on high ground where the cool air and frequent mists foster the growth of many specimens. It is a most interesting collection of trees and shrubs grown for their individual interest and beauty; it owes nothing to design and little to forethought, apart from ensuring, in the main, that every plant had some room to grow. Apart from a tulip tree, magnolias of various kinds, pierises, rhododendrons – particularly *R. thomsonii*, *R. ambiguum*, and a wide-spread hummock of *R. ferrugineum*, over 914 mm (3 ft) high and 7.3 m (24 ft) across – various acers including *A. henryi*, amelanchiers and the like, there is a fine Dawyck Beech and a blue Colorado Spruce of good size. *Eucryphia cordifolia*, *E. nymansensis* 'Nymansay' and *E. llutinosa* are represented by good specimens and flower well in late

68 BELOW The garden at East Riddlesden Hall in 1976, soon after completion. The far wall was transferred from the immediate foreground, thus revealing the garden from the main path, and at the same time making it private.
69 RIGHT Among the many choice shrubs at Emmetts, none is more beautiful than *Zenobia pulverulenta*, from the Eastern United States. Fragrant white bells in May, borne among glaucous foliage.

summer, at which time *Ligustrum japonicum* gives an unusually fine display. *Kalopanax pictus* is represented by a lofty specimen approaching 21.3 m (70 ft); it produces cream flowers in autumn. The coolness and the mists help *Zenobia pulverulenta* to thrive, likewise *Phyllodoce empetriformis*. Its tiny pink bell-flowers appear in spring. Below this lovely assembly of choice woody subjects – there are many more – is a woodland thickly spread with bluebells in the spring. The canopy of russet leaves in autumn vies with the tints of the exotics on the higher ground.

The house was owned by Frederick Lubbock from 1893 onwards; he was a friend of William Robinson who inspired him with a love of trees and shrubs. As a result this little arboretum was laid out mainly with his help and advice and the source of the plants from 1900–8 was James Veitch & Son of Coombe Wood Nursery, Kingston. Many plants were purchased, apparently, from the sale in 1914 when this nursery closed.

ERDDIG
Wrexham, *Clwyd*

Given in 1973 by Mr Philip Yorke, whose family has lived at Erddig since 1735

AREA 5.2 ha (13 acres)
SOIL Lime-free
ALTITUDE 60.9 m (200 ft)
RAINFALL 889 mm (35 in.)
TEMPERATURE 4.5°C (40°F)

1 mile south of Wrexham, off A483

THE APPROACH to the house is through some particularly beautiful undulating meadows, well wooded. The whole area extending beyond the west front of the house was landscaped and planted by William Emes between 1767 and 1789. Apart from planting trees he designed a unique feature known as the Cup and Saucer. It is arranged so that the waters of the Black Brook – the Avon Du – swirl round a circular platform, disappearing into the wide circular central gulf, to dash forth again below, making a curtain of white water when seen through the tunnel underneath. "Cup and Saucer" is perhaps a strange name for this feature, but what else could it be called? It has been repeated, I understand, at Hawarden Castle, Clwyd. The Black Brook was named from the dark water which flushes through coal seams, but it is no longer black.

In one corner of the garden stands a sundial with the coat of arms of John Meller, who laid out the original garden in about 1718, following the sort of schemes which had been popular in England for the previous fifty years or more. It was at the time when Bridgeman and Kent were setting the pointers to a less formal style. With the house dating from 1684, the garden was given firm lines and the area was enclosed by a high brick wall. In 1739 Thomas Badeslade, just after the arrival of the Yorkes, engraved his bird's-eye view which has been invaluable in reconstructing this garden (see illus. 20). The engraving shews the woods to the north, along Wat's Dyke, which still has remnants of the evergreens which lined the formal woodland walks.

The stone front of the house, which sits so proudly on its eminence looking west, is a complete contrast to the brick garden front, so mellow and delicate in colouring. If you stand on the broad steps the eye takes in the entire garden and the impression is of a vast rectangle. But, as in so many old gardens, the apparently regular lines are a delusion. The side walls are not square to the house and the wall at the far end is in two oblique lines.

When I first went to Erddig, before it had actually been accepted by the Trust, the garden was in decay. The only gardeners were sheep; at least they kept much of the grass mown, but did not tackle the nettles. They were much favoured by Mr Yorke for not only did they do the rough mowing but also helped him to control the yew trees. Unfortunately one of these "gardeners" found his way into the house and when confronted by a ram of his own size in a mirror lost no time in breaking the image.

On my last visit everything was much changed. The canals had been dredged and the re-sown lawns were richly green with spring grass. The orchards had been planted and many fruit trees, of ancient varieties specially propagated, had been placed against the walls. It is indeed a return to the planting of the 18th-century engraving.

The garden is divided into three main sections. It is recorded that the broad central walk in 1750 was "gravell'd . . . from the door to the White Gate". This middle section contains a broad gravel walk between newly-planted double rows of *Tilia euchlora*, already having their branches trained sideways along wires for pleaching. These replaced the old beeches which were falling some years ago and had to be clear-felled for safety. We all considered whether they should be replaced with beeches but the garden front of the house being low and long it was felt that trees of lower height should connect the house to the tall double avenue of limes which stand on either side of the central canal. When this was dredged in the early part of this century the soil was used to make two shaped, graded mounds on either side of the long vista in front of the cross wall. By great good fortune a pair of yews stands sentinel too, and by even greater good fortune an early 18th-century screen and gates by the noted Wrexham smith, Robert Davies, were placed here, as a substitute for the White Gate, in 1905.

The section on the left terminates in a lesser canal or fishpond, with a charming niche in the far corner of the angle of the walls. On arrival at this point the diverging lines of the walls are apparent, but what is more

70 The curved gables were added to the old walls at Erddig in 1911.

apparent is the difficulty of replacing the extraordinary – unique, probably – series of yew-hedged scallops which guard Meller's sundial on two sides. For long we pondered on what these shapes represented. Eventually it was considered that they created niches for a series of bee-skeps.

The whole garden – or at least this sunnier side – was given to fruit trees and so five or six good popular sorts are now planted in serried ranks, selected for reasonably uniform growth and suitable for interpollinating. They will be trained into pyramids. We hope that some income will accrue in future years from the resultant crops and that visitors will go home with baskets full of Erddig apples. Perhaps, too, with pears, peaches, apricots and plums from the wall fruit. It is intended to fan-train the stone fruit, while the pears and some apples will be trained as espaliers. Various plants will be grown with them and in particular a collection of older cultivars of daffodils and narcissi given to the Trust by the National Trust for Scotland, from their garden at Threave. A further collection was given by the Rosewarne Experimental Horticultural Station at Camborne, Cornwall.

It must be envisaged that, apart from the two canals and the avenues, the whole area was very much given to fruit production and more fruit trees are in other walled areas. It was a highly productive garden.

There is however a third section, this time on the south side of the central walk. It is divided into three lengths. First there is an avenue of Irish Yews. These had reached very large proportions and were of awkward spreading growth so they were pruned to the ground during the winter of 1975–6 and they are now growing strongly. The next section is given to a flower garden of Victorian style. Here were two raised flower-beds edged with local earthenware curbing; beyond were more flower-beds. In the *Journal of Horticulture* for 1909 a planting of 'Dorothy Perkins' rose and *Clematis jackmanii* growing with variegated *Acer negundo* was described, and this grouping has been repeated in our reconstruction, for summer display. Beyond these is what is known as the Moss Walk, an area much shaded by trees and evergreens. It was originally a bowling green.

If we stand on the steps of the house looking down to the main canal, it will be seen that the new lines of limes for pleaching follow the lines of the two garden pavilions. At one time these were connected by walls to the house, but these walls were taken away in 1861 and the present corner niches made, the garden pavilions being decorated at the same time by the intriguingly curved gables. The northern building was given a clock in 1905, and it is said that in later years in spring and autumn, when British Summer Time came into force, the sundial below the steps was twisted round to conform! Time never stands still in a garden . . .

FARNBOROUGH HALL
Near Banbury, *Oxon.*

House given in 1960 by the Treasury which had accepted it in lieu of death duties; and an endowment given by Mr Geoffrey Holbech

AREA 6.5 ha (16 acres)
SOIL Lime-free
ALTITUDE 75 m (250 ft)
RAINFALL 686 mm (27 in.)
TEMPERATURE 4°C (39°F)

6 miles north of Banbury, $\frac{1}{2}$ mile west of the A423 Banbury–Coventry road

"THERE IS only a grass walk, and a couple of temples. There is no real garden." In these few words

71 Map of Farnborough Hall garden.

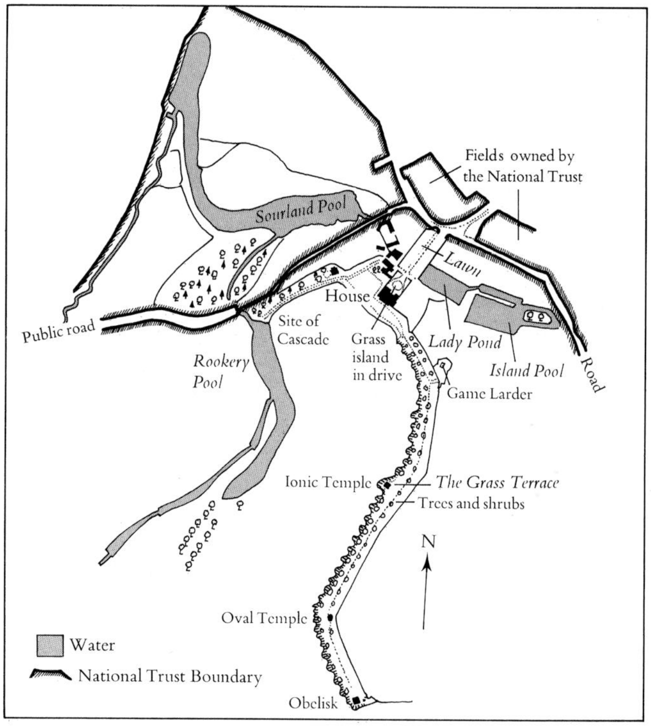

72 LEFT The rare, Oval Temple at Farnborough Hall. Photo 1963.
73 RIGHT The Obelisk at the summit of the long, sloping 18th-century grass terrace at Farnborough Hall. Photo 1960.

Farnborough was dismissed to me by a keen gardener. No doubt he had expected to see some flowery borders and shrubberies, and was not content with the fine Tulip Tree and great Cedar of Lebanon near the house, the ancient Tree Peony and the *Magnolia grandiflora*, planted on the south front of the house in 1778 (it cost half a guinea according to the accounts of the time). I cannot remember whether the rose garden had been restored and replanted at the time; both this small area and that by the old greenhouse have been tidied and replanted since 1960.

There is more at Farnborough than just flowering plants and shrubs. It is an historic layout by William Holbech at the end of the 18th century, and it is recorded that he "was assisted by the advice and taste of his friend and neighbour, Sanderson Miller of Radway", who was by then a landscape designer of some note, mainly in the Gothick taste. It is a most fortunate survivor of the *genre* of the time, untouched by later modifications, unspoiled apart from the falling of aged trees; time adorns it.

But let us approach the place in the proper manner. The north front of the house is first seen from the gate, under spreading trees, across the lawn. It has a small forecourt and the Tulip Tree is on the left, by the verge of the Lady Pond, an almost rectangular piece of water, connected intriguingly from St Botolph's Well with two more formal ponds, one of which is the Island Pond.

Through the garden gate we reach the cedar, with a view across another very large lake known as Sourland Pool. Around this have been planted a number of species of Alder. In the middle distance of the southern landscape is yet another lake, to which Sourland Pool is connected by means of pipes. There is an artificial stone cliff, with the foundations of some sort of gazebo and cascade, approached by a long walk shrouded in ancient yews. This last lake floats away into the distance, and both it and Sourland Pool have been dredged in recent years, so that once again they mirror the light from the sky, as they were intended to do. Directly opposite the south front of the house lies this last long lake, and beyond it trees recede into the landscape. Across the lawn is a ditch marked by a series of bushes clipped arbitrarily into cumulus shapes, making an unusual line of soft contours.

With a map before one, the skilful creation of these lakes can be more easily understood, especially from the rising ground of the terrace, which beckons one for further exploration to the east of the house. It curves in a gentle S-shape ever upwards, perched upon the ridge of the hill (from which it was levelled out), backed by a spinney of large and ancient beeches; under them, in natural abandon in the rough grass, grows the Martagon or Turk's Cap Lily, its shades of pink and mauve blending into the gloom. The grass terrace is 731 m (800 yds) long. Since this sort of thing at any time – and specially in the 18th century – needs some interest for the owner and his visitor, there are two temples and an obelisk to tempt us onwards, while on the lower side is a long series of scalloped promontories, hedged about with laurel. This may well be Sanderson Miller's somewhat Gothick ornamentation. It is possible that Richard Jago in his poem *Edge-hill*, 1767, refers to these promontories as "planted tufts":

> *Her spacious terrace, and surrounding lawns*
> *Deck'd with no sparing cost of planted tufts,*
> *Or ornamental building . . .*

The temples – one Ionic and rectangular, the other exquisitely oval or elliptic in shape, with an upper storey and domed roof – are in the classic taste. An obelisk terminates the walk. From the first temple there is a delightful view back to the house, built of the local brown Hornton sandstone in the 17th century. It passed from the Raleigh family to Ambrose Holbech in 1683.

From this elevated walk the slopes of Edgehill are visible. Hilaire Belloc might have had the place in mind when he wrote: "Here it is possible to linger for many hours alone, and to watch the slope of the hill under the level light as the sun descends." For this we should need his "silence of the air" for every south-westerly gale strikes this walk and its old trees. As fast as gaps occur new ones are planted. The scalloped promontories each were given a tree, an English Elm or a Scots Pine. New elms recently established have been lost through the elm disease, and are being replaced by limes.

On the way back do not miss a visit to the game-larder which lies through the trees on the right; from this vantage point the upper ponds can be clearly seen.

The whole conception at Farnborough is a great achievement, single minded and triumphant, still to be enjoyed as it was conceived two hundred years ago.

FELBRIGG HALL
Cromer, *Norfolk*

Left to the Trust in 1969 under the will of Mr R. Windham Ketton-Cremer

AREA 2.6 ha (6½ acres)
SOIL Lime-free
ALTITUDE 60.9 m (200 ft)
RAINFALL 635 mm (25 in.)
TEMPERATURE 4°C (39°F)

3 miles from Cromer, west of B1436

IF YOU DRIVE through the park at Felbrigg on a still autumn day you will be struck by its expanse and peacefulness, and the mellow tones of trees and buildings. The sea is but a mile away. The house and garden are sheltered by the Great Wood planted by William Windham in the last quarter of the 17th century. Many of the great oaks and sweet chestnuts date from that time. The older part of the house was built in the earlier half of 17th century, and though covered with stucco is substantially in the same style as BLICKLING. It is not until you arrive at the west side of the house that the astonishing change of architecture is visible – a change to the style of the end of 17th century – for this wing was added in the 1680s and the orangery, which houses some remarkably large camellias, was built in 1705.

A short walk will bring you to the walled kitchen garden. In time gone by, when up to a dozen men might have been employed in it, tending vegetables, flower borders, and fruit trees on the walls, it would have presented a wonderful example of husbandry. This extended to the very large dovecote at the top, which housed hundreds of pairs of birds. How the gardeners must have cursed their depredations among the vegetables! Old figs and some fruit trees survive, but in the main this garden has been brought under cultivation again recently by paying lip service to it as a kitchen garden; the rows of Belladonna Lilies remain against the greenhouse wall and flower borders of simple needs against the outer walls. Some newly-planted shrub borders are edged with thousands of *Colchicum autumnale tenori*, a rare form of autumn crocus, making a border one foot wide, a heart-warming sight in the September sunshine (see illus. 76). Another border has standard Tree Mallows, which flower well here in late summer, grapevines trained on timber pyramids, and a collection of culinary herbs. A selection of varieties of lilacs provides early interest and fragrance, and to make use of a large area nearby with a minimum of work a wide range of species of *Crataegus* or Thorn has been planted. Together with some herbs and fruit trees, the whole area is now full of interest from spring to autumn.

Felbrigg was built by a Windham and has been owned by descendants or relatives by marriage ever since. There is a letter extant from Repton to William Windham which he wrote to prove the unphilosophical system of the exponents of the purely picturesque gardeners: "Places are not to be laid out with a view to their appearance in a picture, but to their uses, and the enjoyment of them in real life; and their conformity to these purposes is that which constitutes their beauty." He adds that formality is "in perfect good taste and infinitely more comfortable to the principles which form the basis of our pleasure in these instances, than the docks and thistles, and litter and disorder, that may make a better figure in a picture." I think he would have been happy with today's slogan: "Please take your litter home with you."

FLORENCE COURT
Enniskillen, *Co. Fermanagh*

Given in 1954 by Viscount Cole, endowed by the Ulster Land Fund

AREA 3.6 ha (9 acres)
SOIL Lime-free
ALTITUDE 60.9 m (200 ft)
RAINFALL 1016 m (40 in.)
TEMPERATURE 4.5°C (40°F)

7 miles south-west of Enniskillen, 1 mile west of Florence Court village on A32

ITS DELIGHTFUL NAME commemorates Florence Wrey, a Cornish woman, the wife of the second Cole who owned the property, and who later became the 1st Lord Mountflorence. The house was completed by about the middle of the 18th century.

After suddenly turning a corner in the approach drive you have a splendid view of the long east front, from which the ground slopes gently down, heavily wooded, to Upper Loch Erne. The former walled garden and the park in front of the house belong to the Forestry Commission, with whom the Trust has collaborated in a plan to replant in the English Landscape style. To this end tree planting has already begun and a long haha has been built to give the properly inconspicuous transition from garden to park.

The garden lies on the other side of the house and here the terrain is varied, reaching away to the considerable height of the Cuilcagh Hills. The lush grass is rich with wild flowers and the winding paths provide many impressive views in different directions.

One day in May I was there at a memorable moment. It was pouring with rain, but the majesty of the scene was not lost, for in Ireland the air is always clear, washed through frequent rains. The hills were blue in the distance, the sky was grey; the lawns were of a green from which the Emerald Isle derives its name; an immense copper beech provided a dusky note. The rhododendrons were in flower, clump after clump, mound after mound, the whole spacious plantation dominated by many immense groups of *R.* 'Russellianum' or 'Cornish Red' – the well-known hybrid of *R. arboreum* which is found in so many gardens in the south and west of these islands. These great hummocks of brilliant crimson uplifted the day, some plants exceeding 6.1 m (20 ft) in height. As if this were not enough there are many large, high beech trees of a weeping nature, though possibly not the weeping form that is usually seen. With the weeping skies and weeping bright green beeches – punctuated here and there with grand old Scots Pines by the ice-house and other conifers – the whole was a scene of splendour. (See plate XXV.)

A stream wanders through the lower reaches of the lawns, bridged at one point, and luxuriantly bordered with moisture-loving plants.

In August the views are enlivened by the giant montbretia, *Curtonus paniculatus*, which is more or less naturalised through the garden; it attains 1.5 m (5 ft) in height. Large groups of Rugosa roses in purple or white flower freely in May and June and intermittently later, when their large red hips contrast with the white flowers of *Eucryphia intermedia*, and the yellow of hypericums. Many late-flowering shrubs have been recently planted to augment the display, including *Rhododendron*, *Hydrangea*, *Cornus*, *Myrtus* and eucryphias. In the spring the masses of Lenten Roses accompany daffodils.

It was on the local hills that in 1780 or thereabouts a farmer named Willis, a tenant of the Florence Court estate, found two self-sown seedlings of yew of markedly erect growth. Had he not transplanted one into his own garden, and the other to the Florence Court garden, many British gardens and churchyards would be less full of character. For the plant at Florence Court was propagated and eventually distributed by Messrs Lee & Kennedy of Hammersmith, and from this all the Irish Yews known are descended. Fortunately the tree – which still grows at Florence Court – was a good, female type and bears crimson berries freely in autumn.

GAWTHORPE HALL
Padiham, *Lancashire*

Given in 1971 by the 4th Lord Shuttleworth

AREA 1 ha ($2\frac{1}{2}$ acres)	On east outskirts of
SOIL Lime-free	Padiham; $\frac{3}{4}$ mile drive
ALTITUDE 75 m (250 ft)	to house on north
RAINFALL 1143 mm (45 in.)	of A671, east of
TEMPERATURE 3°C (37°F)	Padiham Adult Centre

THERE HAS BEEN a house at Gawthorpe for a very long time; the foundations have yet to give up their secrets. Much of what we see was completed by 1605, and at that time there may well have been a compact formal garden, probably on the entrance front. The first evidence is a Knyff drawing of the early 18th century shewing many flower borders on the entrance front, enclosed by walls.

When Janet Shuttleworth, whose family had lived at Gawthorpe since its inception, decided to call in Sir Charles Barry to alter the house, much was done to adjust the garden as well. It is reasonable to suppose that the radial beds on the other side of the house, with their raised stone verges, date from the mid- or late-19th century also. Barry also provided a sunken way into the basement; "downstairs" were kept out of sight as at UPPARK and CLIVEDEN. While the level ground of the 18th-century layout remained, high sloping grass banks were made around it, so that, across the lawn from the front door, one has the impression of age-old terraces, receding into the woodland slope above, leading to an avenue through the woodland, which has recently been replanted with limes; from the upper level of the terraces is the finest view of the house with the hills behind. Thanks to many groups of voluntary workers there are now attractive walks in the woodland which wend their way among rhododendrons under old beeches and oaks. The terraces have recently been planted with a pattern of Irish Yews and clipped box.

Around the house is a narrow border where substantial plantings have recently been made, mostly evergreens of compact nature to give a firm base, as it were, to the dominating architecture. Dark green of mahonias, the dense laurel 'Otto Luyken', dwarf berberises and pernettyas, *Euonymus fortunei* 'Coloratus', hebes, *Euphorbia robbiae*, dwarf Periwinkle, heathers and rhododendrons are contrasted by the big round leaves of bergenias and the sword-like leaves of *Yucca recurvifolia*.

GLENDURGAN
Falmouth, *Cornwall*

Given in 1962, with an endowment, by Mr and Mrs Cuthbert Fox and Mr Philip Fox

AREA 10 ha (25 acres)	4 miles south-west
SOIL Lime-free	of Falmouth, ½ mile
ALTITUDE 30 m (100 ft)	south-west of Mawnan
RAINFALL 1016 mm (40 in.)	Smith on the Helford
TEMPERATURE 6.5°C (44°F)	Passage road

SEVERAL OF the most famous Cornish gardens – and there are many – owe their principal interest to numbers of *Rhododendron* species raised from seed brought direct from the Far East. The climate in the deep valleys, for which the county is noted, has proved ideal for nurturing the Himalayan species of *Rhododendron* and all the shrubs that go with them. Glendurgan has glorious rhododendrons and azaleas but does not owe everything to them.

To start with, it is but a short turn off the main road before you are on the lawn in front of the house. The view down the valley to the Helford River is one of the most beautiful I know, and it has been developed and planted by the Fox family since 1820. It is therefore young compared with some gardens in the Trust, but it is difficult to convey a tithe of its beauty by mere words. At what time shall we go? In early spring the valley is cheered with the pale yellow of Lent Lilies and a rhododendron flames here and there under the venerable trees, bursting into growth under the strengthening sun. From then until June there is much to see. Rhododendrons abound – some casting their fragrance afar on the air – lavender-blue perhaps overhung with white cherries, or rosy red seen against the towering masses of creamy *Drimys winteri*. There is another magic moment when the numerous trees of *Cornus kousa* and *C. capitata* flower, casting a cool pale gold colouring through the valley. Later the blue of hydrangeas gives the right contrast to the spires of eucryphias in August. There is then a pause from flowers apart from late eucryphias, hoherias and *Eupatorium micranthum*, but it gives the opportunity to appreciate the numerous shapes and tints of the trees and shrubs which until then have been outbidden by the blossom.

74 A summer view at Glendurgan, shewing a diversity of shapes and the fronds of the New Zealand Tree Fern, *Dicksonia antarctica*.

Spectacular in two places are clumps of the vast, prickly, grey-green leaves of the American Aloe, which, owing to almost complete absence of frost at Glendurgan, thrive unprotected in the grass. Few plants give such a sense of scale. Behind and below are impressive Tulip Trees, the Loquat, *Davidia involucrata*, magnolias of many kinds, *Metasequoia*, *Cryptomeria*, cedars, a Weeping Beech, the Willow-leafed Oak, hardy palms, bamboos, gunneras, myrtles with snuff-brown bark, Tree Ferns, Redwood and *Embothrium* – the Chilean Fire Bush. This little list is but a selection from memory of the many delights, but chief among them is the feeling of freedom; the valley is not choked with growths, and the floor of rough grass and ferns is spangled with primroses, Japanese Primulas, bluebells, columbines and ferns.

Another great joy is to walk down the gravelled footpath which takes us gently into the East Valley among these beautiful things, garnered from all parts of the world, threading its way gradually ever downwards, with vantage points here and there. Eventually deep in the valley we come to the little waterside village of Durgan, with arums, roses and fuchsias, boats and the laughing water and smell of seaweed to refresh us before climbing back to the top again. On this route are more vantage points and seldom does one have the opportunity of standing by *Magnolia veitchii* and *Picea smithiana* and looking down on cedars, *Cuninghamia lanceolata*, and a maze (see plate XXVI). This was laid out in 1833; it is of laurel and the paths describe a strange and asymmetrical pattern.

Still ascending, past more Tree Ferns, and perhaps a waft of sweet scent from *Rhododendron* 'Fragrantissimum', we find a rare and big specimen of *Cupressus lusitanica* 'Glauca Pendula' and then reach the gate of the Wall Garden.

The wall – a noble effort, capped with tiles – was built about 1830, no doubt to produce delectable fruits, and enclosed an orchard and vegetable garden. Gradually this little formal area – comparatively rare in Cornwall – has been given to many tender shrubs and plants including *Clianthus puniceus*, the New Zealand

'Lobster Claw'; *Hoheria sextylosa*; *Acacia longifolia* and *A. dealbata* ('Mimosa' of gardens); *Feijoa*, *Calceolaria integrifolia* and *Ceanothus* 'Trewithen Blue'.

The young tree of *Acer griseum* planted in the grass portion of the Wall Garden arose in my own garden as a self-sown seedling, and after Cuthbert Fox's death was put here in memory of him. Judge of our delight when his grandson William produced a list of 21 kinds of trees which he wanted to plant to commemorate his twenty-first birthday in 1977, in order to enrich the beauty started by his forbears.

By the time that the trees in the valley develop their autumn hues, the conifers and bamboos are at their most lovely green; moreover, among the conifers are some with bluish tints and some with yellow, so that this well-endowed valley is further enriched. At any time of the year and at any time of the day the views are entrancing. It is a place to linger in, so that the changing lights on trees and hills and water may be enjoyed. Never go there in a hurry; it is not a hurrying place. All is quiet. Even so, it does not please everyone; what garden does? My mind harks back to a keen gardener who thought it dull; dull, mark you, in May when all was a-flower; he thought the whole valley should be brightened up with a few hundred orange azaleas. Go there and see whether you agree, or would keep it as made by the Fox family over one hundred and fifty years, and jealously guarded for them and all of us by the Trust. Cuthbert Fox was satisfied with it; he saw it daily in all weathers, and one of my memories of him is the way he would stroll on the lawn looking ever down the valley. Though incapacitated in later life he knew every plant that grew there, and knew what would be in flower at any time of the year.

GREY'S COURT

Henley-on-Thames, *Oxfordshire*

Given by Sir Felix Brunner in 1968

AREA 3.7 ha ($9\frac{1}{4}$ acres)
SOIL Limy
ALTITUDE 75 m (250 ft)
RAINFALL 686 mm (27 in.)
TEMPERATURE 4°C (39°F)

3 miles west of Henley, on right of road to Rotherfield Greys

THE SHORT DRIVE from the lodge by the main road brings you quickly up an incline, with good trees breaking the views over the valley, to the main lawn and it would be a very hardened visitor who could not be touched with the beauty of it all. The house – a comparative newcomer of the 16th century – stands four square and gabled, a study in grey flint, stone and pink brick. Its windows look over the lawn to the assembly of ancient features around it – mediaeval towers and outbuildings of grey flint and stone, portions of wall, and several old Scots Pines; on their rooty banks cistuses and other sun-loving shrubs thrive. The whole gathering of lawn, buildings and trees is delightful, even enchanting. Having taken in these features, the eye instinctively turns to the wide open view to the west, framed by trees, among which is a large Tulip Tree and a Weeping Ash, both planted before 1823. To the east the rising lawn was planted with several Strawberry Trees at the suggestion of that artistic gardener, Humphrey Waterfield; their glittering dark green now gives yet another tint to the assembly, while in the autumn their exquisitely fashioned urn-like flowers give a honied scent, hanging in stiff little pyramids among the orange-red "strawberries" from last year's flowers.

The garden at Grey's Court makes no attempt to be grand or impressive; rather, like GUNBY HALL garden, it is something which has grown up over the years as part and parcel of a home. One little area has a Swiss stone fountain of the 18th century overhung by Japanese Cherries; another has roses; another several Japanese *Wistaria floribunda* of the type with the longest and most elegant flower racemes, up to 914 mm (3 ft) long, of two tones of lavender-blue; another, a walled area at the back of the big tower, has mostly white flowers, grouped along the walls away from the central pool. Here are magnolias, ceanothuses, Californian Poppies and other shrubs. An ancient, very large Common Larch whose branches lie low over the ground leads you to a surprise – a Chinese-style bridge and a moon-gate. Most of the gardened area is contained by a ditch or haha of considerable age.

With its kitchen garden and orchard and all the other features, the garden measures up to the charm of the house. To Sir Felix and Lady Brunner we owe much of this beauty, the newly contrived and the abiding old, preserved by the de Grey family since the 13th century.

GUNBY HALL

Burgh-le-Marsh, *Lincolnshire*

Given in 1944 by Lady Montgomery-Massingberd and Major Norman Leith-Hay-Clark

AREA 2.8 ha (7 acres)
SOIL Limy
ALTITUDE 30 m (100 ft)
RAINFALL 584 mm (23 in.)
TEMPERATURE 3.5°C (38°F)

7 miles west of Skegness, on south side of the A158 Lincoln–Skegness road

IN MANY WAYS a garden has always been an extension of the living rooms so that, comparable to furnishings being enjoyed indoors, the fountains, flowers and fruits were enjoyed out of doors. In Stuart times, as we have seen in Chapter 4, the garden was a place for promenading. Later it became a vast area to ride through, while a hundred years ago it was for the enjoyment of plants once again, and games. Since then the terrace and patio have come much into favour for seats and dalliance. There is no such outdoor room at Gunby, but the walled Kitchen Garden has been cropped and enjoyed for hundreds of years, true to the traditions of gardening. It is essentially a loved home where you go into the garden to pick flowers or fruit, feed the doves, play croquet, or walk to the church. The house was built in 1700 by Sir William Massingberd.

In front of the mellow pink-toned brick of the west front are beds of light yellow roses and purple or blue violas and other plants, while honeysuckles and roses are trained up the walls. This front looks out on to a formal garden laid out about 1900; on a sunken lawn corner beds of lavender and golden privet, and central beds of catmint guarding a sundial, augment the colours under the house. The whole is surrounded by duplicated yew hedges. A picture of 1810 shows a circular walk of sand or gravel in a lawn, unconnected with the gravel before the house. The present design, though not old therefore, fits the house superbly, without being pretentious or self-consciously formal.

Through the windows on my first visit came the sounds of a string quartet. Thus Lady Montgomery-Massingberd allowed the beauty indoors to flow into the garden from the panelled drawing-room. Later she met us in the garden and we said how we felt the music was just another part of the beauty between house and garden – the making of a home. With keen perception, and with a thump of her fist on my chest, she exclaimed, "I know, you're a singer – a tenor from the sound of your voice!" She was right and revealed more than once during the morning that her love of music equalled only her love of the garden and its flowers.

This is what Gunby spells to us who visit it. It is a home fostered for many generations of the family without ostentation. Today it is cared for by Mr and Mrs W. J. Wrisdale. It lies on the last slightly rising ground of the Lincolnshire Wolds, amidst vast areas of farming land. Farming is the main occupation here and gave rise to Gunby Hall.

I have visited Gunby many times and always, from spring to autumn, the walled gardens with their borders

75 The summerhouse at Gunby Hall.

76 The Ghost Walk at Gunby Hall. Photo 1976.

and arched ways have been full of flowers. The surrounding walls and straight paths lined with pyramid fruit trees keep up the long tradition of this kind of productive gardening, enclosing areas of vegetables. Early bulbs are followed by columbines, poppies and thrift; pinks, campanulas, montbretias, anemones and Michaelmas Daisies compete with hydrangeas and roses. Alstroemerias break into orange in June and like *Astilbe rivularis* are apt to run out of space! On the small lawn may well be a white dove, near the little domed summerhouse, which has standard honeysuckles by it. One area contains a herb garden.

On the walls are aged trained fruit trees, clematis and roses; until it was propagated the garden contained the only plant I know of the rose 'Reine Marie Henriette', a fragrant old cherry-red climber raised a hundred years ago. Roses are a speciality at Gunby, and always have been. 'Cupid' has reached a great height on one wall, and in the courtyard 'Lawrence Johnston', 'Gloire de Dijon' and 'Easlea's Golden Rambler' thrive.

To the east of the house stands an impressive Lebanon cedar, planted in 1812, and young ones have been planted to carry on the tradition. The lawn is bounded by roses, in beds and borders; modern and old, quite small, or large shrubs. Cyclamens thrive under the trees. Between the lawn and the walled gardens is a deep stretch of water with a hedged path along one side, known as the Ghost Walk. Was it water to provide fish for the table, comparable with the great pigeonry in the walled garden? Was it a moat, and if so what did it protect? Perhaps we shall never know. It has been there a long time and adds yet another pleasant feature to the garden, advantageous for the display of

XVII OPPOSITE ABOVE Ascott in spring, 1958.
XVIII OPPOSITE BELOW The main view from the east of Blickling Hall, towards the garden temple of 1760. Photo 1975. Directly beyond is the chestnut avenue depicted in illus 181.

XIX ABOVE Two old varieties of *Dahlia*, 'Ella Britten', old gold, and 'Madame S. Stappers', orange red, of matching height and bronzy foliage, replace the hyacinths at Anglesey Abbey in summer. Photo 1967.

XX OPPOSITE ABOVE At Bodnant in May the laburnum archway, laid out nearly a hundred years ago, competes with the beauty of the rhododendrons. Photo 1966.
XXI OPPOSITE BELOW Borders in the Lily Garden at Barrington Court, demonstrating the Jekyllian touch of contrasting foliage of crinums and bergenias against her patterned brick path.

XXII The spring foliage of the 'Brilliantissimum' Sycamore dominates the castellations of the yew hedges at Knightshayes which surround the pool garden, in which grows a Silver Weeping Pear. Photo 1977.

XXIII ABOVE One of a pair of herbaceous borders at Cliveden, replanted in 1971. This soft-coloured border is echoed across the lawns by its companion in strong colours.

XXIV LEFT The Red Borders at Hidcote in 1965. Approximately the same view as illus. 82.

XXV OPPOSITE ABOVE Immense weeping beeches and hybrids of the Himalayan *Rhododendron arboreum* dwarf the landscape at Florence Court. A photograph taken in the rain, in 1965.

XXVI OPPOSITE BELOW The maze planted with Cherry Laurel in 1833 at Glendurgan. Beyond are *Taxodium*, *Cunninghamia* and other trees. *Cornus capitata* displays its annual wealth of pale gold flowers. Photo 1972.

XXVII A view of Charlecote attributed to Jan Stevens (d. 1722). In spite of the alterations wrought by Capability Brown, many of the main lines are extant.

the greater King Cup in spring, and waterlilies in summer.

Pruning, digging, sowing, nursing and gathering have been the main preoccupations for centuries in the walled gardens; the work of an "English home . . . all things in order stored, A haunt of ancient peace". So wrote Tennyson; the whole poem in his handwriting hangs in the dining room for all to see. Written in 1849, it is a tribute correlating what I have been trying to say.

HAM HOUSE
Richmond, *London*

Given by Sir Lyonel Tollemache and Mr C. L. N. Tollemache in 1948

AREA 7.2 ha (18 acres)
SOIL Lime-free
ALTITUDE 15 m (50 ft)
RAINFALL 635 mm (25 in.)
TEMPERATURE 4.5°C (40°F)

South bank of the Thames, west of A307 at Petersham

IF YOU JOURNEY past Ham Common, you will see two rather desultory rows of trees, all that remains of the great avenue that once focused on the south front of Ham House. During the last quarter of the 17th century this was one of the most noted houses in Britain, brought to a splendour within and without by the Duke and Duchess of Lauderdale. Indoors much of the splendour remains.

It was not until 1972 that I paid my first visit to Ham House garden. In the front court the marble busts in their niches were all but obscured by the bay trees. On the south side of the house was an enormous lawn and beyond that what seemed to be a thicket of rhododendrons overshadowed by a miscellany of sycamores and other trees. (This overgrowth obscured the two fine gate piers leading to the avenue to which I have referred above.) But closer inspection showed two things: the vast lawn revealed that it had once been composed of square plats, and the thicket of trees proved to have radiating paths through it. It was obvious that the "bones" of the Duke's garden of about 1672 still existed. The question was how to restore it.

At some time the wall connecting the house to the eastern boundary had been removed, also the impressive semi-circular steps on the south front, but the great gravel terrace was intact, likewise the entire surrounding wall, so disliked by Horace Walpole in 1770. He found the Duke's son living in a close-fisted way: "the gates were never opened . . . you are locked out and locked in, and after journeying all round the house as you do round an old French fortified town, you are at last admitted through the stableyard to creep along a dark passage by the housekeeper's room, and so by a back door into the great hall."

A totally different impression was obtained by John

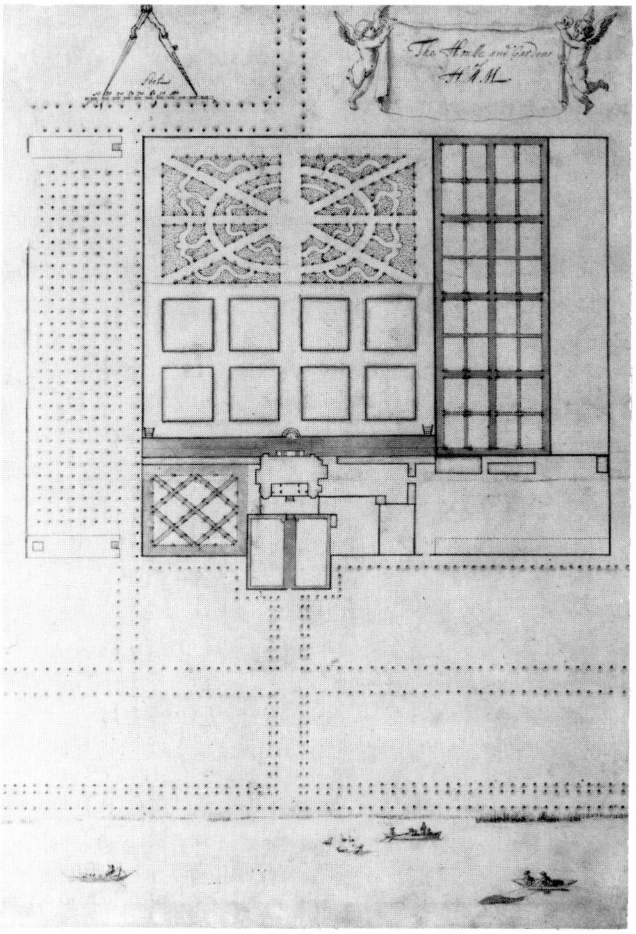

77 TOP A plan of the 1670s shewing the design of the garden at Ham House. The Thames, shewn at the bottom of the picture, lies to the north of the house. Attributed to John Slezer and Jan Wyck.

78 ABOVE A model made in the early 1970s from a bird's eye view of the house and garden at Ham of about 1730. This has served as a pattern for the restoration of the garden which has now been completed.

Evelyn when in the heyday of the 1st Duke's tenure, in 1678, he paid a visit: ". . . the Parterres, Flower Gardens, Orangeries, Groves, Avenues, Courts, Statues, Perspectives, Fountaines, Aviaries, and all this at the banks of the Sweetest River in the World, must needes be surprising."

Fortunately, generous gifts from Mr Kenneth Levy, the Stanley Smith Horticultural Foundation and an anonymous benefactor made the transformation possible and we have worked harmoniously with the Superintendent of the Royal Parks (which organisation looks after the entire grounds) to reinstate the scheme as near as possible to what was there in the 1670s. Ham House may be said therefore to be an authentic period piece within and without.

The enormous expanse of grass was divided once again into the eight uniform square plats in 1976, and the Knot Garden to the east of the house was almost completed in the same year, though less elaborately than originally. It is a pattern of box-edged beds which are diagonally divided and filled with silvery Cotton Lavender. Pyramids of box accentuate the corners and diagonals, much as in embroidery the material is sprigged with French knots in a pattern. The two arts, needlework and knot- or parterre-making, have much in common.

During the winters of 1976 and 1977 the thicket of trees and bushes was clear-felled and the original pattern of paths was traced on the ground and the outlines planted with hornbeam hedges. In this greater design the accents are obtained by small trees, the thorn known as Azarole – introduced from North Africa or western Asia in the 17th century – enclosed by rows of native Field Maple. When this garden was originally designed it followed the formal tastes of the period. Nevertheless, a hankering after the less formal avenues and alleys and straight paths was often apparent, and thus this tree-planted area was called the Wilderness. It was, even so, well ordered, and what today we should call formal; by contrast what it had grown into would be known to us as a wilderness.

There was much to consider in deciding to undertake the restoration of this important 17th-century garden. In favour was the thought of its being a unique example of a garden of the period. Against were the views of some local residents who preferred the modern wilderness and the big lawn. The only real criticism I have ever received during many years' work for the Trust, was an anonymous postcard simply saying: "You have made a mess of Ham House lawns. A total waste of money. None of the people I know like it. I'll never go there again." I very much hope the writer *will* go there again; we should all be interested to have his or her verdict when the plants are established and the bare walls planted with fruits and vines.

John Evelyn was a very great gardener of his time and hence his full approval of Ham House garden. All that he admired has now returned to Ham, except the "fountaines and aviaries"; the orangery still stands and in front of it are two exceptional trees of considerable age. One is *Paliurus spina-christi*, one of the trees from which the Crown of Thorns is said to have been made; it has been grown in this country since 1597. The other is the Pencil Cedar, *Juniperus virginiana*, introduced from North America about 1664. Both plants are likely to have been growing where they stand at Ham since the Duke's time. They now have café chairs around them, a sign of even more conviviality than that of the feast outside the main gates depicted by Thomas Rowlandson in about 1800.

HANBURY HALL
Droitwich, *Hereford and Worcester*

Acquired in 1953 under the will of Sir George Vernon, endowed anonymously

AREA 6 ha (15 acres)	$2\frac{1}{2}$ miles east of
SOIL Lime-free	Droitwich, 1 mile north
ALTITUDE 60.9 m (200 ft)	of the B4090 road
RAINFALL 635 mm (25 in.)	to Alcester
TEMPERATURE 4.5°C (40°F)	

THE WINDING DRIVE is slow to reach the house, but suddenly an abrupt turn brings you face to face with its east front. There is little actual garden at Hanbury but there are two architectural features worthy of note. First, the forecourt is surrounded by incongruous brick pillars with two domed gazebos in the near corners. These were built in the 1870s and represent Victorian taste with an Indian bias – a rare touch in gardens.

Out of sight from the house, owing to a screen of trees and shrubs, is a brick orangery, built, we think, soon after 1732. It is partly covered with wistarias.

Yews, Portuguese Laurels and hollies form the bulk of the shrubberies which with native trees define the outskirts of the wide lawn. A ha-ha guards the southern perimeter, but this is not of ancient construction.

At the beginning of the 18th century Hanbury Hall – which has always been the home of the Vernon family – had a large formal garden with the usual avenues of the time. The birds' eye view of 1732 is extant, showing its general layout and also a small amphitheatre to the north-west. Little remains apart from a long raised path to the north.

79 The orangery of *c.*1732 at Hanbury Hall; it is clad in *Wistaria sinensis*. Photo 1963.

HARDWICK HALL
Chesterfield, *Derbyshire*

Accepted by the Treasury in lieu of death duties and given to the Trust in 1959

AREA 2.8 ha (7 acres)
SOIL Lime-free
ALTITUDE 152 m (500 ft)
RAINFALL 762 mm (30 in.)
TEMPERATURE 3.5°C (38°F)

$6\frac{1}{2}$ miles north-west of Mansfield, $9\frac{1}{2}$ miles south-east of Chesterfield, south of Glapwell on A617.

CHATSWORTH, not Hardwick, has for long been the principal seat of the Cavendish family. Hardwick has thus been little altered to conform with changing fashions. It stands today almost as it was when completed in 1597, and with many of the original contents owned by the woman who built it, the redoubtable Bess of Hardwick, the Countess of Shrewsbury. Her initials ES are carved in the stonework on the top of the building. Her spirit still seems to pervade the place. The stone was quarried locally; water was supplied by a well near the ruin of her earlier house, adjoining the present one. But one needed courage as well as water and stone to build a house on this cold windswept hill. We are used to seeing tall cathedrals from great distances; square-topped Hardwick Hall is a landmark for miles around.

There must have been a garden to the older house; perhaps it lay towards the south-east, near to the stable block and outhouses. But the present garden is in three sections and, unlike the house, has been altered from time to time, though the surrounding walls, garden houses in the corners, finials and gateways, are contemporary with the present house.

One of the approach drives wends its way gently uphill between regular clumps of trees, in avenue formation. To enter the First Court under the imposing archway, framed by cedars, and to be confronted for the first time with the up-towering west front of the house, is a great experience. This court was laid out by Lady Blanche Howard, and she planted, according to the *Journal of Horticulture*, 1875, the Lebanon Cedars in 1832. The grass lawns she used for an elaborate scheme of beds, incorporating the letters ES, for annual flowers. In dry weather the shape of the beds can still be traced in the turf, which, for economy, was extended over all the beds after the First World War.

The Front Court is surrounded by high stone walls, capped by elaborate finials, which support many good climbing plants and shrubs (see illus. 183). Originally filled entirely with herbaceous plants, several shrubs to provide spring flowers were added in the 1960s, to augment the fringe of Mossy Saxifrage, Perennial Candytuft and other lowly plants which spill over the stone edge making pools of colour and foliage. The shrubs include *Syringa josiflexa* 'Bellicent', also the Rouen Lilac, and the rose 'Frühlingsgold'. There are many good herbaceous plants in bright colours, while in the shade of the cedars London Pride, ferns and hostas thrive, *Dicentra spectabilis*, *Kirengeshoma palmata*, rodgersias and *Ligularia veitchiana*.

80 Hardwick Hall with some of its flower borders in 1963. Since then the entire face of the 1597 building has been repaired.

The most impressive way of seeing the garden is now to go into the house and look out from the window on the landing outside the High Great Chamber. From this vantage point can be seen the whole of the Main Garden, laid out by Lady Louisa Egerton, daughter of the 7th Duke of Devonshire. It is about 2.9 ha ($7\frac{1}{4}$ acres), divided into four major compartments by a yew-hedged alley and a crossing alley of hornbeam, meeting at a *rond-point* in the centre, complete with seats and statues. One area has recently been sub-divided with short avenues of *Malus hupehensis* augmenting the old pear trees, and is spread with daffodils and late Pheasant Eye Narcissus in spring. Another has an orchard of plums and apples and a border of old roses, edged with auriculas. Another contains a nuttery and a very large herb garden laid out in the early 1970s by the Trust. It is a four-square design, punctuated by Common Hops on wooden supports, and includes some shrubs to give it solidity. The fourth square until recently had an enormous beech tree, which was blown down three years ago. It was surrounded by magnolias and yews. Three compartments are contained by an outer hedge, and a broad gravel walk between wide grass verges runs round the perimeter, the whole adding up to a very grand formal layout.

What you cannot see from the upper windows are the two long borders, both about 106 m (350 ft) long, which run to right and left on the south side of the wall when you enter by the garden gate. After the brilliant colourings of the forecourt borders, the right border is a contrast with its flowers of cool tints, silvery shrubs, such as Sea Buckthorn and *Elaeagnus argentea*, and the arching load of creamy white bloom of the rose 'Nevada'. Billowy masses of honeysuckles and roses find their way between the finials; ancestral roses like the Yorkist rose, 'Paul Ricault', 'Gloire de Dijon', 'Amadis' and 'Goldfinch', jostle with varieties of *Clematis*. To the left the border contains many more shrubs, *Rosa rugosa*, 'Cerise Bouquet' and others, with *Hemerocallis flava*, pulmonarias, heucheras, and Tree Peonies. Nobody knows whence came the 'Hardwick Hall' Lily-of-the-Valley; it is distinguished by its large bells, and broad foliage which has a markedly pale edge, though by no means variegated.

A gate here will take you into the East Garden, which has a central formal pool – in reality static water in case of fire – with wide borders of shrub roses, a gift in the 1950s. Evelyn, Duchess of Devonshire, designed the pool and the sunk fence and topiary to the east prior to 1900. Thence the eye travels across wide fields to a lime avenue planted about 1936.

But to return to the Main Garden it is interesting to note that its symmetry is broken in an unusual way. Diagonally-sited in two corners are clumps of trees while the south-east corner has a small pavilion to which you are led by a row of Black Mulberry trees and a weeping holly. (This little Elizabethan banqueting house was used by the 6th Duke's private orchestra as a smoking room, since they were not allowed to smoke in the house!) The whole design is an example of late Victorian ingenuity, which shows an enlightened return to traditional ideas. Owing to neglect during the war years the long alley of yews was in need of hard pruning, cleaning of weeds and manuring. The work was done in the mid 1950s and the result is some fine stately hedges. A similar story is attached to the crossing hornbeam hedges (see illus. 184). These were 2.1 m (7 ft) high and 2.7 m (9 ft) through, the growth being almost entirely forward, over the grass alley, from the stems at the back. In 1961 the entire overgrowth was sawn off, and grass was sown in two 2.1 m (7 ft) wide strips on either side of the narrow central walk. By the end of the first summer, after clipping, a splendid new hedge had formed: hornbeam is very obliging in this way and responds quickly. The result here was that the alley was restored to its original width, and the fine seats at either end once again were in scale.

I have been to Hardwick in almost every month of the year, and though spring awakens late on this hilltop, it surely comes and from that moment until early autumn flowers greet us on every side. In the old days many of them would have been growing mixed with fruit trees and herbs; today they are separated and it is to the Herb Garden that most visitors wend their way. There is a fascination in looking at plants whose name one knows from little packets or bottles of dried remains in grocers' shops. Here are the plants, growing, listed and annotated, mostly culinary.

"Accordingly, for salves, his wife seeks ... her garden and fields, before all outlandish gums. And surely hyssop, valerian, mercury, adder's tongue, yarrow, melilot and St John's Wort made into a salve, and elder, camomile, mallows, comphrey, and smallage, made into a poultice, have done great and rare cures." This was written by a priest to the Temple in 1652. Today we do not place such faith in herbs but the interest remains. Many of them are plants of rare beauty of foliage and flower, and many delight the nose as well. They are gaining greater popularity in gardens nowadays, but several remain rare and obscure like their supposed potentials. But one fragrant bush is a continuing source of joy and beauty from its flowers and fruits, and also the fragrance of its leaves. It is the Sweet Brier or Eglantine, *Rosa rubiginosa*, which apart from all its beauty is almost unrivalled for its penetrating prickles, which we find a useful and sure deterrent to those who are tempted to stray from the prescribed way. Bess of Hardwick enjoyed it too; it had been in the coat of arms for generations before her time. It occurs frequently in decoration and embroidery in the house, some of it stitched by her own hands some three hundred and eighty years ago.

HATCHLANDS
East Clandon, *Surrey*

Given in 1945 by Mr H. Goodhart-Rendel

AREA 4.8 ha (12 acres)	East of East Clandon,
SOIL Limy	on north side of
ALTITUDE 60.9 m (200 ft)	the A246 Guildford–
RAINFALL 686 mm (27 in.)	Leatherhead road
TEMPERATURE 4°C (39°F)	

NO DOUBT at one time the garden at Hatchlands was extensive and well cared for but the necessity of letting the house to a school to provide an income has resulted in a lower standard of upkeep than the Trust usually desires. The house, built in 1756, was originally surrounded by a natural landscape, typical of the period, to the east and west, with a lake and grotto beyond the present formal garden; the domestic quarters remain to the north but to the south, strangely enough, were greenhouses and a bothy for young gardeners.

In 1903 Lord Rendel employed Sir Reginald

81 The garden temple at Hatchlands.

Blomfield to build a music room, the ornate facade of which may be seen on the west front. From then onwards at Hatchlands the taste in gardens which Blomfield sought to reinstate through his book *The Formal Garden in England* seems to have obliterated whatever the previous layout may have been. I am not suggesting he was consulted about the garden, but that Mr Goodhart-Rendel in 1919–20 laid out on formal lines the garden we see today. He also demolished the bothy and greenhouses and made in their place a formal rose garden, surrounded by walls and rails and box hedge; the beds are edged with box, too. The fountain, its attendant stone ornaments and the radiating paths are his. These paths extend through the surrounding yew hedges as far as they can go in the four directions, one to the corner by the Music Room, one to a lower flower garden, which has since disappeared, one to a new archway cut in the distant kitchen garden wall, but the fourth ended in nothing.

I think this incompleteness must have worried Mr Rendel, for in 1953 he purchased a garden temple which stood "on a considerable eminence" forming "a pleasing and conspicuous object from the house and lawn" at Busbridge Hall, nearby. The empty path-end needed something of the sort. It was a spot of which his mother was particularly fond, and his inscription on the base of the Temple records this fact.

Just by the Temple is a deep chalk pit and ice-house and a very fine Oriental Plane. Some cedars have been planted partly to shelter the front of the house from cold winds and partly to screen it until one actually comes upon it from the drive. Likewise a young Paper Birch has been planted to replace, eventually, the old specimen opposite the front door.

HIDCOTE MANOR GARDEN
Chipping Campden, *Gloucestershire*

Given in 1948 by Major Lawrence Johnston

AREA 4 ha (10 acres)	At Hidcote Bartrim,
SOIL Alkaline	4 miles north-east of
ALTITUDE 182 m (600 ft)	Chipping Campden,
RAINFALL 635 mm (25 in.)	1 mile east of
TEMPERATURE 4°C (39°F)	the A46

HIDCOTE IS NOT a garden of great size nor has it a particularly long history as gardens go. The estate was purchased seventy years ago by Major Lawrence Johnston, and with the aid of the existing farmhouse, a few walls, a Cedar of Lebanon, and five large beech trees, he created with taste and courage a garden which has become internationally famous. In general it may be summed up as a garden on architectural lines, deriving from Italy and France, with lavish and varied planting; the planting has always been allowed, even encouraged, to soften the firm lines of the design and to exhibit an exuberance at all times. In detail, it is a series of gardens each with definite colour scheme. These separate areas are divided by hedges and walls and are on an intimate scale, whereas to provide complete relief there are two very long narrow vistas extending into the countryside and a splendid large open lawn.

It is one of the most photographed gardens in the country and so everyone goes a little prepared for its style and design. I did, in 1937, on a glorious June day, when all the garden walls in the picturesque villages around were overhung with lilacs and mays. I have never forgotten the impression it made on me. The head gardener took me round from one lovely plant to the next, but underlying all the glories of the day was the impressive design, then in its early maturity. On a later visit I went round with Major Johnston.

The war years played havoc with the Hidcote garden, and, after Major Johnston's death, the garden was gradually restored or re-interpreted by the Trust. Before the war seven or eight men were employed, and one of them, Walter Bennett, continued to work, very skilfully, at Hidcote for many years, thus continuing the tradition of planting. While the design remains as it was, much of the planting had to be started again. Lawrence Johnston was always eager for new plants, and went on collecting trips to the Far East and to Africa, but whatever plants he used the style of planting continued. There would be one plant climbing over another, a group of disparate shrubs united by a continuous underplanting of some lowly flower; there would seldom be a single clump of any herbaceous plant or bulb, rather would it be grouped here and there creating the effect of its having sown itself; the colours were and are mostly blended to separate schemes with occasionally a deliberate clash. Seldom is one plant given one piece of ground; it shares it with others. All this hangs together because of the firm design, which is so much enhanced by the vertical lines of dark evergreen hollies and Holm Oaks.

The taste, skill and courage needed to produce this intriguing garden is often taken for granted. The owner altered his schemes from time to time, improving them, but what he could not alter were two important features. One is the ground that rises gradually up the centre of the main vista from the cedar tree (see illus. 30); the other is the lie of the little stream which sloped downwards, almost from the same spot, and nearly parallel to the first view. The lie of the land was indeed both a major obstacle and also a heaven-sent opportunity in which to indulge in every possible surprise. Large Holm Oaks were imported from France and today bolster up the falling contours. The garden was not expensively laid out; the steps and paving were improvised out of the materials available; their cheapness was disguised by the overflowing plants. Plants were cheap, too, in those days and they came to Hidcote in great quantity – the hedging plants alone must have been counted in thousands. The exuberance of the plants and the intriguing scheme mask the fact that there are few right-angles in the design; it was improvised and grew yearly; no blue-print, we believe, was ever made for it. The various little areas created all sorts of difficulties of levels and transition, but every difficulty was a challenge to ingenuity, which invariably triumphed. The house was not of remarkable quality, and thus it stands aside as it were from the design, and does not dominate any one view, nor does it make any sort of focal point; yet it holds all together. I think we may add that the whole thing was a challenge to Major Johnston and he enjoyed the challenge, as much as he did the assembly of the plants. Various friends, such as Mrs Norah Lindsay, Mark Fenwick, Lord Barrington, Mrs Heather Muir, the Honourable Robert James and the Vicomte de Noailles no doubt contributed ideas.

82 The Red Borders at Hidcote in 1913, with new-planted yew hedge above the wall on the left. To the right can be seen the pair of topiary pieces in the fuchsia garden. Compare with Plate XXIV.

Hidcote has often been described as being composed of a series of cottage gardens. But we must be careful here; this is not a valid statement. Whereas a cottage garden always has an assembly of plants, each area at Hidcote has an assembly of plants for a given purpose. The purpose is a fusion of scale and contrast complete with a blending of colour through the season.

There is another aspect of the challenge. Was it fortuitous that all the long, formal views, ending in an open invitation to explore further, were arranged on ground rising before one? The irresistible urge is in everyone to mount each slope or each flight of steps: a journey ever upwards with the reward at the top. The exception to this upward movement is the view from the extreme end of the downward sloping stream.

83 LEFT Looking into Mrs. Winthrop's Garden at Hidcote, 1957. It had become overshadowed by two large Japanese Cherries. These were removed in 1959 (see illus. 84).
84 BELOW By 1967 the long view was re-opened.

85 ABOVE A photograph at Hidcote in 1913. The fuchsia beds in the foreground are repeated in illus. 86, taken in 1964, but much earlier the sunken garden had been given its raised bathing pool by Lawrence Johnston.
86 RIGHT The same view in 1964.

"There must be no Alleys with Hedges at either End . . . not at the Hither End . . . nor at the Further End for letting your Prospect from the Hedge through the Arches upon the Heath" (Francis Bacon, *Of Gardens*).

Looking back as we can now to over fifty years of the history of garden design in this country since Hidcote first became recognised, it is manifest that it has had immense influence on gardens too numerous to mention. Some of the most notable are Newby, TINTINHULL, THE COURTS, HOLT, and SISSINGHURST. They all owe their origin and style to the first garden of any size which united all the traditions of the English garden into one, and which at the same time showed how to use sensitively the horticultural riches that were in this country at the time. This was the way first indicated by William Robinson and elaborated upon by Gertrude Jekyll, but with its fine ground design and the vertical lines of trees and hedges dividing it, Hidcote first achieved the aim of a garden of boundless variety soberly controlled, a place in which the owner and his visitors could find endless interest in the furnishings.

Most gardens can look well on a glorious June day, but as soon as the lilacs are over, with their accompaniments of peonies, both shrubby and herbaceous, and many a flowering shrub, Hidcote's spell of roses is upon us. The old French roses were much favoured by Johnston, together with species, and there is a wide range of kinds in the garden, at almost every turn. The pinks and mauves in the Old Garden are spread with *Campanula latiloba* and 'Hidcote Amethyst' beneath (see plate VIII), while *Campanula lactiflora* pushes its clouds of lilac blossom through the foliage of *Rosa rubrifolia*. It is not until rose time that the Red Borders awaken to summer; here scarlet and red roses with purple delphiniums and red dahlias accentuate the dusky tones of shrubs and plants with coppery-purple leaves (see plate XXIV). The steps lead up to the gazebos built in 1914 and two long views, one to the Vale of Evesham; to the other we shall return presently.

In a little area under the cedar, white flowers from tulips onwards are blended with silver foliage as an accompaniment, *sotto voce*, to the dark green hedges and dark green topiary; *Tropaeolum speciosum*, the Scotch Flame Flower, a Chilean plant, supplies the *sforzando*. The rose 'Gruss an Aachen' has been grown in this little area since the 1930s. It was raised in 1909, a hybrid between 'Frau Karl Druschki' and another Hybrid Tea, but nevertheless it might be looked upon as a prototype of the Floribundas. From apricot-tinted buds the full-petalled fragrant flowers open to creamy-white, continuously through the season.

Round the next corner is the fuchsia parterre, awash with blue scillas in spring, the whole planting in the box-edged beds lowly, thus showing off the entire height of the multicoloured "tapestry" hedges. Below this garden is the raised, unblemished water of the Bathing Pool, and beyond this the circular green "room". Plants accompany every step.

From the time of early white magnolias, through which is a planting of the blue forget-me-not flowers of *Brunnera macrophylla*, the Stream Garden is alive with flowers and beauty. As you go down the stream the colours change to orange and yellow azaleas and lilies of many types, to white flowers which cool one down, so to speak, as a preparation for the meadow view beyond the ha-ha. Up on the rocky outcrop, which has numerous small shrubs and a remarkable specimen of *Quercus coccifera*, grow two dwarf pines, one propagated from a seedling from a plant I imported when a schoolboy from the Yokohama Nursery Co., Japan: it is *Pinus densiflora* 'Umbraculifera'; the other is *P. sylvestris* 'Moseri' propagated from the remarkable old specimen in Cambridge University Botanic Garden. Its foliage becomes bronzy yellow in winter. We meet too the tall stems of the Japanese Angelica Tree, and in spring the ground is spread with an infinite range of naturalised colour-forms of the Mediterranean *Anemone pavonina*.

The Pillar Garden beckons, the pillars of yews dominating all else, even the funny old double tulip that persists after all these years; *Arum creticum*, Tree Peonies including *P. suffruticosa* 'Joseph Rock', 'Mme Louis Henri' and 'Souvenir de Maxime Cornu'; more old French roses; magnolias, phloxes, *Philadelphus* 'Belle Étoile' and free-flowering yuccas.

If by now you have plant indigestion, or feel a sense of claustrophobia, a great breath of fresh air and an unlimited view awaits you as you cross the Long Walk below the gazebo steps into Mrs Winthrop's Garden. Mrs Winthrop was Major Johnston's mother, and this little garden is kept to blue and yellow flowers; she used to have blue cushions spread on the low brick steps. Yellow doronicums, followed by a froth of Lady's Mantle, *Lilium szovitzianum*, blue veronicas, pansies and aconites provide a colourful foreground to the view down to the stream and up to the undulations of the area known as Westonbirt. The ridges are the remains of ploughing. Many summer flowering shrubs follow the spring display of bulbs and are in turn followed by autumn colour.

This galaxy of small and large garden areas all lie to the south of the Great Lawn, which acts as a further rest to the senses. To the north is the Camellia Shelter. Here the soil was made up with sawdust and lime-free materials, as in stretches of the Stream Garden and the Old Garden, so that camellias, rhododendrons and azaleas could be grown. It is remarkable that beds made up fifty or more years ago should still be effective. Beyond the Camellia Shelter is a small garden with raised beds, devoted to orange and yellow flowers. This was made during the 1960s after the removal of a decrepit greenhouse, and the small bird bath was originally the trough for immersing seed pots. Beyond the Pine Garden and its lily pool was another shelter for plants. This was only a temporary shelter and being built of timber with sawdust filling it collapsed. In front of it were standard clipped Bay Trees which used to be conveyed into shelter for the winter. They eventually became too large to be handled and succumbed to a cold winter. Since then they have been replaced by standard Portuguese Laurels, which are quite hardy. This fashion for standard evergreens emanates from the use of oranges and lemons which were kept in formal shapes in warmer climates.

On one of the outhouses is a wonderful old *Wistaria floribunda* 'Macrobotrys', and in the yard is *Davidia involucrata*. Some highlights in the Courtyard, which was a farmyard originally, are *Schizophragma hydrangeoides* 'Rosea' and *Mahonia lomariifolia*. The latter was introduced by Johnston from western China in 1931; it flowers in November. I have not called attention to *Verbena* 'Lawrence Johnston', the Hidcote Lavender and Hypericum, Rose 'Lawrence Johnston' and 'Hidcote Gold', and hundreds of other plants of note (see plate IX and XIV). If you are looking for plants Hidcote will not disappoint you.

Another visit could be devoted to exploring the avenues (see illus. 181) and the Lime Alley, marvelling at the mind that could translate to Gloucestershire the *palissade à l'Italienne* – the hornbeam hedges on stems at the top of the main vista planted in 1915 which have earned this spot the name of Stilt Garden. The gazebos, the Bathing Pool with its shelter, the gates, finials, iron work and seats form another group of study.

Each separate area deserves a visit and while each could well serve as a model for interpretation for a villa garden, the *tout ensemble* of Hidcote is an achievement which is never likely to be exactly copied nor surpassed.

HUGHENDEN MANOR
High Wycombe, *Buckinghamshire*

Conveyed to the Trust in 1947 by a special trust in which it had been vested by Mr W. H. Abbey

AREA 1.9 ha ($4\frac{3}{4}$ acres)	$1\frac{1}{2}$ miles north of
SOIL Limy	High Wycombe on
ALTITUDE 152 m (500 ft)	the A4128 Great
RAINFALL 762 mm (30 in.)	Missenden road
TEMPERATURE 4°C (39°F)	

THERE IS a particular delight in turning off the main road, going over a small stream and ascending the steep hill, past the little churchyard where Disraeli is buried, and suddenly coming through the trees to the east front of the house. In the foreground is the oval lawn around which the carriage drive sweeps. High banks, grass- or ivy-covered, topped by large yews and cedars, shut out the cold winds. The intriguing graft-hybrid, *Laburnocytisus adamii* grows here; it produces yellow laburnum flowers, mauve laburnum flowers, and the mauve sprays of *Cytisus purpureus*. It occurred originally in 1825 near Paris, when the mauve broom was grafted on to a laburnum root.

Although over a century has passed since the house was remodelled by Disraeli – later the Earl of Beaconsfield – the garden still retains much of its high Victorian interest, and this is being fostered by the Trust. It has however been through hard times; when I first went there in 1958 the west lawn and its attendant paths were, literally, a hayfield. Means were found to employ a full-time gardener, and by patience and diligence the whole surrounds of the house were brought under control, and once again biennial displays of flowers are enjoyed both on the front lawn, and under the terrace walk on the west front, where the statesman liked to pace up and down, thinking out his policies. More often than not, however, his times at Hughenden, freed from city life, were a refreshment deeply enjoyed. He loved the prospect from the house, and used to wander over the extensive park, enjoying the trees in their "burst of spring", noting the "fascination of the sultry note of the cuckoo, the cooing of the wood pigeons and the blaze of rosy may". He planted many beautiful trees. In autumn he observed "the limes all golden, the beeches ruddy brown, while the oaks and elms and pines are still dark and green, and contrast well with the brighter tints. But not a leaf has fallen; they want the first whisper of the frost, and then they will go out like the lamps when the dawn breaks on a long festival." He was fortunate in that the great beeches were still in their prime; many have fallen in recent years, and the depredations of squirrels play havoc with the young. On this chalky hill the Whitebeam thrives and its silvery young leaves offer delight in spring.

It was Mrs Disraeli who designed the terrace with its steps and vases. We hope that one day, copying an old photograph, her rustic arches will be reinstated.

The meek primrose enters our story particularly at Hughenden. It was reputed to be Disraeli's favourite flower, and I think many of us cannot resist its charms today despite the multitudes of newer plants that live in our gardens. The Primrose League, a Conservative society founded in 1883 by other enthusiasts than Disraeli, found in this flower with its five petals a symbol of the British Empire that had extended over five continents. Likewise today it could be held to symbolise the same five continents whence plants have come to grace our gardens.

87 Victorian cast-iron garden vase at Hughenden Manor.

ICKWORTH
Bury St Edmunds, *Suffolk*

Transferred by the Treasury to the Trust in 1956; endowed by Theodora, Marchioness of Bristol

AREA 13.3 ha (33 acres)
SOIL Limy
ALTITUDE 75 m (250 ft)
RAINFALL 610 mm (24 in.)
TEMPERATURE 3°C (37°F)

3 miles south-west of Bury St Edmunds, on west side of A143

HAVING COMPLETED two houses and the Mussenden Temple in Northern Ireland, in 1794 the Earl of Bristol, also Bishop of Derry, started to build this astonishing house. It was completed after his death in 1830; it is over 182 m (600 ft) long with the central rotunda towering to 31.9 m (105 ft). The rotunda is connected by two curving wings to a rectangular pavilion at either end. William Mason in his *The English Garden* (1772–81) might well have inspired the Earl Bishop:

> *High on Ionic shafts he bad it tower*
> *A proud Rotunda; to its sides conjoin'd*
> *Two broad Piazzas in theatric curve,*
> *Ending in equal Porticos sublime.*

It is difficult to appreciate the garden without an idea of the building because the two are embodied in one grandiose scheme. On the north side the curving wings embrace a large oval gravelled court, and in turn a curving flower border confronts a large oval lawn, the whole protected by cedars and a spinney. On the south side the convex of the building is echoed in the curve of the raised gravel walk, enclosing evergreen shrubberries and lawns. Such is basically the design and, being a creation of the early 19th century, it marks a return to compass and set square towards the end of the long interregnum of the English Landscape Garden. But the whole conception would command great interest, even amazement, whatever its date.

Ickworth stands in one of the coldest districts in the south of England. Its record of disasters are many. *Photinia serrulata* was killed to ground level in 1860. The winter of 1880–1 crippled many *Cupressus sempervirens* 'Stricta', and killed figs to the ground. In 1962–3 Hidcote Lavender was completely killed around the south side of the rotunda. The cypresses had been planted in an effort to give an Italianate touch to the grounds of the building which in itself is Italianate. A few lingered until 1962.

There are several interesting points to be explored; Capability Brown is recorded as having worked in the park in the middle of the 18th century though he did not contribute to the house and garden. The walled garden and pavilion some way from the house, beyond the church, date from the 17th century. This is because the original Ickworth, long since demolished, was nearby. A map of 1842 shows an informal layout on the south side and the Albana Walk and other woodland walks were laid out to the west. "Albana" commemorates the wife of the 1st Marquis. The walk was originally margined with clipped box hedges; it has an impressive yew avenue, pines, holm oaks and many walnuts. Throughout the planting of the 19th century at Ickworth the stress seems to have been on creating an illusion of Mediterranean warmth with evergreens. At about this time too some Cedars of Lebanon were planted to the north, and soon after, by 1861, the south curving wall and steps were made, and cypresses lined the walk from the steps to the rotunda. The cedars were interplanted with more, about 1875, this time with *C. atlantica*. It is these which are now failing. In 1881 the Redwood was 15.2 m (50 ft); it is now over 30 m (100 ft); it was found at that time, according to *The Gardeners' Chronicle*, that wellingtonias grown from cuttings grew much faster at Ickworth than those from seeds. *Phillyrea angustifolia* had reached 9 m (30 ft), but only *P. latifolia* now grows there, its cumulus-masses of glittering dark leaves making a perfect foil for architecture. Also at this time the southern area of the garden was filled with evergreen shrubs, now very tall; through them is a long hedged alley. A small domed summerhouse was transferred to the east end of the alley from a position near the west end of the house in 1958, and an urn was placed at the other end in 1973.

One of the pavilions has as its southern face a pillared orangery. Because of the high cost of heating such a building, the Trust planted in it a few years ago shrubs which might give a semblance of tropicality – *Fatsia japonica*, *Fatshedera lizei* and large-leafed ivies among others.

If you go to Ickworth in spring you will be greeted by many bulbs in the grass; by June the large curved border starts its summer display with Rose 'Nevada' followed by shrubs and plants of purple, blue, white and pale yellow colouring. In the garden to the south will be seen a broad collar of Catmint under the rotunda (it replaced the Hidcote Lavender); there is an English Oak, which must have been there long before 1800, a fine Copper Beech, and two young Black Mulberries. The chief claim to horticultural fame is at the east end of the box-hedged alley – an excellent specimen of *Koelreuteria paniculata*, whose panicles of small yellow flowers open, spectacularly, in August. Taking the full blast of the south-west gales in the garden spinney are two Cucumber Trees, *Magnolia acuminata*.

Though not rich in flowers, Ickworth garden can well hold its own with anything in this country by its unique design.

88 The grand, simple, geometric design of the garden at Ickworth. The cross-vista through the shrubberies ends in a domed summerhouse, just visible on the far right. The orangery is on the left of the rotunda, the flower border beyond, framing the oval lawn.

KILLERTON
Exeter, *Devon*

Mostly given by Sir Richard Acland, Bt, partly acquired from his trustees in 1944

AREA 9 ha (22 acres)
SOIL Lime-free
ALTITUDE 60.9 m (200 ft)
RAINFALL 813 mm (32 in.)
TEMPERATURE 5°C (41°F)

7 miles north-east of Exeter, west of B3185, forking left from the A38 Taunton road

ONE OF THE MOST spectacular views in English gardens in May or June is obtained by walking round the front of Killerton house to the foot of the lawn. Acres of neatly-mown grass slope upwards to vast hummocks of rhododendrons of scarlet and other colours, to the spires of conifers of dark green, bluish and yellowish, which spear through a wide selection of other shrubs and trees, right up to the crown of the hill. The display starts much earlier, with *Magnolia campbellii* and many another species, and a generous scattering and grouping of daffodils, including 'Parkinson's Early Straw-coloured Bastard Daffodil'. This was known in 1629, subsequently lost, and reintroduced from Spain in 1882. At this date the whole of the lower slopes of the lawn were covered in native trees, and above the Beech Avenue was a mass of Cherry Laurel, some as high as 15.2 m (50 ft). About 1900 William Robinson, editor of *The Garden*, was called in to advise on the garden. The outcome of his visit was that the wall and terrace garden were made, after clearing away shrubs. John Coutts, with whom I was acquainted in his declining years, took the post of head gardener just as the terrace wall was being completed. In 1946 he wrote to Mr Cowley, then editor of *The Garden*, telling him of this fact and adding that it was "built, if you please, on the advice of the late Mr Robinson; it of course spoilt the park,

89 Beds in William Robinson's parterre at Killerton; these were planted with roses which were unsuccessful, and a change was made in 1957 to dwarf shrubs and plants to give colour and interest throughout the year. Photo 1960.

starting as it does nowhere and ending nowhere. I got into bad odour condemning it. . . ." During his stay of about ten years at Killerton, the paths were made wide enough to take invalid carriages, the rock garden was constructed in the old quarry – which was overgrown with laurel – and the hardy cyclamens were planted, both *C. hederifolium* and *C. repandum*; they are now happily naturalised after three-quarters of a century.

John Coutts left in 1909 to go to Kew, where later he became a distinguished curator. His letter to Mr Cowley is full of reminiscences, including the anxiety over the old Tulip Tree near the house. However, it lasted in a truncated state until 1975, by which time Coutts' replacement tree had grown well. His rock garden is a real period piece, in what Reginald Farrer would have called the "almond-pudding style", with the rocks upended in spiky array.

And so we see today at Killerton, from the end of the house, the great terrace, with its wall, Coade stone vases, and many beds planted with a wide range of dwarf shrubby plants, and the herbaceous border – also originally planted by Coutts; then the sweep of lawn and the shrubs and trees above. Moving up the lawn to the fringe of trees, we look down the slope uninterruptedly, across to the parkland below (see plate XXIX). This is possible because the Trust constructed a haha in 1970 to continue the line of Robinson's terrace wall. The rock garden lies behind the little rustic hut, now known as the Bear's Hut. From here paths lead west to the cross erected in memory of the "great" Sir Thomas Acland (1787–1871), who succeeded his father as owner of Killerton while a boy. After he came of age he did much for the grounds, particularly with the help of nurseryman John Veitch, who had acted as agent for the estate for Thomas Acland's grandfather twenty years before. We may thus date the main founding of this remarkable Devon pleasaunce to 1808, when Veitch was instrumental in planting the original trees of the Beech Walk, the Sweet Chestnuts at its east end and the two Tulip Trees in the Chapel grounds.

Killerton

The progress of the famous nursery firm of Veitch is noted by the transference of the business to Exeter in 1832. From then onwards trees and shrubs reached Killerton regularly. During the next forty to fifty years many of today's great specimens were planted – Wellingtonias, Redwoods, spruces, cedars, Incense Cedar, and probably the old Cork Oak. John Coutts' letter points out that the reason many of the great conifers have high bare stems is because of the thicket of laurels which was growing around them.

Can we visualise the Arboretum – for such it had become – by, say, 1860? The Beech Walk would be well established, many conifers and trees were growing fast, and the conditions were ready for the influx of rhododendrons of which many were raised from collectors' seeds at Killerton – a boon of the firm of Veitch. We can as a consequence look down from the top path through small groves of *R. arboreum* to the Beech Walk; this is quite a magical sight and well worth the long climb (see illus. 29). Dozens of *R. yunnanense* and its relatives give cool lilac shades later, and then there is the moment when the top walk is aflame with 'Coccinea Speciosa' azaleas; in autumn it is the turn of the pink leaves of *Acer nikoense* and the large yellow blades of *Betula maximowiczii* contrasting with the red-brown stem of the Californian Madrona. And from here you can look down between giant conifers to the profile of the house well below the slope, and away to the countryside, occasionally with a glimpse of the English Channel.

To the tree and shrub enthusiast a day spent wandering among species of conifers, of *Tilia*, *Quercus*, *Zelkova*, *Nyssa*, *Acer*, *Ehretia*, *Halesia*, *Eucryphia*, *Embothrium*, *Davidia* and *Magnolia* will be full of interest. Those who are more interested in shrubs will be well content with *Lagerstroemia*, *Vitex*, *Symplocos*, *Cleyera*, *Osmanthus*, bamboos and *Hydrangea*, and of course *Rhododendron*. Some notable specimens include *R. delavayi*, *R. serpyllifolium* and *R. polylepis*.

There is however another impression to be gained. If you walk past the car park to the north-east, you will

90 The thatched Bear's Hut at Killerton.

91 Cork Oaks (*Quercus suber*) thrive and seed themselves at Killerton. One only of the clump of three (here photographed in 1956) remains; it was rejuvenated by soil-injection in the 1960s. The cork of commerce is obtained from the bark of this species in south west Europe.

come to a mellow stone chapel, built in 1841, its stands guarded by two big Redwoods, two vast Tulip Trees, planted *c.*1808, *Ostrya carpinifolia*, two plane trees and a huge Lucombe oak with a girth of 5 m (16 ft 10 in.). The original hybrid was raised at Exeter in 1765, between the Turkey Oak and the Cork Oak.

With such a site – it is a lime-free volcanic hill in an otherwise limy district – a gentle but windy climate and a rich soil, it is small wonder that the growth of the plants encouraged successive Aclands from one planting to the next. The Indian Deodar Cedar produced seed for the first time in England at Killerton and a seedling was sent to Kew. John Coutts recalls in his letter that as a result of this the request came from Kew for two railway truckloads of the beautiful red Devonian soil. This was an indication of the freemasonry which has always been evident between gardeners. Gifts from Killerton have gone to many gardens, and gifts are continually being received. This is what makes an arboretum of some one hundred and fifty years standing so interesting. In no other kind of gardening is the tradition and the year's pageant of beauty so continuous. Even in winter, against the evergreens, the coloured bark of trees and shrubs stand out – the grey-white of *Eucalyptus coccifera*, the flaking browns and creams of *Stewartia sinensis*, the green of *Abies concolor*, the dark brown of Wellingtonia and Redwood, the latter echoed by the brown reverses of the leaves of several species of *Rhododendron*. Woody plants are not only an abiding joy, but refresh us after the surfeits of the flower garden.

KNIGHTSHAYES COURT
Tiverton, *Devon*

Given and endowed by Sir John Heathcoat Amory, Bt

AREA 16 ha (40 acres)
SOIL Lime-free
ALTITUDE 136 m (450 ft)
RAINFALL 762 mm (30 in.)
TEMPERATURE 5°C (41°F)

2 miles north of Tiverton; turn right off Tiverton–Bampton road (A396) at Bolham

THIS GARDEN is on similar rich reddish Devon soil to that at KILLERTON, only a few miles away, and it is equally fertile but less windswept. Fortunately the stone of the house tones well with the soil. Harmonies of this kind seem to come naturally at Knightshayes, for the house sits well above an expansive sloping landscape, firmly fixed over quiet, fine terraces, with majestic trees around. The long straight gravel terrace passes two formal hedged gardens and then mounts a short flight of steps and gently blends with the woodland garden where it eventually takes on soft curves.

And what surroundings they are! Having had an invitation to call at Knightshayes when making my first visit to KILLERTON in 1955, I have watched – every year since then – the "Garden in the Wood" grow from its early overcrowded stages to its peaceful embrace of a much larger area of wood. To achieve this no less than 160 trees were removed during the 1960s and now "view answers view, and every glade has its brother", if I may so paraphrase it. First in this woodland garden are the great trees, left as a broken, overhead canopy. They are fast being overtaken by *Magnolia* species such as *M. sprengeri*, *M. campbellii*, *M. kobus*, and hybrids and forms related to them, rare birches and Southern Beeches; adding to the lofty beauty are roses climbing up pines and larches, 'La Perle', 'Paul's Himalayan Rambler', *Rosa longicuspis* and *R.* 'Polyantha Grandiflora'. Nearer eye level is a selection of beautiful shrubs – shrubs for all seasons of the year. *Corylopsis* are for early spring, followed by rhododendrons and azaleas. These are represented by a choice of good species, and refined hybrids, some with tiny growth and leaves, others giants in every way, and embracing white, yellow, pink, lavender and some strong reds, many with sweet fragrance, like *R. lindleyi* and 'Lady Alice Fitzwilliam'. There are maples and in particular the Coral Bark Maple – 'Senkaki' – and another with coral bark, *A. pennsylvanicum* 'Erythrocladum' whose winter brilliance is remarkable, extending into the spring. Spectacular variegated forms of *Aralia elata* dominate one area; in another are trailing junipers and ivies; here are creamy Dog's Tooth Violets, there are ferns and white foxgloves; elsewhere are *Euonymus tingens* and *Acradenia franklinii*; hybrid photinias show their red-brown leaves, and rose species are on nodding acquaintance with one another.

If you can go there in early summer, *Smilacina* and numerous euphorbias will welcome you and ask you to lower your eyes. It will be difficult to take them off the ground where the peat-edged beds contain all sorts of treasures and garden toys, pleiones, little bulbs, *Ourisia coccinea*, dainty ferns, tiny shrubs, hellebores and hostas in great variety. Early spring – hellebore time – is a wonderful moment when there are for contrast yard-square patches of grey cyclamen leaves. In one spot is a grouping of hardy grasses; in another, moist and cool, *Primula japonica* 'Postford White' grows happily. A surprise, on rounding a corner, are the rapier leaves, steely-grey, of the New Zealand *Astelia cockaynei.* Morning or evening, when shadows lengthen, are often claimed to be the best time of the day for garden visiting, but here in this succession of glades, there are always shadows casting their protective mantle over the soil, preventing the sun's rays from staying too long.

Just above the steps from the main terrace, in the woodland garden is a 'blue cedar'. This was propagated from a plant in the nursery of Henry Morse at Brundall, near Norwich. The parent plant was markedly blue and luxuriant but remained in bush form, a plant of some 7.3 m (24 ft) by 9.1 m (30 ft) wide. This scion from it seems bent on the same lowly habit. I have never seen another like the parent tree.

Knightshayes is a comparatively new garden developed since Sir John and Lady Heathcoat Amory took to gardening soon after the last war. It embodies all that is best in modern gardening, without in any place giving one a surfeit of riches. The spaces see to that, and to the space of the gravel terrace we will return. First below us, is the South Garden, where *Cornus kousa*, Japanese Cherries, rhododendrons (including 'Cornish Cross' and 'Penjerrick', both cream and pink forms), bamboos and other shrubs grow in spacious surroundings. *Sorbus meliosmifolia* grows here, a very early-flowering species. Two young trees of Southern Beeches are growing fast, the evergreen *Nothofagus betuloides* and *N. dombeyi*, together with the Mexican pine, *Pinus ayacahuite*, with long drooping needles. Nearby is the rare Californian evergreen, *Lyonothamnus floribundus aspleniifolius*, some 5.4 m (18 ft) high.

92 A peat-edged bed in the garden in the wood at Knightshayes Court, 1955.

Now for the older parts of the garden, near to the house. The long grass terrace with its pattern of paving was laid out concurrently with the house. It supports a fine Lebanon Cedar, and the terrace walls, facing due south, house many choice shrubs and plants. Lavenders and cistuses, Tree Peonies and *Indigofera* species, and a few old roses established long ago, such as 'Souvenir de Madame Léonie Viennot' and 'Madame Alice Garnier'. This is the spot to stand in June, looking up to the house so high above us; one portion of the walls will be white with a thousand flowers of *Rosa brunonii* 'La Mortola', and another crimson with Rose 'Climbing General MacArthur'; both reach to the eaves and cast their fragrance afar. Under the house walls are many treasured shrubs and bulbous plants: nerines, schizostylis and sternbergias for autumn, when the scarlet *Zauschneria microphylla* tones well with the stone-work. The old rose 'Céline Forestier' and *Clematis rehderana* in light yellow grow behind late blue salvias. Penstemons, yuccas, dieramas and agapanthuses thrive exceedingly. Even more tender plants are grown in the nearby conservatory.

When the terraces were designed, some hedged areas were also made, on the way to the Woodland Garden. They are prefaced by a long raised border devoted to alpine plants, small bulbs and dwarf shrubs. To one little garden we gave a formal paved design, where all the colours are cool, with silvery foliage uniting them to the soft tone of the paving, and uniting also with the great lead tank at the head of the garden, on a dais, hedged around with yew. There is a spring moment here to cherish, when its accompanying pair of standard wistarias contribute their cool colour, or later, when Heliotrope and silverlings flow out of the lead tank. The tank was placed here in the 1960s and came from the Goldsmith's Company.

Divided by the hundred-year-old hedge the adjoining area was designed as a bowling green, but as bowls were "out" and gardening very much "in", a circular pool was added a year or so after the formal garden was designed. A little statue and a Silver Weeping Pear are reflected in the still water (see plate XXII). On the other side of the gravel walk is another hedged enclosure with an urn and stone seats. In topiary the chase runs round the top of the hedge. "Your Gardiner can frame your lesser wood to the shape of ... swift running Hounds, to chase the Deere, or hunt the Hare. This kinde of hunting shall not waste your corne, nor much your coyne." Thus William Lawson, in 1618.

To the west of the house is the oldest and newest

planting. There are azaleas of old types in abundance, and a landscape planting of willows around an enlarged pool; the whole area was, until 1972, covered in coarse shrubs. Willows are not only graceful and add perhaps more different tints during the year than any other genus of plants, but their multitudinous waving branches and leaves of different shapes bring a serenity to the landscape, especially after digesting the riches of the rest of the garden.

It is only a short walk past the car park to one of the most remarkable stands of Douglas firs in the country. This tall conifer, introduced from western North America in 1827, would by 1863 have been a hundred feet high in favoured parts of this country. Perhaps inspired by its rapid growth, John Heathcoat Amory planted the Knightshayes trees when he started building. A few of his trees are already over 45 m (150 ft) high.

In 1889 it was recorded that there was a Weeping Ash by a stream, with *Osmunda regalis*, the Royal Fern, growing nearby, and that among choice shrubs were growing *Desfontainea spinosa*, magnolias, myrtles, *Leycesteria formosa*, *Stauntonia latifolia* and *Azara microphylla*. In common with other gardens which have suffered the passage of two wars, these plants became neglected and perhaps died; but Knightshayes has risen, phoenix-like, from the ashes, and is today a place of pilgrimage.

Soon after embarking on this extensive garden making and planting, the Amorys thought it might help to enthuse their old head gardener to pay a visit to Chelsea Show. On the morrow Lady Amory asked whether he had enjoyed his visit and whether he had noted any special plants which might be added to the garden. The reply came: "No, m'Lady, I don't think there's anything there which we need bother about." It was an answer that could be interpreted in various ways, but there was no doubt about his own impression of Knightshayes garden. (See plate XVI and illus. 170.)

KNOLE
Sevenoaks, *Kent*

House given in 1946 by the 4th Lord Sackville

AREA 9 ha (22 acres)	At the Tonbridge end of Sevenoaks on A21
SOIL Lime-free	
ALTITUDE 75 m (250 ft)	
RAINFALL 762 mm (30 in.)	
TEMPERATURE 3.5°C (38°F)	

JAMES FIENNES, created the first Lord Saye and Sele in 1447, inherited Knole and it passed to his son William; he had a descendant, the celebrated Celia, who, through her enterprise, diaries, and energy – travelling side-saddle from place to place – became the first recorder of houses and gardens. Her delight was a well-ordered garden, of the formal lines so fashionable at the time. We have little to guide us in visualising what the garden at Knole was like in those days, but it is recorded that its surrounding wall of Kentish ragstone was built in the second half of the 16th century. Earlier than this Henry VIII lived at Knole and had a garden made. In 1692 the wages for a year amounted to £10 for a gardener, Mr Olloyndes, who ran up a bill for seeds of "sweet yerbs, sorril, spinnig etc.".

To the east of the house the rectangle enclosed by the wall has a central path gradually ascending from the house to the far wall where there are imposing gates and gate piers. This slope is believed to have been constructed about 1723, by cutting and levelling, and some of the spare soil provided for the mount on which stands an oak tree. The ground is dug out quite deeply towards the house, where stand two brick pillars of later date which may have enclosed a level court. The whole upper enclosed area was known as the Wilderness and is full of great trees and meandering paths, and is a delightful cool retreat, with countless bluebells in spring.

If you walk around the garden boundary wall you will find what must be the longest green alley in the country, hedged mainly with Pontic Rhododendron. You pass a corner grille, the great gates, and another corner grille, all with extensive views over the beautiful tree-sprinkled park. This long, cool, mossy walk is thus punctuated with sudden and lovely relief at one end, while at the other, returning to the south and west, views open up across the garden lawns.

The whole area to the south of the house is bounded on two sides by stone walls, clad with dozens of old wistarias, creating a sight and fragrance of rare beauty in late spring. One portion of the wall has a brick pergola which is given to 'New Dawn' rose and clematises. A short avenue of Leyland Cypress, with attendant shrub roses, lines the central view. There are two Fastigiate Oaks, one of which must be a record in size and height.

On the Orangery wall grows *Magnolia thompsoniana*, near enough to the path for all to savour its sweet scent during the summer months; *Rosa fortuniana*, 'Blush Boursault', and 'Souvenir de la Malmaison' thrive. In a small enclosed area is a herb garden which brings us back full circle to the plants which would certainly have been growing there in the days of Mr Olloyndes. It is also said that the orchard areas perpetuate the planting of the days of Charles I.

LACOCK ABBEY
Chippenham, *Wiltshire*

Given by Miss Matilda Talbot in 1944

AREA 3.2 ha (8 acres)
SOIL Limy
ALTITUDE 30 m (100 ft)
RAINFALL 635 mm (25 in.)
TEMPERATURE 4°C (39°F)

3 miles south of Chippenham, east of A350

IT WOULD BE HARD to resist taking a photograph of the imposing and beautiful archway, towers, and general siting of this edifice on any visit. Today one can photograph almost anything out of doors in almost any light by using the most sensitive cameras and appliances. We are fortunate that such progress has been made since William Henry Fox-Talbot of Lacock Abbey invented photography, as long ago as 1839.

If you can choose a year when Easter is early, a visit to Lacock is specially rewarding. In their many thousands the crocuses spangle the wide lawns and grassy areas, a legacy we inherit from some spirit with a love for flowers and beauty; they are mostly *Crocus vernus*, the more or less wild types, a noted Alpine flower from Southern Europe. From white to purple with every intermediate shade, they are slim and shapely and very unlike the large-flowered named forms which one would have to buy today. This wild type sheeted Miss Willmott's garden at Great Warley, Essex, and from there went to Spetchley Park, Worcestershire. It is possible that the Lacock bulbs are of the same origin.

The other noted plant at Lacock is the Black Walnut, *Juglans nigra*, from the United States; a very fine specimen grows in a walled garden, and a lesser tree near the abbey. There is also a fine *Pterocarya fraxinifolia*, an old Judas Tree, a Swamp Cypress and Tulip Tree, and a *Celtis australis*, the Nettle Tree. Many a good shrub grows about the grounds and on the old walls.

My first visit to Lacock was unofficial; when returning home from Wales one Saturday I thought I would have a look round *incognito*, since I had never been asked to advise there. It was a boiling hot day. Nobody asked me for my ticket at the lodge, and I wandered down to the abbey. No sooner had I passed the lodge than it was realised I had paid no entrance fee and Colonel Burnett-Brown was telephoned at the abbey. As I passed, out he came and I had to confess I was "staff" and spying out the ground. I was welcomed, had tea on the lawn with him and his wife and Miss Talbot, the donor, and then discovered that Mrs Burnett-Brown was as addicted to roses as I was. Thereafter I made regular visits and on one occasion, at lunch, I picked up a tall pepper-mill, gave it a twist, when out popped an earwig. Mrs Burnett-Brown remarked that that was "one less for the garden, anyway"!

LAMB HOUSE
Rye, *East Sussex*

Given in 1950 by Mrs James, widow of the nephew of the novelist Henry James

AREA 3 ha (¾ acre)
SOIL Neutral
ALTITUDE 15 m (50 ft)
RAINFALL 762 mm (30 in.)
TEMPERATURE 5°C (41°F)

In West Street, facing west end of the church

"THE TINY out of door part amounts to about an acre of garden and lawn, all shut in by the peaceful old red wall." So Henry James wrote of Lamb House. At one time laid out by Alfred Parsons, the garden has been altered, enlarged and contracted from time to time, so that it is difficult to say today what is old and who created the different portions. I think we may presume, however, that the small formal borders and beds constituting a rose garden and an area for vegetables and fruit have always been where they are, handy to the sheds and compost heaps.

However peaceful the walls may appear, on windy days – which often occur – the garden is anything but peaceful as the wind buffets the plants; Lamb House garden makes one realise how successful gardening can be even in such places. The pantiled patio in front of the garden door was laid by the Trust in 1969, at which time the beds around the lawn were given a more gentle outline. Our present tenants, Mr and Mrs Graham Watson, have improved the lines and the planting still further and the garden is well stocked with beautiful plants including an assortment of lilies. Peonies include *P. mlokosewitschii*, which is more beautiful than its name and is often affectionately known as "Molly-the-witch".

In the old days there was a greenhouse which contained in it a plant of *Campsis radicans* – then known as *Bignonia*. The greenhouse has gone but this trumpet creeper shares a hot sunny wall with an Australian Bottle Brush, *Callistemon citrinus*, and the pink hybrid jasmine, *Jasminum stephanense*.

A Sweet Gum stands on the lawn and many flowering trees soften the outlines of neighbouring houses. There is a wealth of roses, bush, standard, rambling and climbing, and of especial note are large plants of the old 'Cécile Brunner' and 'Perle d'Or'.

It is said that the garden is on the site of an old fish market; perhaps this is why things grow so well, but I think Mrs Watson would disagree.

LANHYDROCK
Bodmin, *Cornwall*

Given in 1953 by the 7th Viscount Clifden

AREA 10 ha (25 acres)
SOIL Lime-free
ALTITUDE 121 m (400 ft)
RAINFALL 1143 mm (45 in.)
TEMPERATURE 5°C (41°F)

CORNWALL is a very old county, geologically and in terms of man's history. It was not smoothed down by the Ice-Age glaciers and abounds in narrow valleys separated by rounded hills. If you journey north-west from Lostwithiel you go down and down again to the 16th-century Respryn Bridge – itself of great charm and interest – and arrive at the entrance to Lanhydrock; from here onwards we are surrounded by beauty and antiquity. The gate piers are dated 1657 with the initials of John Robartes and his wife Lucy. He planted the avenue of sycamores leading from the gate to the house; many of the old trees remain but were interplanted with beeches during the 19th century and later. New trees are being planted as the old ones fail.

The drive is steep at first, but as it evens out the excitement mounts. Is there any delight of its kind to equal the sight of the gatehouse seen from here with the house and church in the background, the architectural group enveloped with greenery? It is a magical spot in all weathers, but if you are blessed with a brilliant May day as I was, years ago on my first visit, I think you will be entranced.

I spent the morning with Lord Clifden, who gave us the property, and we toured the garden. The granite of the house provides a good home for lichens in the damp climate and I noted how the north wall seemed to reflect the colours of the flowers.

93 The garden at Lanhydrock, noted for its magnolias and rhododendrons, has a circular, hedged enclosure for herbaceous plants. This was redesigned and replanted in 1971.

To find so splendid a formal setting to the house in Cornwall is an exception, in that county of informal valley gardens. Lanhydrock stands high above its avenue, and the broad lawns are punctuated by cone-shaped Irish yews. When I first went there these were infested with jackdaws' nests and untidy with their straw. Originally high walls connected the Gatehouse with the house; these were swept away and the park came right up to the house in the 18th century, until the present terraces and low walls were designed by Sir George Gilbert Scott in 1857. The avenue and buildings therefore, and some of the garden trees, are old, but the garden is the creation of the last hundred years or more, and, like the interior of the house, mirrors the late Victorian taste.

Originally the terrace beds were in a setting of gravel, like the small parterre to the north of the house. This is an exquisite little creation of box-edged flower beds laid out in 1930, surrounded by a low box hedge.

The garden above the house is almost entirely informal, and the walks follow the contours boldly, leading ever upwards to where splendid views open out over the countryside. There is a broad gravel terrace walk right at the top, which commands many of the best views, while very specially at its southern end there is a carefully preserved view down to the gatehouse, framed by rhododendrons, under spreading beech branches.

While so many Cornish gardens specialise in species rhododendrons, the accent here is more on the hardy hybrids and the whole garden is a scene of splendour, colourful and opulent in late May and early June. But before then it is the day of the magnolias. Some are 18.2 m (60 ft) high or thereabouts – *Magnolia campbellii*, *M.c. mollicomata*, *M. veitchii*, and many other early-flowering species, continuing with *M. soulangiana* hybrids, until the later-flowering kinds (*M. watsonii* and its parent *M. obovata*, and *M. thompsoniana* and its parent *M. virginiana*) produce their strongly scented blooms in June. There is one walk to be enjoyed under a long tunnel of *M. soulangiana* 'Lennei'.

Two quadrants of the circular garden hedged with yews were always devoted to herbaceous plants for summer interest. A nondescript shelter stood in its midst, a relic of garden design of a hundred years ago. This was taken away, revealing the granite barn. The Trust completed the circular hedge, and laid out the other two quadrant beds in 1971. The whole contains a liberal selection of hardy plants and bulbs. Many named forms of montbretia are grown, *Canna iridiflora*, *Gillenia trifoliata*, *Cestrum parqui*, *Libertia formosa*, *Cautleya* 'Robusta', penstemons, Clove Carnations, finishing in autumn with Kaffir Lilies.

Camellia reticulata and forms of *C. japonica* grow well on the walls surrounding the park and in beds. A young

Rehderodendron macrocarpum thrives, a gift from Trewithen, while nearby is *Rhododendron* 'Alison Johnstone' named after the donor and raised at Trewithen. The little thatched cottage used to be the dwelling of the gardener; by it is *Magnolia sinensis*, and beyond it the Holy Well, *Cornus kousa* and *C. nuttallii*, two celebrated White Dogwoods.

There is much more than I have mentioned – a very old and venerable *Acer campestre*, for instance, many new young trees, and a slope for summer-flowering shrubs; through the gates at the end of the top path is the Treffry Cross and from here woodland paths lead on under great trees, with rhododendrons and hydrangeas. And everywhere are ferns, covering the banks and open spaces. (See plate XXXII.)

The church is very much part of Lanhydrock. It is embowered in beech trees and stands on the steeply rising ground behind the house, with a terrace walk going right round the servants' quarters.

The Harvest Thanksgiving is and always was a special occasion at Lanhydrock. One lovely wide-mooned evening I attended the service and dined in the house afterwards. On leaving the dining-room we passed by a window to the west where a switch floods with light an outsize thermometer in the outer yard. And thus we knew there might be a frost that night! The owls were hooting on their way home and all was still and perfect.

LEITH HILL PLACE WOOD
Dorking, *Surrey*

Given in 1945 with an endowment by Dr Ralph Vaughan Williams

AREA 4 ha (10 acres)
SOIL Lime-free
ALTITUDE 274 m (900 ft)
RAINFALL 816 mm (32 in.)
TEMPERATURE 4°C (39°F)

3 miles due west of junction of A29 and A24, north of B2126

How sweet the moonlight sleeps upon this bank!
Here will we sit, and let the sounds of music
Creep in our ears: soft stillness and the night
Become the touches of sweet harmony

THESE LINES of Shakespeare's, describing Portia's garden, inspired Vaughan Williams to one of his most exquisite short pieces of music. He spent much of his childhood at LEITH HILL PLACE and who knows but that the woodland planted with rhododendrons and azaleas did not influence him in his choice of words? It later became the home of his brother on whose death he inherited, but he did not again live there. There is no doubt though that the moonlight sleeps upon the banks and, before night driving became such a habit, the soft stillness would have drawn music out of anyone so inclined.

Not far away, LEITH HILL TOWER, built in about 1765 by Richard Hull, stands on the highest point in Surrey and enables anyone who climbs it to ascend to 313.6 m (1029 ft). This whole length of hills is of considerable height and battles have been fought along its escarpment. In spite of the sandy soil, springs and seepage of water occur here and there and it was in one such damp spot that Josiah Wedgwood, a grandson of the famous potter, decided to plant the flowering shrubs. For shelter they have native oaks and other trees, and a number of conifers, some of which may be those planted by General Folliott in the early 18th century.

LEITH HILL PLACE commands a splendid view over the Weald, but one can imagine the relief it was to enter the wood above it, away from the buffeting wind. Originally the drive approached the house from the woodland gate more or less straight down through the area which I am now writing about. There are several very old Scots Pines and also Eastern Hemlocks, one of about 24.3 m (80 ft). Probably of Victorian planting are a Wellingtonia and a Redwood, and *Cryptomeria japonica* which seeds itself here and there. One of the noteworthy clumps of rhododendrons is *R. falconeri*; two plants make an immense mound, 12.8 m (14 yds) through and worthy of a Cornish garden. *R. arboreum* and *R. edgeworthii* are there and many early-flowering species and hybrids. Azaleas include old Ghent and Mollis varieties as well as the Pontic Azalea. Of recent years the Trust has planted several late-flowering kinds to prolong the display to the moment when *Magnolia obovata* spreads its fragrance around. A small pool has been made by the lower fence from where a good view of the house is obtained; a Tulip Tree over 6.4 m (21 ft) in circumference at 1.2 m (4 ft) from the ground stands in the field. At one time apparently the Royal Fern grew freely in this part of Surrey, and was sought eagerly by the Duke of Northumberland at nearby Albury. Mr Wedgwood did his best to preserve plants in the rhododendron wood and the Trust will be replacing these as it clears the overgrown Pontic Rhododendrons which have covered so large an area.

LITTLE MORETON HALL
Congleton, *Cheshire*

Given by Bishop C. W. R. Abraham and his son Mr Rupert Abraham, in 1938

AREA .4 ha (1 acre)
SOIL Lime-free
ALTITUDE 75 m (250 ft)
RAINFALL 625 mm (25 in.)
TEMPERATURE 2°C (36°F)

4 miles south-west of Congleton, on east side of the A34 Manchester–Newcastle-under-Lyme road

FROM THE FLAT surrounding land the 16th-century hall stands up very conspicuously. Its startling black-and-white half-timbering has been much photographed. The most charming view, however, has only recently been made available, simply by the removal of a few low branches off a lime tree in the drive. Such small details are part of the duties of the Gardens Advisory Staff.

In spite of the antiquity of the building, there is no record of a garden at Little Moreton. It is surrounded by a rectangular moat, and has two mounds of soil, presumably taken from the moat, one within and one without it. There is likewise no record of the making of the moat or mounds.

Since there was no garden, beyond a few beds and borders and a short pergola, and the whole place, about an acre in all, needed some attention, the Trust laid out in 1972 a small pattern of grassed areas, outlined in box and with paths of gravel, surrounding it with a hedge of native shrubs in mixed array. The design was taken from Leonard Meager's *The Complete English Gardener*, first published in 1670. The knot garden is enclosed in its own little hedge.

In the accompanying borders there are many old garden plants and herbs, set in a regular pattern and punctuated with English Lavender plants which are being trained into short standards. The old German Iris is there, the Mourning Widow, Thrift and London Pride, Chives and Wall Germander, and the old double red peony. Other borders around the house have similar old-time plants, including Angelica, Christmas Rose, Lemon Balm, Spikenard and Sweet Cicely. On the small lawn are traditional fruit trees, quinces, apples and pears.

Unfortunately the box used for edging the knot garden is not of the approved dwarf box edging (*Buxus sempervirens* 'Suffruticosa') which was unobtainable at the time. It is an increasingly scarce commodity these days, and one yearns for the hundreds of yards of it that used to be in all the old kitchen gardens. The mixed types of box used do however serve the required purpose, but need clipping more often.

94 A knot garden laid out in 1972 at Little Moreton Hall, from a design taken from a book of 1670. The pattern is outlined in box. Photo 1975.

LYME PARK
Stockport, *Greater Manchester*

Given by the 3rd Lord Newton in 1947

AREA	6 ha (15 acres)	On west outskirts
SOIL	Lime-free	of Disley, 6½ miles
ALTITUDE	152 m (500 ft)	south-east of Stockport
RAINFALL	1016 mm (40 in.)	
TEMPERATURE	3.5°C (38°F)	

IT IS OCCASIONALLY stated that though the Trust guards and preserves its possessions, unless the family continues to live in a house, that house becomes cold and lifeless. To some extent this is inevitable, and we should remember that the Trust never asks a family to go; the Trust is after all only a substitute for an owner, invited to take control because its own resources are greater. These thoughts are prompted by this great and splendid house, high on the moorland edge of the Peak District, with hundreds of its own acres surrounding it, together with its impressive garden. Generations of the Legh family have made it what it is, both house and garden.

Gracious living continued in full spate until 1914 in great houses. In those days the Head Gardener and his staff had not only to keep the gardens trim, as we do today, but also to tend the vast glasshouses so that an uninterrupted supply of fruits, flowers and vegetables reached the house. From tall chrysanthemums down to bunches of violets, flowers were loved by all; peaches, grapes and figs were grown together with early and late apples and pears. With a foreman and a staff of about twelve, unlimited fuel and no doubt unlimited manure, this must have been comparatively easy at Lyme. But neglect of all kinds, hastened by disastrous wars and reduction of staff, happened long before the Trust accepted the property. Since about 1969 a vigorous policy of restoration has been pursued with the result that the whole place is now in excellent order once again.

The dramatic lie of the land is scarcely equalled anywhere. The long climb of the drive, deferring till the last moment a full sight of the house, is anticipatory in the extreme. Though obviously debarred from the garden, deer continue to enter the front court, which has two little guard houses; for the warmth of the guards in cold weather fireplaces were built inside and smoke exuded from the curved arch above. This north front of the house, dating back in part nearly four

95 The orangery, built in the late 19th century, at Lyme Park, with summer bedding in the foreground. Photo 1964.

hundred years, gives upon an elegant inner court, whence it is but a short step to the lawns of the south front.

The high rainfall at Lyme, the often cloudy weather, and considerable exposure to the north, makes the south front a special attraction. The warmth reflected by the rosy fawn stone – quarried on the estate – and the shelter of the house and terraces all contribute to creature comfort. The great day of garden design at Lyme was in the late 19th century when the first Lord Newton laid out the steps and terraces, built the orangery with its glass roof, and created the Dutch Garden and fountain below the walled escarpment (see plate XXXI). There is a nice sense of garden history in the creation of what is known today as the Dutch Garden, long before the study of garden history was much to the fore. It was originally known as the Italian Garden and was decorated with vases and statues. Since these had been lost or broken, their places have been filled at least temporarily by neatly-clipped trees.

J. C. Loudon was one of the greatest promoters of the conservatory and during the 19th century every gentleman's house would boast a winter garden, or glass annexe where palms and ferns grew luxuriantly, maybe with pools and fountains, seats and plant baskets. Heating was by means of steam or hot water, and double glazing was an innovation to keep out the cold. It was another world – and was meant to be; a gracious living of a unique kind, and an escape into warmth and a fantasy of perpetual summertime through the winter. Coupled with enormous glasshouses in the great kitchen gardens, a vast range of exotic plants was grown. They later were used out of doors, the result being the summer bedding of annuals in patterned beds on the lawns and terraces. Gardening reached a very high pitch along artificial lines. Much of this style of gardening is fortunately preserved at Lyme by the Metropolitan Borough of Stockport and the Greater Manchester County Council, to whom the property is leased. Two seasons of colourful bedding still contribute to the delights of visitors and I doubt whether any earlier displays could have been better than those I have been privileged to see year after year. Late April and early May, and late July and August are the best times in this climate where spring arrives late and summer does not tarry. Wallflowers, Forget-me-not, tulips and Poetaz Narcissi used in spring; marigolds, *Nepeta*, antirrhinums with phalanxes of tall scarlet *Lobelia* 'Queen Victoria' are some of the memories I have. Equally splendid schemes of bedding are carried up across the lawns to the hedged rose garden. With less staff to manage them the trim herbaceous borders have been replanted mostly with plants that do not require staking, following a colour scheme from end to end. Hollies and yews at the back are festooned with rambling roses and other climbing plants.

But a surprise yet awaits the visitor. Do you see that octagonal Lanthorn Tower in the far eastern distance, on the rising ground? I have heard it suggested (without proof) that in the early 18th century it was removed from the top of the house and erected here to serve as an eye-catcher, its place being taken by the present squat tower, the background for the figure of Father Neptune. He stands ready to spear a fish in the garden pond. Informalised at a later date, this pond is believed to have been rectangular in the 17th century. Beyond it, opposite the south front portico, is a narrow avenue of limes of about the same date. To the east, uphill, is the area known as Killtime.

At the end is an imposing masonry bridge of 1756 under which gushes a little brook to fall down a rocky bed, through the garden pool to the park beyond. Years ago ornamental waterfowl, gold and silver pheasants and cranes, used this whole area, confined by a high deer fence to the south. Today the ravine has been turned into a garden glade with varied views from the old garden paths which thread through it. Something is in flower from spring to autumn in the very varied planting places, warm and sunny, dry, shady, moist and cool. There are *Rhododendrons* such as 'Damaris Logan', 'Susan', *yunnanense*, *luteum* and 'Blue Tit', Japanese Azaleas, Solomon's Seal and primulas for spring. Later, various kinds of *Philadelphus* shed delicious fragrance, *Primula florindae* and astilbes colour the stream banks; then it is the turn of *Rhododendron* 'Polar Bear', *Hydrangea paniculata* and relatives, *Hypericum kouytchense* and hostas. There is a good young tree of the Swiss Arolla pine, and in several places around the area are closely-planted quartets of the Small-leafed Lime, *Tilia cordata*.

Below the west front, looking over the Dutch Garden is an area known as the Vicary Gibbs Garden. Mr Gibbs was a celebrated gardener at Aldenham, Hertfordshire, and being a friend of the family, sought no doubt to add some variety to the conventional garden at Lyme by the gift of choice trees and shrubs.

They include the Algerian Oak, *Cornus kousa* and *Aesculus hybrida*. Today these have been augmented by some plants whose origin was at Aldenham, such as *Malus* 'Gibbs' Golden Gage', *M.* 'Aldenhamensis', and *Aster* 'Climax'.

One of the Legh family, Phyllis Elinor Sandeman, has conjured up the bygone days she knew at Lyme in her little book *Treasure on Earth*. So well does she convey how life for the few was made pleasurable by the many staff. Stripped of their staff, any family in so great a house as this would be lost. It was the staff who warmed the house both actually and metaphorically and made it live, guided by generations of owners, each adding their bit to the whole. Things are not the same as they used to be, anywhere; but there is something to be said for preserving the fabric of a house and garden, and caring for its furniture and plants. Yet again there is something to be said for continuing to add to the beauties of a garden especially when on coming to the Trust it is in sad array. Lyme is a wonderfully beautiful place, at any time of the year. The solid house, the levelled, civilised lawns and terraces contribute a feeling of security and peace to an austere landscape. (See also plate x.)

LYTES CARY
Ilchester, *Somerset*

Acquired in 1949 under the will of Sir Walter Jenner, Bt

AREA 1.2 ha (3 acres)
SOIL Limy clay
ALTITUDE 60.9 m (200 ft)
RAINFALL 762 mm (30 in.)
TEMPERATURE 3.5°C (38°F)

$2\frac{1}{2}$ miles north-east of Ilchester, north-west of the Fosse Way

FROM THE IMPOSING gate piers the drive bends round, passing some trees, and the grey building comes in sight approached by a short avenue of pleached lime trees. But open the garden gate and the eye will not know whether to turn to the old gabled porch or to the grey-flagged garden path. Slightly sunk below the vivid green lawns, the path is flanked by a row, on either side, of comfortable, round, topiary specimens of yew. In early summer these are of burnished green. And beyond are more knobbed gate piers with a large dovecote focussed behind them. To replace an untidy ditch the Trust made a haha here in 1975.

This one view alone makes a visit worthwhile, and is a sober prelude to the brilliance of a long border of shrubs and plants through the next gate. Here are richly-coloured clematises on the walls, spreads of potentillas and pinks, *Penstemon* 'Garnet' and glowing roses, leading away to a little hedged section of white flowers. Accompanying the walk by the border is a series of hedge-buttresses interspersed with small stone vases. The latter are replicas which replaced the broken originals a few years ago. Up some steps there is a long raised walk looking over the one-time orchard. This was planted in 1963–4 with diagonally-crossing walks lined with fruit trees. Four centrally-placed Black Mulberries did not approve of the heavy clay soil and were replaced with Apple 'Sunset' which is not only one of the most colourful in flower, but remarkably good to eat. There are crab apples, medlars, quinces and pears as well. The sundial was added a few years later.

The garden is, as Christopher Hussey described it in 1947, "a necklace of garden rooms strung on green corridors". A yew-hedged alley (see illus. 185) leads to a pool with statues of Flora and Diana and thence to a hornbeam tunnel (see illus. 177) leading to an area with a small ornament enclosed in Variegated Weigela. Hedged squares lead to the oriel window on the south front, and here the double yellow Banksian rose thrives, a Passion Flower, the Tarentum and the Common Myrtles, and the Gum Cistus from which laudanum is obtained. In the old days this gummy substance, a heavily scented perfume, was greatly valued. The gum exudes from the leaves in hot weather. Around the Mediterranean, goats browsing among the bushes accumulated the gum in their beards, and it was found that by cutting off the beards at intervals a large crop was obtained.

Beyond, through the opening in the hedge, there are further formal flower gardens, and a sunken rose garden, in which is planted 'Gruss an Aachen'. Though much in keeping with the venerable building the whole garden was laid out in the second decade of this century by Sir Walter Jenner. Many of the new hedges had achieved an unwarrantable width and have been reduced and re-faced over the past fifteen years or so. The whole scheme has mellowed until with a little imagination it gives the impression of antiquity, which is fitting as Sir Henry Lyte became somewhat famed for having translated De l'Écluse's French edition of the *Cruydeboeck* of Rembert Dodoens. Lyte called his book, published in 1578, *A niewe Herball or Historie of Plants* (see illus. 18). It is much concerned with the medicinal values of plants, Dodoens having been a physician, but Lyte added many original observations: that *Scilla nutans* (bluebell) grew particularly well near Wincanton and Mere "not far from my poore house at Lytescarie"; that the roots of *Campanula trachelium* were eaten in salads near Coventry, and that it was known as "Coventrie bells".

Nothing is known of his garden, but there is a nice little horticultural point about his forbear, John, who owed a large sum of money to the abbot of Glastonbury in 1537 and paid his debt in an "arbour of bay". Henry's son, Thomas, was also a keen gardener and grew black bullace and sloe, Cornishberry and barberry, almond, fig, apples and pears, plums and walnuts. Truly it may be said of the Lytes that "they came of a gardening family".

LYVEDEN NEW BIELD
Oundle, *Northamptonshire*

Bought in 1922 by subscription

AREA Indefinite
SOIL Limy
ALTITUDE 45 m (150 ft)
RAINFALL 610 mm (24 in.)
TEMPERATURE 3.5°C (38°F)

4 miles south-west of Oundle, 3 miles east of Brigstock

BEING A WEALTHY MAN, Sir Thomas Tresham sought to add to his property, the manor house at Lyveden, by designing an extensive garden and crowning it with an elaborate building. The manor house is known as the Old Bield (building) and the hunting lodge or banqueting house the New Bield. He started the work in the late 1590s but died in 1605 before its completion. The remains represent the oldest garden layout owned by the Trust, and one of the oldest in the country anywhere. But do not go there thinking to see an old garden; there is little but mounts, earthen banks, canals and the shell of the unfinished New Bield, in the midst of quiet, open fields.

From the manor house the land slopes upwards to the south, with several banks running east and west, now almost vanished owing to indiscriminate ploughing but once more sown with grass. Next comes a rectangular plot, some 91 m (300 ft) by 152 m (500 ft), in which was a regular pattern of pits containing foreign soil (possibly for fruit trees); these patches have also almost disappeared under the plough. The area is known as the Lower Garden.

Higher up is a much larger stepped bank with a mount at either end, also stepped. This in effect crowns the series of terrace banks, and also serves as a dam to hold the waters of the largest of the canals. Beyond this, approaching the top of the hill, is the Middle Garden, surrounded on almost all sides with canals. At the two southernmost corners of this rectangular area the canals describe three-quarters of a circle, enclosing mounts of considerable size. All the moats were obscured by native trees and bushes, but the Trust's Acorn Campers have done much to clear them.

Sir Thomas placed his banqueting house obliquely beyond all this. It stands looking to the north-east, on a raised earthen plinth, and there are slight traces in the field below it of a diamond-patterned knot, some 60.9 m (200 ft) long by 30.4 m (100 ft). The uncompleted New Bield is a beautiful stone structure, intended as a symbol of the Passion of Christ.

In *The Gardens at Lyveden, Northamptonshire*, by A. E. Brown and C. C. Taylor, published in *The Archaeological Journal*, vol. 129, 1972, the authors give much information on this interesting relic of ancient garden design. They quote a letter to Tresham from his foreman: "We goe forward apace with the west square of your moate, and are now a levellinge of your moated orchards." The moat on the west side of the square was never completed, but the area almost enclosed was described as a water-orchard. We have to remember two things: one, that the lower rectangle looks very like a regular plantation of some kind (it is not likely to have been a vineyard since the land slopes to the north), and the other that the term orchard in mediaeval times merely meant a wort-yard, or place where plants were grown. However, it is evident that the Lower Garden was a regularised plantation, while the Middle Garden, enclosed in moats and decorated with corner mounts, was a very grandiose scheme for those days.

Sir Thomas was ardently religious and a Catholic by conversion, and for this spent much of his time in prison, from which he directed the work by correspondence. With every point of the New Bield governed by religious thought, and its design in the form of an equal-armed cross, is it likely that he looked upon it as the final piece of a considerable scheme, in spite of its peculiar, off-centre siting? The answer is not forthcoming; the only sounds are the soughing of the wind in the trees and the croaking of the moorhens.

MELFORD HALL
Long Melford, *Suffolk*

Accepted by the Treasury from the executors of Sir William Hyde Parker, Bt, and transferred to the Trust in 1960.

AREA 3.6 ha (9 acres)
SOIL Limy
ALTITUDE 30 m (100 ft)
RAINFALL 584 mm (23 in.)
TEMPERATURE 3.5°C (38°F)

3 miles north of Sudbury on A134

WHAT SORT OF impression did Queen Elizabeth get when she stayed at Melford Hall in 1578? There would have been a great concourse to welcome her at Long Melford, and we read that there were 1500 serving men on horseback, and no less than 500 young men, clad in velvet, ready to wait on her and her retinue. As she approached the hall, she would have seen the beautiful brick house over the high wall almost as we see it today, and she would have driven round to the east front and passed through the gatehouse into the central court. The next day she might have walked in the gardens and ascended the steps to the Garden Pavilion to find to her delight that it was heated (see illus. 17). The heat from a furnace below was conveyed through flues in the wall – a Roman device. From its door and windows the whole garden and the village green would have been in view, as would her courtiers playing bowls on the raised green which stretches away from it. In the garden there would have been herbs and flowers and on the walls, no doubt, fruit trees.

Wine would have been produced on the estate and fish would have been procured from the ponds to the south of the house. These are now shut out by the crinkle-crankle wall probably erected in the early 19th century. On one side of the more or less rectangular garden of today, bounded on the other by the raised bowling green – it is narrow and considerable skill is needed to keep the woods from rolling down the banks! – is a dry moat; a wall was built in this in the 18th century.

Gone are the gatehouse and the gardens to the east and north of the house. Gone are the trees which she would have seen, but others are there – an Oriental Plane, a Judas Tree, a Tree of Heaven, a Black Mulberry, and an Indian Bean Tree, trees introduced from Europe, the Middle East, China and America. There is also a good plant of the Chinese *Xanthoceras sorbifolium*, a tall-growing shrub whose flowers, in chestnut-like panicles, appear in May. It is one of the few hardy members of a mainly tropical and subtropical family which includes the Litchi.

On the west wall of the house is the 'Blush Boursault' rose, raised before 1857. It has been propagated and distributed in recent years from this garden. By the sunny wall of the front courtyard grows the rather tender *Vinca difformis* whose blue-white flowers appear from autumn until the spring.

In 1578 there was no doubt a superabundance of knots, beds and borders, and herbs would have predominated. It was with this in mind that, about twenty years ago, the Dowager Lady Hyde Parker designed the little herb garden on the west lawn, complete with low hedge, pool and fountain. Today there is but one part-time gardener, and certainly not 500 young men clad in velvet.

It is amusing to read Gertrude Jekyll's caustic remarks in her *Garden Ornament*, 1918, in which she shews a photograph of the Garden Pavilion with the comment: "The proportions are quite spoilt and details entirely lost by overgrowth of Ivy and other creepers." Perhaps this opinion is the cause of its architecture being wholly revealed today.

MONTACUTE
Yeovil, *Somerset*

Given by Mr E. E. Cook, through the Society for the Protection of Ancient Buildings, in 1931

AREA 4.8 ha (12 acres)
SOIL Limy
ALTITUDE 75 m (250 ft)
RAINFALL 762 mm (30 in.)
TEMPERATURE 3.5°C (38°F)

4 miles west of Yeovil, on north side of A3088

CONSIDERED as a whole, the property at Montacute stands very high in the quality and diversity of its assets. The Mons Acutus was a fortified position soon after the Conquest, seven to eight hundred years before the Folly was built on top of it. This acts as an effective eye-catcher, peeping out of the trees, when seen from the garden. The house is renowned as one of the most splendid of Elizabethan dwellings. Its walled forecourt and two exquisite corner pavilions are a delight to the eye – though Gertrude Jekyll apparently disapproved of them. They are all built of the sandy-coloured Ham stone, quarried locally. There is a great raised terrace walk contemporary with the house, with an 18th-century orangery terminating it; below, a large sunken garden around which runs a continuation of the raised walk. There are yew hedges and Spanish chestnuts of great antiquity, together with other fine trees, and the largest Monterey Cypress in the country. In the original layout, the entrance drive descended to the east side of the house through an exceedingly wide avenue. It was altered in the third quarter of the 18th century when the entrance to the house was transferred to the west side. Since then a number of lesser features and plantings have been added including a garden pavilion. This is surely an impressive list of points of interest.

It is a deceptive garden; it is so much bigger than one can grasp in a short visit and I think this is because the design is so closely allied in scale to the house. This false impression is quickly discounted when one has access to statistics. For instance, there are 2441 m (2670 yds) of grass verges to be kept trim, and 814 m (895 yds) of hedge to be clipped. The west drive is 347 m (380 yds) long and contains 15 pairs of Irish yews, 4.5 m (15 ft) high, which have to be kept annually restricted to size; there are 44 more similar yews in the sunk garden and 22 more on the Cedar Lawn. From the north end of the north garden to the small pool beyond the Cedar Lawn it is 283 m (310 yds). There are several acres of gravel paths and many acres of particularly good lawns. There are of course flowers and shrubs in borders which add to the enjoyment of this great place and to its maintenance.

96 The distance from north to south of the garden at Montacute is 283 m (310 yards).

My first visit was in 1952 before I started my work with the Trust. For a few years Vita Sackville-West of Sissinghurst was looking after the garden for the Trust and she had asked my advice on the planting of shrub roses in a wide border just below the great terrace. I recommended a mixture of old roses, with a few species and Hybrid Musks so that interest would be maintained through the season. The selection included *Rosa gallica* 'Officinalis', originally known as the Red Damask and later the Red Rose of Lancaster or the Apothecary's Rose. "Damask" denotes its origin, Damascus, and it is a pregnant thought that it was introduced from that part of the Holy Land by the Crusaders in the 13th century. The great knight who was the guiding star of the First Crusade was Godfrey de Bouillon and he is one of the Nine Worthies carved in stone on the east front of the house.

The impressions as we visit Montacute today are good. Entry is by what was originally the back entrance, to the south of the house; by it stands a charming gatehouse. The big kitchen garden now serves as a car park and trees have been planted during the last ten years not only to shade the cars but also to screen them partly from view from the upper windows of the house. Along the drive is the immense Monterey Cypress, which finds sunny Somerset and the rather heavy alkaline soil to its liking. It is over 7 m (23 ft) in circumference at 1.5 m (5 ft) from the ground. Though of such a size, and probably planted nearly one hundred and fifty years ago, it still retains the rather conical shape. It has not assumed the windswept, flat top that it does in Monterey, and which many trees in South Devon and Cornwall exhibit. On the opposite side of the drive are some mounds of feathery green which are the result of felling some Redwoods during the last war. By the stable entrance are particularly large golden yews, after which is a short border where the Victorian planting of variegated aucubas dazzles with its spring foliage. For contrast are coppery-purple nuts, blue ceanothus and lavenders. A big Fern-leafed Beech stands opposite.

97 At Montacute in 1960. Reinstatement of lawn verge from which .045m (18 inches) had been pared away over the years. The turf edge is brought forward, the gap filled with soil and sown with grass.

98 An aerial view of Montacute from the north east, shewing the Mons Acutus with folly tower at the top of the picture, above the village and church. The original entrance was by a wide avenue and long drive approaching the walled, east forecourt. To the south is the cedar lawn and above it a cropped enclosure which has since been turned into a car park. To the north is the raised walk and orangery by the house, and the sunken lawn and pool surrounded by clipped Irish Yews and cypresses; the latter were removed in 1964 and replaced by thorn trees. Photo 1948.

The west front of the house looks straight down the drive to the far-away gates. It is lined by wide grass verges, the many sentinel Irish yews, and a continuous line of great trees, cedars, limes, beeches and Wellingtonias. Towards the gate Laurustinus thrives and in late autumn occasionally delights us with masses of indigo berries among rosy buds and opening white flowers.

On going through the garden gate we are on the long raised gravel walk which surrounds the entire north garden; in all probability this is contemporary with the house. The ancient yew hedge to the west was already 4.5 m (15 ft) high and 2.7 m (9 ft) through in 1894.

In the mid 19th century Mrs Ellen Phelips and her gardener Mr Pridham created Montacute garden as we know it today. The historic mount which was in the centre of the sunken lawn was taken away and the balustraded pool was made. It is perhaps more elegant than a mount would be, and makes a good focal point. On the banks are the sentinel Irish yews and above them the rounded heads of *Crataegus lavallei* planted in 1964, whose orange-red fruits catch the light in winter.

Under the terrace is the shrub rose border, spread beneath with *Hosta fortunei hyacinthina* to save cultivation. Among the roses are the Eglantine or Sweet Brier; the Musk Rose; *Rosa rubrifolia, R. moyesii*; old Gallica varieties; the Cabbage Rose; Hybrid Musks and Rugosas, the White Rose of York, the China Rose 'Old Blush', 'Céline Forestier' and the Duchess of Portland's rose. There are many others. The Orangery is unheated, but has ferns and climbing plants on the walls; of particular interest is the mound of tufa rock constantly a-drip with water, in which the Maidenhair Fern is well established.

By 1787 the gatehouse guarding the east court had disappeared. In 1677, in the Phelips papers, is the following record: "Without the gatehouse is another faire large Court walled about and ... with severall walkes and Rowes of Trees ... and variety of pleasant walkes Arbours and Coppices full of delight and pleasure." This must have made an impressive entrance to the east front; we are left today with the two charming garden pavilions ("2 faire Turretts with lodging Chambers") and the wall topped with obelisks, which recall the decorations at HARDWICK HALL. To enter the house one would have mounted the steps of the flagged terrace with its tall lantern-lit pillars.

The morning sun warms the yellow stone of the great house and the gravel paths; this colour is dominant to all floral colours except those of decided tints. For this reason the borders surrounding the walls of the east court were given strong colours by Mrs Phyllis Reiss, the creator of nearby TINTINHULL garden. I remember her pointing this out to me after she had undertaken to replant the borders which had been filled with grey foliage and soft-coloured flowers by Vita Sackville-West. If you go in spring you will find purple aubretias and wallflowers, followed by irises and poppies; then the roses appear, supplemented later by dahlias; compact shrubs with coppery-purple foliage help the effect, contrasting with yuccas, and purple clematises come tumbling down from the top of the walls. Red Hot Pokers, Michaelmas Daisies complete the season with late roses and dahlias. As you go through the gate the fragrance of the dead-white of 'Blanc Double de Coubert' roses greets the nose.

We move next to the slightly sunken Cedar Lawn. The levelling to provide a bowling green took place in the early 19th century; previously it had been known as Pig's Wheatie Orchard. A Cedar of Lebanon and a Blue Cedar spread their branches across the end of the lawn, nearly obscuring the 19th-century garden pavilion. Long before the cedars were planted and the lawn levelled, the yew hedges were there and also the ancient Sweet Chestnuts. Beyond the cedars is a small enclosure which was rationalised during the late 1960s. The little pool, made beautifully with integrated curved stonework, was placed in a central position, the pillars equally spaced, the yew hedge was planted round the west side, and the bed of *Yucca recurvifolia* duplicated by another.

Though undoubtedly the east front of the house is the most beautiful, the splendid building dominates each garden area on each front, and one of the most appealing times of day is on a summer's evening when the north front gets its share of sunshine. Then, with the long shadows of trees across the drive (and most of the visitors departed!) one can feel that here was a worthy endeavour, well nursed through the centuries and that though we may not see it exactly as envisaged originally, the whole concept adds up to a very remarkable home, house and garden. I think Sir Francis Bacon would have approved of the *mille-fleurs* background to the Gothic tapestry in the dining room (see illus. 14); his "wilderness" would have been much enriched by such a prodigality of flowers.

MORVILLE HALL
Bridgnorth, *Salop*

Given in 1965 by Miss A. P. Bythell and endowed by her mother Mrs T. P. Bythell

AREA 1.2 ha (3 acres)
SOIL Lime-free.
ALTITUDE 88 m (290 ft)
RAINFALL 686 mm (27 in.)
TEMPERATURE 3.5°C (38°F)

Between Bridgnorth and Much Wenlock, on the A458

THE ELIZABETHAN HOUSE, built near the site of an old priory, was converted to its present form in the 18th century, when the curving wings and pavilions were added. Standing at the front door these wings and pavilions seem to embrace the church and its trees just across the meadow. The sunny walls are decorated with a variety of plants, and the Summer Snowflake flowers prolifically.

The lawn to the south-west of the house is remarkable for several features. It is enclosed by two rows of tall yews, planted long ago, perhaps marking part of a formal layout of Elizabethan days, or part of the priory garden. They frame the distant landscape – a rising meadow capped by a lengthy piece of woodland. But on crossing the lawn a deep valley is revealed with a long series of rose beds just below the lawn. These are placed on a levelled stretch of ground which extends for some distance across the fields. Below the roses is a canal or formal water, probably deriving from an earlier stew-pond of the priory. Below this is the lush meadow and stream.

Apart from many shrubs and plants in borders around the walls, such as *Deutzia elegantissima*

99 One of the Martabani jars which punctuate the borders at Morville Hall.

'Rosealind', *Potentilla fruticosa* 'Red Ace', *Philadelphus microphyllus, Spiraea nipponica tosaensis,* there are two long borders leading from the terrace to the rose beds. The colours are soft in this garden, not warring with the landscape; here are roses, 'Golden Wings', 'News', 'Lilac Charm' and others, their stems shrouded in a mixed underplanting of winter-flowering heathers, daffodils, small bulbs, bergenias, sedums and lavenders. Breaking the length of the borders is a pair of ancient Martabani jars. These are of a type made in South China, exported from Martaban (a port on the coast of Burma), containing ginger, oil, and other commodities, to the Middle East. They are considered to be of the 17th century, and their dark glaze and patterned sides closely resemble the jar in the White Garden at SISSINGHURST.

Tucked away at the side of the house is a small formal sunk garden and lily pool laid out earlier in this century. The whole garden is devotedly tended by Miss Bythell.

MOSELEY OLD HALL
Wolverhampton, *Staffordshire*

Given in 1962 by Mrs W. Wiggin. The endowment was provided in part by public subscription (organised by the Wolverhampton Centre of the Trust) and in part by annual grant from Staffordshire County Council

AREA 0.4 ha (1 acre)
SOIL Neutral
ALTITUDE 75 m (250 ft)
RAINFALL 686 mm (27 in.)
TEMPERATURE 3°C (37°F)

4 miles north of Wolverhampton, east of the A449 Stafford road

THERE STOOD the house, a dull array of blue-grey and reddish bricks; I had passed it twice, disbelieving that it could be the house I was looking for. And the garden? Apart from a few wind-bitten yews, a few old fruit trees, a variegated holly and an old pear growing up the south wall, there was nothing. Nothing, that is, except the old surrounding wall, some pigsties, hen-coops and broken glass cloches. There was the back gate through which Charles II entered from the fields in 1651, two days after the disastrous battle of Worcester. Since then the house had been encased in bricks, *c.* 1870, completely obscuring its beautiful half-timber work, but inside it is still much as the King would have seen it.

Since there was no garden, the resolve was to create one such as he might have seen. With the advice of Mr Miles Hadfield, and money from a public subscription, organised by the Wolverhampton Centre of the National Trust, and much voluntary help, a scheme was started and most of the work was completed by the spring of 1963 (see illus. 8 and 9).

Throughout the garden only plants which were in cultivation in 1650 have been used, apart from a few fruit trees. In arranging the planting it was at once apparent how few plants in those days flowered after midsummer. But great pleasure was obtained from the fruits which were produced from August onwards, not only because of their value in supplementing the diet, but also because of their beauty and the way they marked the passing of the seasons, which were very much a part of life in those days.

The principal feature of the new garden is a copy of a knot garden which was designed by the Reverend Walter Stonehouse at Darfield in 1640. (This is portrayed in a manuscript in the library at Magdalen College, Oxford; the original garden was still just surviving as late as 1922 according to R. W. T. Gunther's publication *Early British Botanists.*) Different coloured gravels are used in the pattern of beds, edged with Dwarf Box; the whole is surrounded by a box hedge. Stonehouse edged his beds with box, stones and tiles. Alongside is a wooden arbour. The design was taken from one in Thomas Hill's *A Gardener's Labyrinth* of 1577. On it are trained *Clematis viticella*, a native of Europe and a parent of *Clematis jackmanii* and *Clematis flammula*, the Virgin's Bower; both are natives of Southern Europe and have been cultivated in England since the 16th century. With them is the Teinturier Grape, *Vitis vinifera* 'Purpurea'.

This arbour leads to a hornbeam arbour and then to a nut walk, which brings you to a nut *rond-point* and then to the King's Gate. The rest of the garden is taken up by a small herb garden and an orchard whose trees include some varieties grown in the 17th century.

On the wall of the house is *Rosa moschata*, the musk rose of the ancients, and on the garden wall is *R. arvensis*, the musk rose of Shakespeare; the violet, the honeysuckle, the eglantine all grow at Moseley.

Shakespeare conjured up all that is beautiful of an English hedgerow bank. In the corner of the wall you will find the pipe tree, or lilac; ". . . the flours, growing in tufts, compact of four small leaves of white colour, and of a pleasant sweet smell; but in my judgement they are too sweet, troubling and molesting the head in a very strange manner." Thus John Gerard, 1596, dismissed one of the loveliest of late spring flowers in which I find increasing delight, yearly, in contrast to the large-flowered named cultivars, which are stiff and heavy by comparison.

The front garden path is set with box edges; two beds and surrounding borders are filled with shrubs and flowers of the time. The Florentine, the Dalmatian, and the Siberian Irises; Valerian, St Bernard's Lily, Cupid's Dart, Wall Germander, peonies, Solomon's Seal, Periwinkle, Laburnum and, then newly introduced from Virginia, *Tradescantia*, and from China, the Fulvous Day Lily. The White Rose of York, the Red Rose of Lancaster are there together with crimson and blush striped 'Rosa Mundi', and the parti-coloured pink and white 'York and Lancaster'; the old Damask Rose and the Roman Autumn Damask. One plant is there which has been used for centuries for cleansing fabrics, Bouncing Bet or Soapwort. But you must browse through the borders and try to cast your mind back to those momentous years, and the lucky escape of the King to France.

MOTTISFONT ABBEY
Romsey, *Hampshire*

Given by Mrs Gilbert Russell in 1957

AREA 8.5 ha (21 acres)
SOIL Limy
ALTITUDE 45 m (150 ft)
RAINFALL 813 mm (32 in.)
TEMPERATURE 5°C (41°F)

$4\frac{1}{2}$ miles north-west of Romsey, $\frac{3}{4}$ mile west of A3057

JUST AS the monks at the abbey may have gone on a pilgrimage, so hundreds of years later tree-worshippers go to Mottisfont to see the great plane tree. If you can go on a sunny spring day, before the leaves have grown, you will find yourself drawn to that pair of immense trunks, widely buttressed with roots, the rough bark giving way above to the flaking surfaces, cream and green and brown, away upward, till the eye gets dizzied by the twists and turns of the many, sinuous, ascending branches – which at a height of a hundred feet or so shoot out in every direction, like the trajections of a bursting rocket, the outermost branches nearly reaching ground level again, all around the immense canopy. I know of no larger tree of any kind in this country, nor any more impressive, unless it be the Weeping Beech at Knaphill Nursery, Woking. The London Plane at Mottisfont, botanically *Platanus hispanica* (*P. acerifolia*), is approximatly 30 m (100 ft) high, and covers an area of lawn exceeding 1254 m² (1500 sq yds); the twin stems girth 11 m ($36\frac{1}{2}$ ft) at 914 mm (3 ft) from the ground, and a branch of considerable size, rooted in the ground, has produced a third stem some distance from the trunks. A drawing made prior to 1833 shows the two stems separate and of about thirty years' growth. This hybrid tree is a supposed cross between the Oriental and the Occidental Planes, of about 1700.

100 Inside the rustic summerhouse at Mottisfont, 1976.

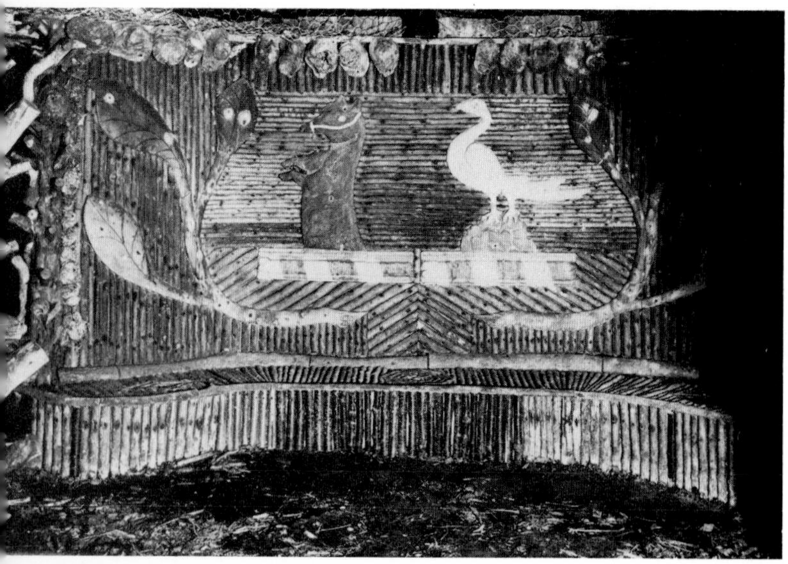

There are other great trees at Mottisfont, including Sweet Chestnuts and cedars, with a strange old gnarled oak, an errant form of the English Oak. They form a canopy of greenery round three sides of the wide, tranquil lawns which slope towards a tributary of the River Test, clear and fast flowing, in which great fish dart. The mellow house fills the other side, benevolently overseeing all. The *raison d'être* of the whole place is nearby – a gushing spring, crystal clear, welling up from the ground, and conveyed through a shady, flint-edged stream to the river; here was the Saxon *moot* or meeting place by the *font* or fountain. The old religious foundations always chose fertile valleys near ample water. We inherit today not only the prodigious tree growths of the past, but many a young tree as well, planted by Mrs Gilbert Russell during the last forty years.

Under the south front of the house, where grows *Feijoa sellowiana*, a native of Brazil and Uruguay, and the apricot-coloured rose 'Climbing Lady Hillingdon', is a small knot edged with box and dwarf lavender, and filled annually with flowers; it was laid out by Mrs Norah Lindsay, whose work is also in the flower garden at BLICKLING.

If your visit is in spring, walk round to the north side of the house where the formal scheme was evolved by Mr Geoffrey Jellicoe in 1936. Here is a pleached lime alley, carpeted below with Flowers of the Snow. The limpid blue and white in the streaked shadow of the branches is a beautiful picture. In August the climbing *Hydrangea petiolaris* and its relative *Schizophragma integrifolia* produce their white blooms on the walls, and *Hydrangea villosa* has lilac blooms on large rounded bushes. The soil at Mottisfont is heavy, limy and full of stones and it is interesting to note what grows well; following the line of the lime alley is a long border filled with hardy fuchsias, free-flowering *Yucca filamentosa*, and *Hydrangea arborescens* 'Grandiflora'. The three plants used repeatedly in clumps give a good effect in late summer. Across the lawn are some shrub beds specially planted for August effect, with such things as Tree Mallows, *Ceanothus delilianus* hybrids, potentillas, hypericums and caryopterises. These beds stand in front of a Gothick-style summerhouse, built of stone and knapped flints in the 18th century partly from material from the old priory (see illus. 3). The complex texture of the flints contrasts well with the simple shape. The evergreen shrubs on the end of the lawn are broken by a series of herms and a remarkable rustic summerhouse is reached by a short walk along the river.

On the east side of the stable block were planted several *Magnolia grandiflora* 'Exmouth Variety'. Supposedly slow growing, they romped quickly up the wall, even faster than the *Cotoneaster* 'Cornubia' with which they were interplanted for quick effect! Magnolias of the *soulangiana* type are nearby, and on the west wall of the house.

For long a great feature of the landscape, the fine circle of old beeches above the stable block at last fell, but before then a new circle had been planted in the early 1960s, whose trees are growing fast. The loss of the old circle revealed the ice-house.

In 1971 Mrs Russell decided to give up her tenure of the walled kitchen garden and this coincided with a desire of the Trust to establish a collection of old shrub roses. No sooner had this been suggested than the Winchester Centre of the National Trust decided to help with the project, and quickly subscribed enough money to purchase all the plants, with sufficient left over for some handsome seats. These, with the old box hedges, the circle of Irish Yews around the central fountain and the layout of paths within the walls make a splendid setting for the rose collection (see plate XXX).

101 The avenue of pleached limes at Mottisfont scattered with Flowers of the Snow in spring, 1963.

102 An old picture proves that two separate London Plane trees were planted close together at Mottisfont. They have coalesced and the result is probably the largest tree of any kind in the country. Photo 1975.

Partly through the co-operation of the Royal National Rose Society (at St Albans) which had already planted a collection embracing all those varieties I had collected over many years, our collection at Mottisfont was speedily brought together. Practically all the old European roses still in cultivation are there – Gallicas, Damasks (see illus. 173), Centifolias, Mosses, and White Roses. These are joined by early hybrids of the China Rose, like the Bourbon and Noisette classes. On the walls some of the Noisettes excelled themselves in the hot summer of 1976; 'Maréchal Niel' and 'Climbing Devoniensis' produced blooms 127 mm (5 in.) across. There is a border devoted to Hybrid Perpetuals and another to Scots or Burnet

Roses. Together with various old ramblers and climbers on walls and pillars there is at Mottisfont a fairly complete picture of the roses grown up to about 1900, with the emphasis on the ancestral species and their early derivatives.

Because these roses produce their main display mainly at midsummer, a number of spring-flowering edging plants are used to provide early interest, and right through the walled garden is a quartet of herbaceous borders filled with summer and autumn flowers.

> *. . . and now the Rose, the garden's Queen,*
> *Amidst her blooming subjects humbler charms,*
> *On every plot her crimson pomp displays.*

So the Rev. William Mason wrote in the late 18th century. I like to think that, though in those days there was no true crimson rose outside China, the rose's pomp will be displayed far into the future at Mottisfont, where my work of some thirty years collecting these varieties together from France, Germany, and the United States, and numerous gardens and nurseries in the British Isles, will not be set at naught. Enshrined in the garden there will be memories of those who treasured them when their cause seemed forlorn – Edward Bunyard, G. N. Smith, George Beckwith, Maud Messel, Constance Spry, Ruby Fleischmann, Murray Hornibrook, A. T. Johnson, Bobbie James, Anastasia Law, Vita Sackville-West, and many others of the fading past. The collection is a tribute to their memory – all of them had considerable influence on horticulture.

MOUNT STEWART
Newtownards, *Co. Down*

Transferred by the Marchioness of Londonderry and Lady Mairi Bury through the Ulster Land Fund in 1955

AREA 31.5 ha (78 acres)	On the east shore
SOIL Lime-free	of Strangford Lough,
ALTITUDE 15 m (50 ft)	5 miles south-east of
RAINFALL 889 mm (35 in.)	Newtownards on A20
TEMPERATURE 7.2°C (45°F)	

IT WAS early June 1949, and fortunately a day of brilliant sunshine.

We walked round the lake with Lord Bury; *Rhododendron griersonianum* and its hybrids were showing colour, also *R. elliottii* in large groups of flaming red. The splendour of the formal prospect, after going through the house, has left a more indelible picture on my mind. Here Lady Londonderry joined us. The grey mansion is surrounded by a generous flagged terrace, from which steps lead down to the southern vista, framed by two immense Irish Yews. The rectangular lawn contains a design of colourful flower beds; here were delphiniums, poppies, peonies herbaceous and shrubby, verbascums and roses. Across the lawn are more steps, with a pair of lofty pillars on either side surmounted by griffins. Further steps take one down to a small lawn and sunken pool, with a bush-grown *Wistaria multijuga* in a pot; both plant and pot were curtained with blossom, weeping to the water. The immediate end of the vista from the house rests on a green-roofed summerhouse, on whose shady walls thrive lapagerias, *Rhododendron rhabdotum* and *R. nuttallii*.

103 *Weinmannia trichosperma*, a native of Chile which thrives at Mount Stewart. Photo 1949.

The view from the west end of the house is quite different and I felt myself fortunate indeed to have been there just when the early summer display was at its best. The square, sunken garden is surrounded by a raised walk and pergola, hedged outside with *Cupressus macrocarpa*. The predominating colour on the pergola is soft light yellow from *Lonicera etrusca*, *Rosa gigantea* (see illus. 172) and *Dendromecon* rigidum, offset by the lavender-blue of *Solanum crispum* 'Glasnevin'. Below this are the four corner beds with a strong L-shaped planting in each corner of *Azalea* 'Coccinea Speciosa'. The splendour of this gorgeous orange colour with the blues of anchusa and the purples and light yellows on the pergola was something to be seen and remembered always.

My impressions of that glorious day, recorded in the *Royal Horticultural Society's Journal* for June 1950, have certainly remained strong, no less than the memory of the kindness and enthusiasm of Lady Londonderry, to whom we owe this great Irish garden. I little thought that twenty years later I should be asked to help to restore it to its former magnificence. It had "slipped" somewhat but with the help of Lady Londonderry's copious notes and diaries, and her daughter Lady Mairi Bury's interest and encouragement, we have gone a long way towards achieving our aim. Once again, it ranks with the most notable gardens in the British Isles.

Owing to the soft mild climate, Mount Stewart garden, started in 1921, has matured quickly, and presents a luxurious appearance. Thanks to the creator's inventive mind, and her catholic taste in plants, the garden is richly adorned in every way – the firm basic designs are fully endowed botanically and artistically, and also architecturally. The several stone animals which decorate in particular the Dodo Terrace are not mere garden whimsies, but reflect a wartime activity in London as may be read in the Guide published by the Trust.

Another wonderful impression I have is of daffodil time. They are everywhere in every colour; drifts of pale ones meet yellows at the lakeside, and huge scarlet hummocks of Arboreum rhododendrons are reflected in the water, the marshy verges strung with yellow King Cups, the grass dotted with Cuckoo Flower. And over all are the trees, burgeoning into new shoots, a soft warm mixture of purplish-grey and brown. Later the azaleas reflect in the water, the coppery purple of Japanese Maples and the shrimp-pink of *Acer pseudoplatanus* 'Brilliantissimum' enhance them and give contrast to the vivid greens that abound. The *Davidia* flowers, and *Weinmannia trichosperma*; later rhododendrons appear, arums, embothriums and eucryphias; silvery willows take on an added beauty against the huge leaves of *Gunnera* and the upright phormiums and rushes. (See plate XXXIV.)

On a clear day in autumn the lakeside comes into another beauty. In sheltered places are *Picconia excelsa*, *Prostanthera*, *Bowkeria*, *Cupressus cashmiriana*, azaras, acacias ('Mimosa'), *Psoralea*, *Clianthus*, *Erica canaliculata*, the Mount Stewart rose and *Arbutus menziesii*; everywhere a rich and involved planting of all that is best in trees and shrubs. Away to the east is the George V Jubilee Glade; various plants contribute red, white and blue colouring through the season; plants include Embothriums, *Rosa moyesii* and fuchsias provide red; white is found in Japanese cherries, *Philadelphus delavayi*, rhododendrons and hydrangeas; blue is from ceanothus, *Solanum crispum* and again hydrangeas, while the white stag and the silver grey stems and bluish foliage of *Eucalyptus globulus* are ghostly in the twilight.

But, glorious though the lakeside planting is, and remarkable the effect of the Jubilee Glade, with dark pines, Holm Oaks everywhere adding contrast to the native trees, it is to the formal gardens round the house to which my steps and mind lead me. Here is Mount Stewart at its characteristic best and Lady Londonderry's imagination most unleashed.

There is first the Mairi Garden with beds in the shape of a Tudor rose, backed by a pretty garden house, a giant *Cordyline* or New Zealand Cabbage Palm, *Pittosporum tobira* and *P. eugenioides*, and *Magnolia watsonii*. Only blue and white flowers are allowed here, from early flowering Chatham Island Forget-me-not to late blue and white African Lilies. "Mairi, Mairi quite contrary" is illustrated by cockle shells around the fountain, Silver Bells and Pretty Maids all in a row. *Eucalyptus viminalis*, *Fuchsia excorticata*, *Sollya heterophylla* and the Giant Lily, white roses and blue clematis add to the effect.

The garden on the south front is completely dominated by the long, low, grey mansion, clumps of *Eucalyptus globulus* over 30 m (100 ft) high at either end, and the towering Irish Yews which by their position gave immediate maturity to the design. The whole area is walled around, divided by a broad grass walk and is given a matching series of beds – a parterre in duplicate. But only the design is matched. As elsewhere the colouring is carefully thought out. Apart from a long series of shrubs on the walls – starting with camellias and followed by *Crinodendron*, *Wistaria venusta*, *Cassia*, *Ceanothus arboreus*, *Carpenteria*, *Feijoa* and *Grevillea* – the colour is provided by the parterres from June onwards. One parterre has flowers of red, orange and yellow, and the other of pink, mauve and white, each with complementary foliage. The beds of the two parterres are gathered around the pools edged with *Hosta plantaginea* and *Iris laevigata* 'Rose Queen'. *Kniphofia snowdenii* is always in flower, and *Hedychium*, *Watsonia*, *Dahlia coccinea*, Madeira orchids, *Boenninghausenia albiflora*, *Salvia fulgens* and *Lobelia vedrariensis* are a few of the delights.

104 The topiary specimens of Sweet Bay which surround the house at Mount Stewart were imported from Belgium. Here they are packed on horse-drawn floats at the nursery of J. P. Hartmann ready for conveyance to the railway station, Ghent, in 1923. The larger specimens were then about 50 years old; the cost was almost £100.

The lower part of the Italian formal garden gives upon the unique Spanish Garden, reached down a long flight of broad, curved steps. The Wistaria I noted in 1949 is still there, with Tree Peonies, 'Souvenir de Maxime Cornu'; the colours here are glaucous-grey foliage with yellow and salmon flowers. The Spanish house has recently been repaired and re-roofed, after untold trouble in securing the typical curved tiles, with green glaze. One of the sad things about Mount Stewart is that, quite naturally at that time, *Cupressus macrocarpa* was chosen for hedging. A quick effect was achieved, as elsewhere with the planting, but the hedges did not withstand the winter of 1962–3 and have at long last been replaced with *Cupressocyparis leylandii.* Nearby through the arched hedges are *Phyllocladus* species, *Sophora tetraptera* and *Cordyline indivisa* from New Zealand, and sweetly fragrant *Rhododendron crassum*.

The south front and the west front gardens are connected not only by the terrace walks but also by the Lily Wood. Here tall trees abound, and some notable items are *Gevuina avellana* with striking, glossy, dark green leaves, bamboos, groves of snuff-brown stems of myrtles (*Myrtus apiculata*), *Nothofagus*, *Stewartia*, *Pittosporum crassifolium*, *Rhododendron* 'Grandex', *R. falconeri* and several whose delicious fragrance wafts through the glades – *R. taggianum*, *R. lindleyi*, *R. polyandrum* and *R. cubittii*. Cyclamens, narcissi, primulas, and various lilies complete a floral succession, while never are we far from giant ferns, hardy palms and eucalypts. The whole garden area on warm days is redolent with the fallen capsules of eucalypts.

The Sunk Garden on the west front boasts many roses, and needless to say it was partly these that brought the prodigal owner to my collection in the 1950s. Here they are however, various yellow varieties and also the extremely rare *Rosa giganta* the parent of the Tea Roses, and with them are vines, *Lardizabala*, *Mutisia oligodon*; *Papaver atlanticum, Calceolaria integrifolia*, *Mitraria coccinea*, *Vestia lycioides*, and the orange azaleas mentioned earlier. Aubrietas and violas contribute to the colour scheme. The four corner beds, hedged with bay and heaths, contain herbaceous plants in the same grading of blue, purple, yellow and orange; the crowning glory is perhaps the purple *Clematis jackmanii* on the central iron hoops.

Gertrude Jekyll was asked for advice about this sunken garden and a drawing of hers, and recommendations for planting, are extant. The design is very much in her style.

We mount the far steps and are confronted by a bed resembling a giant's red hand in the paving – the left hand of the McDonnells. Here again in this Shamrock Garden the cypress hedges had deteriorated and have been replaced, this time, with yews. The borders are given mostly to winter-flowring shrubs. Two vast pots contain *Photinia* fraseri 'Birmingham'. Stretching far away westwards is the Memorial Glade, planted by Lady Bury in memory of her mother, and containing orange-cupped narcissi, *Embothrium*, yellow azaleas, *Cordyline indivisa*, white lilacs, with purple hydrangeas for late summer.

The drive leading to the house is not long, as drives go, but is highly impressive. If you can go in spring when the magnolias and the mighty mound of *Rhododendron macabeanum* in brilliant yellow is in flower, you will be well rewarded. Various other rhododendrons thrive, and another special moment is when the eucryphias flower, grouped with the sword-like leaves of New Zealand Flax, and hydrangeas. It is just as well that there is this dramatic approach, of contrasting exotic foliage backed by native oaks and great conifers, for the north front of the house is large and imposing, seen from the last curve of the drive.

The gravelled court, like the two terraces, is decorated with immense topiary pieces of Sweet Bay, imported from Belgium, at a cost of almost £100, in 1923 (see plate XXXIII). Between them we glimpse the expansive lawn and great trees around – Holm Oaks, English Oaks, Monterey Pine, Wellingtonia – while to the east lies the Rhododendron Wood, the place to wander while spring merges into summer. At its foot is a giant old European Silver Fir, grey-trunked and hoary with age. You will come out of the wood, if you journey through it, near to the Cork Oak and thence to a long glade of ferns from which the White Stag in the Jubilee Glade can be seen. The whole area here on a warm day is redolent of strawberry jam, from the fragrance given off by the extensive groups of Douglas Fir.

Then you can go back to the lakeside and look towards the hill, where, glimpsed between cercidiphyllums and *Nothofagus antarctica* can be seen the roofed corner towers of TIR NA NOG – "the Land of the Ever Young". Here is the private burial ground of the

105 The sheltered walk below Tir na nog at Mount Stewart.

family, where the guiding spirit of the garden rests. A great part of her life she devoted to Mount Stewart, a garden as she wrote "to be lived in and enjoyed"; the time was well spent, for the benefit of us all. Her rose 'Dame Edith Helen' once again grows in the Italian Garden. (See also plates VI and XV.)

NOSTELL PRIORY
Wragby, *West Yorkshire*

Given by the 4th Lord St Oswald in 1955

AREA 4.8 ha (12 acres)
SOIL Lime-free
ALTITUDE 60.9 m (200 ft)
RAINFALL 635 mm (25 in.)
TEMPERATURE 3.5°C (38°F)

West Riding. 6 miles south-east of Wakefield, north of A638

ON THE Wakefield–Doncaster road you pass over a gently humped bridge, built in 1759, which gives you a view of the upper lakes at Nostell, and also shows the great house on a high bank nestling among trees. The whole scheme is basically of the 18th century. The water was there, but it was raised slightly by the garden dam and at the site of the bridge the water tumbles over a low rocky weir. The Trust owns very little land here, but enough for us to see something of what has happened since the Winn family acquired the property in 1654.

There is first the 100-yard-wide avenue, a mile long, approaching the east front; this in 1885 was composed entirely of Dutch Elms and was already slightly past its best having been planted about 1740 while the new house was being built. We get a vivid impression of the lie of the land by taking the steeply slanting walk down to the lake, walking along the dam, and subsequently looking across the water to the trees and west front of the house. In 1829 the whole expanse was more or less devoid of trees; the bridge, the water and the distant clumps and woods were in all probability the work of Stephen Switzer in the 1730s. With so much of the outlook devoted to sport and sporting assignments in those days, its is not surprising to find a cockpit in the grounds, and also a small building which was a menagerie.

During Victorian times, in spite of the poor soil and exposure to wind, the curving paths were planted with rhododendrons, magnolias, other shrubs and conifers. The little menagerie was converted into, or at least used for, a garden house and even at one time housed a gardener. Small beds of azaleas and roses were added around it.

Today, after a considerable combing out of overgrown bushes and trees, something of a garden is materialising, and shrubs and plants have been introduced, many from our other gardens.

106 The Gothick Menagerie in the garden at Nostell Priory.

If you take tea after your walk round, you will do so at the back of the stable block, in the Garden Room, and will see the ancient specimens of Weeping Ash, a Cut-leaf Lime and Maidenhair Tree which were mentioned in *The Journal of Horticulture* in 1885. This *Ginkgo* was then 9.1 m (30 ft) high.

NYMANS GARDEN
Handcross, *West Sussex*

Acquired in 1954 under the will of Lt-Col. L. C. R. Messel

AREA 12 ha (30 acres)
SOIL Lime-free
ALTITUDE 152 m (500 ft)
RAINFALL 889 mm (35 in.)
TEMPERATURE 4.5°C (40°F)

On south-east edge of Handcross, 4½ miles south of Crawley on B2114

DURING THE 1930s my little Austin Seven almost knew the way from Woking to Horsham, the starting point for visiting many of the renowned gardens of the Sussex Weald. South Lodge, Leonardslee, WAKEHURST, Stonehurst, Warnham Court – and Nymans. Glorious days in May and June, filled with the beauty of established trees and shrubs; it was a great change and refreshment for anyone growing them commercially. Here in the Sussex gardens grew all those ravishing shrubs that would not thrive in the frost pockets and open fields of Surrey.

Just before the war I had become interested in the older roses and was asked by Mrs Messel to pay a visit one Sunday to see them. I had acquired several, but was not prepared for the feast that I found at Nymans. There seemed to be roses everywhere, for Mrs Messel was one of the select band who had nursed their favourites through the Kaiser's war, and had gone on preserving them through the years. They knew there was nothing like them in horticulture, a fact which I soon learnt. Accompanied by Colonel Messel and the head gardener, James Comber, we went from bed to border, from border to wild garden, and over the road to a smaller garden where the principal collection was, some in neat beds, others trained over arches, yet more climbing over the hedge and into trees. We lingered over 'Cardinal de Richelieu', 'Maiden's Blush', 'Céleste', 'Charles de Mills', 'Rosa Mundi', and other time-honoured favourites, while 'Flora' and *Rosa mutiflora* hung in festoons from the old apple trees. It was a rare privilege to be introduced to them all by so noted an enthusiast. While tea was being prepared I went to Mr Comber's cottage to see more treasures, and particularly the 'Blush Noisette'. After tea, the three great tomes of Redouté's *Les Roses* were produced and we poured over the lively pictures, checking this and that. Alas! a year or two after the war the house caught fire, Redouté was burnt, and Colonel and Mrs Messel moved to a neighbouring house; the garden, though, was unharmed.

A few years ago Mrs Messel's rose garden was completely refurbished by her daughter, the Countess of Rosse, who now looks after Nymans for the Trust. Here on this rich soil roses do well and late June provides a feast of colour and fragrance. It is the culmination of the long spring season at Nymans.

When you alight in the car park, you are not in the heart of the garden near the house, but at its west end. It is not many steps to the garden's most noted view: between two Dawyck Beeches a large lawn, covered with daffodils in spring, slopes away. It is a sober, uninterrupted setting for the arc of conifers beyond, conifers of all sizes and tints, tight "dwarf" buns and columns to really large specimens, mostly planted some seventy years ago. Pines, junipers, cypresses, thujas and the like, bluish, yellowish, brownish or just dark green. including *Cryptomeria japonica* 'Spiralis' and *Picea abies* 'Nana Compacta'. It is a most impressive assembly. By the time you reach the conifers a garden temple comes into view designed by Alfred Messel in 1907, with a sentinel on either side of it of the Nymans *Eucryphia*, covered in late summer and early autumn with large white flowers (see plate XV).

But possibly we are going too quickly. What does Nymans mean to us gardeners? As you walk from one level area to another, each different from the next, you realise that, in spite of the often steeply sloping terrain around it, the garden is mainly on the flat, with the occasional steps and slope to add interest. This results in the cold air draining rapidly away downhill with a consequent minimum of frost damage, particularly in spring. The two first owners, Colonel Messel and his father, were chiefly interested in cultivating plants, the choice and the rare particularly, and their sights were levelled at the plants and not the landscape. Trees and walls and hedges abound, sheltering the plants. This is no shortcoming; it merely reinforces the claim that every garden is "different", and there is certainly plenty that is different at Nymans. I need only cite the plants that have been raised there, which are mostly household names today, the Nymans *Eucryphia*, *Magnolia* (see plate II) and *Camellia* 'Leonard Messel' among them. The originals still grow in the garden.

107 *Rosa* 'Polyantha Grandiflora' hanging out of tall hollies at Nymans.

You have the choice of two paths on leaving the Pinetum lawn, down the June border, hung with roses, to the rose garden, or earlier in the year taking the other, curved path, which passes by some noted specimens of *Magnolia obovata*. *Cornus kousa*, *C. controversa*, *Sophora japonica*, *Meliosma veitchiorum*, *Cercis racemosa*, *Magnolia campbellii* and *M.c. mollicomata*, *M. sargentiana*, *M. salicifolia* and the hybrids 'Leonard Messel' and 'Michael Rosse' all grow in the neighbourhood. *Eucommia ulmoides*, *Tetracentron sinense*, *Magnolia stellata* 'Rosea', *Eucryphia moorei*, *E. cordata* and *Laurelia serrata* are not far away, and in one shaded spot there is a deep pit where one has the rare experience of looking down on the giant leaves of *Gunnera*.

There is a little, sunny corner by the greenhouse where that most beautiful of crinums grows, *Crinum moorei*, a blush-pink lily of great elegance. A dwarf bush of *Sophora macrocarpa* introduced by Harold Comber steals the thunder from a noble bush of *Cornus florida* 'Rubra' and a huge mound of *Osmanthus delavayi*.

If you cross the drive hereabouts, under a large *Parrotia persica*, which excels in autumn colour, you will find opposite the original *Camellia* 'Leonard Messel'. Lofty Italian Cypresses, *Rhododendron macabeanum*, and pines shade a small glade where in June shoot up the stout stems of the Giant Lily of Western China. It is an annual feature, achieved by growing bulbs of different ages since they may take five years to flower. Looking up into the maroon-throated trumpets is nearly as enthralling as savouring the fragrance and quality of the blooms of magnolias, even *M. watsonii* and *M. sieboldii*.

Tucked away under a shady wall are *Asteranthera ovata* and *Philesia magellanica*, completely at home and

XXVIII The fountain and attendant topiary in the Walled Garden at Nymans in 1973.

XXIX ABOVE Looking down from the slopes of the arboretum at Killerton. A view that would have pleased 18th-century landscape gardeners, achieved by the removal of beds and fence and the creation of a haha in 1970.

XXX OPPOSITE ABOVE In the garden of old roses, laid out in 1972/3, at Mottisfont Abbey. Photo 1975.
XXXI OPPOSITE BELOW A corner of the Dutch Garden at Lyme Park in August 1964, with Catmint, yellow and orange marigolds and scarlet *Lobelia* 'Queen Victoria' on display.

XXXII The 1651 gatehouse
at Lanhydrock.
Photo 306 years later.

XXXIII OPPOSITE ABOVE
Mount Stewart in 1974, with some of the Sweet Bay topiary pieces in illus. 104; *Azalea* 'Coccinea Speciosa' and Tree Lupins in the Sunk Garden.

XXXIV OPPOSITE BELOW
Mount Stewart, April 1976. Scarlet Arboreum Rhododendrons seen across the lake.

XXXV RIGHT
Glacier-smoothed rock outcrop at Rowallane, dominated by the coppery Smoke Bush; Golden Marjoram in the foreground and *Meconopsis regia* on the extreme left. Photo 1974.

XXXVI BELOW
Approaching the central glade at Saltram; Monterey Pines, Japanese Maples, rhododendrons, and self-sown Holm Oaks on the right. Photo 1969.

108 One of the arched entrances into the walled garden at Nymans, with Rose 'Madame Plantier'. Photo 1969.

making us marvel yet once again how plants from all latitudes of the temperate world find a home in Sussex. These two are from Chile, the former introduced by Harold Comber. *Berberidopsis corallina* grows here as well, turning this into "Chilean corner". They all are evergreen, with red flowers of intriguing shape.

Harold Comber was James Comber's son and went collecting plants to Chile whence many choice shrubs and trees were obtained, including the *Sophora* mentioned above and *Desfontainea spinosa* 'Harold Comber'.

The more or less circular Walled Garden built in 1904 is bisected by crossing paths. They cross at the Italian fountain guarded by four old topiary pieces (see plate XXVIII). In early spring one path is a feast of bulbs and small plants; the other waits for summer, being planted with herbaceous plants on the recommendation of William Robinson. It is cunningly backed with summer-flowering shrubs of some size: *Styrax hemsleyana*, buddleias, *Eucryphia glutinosa*, the bush chestnut *Aesculus parviflora*, all of which extend the floral interest upwards and outwards. It would be a good man who could go for the first time to Nymans and name everything in this part of the garden. Evergreen species of *Nothofagus*, stewartias, *Sassafras albida*, *Meliosma cuneifolia*, *Hydrangea sargentiana*, hoherias, *Weinmannia trichosperma*, *Drimys winteri andina*, *Ercilla volubilis* crowd upon one while rose species and 'La Follette' flower on the wall.

The most lasting impression of Nymans is probably the shell of the gutted house standing on the lawn. It forms the nucleus to the whole garden, though it is only partly habitable. Pots of scented-leafed pelargoniums, lilies and *Lavandula dentata* grace the terrace. Across the lawn is a delightful touch: a flower-bed in a wire basket over which is trained Winter Jasmine. It was the sort of thing recommended in books like *The Ladies' Assistant* of 1861. Beyond is a group of very large *Rhododendron arboreum*, some 6 m (20 ft) high, raised direct from Himalayan seed many years ago. Nearby is the original *Magnolia* 'Anne Rosse'. The Cedar Lawn disappears under mounds of historic old Ghent Azaleas planted before Mr Ludwig Messel came to live here, and then we are suddenly in the Sunk Garden with the stone garden house. All around is a coveted assembly of the world's loveliest camellias, including 'Maud Messel'. This leads to the side lawn on which grows one of the original Nymans eucryphias, and thence to the heath garden, the sunken bowling green and wistaria pergola. This whole area was developed in the very early years of this century.

In the heath garden are many shrubs which blend and make a *maquis* effect without being actually heaths; you will find *Hakea sericea*, *Callistemon linearis*, *Pieris* species, noted for white bell-flowers and striking foliage colour, *Hypericum* 'Rowallane' and *Daphne retusa*, dwarf conifers, rhododendrons and rose species, all making one lovely blending thicket through which paths twist. The crowning feature is a mound on which stands a Japanesque wooden structure, hung with *Vitis coignetiae*, and from this vantage point one can look down on the shrubs and smell the warm fragrance of cistuses and *Rosa rugosa*, while through a gap in the trees, away on the horizon are the high South Downs.

Nymans is so filled with good plants in such concentrated array that the uninitiated may by now be getting "plant indigestion". One course is to go home resolved that you will find a place for some new plants in your garden. The other is to take "a breather".

Just as some great gardens have a limitless expanse of water on which to rest the eye, and other may have distant mountains or the fringe of deep gloomy woods, Nymans has yet a surprise in store. From the south-east corner of the heath garden lawn is a long alley, hedged with evergreens. It will take you far up the side of the garden, and rest the eyes and senses. It is an unusually straight walk for Victorian times and is a repetition of a much earlier style of gardening.

On emerging you can make your way down one of the drives to the planted area across the road. So far you have been looking at the oldest parts of the garden, filled with plants from the four corners of the world, many raised from seeds collected in the wild by Forrest and Kingdon Ward. After Harold Comber decided to go on a similar expedition to South America, numerous fresh plants of his introduction were being raised at Nymans and the garden overflowed to this sheltered woodland fringe in 1920. Many young specimens were planted in nursery rows, and there, because of the last war, they remained. It is worth inspection because of the remarkable specimens that

XXXVII OPPOSITE ABOVE *Magnolia campbellii* in flower at Sharpitor in March.
XXXVIII OPPOSITE BELOW Scotney Castle has been reflected in its moat since the 14th century. Photo 1973.

have matured. Species of *Berberis* of Comber's introduction, *Austrocedrus (Libocedrus) chilensis*, the Chinese Lace-bark Pine, *Magnolia globosa*, the Nymans forsythia, *Lomatia tinctoria* and *Stewartia ovata* 'Grandiflora', will all prove rewarding, as well as many rhododendrons. *R. cerasinum* produced its first flowers for one of my earlier visits; I well remember Colonel Messel's delight at this. The best form is named 'Hubert Mitchell' after one of the gardeners; it has plum-crimson flowers each with five black tear-drops in the centre. Tucked away is a rare hybrid Rowan: *Sorbus* 'Leonard Messel', a hybrid between *S. aucuparia* and *S. harroviana*.

If you are a rhododendron enthusiast you will think perhaps that I have been unkind to them. There are many, species and hybrids, at every turn of the path. From earliest spring until midsummer, there are always rhododendrons in flower. In between, neat little *R. roxieanum* produces its tight trusses of pink buds and white flowers; 'Anne Rosse', raised from seed from the wild of *R. sino-grande*, presumed crossed with *R. macabeanum*. A big mound of dwarf species grows on a sunny bank; here are *R.R. hypenanthum*, *saluenense*, *calostrotum*, *campylogynum*, *tsangpoense*, *vellereum* and others, knitted together into a dense canopy as they are in nature. A specially good form of *R. pocophorum* has been named 'Cecil Nice', after the head gardener. A series of hybrids between *R. decorum* and *R. griffithianum* grow in one spot; these are named 'Madonna', and are deliciously scented, a prelude to the late-flowering *R. crassum* in July, whose flowers flood the glade with fragrance, followed by *R. auriculatum*, equally fragrant in August. (See also plate II.)

OSTERLEY PARK
Osterley, *London*

Given in 1949 by the 9th Earl of Jersey

AREA 56 ha (140 acres)
SOIL Lime-free
ALTITUDE 30 m (100 ft)
RAINFALL 635 mm (25 in.)
TEMPERATURE 4.5°C (40°F)

Just north of A4, beyond Osterley station

TOWARDS THE END of the last century, it was claimed that Osterley was the largest park near London, comprising 263 ha (650 acres). Today the Trust owns 56 ha (140 acres), including the house; the "manie fair ponds", recorded in 1596, were subsequently enlarged and landscaped in the 18th century. These and the park were bisected by the construction of the motorway in the 1960s. Such great landscapes and their extensive views are particularly vulnerable in these days of "progress". Factories or other high buildings can utterly ruin the original idyllic conception, and a wonderful landscape and national heritage like Osterley can be torn apart by Philistine planners without due thought – as if the convenience of a car route were held to be of greater benefit to all concerned than the peaceful enjoyment of trees, grass and water. The noise of the motorway alone destroys the peace.

109 Osterley, by Anthony Devis (1729–1817); a pastoral scene from the south west.

Osterley has, even so, much to offer. Apart from the house, the grounds, now in the care of the Royal Parks, have some architectural features of note – the very charming semi-circular Adam Garden House of 1780, the Doric Temple of about 1720 and an ice-house. These all date from the 18th century when the house was remodelled by the Childs, whose daughter married the Earl of Jersey in 1802.

It is something of an excitement to walk from the car park through a grove of large liquidambars. Their autumn colour is both long-lasting and vivid in purple, red and orange; in some years they overlap in colouring with the yellow of the Grey Poplar, which grows with more liquidambars not far away. And from that position the splendid house is revealed by glimpse after glimpse, through the trees. First there are some large-size Silver Limes, and then a grove of mighty Cedars, Lebanon, Blue and Deodar. The house was there long before cedars were introduced from abroad and yet they do not look out of place, for so long have we been used to seeing them adorning old gardens and parks. They bring the dark winter-green of warm climates without the upsetting outline of a conical conifer.

From the portico is a splendid prospect of mown grass, distant water and great trees. The bulk of the planting dates from the last hundred years or so and, as at Kew, the soil is gravelly and has a high water table, two factors that foster good growth. An equally splendid prospect is from the steps of the west front; here we see a Golden Cedar, a Copper Beech, a Montpelier Maple and many natives in all shades of green.

By the Adam Garden House stand two paulownias; in a gentle spring these will astonish by their erect trusses of lilac-coloured tubular flowers, and later by their large rounded leaves. Tall Common Limes – easily distinguished from other limes by the masses of adventitious shoots which arise from great carbuncles of bark towards ground level – and other trees lead us to what might be described as an American garden, a mere shadow of its former self, but containing more cedars, *Pinus cembra* and *Abies concolor*, and some groups of rhododendrons and Japanese Maples. Partly screened by a catalpa, the Doric Temple then comes into view.

Beyond the extensive greensward which stretches away from the west front, is a narrow wooded spinney terminating all views. A considerable time ago this was provided with a park fence and a long straight walk hedged with evergreens. Some fine specimens will be found, particularly of *Quercus frainetto (Q. conferta)*, the Hungarian Oak, so striking in its large leaves and also the upthrusting array of branches, all ascending at about 45°. One is 30 m (100 ft) high. Also there are the Algerian Oak, *Quercus canariensis*, together with the Red Oak, *Q. rubra*, and the Pin Oak, *Q. palustris*, both from the other side of the Atlantic, and splendid with their rich colouring in autumn. *Sorbus torminalis* and *Carya laciniosa* will also be found.

About half-way along the walk is an opening specially designed so that the distant west front of the house can be enjoyed; it is particularly good when standing in the shade of the trees to see it lit by the evening sun. Here are some *Juglans nigra*, the Black Walnut, and several Norwegian Maples. Farther along we meet the arm of the lake which extends to the cedar grove and car park, and here is a group of Flowering Ash trees. Just before the cedars are reached there is a distinguished southerner, the Cork Oak, a venerable, luxuriant, rather weeping specimen. Several *Taxodium distichum*, Swamp Cypress, contrast with the Lombardy Poplars by the water. Though there are many good Oriental Planes, the tallest is its hybrid, the London Plane, an inspiration in tree architecture in the winter.

The whole of the landscape is flat, but the height of the trees and the wide spaces between them relieve the flatness, to give this great building, so noble and so square, a fitting setting.

OXBURGH HALL
Swaffham, *Norfolk*

Given in 1952 by the Dowager Lady Bedingfeld, with help from the Dulverton and Pilgrim Trusts

AREA 7.5 ha (18½ acres)
SOIL Limy
ALTITUDE 30 m (100 ft)
RAINFALL 635 mm (25 in.)
TEMPERATURE 3.5°C (38°F)

7 miles south-west of Swaffham, on south side of Stoke Ferry road

THERE IS a very special chapter in garden history to be enjoyed at Oxburgh. I had been told that there was "an 80-ft medieval tower, a moated house, and some flower-beds on the lawn". Judge of my surprise to find some 10 acres of lawns, moat, flower-beds and borders, all tended by one expert man; the "flower-beds" proved to be arranged in an intricate parterre on the lawn; there were even some traces of coal and cement used as colour-facing for some of the beds instead of plants. I was interested to learn from the Dowager Lady Bedingfeld that this extensive parterre had been copied from a French example about 1845 by Sir Henry Paston-Bedingfeld, the 6th Baronet, and his wife Margaret Paston (see illus. 13). This was while the dwelling was receiving its Gothick character and it is an interesting piece of history that the garden, perhaps unwittingly, was being given a similar touch.

In recent years the pattern has been made more decisive; fresh gravel has been laid, the gaps in the box edges have been filled, the small grass plats have been squared. Since all the thousands of plants needed annually were raised in the one little greenhouse, we filled certain of the beds with silvery Cotton Lavender, and others with Blue Rue. This eased the annual production of plants considerably.

Some years later on browsing through *The Garden* by Judith S. Berrall, I came across this same design, though the plan at Oxburgh has become slightly blurred in some respects. The design was first published by John James in 1712, in his translation of A. J. Dezallier d'Argenville's *La Théorie et la Pratique du Jardinage*; it was described as a *Parterre de Compartiment*. And so we have a French formal garden of unusual interest being copied over a hundred years later in England; moreover, this design, withstanding the Victorian age of in-and-out bedding, has survived untouched for one hundred and thirty years more; surely a remarkable achievement.

Whether seen from the raised terrace walk which runs along the whole length of the garden to the north of the house, or from the top of the 80-foot tower, it leaves an indelible impression. So far as I am aware there is no such scheme extant anywhere else in these islands.

Beyond the parterre is a yew-hedged walk, with a long herbaceous border against the wall. Here grow many treasured plants including *Hemerocallis flava*, the sweet-scented earliest-flowering Day Lily from Southern Europe, poppies and lupins, delphiniums and campanulas, all united by an edging of Catmint. On the wall behind are escallonias, honeysuckles, clematises and roses; among the latter is 'Alister Stella Gray', the perfect buttonhole rose, a yolk-yellow Noisette. Beyond is a shrub border containing a Judas Tree, *Acer griseum*, and standard pink *Wistaria floribunda*, fronted with irises and Japanese anemones, leading to a large copper beech. The walled kitchen garden has recently been given a formal pattern of mulberries, quinces and medlars, and climbing plants; it is contained by the Gothick-style brick walls, also mid 19th-century.

Oxburgh is a windy place. Trees have been planted to help its appearance, and to give it shelter, in the future. A great house without trees is a poor thing and the old oaks and beeches are thinning but replacements are immediately provided when one falls. The Wilderness, an area so-called beyond the Chapel, has recently been cleared and an interesting array of box hedges and walls to an embrasure have been revealed.

PACKWOOD HOUSE
Hockley Heath, *Warwickshire*

Given in 1941 by Mr G. Baron Ash. Three acres to the east given in 1943 by Col. J. L. Mellor

AREA 2 ha (5 acres)
SOIL Limy
ALTITUDE 75 m (250 ft)
RAINFALL 686 mm (27 in.)
TEMPERATURE 4°C (39°F)

14 miles north of Stratford-upon-Avon, 1 mile east of Hockley Heath, off the A34

BEFORE THE DEVELOPMENT of hardy efficient lawn mowers, grass was kept smooth by the skilful use of the scythe, a laborious process for large areas, and difficult in places where a good swing of the scythe could not be achieved. As a consequence topiary work was often surrounded by gravel in parterres and the like. This made an excellent colour contrast to the dark green of the topiary stands; on green grass, as at Packwood, the contrast is not so satisfying. There is a space of a few weeks in early summer, however, when the young yew twigs break into fresh bronze leaf and that is a glorious moment to visit Packwood. Soon after the clipped shrubs begin to look shaggy until they have been clipped which is usually in August or early September.

110 A view from the north east of the box hedges around the spiral walk to the mount, crowned with a tall conical yew, at Packwood, dating from the mid-18th century or earlier. Photo 1966.

111 A corner at Packwood where brick, tile, wood and iron, plants and lawn contribute to an intriguing whole. The vine is trained around two circular windows in the 200-year-old building.

Thereafter, until the following summer, they provide a very dark green tint. If, therefore, you can catch that June moment at Packwood when the lawns are bright green and the yews bronzy, you will gain a lasting impression; but if you go later the majesty of these trees will stand out in your memory. They are all of a tapering conical shape, some as much as 6 m (20 ft) high.

For so long has the legend of the yews having been planted at Packwood during the Commonwealth been offered to us – and that the planting represents the Sermon on the Mount and the Multitude around – that it will come as something of a shock to find that much of it is untrue. The earliest reference I have found about the legend is in no less a book than Sir Reginald Blomfield's *The Formal Garden in England*, 1901, though he admits he was given the story by the gardener. And all the time proof to the contrary was in records in the house. The true historical sequence goes something as follows.

The house dating from Elizabethan times was altered in the 17th century by John Fetherston.

Originally the garden on the west side was known as the Fountain Court, since it contained the strange little sunken feature known as the Roman Bath; I should think twice before dipping into its waters unwarmed by the sun. This is shown as existing in 1723. The area was surrounded by hedges and was used as a drying ground. By 1756 the garden to the south – the principal part today – had been further developed, with the gazebos, the raised walk or terrace, the gate and also the bee-boles in the south side of the terrace wall. It is clear also that at this date the present arrangement of yews had not materialised though the highest terrace and the Mount were there, with a line of yews which has for long been known as the Apostles. The main planting of yews did not occur until after 1850, when they were put in as small topiary specimens to surround the newly-planted orchard, the original 18th-century orchard having died of old age.

The donor of the property, Mr Baron Ash, tidied up the Yew Garden by removing the fruit trees but left the surrounding box hedge; he also altered the house, laid out the garden area to the north of the house, and created the sunk garden. By a curious chance, long before I had ever visited Packwood, but knew of it by repute, Mr Ash had ordered the yews from the nursery of which I was then manager.

The little flight of iron steps by the north-west gazebo is a beautiful example of 18th-century iron work, though the gazebo was reconstructed by Mr Ash; he also inserted the gates on the west side of the walled garden.

In the 17th century Packwood was well supplied with avenues and some of the trees remain. More interesting is the presence of the kitchen garden, surrounded by walls, on the far side of the road, where it was as long ago as 1723.

But I have said nothing about the flowers and shrubs at Packwood. The tradition for some twenty-five years or more is for massed colour where it can be accommodated: that is to say, in a herbaceous border along a south facing wall, in two lines flanking the path on the terrace walk and in the sunk garden. Colour schemes are changed annually and a continuous effect is skilfully maintained from spring to autumn by means of small groups of each kind of plant, rather than large groups which create such a gap after flowering. To be able to stand on the terrace – or raised walk – looking along bands of colour to the garden house opposite, and down into the sunk garden or through the immense clipped yews is to savour a type of garden and gardening that cannot be found elsewhere. No doubt the raised walk was originally constructed partly because of the advantage it gave on looking down into the walled garden where garden knots might have been. We have no knots at Packwood today but there is much satisfaction to be gained from the ancient brickwork, the velvety darkness of the yews, and the brilliant-coloured flowers. While today there are several attractive shrubs and roses trained on the walls, in earlier centuries they would have been covered with fruit trees; indeed some 18th-century walls have flues or pipes in them for the provision of additional warmth.

112 Bee Boles in the 18th-century garden wall at Packwood House.

113 The "Roman Bath" at Packwood House.

The yews at Packwood, like many others in the Trust's care, were infested with scale insects. They are now clean, but the cause of continual worry. In the first place they are on heavy clay soil, which is never chosen by yews in nature; and you and I and all the multitudes of visitors compact the soil so that roots become starved of air and nutriments. Some yews have died as a result, but the Trust has drained and aerated the ground. For many years we have kept strong young specimens in the kitchen garden ready to replace those that occasionally fail.

PECKOVER HOUSE
Wisbech, *Cambridgeshire*

Given in 1943 by the Hon. Alexandrina Peckover, whose family had owned the house since the second half of the 18th century

AREA 0.9 ha ($2\frac{1}{4}$ acres)
SOIL Lime-free
ALTITUDE 30 m (100 ft)
RAINFALL 533 mm (21 in.)
TEMPERATURE 3.5°C (38°F)

In North Brink by the river Nene

I USED TO THINK of this part of England as flat, bleak and windswept, but given the rich alluvial soil, you only have to grow a few dozen trees, and the shelter they afford makes an ideal microclimate for a garden. There is usually ample sunshine and enough rain. The trees around Peckover House have made gardening fairly easy, and for a hundred years or so the garden has been, as one writer put it, "the product of prudent tidiness, a period piece, and for that reason, particularly worthy of a close look. It is a memorial to the nineteenth century; formal, immaculate, full of carefully spaced trees and tidy curving paths." In 1898 Frederic John Gardiner, writing in *The History of Wisbech*, gave his impression of the garden at Bank House as it was then called: "It contains some curious trees, among them the Maidenhair Tree, one of the largest in England, planted by Mr Peckover's grandfather about 100 years ago, and hardy palms which flower every year, one being about 15 ft in height. In the orange house is a tree bearing sweet oranges, purchased at the famous sale at Hagbeach Hall, and at least 200 years old."

Whenever you go, you are likely to see oranges ripening on the old plants in the Conservatory, though I should warn you they are far too bitter to eat! With them are growing numerous exotic plants and flowers, fuchsias, begonias, *Billbergia*, *Datura*, *Monstera* and others, while round the corner is a small house given to tender ferns. All the flowers and plants for the house and for bedding the front garden borders are raised in the garden, and this is one of the many ways in which the house and garden at Peckover unite in such an entity; two summerhouses contribute to this feeling of people living here and enjoying the place to the full.

Several sizeable trees are to be found, all contributing not only their quota of height and shelter, but also the Victorian taste: a fine large Maidenhair Tree, a Fern-leafed Beech, Tulip Tree – in a poor state – variegated hollies, a hardy palm, a Wellingtonia, Lawson's Cypresses, a yucca and spotted-leafed aucubas. An intimidating assortment perhaps to start with.

But, divided as the garden is with walls, and plentiful paths lined with flower borders, every opportunity has been taken over the years to provide flowers for all seasons, from bulbs, herbaceous plants, shrubs and climbers. These may be looked upon as the 20th-century contribution to this garden, the detail of the picture within the framework. One border which used to be filled with herbaceous plants has been given a novel idea: an imitation of Victorian carpet-bedding done with compact dwarf perennial plants. Another border is mainly for autumn, where hardy fuchsias and Japanese anemones thrive, with *Kirengeshoma palmata* and the Willow Gentian not far away, for company.

114 The white-painted Victorian summerhouse at Peckover House, with green design.

Two matching borders, edged with pinks, flank the walk from the conservatory to an elegant painted summerhouse. These borders used to be nursery beds, but we found some delicate metal pillars laid away in a rubbish corner; these were duly erected to line the walk and they serve as points from which hedges of flowering shrubs divide the borders into compartments, each filled with a different mixture of plants. From the earliest flowers of the perennial Honesty, doronicums, euphorbias and Day Lilies; through Hyssop, white roses, *Perovskia* and *Caryopteris*; through *Agapanthus* and Michaelmas Daisies of the star-flowered kinds, there is always something in flower. And everywhere on the walls are honeysuckles, clematises and roses; roses old and new. In a ferny corner is the other summerhouse, a rustic one, overshadowed by a Holm Oak; it was restored in 1970–1. The little pool with waterlilies in front of the other painted summerhouse was brought from the main lawn in 1957.

Peckover's garden is a flowery paradise, and still has the intimate charm of a garden tended with "prudent tidiness", and a "close look" will reveal many an unexpected treasure.

PENRHYN CASTLE
Bangor, *Gwynedd*

Given in 1951 by the Treasury which had accepted it in lieu of death duties, after the death of the 4th Baron Penrhyn.

AREA 19 ha (47 acres)
SOIL Lime-free
ALTITUDE 45 m (150 ft)
RAINFALL 1143 mm (45 in.)
TEMPERATURE 5.5°C (42°F)

1 mile east of Bangor
between A5 and the coast

"There is no garden at Penrhyn Castle." This had often been said to me, partly in ignorance, partly because the actual ornamental garden is small in comparison with the size of the property and castle.

For years I had seen from the A5 what looked like the turrets of a toy castle rising from the rounded tops of trees in the beautiful countryside approaching Bangor, with the sea in the distance. You enter the long drive under the forbidding gateway, passing a grove of Redwoods, the church tower, several large conifers, Red Oaks and clumps of rhododendron. The Trust only owns the drive and a few feet of verge on either side; the woodlands are still owned by the donor's family. Suddenly, on rounding a corner, there is the stupendous keep of the castle, standing on a knoll. It is obvious this is no "toy castle"; it was built in about 1830, in Norman style, and from whichever side it is seen it is nothing but majestic. This first view has been given a group of Austrian Pine for the future; no other pine gives that dark tint of green coupled with a picturesque habit and it is hoped that they will enhance the building with true Claudian gloom. If you are fortunate in the weather and there are some dark violet clouds about and dazzling sunshine on the castle, the stone – Mona Marble, pale grey, from Anglesey – will appear almost white.

The next view along the drive is also of the keep, but this time it has for contrast Copper Beeches. From here onwards the planting becomes richer from early daffodils, white Pheasant Eye Narcissus and bluebells, to Meadowsweet in July. And then the south front appears, above its rising foreground of rhododendrons and fuchsias; approaching the entrance are particularly fine Japanese Maples and a *Paulownia*. The view across Beaumaris Bay embraces Anglesey and Snowdonia. Everywhere great beeches and oaks abound with a sprinkling of conifers, in fact many specimens were planted during visits of different members of the Royal Family, from 1859 when Queen Victoria and Prince Albert paid a visit and planted a Turkey Oak and a Wellingtonia. The views through the trees, all quite dwarfed by the impressive castle, are varied and expansive; a favourite moment to go is at bluebell time when the trees are pale green or raw sienna, or again in autumn.

There is quite a lot to be seen in the grounds around the castle. Away to the north is the Gothic Chapel which in itself adds to the study of garden history. Built originally near to the 14th-century manor house, it was moved to the present position during the 18th century. Since the present castle has a chapel of its own it eventually became redundant, but was retained for the sake of its picturesque character. It has therefore spent a hundred and fifty years of its life serving as a "folly" or "eye-catcher", in the true tradition of landscape gardening.

All around the northern slopes of the eminence on which the castle stands are good trees and shrubs: a Wellingtonia, Nootka Cypress, Sweet Gum, a large grouping of winter-flowering heaths and Tree Heaths, as well as *Eucalyptus gunnii* from Tasmania, *Griselinia* from New Zealand and Strawberry Trees. If you take the gravel walk to the camellia bank you will arrive at the gate to the walled garden.

This is always a surprise to people. Inside there is complete contrast to what we have already seen. We must try to imagine the setting to appreciate all that has been done here, inside the walls, since they were built about 1840. It was a formal terraced garden well protected by woodland. Containers were built behind the wall in several places so that young trees could hang

115 By the steps in the flower garden at Penrhyn Castle a leaden peacock poses for the camera beside pink hydrangeas.

over the wall. The microclimate was very mild, in fact no other place could have provided a more sheltered setting for the numerous schemes of bedding and subtropical bedding that was so popular then. A long straight path ran from end to end of the upper terrace, decorated with lozenge-shaped beds enclosed by gravel and clipped box in parterre fashion (see *Garden Ornament* by Gertrude Jekyll, 1918). The central semi-circular promontory had radial beds and a metal pergola, with chains hung with rambler roses. Lady Penrhyn altered this after 1928 to the present scheme, built the loggia and added the pools and fountains. From this time onwards most of the trees and shrubs were planted.

On a visit in 1967 I was shown a heap of old iron arches outside the wall, which the head gardener told me used to flank the central walk from the promontory, covered with fuchsias. Since this walk is lined so beautifully with *Eucryphia glutinosa* whose white flowers appear in August, we decided to use the arches along the lower walk; they are now covered with honeysuckles.

This west-facing garden with its sheltering walls provides congenial homes for a number of tender shrubs. For instance, one would not expect to find the fragrant yellow broom which is sold by florists at Easter growing outdoors; but here is a large plant smothered with bloom every year. With it grow *Jasminum polyanthum*, so sweetly scented and always in flower, *J. primulinum*, *Camellia reticulata* 'Captain Rawes', *Berchemia racemosa* and *Smilax aspera*; *Rhododendron* 'Lady Alice Fitzwilliam' sheds its delicious fragrance in early summer.

The garden lost its bowl-like effect as well as its shelter after the surrounding woodland had been felled but this is slowly maturing again. The ancient, gaunt Maritime Pine gives the area an air of distinction.

Approaching it in height is *Eucryphia cordifolia* from Chile; in fact August is a lovely time to visit the garden when all the eucryphias flower. Dotted about are many other fine trees and shrubs: *Kalmia latifolia*, *Cornus kousa*, *Crinodendron Hookeranum* or Chilean Lantern bush; *Drimys winteri* (Winter's Bark, an antidote to scurvy), *Styrax obassia*; there is also a large *Magnolia tripetala* 9.1 m by 9.1 m (30 ft by 30 ft); *M. stellata* over 5.4 m (18 ft) high and nearly as much through, and a good *Sophora japonica*, which resembles a laburnum with white flowers in August. Here and there are fuchsias and hydrangeas, azaleas and ferns. Charles Maries, after having seen many hydrangeas in the Far East, expressed surprise at the brilliant blue colouring of them here. Altogether this is a remarkable planting, much rare beauty concentrated into a small area, which is threaded by a pattern of paths.

Below this sloping garden is the honeysuckle pergola, and below again what at one time was a stream garden, created by Lady Penrhyn also in the early 1930s, and at that time highly decorative with spring bulbs, primulas, astilbes, hostas, Japanese maples and the like, together with *Gunnera manicata* and bamboos. Unhappily this garden was abandoned during the 1939-45 war, and, also unhappily, most of the bamboos put in were *Arundinaria anceps*, one of the most graceful but of an abounding, colonising vigour, so that the whole area was covered with it by 1960. Ten years later it had been dug out by the one and only gardener, and the gunneras and maples once more became the star performers. And the surprise was that along the marshy stream site *Primula japonica* germinated from dormant seed and flowered freely the following year. The big ornamental grass is *Cortaderia richardii*, a New Zealand relative of the South American Pampas Grass.

Once again this pretty Victorian effort at gardening with its subsequent adjustments has come into its own. Spring and summer bedding flowers annually decorate the box-edged beds on the gravel terrace, and roses and catmint add their quota of blossom. In the old days, when a large staff of gardeners was kept, all the beds would have been planted with every exotic plant imaginable for summer display, grown in the large kitchen garden some distance away.

Penrhyn was one of the most noted gardens where young men received training before moving on to more responsible posts elsewhere. One John Elias Jones returned in the 1960s as head gardener, after having received his training here. The hours were from 6.00 a.m. to 6.00 p.m., with a rota for fire stoking, locking up and other duties outside these hours, and all attention necessary was given to the flowers and plants for the castle before Lord and Lady Penrhyn came down to breakfast. From what he has told me the garden was excellently run and everyone was happy. Produce for the family included every fruit and vegetable and flower that could be grown either out of doors or under glass. Entry after entry in *The Gardeners' Chronicle* during the 1870s stresses this, recording *Lapageria rosea* with 200 flowers out at one time, and *Platycerium alcicorne* growing naturally on the local mountains, having been transplanted as an experiment from the greenhouses. *Euonymus radicans* 'Variegata' on a wall was spectacular when threaded by the scarlet Scotch Flame Flower; *Fuchsia* 'Riccartonii' was 3.6 m (12 ft) high; *Metrosideros florida* and *Caesalpinia japonica* thrived at Penrhyn. There is no reason why they should not do so again.

PETWORTH HOUSE
Petworth, *West Sussex*

Given with an endowment by the 3rd Lord Leconfield in 1947

AREA 4 ha (10 acres)
SOIL Lime-free
ALTITUDE 60.9 m (200 ft)
RAINFALL 635 mm (25 in.)
TEMPERATURE 4.5°C (40°F)

In Petworth, 5½ miles east of Midhurst, at junction of A272 and A283

TO THOSE OF US who spend more time in appreciation of the outside of great houses, and in particular their setting, three impressions of Petworth compete in our affections. There is the majestic west front of soft grey stone, 97.5 m (320 ft) long, rising directly from a vast greensward; there is the opposite view – one of Capability Brown's finest parkland views – complete with serpentine lake, tree clumps and undulating landscape; and there are the Pleasure Grounds with trees of great size, both native and exotic, and shrubs both rare and common. That is as we find it today. Turner was inspired to commit the landscape, immortally, to canvas in the 1830s. Not one of the least excitements for us is to compare these views with their reality today. But there is more at Petworth than at first meets the eye.

If you stand on the knoll just north-west of the west front, you may detect depressions in this noble greensward, marking out the 18th-century walled court and also similar depressions on the slopes of the knoll which denote the lines of terraces or ramparts. The knoll has on one side of it a splendid urn, and on the north-east side a Spanish Chestnut of great size; its bole measures 9.5 m (31¼ ft) at about 1.2 m (4 ft) from ground level.

On arrival at Petworth you will enter the garden via the east court, wherein are good magnolias, camellias, and roses – 'Paul's Lemon Pillar' has ascended to about 4.5 m (15 ft) – and pass under two Pyramid Hornbeams, to reach a flat lawn. Here are old sycamores and other trees, also two young trees of the Large-leafed Beech, with the Hop Hornbeam on the side border. Though they look very old these sycamores are post-Brown,

116 A modern photograph of one of Capability Brown's masterpieces – the park at Petworth – now considered as a possible site for a by-pass. Photo 1975.

since originally there was – as early as 1610 – a formal area here, with straight paths, running into what are the present Pleasure Grounds as far as the point where the Doric Temple now stands. It is thought that George London at the end of the 17th century adapted a much earlier formal layout and carried a straight walk through the area as far as the site of the later Ionic Rotunda. All traces of these formal lines have vanished; it is tempting to try to attribute some of the old Sweet Chestnuts to the earlier planting, but not more than two trees are in line anywhere. The straight walks gave way, under Brown's direction, to the boldly curving gravel walks of today.

As at KILLERTON, the Pleasure Grounds (which are the principal horticultural delight for visitors, since the remainder of the garden lawns and Walled Garden are private) form a complete contrast to the predominantly limy countryside. Sandstone occurs locally, and seams can be seen in the tunnel which creates an access from the estate yard to the park. The slope is mainly to the north-east; centuries of fallen leaves have enriched the soil, and the cool and shade make ideal conditions for numerous shrubs. Just around the Doric Temple, for instance, will be found *Parrotia persica*, *Acer negundo*, *Fagus englerana*, *Prunus serrula tibetica*, *Magnolia tripetala*, and *Stewartia pseudo-camellia*, *Cornus kousa* and *C. nuttallii*; the grassy slopes are first scattered with daffodils and primroses, succeeded by bluebells, and later by blue from Bugle, Speedwell and Ground Ivy.

Many of the walks are lined with rhododendrons, species in considerable range, including *R. bureavii* and *R. campylocarpum*, *R. arboreum*, *R. decorum*, *R. schlippenbachii*, with hybrids like 'Loderi', 'Pink Pearl' and others. One of the last to flower is a form of *R. ponticum*, with mauve flowers and white variegated leaves.

During the summer, when few woodland shrubs flower, one is not distracted by blossom and low growths and can wander with eyes aloft, marvelling at the height of the trees. Many natives must exceed 30 m (100 ft) and there are tall firs – the Oriental Spruce and the Noble Fir for instance – and a Lebanon Cedar which at 40 m (132 ft) is the tallest in the country. A Horse Chestnut shares this distinction and an Indian Bean Tree has grown to unusual height. Over and again you will find yourself staring up into the lofty canopy of foliage and gauging the height of the immense trunks of beech and other trees.

In October numerous Japanese Maples, both the wild species and the cultivated forms, turn scarlet, succeeded by many *Photinia villosa* and *Enkianthus perulatus*.

But at whatever time of year you make your visit you should look again at Brown's landscape before leaving. That master knew well the shifting lights that make a landscape a vibrant, living thing; a thing of moods both gay and sad, sharply outlined or soft, of green unrelieved or accentuated by bare trees and dark shadows. It is this landscape, a work of art comparable to any hanging in the house, together with the Pleasure Ground full of majestic trees, which the planners have thought fit to recommend for the making of a by-pass!

117 The Doric temple at Petworth House.

PLAS NEWYDD
Llanfairpwll, *Isle of Anglesey, Gwynedd*

Given in 1976 by the Marquess of Anglesey

AREA 12.4 ha (31 acres)	1 mile south-west of
SOIL Lime-free	Llanfairpwll and A5
ALTITUDE 30 m (100 ft)	on A4080
RAINFALL 889 mm (35 in.)	
TEMPERATURE 6°C (43°F)	

SPLENDID WESTWARD VIEWS along the shore of the Menai Straits, a landscape sculptured by Humphry Repton, a house re-shaped by James Wyatt and a stable block of mansion-like dignity – join all this to a garden planted specially for spring and early summer effect during the last sixty years by the Marquess of Anglesey and his father, and you have an impression or miniature portrait of the delights of this splendid property.

The garden by the house is mostly given to lawns, sloping down to the straits, protected by sycamores of considerable size, and Irish Yews. It is not far to the terraced formal garden which was created earlier in this century around and below the foundations of a conservatory. This little area is gay for many months of the year, partly from the close-clipped hedges of *Potentilla fruticosa* forms and coppery-purple *Berberis thunbergii* 'Atropurpurea'. There is a wide assortment of plants: *Clematis armandii* and *C. montana* 'Rubens', honeysuckles, *Rosa hugonis* and 'Canary Bird', 'Nevada', and the little miniature China rose 'Climbing Pompon de Paris'; also the August-flowering climber related to the hydrangeas, *Schizophragma intergrifolia*. One spring I remember the yellow roses made a lovely foil for a mass of blue Bugle. Several small bushes include *Daphne burkwoodii, D. retusa, Erica carnea* and *Picea abies* 'Gregoryana'. This recital of names does little to knit together an effective piece of planting enriched by several garden ornaments and a squad of Italian cypresses standing sentinel below it all.

Plas Newydd is a windy, sunny, mild place and the shrubs and trees are all compact and clean in the open here, many sun-lovers like *Genista hispanica, Iberis sempervirens, Cotoneaster conspicuus,* and *C. humifusa* clothing the banks to the west of the house. There is a neat hedge of *Corokia cotoneaster*, its tiny yellow starry flowers exhaling a delicious vanilla scent as you walk past.

From the house and its garden fronts it is but a short walk to the feast of spring beauty in the woodland glades known as the "West Indies". One wide expanse of sloping lawn boasts a very large group of *Magnolia soulangiana* 'Lennei'. There are azaleas everywhere. A grove of the primrose-yellow Japanese Cherry 'Ukon' has dark conifers as a background. There are Blue Spruces and Blue Cedars, the coppery-barked birch *Betula albo-sinensis septentrionalis*, tall magnolias of several kinds, *Styrax japonica* and *S. hemsleyana* for later interest until the eucryphias start flowering with the hydrangeas; before they have faded autumn arrives with brilliant tints from *Cercidiphyllum*, Japanese Maples, azaleas and Red Oaks.

In the next glade is a tremendous sweep – almost a hedge – of *Viburnum plicatum* 'Mariesii', whose spreading tabular branches are clothed with vast numbers of white flowers in June; the bushes also contribute to the autumn colour display. This sloping lawn with the viburnums all around is an example of the success of bold planting in a large area. Beyond is something else that is unique, so far as I am aware – an avenue of *Chamaecyparis pisifera* 'Squarrosa', a feathery blue-grey conifer with rich brown stems; this avenue slopes abruptly down to the water.

On the way back you can divert to a little knoll where a seat built round the huge bole of an old oak gives a view into a deep dell, filled with camellias and *Osmanthus delavayi*. Nearby is *Schima argentea* and some stewartias. Later there is an iron seat with vine leaves round a Tulip Tree, and we come back to the group of *Magnolia soulangiana* 'Lennei', the sculptured globes of deep lilac-pink offset by the grey lichen on the stems and the seemingly endless carpet of primroses and daffodils, followed by bluebells.

The mild climate is conducive to good growth particularly of rhododendrons, wherever there is shelter from trees. For this reason another clearing was carved out of old woodland of Repton's planting, some distance from the house, in a north-easterly direction following the straits; it is known as Lady Uxbridge's Walk. It is a sheltered place where early flowering species such as *Rhododendron praevernum, R. thomsonii, R. fortunei* and *R. shilsonii* have made very large bushes. There is a magnificent specimen of *R. mollyanum*. Since the last war this area has been extended, and enriched by many a gift from Bodnant. Many of the scented rhododendrons, such as 'Fragrantissimum', 'Lady Alice Fitzwilliam', with *R. crassum* and 'Polar Bear' are planted keeping up the display from spring to late summer. I was fortunate to find the peerless *R. soulei* in

118 The seat with views in all directions at Plas Newydd.

fine form. This area is a mecca for the rhododendrologist, but whether of this category or not, the visitor is likely to return again and again to Anglesey to enjoy its peace and beauty, knowing perfectly well that if the eye tires of plants there are always the expansive views of Snowdonia to be enjoyed.

PLAS-YN-RHIW
Pwllheli, *Gwynedd*

Given between 1950 and 1966 by the Misses Eileen, Lorna and Honora Keating

AREA 4 ha (1 acre)
SOIL Lime-free
ALTITUDE 30 m (100 ft)
RAINFALL 1000 mm ($39\frac{1}{2}$ in.)
TEMPERATURE 5.5°C (42°F)

On west shore of Porth Neigwl (Hell's Mouth Bay), 10 miles from Pwllheli on south coast road to Aberdaron

THE TRUST engenders enthusiasms of widely different character. There is a very special kind of enthusiasm at Plas-yn-Rhiw, where over a period of thirty-five years the Misses Keating pieced together by separate purchases an area of some 400 acres of superb coastline for the sole reason of preserving it from despoliation and giving it to the Trust. This in itself is a great achievement. They started with the old manor house, part Tudor and part Georgian, with its own firm foundation of reputedly Roman cement joining huge boulders together. From here you look out to the graceful curve of Hell's Mouth Bay – though the peace and utter quietness of this remote spot seems disturbed by this unfortunate name. As you walk round the garden your eyes keep catching glimpses of this beautiful shore line and even the spread of the Welsh mountains beyond.

The garden is small but full of treasures. Old plants of Sweet Bay, Cherry Laurel and trees break the main force of the winds, supplemented by newer hedges. The garden is in fact broken by hedges and old walls into a series of compartments, in one of which water from the spring gushes into an old trough. The planting of the garden owes its varied collection of plants chiefly to Miss Honora Keating and she made her choice well and wisely. Magnolias and camellias are represented by rare and beautiful species and hybrids, likewise rhododendrons. At every turn of the path something choice meets the eye: *Embothrium*, *Desfontainea*, *Eucryphia*, *Crinodendron*, *Daphne*, *Lapageria* or *Philesia*. In early summer *Pieris formosa forrestii* sheds its white bells, while the new leaves turn to scarlet; hydrangeas and fuchsias enliven the garden in summer and *Hypericum* 'Rowallane' is some 2.4 m (8 ft) high and wide, and was laden with bloom when I was last there.

From snowdrop time to autumn there is always something to see (by appointment only), a tribute to skill and a love for Wales and beautiful things.

POLESDEN LACEY
Dorking, *Surrey*

Acquired in 1944 with an endowment under the will of the Hon. Mrs Ronald Greville

AREA 12 ha (30 acres)
SOIL Limy, but overlaid in parts by lime-free soil
ALTITUDE 91 m (300 ft)
RAINFALL 762 mm (30 in.)
TEMPERATURE 4°C (30°F)

$1\frac{1}{2}$ miles south of Great Bookham, off the A246 Leatherhead–Guildford road

"SPACIOUS EDWARDIAN DAYS!" How often we have heard that phrase, sometimes applied inappropriately to houses and gardens. It is however especially applicable to Polesden Lacey, where for nearly forty years the Honourable Mrs Ronald Greville lived, adapting and adjusting the house and garden to give to both the luxurious touch that we enjoy today. From the gilded and mirrored drawing-room her influence extended to the farthest ends of the garden, east and west.

Having gradually mounted the long approach drive through an avenue of beech trees, on reaching the crest of the North Downs you suddenly drop down between high grass banks to the forecourt and sloping lawns – sloping down to a deep valley whence the eye is again carried up to the heights of RANMORE COMMON, also owned by the Trust. Thus this whole landscape is preserved as one entity.

The collonaded south front still annually receives its colourful bedding plants, and leads us along the terrace to the Ladies' Garden where lies Mrs Greville's tomb hedged with ancient yews. From here it is but a step to the rose garden (see illus. 7). In summer the walls are covered with 'Mermaid' rose and lavender-blue and purple clematises; the outer borders filled with early and late shrub roses; the paved paths edged with purple Hidcote lavender. The area is divided into four by paved paths, meeting at a marble well-head; the crossing paths are covered with a delicate wooden pergola. It is a particularly Edwardian touch to find these pergolas covered mainly with 'Dorothy Perkins' and 'American Pillar' roses, raised in 1901 and 1902 respectively, two of the most popular varieties ever to come out of the United States. They were taken to heart in this country before and after the First World War, and we like to retain this particularly Edwardian touch. With them are 'Excelsa' and 'François Juranville'. Because they rather quickly go out of flower, two ramblers of the same style, 'Crimson Shower' and 'Sanders' White', have been given to some of the uprights to prolong the display.

It is not a happy spot for a rose garden. The soil is shallow and about a foot down pure chalk was found. This was taken out to a depth of 457 mm (18 in.) and the beds were made up with good soil. Even so the life of

119 Started in 1761, the long walk at Polesden Lacey was enlarged by Richard Brinsley Sheridan at the end of the century. The columns were added in this century. Photo 1964.

the roses is not long and beds frequently have to be replanted. It is a large rose garden, containing about 2000 plants of about forty varieties, some of them old kinds like 'Ophelia', 'Home Sweet Home', 'Mrs John Laing' and 'Etoile de Hollande', but more modern ones such as 'Peace', 'Frensham' and 'Rose Gaujard' are included. The Rose Garden is bounded to the north by a greenhouse in front of which is a warm border for tender shrubs and agapanthus, and a water tower on which grows a very old wistaria.

Probably the walled gardens which are now filled with roses were originally the kitchen gardens. In the second section is a pair of small gardens, hedged with yews, one containing lavenders and the other irises. Dutch and English Lavender, also white and pink lavender and Hidcote varieties give off a lovely scent in July. The Iris Garden is a special gathering of kinds popular earlier in this century, before the tall, large Bearded Irises became so interbred and magnificent. There are the old 'Germanica' in lavender-blue and purple; 'Kochii' in royal purple, and *I. pallida dalmatica* in lavender. Also 'Lorelei', 'Prosper Laugier', 'Iris King', 'Gracchus', 'Aurea' and others. These make so many flower spikes, so close together, that it is difficult to see the foliage.

Early in the year, the velvety brown buds of *Parrotia persica* open to reveal crimson stamens. Four very large plants grow in a distant enclosure, covering 15 m by 15 m (50 ft by 50 ft) and they approach 12 m (40 ft) in height. Under them is an ever-growing assortment of winter-flowering shrubs, plants and bulbs – hellebores, sarcococcas, snowdrops, viburnums, mahonias among them. By the end of June the first autumn colour appears at the end of the long *Parrotia* branches; if one can catch this species at the right moment one can often see a remarkable effect when the inside leaves are bright yellow and those on the outer branches are orange-, red- and purplish-toned.

To the south of these gardens, all along the old wall, is a herbaceous border, 137 m (450 ft) long in four sections. Each section builds up to a firm group of colour around yellow achilleas and purple salvias, while at each end firmness is likewise given by yuccas and santolinas. There is a considerable collection of plants, all of them being chosen for their tolerance of hot limy soil and for their short self-reliant growth.

Across the grass a statue of Diana beckons us to the rock garden, built between the wars. It merges into a long bank of chalky soil where the Smoke Bush and *Perovskia* thrive, berberis and Willow-leafed Pear, and towards the main steps is a vast spread of *Juniperus media* 'Pfitzerana', a nice reminder, in its size – covering about 11 m by 11 m (36 ft by 36 ft) – to those who plant it in small gardens. Lilacs love chalky soil and when these are in flower below they blend happily with the pear, *Pyrus nivalis*, growing in the grass, whose silvery foliage is as bright as the willow-leafed species. A very good contrast of shrub growth is found here in all these spreading specimens, the broad leaves of *Viburnum rhytidophyllum* and the distant tall conifers and lime trees.

Throughout the garden are evidences of Mrs Greville's taste in ornaments, all of which she placed. There are griffins on the terrace, a Roman bath, sundials, vases, urns and statues at various vantage points in the long views from lawn to lawn, from grove to grove.

If we cross the wide sloping lawn in front of the house two slender stone columns will be seen to guard the entrance to a long grass walk, 425 m (480 yds) long, beautifully sheltered from the north by a long spinney of trees filled below with yews, box and hollies. This was begun in 1761, but was greatly enlarged by Richard Brinsley Sheridan after he acquired the property in 1796. It is certainly a lovely walk in cold weather. It is moreover an interesting survival of a formal feature existing and being enlarged at so late a date. It is also noteworthy in that the natural lie of the land was utilised, and not levelled; the effect is the more intriguing. Some twenty years ago the yew hedge on its outer side was 2.1 m (7 ft) high and 2.4 m (8 ft) through, but it was skilfully reduced to its present height in 1957, and thus the deep valley and wooded hills came into view. There is a delightful effect on the woodland side of the walk where St John's Wort is allowed to spread out into the grass by the yard in scallops and billows; at all seasons it rests the eye and its large yellow flowers in summer enliven the green carpet.

At the far end of the walk is a peristyle composed of the Doric columns which used to form part of the front of the house.

I have already called attention to the hungry limy soil in this garden. When the North Downs and the South Downs were united in a great dome of chalk over what was to become the Weald, a thin layer of lime-free soil got left behind, so to speak, and this is probably the reason why, round the entrance drive and car park, not only conifers thrive but also Sweet Chestnut and rhododendrons. We should expect to see yews thriving, but the plantation of conifers between the open-air theatre and the house provides an excellent guide as to what will succeed on chalky soil. There are good Redwoods, Lawson's Cypress, junipers and thujas, *Podocarpus andinus*, also *Pinus parviflora* and Atlantic cedars. Young Lebanon Cedars have been planted to replace one old tree that broke in gales.

POWIS CASTLE
Welshpool, *Powys*

Given in 1952, with an endowment, by the 4th Earl of Powis

AREA 9.7 ha (24 acres)
SOIL Lime-free except for the hill on which the castle stands
ALTITUDE 75 m (250 ft)
RAINFALL 762 mm (30 in.)
TEMPERATURE 4°C (39°F)

West of the A483 Welshpool–Newtown road

FROM A PLANT LOVER'S point of view the garden here is specially interesting because the castle and terraces are built on a sudden hill of pink limy rock while the rest of the garden and woodland is on lime-free soil. As a defensive position the hill was unrivalled, overlooking as it does a large area of countryside towards the Severn valley. The garden is also unrivalled in its soils, terrain, layers of history and vegetation.

We all wish we knew just when the terraces were designed and by whom. Miles Hadfield has suggested William Winde, who built the terrace at CLIVEDEN, but there is no proof. What is fairly evident is that they were designed by an Englishman somewhere between 1688 and 1722. Besides forming such an imposing line below the castle, the three terraces, about 152 m (500 ft) long, are as they were made, untouched apart from the addition of the portico to the orangery. This was moved here from the castle entrance early this century.

Powis Castle has a long recorded history; built by the Princes of Powis, it was inhabited by them until William III's reign when he gave the castle to his favourite, the Earl of Rochford. During his period of tenure the terraces were laid out; later when Lord Clive married into the Herbert family, again Earls of Powis, the leaden peacock on the Orangery Terrace was brought from CLAREMONT.

I had been travelling up to North Wales yearly for a long time before I first visited Powis. I had been told there was nothing there but oaks and clipped yews, but anyone who has walked from the forecourt with its leaden central figure of Fame to the top terrace can hardly fail to be impressed beyond anything the imagination could suggest. The castle stands on one arm of a U-shaped hill; to the right are the wooded slopes of the other arm, the "wilderness" of the garden. Below, steeply out of sight, are the terraces, and from them the eye can range afar to the dramatic line of the Breidden Hills and also to the gentle chequering of fields over the vast slope of the Long Mountain. In the spring the golden-green of oaks is contrasted by the emerald of the meadows; something of this colouring is repeated in the autumn. On a sunny day the prospect is breathtaking (see plate XL).

One would not expect the limy, rocky hill to give rise to prodigious growth in trees, but the rest of the estate does. Admiral Rodney specified oaks from Powis for his ships in the 18th century. The tallest Douglas Fir in the British Isles grows not far from the castle.

If the view from the terraces outwards is magnificent, that obtained from the wilderness back to the castle is unparalleled. The whole majesty of castle and terraces is before us, and one can only be thankful that this masterpiece of design was never swept away when such formality was out of favour, a fate which

120 Photographed from the air (1949), the remarkable terraced garden at Powis Castle, laid out about 1700. In the right foreground is the site of the old kitchen garden, outlined by the 80-year-old pyramid apple trees.

happened so often with formality on flatter terrain. By tradition, Capability Brown paid a visit and suggested that the terraces should be simply put back to the natural rock. In an engraving of 1742 by Samuel Beck the entire terraces are shewn together with the site of the present lawn in the valley laid out with formal pools. All the terraces and the pools were decorated with topiary in the engraving, but the Irish Yews on the terraces are a much later addition. Looking at the prospect today, it is difficult to imagine the 9.1 m (30 ft) high clipped yews above the top terrace were slim little cones about 1.8 m (6 ft) high, some two hundred and thirty years ago. There is a comment in *The Gardeners' Chronicle* for 1893 that the big yew towards the west had just been cut away to provide a spot for a rustic seat; it, or its counterpart, is still there, snugly ensconced.

The prospect has altered from time to time; for some reason one of the yews had been left unclipped until about twenty years ago and they were all less uniform than they are now. The statues in the niches were not added much before 1875. The Loggia or Aviary Terrace used to have, in 1874, slopes of grass at either end; when labour became more expensive after the last war these slopes were planted with St John's Wort and other dwarf shrubs. With the advent of mowers which will easily tackle slopes the grass has been reinstated. Likewise the orangery became debased into a store for tools and canes, but no sooner was the toolshed built by the Trust, out of sight to the west, than the orangery was restored, busts of the Caesars were brought from the house to decorate it and some evergreen plants were added. It is once again open for the public's enjoyment. The lowest slope was once all fruit trees, but during this century many exotic trees have been planted, particularly for autumn colour, and most of the old apples have gone. The walls are being rebuilt or repaired as necessary for they bulge with the weight of soil above. When one was taken down recently fireplaces were revealed at the base, with ashes still in them proving that they had been used for fruit culture, as at PACKWOOD HOUSE and TATTON PARK.

The terraces face south-east, and, owing to the sharp drainage and comparatively low rainfall, provide congenial homes against the old walls for a number of rare and tender shrubs. If you go there in early spring or autumn, the architecture, the leaden statues, layout and views will gain all your attention, but in the summer months you will be distracted by many plants. The actual pink rock on which the castle stands is exposed at either end of the top terrace, the one as a rock garden, and the other as a sheer escarpment, holding up a formal bowling green above. The second terrace with the loggia has a narrow border to the west with irises and cistuses and a beautiful white variety of *Wistaria floribunda* which looks entrancing against the pink brickwork. If you pass by the arches of the loggia in

121 'Striped Beefing', raised in 1794 at Lakenham, Norfolk, is one of the old Apple varieties preserved at Powis Castle. The trees are about 80 years old, trained into pyramids. 'Striped Beefing' fruits are recorded to weigh as much as $12\frac{1}{2}$ oz. each.

early summer, fragrance will reach you from inside where sweetly-scented tender rhododendrons have been planted in troughs of prepared soil.

The orangery, also sometimes called a conservatory, used to have ferns and oranges inside; the oranges would have been trundled outside to the standing-ground in front for the summer months. Until recently beds of fuchsias with a box edge decorated the front of the orangery, but a few years ago a return to quiet formality was approved, though there are no oranges. The wall of the orangery proves suitable for Rose "Gloire de Dijon", whose deep colouring is not bettered elsewhere; the double white and the double yellow forms of the Banksian rose flower freely, also the red, the orange and the yellow forms of *Eccremocarpus scaber*.

The borders of the Orangery Terrace and that below it are given mostly to herbaceous perennials, with shrubs on the walls. Every now and again is a metal hoop covered with purple clematis; in 1879 these were called the "Jackmanii balloons". On the walls will be found *Hydrangea heteromalla*, *H. anomala*, *Jasminum fruticans*, *Viburnum macrocephalum*, *Punica granatum*, the Pomegranate (a double red form), *Indigofera gerardiana*, *Buddleia alternifolia*, *Schizandra grandiflora rubriflora*, together with magnolias, ceanothuses, roses, clematises and escallonias. *Arauja sericofera* grew for many years and has been replaced recently. This, the "Cruel Plant", is so called because night-flying moths are entrapped by the flowers until daylight, thus effecting pollination.

The whole of the orangery borders are edged with a foot-high hedge of box. Therefore when replanting these we were unable to use the many customary low plants, nor did we wish to plant things which need a deal of staking. The medium-height plants chosen are graded in cool colours at the west end but the tints change to vivid tones after the slight curve in the path. Besides a general selection of floriferous and popular plants, a number of less-known species have been included such as *Selinum tenuifolium*, *Veratrum nigrum*, *Adenophora tashiroi*, *Marrubium candidissimum*, *Crambe koktaibelica*, *Centaurea atropurpurea* and *C. salonitana*, *Agastache anisata*, *Nepeta sibirica* and *N. govaniana*, *Eremurus* species, *Aconitum napellus* 'Carneum', *Thermopsis lanceolata*, *Lepachis pinnata* and *Galega orientalis*. They are interspersed with various bulbous plants and a few shrubs, particularly some huge old plants of *Rosa moyesii* and its relatives which are so vivid in flower and later when in fruit.

The walk from the orangery disappears into a high buttress of clipped yew and thence turns left into a curving walk with an exceptionally high box hedge, or straight down the steps to the lower garden. But I must first hope that you will go to Powis in spring when at the other end of the walk stand several 'Brilliantissimum' maples, whose shrimp-pink young foliage makes a unique contrast for the lavender-blue *Rhododendron augustinii*, and later, as the foliage fades to pale yellow-green, with the purple of *R. pseudoianthinum*.

Towards this end of the terrace a stairway leads up to the rock garden; the rocky outcrop is a home for various small plants, particularly *Erigeron mucronatus*, a pinky-white daisy which seeds itself everywhere.

While it is probable that the pools shown in the engraving of 1742 were never made, there are some depressions west of the great lawn indicative of another water garden. All around is marshy meadow, thick with native flowers in spring, including the Mourning Widow, *Geranium phaeum*. From the ends of the terraces the walks all gather into one by the pond and thence into different levels of the Wilderness. On a specially cold dank bank is situated the Ladies' Bath, surrounded by ferns and rocks while over every sloping bank are rhododendrons, overtopped by the oaks for which Powis is so noted, conifers planted during the last hundred years or so, and a sprinkling of exotic trees – davidias, Tulip Tree, *Acer carpinifolius*, *Populus lasiocarpa*, *Koelreuteria paniculata*, *Ilex glabra* and *I. yunnanensis*, *Magnolia campbellii* and *M.c. mollicomata*, *Nothofagus obliqua*, with two magnificent Redwoods and *Tsuga mertensiana*. Bluebells drift into azaleas, contrasted by the great oak trunks; rhododendrons flower from early spring with *R. sutchuenense*, *R. barbatum*, and *R. cinnabarinum*, to mid-season when the yellow bells of *R. concatenans* are so conspicuous; *R. discolor* and *R. decorum*, and many more continue until *R. auriculatum* closes the season.

Following down the slope you come to the end of the lawn and the yew alley; the neat hedges carry on ever upwards almost to the castle. Below is the old kitchen garden, surrounded by thick castellated yew hedges; its walks are lined with superb old pyramid apples about eighty years old. There are borders of phloxes, delphiniums and roses, and a series of arches with vines growing on them bestride the lawn. The story goes that here is the site of the original grape houses, marked by arches, one of which is covered with *Vitis coignetiae* whose autumn leaves of brilliant red make a wonderful foreground to the slopes and terraces of the castle, so supremely well placed above, guarded by the clipped yews in their faded dark velvet tints. It was confident of withstanding the foe in old days and is equally confident of enthralling visitors today.

ROWALLANE
Saintfield, *Co. Down*

Given and endowed by the Ulster Land Fund in 1955

AREA 20 ha (50 acres)	11 miles south-east of
SOIL Lime-free	Belfast, 1 mile south
ALTITUDE 60.9 m (200 ft)	of Saintfield on
RAINFALL 889 mm (35 in.)	west of A7
TEMPERATURE 5.5°C (42°F)	

THE COUNTRYSIDE at Saintfield is composed of small hills patterned with hedged fields and small groups of trees. Though not at great altitude, it is open and windswept. But this is not the impression one gets when one goes up the splendid drive under great beeches, Scots Pine, Wellingtonias and huge rhododendrons. Immense outcrops of whinstone rock, smoothed by glaciers long ago, occur here and there (see plate XXXV) and suddenly conical piles of giant's marbles appear. These were erected by the Reverend John Moore over a hundred years ago.

After his death in 1903, his nephew Hugh Armytage Moore came to live here and for fifty years, by dint of his enthusiasm, growing knowledge and tasteful planting, continued to develop the 50 acres of garden. His was a rare touch – an unlimited enthusiasm for the choice and beautiful among trees and shrubs, tempered by an eye for good placing. He of all men sought to choose a plant for a place rather than finding a place for a plant, as if, in Francis Bacon's words, "gardening were the greater perfection" than building finely. He described himself as a selector, not a collector. Just before his death the government of Northern Ireland purchased Rowallane and gave it to the National Trust. Owing to the war years the garden had become rather run-down, but has been nursed back to its full health by the Trust, largely through the efforts of Lady O'Neill of the Maine, and two devoted head gardeners, father and son, and the collection of plants has greatly increased.

The most characterful area of Rowallane is the splendid panorama which greets us just inside the gates of the Spring Garden. A foretaste of what is to come can be seen by the house where some old Deodar cedars and two large groups of rhododendrons lie comfortably over the contours of the grassy slopes. But the same effect is doubled in the Spring Garden. Let those who disparage rhododendrons for their short flowering

122 The Yunnan form of the Giant Lily (*Cardiocrinum giganteum yunnanense*) in the Walled Garden at Rowallane in 1937. Descendants of the same bulbs still grow there.

season hold their peace until they have visited Rowallane from early April to late June! For here are landscape clumps of species and hybrids of every sort, small and large, early and late; with a little segregation of types apparent, they may be described as mixed plantings. Not the haphazard 'Cynthia', 'Pink Pearl' and yellow azalea of many a lesser garden, but the deliberate mixing of like sorts to create what was I believe Mr Moore's deliberate desire: to echo the subtle yet infinite variation of tint and form that one finds in the hawthorn or Pontic rhododendrons in our great parks and gardens. His mind may well have travelled back to the belts of varied greens achieved by 18th-century planners, or to descriptions of the vast tracts of rhododendrons in the west of China and the Himalayas.

And so today we own this barren land – "not fit", he was told by his uncle, "to graze a goat" – where solid rock is never far from the surface, and where all the loose stones have been used to make cairns and walls.

I first went with a friend to Rowallane in 1937. Mr Moore greeted us at the front door: "Delighted to see you, and you've brought a lovely day. I'm afraid I have a rather busy morning and must just go over to the potting shed, but do go into the garden and I will join you as soon as I can." With a wave of seed packets, labels, trowel and string, the spare figure trotted down an avenue of Irish yews, and my friend and I walked into the walled garden.

The Walled Garden in those days was very much a kitchen garden and nursery ground, where young plants were brought into condition for planting in the other areas. But in particular there was a liberally-planted pair of borders along the west side where many a plant delighted us. *Paeonia lobata* 'Sunbeam' in blazing scarlet, soldier-like *Dactylorrhiza* (*Orchis*) *elata*, brilliant pink *Rodgersia pinnata* 'Superba', the 'Rowallane' *Viburnum*, and, flooding the air with fragrance, *Magnolia watsonii*. *Meconopsis betonicifolia* was in full flower by the side of a great leafy clump of *Kirengeshoma palmata*. Standing like sentinels on either side of the path was the impressive *Cardiocrinum* (*Lilium*) *giganteum yunnanense*, some 1.8 m (6 ft) high. All of these plants still grow happily there.

We had been somewhat dashed by our brief encounter with Mr Moore but he joined us in about half an hour, and at once took us to see three rather rare plants. We passed the test, named them, and learnt much later that this was his method of ascertaining whether visitor, who, no matter what he was shown, always were, and spent a wonderful day in his company.

Garden visitors can be such a nuisance if the owner is very busy – as Mr Moore undoubtedly was because he designed and planted gardens professionally from time to time, besides working at Rowallane. He once related to me how he dealt with an impossibly bumptious visitor who, no matter what he was shown, always made out that his own specimen was bigger or better. At last, having shown him specimens that he knew were remarkable, Mr Moore said: "Tell me, do you grow *Hydrangea sargentiana*?" "Why, yes," said the visitor, "I have a fine specimen; it is about 1.5 m (5 ft) high and wide and is a magnificent sight, covered with flower heads at the moment." "Ah, yes, that's interesting. I was wondering whether it would grow in the crevices of an old brick wall," said Mr Moore. "My dear sir," said the visitor, "that would be the last place; it likes cool woodland treatment, a sheltered position, and lots of humus in the soil." His host thanked him, and they moved on past a huge clump of *Philesia buxifolia* and a large bush of *Pseudowintera* (*Drimys*) *colorata* and came later to a shrub whose flowers appear in the middle of what seem to be leaves, which the visitor did not know, *Helwingia japonica*. "And there", said Mr Moore, "is my *Hydrangea sargentiana*; I measured it the other day; it is 8 ft (2.4 m) high, 14 ft (4.2 m) across, and you see it is seeding itself into the brick wall . . ."

The walls at Rowallane are unique. They were built soon after the Rev. John Moore bought the property in 1860. Horizontal bands of pierced tiles project, a foot apart, along their length; the Rev. Moore was not a plantsman and the walled area was his kitchen garden. The pierced tiles would take wires for training fruit trees – an ingenious solution of an old problem, avoiding the use of nails. The area known as the Pleasure Grounds is his also, including the "bandstand", but the whole of the rest of the garden as we know it today is the creation of his nephew Hugh.

Thus, three-quarters of a century ago, we find Hugh inspired to start gardening along different lines. His first effort was in the farthest enclosure where he created the only rock garden of its kind that I know – a knoll out of which appear rocks lying in their primeval state, relieved of their immemorial turf and scrub and having as their winding sheet today a covering of shrubs and plants of beauty and rarity. Soil was so scarce on the rocks that cartloads had to be brought to make beds for plants around the outer groups of stone.

Several species of those snow-white New Zealand daisies thrive, species of *Celmisia*, with South African *Euryops acraeus*, South American fuchsias, Chinese primulas, gentians and meconopses, Japanese *Nephrophyllidium crista-galli*, North American violas and erythroniums – in fact plants and shrubs from all round the world. *Berberis hypokerina* with its large leaves so bright in their glaucous tint underneath, the scarlet *Grevillea rosmarinifolia* from New South Wales, the lacy fine leafage and dainty blooms of *Hypericum uralum* delight the eye, and into many a corner are tucked dwarf rhododendrons: *R. lepidostylum*, noted for its almost turquoise young leaves, *R. ludlowii*, *R. sargentianum*, *R. pemakoense* and a number of hybrids like 'Pink Drift', 'Sarled' and 'Sapphire'. This great knob of rocky outcrops is dominated by a huge clump of *Cotinus coggygria* in smoky purple-brown, and the stems of neighbouring pines; from the earliest dwarf bulbs until the last gentian wanes amidst autumn tints it is a place of interest and beauty. There is a hallowed spot near the topmost slope of rock where the original seedling of *Hypericum* 'Rowallane' was found (see plate XII); this is believed to be a hybrid between *H. leschenaultii* and *H. hookeranum* 'Rogersii' and throughout the milder counties of these islands is acknowledged to be the most handsome of all St John's worts.

Although it is many years since that troublesome visitor gaped, astonished, in front of *Hydrangea sargentiana*, and all the specimens have put on much growth since, one can well imagine a little of the disappointment of his host, having walked him through the Spring Garden. Besides the great banks of rhododendrons there are trees and shrubs galore. In places they pretend to be natives, gracing the contours and blending with the native trees and the old walls, and in some of the parts where the soil is deeper some impressive groups are found. An immense *Acer capillipes* vies in magnificence with a fine *Cladrastis sinensis*, *Nothofagus cunninghamii* and a *Desfontainea spinosa* – a holly-like shrub from Chile hung with orange-red bells in summer – over 7.6 m (25 ft) across. The Handkerchief tree (*Davidia*) is there, *Cupressus duclouxii*, *Austrocedrus (Libocedrus) chilensis*, *Styrax japonica* and *Eucryphia glutinosa*, all represented by impressive specimens. *Pseudowintera (Drimys) colorata* 1.5 m by 2 m (5 ft by 6½ ft) across, a low shrub with strangely-coloured leaves and the renowned clump of *Philesia buxifolia* 1.5 m by 4.4 m (5 ft by 14½ ft) across cause surprise. Young specimens recently established include *Sorbus hedlundii*, a whitebeam with spring foliage of grisaille and gold, and rare birches.

With such a collection distributed over undulating ground, but at the same time granting peeps through the trees to distant landscapes, it is not hard to visualise something of the unfolding blossom in spring, sweeps of daffodils giving way to rhododendrons and azaleas, but it is a new experience to find the autumn pageant of coloured leaves so spaciously disposed, heralded by the tremendous cloud of scarlet from *Prunus sargentii* through every tint of orange to the butter yellow of *Cladrastis*; this final flare is accentuated by the subdued tones of conifers and evergreens.

Rose species, old roses, clethras, hydrangeas and fuchsias keep the garden interesting between its spring and autumn glories, and in summer a cloud of white fluff may assail you from the catkins of *Populus maximowiczii*, one of the first trees to produce leaves in spring.

Mr Moore raised many a packet of seed from collectors abroad and the first flowering of *Viburnum plicatum tomentosum* in the British Isles was at Rowallane. The plant was subsequently named 'Rowallane' and is much more compact than other forms. It originated from seeds sent from China by E. H. Wilson and the original grows in the Walled Garden in an honoured place in the centre of a small paved area shaped like a Celtic cross. This was made about 1937. The original 'Japonica', *Chaenomeles* 'Rowallane' is still a good bush (see plate I), while *Primula* 'Rowallane Rose' has been grown and distributed by division ever since the first plant appeared in the Walled Garden. (See also plates V and XIV.)

ST JOHN'S JERUSALEM
Dartford, *Kent*

Given in 1943 by Sir Stephen and Lady Tallents

AREA 3.2 ha (8 acres)
SOIL Limy
ALTITUDE 30 m (100 ft)
RAINFALL 686 m (27 in.)
TEMPERATURE 3.5°C (38°F)

3 miles south of Dartford at Sutton-at-Hone

THE ACTUAL GARDEN – for flowers, vegetables and fruits, with accompanying paths and lawns – was

123 The moat around the garden at St John's Jerusalem, taken from a map of *c.* 1840. The moat now only contains water during wet periods.

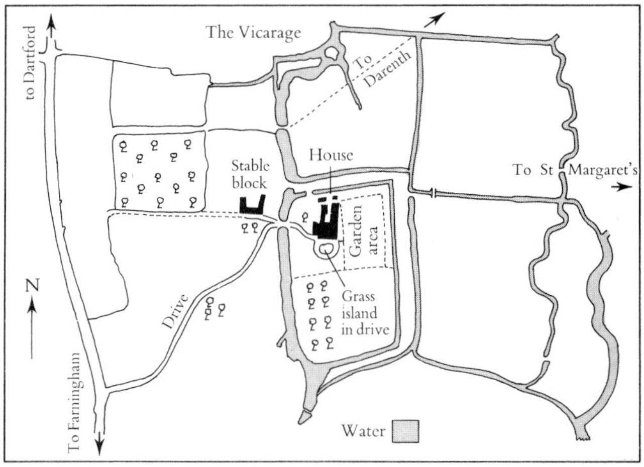

probably brought to its present pitch by Sir Stephen and Lady Tallents, but as likely as not followed a much older design. In spite of its trees, distributed seemingly informally, the garden and grounds enclosed by the moat are controlled by roughly rectangular lines, as might be expected from the surrounds of a mediaeval house. It acquired its present name when given to the Knights Hospitallers of St John, whose headquarters were in Jerusalem. It has a long and varied history; Henry VIII disposed of it in a light-hearted way after the Dissolution. It passed through several hands until leased to Thomas Ebbot in 1645, with the stipulation that he should plant an orchard, and plant twenty other trees (elm, yew or oak) every year. In 1667 Abraham Hill bought the property and it remained in his family for nearly a hundred years.

Presumably Thomas Ebbot did not fulfil his obligations because we read that Abraham Hill, about 1670, was planting an orchard adjoining the manor. He was anxious to introduce cider apples and perry pears from Devon and Herefordshire to Kent. 'Red Streak' was a cider apple he was specially interested in. Nothing of this planting now remains. In fact St John's is rather a sad place in summer, because the moat fed by the River Darenth tends to become completely dry due to local gravel workings which have lowered the water table. Trespassers with two and with four legs are no longer automatically excluded.

Abraham Hill probably planted the Lebanon cedar near to the house. (Mr Christopher Hill, his descendant, informs me that Abraham's firm of merchantmen plying between England, the Near and the Far East, was one of the first to import seeds commercially.) Abraham's great cedar stands boldly before the house as you approach it; crossing the moat, the view to the south is one of undulating lawns with a broad avenue of chestnuts. These are old and are continually falling but young ones have been planted. Lime trees are being replaced all round the moat. There is a rectangle devoted to a nuttery and a small orchard.

The flower borders are bright in spring and summer with a variety of flowers from bulbs and herbaceous plants, dahlias and buddleias.

ST MICHAEL'S MOUNT
Marazion, *Cornwall*

Given and endowed by the 3rd Lord St Levan in 1954

AREA 2 ha (5 acres)
SOIL Lime-free
ALTITUDE 18 m (60 ft)
RAINFALL 889 mm (35.)
TEMPERATURE 7.2°C (45°F)

½ mile south of Marazion (A394); access on foot over the causeway at low tide or by ferry.

WHEN THE TIDE is up, this rocky pyramid-shaped island appears to be floating on the water and only at low tide

124 On the south side of St Michael's Mount the natural rock outcrops are dramatic and provide homes for many tender plants. Photo 1974.

is it possible to walk across the causeway from Marazion. In spite of being so windswept it is surprising what grows on the island, for wherever there is the least shelter, bushes and pines establish themselves. On the south side of the island, fully exposed to the winds of course, but also gaining the benefit of the sun, there are some little terraced gardens, overhung with giant rocks. Here many succulent plants grow, including *Aloe aristata*, aeoniums and mesembryanthemums. A clump of *Fascicularia bicolor* is several feet across. In the tiny terraced gardens, each with its wall or hedge, there is enough shelter to enable *Sparrmania africana*, a native of South Africa, to thrive, as likewise do *Datura chlorantha*, pelargoniums, and *Medicago arborea*, the Moon Trefoil. Callistemons are of course in their element and blue African lilies seed themselves about. It is a wonderful spot on a good day.

SALTRAM
Plympton, *Devon*

Given in 1957 by the Treasury, which had accepted the property in lieu of death duties, after the death of the 5th Earl of Morley, who provided part of the endowment; maintained by an annual subvention from the Historic Buildings Council

AREA 8.5 ha (21 acres)
SOIL Lime-free
ALTITUDE 30 m (100 ft)
RAINFALL 1016 mm (40 in.)
TEMPERATURE 6°C (43°F)

South of A38, 2 miles west of Plympton

THE GARDEN at Saltram today is largely the creation of the 3rd Earl of Morley, who lived there from

1884–1905, and his son who died there in 1951. The fact that they were related to the Holfords at Westonbirt no doubt had an effect on their gardening activities, though their old diaries record very few gifts; most of the trees, shrubs and plants having been purchased. Since the death of the 4th Earl in 1962, the Trust has refurbished the garden. Because animals from the park had access to the gravelled forecourt and the portico on the south front, a haha was constructed in 1963, to exclude them (see illus. 186 and 187). Apart from the desirable cleanliness of the front, it allowed the removal of a fence, hedge and gate at the west corner of the house. This has had the result of re-uniting the whole area round the house into one.

We can fairly easily visualise what has happened since 1811, when the orangery, built in 1775, and the Chapel, 1776, were not included in the garden, whose axis lay in a long walk or terrace leading to the "Castle" (the octagonal pavilion) built in 1743 at the far end. The avenue of limes, astride the long walk, was probably not planted until after 1884 (see illus. 179). It is a unique example of a long avenue inside a garden; it is 237 m (260 yds) long and a delight at all times, but specially in spring when it is ribboned with old varieties of narcissus and again in September when *Cyclamen hederifolium* flowers in various patches. In 1903 *The Gardeners' Chronicle* recorded that a large *Cycas* was established outside in the garden (with winter protection), its leaves making a circle 3 m (10 ft) across. The strange old twisted oak at the west end was already growing polypody ferns on its branches in 1903, as it does today.

Old diaries give us details of the conventional plants used from the 1880s onwards. The garden proper was a series of beds under the west front decorated with annual plants and encompassed by pillars and chains covered with ivy. There was another bedding scheme, star-shaped, nearer to the orangery.

125 The 1771 Orangery at Saltram was partly destroyed by fire in 1932 but was reconstructed by the Trust in 1961. Tubs of Blue African Lily decorate the front and oranges and lemons grow inside.

126 The Gothick Castle at the top of the garden at Saltram House.

From 1888 Lord Morley was busy bringing the chapel and orangery into the garden, cutting down the mass of laurels which covered the fringe of the wooded northern slope of the garden and planting good trees and shrubs. He frequently referred to the Laurel Walk, which is now usually called the North Walk. We think several shrubs including the *Eriobotria*, *Griselinia*, and some camellias, were planted by 1890, together with numerous tender shrubs. The lists read enticingly, but show how quickly things alter in gardens; there are as many records of death as entries for planting, and no doubt 305 mm (1 ft) of snow in March 1891 did not help. The escallonia hedge at the east end of the lime avenue was planted in 1888, and, like the avenue, has protected the garden from south-west gales ever since. The exposed ridge of poor soil filled with slaty particles was hardly conducive to good gardening until the avenue had grown. The garden has always been protected from the north by natural woodland on the steep slope down to the river.

Much of the park woodland was replanted in the 1880s and 1890s, with thousands of plants from nurseries in the north of Scotland. As you drive through the park spare a moment to appreciate the large trees and lovely views. There used to be a remarkably good *Pinus patula* in the park; no sooner had I published its portrait than it fell over – a fate not uncommon in specially good specimens, I find! By the end of the century Lord Morley was becoming known as a keen gardener and received gifts from Kew and Veitch's London nursery and the garden was well on the way to being established. Further planting was done from 1909 by his son, who particularly contributed to the big clump on the lawn, where he planted the rhododendrons, including *R. yunnanense* and a *Photinia serrulata* which is always such a wonderful colour in its red-brown young foliage in spring. This big tree died in the 1976 drought but has been replaced. In the North Walk we can attribute to him *Pieris formosa*, *Cercidiphyllum*, *Pittosporum tenuifolium* 'Silver Queen',

Myrtus apiculata, *Eucryphia glutinosa* and the big procumbent specimen of *Umbellularia californica*. The extra pungent smell from crushed leaves of the latter, when inhaled deeply is supposed to have an intoxicating effect. This does not apparently prevent some Parisian vendors from selling its dried leaves as Sweet Bay, of which it is a relative, but it accounts for the fact that some dishes are ruined by its potency.

As you go round the house the long, narrow lime avenue invites you, as also does the lawn sloping gently up towards the once-ruined chapel, now repaired and in use as the assembly hall and gallery of the Trust's Plymouth Centre, and to the plane tree standing over its bluebells in May. The various walks are bordered by specimen trees or arrays of shrubs all adding their quota to the delights of the garden. Magnolias, camellias and early rhododendrons interspersed with daffodils, and the young foliage of Japanese maples is one memory I have (see plate XXXVI). The central glade is a place of special delight; it is framed by big trees, pines, *Picea smithiana* and oaks standing singly, with the fringe on one side leading the eye upwards to the lime avenue and on the other to the native woodland. Later rhododendrons and azaleas follow, *Styrax*, various brooms, both *Cytisus* and *Genista*, and before long the sweet fragrance of mock orange is noticed. From July onwards the garden had little to show, but during the last fifteen years many late-flowering shrubs have been added, *Rosa rugosa*, *Indigofera*, *Hypericum*, *Fuchsia*, *Aesculus parviflora*, *Ligustrum*, *Hydrangea*; the old *Oxydendrum* is the final note in September, when autumn colour starts. One sunny border has *Illicium anisatum*, an unusual Japanese evergreen, *Osmanthus yunnanensis*, hoherias, the striking yellow variegated holly 'Lawsoniana', *Acer palmatum* 'Ribesifolium', a remarkable form of almost fastigiate growth and small gooseberry-like leaves and the prickly *Photinia davidsoniae* which is about 4.2 m (14 ft) high.

If we return by the North Walk we pass several old camellias and approach the orangery. This was partly destroyed by fire in 1932, but was reconstructed by the Trust in 1961. Orange and Lemon plants were imported from Portugal and Italy and planted in wooden tubs made to measure specially. Owing to the mild climate at Saltram these and other tender plants are sufficiently protected by the building in winter, but oil stoves are kept for emergency use in very cold weather; the building used to be heated by a furnace at the back and the hot air was conducted through flues in the floor and walls.

Every year the oranges and lemons were transferred to the standing ground nearby on Oak Apple Day (29 May) and brought under shelter again on Tavistock Goose Fair Day, which was held on the second Wednesday in October. Thus were the seasons duly observed. The original plants, purchased in 1811, had reached 3.6 m (12 ft) in height ninety years later and required elaborate contraptions for transference. Today, even with smaller plants and a handy tractor, it is still a considerable job. The place for summer airing is a little grove to the east, which has a small fountain and pool in the middle, surrounded by a rockery; all these were additions in 1893. Some of the alpine plants were a present from Batsford Park, Gloucestershire. The palms were planted two years before. The 4th Earl put in a lot of new plants around the Orange Grove after 1909, including *Crinodendron hookeranum*, *Camellia japonica* 'Holfordiana' (raised at Westonbirt), *Magnolia stellata* and *M. liliflora* 'Nigra', and *Eucryphia cordifolia*; at that time the loquat (*Eriobotria*) was 6 m (20 ft) high and a palm 4.5 m (15 ft). Camellias and *Rhododendron* 'Cornish Red' make this a scene of splendour in May, quickly followed by other flowering shrubs. A Cork Oak and a Black Walnut of good size grow in the background. Lord Morley's diaries and lists show a remarkable collection in 1910 of 479 different trees and shrubs, most of them species; some came from V. N. Gauntlett of Chiddingford.

If we go to the East Lawn we find it dominated by a large red twigged lime. The laurel hedge around the iron railings used to be 6 m (20 ft) wide, but this was reduced to a single row some years ago, and several shrubs were planted including a group of the Chinese *Ligustrum chenaultii*. The Tulip Tree is gradually absorbing an iron stake in its trunk. Behind the lime and a mass of Golden Yew is a deep dell with several remarkable plants in it. First, *Acer griseum*, a beautiful tree of considerable size; *Pittosporum tenuifolium*, the Nymans *Eucryphia*, *Drimys winteri*, *Rhododendron arboreum* and hybrids, camellias and *Chamaecyparis pisifera* 'Squarrosa' whose feathery soft grey-green foliage makes such a complete foil to the huge leathery green leaves of *Magnolia delavayi*. *Elaeagnus macrophylla*, planted in 1911, has made a huge plant and is climbing to a height of 12.1 m (40 ft) into sycamores.

The central block of the west front is very old but other fronts date from the 1700s. About two hundred years ago Fanny Burney, Keeper of the Robes to Queen Charlotte, came with the Royal Family to stay at Saltram; her diary records many details of the visit, which included a fireworks display from the Amphitheatre. This lies some distance away from the house and garden, but the little stone temple known to this day as "Fanny's Bower", is in the woods below the orangery. Miss Burney, who later became Madame d'Arblay and had a rose named after her, spent much of her spare time during the visit in the bower, reading *The Art of Contentment* which she had found in the library. It seems to me that anyone who visits Saltram would find contentment in the splendid house, the views and the garden.

SCOTNEY CASTLE GARDEN
Lamberhurst, *Kent*

Acquired with an endowment under the will of Mr Christopher Hussey in 1970

AREA 7.6 ha (19 acres)
SOIL Lime-free
ALTITUDE 75 m (250 ft)
RAINFALL 762 mm (30 in.)
TEMPERATURE 3.5°C (38°F)

½ mile south-east of Lamberhurst on A21

THE 12TH-CENTURY dwelling at Scotney developed over the years into a moated fortified house or castle late in the 14th century. A larger dwelling was added in the 17th century, which was lived in until 1816. After an interval Edward Hussey, whose antecedents had bought the place at the end of the 18th century, decided to build a new house; it was conceived in 1835 but not finished until 1842. Very often in such circumstances the old dwelling would be pulled down and the material used for building the new. This did not happen at Scotney, partly because it would have meant carting the stone uphill to the new site, partly because there was ample new stone in the side of the hill, but largely because of the influences at work in gardening taste.

Towards the end of the long period of the English landscape garden, as has been noted in Chapter 5, the *avant garde* of garden writers, notably Sir Uvedale Price and Richard Payne Knight, were leaning evermore toward the picturesque, rather than Brown's suave landscapes. Humphry Repton's work showed this in his return to gardening as opposed to pure landscape design. The awakening to the manifold beauties of nature, idyllic, sublime or savage, fastened upon ancient stag-headed oaks, gushing water falling over rocks, and ruined buildings which were somehow to be contrived to make the garden landscape "picturesque". William Gilpin and his son William Sawrey Gilpin were to the fore in this influence and what did Edward Hussey do but call in the latter for advice on handling the view from the new house, perched on its level terraces, above the quarry slope, and looking down on to the old castle towers and crumbling manor house. It was a heaven-sent opportunity. Few sites today or then had so much magic and provided such play for the senses. The 17th-century portion was adjusted so that the older castle walls predominated. So it remained for about a hundred years, slowly maturing until the late Christopher Hussey inherited in 1952, to whom we owe much of today's beauty (see plate XXXVIII).

It is therefore a "picturesque" garden in the true sense of the word, and the timeless view from the upper lawn and bastion depends on the interplay of dimensions – distance, nearness, width and height, lines upright and horizontal, decay and growth, undulations of the terrain and expanse of water. The view beckons more persuasively than most, and it is a further delight to be lost in shrub walks before arriving on the level land below by the castle. Here the gloom of yews and vast piles of dark rhododendrons enhance the sheet of water wherein the crenelated towers are reflected, broken here and there by waterlilies or an agitated moorhen. Dragonflies dart about the waterside flowers in summer, and the woodpigeons coo comfortably all day long.

High summer is the moment to visit. You can feel the enchantment of *A Midsummer Night's Dream* and have no need for floral colour. The little circular Herb Garden across the bridge adds a quiet gardening touch; it was contributed by Mr Lanning Roper (see illus. 31).

But in May and June the whole bank down which we have come is alight with azaleas in yellow and orange, and in rhododendrons of all colours, including the huge groups of the late-flowering Pontic Rhododendron which are so sympathetic to woodland greenery. Before they have finished the broad groups of *Kalmia latifolia* come into flower, their scintillating pink and white buds like icing on a cake. Soon after the old buildings become embowered with soft-coloured roses, and the air is sweet with their fragrance and that of Mock Orange. Later buddleias attract butterflies and Day Lilies shine each for a day, and then it is the turn of the Willow Gentian approaching the quarry. After so much colour the eye can note again the mastermind who planted the Lebanon Cedar beyond the castle, and the vertical dark green cypresses, which together remind us that this is a created picture and not simply a piece of English landscape. And the dark greens of the conifers and rhododendrons are so appropriate a foil for the brilliance of the autumn colour; brilliance of red and yellow of exotic shrubs and trees, sobering gradually to the russet of oaks and beeches as autumn advances; a deep snuff brown remains in the huge clumps of Royal Fern by the water's edge. These in turn, in spring, are intriguing with their fronds shaped like croziers, gradually infolding glaucous and pale brown tints. But go to Scotney; no words can truly convey it. The Hussey family motto "I scarcely call these things our own" exactly voices the reverence accorded to Scotney by them all and by the National Trust.

SHARPITOR
Salcombe, *Devon*

Acquired in 1937 under the will of Mr Otto Overbeck

AREA 1.2 ha (3 acres)
SOIL Limy
ALTITUDE 30 m (100 ft)
RAINFALL 1016 mm (40 in.)
TEMPERATURE 6.5°C (44°F)

1½ miles south-west of Salcombe, signposted from Malborough and Salcombe

IT IS QUITE an adventure getting to Sharpitor; Salcombe has such steep hills and dramatic terrain. You go up through narrow streets and then traverse an ever-rising bumpy road until you are confronted by the shrubs and tall trees that grow in the lowest corner of the garden. Following the coombe, bamboos, gunneras, palms and all the signs of a mild climate greet you. Hydrangeas and fuchsias flourish.

The house stands on a high shelf of shaly rock and has a superb view of Splat Cove and the hills beyond, mostly owned by the National Trust. There is sharp drainage, abundant sunshine and wind, and the garden faces south-east. It is sheltered from the east by a belt of trees which are not owned by the Trust.

The garden slopes steeply and was firmly terraced with masonry and retaining walls in 1901 by Mr Edrick Hopkins. He and Mr and Mrs Vereker who followed him in 1913 were keen gardeners and most of the shrubs, trees and plants therefore were planted during the first quarter of the century, though probably Mr Overbeck also planted many between 1928 and 1937. One of the highlights at Sharpitor at that time was a long row of *Eucalyptus globulus* below the main garden, but frost killed them all soon after the Trust accepted the property in 1937.

By the gate is the variegated form of *Azalea microphylla* and *Ligustrum lucidum* 'Tricolor'. Descending the avenue of Chusan palms we come to a lawn which has moist cool borders on one side where hostas and fuchsias thrive, including *Fuchsia magellanica* 'Sharpitor', a white variegated form of *F.m. molinae*; it first grew here in 1973. A low hedge of *Euonymus japonicus* 'Ovatus Aureus' adds further shade. On the high banks above the walls fuchsias and cistuses grow. *Euonymus lucidus* (often known as *E. fimbriatus* in gardens) is a spectacular sight in spring when its new shining foliage is a brilliant red. Wherever you go are palms – they even seed themselves, and a short avenue leads to the garden gate above. When you come to the upper lawn it is quite a change to walk on level ground. Against the retaining wall are *Iris wattii*, *Francoa sonchifolia*, *Jovellana violacea*, *Nerine flexuosa* and amaryllises, which all flower freely. On the bank above one can have the luxury of observing *Eucomis punctata* at eye-level and admire its glistening pale green flowers and violet berries. The tender prostrate rosemary flows over the wall while behind numerous good shrubs include the Camphor Tree, *Cinnamomum camphora*, and an old-established Olive. A young olive has been planted, grown from a cutting from the old tree in Chelsea Physic Garden, London.

There are many rare and tender herbaceous plants in the lawn beds and elsewhere in the garden, agapanthuses, crinums, crocosmias, watsonias, libertias and the like, and on the brick pergola which surrounds this and other vantage points, many "windows" have been created under roses and wistarias, vines and other climbing plants. In spring you may catch the amazing display of flamingo-pink blooms on *Magnolia campbellii* (see plate XXXVII). A very large, low-branched tree grows in the lower garden and you can have the incredible luxury of looking down on hundreds of great flowers. Near it grows the hardy banana, *Musa basjoo*, callistemons, *Carmichaelia platyclada* and several species of *Acacia*. Elsewhere there are hundreds of fuchsias and hydrangea, purple-leafed and variegated *Phormium tenax*, *Syringa emodi* 'Aureovariegata', *Buddleia colvilei*, *Feijoa*, *Cornus capitata*, while the palms and cordylines make us think we are on the Riviera.

On the east side of the garden it is cooler and more shady. Here cyclamens and early bulbs have established themselves among the primroses and violets; several magnolias and other trees thrive – *Cornus controversa* 'Variegata', *C. kousa*, *Styrax japonica*, *Daphniphyllum macropodum* and species of bamboo.

Whenever you go to Sharpitor, unless you live in equally mild districts, you will find a wealth of unfamiliar shrubs and plants in flower. And every now and then your eyes will stray from the riches on the ground to the expansive view, alive with little boats and the cries of the gulls.

SHEFFIELD PARK GARDEN
Uckfield, *East Sussex*

Bought in 1954 with money from the Penfold Fund and supported partly by local authorities' grants, and partly with subscriptions obtained after a public appeal

AREA 40 ha (100 acres)	½ mile from Sheffield
SOIL Lime-free	Park station, midway
ALTITUDE 91 m (300 ft)	between East Grinstead
RAINFALL 889 mm (35 in.)	and Lewes, 5 miles
TEMPERATURE 3.5°C (38°F)	north-west of Uckfield

"IF STONES could speak what tales they could tell!" is a phrase we sometimes hear. As far as our gardening goes we might wish that trees could give us their memories. At CROFT CASTLE and Sheffield Park it is generally considered that the Sweet or Spanish Chestnuts exceed three hundred and thirty years of age and those years have seen the development of the English garden from the little plots and beds of herbs and the like to the complex art or hobby that it is today.

If the chestnuts at Sheffield Park could speak they would first tell us of the felling of oaks for the smelting of iron in the 17th century and the continuous search for the strong, elbowed branches needed for the King's navy. Some of the oaks would have nearly as long memories; the area has been famed for oaks for all time. In 1777 two giants were felled, each needing 24 horses to haul them four miles per day to Lewes and thence to Chatham for shipbuilding. Either the oaks or Sweet Chestnuts might have heard, somewhere about 1775, John Baker Holroyd, who later became the 1st Earl of Sheffield, discussing with Capability Brown the shape

127 ABOVE The north side of the first lake at Sheffield Park, photographed in 1938.
128 RIGHT A temporary causeway was built through the site of the third lake at Sheffield Park in 1973 in order to extract thousands of tons of mud, through which rushes and reed-mace were rapidly creeping. Recently a new walk has been opened along the eastern shore, thus increasing the ambit and providing some new views.

of the lakes – two of which Brown designed for him. In the heyday of their magnificence the chestnuts might have heard his Lordship's grandson urging on his team of cricketers in the first Test Match – played at Sheffield Park – against the Australians a hundred years later. Perhaps, too, they would conjure up the shade of Mr Pulham, landscape gardening expert, who, we believe, designed the second lake and the rocky waterfall connecting it with the first (see illus. 191), and also the stonework over which the water flows to the third lake.

They might have looked across the lakes and have seen the 3rd Earl instructing his gardener where to put some little conifers. In their already declining years they may have looked with some disdain at the tiny foreign evergreen conifers, little knowing they would double the height of their own lofty branches in a hundred years or so – the tall Maritime Pines and cedars, Wellingtonias and Redwoods which today dominate the scene.

They would have seen Mr Arthur G. Soames making full use of their picturesque old trunks, Brown's lakes, Pulham's lakes, and the dark green conifers, for the setting of his transformation plan for Sheffield Park – to create the most superb collection and display of autumn-colouring trees and shrubs. They might have heard the haggling over the price for the property and seen the sad division of house and garden, and transference of the latter to the Trust. Since then, sadly depleted in branches and stature by old age, but ever bravely throwing out new shoots, they would have watched the winter work of felling decrepit and dangerous old comrades, skilful tree surgery on many more, the removal of a rickety stone bridge between the second and third lakes, and the substitution of an iron one, and much pruning and planting. From spring to autumn they would wonder how many *more* visitors could be accommodated annually and have watched several muddy stretches of path being given good gravel surfaces. And they would have heard for months the clanking of big machines in their work of dredging the third and fourth lakes. Perhaps too, as eavesdroppers, they would be able to tell of further work discussed by the Trust on the spot.

This fanciful picture of the sequence of events which make up the glories of Sheffield Park today is merely a repetition of the sort of things that unwittingly contribute, decade by decade, to the famous gardens of this country. And what is so wonderful is that few of Arthur Soames's exotic trees have yet reached maturity and so the garden is a vibrant living thing full of health and beauty, composed of the traditional elements of the English landscape garden – trees and shrubs, grass, and water, with the added attraction of the three bridges, cascade and falls and the fairy-like edifice so compellingly sited above the top lake, melting away in its Gothick dream (see plate XLII). To see this in October from the bridge, mirrored in the water when the maple's scarlet leaves are partly fallen on the bank and the bright tints of the trees stand out from the dark conifers, is a moment of rare beauty. The eye then wanders to the silvery Pampas Grass, the creamy birch stems. Or turn round for a moment to the opposite view, where Lord Sheffield's pines rear high their heads over the mixture of shapes and colours, the golden pencil of the juniper is like an exclamation mark and the Tupelo Trees vie with all the others in their brilliance. Take in, also, the third lake whose one shore is open and spacious, softened by the yellow shower of Weeping Birches; opposite there is a veritable backdrop of dark green columns to the orange-brown, scarlet and gold from the deciduous trees. If your eye tires of this wedding of horticulture with a historical pleasaunce, go to the cascade and enjoy the glittering, chattering water and let the eye travel across the expanse of the fourth lake to the distant native trees. Or you may wander round to some beds where a thousand blue Chinese gentian trumpets stare

129 Every breeze causes the long thin needles of the Mexican *Pinus montezumae* to shimmer at Sheffield Park.

up to the yellowing leaves of a sweet chestnut, or enter the gloomy walk of conifers, upright or drooping, broad or narrow, green or blue or yellow. Or again you may cross the bridge, espy some palm trees below, and later enter an avenue of them leading to nowhere but returning to fading hydrangeas. This is all yours for several weeks, while the exotic maples, the Tupelo Trees, the Sweet Gums, Mespiluses, Blueberries, fothergillas, the sentinel Swamp Cypresses, rowans and birches develop their most brilliant tints. It is not a case of just one of each; there may be a dozen, fifty or a hundred of each. I know no other place where one can wander through groves of Tupelos, for instance. When the exotics have had their fling, and their leaves have fallen, then is the time to enjoy the russet of the oaks, and their companions the great conifers which assume even greater importance. Serbian Spruce, Tasmanian *Athrotaxis*, Japanese *Cryptomeria*, Lebanon Cedar, Blue Cedar, Monterey Pine, Eastern and Western Hemlocks and Western Arborvitae from North America, Nootka Cypress, Californian Redwood and "Big Tree", Chinese Juniper, Arizona Cypress, Japanese and European Larch, Indian Cedar, Japanese Umbrella Pine – they are all there, and many more, many of them of great size, providing valuable timber in their native countries and here contributing to a painter's landscape.

Through the autumn these glories are apparent. As the eye travels round you take in the great rounded hummocks of dark green rhododendrons; these contribute nobly in a passive way at this time of the year. But in May and June they steal all the thunder. Many of them are in groups a hundred feet across and twenty feet high, their flowers in pink, red, white and mauve, touching the water in some places and covering the bushes all over. One glade is mostly given to purples, lavenders and light yellows; in another, orange azaleas are grouped around a copper beech; in another, yellow azaleas are found accompanied by trees and shrubs of yellowish foliage. Here may be scarlet early Himalayan rhododendrons while there may be fragrant late American azaleas; in several areas and groves Captain Soames's own hybrid strain of *Rhododendron* "Angelo" casts its lily-like fragrance from lily-like flowers of white, blush and pink. *Kalmia latifolia* follows the later rhododendrons into June.

Camellias for early spring anticipated by the little Lent Lily in its thousands are quickly succeeded by drifts and drifts of daffodils and narcissuses – old favourites like 'Sir Watkin', 'Barri Conspicuus', 'Emperor' and some of Captain Soames's hybrids. It is when these are in flower that all the deciduous shrubs and trees begin to develop their leaves, brilliant green, or yellow or bronzy, opening out more fully later to balance the sweet fragrance of the bluebells.

In summer all is quiet and green, with a few shrubs. The admiration is all for the lakes, now dappled with the green pads of waterlilies and their flowers in pink, white and yellow, with very large groups of 'Escarboucle' in rich crimson. There may be as many as 500 blooms open on one day, competing with the patches of pink and crimson astilbes by the waterside and merging with the young flowers of blue hydrangeas, stewartias and eucryphias.

When you arrive at Sheffield Park you immediately have a choice of paths. The main one goes direct to the head of the top lake; another wends its way to the storage lake, which is not scenically planted. Another will take you to a grove of rhododendrons. If you take my advice you will first go to the head of the lake and make the traditional figure-of-eight circuit of the two upper lakes. Thereafter, if you have all day to spare, you can enjoy the other walks which take in many outlying parts, and give you a fine sight of *Pinus montezumae* for instance, *Magnolia kobus*, *M. tripetala*, or *Nothofagus antarctica*. In addition, the Queen's Walk round the third lake, made in Jubilee year, provides some entirely fresh views. But whatever circuit you make, spare a moment before leaving to look at the two great Cider Gums, *Eucalyptus gunnii*, from Tasmania, which approach 30.4 m (100 ft) in height and prove yet again how British gardens absorb happily and readily trees from all over the temperate world.

SHUGBOROUGH
Stafford, *Staffordshire*

Accepted by the Treasury in lieu of estate duty and given to the Trust in 1966. An endowment was given by Lord Lichfield's trustees

AREA 7.2 ha (18 acres)
SOIL Lime-free
ALTITUDE 30 m (100 ft)
RAINFALL 686 mm (27 in.)
TEMPERATURE 3°C (37°F)

5½ miles south-east of Stafford on the A513 Rugeley–Stafford road

BOTH THE drives approach the house obliquely and I think this makes the building appear more impressive.

130 ABOVE The scene in 1966 around the Chinese House at Shugborough.
131 RIGHT The transformation at Shugborough in 1968: the same view as Fig. 130.

It was a cold day when I first visited the property and the imposing portico was already partly hidden by scaffolding. This was in preparation for the renovation of the eight massive Ionic pillars. Though seemingly of stone, each one was a tree-trunk encased in thin panels of slate; water had entered the tops and as a consequence the timber was rotting. Surely this was one of the most distinguished uses of tree trunks in comparatively modern times? The portico was added in 1794, as an embellishment to the 1693 house. The garden as we know it has developed from the earlier date. Most of the magnificence that is Shugborough's is due to George Anson and his brother Thomas. George, later Admiral Lord Anson, returned from a four-year voyage round the world in 1744, bringing with him a captured ship worth a fortune, and on this fortune the brothers enlarged the house, and built the numerous monuments in park and garden.

During the long sea voyage the sailors were glad of green food and they found a pea in pod at Port San Julian, Patagonia, which was acceptable. Lord Anson's cook brought some seeds home with him. It produced fragrant blue flowers and was subsequently named *Lathyrus nervosus* and has always been known as Lord Anson's Blue Pea. It has been in cultivation in England from time to time between long spells when it has died out. For many years I sought for seeds, and at last through the kind offices of the Royal Horticultural Society plants were made available and it is once again growing at Shugborough. (See plate XI.)

A third Anson, Thomas William, son of the Admiral, added considerably to the park. His ambition was to emulate his father-in-law, "Coke of Norfolk", at Holkham, where revolutionary ideas were altering the traditional processes of farming. Thomas William stopped at nothing; a village was removed from the park and new houses built at Great Haywood in compensation, and the park much enlarged.

The entrance drive wends its way up rising ground, well wooded with beech and other native trees, with extensive plantings of Pontic Rhododendron. Suddenly you come out of the trees and look over the wide, flat, tree sprinkled valley. First to left and then to right are the Lanthorn of Demosthenes and the Triumphal Arch; the Tower of the Winds is farther along and used to be mirrored in a large lake, which is now dry. It so happened that a disastrous flood in 1795 caused tremendous havoc in the grounds, sweeping away the Chinese Pagoda which is illustrated in plate XLIII.

Another drive enters the park near the old stone Essex Bridge; it curves gently towards the house whose grey stone is just right for the billowy masses of Pontic Rhododendron. Glimpses are obtained of the Doric Temple in the garden, and wide expanses of grass with cedars, limes, beeches and a good Weeping Holly. This drive is entirely on flat ground; in fact, while the perimeter of the land in view is raised, the whole place may be said to be on the level, which adds height to the many great trees.

Some paragraphs occurred in *The Journal of Horticulture* for 1872 bemoaning the flatness of the terrain, but extolling the beauty of the crisp green of a bed of parsley, the majesty of rhubarb leaves, the colour of red beet and the excellent ferny greenery of the carrot, "while the Cabbage and Onion give a diversity of form fully equal to all the far-fetched rivals in the parterre". The vegetable garden at Shugborough was justly famed in those days and lay in the walled enclosure in the park; it was noted as "a kind of Academy for the study of Horticulture" as early as 1817.

By 1872 the Victorianising of the garden had been started; the terraces on the west front had been made, punctuated by Irish yews and small round-headed trees, probably Portuguese Laurels, but the Golden English Yews had not been planted. These, like much of the rest of the garden, were in a poor state in the 1960s but have been nursed back to shape. The terrace rose beds were replanted and a few desultory rose beds on a lower terrace were redesigned and turned into a Victorian-style rose garden to the Trust's design in 1966. All the work has been done with the co-operation of the

Staffordshire County Council to whom the property is leased. Here are roses of white, pink, crimson and mauve, both bush and standard, and many ramblers which with clematises are trained over arches, pillars and swag-ropes. Pools of silver foliage from Cotton Lavender are under the clematises on their hoops, making good contrast to the grass paths, one of which leads from a pleached green arbour to a central sundial.

To the south of the house is the Wild Garden, where gentle paths meander among big trees and banks of rhododendrons, turning at the end for the long walk back by the River Sow. In this area are several groupings of dark purple rhododendrons and creamy yellow azaleas which blend well with the common purple, and thus there is one colour scheme, avoiding the usual pinks and scarlets. Spread with daffodils in spring, followed by bluebells, this whole area is a pleasure for many weeks. As one reaches the terraces by the house shrub roses, early 'Frühlingsgold' and late *R. multibracteata*, enliven the scene, and in July dwarf purple *Lavender* 'Hidcote' and yellow roses, with, usually, purple petunias in the big stone troughs, contrast with the massive cones of golden yews.

You can walk as far along the river in the other direction. The first important feature is the Chinese House, erected by the Admiral in 1747, from a sketch made in China by Sir Percy Brett, one of the officers in his flag ship, the *Centurion*. It has exquisite Chinoiserie decoration inside, and only Chinese shrubs have been planted around it, including a Pagoda Tree. Its original bridge, of wood, disintegrated; the present cast-iron bridge, painted in Chinese lacquer-red, was erected in 1813, and the two, at the bend of the river, make a pretty grouping. Thence the river enters a long straight reach to the Essex Bridge overhung in places by trees of some size. Nearby is the Shepherd's Monument, with its enigmatical incised lettering, also an immense English Yew. Figures are not easy to grasp but I must ask you to visualise a tree 21.9 m (72 ft) high or more, whose skirt lies on the ground, all round the central growth, to a height of about 2.4 m (8 ft) and covers, in all, nearly an acre.

132 Design for the Victorian-style rose garden laid out at Shugborough in 1966, planted with roses of the colouring of the period, and clematises.

133 The Shepherd's Monument at Shugborough, embowered with rhododendrons.

In addition to his essays in architecture and agriculture Thomas Anson made an alternative channel for the River Sow. This resulted in a broad stretch of water below the terraced garden. Shugborough is particularly rich in its associations with the one family and their tastes, and we may be thankful that so much beauty is ours today, owing to the capture of the galleon in the Pacific over two hundred and thirty years ago, by the ancestor of the present Earl of Lichfield.

SISSINGHURST CASTLE
Cranbrook, *Kent*

Accepted by the Treasury in lieu of estate duty, given to the Trust in 1967. Funds for endowment and capital expenditure given by Mr Nigel Nicolson

AREA 4 ha (10 acres)	2 miles east of
SOIL Mainly lime-free	Sissinghurst village,
ALTITUDE 60.9 m (200 ft)	off the A229 Maidstone–
RAINFALL 686 mm (27 in.)	Hawkhurst road
TEMPERATURE 3.5°C (38°F)	

IT WAS a glorious day in June. I had been to a luncheon party at Winkfield Place, the home of Constance Spry. Among others Vita Sackville-West (Lady Nicolson) was present. After lunch we visited the rose garden, for it was roses – old roses – which had already brought me in touch with Constance. We lingered among the blooms, enthralled, but picking our way through the weeds, for which Constance apologised but explained as was her wont that such heavy clay-soil broke the tools and the spirits of those who tended the garden for her. "It is just the same at Sissinghurst," exclaimed Vita, "I ought to be there now, weeding, ever weeding. I can't keep up with them." How I wish they could both see their gardens today, well tended, floriferous and beautiful; how they would have enjoyed seeing the cultivation under control!

There is little need for me to describe in detail the garden at Sissinghurst Castle (it is not really a castle though there is a tall tower of the sixteenth century). The garden is one of the most photographed and visited in the country, and countless references to it have appeared in print. Its history is recorded in several books. Put very briefly it is a group of ancient buildings around which Sir Harold and Lady Nicolson created a garden in the 1930s, he being mainly the designer, she the planter. By degrees she developed colour schemes for the various enclosures, which have been carried on faithfully ever since, each enclosure having a different set of plants, but remaining in beauty throughout most of the growing season, except special areas where the planting is for one season only. It is a firm formal design, informally planted with good things and what Vita Sackville-West wrote about HIDCOTE in 1949 applies as much to Sissinghurst: "a rumpus of colour, a drunkenness of scents". HIDCOTE remains the first garden which was created and brought to perfection after we had absorbed Jekyllian maxims and examples and begun to use plants as a painter uses the colours of his pallette. But there the comparison stops. No doubt Lady Nicolson profited from her visits to HIDCOTE, just as Phyllis Reiss did, and many more. The mainspring was there ready to be adjusted to the different needs of the Kentish site.

Soon after the Winkfield meeting I was invited to Sissinghurst; it was the first of several visits before it was given to the Trust in 1967. We made our way, of course, to the rose garden where the quality was, as always, superlative and where many of my own treasures had found a home. The old French roses like 'Charles de Mills', 'Cardinal de Richelieu', 'Gloire de France', 'Céleste', 'Coupe d'Hébé', 'Fantin Latour', 'Tuscany', 'Hippolyte', 'Camieux', 'Duc de Guiche' and 'Nuits de Young' thrive in the heavy Wealden soil; on a wall by the tower was in full flower 'Souvenir du Dr Jamain', saved by Lady Nicolson from a Groombridge nursery after the last war. But it is one thing to have luxuriant roses and quite another to know how to dispose them and what to grow with them. At Sissinghurst they are free-grown bushes, or trained round supports if they are of lax habit; or trained over long hazel wands if they are too tall, or trained into old trees so that their flowering shoots fall down in cascades. And with them are grey iris leaves, amethyst alliums, *Crucianella stylosa*, and other plants and shrubs of subdued colour, aiding and abetting the whites, pinks, mauves and maroons of the old roses. It is indeed a "rumpus of colour" in June, and other plants continue into the autumn. One of the best views is from the top of the tower, looking down onto the yew Rondel in the middle of the rose garden. Roses are everywhere round the garden; the White Garden has a central arbour of metal to support white roses. This was constructed in 1972 by the Trust after the old almond trees in which the roses grew had collapsed. 'Iceberg' and 'Gruss an Aachen' are in some of the beds. On the cottage 'Mme Alfred Carrière', raised a hundred years ago, flowers more profusely every year than any other rose in the country. There are roses in the Orchard – Scots Briers, species, great mounds of ramblers like *R. longicuspis*, Rugosas and one that is very old and called 'Sissinghurst Castle' for want of a name (see illus. 174). It was growing next to old house foundations and I have only seen it in one other old garden. At one time it was erroneously given the name of 'Rose des Maures'.

But I must stop writing about the roses. A time of great beauty at Sissinghurst is the spring, when the pleached lime walk is a feast of every small spring bulbous plant that you can think of – narcissi, tulips, scillas, crocuses, fritillaries, anemones, and many another dainty flower. Here the walk had been paved with concrete slabs which had not settled well; the lime trees were the Common Lime which persists in throwing up shoots from the root, and also casts stickiness around in summer. We resolved to replace the limes with non-suckering trees. The alteration to the trees and the paving were made in the winters of 1976 and 1977.

Beyond the lime walk is the Nuttery, so famous for years with its carpet of mixed polyanthus. Alas, the soil became polyanthus-sick and more than half of the crop died every year, and as a consequence this shady area now has an assortment of plants to cover the ground and provide flowers for a long time.

It is only a few steps to the Cottage Garden, which is always a heart-warming sight from spring to autumn, even on a dull day, because of its rich assortment of yellow, orange and dusky red flowers grouped around a verdigris-tinted old copper. The concentrated colour from early euphorbias and tulips, tree peonies and day lilies, aquilegias, Oriental poppies and irises, to Tiger

134 In the Herb Garden at Sissinghurst Castle.

Lilies and dahlias, *Bupleurum falcatum*, mimulus, snapdragons and gazanias is a vivid symphony, finishing with *Salvia confertiflora* from Brazil, which has to be given shelter in the winter. In July the Mount Etna broom hangs over everything in a shower of tiny yellow flowers.

Down a flight of steps, and a long rosy-red brick wall provides little spring flowers in the mortar, and a long border for *Aster frikartii* 'Mönch'. This is a deep grass walk, with a bank on the opposite side covered with azaleas, *Lilium pardalinum* and *Gentiana asclepiadea*. You are actually standing in a drained and dry part of the moat, constructed in the 12th century. The water-filled parts reach from the neat Herb Garden, all round the orchard to the White Garden.

The fact that Sissinghurst has always been so popular with the public has presented problems, one of which is overcrowding at weekends. The other is the wear and tear of grass paths on sticky wet soil. Over several years one or another area has been paved in vernacular style by a craftsman builder, using stone, bricks, tiles, cobbles, setts and the like. It pleased me no end to hear one visitor saying to another, how much she liked the "old world paths" in the herb garden; "they must have been here a long time". This was in the first summer after laying, which says a lot for the skilled work and old materials used.

With the courage needed to conceive the Cottage Garden colourings it is no less surprising to find a big border backed by a high wall, being given to purple and blue colouring. Every tint is there from the flaming magenta of *Geranium psilostemon* to the darkest purple clematises, which give a velvety back drop to the *Rosa moyesii* of flaming flower and hep, *Baptisia australis*, nepetas, delphiniums, campanulas, monkshoods, salvias and lavateras – including *Lavatera maritima* – which help to keep up the display from June to autumn.

I will leave you to go at different seasons of the year to find for yourself the innumerable treasures that cover the old walls; the nook where the Blue Poppy grows; the long yew alley and the rosemaries pouring over the path; the variety of urns and vases that are placed at vantage points and as like as not filled with plants, of the appropriate colour; and to stay till evening when the flowers become luminous in the dusk in the White Garden, when, too, the leaden statue recedes into nothingness under its canopy of silver pear leaves, and the white spires of delphiniums and the statuesque Scots Thistles seem to burst out of the grey froth of gypsophilas and Masterworts.

Some trees and spinneys have been planted around this rather exposed property to minimise the cold winds. Sometimes if an icy spring east wind is blowing it is quite a job to open the wooden door to the area known as Delos. This was the last portion of the garden to be laid out, in a series of raised rectangular beds. Neither Nigel Nicolson nor the Trust found them satisfactory and so the present path was laid in 1974, leading to the well; the planting is mixed for all seasons, hellebores under magnolias in spring, with *Polygonum equisetiforme* for autumn and many things in between. In particular the little holly-like bush should be noted; it is an oak, *Quercus coccifera*, a native of Greece and other countries of the Mediterranean; it has been in cultivation since the 17th century and was adopted as the insignia of the Dyer's Company for an interesting reason. It is the host plant of the Kermes insect – and therefore also known as the Kermes Oak – from which true cochineal used to be obtained. This is therefore a historical link with Delos, ancient industry, and the travels of the Nicolsons, and it is appropriately well suited to the soil at Sissinghurst besides being well sited.

SIZERGH CASTLE
Kendal, *Cumbria*

Given in 1950, with an endowment, by Mr and the Hon. Mrs Hornyold-Strickland and Lt-Cmdr. T. Hornyold-Strickland. The home of the Stricklands for 700 years

AREA 5.6 ha (14 acres)	3 miles south of Kendal,
SOIL Neutral	on west side of the A6
ALTITUDE 60.9 m (200 ft)	Lancaster road
RAINFALL 1143 mm (45 in.)	
TEMPERATURE 4.5°C (40°F)	

AS YOU APPROACH the castle from the drive it is worth noting the large size of several Field Maples on the left, just before the rocky knoll is reached. Thereafter the castle comes into view.

The substantial pele tower was built about 1350, and the earliest approach was from the great gates at the far side of the main lawn. Ancient beeches lined it, but were felled for safety, and eventually replaced by limes by the Trust in 1963 and a final stone seat was added in 1968, closing the vista. Spread around this area with its dark yews as a background are thousands of pheasant-eye narcissi; no sooner are they over than the big grey leaves of hostas unfold in the shade, sheltering *Lilium pyrenaicum* and *L. martagon*, while beds of rugosa and other shrub roses and lilacs fill the sunny areas, carpeted with hardy geraniums. A young *Davidia involucrata* should soon start flowering.

If you are visiting Sizergh in April, you will have missed the widespread Lent Lilies on the slopes above the lake, but in all probability, below the pele tower a narrow border will be a ribbon of vivid blue from *Gentiana acaulis*. Or, in October, the tower will be robed in the scarlet leaves of Boston Ivy. Above the lawn is a stone wall, fronted with brick, facing east. The bricks hold warmth longer than stone and this was a method of helping fruit trees to set and ripen their fruit long ago; now there is a goodly selection of shrubs:

135 18th-century garden niche at Sizergh Castle.

Osmanthus delavayi, *Viburnum juddii*, olearias, ceanothuses, escallonias, *Solanum crispum*, Sweet Jasmine, clematises and pyracanthas, with hebes, *Ceratostigma* and *Caryopteris* spilling out on to the path below. This terrace and wall are believed to be of mid 18th-century construction, but the garden pond is of earlier origin, and was enlarged and given its island when the flight of steps and their retaining walls – over which cascade clematises and *Vitis coignetiae* – were made in 1926.

Impressive though all this is, it is to the quarter-acre rock garden we turn for the main horticultural delights of Sizergh (see illus. 190). Like the steps it was constructed for the late Lord Strickland in 1926 by T. R. Hayes & Son, the noted nurserymen of nearby Ambleside. Thus it is a lakeland rock garden made of typical lakeland stone – so different in feeling from gardens in the south where Cumbrian limestone, however beautifully fretted by water over the centuries, never seems at home.

The water-course derives from the lake above the castle, and flows through pools and down little falls in the rock garden eventually to reach the garden lake. Since 1926 many of the conifers put in for background effect have grown to large size, among them the Bhutan Pine, the Swiss Arolla Pine and the Japanese *Pinus parviflora*, so picturesque in the way it holds its old cones. Many visitors exclaim at the size of some of the true dwarf conifers. After all if you leave a dwarf conifer in a suitable place it is apt to get big, for the simple reason that there is nothing else for it to do. There are some remarkable specimens of dwarf spruces, some 8 feet or more through and half as high, dense, splendid hummocks. The Noble Fir is represented by a prostrate blue form over 4.5 m (15 ft) wide, the Eastern Hemlock by a very large plant, and there are dense bushy cypresses and thujas, Mountain Pine, Golden Dovaston Yew and junipers. Many rare little forms of cedars, pines and other genera have been planted recently to carry on the tradition. When the Japanese Maples – green, copper, and in a variety of leaf-patterns – are scarlet with approaching autumn, then the conifers look their best.

In early summer the young maple foliage vies with many a good rock and bog plant, among the rocks and in the moist soil beside the pools. Globe Flowers, primulas, rodgersias, astilbes, keep it gay for weeks, while in September the Willow Gentians and pink spikes of *Polygonum vacciniifolium* and *P. affine* are much in evidence; the gentian seeds itself in many corners and by great good luck among them are various shades of blue, from dark to azure, as well as white. They contrast particularly well with the yellow fruiting sprays of *Coriaria terminalis xanthocarpa*.

Apart from the rock plants and noted conifers the rock garden houses what is perhaps the largest selection of hardy ferns, species and forms, found in any garden in these islands. There are forms of the Royal Fern, seldom encountered, the Ostrich Plume Fern, the Sword Fern of North America; broad and curled Hart's Tongues, and unusual Polypodies. Then the ordinary Male fern and its striking relatives *Dryopteris pseudomas* and *D. wallichiana* catch the eye, and numerous forms of the Lady Fern and the Shield Ferns, so lacy and dainty in their segments. In the rocks are the spleenworts; in one corner the hardy Maidenhair Fern, in another the grey leaves of the Japanese Painted Fern or the red-backed fronds of *Dryopteris erythrosora*, down to tiny, running, Beech and Oak Ferns and *Blechnum penna-marina*. Few would be able to spot them all and fewer still would be able to name them; "they do not flower", it is complained, but they add a gentle foil of greenery to the general scene of rocks and water plants and shrubs, and are, like the British Pteridological Society, gradually finding more and more devotees.

SMALLHYTHE PLACE
Tenterden, *Kent*

Given in 1939 by Miss Edith Craig, Ellen Terry's daughter

AREA 0.8 ha (2 acres)	2 miles south of
SOIL Limy	Tenterden, on east
ALTITUDE 30 m (100 ft)	side of the B2082
RAINFALL 686 mm (27 in.)	Tenterden–Rye road
TEMPERATURE 4.5°C (40°F)	

THIS CHARMING timbered house, built about 1480, has a small garden consisting of several separate areas, and for historic interest has one unique feature though not of a horticultural category. It has a dry dock for the repair of boats, reputedly dating from Henry IV's reign, at which time the sea came far inland. The dock was recently dredged and its shape corrected, thanks to an appeal launched by the Trust, which was quickly subscribed.

Ellen Terry lived here for thirty years and fortunately the rose named after her 'Ellen Terry' (1925) has always been growing in the garden, a shapely Hybrid Tea of creamy sulphur with soft peach shadings on the outer petals. This was labelled when I went there first, and has since been propagated. But what intrigued me even more was to find a rose exactly resembling 'Souvenir de la Malmaison' but with white flowers shaded with sulphur yellow in the centre. This proved to be an almost non-existent rose, 'Kronprinzessin Viktoria', which occurred in 1888 in Germany, a sport of the Malmaison rose. This has also been propagated and distributed. The small rose garden contains other contemporary varieties and is gay in spring with ground-cover plants. Ancient fruit trees contribute just the right touch elsewhere in rough grass, where spring bulbs abound.

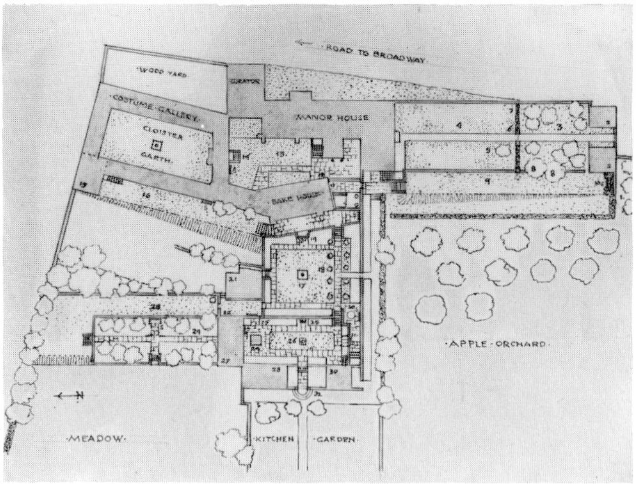

136 TOP Charles Wade's design for the garden at Snowshill Manor.
137 ABOVE Evening light at Snowshill Manor. Photo 1961.

SNOWSHILL MANOR
Broadway, *Gloucestershire*

Given in 1951 by Mr Charles Paget Wade

AREA 0.8 ha (2 acres)
SOIL Limy
ALTITUDE 228 m (750 ft)
RAINFALL 675 mm (26 in.)
TEMPERATURE 3.5°C (38°F)

3 miles south of Broadway

MR WADE left to us copious notes about the creation of his garden. How that the house in 1919, when he came to live here, stood "sad and desolate in the midst of a wilderness of chaos. What is now the Courtyard was a jungle of rampant nettles with narrow tracks trodden to the various doors. Nettles covered the slope from the very walls of the House right down to the kitchen garden, strewn with old iron, bones, broken crocks and debris". It was the story of SISSINGHURST repeated, but on a lesser scale, and no doubt it also repeated what had gone on long before at HIDCOTE. In fact the three gardens have much in common: all three were developed in this century in a style in which the new-found English gardening shone forth. In 1919 HIDCOTE was in its infancy but possibly an early visit started a friendship with Lawrence Johnston.

The creators of both were faced with steeply sloping ground and Wade wrote that terraces and retaining walls are necessary to provide a sound base for the house "to lose the feeling it gave of being about to slide into the depths of the vale far below", where "springs had formed a treacherous swampy morass in what is now the lower garden – it had been the cattleyard". To him the ancient dovecote and the two old stone cow byres at once suggested the design, and he created a garden of great charm.

One of his maxims was that the plan of a garden is more important than the flowers; another that mystery is most valuable in garden design and that the visitor should be enticed beyond what is immediately seen. He valued the light and shade of sun and shadow and of light foliage against dark.

Although so small, it is a continual joy to walk through the different garden "rooms" on so many levels, separated by walls, arches and steps; and though so varied, its scale is carefully arranged so that, richly ornamented architecturally though it is, it never feels claustrophobic or cluttered. The tinkling of water into cisterns and little ponds adds charm on different levels; roses and clematises billow over the walls, and many a small plant in the borders delights the eye. Well-head, armillary dial, seats in niches, dovecote, stone troughs, various types of walling and paving – it is all there, assembled by the collector Wade at a time when traditional things were suddenly seen to be disappearing.

Snowshill garden is the product of a mind trained in architecture, history, art and poetry. The first two are at every turn; the last two gleam out from his notes. How he liked best in the garden – as a contrast to the stonework – flowers of blue, mauve and purple to predominate, with some other tints to enliven them.

His selection of colour extended to the paint used for doors and gates; he found the rather strong blue-green (actually marketed in the past as "Wade Blue") was the ideal contrast to stone and to the garden greens, not warring with either.

But it is not the separate features that stand out in one's mind after a visit; it is, to me at least, the welding of them all into an intriguing and coherent whole that is the essence of Snowshill. The shady, walled approach to the flat lawn and upstanding regular south facade of the house is a complete contrast to the garden proper, where every whim is indulged, but in seemly manner.

Realm of infinite delight
With thousand beauties dight,
Inspiration, day and night

SPEKE HALL
Liverpool, *Merseyside*

Given in 1944 by the Trustees of the Speke Estate with the consent of Mr T. P. Watt Norris, under power contained in the will of Miss Adelaide Watt

AREA 6 ha (15 acres)
SOIL Lime-free
ALTITUDE 30 m (100 ft)
RAINFALL 813 mm (32 in.)
TEMPERATURE 4.5°C (40°F)

On north bank of the Mersey, 8 miles south-east of the centre of Liverpool, on east side of the airport

MANY GARDENS become more grand and are enlarged as the centuries pass. The garden at Speke has lost its former splendour and has shrunk, swallowed up by the incursions of urbanisation, factories, roads, and an airfield. It is an oasis of history and culture in a woebegone region. If you can forget its surroundings, you may yet enjoy the impact that is given by the low half-timbered house that has stood there since its first portions were built in the early 14th century, with a moat enclosing a garden of about 2 acres, with, later, a walled kitchen garden to the east.

Today it is leased to the Merseyside County Museums and, while the interior is well cared for, the garden has not yet received the same expertise and attention. It is a long melancholy story: part of the moat was filled in about three hundred and fifty years ago, and the rest of it was drained, probably towards the end of the 17th century or in the early 18th century. In 1795 it was described in glowing terms "with Gardens, Orchard, Plantations, and Pleasure Ground", but it rapidly deteriorated. A hop yard is mentioned, surely a far northern example. A stream from a pond to the north-west flowed through a part of the moat to the small wooded valley.

After 1855 it entered into a period of greater prosperity under the fourth Richard Watt, and the garden as we see it today was then created. Across the lawn to the north can be seen the picturesque lodge, thanks to the track across the middle distance having been sunk, well out of sight. The stream was diverted into the West Wood, leaving the moat completely dry, but its banks were graded and terraced in an impressive fashion, making a large sunken grass lawn. One of the most urgent matters in recent years was to plant trees around the south lawn to screen the high bank made by the airfield to help to shut out the roar of planes.

The little garden to the south of the house, walled on two sides, also has a long history. The garden gate bears the date 1605, and the elaborate finials remind us of those at HARDWICK HALL. In Miss Watt's time, around 1911, the whole place was beautifully tended, and the little garden was a mass of flowers; lawns were immaculate and many evergreens, hollies, rhododendrons and Irish Yews planted around the house and elsewhere. The curious, especially those with nostalgia for Edwardian days, can prove this for themselves by referring to *The Gardens of England* published by *The Studio* about 1910, which has photographs and a water colour by George S. Elgood who immortalised the extravagant scenes of so many gardens at that time.

If neither nostalgia nor the appearance of the garden today satisfies you, and no matter what impression you get of the place as a whole, there is an experience yet in store for you which is different from any other in our gardens.

Pass over the bridge with stone parapets which gives access across the dry moat into the old dark house. Beyond the entrance hall is a door leading into a central courtyard, cobbled and of some size, surrounded on all sides by the timbering of walls and windows. It is neither bright day, nor dark night in the court, but an unexpected twilight. A permanent twilight, with the sky obscured by a high tracery of branches, for long ago somebody planted two yew trees there. They completely overhang, loftily, the entire court. It has been guessed that they are as old as the house. Who knows?

SPRINGHILL
Moneymore, *Co. Londonderry*

Acquired under the will of Capt. W. L. Lenox Conyngham in 1957

AREA 18 ha (45 acres)
SOIL Lime-free
ALTITUDE 30 m (100 ft)
RAINFALL 889 mm (35 in.)
TEMPERATURE 4.5°C (40°F)

Just outside Moneymore on the B18 Moneymore–Coagh road

THIS IS ANOTHER of the gardens which have no real pretence at grandeur or impressiveness, but where one can feel the subtle touch over the years of the Lenox Conyngham family whose home it was. It has a long history. It is said that Lord Macartney, of the Co. Antrim family, gave a plant of his new Chinese rose, *Rosa bracteata*, to Springhill around 1793, but I doubt whether the present plant is the original.

Other old roses grow well here, too: on the buildings which flank the approach to the entrance front of the house, "Félicité et Perpétue", raised in 1827, and an old Boursault variety in the basement area. Walled areas have proliferated, but today each one is used for a different style of gardening. A little summerhouse is built into the angle of the wall in one; its walls are covered with shells. It looks across a small lawn to a border richly planted. Here is *Polygonum milettii*, whose crimson spikes are generously produced over a long summer period, also hostas and primulas, rodgersias and the like.

A small courtyard has a recently-planted short avenue of *Sorbus scopulina*, a slow-growing columnar Rowan or Mountain Ash, whose dark green leaves admirably foil the scarlet fruits in early autumn. To add point to a long narrow enclosure Irish Junipers have been planted.

Springhill lay, so the histories tell us, in a large wooded area extending to Loch Neagh, and old beeches, other native trees, and fine old yews are scattered around, interplanted in an informal way to the east of the house with *Hoheria glabrata* and rhododendrons. The former spills its white flowers over the wall into the Bleach Green. Among rhododendrons I particularly remember 'Boddaertianum', because this plant is tall enough to be seen above one's head; thus the beauty of its nearly-white flowers is enhanced by the rusty brown of the undersides of the dark green leaves. Beyond this small woodland garden the Trust has recently made a short ha-ha to contain the garden, and new trees have been put in to replace the old beech avenue, which leads to a tower or folly.

Herbs have returned to favour of late and so are represented in a small garden, an assortment planted around a tiny camomile lawn. They are of course plants which have always been associated with the home, both for medicine and the pot. The legends attached to them and their curative powers are carried to extreme lengths. But at Springhill a new legend has been started. *Artemisia angustifolia* is a silvery sub-shrub which gives off in warm air a distinct fragrance of curry – a character which is only known to the more experienced botanist and gardener. "Do you smell anything special just here?" asks the very Irish guide. The visitor sniffs appreciatively and says, "Why yes! curry, I think". "Ah," says the guide, "I have often wondered about it. They tell me there was once an Indian cook at the house. He died one day and nobody seems to know where he was buried ..." Irish embroidery is not necessarily worked with needle and silks.

STANDEN
East Grinstead, *West Sussex*

Bequeathed to the Trust in 1973 by Miss Helen Beale

AREA 4 ha (10 acres)
SOIL Lime-free
ALTITUDE 60.9 m (200 fet)
RAINFALL 686 mm (27 in.)
TEMPERATURE 4°C (39°F)

1½ miles south of East Grinstead, signposted from B2110

HERE THE TERRAIN, dramatically sloping, and the desire to grow plants have prompted the style of design, known as the Gardenesque. In spite of his living so near there is no evidence that William Robinson had anything to do with the design and planting, though both owe something to his precepts. As at CHARTWELL, the slope is downhill from the house and then across the valley to rising wooded ground beyond. It is a beautiful setting and the appetite is whetted when you descend the entrance drive, so forcefully bounded on one side by a high dank cliff of sandstone. The house comes into view accompanied by old Scots Pines, hollies, *Phillyraea latifolia* and rhododendrons, including *R.* "Boddaertianum", with its rusty leaves and blush-white spotted flowers.

It is pleasant to go round to the side of the group of buildings where a cottage faces the Goose Green complete with plane trees; but your eyes will probably travel to the view across the valley.

On the east side of the house there is a mulberry in a square lawn, surrounded by Dutch lavender. The south walls of the house, on which grow double white and double yellow Banksian Roses, *Smilax aspera* and white jasmine, look towards Philip Webb's garden fence. Hereabouts are fragrant plants: 'Zéphirine Drouhin' and 'New Dawn' roses, Virgin's Bower, Hidcote Lavender. The main border, devoted principally to blue

138 The walk to the gazebo, Standen.

and lavender flowers with grey-leafed plants, is punctuated with the sweet-smelling evergreen, *Osmanthus delavayi*.

If you are there in September you may espy the little Ladies' Tresses Orchid in the upper lawns. Hydrangeas give colour, together with fuchsias and various other shrubs; rhododendrons, azaleas, kalmias and *Prunus tenella* are grouped around different portions of lawn; these lawns take you ever downhill under a *Davidia*, a mighty Monterey Pine and tall Tulip Tree to the old orchard, now replanted, where rhododendrons are grouped in the form of a bower. Among the shrubs are several forms of Japanese Maple, coppery, cut-leafed and others; one especial pride and joy is a fine bush of the Coral-leafed Maple. Its foliage in spring is a warm rosy coral.

Above and beyond the house, under the main hill, is a little rocky dell, partly of natural stone and partly built, where epimediums and ferns are grown. *Blechnum penna-marina*, a dwarf evergreen fern, has made wide groups and the citron Hoop Petticoat Daffodil and British native flowers have seeded themselves. They are overshadowed by *Magnolia soulangiana* and its relatives and also by *M. obovata* which delights us with its handsome leaves and is so gloriously fragrant in June; purplish seed cones develop later. Camellias add to the spring delights when primulas and anemones begin to show, and in moist places the fronds of the Royal Fern unfurl, crozier-like, covered with buff-tinted scales.

If you tire of so much concentrated horticulture there is a delightful escape route – a long level walk beyond the Fern Dell. Blue Cedar, azaleas and Tree Heaths accompany you for most of the way, but from the little gazebo at the end the eye leaves the garden planting and can enjoy wide and restful views.

STOURHEAD
Mere, *Wiltshire*

Given in 1946–7 by Sir Henry Hoare, Bt

AREA 16 ha (40 acres)	At Stourton, west
SOIL Lime-free	of the B3092
ALTITUDE 152 m (500 ft)	Frome–Mere road
RAINFALL 889 mm (35 in.)	
TEMPERATURE 3.5°C (38°F)	

SOME PEOPLE go to Stourhead to enjoy a constitutional walk round the lake. Others are particularly interested in the architectural features. Many go to see the great trees and shrubs, native or exotic, or to rejoice in the appearance annually of native flowers. Some think of Stourhead as a home for birds. Others go in May and June to glory in the great banks of colour from rhododendrons; others, again, go at any time but this in order to enjoy a more peaceful visit. Some consider that October and November give best the welding of colourful beauty and comparative quiet. They all go, whether consciously or unconsciously, because the place as a whole is beautiful and the detail is composed of beautiful things. It is in fact a unique work of art, and one of the most precious, involved and all-embracing of the several great landscape works of the 18th century. It is as valuable to the nation as a Gainsborough or a Turner, but does not remain static; as unique as a great musical work, but it cannot be reproduced. Crowds come yearly to see it in its many moods. I have been there several times a year for over twenty years, in every month and in all weathers, in broiling sun, in rain, in fog or wind, when the lakes are alive with life or sibilant with broken ice, or all is frozen hard. It never fails to please.

Its history is well known; a wealthy London banker, Henry Hoare, purchased Stourton House, pulled it down and started to build the new one in 1718; his son, also Henry, a highly educated man, versed in the classics, came to live there in 1741, and during the next forty years impressed his thoughts on the landscape and created much that we see today (see illus. 22). The mainspring was the study of the classics, both in words and pictures. He was driven in upon himself by the sad losses over the years of his wife, son and two daughters, and devoted himself to the great endeavour of making a work of art out of an almost unlimited landscape. He left his estate and work to his grandson, Richard Colt Hoare, who added to the house and garden landscape in both elaboration and planting. Thereafter various members of the family succeeded to the property, each adding their quota to the planting. Throughout it is a long story of bereavement for the family, but with the beauty of Stourhead acting as a salve and outlet for their energies. The love of growing things was inherited by the first Henry from his grandfather Richard, who tried to import evergreens for his London garden from Holland around 1701; they were lost to the French in transit.

If you approach Stourhead from the east the remarkable transition from a landscape of long, low, smooth chalk hills to a wooded valley of rich lime-free greensand becomes the more apparent. It can be appreciated even more from the east front of the house, which is a prospect of particular beauty. Thereafter you may walk round the house taking in the later extensions to the original building, and enjoying the large lawns fringed with rhododendrons and trees. Tulip Trees grow extremely well at Stourhead and one of the largest is beyond the lawn enlivened by extensive carpets of Lent Lilies in spring, and later by bluebells which flower with the scented, yellow Pontic Azalea. A little *Carya* or Hickory grows nearby; it is from this tree that the best rollers for lawn mowers are made. On busy weekends the gate we come to is opened, at other times closed, but it is the best route to take, revealing

139 The interior of the Grotto at Stourhead: a water-colour impression by F. Nicholson, 1813/14.

that wonderful glimpse, shortly, of the Temple of Apollo, serene and riding, as it were, on a sea of greenery on the hill across the valley. The Fir Walk to the Obelisk has recently been cleared of seedling trees and rubbish and will in time provide a diversion again. Meanwhile the so-called Sand Walk leading you to the Shades provides some glorious views down to, and across, the main lake. It is useless to try to put one's experience and delight into words; the moods are so variable and the variety of views too extensive, but there is no doubt that this is the best way to approach the lake.

On the other hand, on leaving the car park you can descend the valley and enter the garden landscape by the gate on the village green, with the much-photographed view before you of the cross brought from Bristol in 1765, the Stone Bridge built in 1762, with the distant view of the Pantheon (1754) across the lake (see plate XLV), thence to walk along the path to the right joining the route from the house farther along.

Henry Hoare had a wooden bridge across the lake part way along the eastern shore. His grandson, Richard Colt Hoare, laid out the sequence of paths and in doing so brought into the tour the little lake known as Diana's Basin, and the Lily Lake above it. This again is a spot for extensive and beautiful views, especially in autumn when, beyond the Lily Lake, the next piece of water has banks overspread by beeches and covered by the russet of their fallen leaves. Here we may pause and remember that, with the church, these smaller lakes – and some more engulfed by the main lake when the encircling dam was made in 1744 – are of mediaeval origin.

Thereafter it was Henry Hoare's intention, which has again been followed by the Trust, that the approach to the Grotto (the next point of interest) should be overgrown and shaded by trees and evergreens or "lost in a wood". You first come to a small arch of rough rock and enter a gloomy cavern, to the sound of running water, where the Nymph of the Grot lies sleeping. This is where the waters are gathered from the bank and flow out into the lake, so flatly brilliant when seen at this low viewpoint. Horace Walpole, in 1784, described it as the "most judiciously, and indeed the most fortunately placed grotto ... where the river bursts from the urn of its god and passes on its course through the cave". Beyond is the statue of the River God and thence steps will take you up to the high bank and presently the Watch Cottage comes into view. Just beyond is the next view of the Pantheon, and the Iron Bridge. The walk here approaches the bridge and takes in a wide sweep of countryside; next a view of the plunging, splashing cascade of 1765, falling into the lower lake. Ascend the Rock Arch, which will take you up a zig-zag path past the site of the Hermit's Cave, to the Temple of Apollo. From the Rock Arch and the Temple of Apollo some superb panoramic views are obtained, of the whole terrain, the lake and its islands. Shortly after descending the grotto tunnel – which means you have crossed the main road twice – the Temple of Flora (see illus. 23), and the Stone Bridge appear again from a different angle, and you are at the exit.

This rather prosaic description of the whole *raison d'être* of the design at Stourhead is at best a mere introduction to the wide variety of the sequence of events devised mainly by Henry Hoare, with extensive and ever-changing views. No words of mine can convey half of the magic and size of the place. It has always been, and always will remain a source of inspiration. You have to be well versed in history to appreciate to the full the classical overtones, and the varied architecture: the Roman-style seats in the Temple of Flora, the grass-covering of the Stone Bridge, the golden light and rich echoes of the Pantheon and its statues; the intimate touch of the cottage; the crowning glory of the Temple of Apollo, from where can be seen the gilded star of the Obelisk shining from the far side of the lake, carrying one's mind back to the first view of it from the west front of the house. The Obelisk commemorates the Hoare Family to whom we owe all this beauty.

The Temple of Flora is one of the first buildings we see today as it is in the extemporised route from the village gate. In a quotation from Virgil over the door, Henry Hoare sought to warn visitors that unless they were "initiated" into the classics and mysteries of the past they should not enter. But Flora, the goddess of flowers, beckons us on, initiated or otherwise, to taste the beauties assembled in the grounds. Once again on a historical basis we may recall the huge old Sweet Chestnuts on the approach to the house; in all probability they are pre-Hoare. Throughout the grounds there are splendid trees; beeches, for instance, planted over two hundred years ago and still in the glory of their lofty smooth boles and spreading canopy of branches. Particularly fine ones are in the Shades, and most or all would have been planted by Henry Hoare; he wanted light green to blend in great sweeps with the darker greens of firs in the way of the painters of "landskips". It was his grandson Colt Hoare who started adding exotic trees such as the Norwegian Maple, Variegated Sycamore, Pink Chestnut, the picturesque Weeping Ash by the water, variegated hollies, Tulip Trees, planes, and some Lebanon Cedars. He was in control from 1783 to 1838. The next big planting period was from 1894 to 1947, by the 6th Baronet. He contributed many conifers, particularly to the north-west of the lake, and the bulk of the named varieties of rhododendron. The background evergreens, Cherry Laurel, and Pontic Rhododendron, had been in command of many shaded areas since the late 18th century, when the rhododendron gradually replaced the laurel as a "choice" evergreen. Further trees have been put in by the Trust, notably those which reinstate older vanished plantings such as those by the garden entrance and on the green by the church.

Whatever may be our principal appreciation of Stourhead, we cannot escape the riches Flora has brought to the scene, mirroring the tastes of several generations. If you are fortunately there in earliest March you may catch the reflections of millions of tiny daffodils in the lake, against the parchment tint of last year's rushes and the warm maroon-red of the Dogwood. Soon the red bells of *Rhododendron* "Shilsonii" will be sounding out their telling colour to be followed by numerous others, *R. cinnabarinum* and its hybrids, *R. arboreum* and hybrids, *R. yunnanense*, hardy old hybrids of the Waterer class, newer ones in strange colours; all colours were planted in this century around the lake, dotted indiscriminately. Many of the more strident clashes have been combed out and a few dozen of the scarlet 'Britannia' have been gathered together in the shade, out of sight, where their colour can glow without harm. 'Loderi', 'Kewense', *thomsonii* and others are there until late maroon 'Impi' opens its flowers, and the season eventually closes with 'Polar Bear' and *auriculatum*, in July or even August. For many of the May-June weeks the fragrance is not only from 'Loderi' and its relatives but also from the Pontic and other Azaleas.

If you are looking for conifers you will not be disappointed. By the entrance is a wide-spreading specimen of *Picea abies* 'Clanbrasiliana' and beyond the Temple of Flora *Chamaecyparis obtusa* 'Nana Gracilis' almost 9.1 m (30 ft) high; it is usually a rock garden plant. Green and blue and Deodar cedars, together with spruce and fir trees from Europe, China and America abound. The Japanese *Pinus parviflora* at 21.3 m (70 ft) is the tallest recorded in Britain. Lofty Noble Firs dominate several views and the Macedonian pine at 33.5 m (110 ft) is another record in height. There is a small grove of Dawn Redwood and a *Torreya californica* of 14.3 m (47 ft).

During the summer the most conspicuous trees are two large Copper Beeches and the silvery White Willows; these are all notable specimens. Less conspicuous until in flower or autumn colour are younger catalpas, davidias, rowans, eucryphias, *Aesculus indica* and magnolias. In May the group of magnolias along the southern shore of the lake brings to this walk pink and white flowers of great sculptural quality, abundance and fragrance. In the autumn the Japanese Maples are the first to turn to scarlet, followed by many another exotic plant in red and orange and yellow, leaving the natives, the stalwart, resistant beeches, oaks and Sweet Chestnuts, to carry on in brown, ochre and yellow; if you are fortunate you may find a view where their colours are interspersed with the silver of the willows. There is one memorable moment when, standing near the Weeping Larch on the south shore, one sees the westering winter sun light on the orange-twigged willows on one of the islands, while the woodland beyond is in black shadow.

But no beauty, architectural or floricultural, quite equals that first glimpse of the Temple of Apollo from the path from the house. This is worth a long journey to see. (See plate XLVI.)

The war years resulted in neglect at Stourhead as they did in almost every garden. The Trust's task in the 1950s and 1960s was first to care for the trees which make the framework of the garden. Thousands of young beech trees have been planted to replace old trees that had fallen or had to be felled. In spite of the depredations of squirrels among beeches, chestnuts and sycamores, there are many trees coming on for the future. It is recognised that at places like Stourhead, while obviously the main historic views must be kept open, other views will come and go over the many decades in the growth and development of trees.

One of the biggest and abiding jobs is the control of the undergrowth. Common laurel, which can grow almost a metre (3 ft) in a year, and Pontic Rhododendron which is half as quick, are voracious consumers of ground, particularly in the shade; they are very much part of the landscape at Stourhead, the laurel having been planted extensively in the 18th century, but many paths would be completely obliterated if they were not kept in check annually. Likewise the bramble is a cause of much winter work. And always there lurks in the ground the deadly fungus, *Armillaria*, whose black "bootlaces" fasten on to the roots of trees and shrubs with disastrous effect. It is probable that this disease was present in Henry Hoare's time but it is fostered by old woodland stumps and particularly beech stumps which decay quickly. We may take heart however in the knowledge that the history and landscape delights of this renowned place are being carefully watched and fostered for the benefit of us all in what has been called "Henry Hoare's Paradise". Paradise is but another name, long acknowledged, for "garden".

SUDBURY HALL
Uttoxeter, *Derbyshire*

Accepted by the Treasury in part payment of estate duty and transferred to the Trust in 1967. An endowment was given by Lord Vernon

AREA 6.8 ha (17 acres)	6 miles east of
SOIL Lime-free	Uttoxeter on A50
ALTITUDE 45 m (150 ft)	
RAINFALL 635 mm (25 in.)	
TEMPERATURE 3.5°C (38°F)	

THIS RENOWNED Caroline house had at one time a great formal garden to the south, the subject of a painting in 1700. During the 18th century this was swept away and several formal lakes were turned into a "natural" one, with an arched stone bridge at one end. The big grass banks and terraces below the south front of the house were constructed in the 1820s to the design of William Sawrey Gilpin. Since it acquired the property the Trust has decorated these top terraces – which had become featureless – with some formal, Victorian-style, star-shaped beds planted with Hybrid Musk Roses and edged with Cotton Lavender. These edgings in turn are rimmed with gravel and an outer box edging. Balls of box decorate the points of the stars. The terraces run into tree plantations at either end, reinforced by a quincunx of lime trees on the top terrace which has been planted with the intention of focussing the eye on the main house. The second terrace has a pool; the paths are picked out with standard hollies and the plats with two yews, intended to be clipped into geometric shape. These embellishments were inspired by John Fowler, who helped the Trust with the interior of the house.

TATTON PARK
Knutsford, *Cheshire*

Bequeathed to the Trust by the 4th Lord Egerton of Tatton

AREA 20 ha (50 acres)	2 miles north
SOIL Lime-free	of Knutsford,
ALTITUDE 60.9 m (200 ft)	13 miles south-west
RAINFALL 711 mm (28 in.)	of Manchester,
TEMPERATURE 3.5°C (38°F)	off A537

A STRAIGHT DRIVE bordered by very old beech trees was at one time the main entry; it now is embodied in the garden. At the very end of the 18th century, Humphry Repton recommended that it should be made to curve and the trees be distributed into clumps. His advice was fortunately not taken since today it makes an impressive, firm feature. He did design a new drive, which lies within sight of Tatton Mere, a large sheet of water, and he asked for a second sheet of water but this was also refused. In recent times a depression occurred due to extensive salt extraction, and a lake has formed more or less where he had intended. Today one arrives either by this drive or by a gentle curving one, also of about his date, lined by two rows of trees – beeches, limes and sycamores. The tall trees, mostly beeches, scattered through the garden areas, survive from this period.

140 Lawns and terraced garden at Tatton Park. Photo 1961.

The porticoed south front of the house looks over the large landscape away to the mere, across wide sloping lawns, taking in below its gravel terrace the formal garden, fountain and beds and marble vases designed by Sir Joseph Paxton in 1856. The colours of the roses and plants, pinks and mauves, blues, white and pale yellow, are soft enough not to detract from the distant view. If you walk west you will come to a big L-shaped border filled with shrubs and plants. It is divided into sections by buttresses of yew and each section is devoted to a different colour scheme. But apart from the colours there are some unusual shrubs of long standing, such as *Eucryphia intermedia*, *Cytisus battandieri*, *Olearia virgata*, *Itea ilicifolia*. Out of the shaped hollies tumble rambling roses and clematises. The vases on top of the wall are in reality chimneys because the wall was at one time heated by flues to assist in the growing of fruit trees against it. Opposite, on the lawn, are *Magnolia kobus*, *M. obovata*, *M. tripetala*, *Cornus controversa* while Lady Charlotte's charming bower invites you to dally.

The L-shaped path following the wall borders leads straight into the long Beech Walk, but let us step aside between tall topiary – with a peacock about to "take off" – into a small formal garden complete with garden shelter, sunken patio, formal pool and fountain, and flanking pergolas. Roses of soft colours, 'The Fairy' and 'Pink Parfait', 'Frances E. Lester', 'Zéphirine Drouhin', Mock Orange, honeysuckles and jasmines contribute to the scent in this enclosure. Yet another small garden adjoins it; here is the old brick tower from which a watch was kept for sheep-stealers in the park. Now it looks down on flowers and rare shrubs: *Decaisnea fargesii*, *Emmenopterys henryi*, *Distylium racemosum* and the Kentucky Coffee Tree, *Gymnocladus dioicus*.

If you go to Tatton in May and June you will find a very wide selection of rhododendrons and azaleas in flower. The latter embrace the evergreen Japanese types, old Ghent and Mollis varieties and many Knaphill and Exbury hybrids. In rhododendrons there are tiny dwarfs like *R. ferrugineum* and *ovatum* of gardens, the exquisite grey-leafed *R. lepidostylum*, *R. williamsii*, to many a popular hardy hybrid including the inevitable 'Pink Pearl' and all the stalwart Waterer breed, later 'Moser's Maroon', 'Azor' and *R. auriculatum*. These are grouped and scattered in many places, mirrored in pools and the Golden Brook, contrasted by great ferny beeches, and the dark green of many a good conifer. Compact *Tsuga mertensiana*, *Austrocedrus chilensis*, *Pinus pumila*, *P. cembra* and *Abies koreana* give inspiration to owners of small gardens, while the graceful *Picea smithiana*, *P. brewerana*, *P. likiangensis*, the tall *P. orientalis* and Wellingtonias tower above them. There is a small grove here also of Dawn Redwood. Among some of the "blue" conifers, spruces and cypresses, the blue *Lactuca bourgaei* is allowed to grow – not that one can ever get rid of its invasive roots! All this exotic beauty stems from the impassioned planting of the last Lord Egerton between 1940 and 1958.

If you walk along the Golden Brook, past several commanding Swamp Cypresses of considerable age and size, pale green in spring and foxy-brown in autumn, past waterlilies and yellow Flag Iris and Purple Loosestrife, you will come to a unique feature. It is a Japanese garden laid out in a traditional way by Japanese workmen in 1910. I do not know of another

141 In the Japanese Garden at Tatton Park.

142 New Zealand Tree Ferns (*Dicksonia antarctica*) and *Woodwardia radicans* in the Fernery at Tatton Park in 1961.

garden of its size and kind in the country which so nearly approaches what was understood as a Japanese garden of that date; it was long after the Chinese influence came to England – more than a hundred years in fact – and connects most closely with the *art nouveau* movement. There is, to start with, a Shinto temple which is linked to the garden by a pretty, typical, arched bridge. Thence there are numerous views governed by the etiquette perfected over centuries of Japanese civilisation, concerned with contemplation and the sipping of tea. So we have stones and water of important significance in the scenes, a miniature Mount Fuji Yama and pagoda, stone lanterns of various shapes and purposes, such as the broad-topped Snow-scene lantern, the valley-scene lantern on arching support, and lofty domed Enshiu shape. With the bamboos and pines, and solely Japanese plants which are used, meandering waters and slab-bridges, it conveys enough of what is intended to make us wish it could be maintained by Japanese gardener-craftsmen.

What we have passed through lies to the west of the Long Walk; to the east are more and more rhododendrons with an occasional rare tree or shrub; *Acer carpinifolium*, which usually defies identification; *Kalopanax pictus* which looks much more like a maple, and the rare *Oplopanax horridus* or Devil's Club. We pass a thatched shelter and come to another pool and fountain embowered in azaleas; not far away is a beech maze, a *Pterocarya* and a Dawn Redwood, and thence you can return to the lowest approach to the Italian garden, below the house; on mounting the steps the full majesty of terrace and vases, steps and portico come upon you.

This is not all. The orangery, designed by Lewis Wyatt and built in 1811, has many fascinating plants in it: *Dipladenia sanderi* from Brazil with large pink trumpet-flowers, mandarin and Seville oranges and lemons, some in decorative Chinese pots or standing by Chinese porcelain stools. And if ferns are your special ploy do not fail to visit the Fernery in which New Zealand Tree Ferns stand loftily above you, but never reach the glass roof, simply because when they get too tall, their stems are sawn off and they are planted deeper. Among them are some that may well have been brought to England by Captain Egerton, RN over a hundred years ago. Here in Cheshire they need artificial warmth; in Cornwall they grow in the open air, likewise that most graceful and large of semi-hardy ferns, *Woodwardia radicans*, whose fronds achieve 2.4 m (8 ft) in length. With them all, contrasting with the green filigree, are time-honoured aspidistras, and the walls are covered with self-clinging, small-leafed fig, *Ficus pumila* from the Far East. Tatton I think may be briefly described as a very great garden with numerous separate attractions superimposed on an old plan, a palimpsest of nearly two hundred years' development.

TINTINHULL HOUSE
Yeovil, *Somerset*

Given in 1953 by Mrs P. E. Reiss

AREA 0.3 ha ($\frac{3}{4}$ acre)	5 miles north-west
SOIL Limy	of Yeovil,
ALTITUDE 30 m (100 ft)	1 mile east of A303
RAINFALL 762 mm (30 in.)	
TEMPERATURE 4°C (39°F)	

WE SEE AT Tintinhull a garden in the Jekyll tradition, brought to its high state of perfection by Phyllis Reiss, who first worked in this modern style of gardening in a garden near HIDCOTE where she and her husband lived. Those experiences and others of her youth when she used to stay not infrequently at Warnham Court, Sussex, served her in good stead on arrival at Tintinhull. She lived there for twenty-eight years, tending and developing the garden and continually polishing her planting schemes. In design, proportion and colour they followed the Jekyll pattern. I do not mean by this that they were anything but original, and she was always on the look out for a new (or old) good plant which might be an improvement on the one she grew, so long as it would conform to the overall scheme. In 1965, in *The Field*, Margery Fish, her friend and neighbour, put the matter very clearly: "Many gardens are interesting and beautiful, but few have this blessed feeling of serenity, for, whatever the season, the garden is lovely, with different flowers and shapes but always in harmony. This is achieved by choosing plants that fit in with a preconceived plan and not because of their individual attraction. This does not mean there are not unusual plants in the garden. There are many, but they have been chosen so cleverly that one sees the garden as a whole first and discovers the many treasures in it afterwards."

Mrs Reiss, in a broadcast in 1939, said: "As the garden is flat and overlooked from most of the rooms in the house, my main object in planning and planting is to make it as interesting as possible all the year round."

Though the soil was not ideal – it is rather sticky and ill-drained and also limy – there were certain things to aid her. The house, mainly built about 1600, has a garden front of over a hundred years later and it is this which gives such a satisfying background to the series of rectangular areas, enclosed in brick walls, leading away from it. These walled gardens were built soon after 1900. In addition there is a majestic Lebanon Cedar and a pair of Holm Oaks; these are the only trees of any height within the garden. Mr and Mrs Reiss nearly doubled the size of the garden by adding two areas at right angles to the main vista which leads through the walled gardens.

So that the Trust could feel that it really was caring for Mrs Reiss's garden and planting schemes, a complete inventory was made of all the plants, border by border, after her death. This list is available to you for a few pence, to aid you in studying and profiting by her skill achieved over the years. Since her death the Trust has been fortunate in its tenants, first Miss Katherine Bevan and now Miss Molly Ware, who both appreciate so much what is meant by Tintinhull.

Whenever you go to Tintinhull you will find each section of the garden presenting a different selection of plants, through the seasons. If it is not the time of yellow "Mrs Moon" tulips and green hellebores, it will be Tree Peony time, or that of lavenders and Regal lilies, or in autumn pink nerines and *Gladiolus callianthа (Acidanthera)*. Elsewhere there are beds of special soil where azaleas thrive and hydrangeas of the grander kind grow in the shade of a wall. Fritillarias and erythroniums come in spring with the dainty blooms of epimediums.

Enclosed by dark yew hedges, not by walls, the little fountain and pool are only given white flowers and silvery foliage – white roses, anemones, irises, lilies, colchicums and the Summer Hyacinth. Turning off to the kitchen garden with its rows of vegetables and flowers for cutting and cross vista of espalier fruit trees, one is again struck how everything fits together.

The main cross vista is towards a pillared garden shelter seen at the far end of a long rectangular pool. The borders on either side go far with all visitors in summer, for they are perhaps the most polished of Mrs Reiss's efforts. Perhaps unwisely today, I dub the one a masculine border – its colours are daring and unusual, scarlet, yellow, white (see plate XLI) – and the other feminine; here the tints are soft, pink, mauve, blue, and light yellow. The two are made into a pair by clumps of sword-like leaves and also of grey foliage; both are backed by dark hedges and are some 3.6 m (12 ft) wide, edged with flagstones along the grass verge. Grey eucalyptus, white philadelphus, yellow Mount Etna Broom, coppery prunus, and the lofty cedar carry one's eye upwards.

In the cedar tree garden is a border given to red flowers and copper and yellow-leafed shrubs, which is as tellingly different in its spring delight as in full summer colour. If I say that every area has its spring bulbs, every wall its climbers, and every plant its bloom in due season, I can stop writing and leave you to explore and learn, as I have done for many years, this first-hand garden expertise. None other than Dame Sylvia Crowe, in her book *Garden Design*, cites Tintinhull many times, and repeats the theme that all writers accent: "Its planting is probably unique, because it combines a use of very varied species grown naturally, and yet used strictly as elements of design."

TRELISSICK
Truro, *Cornwall*

Given by Mrs Ronald Copeland with an endowment in 1955

AREA 10 ha (25 acres)
SOIL Lime-free
ALTITUDE 30 m (100 ft)
RAINFALL 1016 mm (40 in.)
TEMPERATURE 6.5°C (44°F)

4 miles south of Truro on the B3289 Truro–St Mawes road

FOR MANY YEARS it was a well-known thing that my once- or twice-yearly visits to Trelissick heralded rain. In times of drought I have actually been prayed for, at others sentiments were different. It always appeared a little unfair to me (it is so difficult writing notes with one hand holding an umbrella to shelter the papers) because there seems no doubt that the visitation of rain was merely retribution on the head gardener, who years ago, as garden boy, inadvertently sprayed the then head gardener with whitewash!

Though I had visited Cornish gardens before doing so officially for the Trust, it was and always is like setting forth into a new world – the soft climate, general absence of frost, the lush growth in the sheltered places usually chosen for gardens, all producing a sense of wonder. The excessive planting of rhododendrons in overgrown array characterises so many of the Cornish gardens, and often there is little else but hydrangeas, eucryphias and hoherias for late summer. Trelissick is blessed with wide lawns sloping down to the valley, not rough mown areas but closemown greensward, and it is this which makes it so different from many Cornish shrub gardens. The garden is on either side of a valley down which runs the road to the King Harry Ferry.

Those who possess beautiful Spode plates decorated with flowers may like to know that, from 1937 at least, many of the subjects came from Trelissick; Mr Copeland was managing director of the Spode china factory until 1955. He planted most of the choice shrubs in the garden and thus it may be called a modern garden. Before Mrs Copeland inherited the place, members of the Gilbert family had been busy putting in most of the clumps of trees in the park and also some conifers in the garden, including the large Japanese Cedar on the main lawn, the Maritime Pines, Holm Oaks, Himalayan Spruce – this is now about 21.3 m (70 ft), but one was recorded as being 18.2 m (60 ft) in 1894 – the plane, Deodar, and several Atlas Mountain Cedars. These had all reached considerable size, and with the native oaks and beeches provided a ready-made background for the new plantings of rhododendrons and other shrubs.

It is remarkable to record that for my first visit, in May 1959, the sun shone brilliantly. The weather had not got into its stride! Though it is not in the garden, the view from the house to the River Fal held me spellbound. The lie of the land and the shining water are spacious and lovely, huge trees frame the view and the porticoed house fittingly closes it. We resolved then and there that the garden should be spacious and lovely too, throughout the growing season, and not just a formless botanical collection.

But first there were several winters' work in attending to trees, felling the unsafe and pruning others. Trees which the head gardener had climbed for fun as a boy were now needing expert attention aloft. New trees needed planting for the future, and shelter-belts needed establishing. All this has been done, together with the construction of a haha to the west so that the fine view of the river and park is unimpeded.

Many shrubs were overgrown and some needed moving to fresh quarters. What a rich assembly of rhododendrons there were – to which we have added late-flowering kinds like 'Aladdin' and 'Bustard' to prolong the display. From spring onwards the garden is full of bloom. One of the first things to flower is the evergreen magnolia-relative *Michelia doltsopa* from Tibet, with white sweet-scented flowers. Planted in 1946, it is now 10.6 m (35 ft) high and 8.5 m (28 ft) across. Then the rhododendrons start, with white *R. leucaspis*, blood-red *R. thomsonii*, blush *R. sutchuenense*, and pretty pink *R. williamsianum*, with its hybrids 'Bow Bells' and 'Cowslip', and pure yellow *R. wardii*. There are several of *R. cinnabarinum* with long, narrow tubular flowers, 'Roylei', 'Lady Chamberlain', and 'Full House'. At one corner of the main lawn is a most beautiful blend of colours: mauve *R. concinnum*, pale yellow 'Mary Swathling' and an orange *R. cinnabarinum*. Tall rhododendrons are above us on banks and small ones by our feet, several casting delicious fragrance from their glistening lily-like trumpets: 'Lady Alice Fitzwilliam', *R.R. bullatum*, *iteophyllum*,

143 *Hydrangea* 'Ayesha', closely related to *H. macrophylla normalis*, but with incurved petals, usually of lilac-grey. One of the great collection of species and cultivars at Trelissick.

lindleyi and *polyandrum*. They thrive at Trelissick without protection.

There are also many tender hybrids of great luxuriance raised in different Cornish gardens, such as 'Beauty of Tremough', 'Glory of Penjerrick' and 'Penjerrick' itself, 'Richard Gill', 'St Probus' and 'Trewithen Orange'. Two originated at Trelissick, 'Trelissick Port Wine' and 'Trelissick Salmon': the latter was a self-sown seedling. On the other hand there are many well-tried old hardy hybrids like 'Mrs G. W. Leak', 'Mrs A. T. de la Mare', 'Sigismund Rucker', 'Strategist' and others, besides the inevitable 'Pink Pearl' and 'Cynthia'. Mr Copeland particularly liked red rhododendrons and there is a long succession of gorgeous varieties: 'Little Bert', 'David', 'Earl of Athlone', 'Gwillt King', 'May Day', 'Elizabeth', 'Fusilier', 'Tally Ho' and 'Romany Chai'. There are also many deciduous and evergreen azaleas. These with many *Camellia japonica* forms, *C. williamsii* crosses, *C. reticulata* 'Captain Rawes', and, for autumn, *C. sasanqua*, keep up a long display augmented with hellebores, daffodils and narcissi naturalised in the grass in many places together with *Anemone nemorosa*, large blue 'Allenii' and the neat double white 'Vestal' (see plate XXXIX).

There is one very fair spot where on rounding a corner obscured by *Rhododendron* 'Russellianum' or 'Cornish Red', the fine Japanese Cedar comes into view and away in Carcadden, beyond the road to the ferry, are cherries and flowering shrubs of all kinds. The sloping lawns at one time had two long straight borders but these were adjusted to a line more sympathetic to the rest of the garden in the early 1960s. In the far corner, in brilliant shrimp-pink spring foliage, is the variety of Sycamore known as "Prinz Handjery", against Japanese maples. For the long summer months this whole lawn is bordered with pink and white crinum lilies, shining through a mist of tiny mauve flowers of the stately *Thalictrum delavayi*, with hybrid ceanothus, crimson and purple hebes, hardy plumbago, rare fuchsias, cannas, *Abelia grandiflora* – a very large bush – and backed by a climber-covered wall. Pale green leaves of *Hosta plantaginea* contrast with dark green of *Acanthus*, as a foreground to *Crinodendron hookeri* hung with scarlet bells and, later, the mauve of *Hydrangea villosa* and the unusual *H. macrophylla* 'Ayesha' with cup-shaped florets.

Another lawn has greeny-orange *Kniphofia rooperi* and white hydrangeas of various kinds leading up to stately eucryphias and the leaden green of *Eucalyptus gunnii* and *E. subcrenulata*. From this lawn is a captivating view of distant Tregothnan House, a Gothick fantasy, often with modern ships in the backwater below; the view is framed with wide-spreading branches of *Cornus capitata* covered with soft butter-yellow flowers in June.

Carcadden, the ground over the bridge beyond the road, has been transformed from a poor sort of orchard and nursery ground into an extension of the garden, worthy, the Trust hopes, of Trelissick. It had all to be kept tidy in any case, and so the new plantings have made little extra work. One is never far from hydrangeas at Trelissick; here in Carcadden are dozens of Hortensia and Lacecap cultivars of *Hydrangea macrophylla*, together with several of *H. serrata*. All together in the garden there is a fairly complete collection of species and cultivars numbering well over a hundred. In autumn *Acer platanoides* 'Cucullatum' is conspicuous; young magnolias of the tree type are rapidly growing; *Magnolia globosa*, both Indian and Chinese forms, and *M. wilsonii* thrive. Against the gloom of evergreens the 'Silver Queen' *Pittosporum* shines forth, and orange azaleas are grouped round some coppery-leafed nuts and maples.

As you recross the bridge, note the deep dell, spread with ferns and astilbes, Willow Gentian and *Kirengeshoma palmata*, cimicifugas and primulas, with a striking backcloth of true *Rhododendron arboreum* – erect trees, clad in dark narrow leaves, a curtain of scarlet and pink in spring. In this sheltered spot, overtowered by the Gilbert's plane tree, are several New Zealand Tree Ferns and a Banana, contrasted by delicate bamboo foliage. I have seen frost and snow on the crowns of the ferns but it has not harmed them. Opposite is an impressive group of the large evergreen fern, *Blechnum chilense* from Chile.

It has long been the tradition at Trelissick to grow Heliotrope in the border near the entrance gate. Its scent is a welcome as you come in and a reminiscence as you go out. Usually around it are fuchsias of many colours, while entwined in *Hoheria sexstylosa* from New Zealand are the white flowers of the Potato Vine, *Solanum jasminoides* 'Album' from Brazil. Next to the shop is a little garden which bears the name of Parsley Garden, being near to the kitchen; it now contains many choice and tender shrubs. Among them you may find the intriguing greeny-yellow bells of the Chilean *Vestia lycioides*, the luscious fruits of *Myrtus ugni* (not for tasting), the so-called "Chilean Guava", *Cestrum* 'Newellii', the lavender-blue cups of *Abutilon suntense*, and the unusually effective daisy flowers, in cool lilac with dark centre, of *Olearia semidentata*, a native of the Chatham Isles, which lie some 370 miles east of New Zealand. Plants from the four corners of the earth certainly grace Trelissick – the four corners pointed out by the weather vane on the water tower, above which the Gilberts' crest, a squirrel, twists and turns. (See also illus. 171.)

TRENGWAINTON
Penzance, *Cornwall*

Given with an endowment by Lt-Col. Sir Edward Bolitho in 1961

AREA 6 ha (15 acres)
SOIL Lime-free
ALTITUDE 75 m (250 ft)
RAINFALL 1011 m (40 in.)
TEMPERATURE 7.2°C (45°F)

2 miles west of Penzance, ½ mile west of Heamoor on Penzance–Morvah road (B3312)

IT IS WELL KNOWN that we in these islands always want to grow things which are not really hardy in our own gardens and this can be attributed to two reasons. The first is that there is little to the north of this country which we might wish to grow and the other is that we all hanker after warmth for our bodies and evergreens to cheer the winter days. And evergreens come mainly from warmer climates than ours. We give any tender plants, therefore, the shelter of sunny walls, which is why, in the series of walled enclosures built at Trengwainton around 1820 by Sir Rose Price, the south-west facing walls have high sloping beds of soil to catch every hour of sunshine possible.

The Bolitho family did not come to live at Trengwainton until 1867. When he inherited, Lt-Col. E. H. W. Bolitho, later Sir Edward, found these gardens just the place in which to accumulate one of the most remarkable collections of tender and half-hardy trees, shrubs and plants growing out of doors in England.

Here in these walled gardens, three out of the five of which were filled before I visited the garden on behalf of the Trust, each square has a few big things like magnolias, and then an assortment which it would take an expert to recognise, unless one were versed in plants which are frequently grown under glass elsewhere in these islands. Throughout the enclosures there are species of *Callistemon*, *Acacia*, *Leptospermum*, *Fuchsia*, *Hypericum*, together with camellias and rare southern hemisphere conifers such as *Dacrydium*, *Taiwania*, *Athrotaxis* and *Podocarpus*.

In the first enclosure *Magnolia veitchii* dominates all else, but when you have taken in its majesty you will find yourself drawn to the rest of the area where rarities crowd upon one another. Where else would you find such things as *Melaleuca hypericifolia*, *Acradenia frankliniae*, *Erica canaliculata*, *Vestia lycioides*, *Correa alba* and *Lomatia ferruginea* growing together out of doors? With *Mitraria coccinea* on the wall, overshadowed perhaps by *Rehderodendron macrocarpum*, tender eucryphias and the like? The range of plants is drawn from countries all round the North and South hemispheres.

The second walled garden has a great dark green tree of *Podocarpus salignus*, also *Michelia doltsopa*, *Manglietia hookeri* and numerous smaller things. To get to the third garden you will pass under a huge *Styrax japonica* and be confronted with a huge *Styrax hemsleyana*. They are both hardy in England but their size and the clean bark will astonish you. A splendid *Magnolia campbellii* and *M. cylindrica* grow here as well as *Cassia corymbosa*, *Pentapterygium serpens*, *Gordonia chrysantha*, *Magnolia campbellii mollicomata*, *M. sprengeri diva*, *M. nitida* and *Grevillea sulphurea*. On the wall is *Mandevillea suaveolens*. The last two areas are smaller and were empty when the property was given to the Trust. Sir Edward and I placed several rather special things and I felt very glad to be able to suggest a magnolia new to him. Every species that could be obtained he had already established, and so in the fourth garden a space was given to *M. thompsoniana*, a hybrid which flowers into June, when most are over. Large-flowered fuchsias, *Solanum aviculare* and *Wachendorfia thyrsiflora* are in evidence here, with *Adenocarpus decorticans*, *Dodonaea viscosa* 'Purpurea', *Rhaphithamnus cyanocarpus* and that rare spring flowerer *Myosotideum hortensia*, whose large blue forget-me-not flowers are so remarkable. *Banksia serrata*, *Debregaesia longifolia* and *Melicytus ramiflorus* are a few more rarities. Every year there is a splendid group of the big biennial *Geranium palmatum*, a native of Madeira.

All of these brick-walled gardens have a retaining wall of stone (a Cornish "hedge") on their south-west side and of late years many plants have been established both on and in it. Tucked into crevices are *Fascicularia* and *Lewisia*; tumbling down from the top are the prostrate rosemary, cotoneasters, *Sequoia sempervirens* 'Prostrata', *Lithospermum diffusum*, the fascinating hair-tresses of the Pheasant Tail Grass, and fuchsias. Hanging overhead are the mauve bells of dieramas.

I have not drawn attention to numerous camellias in the walled gardens, nor to the special delight, the sweet-scented rhododendrons. If you go to Trengwainton in late spring your nose will be titillated on every path with the delicious fragrance of species and hybrids of the Maddenii Series, beautiful white flowers some with yellow throats, others flushed or striped with pink, and the giant of all *R. nuttallii*, in creamy yellow; not only do many of them resemble lilies in shape but their fragrance is amazingly pervasive and like that of *Lilium auratum*. The garden has a big selection, *R.R. maddenii, megacalyx, polyandrum, lindleyi, cubittii, taronense, iteophyllum, ciliicalyx, carneum, manipurense, brachysiphon, rhabdotum, johnstoneanum, taggianum, parryae, dalhousiae* ... and hybrids 'Countess of Haddington', 'Tyermanii' and 'White Wings'; also the beautiful lime-tinted yellow 'Laerdal', raised at Trengwainton (see plate VII). They are not only in the walled gardens, but scattered through other parts of the garden. They are all natives of the moist mountain valleys of the eastern Himalayas, Sikkim, Bhutan, Assam and Burma. Several were introduced by Kingdon Ward in his expedition to Assam and the Mishmi Hills in 1927–8, in which Sir Edward took shares. In fact the results of this expedition form the basis on which he built his collection of species.

144 A rare Japanese azalea, *Rhododendron nipponicum*, grows at Trengwainton. White flowers and brilliant autumn leaf-colour.

Having introduced you to the congested collections of plants in the walled gardens I must explain that this is only one section of Trengwainton. The next section is the impressive scenic drive (see plate XLVIII), complete with stream and stretches of grass, and at the top is the garden around the house. The new drive was made in 1897 and the whole garden development of it was made by Sir Edward, the planting on both sides and also the bringing of the stream out of its culvert so that the sound of the water delights the ears while its moisture provides the right conditions for primulas in spring, followed by rodgersias, scarlet lobelias, arums white and yellow, astilbes, and the pale yellow of *Primula florindae* which carries on until Kaffir Lilies start to flower. By then, in late summer, the whole woodland background of the stream, planted with beech and oak trees in the early 19th century, is a wash of pale blue from hundreds of hydrangeas. In the sheltered damp ground are many New Zealand Tree Ferns, hedychiums, meconopses and dianellas, and rhododendrons are within touch everywhere. Here and there are extra sheltered places for *Magnolia rostrata*, and the large-leafed rhododendrons *R.R. grande, falconeri, sino-grande, macabeanum, magnificum, arizelum* and others. Later in the rhododendron season blazing scarlets will be found in several places, *R. eriogynum* and *R. elliottii*; the last species Sir Edward used to create late flowering red hybrids like his renowned 'Morvah'; also 'Bulldog' and 'Lanyon'; 'Cherubim', 'Ding Dong' and 'Nanceglos'. In the same endeavour to pro-long the flowering season is *R. griersonianum*. It grows so fast here that it is usually clipped over after flowering which keeps it compact and floriferous. 'Cornish Cream', a hybrid of *R. campylocarpum*, pleases in its own way earlier.

On one visit to Trengwainton I was invited to provide a list of late-flowering rhododendrons. It contained a number of hybrids raised at Exbury, and Sir Edward quickly brushed it aside with the remark that he didn't want "any of Rothschild's bastards here". I have told several horticulturists this little story through the years, because it amused me very much. What I didn't know was that it must have amused Sir Edward equally, for a year ago it was related to one of my colleagues by Lord Morley at Saltram!

Nothofagus species are much in evidence at Trengwainton; they are some of the new trees which will eventually replace the aged beeches; in addition several long belts of pines have been put in to break the south-west gales. You may walk to the house either up the drive, or via the Long Walk which is over the stream. It was, until 1897, the drive to the house, but it was tortuous and narrow, and led to disasters on dark nights when the drivers of carriages collided with the tree trunks and boulders after being well entertained in the house. Whichever route you take you will find unusual plants: *Schima argentea, Myrtus bullata, M. lechleriana*, acacias and callistemons, *Gevuina avellana, Eucryphia lucida, Stewartia pteropetiolata, Vaccinium retusum*; *Magnolia virginiana* and *Pinus wallichiana* are opposite, in the Queen Mother's Meadow.

Sir Edward gardened, as he used to say, "above the knee", which was his way of informing one that lowly plants did not interest him. In fact he would walk regardlessly through primroses, cyclamens and daffodils to point out to me yet another of his special treasures. After lunch he would probably fall asleep over his coffee and I would creep out, glad to find myself in the heart of the Upper Garden. Here are two widely disparate views. One is of ST MICHAEL'S MOUNT, seen through an arch of beech trees, another is broader, from a long gravel walk raised prior to 1820; all around are beautiful plants. On the house walls for instance are lapagerias, *Kennedya rubicunda, Schizandra sphenanthera, Dendromecon rigidum* 5.4 m (18 ft) high, *Tibouchina semidecandra* 'Grandiflora', *Berberidopsis corallina, Callistemon citrinus* 'Splendens', *C. pithyoides* and *Datura sanguinea*. Across the lawn in autumn the yellowish blooms of *Schima khasiana* look down upon you and *Eucryphia* 'Penwith' – Sir Edward's hybrid between *E. lucida* and *E. moorei* – will be found (see illus. 175 and plate VI).

But come past an old gate bearing the date 1692,

wreathed with *Jasminum polyanthum*, noting dwarf rhododendron species and a luxuriant clump of *Philesia buxifolia*, to a sheltered spot behind laurel hedges where is Trengwainton's crowning glory – an immense tree of *Magnolia sargentiana robusta*. To see this covered with large pink flowers in spring is worth a long journey. The plant is about 15 m (50 ft) high and 18 m (60 ft) broad. Behind it is a tall *Eucryphia cordifolia*; *Rhododendron nipponicum* is by the hedge and there is a grouping of *Camellia williamsii* 'November Pink' around it.

Trengwainton is lucky in that Major Simon Bolitho has inherited his father's love for the garden and its plants and carefully superintends the annual work, with an eye, like the Trust's, on the future.

TRERICE
Newquay, *Cornwall*

Bought in 1954 with money bequeathed by Mrs Annie Woodward

AREA 2.4 ha (6 acres)
SOIL Limy
ALTITUDE 30 m (100 ft)
RAINFALL 940 mm (37 in.)
TEMPERATURE 6°C (43°F)

3 miles south-east of Newquay via A392, west of A3058

A LITTLE GARDEN which is nearly unique in Cornwall, for it is a series of level terraces, walled either in the form of a Cornish "hedge" or retaining wall, or with masonry. The front court was painted in 1818 by George Shepherd and the water colour shews the masonry wall on the south side but nothing on the north apart from the natural rock bank, whence came the spring providing water to the house. The house was largely rebuilt in 1573 by Sir John Arundell and remained in the hands of that family until 1768, and in 1802 passed to Sir Thomas Dyke-Acland of Killerton. Although we have no proof it is likely that he or his descendant built the garden walls.

Though the terracing had remained intact, the garden was in a neglected state in 1969 when the Trust assumed control and since then it has been replanted. The two borders in the front court are planted with shrubs and climbers, choosing plants with purple, blue and yellow colouring to blend with the colour of the stone of the house – surely one of the western-most examples of a building with Dutch-style gables. Some purplish colouring is added by the use of foliage shrubs such as *Hebe* 'Mrs Winder', *Cotinus coggygria* 'Foliis Purpureis'; good blues and purples are provided by the flowers of *Hebe speciosa* hybrids, ceratostigmas and clematises. *Hypericum* 'Rowallane' provides magnificent yellow flowers.

Above is the bowling green created since 1818, a long narrow raised lawn leading to a seat. Here the colouring is different, long stretches of the pair of narrow borders being filled with the grey of *Hebe albicans* backed by pink fuchsias, each strip divided from the next by buttresses of *Drimys lanceolata*, a dark small-leafed evergreen with rich brown spring foliage.

On the other side of the front court is a warm sunny wall wherein *Erinus alpinus* and *Linaria cymbalaria* seed freely; here are more clematises, roses, cistuses and the like. Below the great bowed gable on the south front are further sun-loving dwarf shrubs and the rest of the area is given to orchard trees planted in a quincunx. There are many other good plants but it is the design of the garden which is the overriding interest for the county of Cornwall.

UPPARK
Petersfield, *West Sussex*

Given in 1954 by Admiral the Hon. Sir Herbert Meade-Fetherstonhaugh and his son Richard. Money for maintenance given by the Pilgrim Trust, the Dulverton Trust and anonymously

AREA 3.2 ha (8 acres)
SOIL Limy
ALTITUDE 152 m (500 ft)
RAINFALL 940 mm (37 in.)
TEMPERATURE 4.5°C (40°F)

1 mile south of South Harting on the B2146 Petersfield–Chichester road

"THIS UP PARK is a handsome great house looking southward, with beech woods and bracken thickets to shelter the dappled fallow deer of its wide undulating downland park. Up Park was built by a Fetherstonhaugh and it has always been in the hands of that family." So wrote H. G. Wells in his autobiography in 1934. Thinking again of it as Bladesover, he wrote: "There were corners that gave a gleam of meaning to the word forest, glimpses of unstudied natural splendour. There was a slope of bluebells in the broken sunlight under the newly green beeches in the west wood that is now a precious sapphire in my memory." It came as something of a delight to me to find these impressions by Wells, because his father Joseph had worked in some noted gardens such as Penshurst Place, Trentham Park, and Redleaf; the last is mentioned in the autobiography. But, sadly, no horticulture seems to have rubbed off onto H.G., and so the only reasons for mentioning him now is that he has recorded some of his early life in this house in his autobiography, also in *Tono Bungay* and perhaps in *Bealby*, and that his mother was for thirteen years housekeeper at Uppark.

There is nothing remarkable about the garden at Uppark, but various points of interest add up to a most unusual history. In the first place the house, built in or soon after 1685, was placed on its high downland because the grandfather of the builder, Lord Grey, was

145 The Soapwort has special associations with Uppark. It was depicted in Lyte's *Herball* of 1578 (see illus. 18).

146 An 18th-century summerhouse of wood on a mound at Uppark. The Soapwort grows on the left border. Photo 1977.

the scientist who had contrived to pump Thames water up to rising ground in London for Cromwell. His water wheel is still at Uppark. Practically all earlier houses had to be sited in valleys or where water was available from springs. The approach to Uppark was to the east side of the house, past two pavilions, as depicted by Johannes Kip about 1720 and observed by Celia Fiennes. In about 1750 these pavilions were demolished and replaced by the existing buildings which flank the house, set back from it to east and west. That to the east was originally termed a greenhouse, or plant shelter.

There is also an impression in a letter to Sir Harry Fetherstonhaugh from Humphry Repton in 1810 who found no place with such "olfactory joy as Uppark – every window has its Orange Trees or Tuberoses – and admits perfume from the surrounding beds of Mignonette and Heliotrope – till the whole is an atmosphere of sweets"; and that "the lawns and woods are open to the holiday visitors of rural felicity". Sir Harry commissioned from him the pillared portico on the north front and a new entrance behind it. He added the delightful game-larder of knapped flints with its paths appropriately paved with knucklebones of deer, and probably also the beautiful little dairy. He created two mounts, one of which has a noble vase on top; the other has a Reptonian Gothick summerhouse brought from elsewhere in the park after Sir Harry's death. We can also attribute to him the placing of the gates and drive – in a gentle curve, quite at variance with the date of the house – and the gentle sweeps of lawn.

If you are able to make your visit in August or early September, go round the house to the west lawn and the grass will be dotted with ladies' tresses orchids. Some years ago it was impossible to stand away to the south of the house to gather the whole assembly of buildings into view, but recently the grass terraces have been brought into the ambience of the house by providing a ha-ha to exclude cattle. After much thought we also removed a laurel hedge across the west lawn which had been placed by Repton. And so today the whole prospect of the rolling countryside and a glimpse of the sea from the house and lawns can be enjoyed – but a balloon is required for quiet contemplation of the setting of the buildings nestling among their old beeches.

Buddleia crispa thrives on one of the garden walls, and the tender *Olearia macrodonta* and *Pittosporum tenuifolium* are quite at home. The surprise is to find an old specimen of *Picea smithiana* withstanding so much wind on the chalky hilltop. *Polygonum baldschuanicum* provides a mass of fragrant pinky-white bloom in autumn, threading its way through yews and hollies; beyond is a fine Chinese maple, *Acer griseum*.

By Repton's summerhouse are growing plants of Bouncing Bet or Soapwort – from which plant a soapy solution is obtained. Lady Meade-Fetherstonhaugh used this to clean the 18th-century curtains in the house.

UPTON HOUSE
Edgehill, *Warwickshire*

Given with an endowment by the 1st Viscount Bearsted in 1948

AREA 7.6 ha (19 acres)	7 miles north-west of
SOIL Neutral	Banbury, on west side
ALTITUDE 213 m (700 ft)	of the A422 Banbury–
RAINFALL 685 mm (27 in.)	Stratford-upon-Avon
TEMPERATURE 4°C (39°F)	road

EDGEHILL stands on the north-west escarpment of a plateau of brown sandstone – hence its name – and the sandstone, known as Hornton stone, is never far from the surface hereabouts. The hill top slopes away into several valleys gouged out glacially, towards Banbury, but the level drive to the north front of Upton House gives little indication of this, nor does the level lawn on the south front.

Hornton stone was used by Sir Rushout Cullen in 1695 for the house and again for the extensions and comfortable balustraded terraces, designed by Mr P. Morley Horder for the 1st Viscount Bearsted in 1927–9. He made the terraces extend west to include a small formal garden reached by steps and surrounded by walls. A very appealing time to visit Upton is in early summer when the brown of the stone is delightfully contrasted by 'Williams' Double Yellow' Burnet Rose – which was raised at Worcester in 1828 – and the cool lavender colouring of Catmint.

The long low house overlooks a wide lawn and away to the gentle hills in the distance; the lawn is framed by native trees on the left and tall Lebanon Cedars on the right. One of these fell recently and its growth rings were counted, proving that it was planted about 1740. Under the native trees the local rock was again called upon for a rock garden, made by the late Lady Bearsted; on it are several good shrubs and plants and Tree Peonies.

Quite a different impression is gained if you walk across the lawn when suddenly the ground recedes into a long valley completely cutting off the lawn from the rest of the landscape. Obliquely to the left, down below in the distance, is a small lake with a classical temple at the far end. It takes an effort of imagination to relate the picture in the house, painted by Anthony Devis about 1800, to this view. The artist used his licence with considerable aplomb for not only did he depict a temple of different outline, but showed it at the opposite end of the lake! However the picture also suggests that the hilltop around the house was considerably more bare of trees than it is now. The lake was altered from a rectangle to an irregular outline around 1775, by the then owner, Robert Child. If you move a little nearer to the edge of the lawn you will find another lake directly below, and it is on the warm sunny slope that all the gardening was done during the recent centuries.

147 The splendid garden stairway of brown stone, constructed in the early 1930s, at Upton House. It is embowered in wistaria, laburnum and *Rosa hugonis*. Photo 1959.

148 At the top of the garden stairway, Upton House.

It is obvious that the presence of the distant lake and its temple drew the eye and the footsteps to the east corner of the lawn, because from here the access to the garden was always made. The walls in this part of the garden are considered to be of late 17th-century construction. The steep banks reveal the crumbling layers of rock and one wonders how plants survive. Those that like it do well. I remember one terrace where at midsummer the warm carmine of the dark-tinted Valerian is accentuated by the pale straw yellow of *Sisyrinchium striatum*, while above the cool tints of Tree Lupins give way to the purple spires of *Linaria purpurea*. There are long borders of perennials of many sorts, including delphiniums, *Veronica gentianoides*, phloxes, peonies, anemones, erigerons and the like. Shrubs are on one of the steep banks, for flower and autumn colour, laburnums, lavenders, brooms, *Mahonia aquifolium*, Jerusalem Sage, Rock Roses, *Senecio*, the Tatarian Maple, Snow-in-Summer, irises, *Lithospermum diffusum* and aubretia. This big slope is a good reminder of what will thrive on a hot, hungry bank.

But the real reason for cultivating this bank was to obtain early fruits and vegetables. A sloping rectangle produces excellent crops and the whole prospect from across the water has great appeal. Waterlilies grace the placid water, and mirrored in it are the sloping flower borders, trees, the white and yellow of Mock Orange and Golden Privet, and the neat rows of crops.

Much of the skill of the colour schemes at Upton, and the choice of plants no less than the design of these later parts of the garden, may be attributed to Miss K. Lloyd-Jones who for many years advised the late Lady Bearsted. Together they devised another way down to the lake. Originally the thought was to take it down the middle of the slope, but the present Lord Bearsted and his father managed to have it pushed to the far west end. Here a grand garden stairway was devised by the two ladies in the early 1930s or thereabouts; the greenhouses were swept away below it, and the yew hedges which enclosed them were allowed to guard areas of formal beds, mainly containing roses. The architecture of the stairway, broken by landings and balustrading, conforms very closely to the style and scale of the terraces below the house. When overhung with wistaria and *Rosa hugonis* in May the effect is delightful.

From this point you can walk along the steep bank below the cedars, where more ancient yews and their self-sown progeny mark some of the ancient terrace paths. If you follow on round the lawn at the bottom, the valley scheme unfolds. There were originally three formal lakes here, no doubt of 17th-century origin, fed by clear water gushing out of the natural rock in a small brick grotto. When the first Lord Bearsted came to live here, the top lake, just below the late 17th-century arcaded building which is now the head gardener's cottage, was a marsh, and the present Viscount remembers helping to design the concrete water courses creating the Bog Garden. Here are many good shrubs, cercidiphyllums, spiraeas, bamboos, with numerous groups of spring- and summer-flowering moisture-loving plants, primulas, astilbes, Chinese crimson-flowered rhubarb, and a sheet of *Symphytum grandiflorum*.

The original banks of this first lake are still visible; the second lake, which fifty years ago was a flower garden, is now clearly marked with grass banks but is planted with flowering cherries; the water is piped to the third lake and thence again to the temple lake.

The very early history of this place is still obscure, but these rectangular lakes point perhaps to fish tanks for a large establishment, and form an interesting point for conjecture.

THE VYNE
Basingstoke, *Hampshire*

Acquired with an endowment under the will of Sir Charles Chute in 1956

AREA 4.8 ha (12 acres)	4 miles north of
SOIL Neutral	Basingstoke, off
ALTITUDE 60.9 m (200 ft)	the A340 Reading road
RAINFALL 762 mm (30 in.)	
TEMPERATURE 3.5°C (38°F)	

APART FROM the large walled garden, which is not open to the public, The Vyne's original garden has disappeared, swept away by Mr Wiggett Chute who lived here from 1840 until 1872. Before then John Chute had enlarged the water, creating the semblance of a lake, and built a wooden bridge which would give

149 It is appropriate at The Vyne that grapes should be grown. On the west front the Teinturier Grape is trained on cone-shaped supports. In autumn its foliage assumes glowing colours in contrast to the very dark fruits.

access to the far shore where he had a bowling green and garden enclosed in yew hedges. No vestige remains, and the wooden bridge was replaced in 1860 by the present iron bridge. It was the old story of clearing away formality and substituting the delights of a natural landscape.

Standing under the north portico of the house the full impact of the graceful old White Willows will meet you, also the clump of Scots Pines, the cedar and the light green of False Locust or *Robinia*. Towards the east is an avenue of Red Twig limes leading from a charming little garden house, built in the second half of the 17th century. Its more modern replica lies to the west of the house, another addition by Wiggett Chute.

The lawns gradually blend into rough grass to the west, beyond the willows; here walnuts thrive and the St Lucie Cherry, the White Mulberry and Sweet Gum. Numerous shrub roses are growing, some, like species of the Synstylae section, ascend into trees and spread their fragrance around. *Rosa virginiana* has made an excellent thicket, providing vivid autumn colour; 'Cerise Bouquet', nearer to the main water, is spectacular in July and again later. Lord and Lady Chandos, until recently the Trust's tenants, did much to refurnish the garden. The herbaceous border near the house contains many good things, and tends to enclose the west lawn; here, by the door of the Stone Gallery, are two Claret Vines trained into formal shapes, a reminder that "Vyne" probably indicates a vineyard of days gone by.

If you can time your visit to The Vyne in the late afternoon on a beautiful late June day, the roses will be at their best, and the sun will be getting round to the north front. The pink brick, mirrored in the water from the far bank, will provide you with a scene of beauty hard to equal. The masonry of the chapel is contrasted strongly by the rounded masses of glittering dark green from some old specimens of *Phillyrea latifolia* and the willows softly screen the other end of the house.

WADDESDON MANOR

Aylesbury, *Buckinghamshire*

Bequeathed to the Trust in 1957 by Mr James A. de Rothschild, with an endowment

AREA 64.7 ha (160 acres)
SOIL Limy
ALTITUDE 75 m (250 ft)
RAINFALL 635 mm (25 in.)
TEMPERATURE 3.5°C (38°F)

6 miles north-west of Aylesbury, on the A41 Aylesbury–Bicester road

IT IS RECORDED that Baron Ferdinand de Rothschild, when hunting from his house at Leighton Buzzard, noticed "a small steep hill – a misshapen cone – with a farm on top" and decided he would like to build a house on it. We know nothing of the appearance of the hill but a few native trees remain of what was there. The building of the house started in 1877 and was more or less complete by 1883, mainly derived in style from French architecture of the 16th century. For the design of the grounds and park the Baron employed a Frenchman, M. Lainé. While the influence of French chateau gardens is felt in the approach drives to the north of the house, much of the rest of the grounds echoes the Victorian interpretation of the English Landscape Garden. It was desired that the house should stand in a commanding situation on high ground, that it should have a long level approach when once the high ground had been reached, and that the terrain should be terraced in front of the house, and otherwise modelled so that drives and separate features could be suitably enjoyed; also that eventually the house should be framed in trees. The soil is of a heavy nature.

With these thoughts in mind we can see how well all was achieved, but not without great difficulty. In the first place, having arrived, by means of a scenic drive, at the plateau whereon stands the mansion, the immensity of the task of reducing by some 2.7 m (9 ft) an area of 4 ha (10 acres) of hilltop is at once apparent. The fountain in a wide circle of the gravelled drive is surrounded by large trees including Silver Limes and Blue Cedars. Thence no less than five parallel drives lead to the north front, the centre one being widest. Lord Beaconsfield, having visited Waddesdon when this transformation was taking place, is reputed to have remarked later that if the Almighty had had the assistance of a Rothschild, the making of the world would have been achieved in less than seven days. The one failure was the double avenue of English Oak – recorded as then being forty years old – lining the side drives, their "ultimate success being debated anxiously", for the two reasons that they had been brought in as large trees for an early effect and that there was insufficient depth of soil over the native limestone. Of those that remain many are unhealthy. But there are some excellent trees and shrubs in this area, notabilities being a fine Maidenhair Tree, from China, where it has been treasured for hundreds of years around monasteries, and two autumn-flowering evergreens, a large-leafed Privet, *Ligustrum lucidum* also from China, and a Strawberry Tree.

150 A photograph of 1875 shewing the grading of the hilltop at Waddesdon in process, to the north of the house.

The selection of shrubs in this garden includes many variegated forms, particularly yellow-tinted yews and cypresses, which are kept trimmed by knife and secateurs in the several hedges around the house. One of the most gratifying views is from first floor windows looking over the formal, Italian-style terraces, with the central marble fountain of Pluto and Proserpine, surrounded by small paths. It is worth noting that these paths are of a narrow width for walking, whereas the rest of the grounds are traversed almost entirely by carriage-width drives. The Baron laid out these noble terraces himself, aided by his bailiff and head gardener. The architect of the house, Destailleur, had provided some original ideas which were not followed apart from some steps below the main garden terrace.

Until 1931, the year of the recession in world trade, there were many beds of flowers on this garden terrace and in many other parts of the garden. The terrace remained flowerless until the Trust restored some of the larger beds in the early 1960s (see plate XLVII). The main beds take annually 3500 pot-grown geraniums (Zonal Pelargoniums) and the same number of ageratums. They are prepared, ready for planting at the end of May, and the head gardener tells me that, given fine weather, he manages to plant this whole quantity in less than three days. The plants are of course brought and handed to him as he works. For spring display 4000 wallflowers and 5000 tulips are used, the colours varying from season to season. Several thousand more plants are used elsewhere in special beds through the garden.

Beyond the Fountain Terrace the view extends down sloping lawns and away to the countryside. In May the many Horse Chestnuts give a note of floral beauty.

The apparently natural outcrop of rock on the west side of the levelled approach to the house is in fact bogus. *The Gardeners' Chronicle* of 1885 states that the rock was found when the top of the hill was razed, and this has since been proved – it is Portland Beds stone of which the hill is composed. It is built in the manner typical of Messrs Pulham & Son of Bishop's Stortford who built the waterfall at SHEFFIELD PARK. The tell-tale artificial stratum of "soft" stone (concrete) is an indicator of this firm's work. At one time Pampas Grass, ferns and palms decorated it. No doubt some of the spare soil from the levelling of the approach drives forms the bank of the outcrop and the hillock which has a cavern at the back, and also creates the high background to the Aviary. The cavern was originally designed as a retreat for a small flock of mountain sheep but Mrs James de Rothschild has recorded that the effluvium was not appreciated so near to the house and the sheep were given a new home far away in the valley. The cavern does however provide a most useful and handy recess nowadays for mowers and tools.

The Aviary is a very splendid affair, of considerable size and dignity, with a great variety of birds, some of which fly about outside (see illus. 28). Frequently gawdy macaws chatter at you and alight on trees around. The grey paint of the intricate metalwork is echoed in the white rose 'Iceberg' enclosed in hedges. The design of the Aviary is very much in accordance with French garden architecture of the 16th century; it was built in 1889 but the designer is unknown. It was restored to its present beauty in early 1966 and the planting was devised by Mr Lanning Roper.

Apart from many Horse Chestnuts, limes, hornbeams and other native trees there is a good sprinkling of conifers as one would expect of a garden of this period; Pines of various species, including the Spanish, Crimean, Macedonian pines, and the Arolla pine, 18.2 m (60 ft) high; Lebanon and Blue Cedars, Wellingtonias, Chinese Arborvitae and cypresses, and several spruces and firs – the Noble Fir, Norway and Serbian Spruces. Many of these add tremendous height to the rim of the great bowl that is the Daffodil Valley. With native deciduous trees just breaking bud interspersed with the black-green of the conifers, the huge expanse of thousands of daffodils is a breath-taking sight if you come across it suddenly on a bright April day.

We can attribute this kind of enrichment of the grounds to Miss Alice de Rothschild, Baron Ferdinand's sister, who lived here long after his death in 1898. In her day the garden was renowned for its beauty and the range of greenhouses of great size and variety below the drive was joined to a 7-acre kitchen garden, a rose garden and a large rock garden. Europe was scoured for new species of exotics, fruits and vegetables, and for sixty years the head gardener, G. F. Johnson, reigned supreme over a large staff.

It was in the rose garden that the delightful Victorian fantasy – a gem in fact – the Pergola was sited; it was placed in its present position not far from the Aviary in 1966. It is a circular metal confection with the amusing addition of wire baskets attached to the tops of the uprights so that climbing plants can ascend over the dome-shaped roof, while over 100 fuchsias hang down at you.

It is a long way from the ornamental areas around the house and Aviary, where so much annual flower gardening was practised in the first thirty years of this century, to the huge range of glasshouses which stood below the house, to the north-east. From there the many thousands of plants had to be transported on hand-barrows upwards through a service path (though crossing the drive) to the east end of the house. Mr Johnson did not allow his staff to use either carts or the main drives for transport of his precious productions, whether for the garden beds or for decorating the house. It is on the path used to the north of the drive that a unique cromlech-like grotto may be found; it was one of the resting places built for the mountain sheep.

I should have invited you to look down from the west end of the terrace; here can clearly be seen the artificial shaping of the ground, the deepened drive, graded banks and hillocks. All this was of course done by men with shovels, carts and horses. One hillock has a clump of Silver Weeping Lime, the only example I have ever seen of a grouping of this particularly graceful tree. In the autumn, if you get there the day before the staff sweeps that particular area, the ground under them will be a dappled pattern of fallen leaves, showing either their yellowed upper surface or the grey underneath. The hillock and its limes can be seen again from the exit drive (originally the main drive) which is scenically impressive with repeated glimpses of the countryside between belts of trees.

We are enjoying today at Waddesdon the glory of the extensive tree planting of the 1890s and later. We read that many large specimens were put in for early affect, being lowered by machinery with stout chains into their places – no doubt by the only firm that specialised in such work, William Barron & Sons of Borrowash, Derbyshire.

XXXIX OPPOSITE The double white *Anemone nemorosa* 'Vestal' is naturalised under trees at Trelissick; Arboreum Rhododendrons and 'Prinz Handjery' Sycamore add colour to this spring view. Photo 1971.

XL ABOVE Rose 'Buff Beauty' enhances this view of the Orangery terrace at Powis Castle. Photo 1976.

XLI OPPOSITE ABOVE Scarlet, yellow and white flowers, with silvery foliage, are the main ingredients of this border at Tintinhull.
The Tasmanian *Eucalyptus gunnii* gives height behind Mock Orange and Spanish Broom. The opposite border of the pair is in soft colours. Photo 1968.
XLII OPPOSITE BELOW Sheffield Park house, from the First Lake, in 1976.
The Monterey Pine and taxodiums are also seen in illus. 127.

XLIII A panoramic painting of the house, park and monuments at Shugborough by Nicholas Dahl (d. 1777). The Essex Bridge over the River Sow is to the right.

XLIV LEFT
A concentration of autumn colour in the Bowl at Winkworth Arboretum in 1967. Liquidambars, larches, cherries, maples and nyssas vie with the Blue Cedar.

XLV BELOW
An autumn view of the Pantheon built at Stourhead *c.*1754. Photo 1972.

XLVI OPPOSITE
The Temple of Apollo at Stourhead; a view from the Temple of Flora. Photo 1966.

WAKEHURST PLACE
Haywards Heath, *West Sussex*

Bequeathed to the Trust in 1964 with an endowment by Sir Henry Price

AREA 68.7 ha (170 acres)
SOIL Lime-free
ALTITUDE 60.9 m–136 m (200–450 ft)
RAINFALL 813 mm (32 in.)
TEMPERATURE 4.5°C (40°F)

1½ miles north-west of Ardingly on B2028

MY FIRST VISIT to Wakehurst was in 1938. Its renown as a garden had reached me many years earlier while still a student at the University Botanic Garden at Cambridge. It so happened that one of my colleagues was the son of the head gardener at Wakehurst, Mr Alfred Coates. Therefore no sooner did I acquire a car than a visit to the legendary garden was fixed up with Mr Coates. I say legendary because his son, Gordon, gained considerable prestige at Cambridge by dropping the remark that *all* the tools at Wakehurst were of rustless steel! I was completely bewildered by a long afternoon visit, and saw more things new to me in one garden than ever before, excepting Kew. My notebook records *Machilus (Persea) ichangensis*, *Pseudopanax arboreus*, *Libocedrus bidwillii formosana*, *Eucryphia milliganii*, *Euonymus fimbriatus (E. lucidus)*, *Hartia sinensis (Stewartia pteropetiolata)*; it was October and *Escallonia montevidensis* was still in flower, covered with butterflies. Some of these plants still grow at Wakehurst, but are a mere handful of the 7500 growing there today.

Tracing its origins back for centuries, Wakehurst first made its mark horticulturally through Lady Downshire, in 1869. It was she who planted the Wellingtonias and Redwoods which have reached a great height today. The place was owned by Sir Thomas and Lady Boord from 1890 to 1902; Lady Boord created the first rock garden by the garden lake, which was later adjusted. Sir Thomas started the rhododendron collection from seeds from Asia. From 1902 to 1937 it was owned by Gerald Loder, later Lord Wakehurst, and then by Sir Henry Price; Lord Wakehurst gathered together a vast collection of plants, enlarging the garden considerably, and Sir Henry did not spare himself to continue its development. Shortly after its being accepted by the Trust it was leased to Kew. The mere fact that Kew was desirous of leasing it proved its value; this same fact makes it obvious that new life would be given to the garden. I have watched it for fifteen years, and each year some vast improvement or elaboration has been made.

XLVII OPPOSITE ABOVE Seven thousand plants are annually used to create this colourful display on the terrace at Waddesdon, with the Italian fountain by G. Monzani. Photo 1977.

XLVIII OPPOSITE BELOW The long drive at Trengwainton, connecting the walled gardens with the house and lawn. Here Chinese *Primula helodoxa* and Japanese *P. japonica* throng the stream-side, with Japanese Azaleas and Maples opposite, in 1971.

151 In the Pleasaunce, Wakehurst Place.

With such a succession of owners it is natural that it should be one of the foremost gardens in the land. It is on excellent soil, standing high but with deep moist valleys, well sheltered, with extremely variable terrain and massive sandstone outcrops (see illus. 192), the whole crowned by the grey, weather-beaten Elizabethan mansion. It is small wonder that it is a horticultural mecca, a place for pilgrimage at all times of the year.

Its speciality is trees and shrubs, but even so a walled garden has been made into a memorial to Sir Henry, and contains a wide variety of silver-leafed shrubs and perennials, coupled with coppery purple-leafed plants; the flowers are all of soft colours from white to pink and mauve to wine colour. This planting presents a cool and restful effect and is at its best in summer. Rosemaries, rue, sages, senecios, lavenders, *Ballota acetabulosa*,

152 At Wakehurst Place in 1959; the main view to the house.

153 In the Heath Garden at Wakehurst Place, *Pieris formosa forrestii* 'Wakehurst' on right, *Hakea epiglottis* in centre.

artemisias, *Chrysanthemum haradjanii*, clematises, indigoferas and Rugosa roses all contribute to the scheme, which is worth long study. The next walled enclosure, the Pleasaunce, further divided by hedges and topiary of yew, planted before 1900, is a sheltered place; the north wall is hung with crimson flowers of *Berberidopsis* and the west with the creamy white of *Decumaria*. Against the south wall stands a marble Roman bath, similar to one at POLESDEN LACEY.

The gate leads to a long border devoted to plants belonging to the Lily, Iris, and other botanical Families known as Monocotyledonous plants. Here are species of *Agapanthus*, *Eremurus*, *Nerine*, *Hedychium*, *Cautleya*, *Eucomis*, *Cyrtanthus* and *Fascicularia*. There are thriving colonies of the rare little double daffodil *Narcissus pumilis* 'Plenus', and *Camassia leichtlinii* 'Eve Price'. On the sheltering wall *Pittosporum bicolor* produces its tiny yellow flowers in spring.

One is always drawn to water and the glimpse of the pond to the east will entice you that way. The reflections in autumn are particularly fine and colourful, and the rock garden at its side will show tumbling masses of the little pink spikes of *Polygonum vacciniifolium* and wide spreads of *Gentiana sino-ornata*. A long established clump of the yellow-flowered *Dicentra macrantha*, a Chinese rarity, thrives on a shady slope, and *Oxalis purpurata bowiei* from South Africa is equally at home. To one side is a large sheet of *Geranium procurrens*, introduced from Nepal by Dr Geoffrey Herklots in 1972; it bids fair to be the most prolific and popular of the greater ground-covering plants. *Arisaema candidissimum* and other species, *Meconopsis* species and many delights are tucked away in shady places. A splendid plant of *Rhododendron pseudochrysanthum*, one of the true gems of the genus, scarlet *R. pocophorum*, *R. bureavii* whose foliage is dark green above and red-brown beneath, and *R. degronianum* "Gerald Loder" are are nearby, with plants of the scarlet-leafed *Pieris formosa forrestii* named "Wakehurst" (see plate v). In the sun are the silvery grassy tufts of *Astelia* and Fascicularia species; behind them grows the Tea Plant, and *Pittosporum colensoi*.

The Heath Garden was one of Lord Wakehurst's particular joys and its open situation and good drainage from raised beds are conducive to the ripening of the stems and consequent thriving of numerous shrubs, many from the southern hemisphere. I like to stand near the big *Hakea epiglottis* and let the eye wander over the long beds closely set with dwarf rhododendrons and conifers, grevilleas, leptospermums and *Richea scoparia*, while above them tower columnar cypresses, *Embothrium coccineum* in flaming scarlet, white *Hoheria sextylosa*, *Lomatia tinctoria* and the astonishing *Telopea truncata* from Tasmania. It is well worth a special visit to see this rare beauty freely set with its intriguing dark red flowers in early summer. One can have the privilege, too, of standing just here to admire the yellow forms of Lawson's cypress, one named 'Winston Churchill' and the other 'President Roosevelt'. For some reason the third of the trio, raised just after the last war, named 'Joseph Stalin', suffered an early demise – or so they tell me . . .

Two species of *Chusquea* grow here, both introduced by Harold Comber, *C. culeou* and *C. breviglumis*. They are solid-stemmed bamboos from Chile, the first, a tall, luxuriant, and graceful plant; the second, a lowly spreader. Leptospermums from New Zealand and Tasmania are much in evidence in the Heath Garden, lighting it with a variety of tints from white to crimson in early summer; *Nothofagus cliffortioides* also from New Zealand and *N. betuloides* from Chile, relatives of our native beech, give height coupled with fern-like greenery, and the feathery columns of the Bhutan Cypress punctuate the general beauty of the shrubby hummocks.

The Heath Garden was laid out to take just a few visitors. It soon became apparent that its narrow walks would not suit the thousands who now visit the garden and so it was necessary to remove one long narrow bed. But by adding in later years several large beds towards the south-west a more extensive heath garden has been achieved, open to the sun and air and it will not be many years before the whole scheme blends together.

One of the richest parts of Wakehurst has always been the series of beds which now lead us east or west. West is tempting; you reach the steps from which a superb glimpse is obtained down Westwood Valley, but we will leave this till later and concentrate on the beds themselves making our way gently east to the water garden. This whole area was vastly overgrown and has been thoroughly combed out so that each plant can be better appreciated. In one spot in May a lovely grouping of light lavender-blue *Rhododendron augustinii* and others contrasts with light yellow species and varieties. Several large evergreen shrubs break the views, uncommon and beautiful. *Quercus phillyreoides*, *Q. glauca* and *Osmanthus yunnanensis* from the Far East and *Maytenus boaria* from Chile are large shrubs; the Black Beech of New Zealand is much taller, and always provides a dark note, likewise *Torreya californica*, a conifer relative with plum-like fruits. Two species of sumach, again from the Far East, are *Rhus sylvestris* and *R. verniciflua*, both noted for their autumn colour. The latter is known as the "Varnish Tree" because it provides the main ingredient of the Japanese lacquer. *Zanthoxylum ailanthoides* is another rarity, aromatic to the point of being pungent. And look aloft, the skyline is broken by the Tasmanian *Eucalyptus gunnii*; I often think that this tree, which is proving to be quick growing and hardy, will have as much effect in our landscapes as the Holm Oak. Both species blend well with our native trees, are evergreen, and thus give winter density and screening without having to resort to the upsetting slender outline of many conifers.

The experts at Kew and Wakehurst are fully alive to the value of ground-cover plants, and also their complementary beauty which provides a quiet floor above which single specimen trees and shrubs grow; it unites them into an interesting whole. There are wide mats of dwarf shrubs, *Geranium macrorrhizum*, *Meehania urticifolia*, *Pachysandra* species; in one shady spot is a mat of *Ercilla volubilis*, an evergreen climbing plant.

Magnolias grow freely in this part of the garden, including *M. campbellii* and 'Wakehurst' whose rich pink flowers in April need to be seen to be believed. Years ago the head of the valley here, known as the Slips, used to be a thicket of azaleas; the water-course has been opened out and gives a foretaste of delights lower down. Above it all towers the large-leafed American Beech, an exceptionally tall specimen, while nearby is the rosy-budded Laurustinus named 'Eve Price'.

Old alders and limes cast a lot of shade here, at the beginning of the water garden area. This has a complicated water system, two springs being supplemented by a pump lower down, so that a tall cliff of sandstone could be made in one corner, over which descends splashing water, to be lost again in little pools and rivulets and boggy beds. In May the daffodil-yellow leaves of *Hosta fortunei* 'Aurea' lighten a dark corner; the woolly fronds of *Osmunda cinnamomea* unfurl, primulas of all colours flower. One of William Robinson's favourite bamboos for landscape planting, *Sasa veitchii*, has made a large clump; its dwarf habit and large dark green leaves edged with parchment-white are effective at all times. Its spreading underground stems travel like couch grass but are as hard as steel wire. Two remarkable trees are here, a very large Japanese Varnish Tree, noted above, and *Stewartia sinensis*, whose bark, flaking and revealing different tints, rivals the beauty of any other tree grown for bark colour, to say nothing of its white flowers in July and resplendent autumn colour. Behind it a dell has been suitably prepared to grow the Himalayan species of *Primula* (especially those of the Petiolares Section) and meconopses. In the bog beds are sheets of astilbes, irises, and the dwarf form of *Peltiphyllum peltatum*; *Scopolia carniolica*, a relative of the potato, produces reddish bells in early spring; but I prefer the yellow form of *S.c. hladnikiana*, in spite of its tongue-twisting name.

With so much on the ground, so to speak, one is apt to forget that whenever you go to Wakehurst you will be passing rhododendrons in flower of one kind or another from early spring to midsummer and even later. There is for instance the special form of *R. uvarifolium* named 'Reginald Childs' in 1974. Many species, some old-established, some brought in large size from Kew, some young and newly-planted, throng the cool slopes, or warm sheltered corners as their preferences demand. Many would hardly be seen outside of Cornwall. There are too many to mention in detail, but some noteworthy species include *R. argipeplum*; a red form of *R. arizelum*; *R. longisquamatum* and *R. mallotum*; *R. lacteum*; *R. stamineum*, *R. valentinianum* and *R. zeylanicum*. Their colours range from white to pink and crimson, scarlet and yellow, and from palest lilac to dusky purple; the tints peep out from the surrounding greenery, here and there, from week to week and month to month, according to their flowering periods.

If you take the path which runs along the left escarpment of the valley, you will be amidst trees which for rarity and size in one group can seldom be equalled, at least in the gardens of the National Trust. Just listen to the recitation: a columnar Dawyck Beech, about 24.3 m (80 ft); the Cucumber Tree of the same height; *Magnolia campbellii*, 18.2 m (60 ft); the Chinese Tulip Tree with narrower leaves than the usual American species and glaucous beneath; *Liquidamber formosana monticola* – hardier than the Formosan species itself; *Photinia serrulata*, noted for its colourful young foliage; *Persea ichangensis*, a relative of the Avocado Pear; a splendid *Davidia involucrata*, or Handkerchief Tree; the bush *Betula medwediewii* whose large leaves turn to yellow in autumn and *Pittosporum patulum*, whose leaves are so variable in shape that extremes would confuse a good botanist. And rhododendrons are on every side, including a form of *R. arboreum roseum* which was named 'Tony Schilling' in 1974.

But come with me back to the forking of the paths, and take the one on the right of the valley; the little stream glints deep down below the steep slopes. You will come to *Pseudopanax crassifolius*, a New Zealand tree whose juvenile foliage – long, slender and coarsely toothed like a saw – differs so much from its broader, even three-lobed adult foliage, that it leaves the pittosporum well out of comparison. Far away down the valley can be seen the top of one of the tallest Western Hemlocks in the country – about 39.6 m (130 ft).

Don't be tempted to rest on the seat of unusual design, but go on a short way until a new scene greets you. This is our first sight of the impressive outcrops of sandstone which abound at Wakehurst. Enveloping growth has been cleared away to reveal them and a Himalayan planting of *Berberis wilsoniae*, *Potentilla cuneata*, *Polygonum vacciniifolium* and *P. affine*, *Cotoneaster microphylla* forms and a few other things have been provided.

From here the valley extends to Westwood Lake, created prior to 1850, with a weir being added later, and as complete a collection as possible of *Rhododendron* species has been planted, grouped in their botanical series, for future reference. We have the choice now of going back to the house through the Pinetum or going down to the lake. Let us enter the Pinetum on our shorter tour.

Conifers have been brought together here, mainly by Lord Wakehurst, from all corners of the world. The lacey green of the Mexican pine, about 12.1 m (40 ft) high, Californian Bishop Pine and the Knobcone Pine will show a great range of growth and colouring. Some of the pines' cones provide regeneration only after a forest fire has cracked them open, the branches carrying them unopened for thirty years or more. The Cilician Fir and *Larix griffithii*, a Himalayan larch with very long cones, *Picea lichiangensis* from western China – whose young cones are rose-red – and the New Zealand *Libocedrus plumosa* are there. *Keteleeria davidiana*, *Abies* species including *A. bracteata*, *A. nephrolepis*, *A. magnifica* and *A. numidica*; *Taiwania cryptomerioides* and *Thuja koraiensis*, are just a few more names to whet the appetite of Conifer enthusiasts. And then suddenly you may come upon a Scots Pine and realise once again that our native can be as beautiful as any exotic.

If we decide on a much longer tour another day we can omit the Pinetum and carry on downhill to Westwood Lake – a peaceful spot, alive with birds and insects – and walk through Horsebridge Wood, an extensive area of oak and larch in which many trees have been planted. In October one glade is livened with the Golden Larch. Bluebells abound in countless numbers, a beautiful flooring for the white and pink of magnolias, for a new collection of these species has been planted here, and numerous species of *Acer* have been included not only for their spring bloom, but for their brilliant autumn tints.

If you are by now getting horticultural indigestion, be comforted because suddenly a grassy glade of several acres opens out, sloping, and ensconced in woods and trees. It is sheeted with the native Lent Lily in spring. There are some views of rare beauty. It is known as Bloomer's Valley. While Horsebridge Wood is a name easily understood, from probably a packhorse bridge over the brook, and the Slips are self-descriptive also,

154 Cones of *Abies procera* 'Glauca' at Wakehurst.

Bloomer's Valley dates back to the blooming of iron by smelting, in the days when the Sussex Weald provided much of the commodity. Bethlehem Woods, which we come to presently, is plausibly explained in several ways but without confirmation. In Bloomer's Valley, apart from the surrounding native trees and daffodils, there are cedars, cypresses and larches, and a group of Monkey Puzzles whose characterful futuristic lines for once seem to blend in with the vegetation.

The outstanding exhibit – if we may look upon it as such – at Wakehurst is the sandstone outcrop which runs along the south brow of the valley for three quarters of a mile. Here immense blocks of stone overhang the steep bank, and are overhung in their turn by yews and other trees. The whole is shady, particularly dark and gloomy under the yews, cool and dank. This sandstone, though hard on exposure – it is of course used freely for building – is comparatively soft and absorbs and holds several times its own weight of moisture; as a consequence roots of any plants enjoy its proximity. Some of the yews' roots resemble the tentacles of an octopus, clasping the rocks as if to stay them from falling down. Even in the hot summer of 1976 the rocks remained sufficiently cool and moist to sustain the life of the several patches of *Hymenophyllum tunbridgense* which grow upon their surfaces. This is the native Filmy Fern – though it more closely resembles a Liverwort to the inexperienced eye; a plant which shrivels and dies if it gets too dry, having no epidermis. It is a very special experience to walk along this great irregular shelf of rock, and also to look down the valley from various vantage points.

And so we return to the house and car park, through Bethlehem Woods. This area will be mainly noted for its collection of Birch species in the future, grouped according to their natural distribution.

If your eye is not tired with arboricultural delights you may like to linger in the grounds at the entrance, alongside of which the car park is made, and through which thread the main walks to the garden. And here you will find many unusual trees and shrubs, a collection in itself which would do credit to many a lesser garden. By their diversity alone can be gauged the magnificence of Wakehurst.

WALLINGTON
Morpeth, *Northumberland*

Given by Sir Charles Trevelyan, Bt, in 1942

AREA 17.8 ha (44 acres)	12 miles west of
SOIL Lime-free	Morpeth, along B6343;
ALTITUDE 152 m (500 ft)	1 mile south from
RAINFALL 787 mm (31 in.)	Cambo, off B6342
TEMPERATURE 3°C (37°F)	

APART FROM the ponds, the one strong feature of the garden at Wallington, that has remained inviolate is the broad gravel terrace which runs along the south front of the house. Here it has remained through changes of fortune and fashion since the early 1700s, a strong line, deeply ditched in front, in fact an echo of the raised walks of the previous century. It is a splendid vantage point from which the eye can turn west or east to handsome urns placed by the Trust in 1974, or south over the countryside to Bobby Shaftoe's crags. The view to the west along the path has been given an avenue of limes in place of an indeterminate grouping of sycamores and beeches. If you go round to the east lawn, there is a lovely glimpse of the Clock Tower through the gateway, framed by big trees, golden yews and a flower-bed of large size which produces bloom from spring to autumn. Tulips, Madonna Lilies, campanulas, delphiniums and phloxes do their bit in keeping up the display.

The main garden, however, lies on the other side of the road and this is where, to understand it, we need to look into early schemes for the whole garden. As I said earlier, the ponds remain, also inviolate; they are to the west and the east, remnants of a grandiose scheme of about 1737 with radiating views separated by serpentine walks, canals, and the ponds. It is the two ponds to the east with which we are concerned, and some of the serpentine walks remain. If we cross the road we can go to the China Pond. This is in woodland, planted at the same time, though the great beeches are gradually falling and being replaced. The wild fowl, waterlilies, rushes, mossy-rooty banks under the beeches, the larches planted in 1738 and Chinese Juniper, a plant much in vogue at the time, all contribute to the picture.

There are alternative routes to the garden proper; both eventually look down on the Garden Pond. Apart from the wildlife, in spring and through to late summer, this is beautiful with native vegetation, King Cups, irises, Giant Water Dock, Willow-herbs and Purple Loosestrife. If we take the right fork we shall see all this from a vantage point directly opposite to the Portico House, built in 1740. At first sight it seems an important building to be so isolated, but it is in reality in the middle of a very high brick wall; the slopes between it and the Garden Pond were initially used by Sir Walter Calverley Blackett as a kitchen garden. This in his day would have been a sheltered south-facing slope, but possibly it was found to be a frost pocket, because towards the end of his life, in 1760, he built the new kitchen garden and abandoned the old one, which was then planted with trees. In the new garden, though the ground slopes to the south, it also slopes to the east and thus cold air would have drained away.

Let us go through the handgate and stand on the upper path decorated with lead statues. The ground is terraced, and the overflow from the ponds is caught in a pool in a stone niche built in 1938 by Mary, Lady Trevelyan. In the middle distance of the garden is a paved *rond-point* made by the Trust in 1962. This connects two important paths, the one along the big border and the other from the double borders, and thence the lower garden is reached.

My first sight of Wallington was on a January day when all was covered with snow. None of the hundred and one weeds was visible. Over the years, since 1958, the entire garden has been cleaned and restored, the lawns cultivated and resown, the paths newly gravelled, the walls and greenhouses repaired; the stream which travelled for much of its length through this large walled garden through a culvert, was brought to the surface and its tiny chatter can be heard as one walks down the path.

There is no doubt that this garden produced good crops. It is sheltered from every side except the east (where trees have been planted) and catches the sun at all times. Its walls would have provided all help possible in ripening fruits; today on them are numerous roses, honeysuckles, clematises, and sun-loving shrubs. In the joints of the lichened bricks the mauve *Erinus alpinus* seeds itself. Though a cold district with a comparatively

155 The main garden at Wallington in summer, after restoration and replanting. Photo 1969.

156 The rocky stream at Wallington constructed in 1962, photographed a few years later. Many alpine plants and dwarf shrubs find conditions to their liking here.

short summer it is surprising what thrives. The Mediterranean Heath for instance – which is damaged but not killed in hard winters – the Moroccan Broom, *Rosa soulieana*, *Lonicera splendida*, and Rose 'Climbing Lady Hillingdon'.

The border along the top path gives a soft effect of grey and purplish foliage – irises, *Stachys*, Seakale, Corsican Hellebore, with pale yellow and blush roses, white and lavender clematises, Catmint and Armenian Geranium. On the opposite side of the path, just under the wall, is a series of clumps of ornamental ferns, their rich green tint in contrast to the subdued border colours; over the ferns spill the climbing roses from below.

As you walk along your nose will catch a waft of fragrance from the conservatory. Right through the growing season it is a wonderful change of climate to enter its doors and drink in the sweet scent of the Heliotrope. A very pale lavender type is trained up a central support, like some of the aged, giant fuchsias. Fragrance and brilliance meet you all around.

157 The marble fountain in the Conservatory at Wallington with *Fuchsia* 'Rose of Castile Improved', of which there is a very old plant with trunk 230 mm (9 ins) through.

If we look over the wall again we can enjoy the broad sloping border on the other side of the garden where a gradation of colours from pale to dark in the soft tints changes to full oranges and reds lower down. Some quite large shrubs such as *Magnolia wilsonii*, *Kolkwitzia*, the Highdown rose, coppery Sumach and maple, white variegated dogwood, *Hydrangea villosa*, and the white *H. cinerea* 'Sterilis' all make a background to the phloxes, lilies, hostas and fuchsias.

We can also look over the hedged square which was originally a vegetable garden, but now contains a selection of small ornamental trees in the semblance of an orchard. The double borders sloping down the near side are given purple, blue and yellow flowers and meet the paved *rond point*. The land beyond contained a mass of weeds, spruce trees and broken-down greenhouses. All was cleared in the early 1970s and the present grouping of trees, climbers on the wall, and the pool – a further use of the underground stream – was laid out. At the bottom is an imposing pair of wrought iron gates, and from here we can now look up the whole garden noting, above the greenhouses, the Owl House, a dwelling in old days for the head gardener.

Much hard work by patient men has gone into the rejuvenation of this garden. The initial cleaning and replanting; the raising of seeds and cuttings; the building of the stream banks and waterfalls; many interests and skills combined. But the result must have given them and many visitors pleasure and caused them to re-read, with thought, the inscription in the conservatory: "When wearied and overwrought by study or affairs of business, repair to these haunts and refresh your mind by a stroll amid the flowers." This is from an original on the Pincian Hill at Rome; ancient amphorae stand nearby. On the staging and in the garden are flowers of all ages, all combining to delight us.

THE WEIR
Swainshill, *Hereford and Worcester*

Acquired under the will of Mr R. C. Parr in 1959

AREA 4.4 ha (11 acres)
SOIL Lime-free
ALTITUDE 60.9 m (200 ft)
RAINFALL 766 mm (30 in.)
TEMPERATURE 4.5°C (40°F)

5 miles west of Hereford, astride the A438 Hereford–Hay road

IF YOU GO to The Weir looking for a garden you will probably be disappointed. But the view from the east end of the long, curving, steeply-sloping bank on the

River Wye is alive with daffodils, bluebells and other native flowers in spring and early summer, and presents a glimpse of the house above among trees. The view from the house lawns and upper walks is of the finest, across the river and over gentle farmland. The steep banks have to be mown in summer which is a dangerous and difficult job, but when once it is done the banks take on a new note for they are sprinkled with substantial bushes of yew and Common Privet, while between them the Perennial Pea in pink or white, and Evening Primrose provide a little colour. From summer onwards the air is redolent with the soft smell of balsam, from the thousands of *Impatiens roylei* covered with pink flowers of intriguing shape – and still more intriguing seed pods. Its floral shape is well worth a study. Though it is a native of the Himalayas, it has adopted England wholeheartedly. In September the colchicums begin to flower and from then onwards the evergreens come into their most important role, that of a foil to the weekly increase of autumn colour, from old beeches, great planes, and a sprinkling of exotic trees and shrubs. At one point the underground moisture seeps through soil and erodes the banks; a river wall was built in the early 1930s and strong cuttings of willow and privet are inserted straight into the bank above to hold it together.

We owe all this to Mr R. C. Parr who bought the property in 1922. At that time the steep banks were a tangled mass of brambles, thorns and native trees. By degrees, aided by Mr R. V. Morris, order was restored, the winding walks made, the shrubs and trees planted and the small rock garden of Cheddar limestone, with its pool, was built.

WESTBURY COURT GARDEN
Westbury-upon-Severn, *Gloucestershire*

Given in 1967 by Gloucestershire County Council; endowed by means of a public appeal, an anonymous gift and a grant from the Historic Buildings Council

AREA 1.6 ha (4 acres)
SOIL Limy
ALTITUDE 9 m (30 ft)
RAINFALL 686 mm (27 in.)
TEMPERATURE 4.5°C (40°F)

By the church in Westbury-on-Severn, 9 miles south-west of Gloucester on A48

LIKE MANY another famous garden, Westbury was vaguely familiar to me through *Country Life* books before I went there first in 1960. But instead of the trim lawns, neat hedges, sheets of placid water and flower beds in the Edwardian pictures, a scene of utter desolation greeted me. The lawns were hayfields, the hedges mostly dead and covered with brambles, the water was either covered with reeds or sunk to the mud and apart from half a dozen pathetically struggling roses there was not a flower to be seen. We all thought it

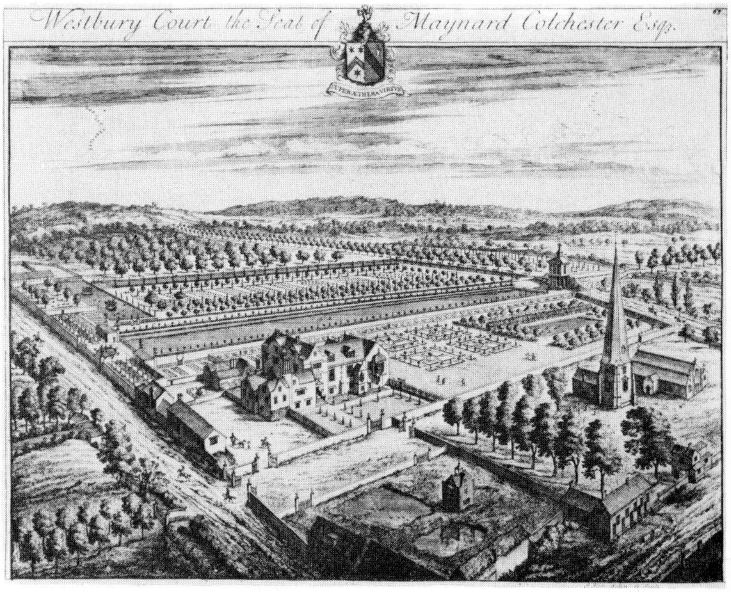

158 Westbury Court in 1717, after an engraving by Kip. The church still stands and the garden pavilion to the left of the spire has been reconstructed and still looks down the long canal. Above it is the T-shaped canal. The house vanished long ago. Inventories of the original plantings are extant.

a daunting task to take on such a place. But gradually, owing to generosity from several quarters, it became possible to envisage complete restoration – and by this I mean reinstating lawns, hedges, walls, water, and the plants. By a stroke of incredible good fortune, the 1696 to 1705 account books of Maynard Colchester, the original creator, were discovered, disclosing the exact numbers of plants he used; they included thousands of yews and hollies, fruit trees and plants. With the historical information uncovered from various sources and these lists it has been possible to re-create the original garden in great part.

The first things that were tackled were the removal of dead hedges, the dredging of the canals and the rebuilding of their retaining walls, and the demolition and reconstruction, brick by brick, of the derelict garden pavilion. During the last operation the original

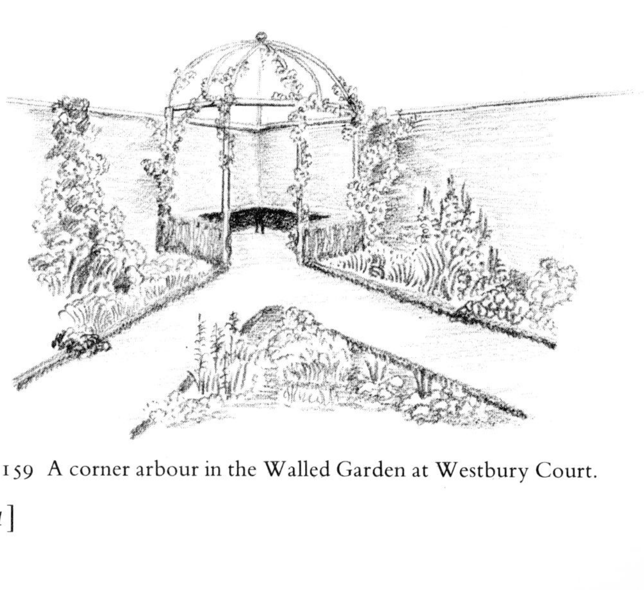

159 A corner arbour in the Walled Garden at Westbury Court.

160 TOP LEFT Westbury Court in 1963. The sorry state of the long canal and pavilion.
161 TOP RIGHT During dredging.
162 ABOVE LEFT The state of the east end of the T canal at Westbury when it was offered to the Trust. The garden house is shewn enclosed in its garden wall.
163 ABOVE RIGHT The garden house and little walled garden at Westbury after restoration and planting in 1975.

pillars and their capitals were freed of their encasing of fletton bricks – a most exciting revelation. Now the pavilion once again looks down the long, narrow, uninterrupted canal, lined by yew hedges.

The vast amount of silt dredged out of this canal and the much larger T-shaped canal resulted in having to cover the spare ground to the west, an area of about 0.8 ha (2 acres), with about 914 mm (3 ft) of mud. The Kip engraving of the garden, *c.*1707, shows a pretty parterre near the vanished dwelling house; two sections of the rectangle have been redesigned on the fine mat of greensward which germinated on the raised ground. The plants used are all old garden favourites, as indeed they are in the rest of the garden, along the walls and in the small walled garden by the gazebo. Here are traditional herbs and medicinal plants, ancestral roses, vines, pomegranate, rosemary and yuccas, violets, primroses, auriculas and numerous bulbs. In all several hundreds of old cultivars of trees, shrubs, fruit trees, herbaceous plants and bulbs are to be found in the garden. The original Musk Rose is there and the Christ's Thorn from Europe, the Fox Grape from America, Himalayan Sweet Jasmine, lavenders, old cultivars of irises from Turkey, ancient tulips, and apples, pears and plums of pre-1700 derivation, together with the Apothecary's Rose, Damask Rose, the White Rose of York and *Rosa centifolia*, which was then fairly new to cultivation. Many details and dates are to be found in the garden guide.

We know the date of the garden and what it

contained; its history has been written several times. We know too that it is about the most complete survival of a Dutch-style water garden of the late 17th century, with perhaps additions later in the 18th century by the second Maynard Colchester. We know that it now, once again, shows something of its former quiet beauty, and will grow in interest as the hedges, trees and plants mature. What we do not know is whether the old Holm Oak to the north of the canals has stood there witnessing all these changes. It is the largest tree recorded in these islands but until it falls, nobody will be certain. And, standing under its knotted branches and umbrageous dome, we should like to remain uncertain as long as possible.

WEST GREEN HOUSE
Hartley Wintney, *Hampshire*

Given by Sir Victor Sassoon in 1957 and endowed by Miss Yvonne Fitzroy

AREA 1.4ha ($3\frac{1}{2}$ acres)	1 mile west of
SOIL Lime-free	Harley Wintney, 5 miles
ALTITUDE 60.9 m (200 ft)	south-west of Camberley,
RAINFALL 686 mm (27 in.)	1 mile off A30
TEMPERATURE 3.5°C (38°F)	

OF THE EARLY HISTORY of this garden we know little, but there are three important periods in its development. The first is when an earlier owner, General Hawley, built the little stone garden house in the late 18th century, in which is a memorial to his favourite spaniel, named Monkey. For this reason it is always known as the Monkey House. Probably he also built the garden walls, thus providing the setting for Evelyn, Duchess of Wellington, to embellish in the early part of this century. Miss Yvonne Fitzroy for many years until her death preserved the atmosphere and the many trees,

164 The Nymphaeum at West Green House.

165 There is a rich assortment of roses, bulbs and perennials at West Green; in the borders in summer *Veratrum nigrum* produces its spikes of maroon flowers.

shrubs and plants, since when the Trust's tenant, Mr Alistair McAlpine, has given it new life.

Today it is a garden well endowed and enriched with a great variety of plants giving flower and interest from earliest spring onwards. The entrance to the house has recently been restored to the south side, which released the east side for a new scheme. A short avenue of hollies leads to a long avenue 329 m (367 yards) of limes at the end of which is a stone column surmounted by an elaborate finial. It was erected in 1976 and its inscription in Latin states that a large sum of money was needed for it, "which would otherwise have fallen, sooner or later, into the hands of the Inland Revenue".

If you enter the garden through the arched brick wall, you will find a terraced lawn finalised towards the skyline by clipped hornbeams. But resist the temptation to ascend the terraces – probably the work of the Duchess, or even earlier – and instead choose the back path behind the evergreen hedge. This will bring you to the small orangery, and then on, upwards to the Monkey House in the top far corner. The gravel terrace runs along a ha-ha, through two hornbeam tunnels with, in between, a delightful view of the house, supported by its arched, wing-walls on either side. Here you should take the opposite evergreen alley, downhill, but I think it unlikely that you will be able to resist the temptation, half-way down, of turning right into the main flower garden, encompassed on three sides by old brick walls.

This has been entirely replanted of late years, and has

been given a spaciousness which it never had before, due to four considerable plats of grass, which replace some of the areas where vegetables at one time were grown. Here then are the old box-edged borders with their flowers and shrubs, picked out with sentinel topiary pieces of box and holly; old fruit trees remain in avenue fashion or trained on the walls, with young ones newly planted to continue the tradition. Two charming wooden arbours are against one wall and all of a sudden one catches sight of two large replicas of them used as fruit cages – surely the most ornamental way of designing these usually unsightly adjuncts to a kitchen garden. These were the work of Mr Oliver Ford in 1975. Herbs of numerous kinds and vegetables are planted radially from them. Elsewhere in the borders as winter gives way to spring, bulbs and lily of the valley, irises and asphodels give way to roses, veratrums, phloxes and Michaelmas daisies in the old tradition but augmented with many a new plant.

Beyond the fruit cages is a circular opening in the wall – an idea adapted from the Japanese moon-gates – which entices you up some steps. Here are two pools and beyond them is – but that would be telling. You must discover the Nymphaeum for yourself. Both it and the column are to the design of Mr Quinlan Terry. In the grass of the Wild Garden grows the Elecampane, a native of Hampshire and a very grand plant indeed. It is related that Helen of Troy was carrying a bunch of this plant when borne away by Paris, perhaps to flavour barley sugar for which its roots have been valued throughout history.

WEST WYCOMBE PARK
High Wycombe, *Buckinghamshire*

House and land given in 1943 with an endowment by Sir John Dashwood, Bt

AREA 18.5 ha (46 acres)	2 miles west of
SOIL Limy	High Wycombe,
ALTITUDE 75 m (250 ft)	off the A40
RAINFALL 762 mm (30 in.)	London–Oxford road
TEMPERATURE 3.5°C (38°F)	

IT WILL BE BEST, I think, when arriving at the park from the High Wycombe side, to bear in mind the two lodges by the roadside, and to walk direct to these after purchasing a guide at the house. The fundamental alterations to the house and park in the 18th century become thereby more easily grasped.

On arrival at the two "lodges" it will be seen that one only is a lodge – Kitty's Lodge – and that the other is in reality a temple – Daphne's Temple – which faces the lake. These two buildings stand at either side of the original entrance to the park, at the beginning of a long almost straight drive to the south. If we had been there

166 The Music Temple appears to float, a miniature, on the water above the 18th-century cascade at West Wycombe Park.

in the mid 18th century the prospect would have been pleasantly wooded, not a formal avenue but a way through trees. As we moved up the drive the lake and its islands would have come into view through the tree stems on the right, and later we should have passed between lake and stream. The water went under the drive and through an arch in an imposing and rather terrifying compilation of rocks, with a leaden River God on top, and then gushed its way down the cascade to the long straight reach of river. We should surely have paused here because at the same point, across the lake, the open, Broad Walk through the wood beyond the lake stretched away to the west. But the rock arch dominated this spot. Continuing the long straight drive up the gentle gradient, a building would have come into view where now stands the Tower of the Winds. Here we should have turned right through the trees and followed the line of the ha-ha over which a view up the hill was freely open. And then the portico of the house could be seen, set down the slope a little, with wide lawns about it from whence were beautiful views uphill to the south, across the water to the north, with the light picking out the shades of greeny contours of the trees, to the church and mausoleum on top of the distant hill, all devised by Sir Francis Dashwood, the 2nd Baronet. The hill, only, is owned by the Trust, not the buildings. Below the lawns were serpentine walks threading their intriguing way through the trees and crossing the two streams that passed over weirs and under bridges on their way to the lake.

For some reason this distinguished landscape park has never caught the attention of gardening writers in this century and remains little known. This may be partly because when it first came to the Trust in 1943 the park and lakes showed signs of neglect and it is only during the last few years that a vigorous policy of rehabilitation has been adopted. Whatever its condition, it is however one of the outstanding examples of the Landscape School and is doubly interesting in exhibiting more affinity to the influence of Bridgeman and Kent than to later exponents. It is interesting to recall that it was being laid out well after the essays in landscape design of these two noted figures, but still had not launched itself into the much bigger and more lavish strides of Brown. The drives and views were yet straight and directed forcefully on to the architectural features, the Tower of the Winds being one of the very first reproductions in England of an ancient monument.

Later in his life, about 1770, Sir Francis decided on a complete reversal of the route approaching the house. The entry from the main road was made much farther west, and cut across the end of the Broad Walk, reaching the house at the west end. Another portico was built on this face of the house but the strong architectural feature was as much a part of the landscape park as an entrance to the house. As a temple it was dedicated to Bacchus, and reminds us of the lavish *fêtes*, processions and outdoor entertainments for which the owner was noted.

So now, from the house we can see the late 18th-century developments in the park. First there is the delightful note struck by the view down the sloping greensward to the lake and islands, on the largest of which is the elegant Music Temple. The pillared portico being rounded, there are many angles from which the pillars stand free from the building, reflected in the lake. And away in the distance, by felling trees on the far side of the lake, Daphne's Temple is brought into view as an eye-catcher. The Tower of the Winds is reached by the green drive through the trees and becomes a landscape feature of surprise in the park.

When we get to the cascade we find its rock arch and its statue gone, but the water rushing over the steps as before. The steps have a regular array of knobs to break the water into light-catching sprays, reminiscent of the cascade at SHEFFIELD PARK. I think one of the most intriguing views is from the south bank of the river, looking up to the cascade. From there the Music Temple appears to float, a miniature, on top of the waters, an illusion fostered by the rough flint work of the piers flanking the cascade in such contrast to the stone of the temple, smooth by nature and softened by distance.

There are further temples to be seen, all adding their quota to the varied beauties of the place, and in the late 18th century the park was extended considerably to the east and more architectural features were added. It is thus a remarkable example of the times, and is possibly unique in having experienced, during a space of less than fifty years, a complete reversal of its original design. The handling of the whole transformation was by Nicholas Revett, and does not owe its success to Brown or Repton, though the latter gave a little advice towards the end of the century. Today the groves of trees are thin in places, but this does not lessen the appeal of the flowery stream banks and the white Horse Chestnut flowers which are so prodigally produced every year, offset by the gloom of the native yews.

WIGHTWICK MANOR
Wolverhampton, *West Midlands*

Given in 1937 with an endowment by Sir Geoffrey Mander

AREA 4 ha (10 acres)
SOIL Lime-free
ALTITUDE 75 m (250 ft)
RAINFALL 686 mm (27 in.)
TEMPERATURE 3.5°C (38°F)

3 miles west of Wolverhampton, up Wightwick Bank (A454)

THE GARDEN at Wightwick is one of associations. It is not a famous garden nor is it extensive but it brings together many facets of interest and is about as near as we can get to pre-Raphaelite taste in gardens, a medium in which the expression finds few outlets.

All the upper, more or less formal parts around the house were designed by Alfred Parsons, RA, famous horticulturally for his exquisite portrayal of roses in Ellen Willmott's monumental work, *The Genus Rosa*. It would not necessarily follow that an artist of that calibre and predilection for flowers would make a good garden designer, but he had painted many pictures of Miss Willmott's garden and therefore knew what he would like to achieve. Together with a later addition by T. H. Mawson, of the famous Lakeland firm – a broad stone terrace and delicate oak balustrade supported by detailed masonry pillars – the succession of yew-hedged enclosures leads you on, up to the rose garden or down to the ponds. Bright herbaceous borders flank the entry into the rose garden which has a circular arbour in the centre covered with pink roses and purple clematises; the whole is brought to attention, smartly, by a large drum-shaped piece of topiary in golden yew. Some vast green drum-shaped yews are below the terrace and scattered around the lawns a selection of trees planted by royalty and political notabilities.

On the way to the ponds a very striking effect is achieved by a row alongside the path of 'Golden Queen' Holly alternating with the very dark green Irish Yews. In the cooler, moister areas rhododendrons of many kinds flourish, reflected in the waters. There is another point of interest, nostalgic to Cambridge men, and that is the replica of the wooden bridge at Queens' College. And if it should be pouring with rain, which does happen even in the best regulated gardens, be sure to go into the house, where many hours can be whiled away trying to put scientific names to the plants portrayed by William Morris – some of them easily recognisable, and others which go beyond, just into the world of fantasy.

WIMPOLE HALL
Arrington, *Cambridgeshire*

Acquired in 1976 with an endowment under the will of Mrs Elsie Bambridge

AREA 8 ha (20 acres)
SOIL Limy
ALTITUDE 30 m (100 ft)
RAINFALL 584 mm (23 in.)
TEMPERATURE 3.5°C (38°F)

At Arrington on A14 near junction with A603 Cambridge–Sandy road

THE ENGRAVING by Kip of Wimpole Hall in *Britannica Illustrata*, 1707, is in some ways untrue, but it at least gives us an impression of great formal magnificence. Long avenues command the approaches to the house from all four points of the compass. Charles Bridgeman had a great octagonal "bason" in the South Avenue of *c.*1720 – an avenue which is no longer in existence owing to the ravages of elm disease. The width, 152 m (500 ft), is however clearly visible. The house was first built about 1640 but was altered and improved by the numerous successive owners; many landscape designers have left their mark too.

Some landscaping to the north-west of the house was undertaken between 1752–4. Sanderson Miller was adviser at one time and designed the present walled garden, also producing an imaginative drawing for the folly to the north (see illus. 25). What little was left of the formal lines, apart from the majestic South Avenue, was altered by Capability Brown between 1767 and 1772. The formal 17th-century fishponds were "serpentined" and a third was added to the east. He also brought into the park Johnson's Hill to the north-east and planted the area with his usual effective belts and clumps. It is interesting to find that during this period the Sanderson Miller folly was built. It is a remarkable piece of work, built of brick and rubble but faced with clunch which has weathered to a hard exterior. Unfortunately it can only be approached across rough fields. Another designer, William Emes, also produced a plan of the park.

What we see today is the house, finalised in 1795 (some additions were removed in this century) by the Earl of Hardwick, with further alterations to garden and park by Humphry Repton. Repton's Red Book is dated 1801. In it he refers to the "avenues which are on too vast a scale to be destroyed by the new system and therefore it remains as a specimen of former magnificence". He thought the folly to be "one of the best of its kind extant". Looking from the house a considerable clump of trees had grown up partly obscuring the Folly from view; he advised the removal of the trees. On the same page is Lord Hardwick's comment: "Removing the clump deferred for the present tho' the principle admitted." Two rather nice little touches of Repton's were to have an iron railing enclosing the north garden to counteract the "absurd fashion of bringing cattle to the windows of the house", and, since the water of the ponds was not visible from the house owing to the lie of the land, to have a ship permanently in the pond so that its sail could be seen moving about, indicating water. Repton felt that cattle and boats were essential decorations for lawn and water.

Repton's railings still enclose the north garden, but the fountains have gone. If you walk round the house to the west in early August a fine old Indian Bean tree will be in flower; earlier the Flowering Ash puts forth its fluffy cream flowers. There is an immense bush of Common Box and an intriguing large lump of stone by a yew tree.

To the east of the house a 19th-century shrubbery extends as far as the walled garden, enclosed by its 17th-century ha-ha. In spite of the heavy clay soil some good specimens of conifers will be found, a golden Chinese Juniper, the Bhutan Pine, a blue Colorado Spruce, some remarkable native trees and a very large specimen of the Cornelian Cherry whose yellow flowers in early spring are followed in summer by red cherry-like fruits.

Over this whole area have been planted different kinds of *Narcissus* and daffodil, a yearly addition being made by using best quality bulbs after forcing for the house during Mrs Bambridge's period of tenure. Old varieties like 'King Alfred' (1899), 'Mrs E. H. Krelage' (1912), 'Mary Copeland' and 'Bath's Flame' (1914), 'John Evelyn' (1920), 'Mrs R. O. Backhouse', 'Fortune', 'Beersheba', 'Cheerfulness' (1923) are included, with many kinds of later raising such as 'Golden Harvest' and 'Carlton' (1927), 'Rembrandt' and 'Geranium' (1930), 'Mount Hood' and 'Sempre Avanti' (1938), 'Red Rascal' (1950) and 'Mrs Barclay' (1954). A further dozen or so kinds are mixed with them, and it will be an interesting example of what will thrive in grass in heavy soil in years to come.

The association of the successive owners of Wimpole with other properties of the Trust is remarkable. Thus twice have links been made by marriage or sale with the Robartes family who gave LANHYDROCK to the Trust; also to the Yorkes of ERDDIG; more recently with Kipling of BATEMANS, whose daughter became Mrs Bambridge.

WINKWORTH ARBORETUM
Godalming, *Surrey*

60 acres given in 1952 by Dr Wilfrid Fox;
35 acres bought in 1957 from the Dibble Fund.
Maintained by Councils of Surrey and Waverley

AREA 39.5 ha (99 acres)
SOIL Lime-free
ALTITUDE 60.9 m (200 ft)
RAINFALL 762 mm (30 in.)
TEMPERATURE 4°C (39°F)

3 miles south-east of Godalming on east side of B2130

THE ARBORETUM lies in the heart of the most beautiful part of Surrey, on one side of a valley, down which flows a stream, which has been dammed in several places, making a string of lakes. There are two lakes in the property; the lower one, known as Fish Pond, was there before 1898, but was enlarged later to be called Phillimore's Pond and by 1920 both this and Rowe's Flush, the upper lake, were in being. There is a considerable flow of water, and lower down it serves to fill the lake at Bramley House. Here Gertrude Jekyll spent many years as a girl.

The high banks and low hills on both sides of this valley are sandy and dry, but support a varied flora. Huge clumps of the Greater Tussock Sedge grow in the swampy ground around the south end of Phillimore's Pond. From the marshes to the hill tops there is a great range of native plants and Miss Jekyll recalled how she had, as a girl, enjoyed roaming through acres of this countryside with its high-hedged lanes, and uncultivated scrub and woodland – much of it too steep for farming. In all probability she traversed the woodland of scattered oak, birch and pine, beech and hazel, which now is the arboretum.

If you walk along the top land from the upper car park, or ascend from the lower one, to the pine-clad hill to the south, I think you will be well rewarded by the view at any time of the year. This is the spot to which Dr Fox came daily in his walk from his nearby house. You can look down towards Bramley, with high, farmland on the right of the valley. There is the main lake below you, with its rustic boat-house at the far end; beyond is a glimpse of the lower lake – revealed only in recent years – and all around, is the Bowl of the arboretum (see plate XXXIV).

At any time of the year, as I say, it is a rewarding sight but in October and early November, particularly when lit by the morning sun, it is of very great beauty, for the arboretum was planted mainly for autumn colour. It is not a planting of single specimens; almost every genus, and sometimes each species, is represented by a group. Thus the flaming colours of low bushes like azaleas and fothergillas run into the brilliant yellows and reds of Japanese Maples and stewartias, the coral pink of cherries, scarlet berries of cotoneasters, dark blood-red and bronzy-purple leaves of Sweet Gum; the whole glowing array is touched up by the more distant curtain of yellow from a group of larches and the steely grey of the Blue Cedars by the lake.

167 One of the longest stairways in British gardens; the 93 steps at Winkworth Arboretum, lined with Japanese azaleas and autumn colouring Japanese maples. Photo 1964. The fir trees have since been felled.

It was mainly neglected woodland when Dr Fox started work on it just before the last war. It is, I think, a wonderful thing, a magnanimous gesture, for someone to develop and plant such an area during the evening of his life, with the sole object of creating beauty and to hand it to the Trust for the benefit of us all. While he loved all growing things – and among them the Muscat Grapes from his own garden with which he used to regale us after lunch – his passion was for autumn colour. I remember writing in some magazine about a few uncommon autumn-colouring trees; among them I mentioned *Sorbus aucuparia* 'Beissneri' (which was then called S. moravica 'Laciniata') whose leaves turn to a pale fawny-yellow; he was in touch by telephone almost at once. He visited the nursery of which I was then manager, with Mrs Madeline Spitta, who acted as secretary, aide and abettor, and one could feel the enthusiasm they both had for autumn colour. He could not resist adding several trees to his collection. He bought from far and wide, and planted group after group of lovely things with just enough segregation to make you feel you are in a botanical collection, but not enough to detract from the natural beauty of the place. In fact apart from a few Japanese Maples, he left the oak wood untouched, partly because any interruption of the extensive woodland floor would not only have

168 The memorial to Dr Wilfrid Fox, framed between two *Eucryphia* 'Nymansay', at Winkworth Arboretum.

warred with the noble tree trunks, but would have obscured the solid carpet of bluebells in May.

Unfortunately Dr Fox did not prune nor did he thin. As a consequence many of the trees are not perfect specimens and many of the shrubs were overcrowded, but during the last ten years or so the Trust has had an expert staff and with the help of adequate modern machinery the whole arboretum is now in good order. Some income is obtained from the belts of timber trees which he planted with this need in mind.

The rising panorama is best appreciated from the lakeside near the lower car park; you have easy access to the Bluebell Wood and the azalea steps. There are 93 of these steps – surely one of the longest stairways in British gardens. I was there one wet day in October with some members of the International Dendrology Society. Leading the party from the top, I was down first and looking back up the steps a Japanese fairyland seemed to materialise, brightly coloured umbrellas and mackintoshes vying with the maples' brilliance.

From the upper car park you have a choice of areas for exploration: the Winter Garden, where Witch Hazels, rhododendrons, Autumn Cherry and camellias delight the eye in the earliest months of the year; the Foliage Glade, complete with variegated chestnut, *Populus lasiocarpa*, *Idesia*, *Fatsia*, and other plants with handsome leaves; thence to Dr Fox's Memorial Garden which contains a plaque set into a Bargate (local) stone plinth, inspired by Sir Hugh Casson. For this we had a gift of two fine *Eucryphia* 'Nymansay', and have since added some evergreens to make a little enclosure with seats. Then there is an area devoted to summer-flowering shrubs, also a considerable hazel wood in the shelter of which numerous magnolias grow. A collection of holly species and cultivars nearby leads you to the escarpment view-point, where, over maples and parrotias, the idyllic Surrey landscape lies away on the far side of the valley, a pretty chequering of fields and hedgerows.

Two of his early specialities were the genera *Acer* and *Sorbus*. The acers thrive; the sorbuses, some 80 species and varieties, are suffering from various troubles; but they both contribute well to the whole. In different areas will be found *Malus trilobata* from the Mediterranean, *Pyrus ussuriensis* from China; *Quercus laurifolia*, the Laurel Oak from eastern United States; *Q. schochiana*, a rare hybrid between *Q. palustris* and *Q. phellos* and 'Rubrifolia' a form of *Q. velutina* with gross foliage; *Nothofagus dombeyi* and *N. procera* from Chile; *Betula albo-sinensis* from China; *Cladrastis* and *Oxydendrum*, hybrids such as *Crataegomespilus*, and *Sorbaronia*; new hybrid viburnums from the United States: the list is long, the range is great, the enjoyment and instruction incalculable.

169 An early spring-flowering rhododendron raised at Bodnant prior to 1933, 'Seta' is very free flowering with white flowers vividly flushed with clear deep pink on the lobes, well contrasted by chocolate coloured anthers. *R. moupinense* × *R. spinuliferum*.

The flowers in illustrations 169–176 are reduced to four-fifths of their actual size.

170 *Trillium chloropetalum*, which flowers in early spring, is variable in colour, from maroon to almost white, stained with pale maroon. It is a native of the western States of North America, and was sketched at Knightshayes. Sweetly fragrant.

171 ABOVE *Rosa bracteata*, sketched at Trelissick, was introduced by Lord Macartney from China in 1793. It is a climber for a warm wall, and produces its lemon-scented flowers from July until autumn; they are pure white, silky, with orange yellow stamens. Glossy dark green leaves. A parent of the rose 'Mermaid'.

172 RIGHT *Rosa gigantea*, a tender tea-scented climber of pale yellow colouring, sketched at Mount Stewart. In that mild climate it has grown for many years unprotected on a pergola. The long, recurved petals and unique fragrance were transmitted to the old European strains in the 19th century and gave rise to the sophisticated shapes of modern roses.

173 ABOVE The Autumn Damask Rose, known and grown since Roman times. Considered to be a hybrid between *Rosa gallica* and *Rosa moschata*. Flowers of clear soft pink, sweetly fragrant, produced from summer until autumn. Sketched at Mottisfont Abbey.

174 RIGHT The Gallica rose named 'Sissinghurst Castle' because it was found growing there when the Nicolsons bought the place in 1930. Old-established plants also grow at Wotton Place, Woodstock. The colour is a rich plum-crimson, flushed and flecked with maroon-crimson, with light magenta-crimson around the edges of the petals. Sketched at Sissinghurst.

175 The hybrid *Eucryphia* 'Penwith', raised and sketched at Trengwainton. Flowers white, with creamy anthers; the foliage dark green.
This particular cross between *E. lucida* and *E. moorei*, sometimes known collectively as *E. hillieri*, shews the influence of the former species in its entire, not pinnate foliage and is therefore likely to be more hardy than other named crosses which may have pinnate leaves, inherited from the tender *E. moorei*. Sketched at Trengwainton.

176 Felbrigg Hall has two long borders of the rare *Colchicum autumnale tenori* which bear thousands of rosy-lilac flowers in September. With it are shewn for comparison *C. speciosum* 'Album' (large, white, at top), *C. aggripinum* (lilac-pink with tesselated segments), and 'Water Lily' (double flowers of lilac-pink).

PART IV

Features of Garden Design

177 Stone vase and pleached hornbeam alley
at Lytes Cary.

7

AVENUES AND TREES

THE WORD "AVENUE" simply means "the way of approach" and what more natural than it should be marked by a row of stakes? And if those stakes happened to grow, they would form trees bordering the way, at least on one side. Or if the way were cut out of woodland or open forest, the trees left would equally well mark the route. Avenues had their great period of fashion in England in the 17th century, derived from their popularity in France, where on some of the flatter land around Paris they were a triumphant success, marching through clearing and woodland alike. Their very length obscured defects, such as the failure of trees in certain spots. In England the fashion grew speedily after the Restoration. Some were no doubt cut through woodland, but probably as many were actually planted, and this was for a variety of reasons. One was that the English nurserymen were beginning to produce quantities of trees; until then as far as one can gather the cutting down of trees and the making of clearances was common and the replacement of trees was not taken seriously until John Evelyn strove to call attention to the decreasing woodlands. There was a general imposing of man's will on the landscape, a proliferation of tree-lined vistas from the great houses of the nobility, and also the added discovery that looking down a long vista appeared to increase the length, whereas looking upwards to a house tended to belittle the building. All this could be exaggerated by false perspectives, and, in more intimate areas by the use of the *trompe l'oeil*.

The most popular trees were those which grew well and could be produced quickly and in quantity. It was easy to raise beech trees and chestnuts from seeds; oaks also grow well from seeds but are slow in growth in early years. The English Elm is prolific of its underground suckers, but like many plants with this propensity, it seldom produces seeds. Today, apart from the dreadful loss of millions of trees through disease, it is seldom seen as a woodland tree, but nearly always in hedgerows. This can be attributed not only to its ease of rooting and readiness to be transplanted to make a boundary, but also to its liking for good deep soil which would have been cleared for farming. The Lombardy Poplar, so beloved in France, was not introduced to this country until too late for the fashion for avenues. The lime has however always been the most popular tree for avenues, partly on account of its fragrant flowers. The Dutch had found that the Common Lime was easy to reproduce from its prolific basal shoots. (It is open to question whether this is the *cause* of this unfortunate habit, perpetuated over hundreds of years.) It is a sterile hybrid between the Small-leafed Lime and the Red Twigged Lime.

It is normal for trees to grow in close proximity to others, in fact though they produce very handsome

178 The protection of a tree against stock and deer in parks and meadows costs several times more than the tree itself.

specimens when grown singly in conditions to their liking, they do not really give of their best in exposed windy positions. We are apt to judge trees by single specimens, not by attenuated trees in woodland, where, closely pressed by their neighbours, they tend to develop tall stems and small heads. This is exactly what the Common Lime does when grown singly or as an avenue. Perhaps this is why it was so popular, but I think its uniformity from being vegetatively propagated, especially by the astute businessmen of Holland, was a factor of equal importance. Whatever may be the cause, it was the Common Lime which was almost always the tree used in very old avenues. Today with shortage of labour we do not use it, mainly because of its prolific basal shoots which have to be cut away every winter, or treated with a hormone growth-inhibitor; sometimes these basal shoots are clipped into a sort of basal hedge below the avenue, as at Hopetown House, West Lothian. Examples of old common lime avenues are at CLIVEDEN, HAWKWOOD and CHARLECOTE. Two very old avenues are at CROFT CASTLE (Sweet Chestnut) and LANHYDROCK (sycamore and beech). Our old elm avenues are, alas, no more.

With the advent of the landscape movement of the 18th century, avenues were outmoded, and also the use of the Common Lime, whose narrow outline was useless for the comfortable contours desired of specimen trees, though it was still useful in woodlands. William Kent still used avenues; to Capability Brown they were anathema; Humphry Repton allowed them so long as they were not straight, indeed it was on his recommendation that one of the country's longest avenues – double rows of Common Lime which wind their way for three miles through CLUMBER PARK – was planted in 1840. As a rule he would have subscribed to the precept that turns and twists should follow the contours of the land, and are not usually acceptable on flat ground. *Tilia platyphyllos* at times develops a narrow outline and has been increasingly used as an avenue tree through the last hundred years or so. *Tilia cordata* reliably makes a fine rounded crown and a number of isolated trees in our parks prove its popularity – notably at SHUGBOROUGH and at CLUMBER PARK – apart from its being so much more conspicuous when in flower than any other species owing to its habit of bearing its flowers above the branchlets instead of hanging from them.

Avenues are best on flat land where the soil does not vary much. This is amply demonstrated by the disparity in growth of some of the avenues at BUSCOT PARK, where the land is undulating. Even flat land is not always reliable; we only have to look at the quadruple avenue of Horse Chestnuts at ANGLESEY ABBEY to realise how growth is controlled by the soil, subsoil and water table.

If we think that avenues first were the outcome of a row of stakes which took root, or forest clearance, or the deliberate planting of trees, we next come to the orderly mind which inaugurated planting at regular intervals. Only in this way can the avenue exert its tempting power to lead one along; there is even a feeling of compulsion to get to the end to see what is there. It may be an object, or an open view, and its terminus – no less than its beginning and length – dictates its most suitable width. Some avenues would be too wide for their length, such as those at NOSTELL PRIORY, HARDWICK HALL and MONTACUTE (all to the east of the dwellings), were they not based on the width of the building. Others may be considered too narrow, as at SALTRAM HOUSE, THE VYNE, HAWKWOOD and LYME PARK (south of the house). In fact it takes a Repton to decide on the planting of an avenue, someone who has some knowledge of trees and their growth, for there are many things to be considered, apart from the suitability of trees to the local soil and conditions.

The trees must be so placed in their rows that they have enough light and space to allow good growth. The rows must be placed wide enough apart for the same purpose. These are the practical considerations, after which it is a matter of aesthetics. An avenue should lead to something, as I have said, and on that something depends its width, but here we have to think

179 The avenue of limes within the garden at Saltram, under which grow old cultivars of *Narcissus* and Neapolitan cyclamens. The walk was designed as a principal approach from the house to the "Castle", some 240 years ago; the trees were added after 1884.

180 The chestnut avenue at Blickling. The wide spacing creates the opposite of a Gothic arch. Photo 1960.

of the normal width of the tree chosen. Extremes are the very narrow Gothic-arch effect which will be the result in an avenue where trees of normal growth are planted in lines close together, or where the same trees are so spaced that with normal growth each can develop into a specimen, as at the GIBSIDE CHAPEL or BLICKLING HALL (east of the garden). But the pitfall with the narrower spacing is that for the first fifty years or so the view along the avenue will be closed by overlapping branches, unless they are high-clipped after the French fashion, or until the under branches can be pruned away, accelerating the natural process which produces the pointed arch.

The most beautiful Gothic arch I have ever seen was Brooklands Avenue, Cambridge in the 1920s and 1930s. Having the same tree – the Huntingdon Elm – at much the same spacing at HIDCOTE, for some twenty years we have been pruning away the under branches to achieve the same effect, sadly to no avail as the avenue, just fifty years old and in its prime, has succumbed to the bark disease, in spite of the large sums of money spent on preventive treatment. This avenue at HIDCOTE in particular would have merited Repton's approbation, for it "climbs up a hill and, passing over the summit, leaves the fancy to conceive its determination".

With wider spacing between the rows, a Tudor arch can be achieved, lower and wider than the Gothic. And of course by choosing different species an infinite variety of shape and quality can be envisaged; by the use of tapering, fastigiate trees, such as the Fastigiate Oak at BUSCOT, Dawyck Beech at Stowe, Buckinghamshire, or Lombardy Poplar at Madresfield Court, Worcestershire, a wide glimpse of the sky is seen even with close spacing.

From what I have written it is obvious that any effect can be achieved by the use of the right plants, at the right spacing. Your wide view should be approached by a wide avenue perhaps, your substantial vase or statue by a broad arch, your obelisk by a narrow one and your house perhaps by trees so spaced that their branches sweep the ground. Two splendid Red Twigged Lime avenues are at POLESDEN LACEY and CASTLE WARD. Smaller schemes or smaller parts of gardens may have sentinel cypresses, or clipped box as at TINTINHULL, or huge trim Irish Yews as at MONTACUTE or LANHYDROCK. They can all be described as avenues and so indeed can rarities such as the remnants of the Monkey Puzzles at ARLINGTON COURT, the Hardy Palms at SHEFFIELD PARK and SHARPITOR and the cordylines at MOUNT STEWART.

If the planner of an avenue has plenty to think about, conundrums of a different kind plague those of us who are faced with decaying avenues, and have to decide how they can be replaced. An avenue properly spaced originally is impossible to replace effectively except by clear-felling, and this is not always possible nor desirable. Think for instance of the double avenue of old sycamores initially planted in 1657 at LANHYDROCK, and subsequently patched with young trees and beeches. We continue to patch it as trees fall for the simple reason that its width is ideal and a new avenue could not be planted either inside or outside of it. The same may be said about the avenue of beeches at KILLERTON. At CLIVEDEN the width of the lime avenue is governed by the width of the house; does one wait till all have fallen and plant on the same lines, or plant a narrower avenue to prepare for the sad day? The problem has been solved at CLUMBER PARK where entirely new avenues have been planted so that when one fails another will be in its full beauty.

Informal types of avenues are to be found in one of the approaches to HARDWICK HALL, where the trees are planted in clumps (as at Castle Howard, Yorkshire), and the gently curving row of Sweet Chestnuts at CROFT CASTLE. The former is easy to patch as trees fail; the latter can be replaced elsewhere; CROFT in fact has a new avenue of limes leading across the park from the west of the Castle. The old beech avenue in the approach to POLESDEN LACEY is slowly being replaced with limes, while outside the avenue young beeches are already taking shape. Other young lime avenues are at WALLINGTON, BENINGBROUGH HALL, ANTONY HOUSE, SIZERGH CASTLE, MELFORD HALL and WEST GREEN HOUSE. *Tilia euchlora* or *T. platyphyllos* have been used in these projects according to the effect required, while at POLESDEN LACEY the Common Cherry or Gean has been planted in crossing avenues.

Though many other trees are suitable, the lime remains the favourite tree for avenues. As with hedges, preference is given to trees propagated vegetatively, on their own roots (not grafted or budded), since these make uniform growth, whereas seed-raised stock is likely to be very variable in growth. However even the Broad-leaf Lime (Red Twig) is seldom produced from layers these days, and seed-raised stock is more readily available. With some of the choicer trees propagation is by cuttings. Small trees are generally the most successful though in the past records show that large trees were moved in for immediate effect, as tall as 18.2 m (60 ft). This was in the days of men and muscle, horses and wooden conveyances.

Apart from the splendour and wide variety of its avenues the Trust probably owns, throughout its properties, a greater collection of specimen trees, native and foreign, than is to be found elsewhere in these islands. I hoped to have been able to include some lists in this book but the time is not ripe for two reasons.

181 OPPOSITE Yet another type of avenue is found at Hidcote, where young beeches were planted closely together in French style. They have been thinned since this photograph was taken in 1960.

One is that thanks to the Thomas Phillips Price Trust and the co-operation of the Royal Botanic Gardens at Kew, the Trust is having all its trees and woody plants checked botanically and catalogued; the results will be recorded at Kew and anyone wishing to see good specimens of any particular species will thereby have direct reference to them. The other reason is that for some years Alan Mitchell of the Forestry Commission at Alice Holt Lodge, Farnham, Surrey, has been busy recording the heights and girths of notable trees throughout the country. He has published several lists to date in the Royal Horticultural Society's *Journal*, now *The Garden*, and *The Quarterly Journal of the Royal Forestry Society* and elsewhere, but such is the immensity of the task that it can never be up to date.

Therefore neither of these projects is complete and I think it best, since word-space in this book is running out, to leave the publication of definitive lists until, perhaps, a later edition.

8

BOUNDARIES AND BARRIERS

IN DAYS LONG AGO, having built your house, which would safely contain you and your family – and livestock at night – the next need was an area safe from the intrusion of wild animals or roaming stock, and so the garden was born. It had to be surrounded by a barrier. In the stone-belts this was easy – there was plenty of stone lying on or just under the soil and it helped the early farmer to have the topsoil free of stones. Walling material was there for the taking. When the stones were large and rounded, the walls were correspondingly thicker, a fact which accounts for the immense gate piers found in parts of Northern Ireland, for instance near ROWALLANE.

In other areas the trees provided fencing material – after the needs of building, seating, warmth, utensils and arms had been satisfied. The fence, however, has never been a popular boundary in greater gardens, walls and hedges being preferred, though the fence continues to surround thousands of small gardens today, and in parks open rail fences are also common.

The use of living plants for a boundary probably came later. There were no nurserymen in very early times, and the best and most popular hedging plant ever since hedges were planted – the hawthorn or may – has the disconcerting habit of holding its seeds dormant for a year or more before germination (like the holly and the wild roses). But once this fact was grasped its use was widespread. Elm and Blackthorn suckers would also have proved useful, and the Common Privet and Box from the chalk hills would grow from cuttings in the open ground; beech and hornbeam germinated promptly and freely. It was not until the 17th century that the English Yew, released from its specially favoured position of being the supplier of branches for spears and bows, came into use in gardens. Its poisonous effect on stock would have led to its extermination in grazing or browsing areas, and also in hedges, and hence perhaps came the idea of planting it safely in churchyards. After John Evelyn's time it has assumed great importance for hedges. It provides a dark velvety background for flowers, and though the holly may rival it in its glittering beauty of leaf, the holly is an unpleasant neighbour when gardening.

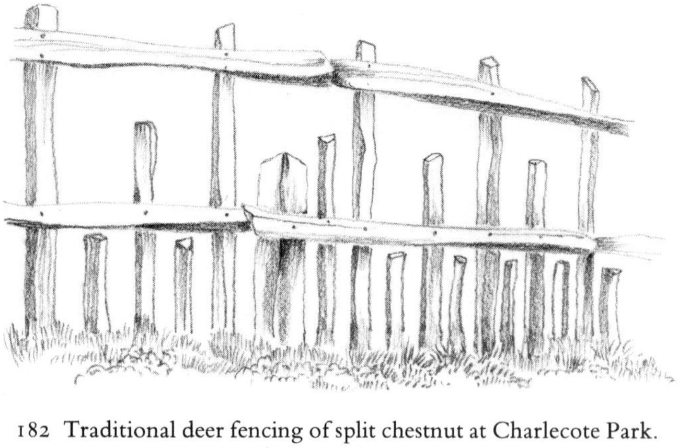

182 Traditional deer fencing of split chestnut at Charlecote Park.

Our garden design has gradually become so involved that, apart from suitability of soil, and local availability of stone or, later, brick, no prevalent use of one or other material over any district can be detected. As a rule the grander the house the more likely were the garden areas to be outlined with walls. These in any case usually joined the house to create a forecourt, or were made into a rectangular enclosure for the production of fruit, herbs and vegetables. Hedges would form a boundary where the garden met the countryside, or were used for subdivisions of the garden. I do not want to go into architectural details in what is a garden book but garden walls have assumed infinite variety over the centuries. From the retaining walls of rough stone in Gloucestershire or Cornwall, the flints of the chalk belts, to the masonry of the hard sandstones and limestones, there is a wide difference of style and finish, culminating in the high, buttressed and capped walls of MONTACUTE and HARDWICK – with tall elegant finials to boot.

When bricks were made in quantity in Renaissance times their regular use for houses, in stone-less districts,

183 Stone finials on the garden wall of 1587, at Hardwick Hall.

would have taken precedence over their use for garden walls. But as their manufacture increased, highly elegant walls grew up – at HAM HOUSE for instance – and they had the added value that their surface retained the sun's warmth longer than cold stone. While low retaining walls would use up unwanted stone, nearly all the huge walls of the 17th-century ornamental gardens, and the kitchen gardens of later years, were principally built to aid the production of fruit – apples, pears, plums, apricots and peaches, grapes and figs. For this reason some stone walls were faced with brick, as at SIZERGH CASTLE. The bricks in the Walled Garden at ROWALLANE have glazed flanges through which wires could be threaded, on which to tie branches. Elsewhere old kitchen garden walls are likely to be pock-marked with thousands of nail holes, the evidence of the constant adjustment needed for training the young wood of peaches and other trees. In more recent times, "vine-eyes" were inserted at the time of building to avoid this yearly damage to the ashlar or bricks.

The wall therefore has several uses, the linking of house to garden, protection from animals and wind, provision of sites for training fruit trees – some like the Morello Cherry seem to prefer a north-facing wall – and also for the ease of covering the fruits against depredations of birds; while today, when small-scale production of fruit is no longer economic, we all covet the luxury of wall protection for our half-hardy shrubs and climbers and for nursing those which prefer shade. Thus the masonry of a garden wall is often obscured, but in general, if it is a good wall, some portions should be free of growth. Particularly does this apply when the wall is venerable, clad with tinted lichens or moss, and little plants have seeded in the old mortar and interstices. Most stones provide a good background for plants though some of more yellow tone, like Ham stone, are somewhat difficult when it comes to flower colours. Like some red bricks, only the strong colours, or white and yellow, will be happy against them.

We are apt to think of a neatly-clipped hedge as a static object, much like a wall. They last for a long time if the ground is suitable for the species chosen, but like any other plant will eventually fail. The Japanese have proved that by suitably nourishing them, *bonsai* plants can be kept in health for an immense time; the care lavished upon them would ensure their longevity. Compare this with the complete lack of care given, normally, to hedges: every year their young growth is clipped away, depriving them of nourishment, and their roots and stems are often smothered with weeds and ivy. While flowerbeds are given manure, and water in times of drought, the hedges go without any attention. Their dense vegetation, often unwashed by rain, makes a breeding ground for pests, such as aphides and scale-insects. Some twenty years ago I could go into almost any garden inherited by the Trust and with one glance at a yew hedge, detect the blackish tinge of the foliage denoting the presence of scale-insects, steadily sucking out the sap. Some years of spraying have resulted in our hedges being clean once again, but aphides, being gifted with wings, continue to affect box and beech hedges.

However closely it is clipped, a hedge or topiary piece always gets larger. This is all very well in some ways; there is a charm about an ancient overgrown topiary peacock or other object, but the time taken and difficulty encountered in clipping them annually has to be balanced against their aesthetic value. Very large hedges, perhaps 2.1 m (7 ft) wide, are almost impossible to clip on top. Fortunately most hedging plants respond to hard pruning and particularly is this so with privet, thorn, hornbeam and yew; holly and box are slower, and beech is very slow and, unless in good health, is sometimes unresponsive.

Some very old high hedges become so much part of one's life that it does not immediately register that they have grown out of all proportion to their surroundings, and that the time taken with ladders and trestles for their clipping is simply not worth it. Time was when the great yew hedges on either side of the approach to BLICKLING HALL had their branches supported inside the hedges with innumerable props, to ensure that the clipped front maintained a close appearance. They are now left to sag as they wish, and look surprisingly little worse for the neglect! Venerable yew hedges at MONTACUTE and CLIVEDEN have reached an immense

184 TOP The main cross-vista at Hardwick Hall shewing the hornbeam hedges in 1963, after the excessively wide growths had been reduced. The growths covered two-thirds of the grass alley.
185 ABOVE A yew hedge at Lytes Cary in process of being reduced and rejuvenated. The top and one side have been pruned away to encourage new compact growth. Photo 1963.

size and are in the process of being reduced on one side and heavily mulched with manure to promote their growth.

When hedges have to be reduced to restore balance, proportion and health, and also to reduce work, it is usual where possible to cut one side and the top hard back to the mainstems. By cleaning out rubbish from the base, feeding them, and admitting light and air new growth will soon appear. When it has been clipped and produced a good new surface the remaining side is treated likewise. Many hedges in the Trust's gardens have been treated in this way over the years with a consequent saving in annual clipping. The sides are always easy; it is the wide top that is so difficult. The space taken up by an overspread hedge is amazing; the record was, I think, at HARDWICK HALL where the pair of hornbeam hedges had each absorbed about 2.1 m (7 ft) of the grass alley between them. Many other hedges in our gardens have been reduced to good and manageable proportions, particularly at LYTES CARY, HIDCOTE, ASCOTT, POLESDEN and SISSINGHURST; after a few years it is difficult to detect that anything has happened. William Mason, in the 18th century, had some definite ideas about hedges.

Select the shrubs that, patient of the knife,
Will thank thee for the wound, the hardy Thorn,
Holly, Box, Privet or Pyracanth.
They, thickening from their base, with ten-fold shade
Will soon replenish all thy judgement prun'd.

Returning to topiary, it is a much more difficult job to reduce the shapes without spoiling the outline for many years. It is likely that the yew pyramids on the Top Terrace at POWIS CASTLE started life as quite small "Noah's Ark" trees; some are now 9 m (30 ft) high. But on such a majestic scale are the castle and terraces that they do not seem out of proportion – and will remain, no doubt, so long as we can afford to continue tending them.

While it is unfortunate that through too gentle clipping hedges get wider, they can usually be reduced without too much distress. But if, when clipping topiary, so much as a quarter of an inch of growth is left annually at clipping time, in half a century this will result in the shape being widened by a foot in every direction. This is always a disaster; shapes are lost and a clumsy unrecognisable lump of greenery slowly develops. For instance, when the birds-on-obelisks were planted between the fuchsia parterre and the Bathing Pool at HIDCOTE they were the same height – approximately – as now, but the obelisks were only about 305 mm (1 ft) wide. They are now over 914 mm (3 ft) wide and the birds had grown out of all proportion and had to be reduced. They are very slow in recovering in spite of every care and feeding.

The haha is a means of making an effective boundary which does not interrupt the view. And views were all important during the long period of the landscape garden or park, where the eye sought to bring the countryside into the ambience of the dwelling. The haha could be just a wide ditch with prickly bushes planted at its lowest part – the bushes being kept below the level of the surrounding ground by pruning – or a ditch with one sloping side towards the field and a vertical, walled side, holding up the ground, on the house side. Something of the former, more rare, type may be seen at BLICKLING HALL, while most of the hahas in the country belong to the latter type, such as Brown's efforts at CHARLECOTE and PETWORTH, and those of the Trust's construction at SALTRAM, KILLERTON, LACOCK ABBEY and TRELISSICK. The cost of construction today, thanks to machinery, is not high in relation to the benefit that accrues.

Finally there is water. Great houses and castles often relied much upon this as a barrier and interesting examples are the moats which completely surround OXBURGH HALL, LITTLE MORETON HALL, SCOTNEY CASTLE and BODIAM CASTLE, and the entire garden at ST JOHN'S JERUSALEM.

186 ABOVE The construction of a haha at Saltram in 1963.
187 BELOW The finished haha in 1965, protecting the front of the house from animals and permitting the removal of fence and hedge which obstructed access and the view into the garden.

9

STONE IN GARDENS

ONE OF THE FASHIONS of gardening in Britain which reached considerable popularity during the first half of this century was the rock garden. Its popularity has declined, due to three reasons – the cost of gathering and transporting suitable rocks, the time consumed in hand-weeding the gardens, and the increasing knowledge that alpine and other dwarf plants will grow successfully in less pretentious environments. The origin of the cult of the rock garden is not difficult to trace, but it has varying degrees of relevance to other garden fashions.

First there is, of course, the stone itself. Most of the great architecture in England is due to the limestone belt which extends from Yorkshire down to Dorset. It is of various quality, soft or hard and indeed some of its beds not only provide our finest building stone but also our best cement, such as the beds at Portland. Together stone and cement have been carted about all over the country, and even to Ireland, to build abbeys, churches, cathedrals, castles and mansions, bridges, orangeries and all manner of garden buildings. In colour these limestones vary from cold grey to warm yellowish brown. Carboniferous limestone, which unlike these later limestones gives off little lime in the soil, is found in Derbyshire and in Cumbria, and is mostly of a grey colouring. There is also a great range of older sandstones, mostly to the west and north, and mostly of darker colouring, to say nothing of the really old rocks, the slates and granites and igneous foundations of our islands. To the east and south of the great limestone belt, stone does not occur so freely; much of it is well below the silts and sands of later geological layers, but some younger sandstones and limestones do occur in Sussex, Surrey and Kent, apart from clunch and chalk. It is mainly in chalk deposits that flints are found. There is however another hard stone from the south-east, pieces of which are known as sarsen stones; as the chalk and gravel ridges of the south-east gradually wore down, this young hard sandstone became exposed. Immense lumps were used for the construction of Stonehenge and today it is not uncommon to find lumps in road excavations. Over hundreds of years this stone, requiring little quarrying, was broken and cut and used for building, or was broken further and used in all sorts of other ways. The ground in front of ASHDOWN HOUSE is littered with sarsens, and the same material was used for parts of the grotto at CLAREMONT.

In the earliest days of gardening, local rock which could be spared from the construction of dwellings would have been used for edgings to garden beds. Bones, timber or shells were used in less fortunate areas, but where good stone was available, as the expertise of quarrying and cutting progressed, and as the design of gardens advanced, it was used for garden walls, steps, paths and other features.

When the Picturesque movement gathered way in the 18th century, and the inclusion of the "awful" became a diversion and a delight in the landscape, ruined buildings, hermit's caves and natural-looking waterfalls (as opposed to fountains, pools and rills of the previous century) became a new fashion.

From an artist's point of view rocks provide just the right immovable solid needed as a foil to playful water or swaying greenery; in their own right, too, they have immense appeal in their colour, size, shape and texture. However, before this period there is a mention of a grotto at Wilton in 1615, but it disappeared in the 18th century. It was of a "folly" nature outside and thus bore some resemblance to the much later building at CLANDON PARK which is of brick and flints outside, but of rough work inside. Both this and the 19th-century effort at CLIVEDEN are not far removed from the elegant flint summerhouse at MOTTISFONT ABBEY. They all perform the same function; they form a cool, covered, dark retreat.

There is much stress on shady alleys in old garden descriptions, and coolth was also obtained from caves – from which grottoes derive. Examples are at WEST WYCOMBE. Sir Walter Scott wrote in *The Garden*

Where midst thick oaks the subterranean way
To the arched grot admits a feeble ray,
Where glossy pebbles pave the varied floors
And rough flint walls are decked with shells and ores.

We have for comparison grottoes at Pain's Hill and CLAREMONT (early 18th century) a-glitter with coloured spas; STOURHEAD (mid 18th century) with stalactite-hung interior, gushing water and a sleeping beauty; a suggestion of one at LACOCK ABBEY and also at CLUMBER PARK (late 18th century) and a fascinating affair, a roofed cromlech, at WADDESDON (late 19th century). All of these, except the remnants at LACOCK and CLUMBER, are of the truly gloomy, horrific and picturesque style, and water is associated with all but the last.

Grottoes, apart from their connection with caves, were a creation entirely on their own, and the rock garden of the plantsman of today has little in common with them, except in its more scenic effects.

It is believed that the first rock garden constructed in England was in the Chelsea Physic Garden. As early as 1772 basaltic lava was brought from Iceland to the garden by Sir Joseph Banks, and was added to a collection of flints and chalk and 40 tons of old stones brought from the Tower of London. This assortment was arranged round a lily pool inside a greenhouse of some sort built as early as 1685 when it was noted by John Evelyn. The greenhouse has long since gone. It was a common fallacy of 19th-century gardening that choice exotics needed the warmth of a greenhouse for their cultivation. The rock was used to help with the cultivation of plants from the Alps and elsewhere, and the lava forms the bulk of the rockery remaining today. It had no pretence of being of scenic quality and it was scarcely allied to the grotto.

Innumerable rockeries sprang up during the last century, built with flints, brickbats and broken stone of various kinds where good stone was not available, and these efforts were in great part due to the craze for growing ferns, which was at a peak for about twenty years from 1850. Though ferns declined in popularity, Alpine plants became increasingly popular during the late 19th century and have never lacked their devotees since.

The remnants of George Maw's rockery which he made around 1875 can still be seen at BENTHALL HALL, in which garden there are rock beds growing alpines today. At COTEHELE pink-tinted alabaster was used some eighty years ago in the valley garden; local Hornton sandstone forms the rock garden at UPTON HOUSE, Sussex sandstone was used at WAKEHURST PLACE, while imported Cheddar limestone was used at THE WEIR, and tufa at ASCOTT for a tiny grotto and also a rock garden. ARLINGTON COURT and CASTLE WARD have rock banks fashioned of local stone, and at DUDMASTON the old red sandstone outcrops have been used with effect. Taking the above as a group they were constructed over the last one hundred years as homes for plants.

188 The grotto at Claremont needed restoring and the arches strengthening. Here the temporary causeway is shewn which enabled the work to be carried out; the crane was used to transport fallen rocks. Photo 1977. Before work started self-sown sycamores and alders of some size had to be removed.

189 The late 18th-century grotto at Clandon Park, built of flint, stone and brick. The figures of the Three Graces are a later addition.

It is worth noting here the numerous plants mentioned by Mawe and Abercrombie in *Everyman his own Gardener* of 1776: auriculas, pinks, double saxifrage, also *Saxifraga pyramidalis (S. cotyledon)*, *Gentiana lutea* and *G. acaulis*, which they called the gentianella, a name which Reginald Farrer tried to revive early in this century. By 1817 Abercrombie in *The Practical Gardener* listed many an alpine plant such as species of *Draba*, *Gentiana acaulis*, *G. cruciata*, *G. asclepiadea*, *G. pneumonanthe*; *Helonias bullata*, *Saxifraga oppositifolia*, *S. lingulata*; *Pyrola* species, *Trifolium alpinum* and *Onosma echioides*. *Trillium grandiflorum* was also included. The desire for a rock garden therefore was two-fold: to provide rocky homes for rock-loving plants and to bring these little plants nearer to the eye and hand for appraisal and attention. They could not be left to the spade-wielding garden staff. The title of the first book calls attention to this.

Partly because cartage was cheap, it became as commonplace to bring limestone from Westmorland or Somerset to the Home Counties to make rock gardens as it did to cart building stone as necessary from county to county. But whereas the building stone was brought to create something artificial, as time went on the stone used in rock gardens was laid in an effort to make it appear part of nature. And one cannot make the beautiful waterworn limestone of Cumbria look really at home in, say, Cambridgeshire or Sussex. But this thought, quite apart from the sacrilege of denuding the mountain slopes of their beauty, did not occur to such as myself, lately out of school, nor to the many exponents of rock garden building during the second quarter of this century at Chelsea and Southport shows. The Trust owns one of these great rock gardens, built at SIZERGH CASTLE in 1926 with Westmorland limestone. The same may be said of the pseudo-natural effect of the same stone at POLESDEN LACEY.

190 The rock garden at Sizergh Castle soon after construction, about 1927/8.

All of these creations, fostered by the writings of William Robinson at first, and later pushed forward by the force and persuasiveness of Reginald Farrer, were made with the express idea of cultivating alpine plants, and so have really no connection with the grotto. The scenic rock garden, on the other hand, goes arm in arm with the 18th-century efforts.

So far as I can trace, the Thornery at Sezincote, Gloucestershire, laid out about 1804, is the first time that rock was used to give a more or less natural effect. It is used in the creation of outcrops and waterfalls all down the stream. The large rocks are still exactly as originally placed. They were then graced by a few ferns and weeping trees; now there is an elaborate modern planting all around.

Another early effort was at Redleaf, Kent, where a garden was made, unique for the times, with shrubs and rocks disposed about the lawns to give a "natural" effect. In 1847 the rock work, more or less erect against a wall, was started at Lamport Hall, Northampton; it was in the form of an escarpment, complete with small caves and gnomes.

The three uses of rock – the grotto, the rockery and the scenic rock garden – are linked together by the efforts of one famous firm, Pulham & Son, which was in being from 1820 to 1939. For many years they operated from Bishop's Stortford, Hertfordshire. A character of their work was the "craggy" effect achieved by the stratification of big rocks overhanging thinner receding strata, and most of their bigger jobs included a cavern; thus the work clearly links with the grotto. The great, tipped outcrop and cavern by the house at WADDESDON is attributed to Pulham, and was built of the native rock in 1874. Authentic examples are at SHEFFIELD PARK (the waterfall) *c.*1895, and Leonardslee, Sussex, 1890; the Royal Horticultural Society's garden at Wisley is constructed of Sussex sandstone and also includes a cavern, but has been much altered of late years. Some of the firm's most famous work is made of Pulhamite stone – a clever method of building first the main outlines of the outcrops, and facing them with what today we should call reconstituted stone, tooled and shaped to look like rock. The deception is remarkably good; examples are at Bearwood, Berkshire, and Madesfield Court, Worcestershire.

After Pulham's major work, mainly before 1930, many exponents of the more natural style of rock construction – where the effect of the rock was more important than the plants – came forward, and exhibited freely at Chelsea and other shows. B. H. B. Symons-Jeune, who wrote the only book which explains the placing of rock in strictly geological formation, was one of the first, but the firm founded by Gavin Jones brought this art to its greatest height. They usually used Cheddar limestone, Welsh granite, or Forest of Dean sandstone.

191 ABOVE The waterfall between the First and Second Lakes at Sheffield Park was repaired and a continuing flow of water ensured by installing an electric pump. Photo 1974.
192 RIGHT Sandstone outcrop at Wakehurst Place embraced by roots of yew.

It is amusing to note that while Pulham used concrete to look like stone, for the grotto at Ashridge Park Repton used a conglomerate stone with the appearance of concrete. This also occurs on the grotto at CLAREMONT.

But to return to the rockery. Some of its excesses were shot down by Reginald Farrer and others, in their keen desire to place the rocks so that the greatest number of alpine plants could be grown. At KILLERTON in the quarry, just below the ice-house constructed *c.*1808, John Coutts, later to become a famous curator of the Royal Botanic Gardens, Kew, had a hand at placing rocks to turn the quarry into a garden. He placed many of the rocks upright in what Farrer ridiculed as the "almond-pudding style". It was but a striving towards the horrific. Another charming but small example is at CLEVEDON COURT.

Much of the rock at KILLERTON lies in its natural bed, as it does in the two areas of rock garden at ROWALLANE. This Irish rock was smoothed by the glaciers aeons ago and pokes out of the thin covering of soil here and there over the rather barren local landscape. Good use of it has been made to provide nooks for plants of all kinds, but unfortunately some extra stones have been added which spoil the real effect. Another outcrop occurs at MOUNT STEWART.

By uncovering some of the steeply sloping slaty rock much has been done at BODNANT to increase the majesty and beauty of the dells. The limy pink rock hill on which stands POWIS CASTLE provides a home for *Erinus alpinus* and *Erigeron mucronatus* without spoiling the quarry-like face. Sometimes great natural rock outcrops can be enjoyed in their unadulterated beauty and first among such examples must come the escarpment of sandstone at WAKEHURST PLACE. It is there unadorned except by ferns and gloomy yews and captures what many rock-builders have striven for during the last one hundred and seventy years – the sublime. This Sussex sandstone is very conducive to plant life, being very absorbent and thus always cool and moist. Even filmy ferns grow naturally on the north-facing rock at WAKEHURST. The same rock occurs at STANDEN, and also in the quarry at SCOTNEY CASTLE, while native igneous rock outcrops with dramatic suddenness at ST MICHAEL'S MOUNT where it makes dry hot homes for succulent plants. There is natural rock in the back of the grotto at STOURHEAD and the waterfall at SHEFFIELD PARK; in both places it has been used as the foundation on which to build. Recently, in order to make it more enjoyable for our many visitors, the waterfall at SHEFFIELD PARK has been given a causeway of Forest of Dean sandstone, being harder than the Sussex sandstone and thus taking both wear and frost better. The same has been used to supplement the sarsen stone at CLIVEDEN; the two are very similar and the latter is not readily available today.

Bargate sandstone outcrops at WINKWORTH ARBORETUM but no use is made of it, whereas at HIDCOTE, during his levelling of the main vista, Lawrence Johnston unearthed a quantity of limestone which he fashioned into a natural-looking rocky bank. It was a case of unwanted surplus material being used to good effect. This brings us to the lowest form of rock garden, which is what some unfortunate owners of new gardens today have to cope with – the heap of builders' rubbish disguised with a thin skin of soil! Fortunately the true gardener today is not daunted by such a discovery; there are so many different plants in cultivation today that a selection can be made for any untoward site.

Garden Specialities

	ORANGERY	CONSERVATORY	BRIDGE	STATUARY	ORNAMENTS	FOUNTAIN POOL	FORMAL WATER	MOAT	NATURAL WATER	TERRACE	RAISED WALK	HAHA	MOUNT	ICE HOUSE	WALLED GARDEN	TEMPLE	GARDEN HOUSE	DOVECOTE	GROTTO	FOLLY	ROCK GARDEN	GREAT TREES	PLEACHING	AVENUE	HEDGES	MAZE	TOPIARY	KNOT GARDEN	PARTERRE	FORMAL BEDS	BORDERS	ROSES	ROSE GARDEN	RHODODENDRONS	WOODLAND GARDEN	HERBACEOUS BORDER	MIXED BORDER	NATURALISED BULBS	NOTABLE SHRUBS	BOG OR WATER PLANTS	HERB BEDS OR GARDEN	FRUIT AND VEGETABLES
ACORN BANK		●			●	●			●						●							●								●		●				●	●	●			●	●
ALFRISTON CLERGY HOUSE					●				●	●															●		●			●		●						●				
ANGLESEY ABBEY				●	●	●			●							●						●	●	●	●					●		●				●		●	●			
ANTONY HOUSE			●		●				●	●												●		●	●		●			●		●		●				●	●			
ARDRESS HOUSE																																●		●			●	●				
ARLINGTON COURT					●	●			●	●		●					●			●	●	●								●				●		●		●	●	●		
ASCOTT				●	●	●				●		●					●		●		●	●		●	●		●			●		●				●		●	●	●		●
ASHDOWN HOUSE					●																			●	●				●									●				
ATTINGHAM PARK			●						●			●		●								●												●				●	●			
BARRINGTON COURT			●	●	●	●		●		●					●							●	●	●	●		●			●			●			●		●	●			●
BATEMAN'S				●		●			●	●					●								●		●					●			●			●		●	●	●	●	●
BENINGBROUGH HALL		●			●					●		●										●		●	●		●			●		●					●	●				
BENTHALL HALL					●	●				●		●						●			●				●		●			●		●					●	●	●			
BERRINGTON HALL									●			●			●							●			●							●		●			●	●	●			
BLICKLING HALL	●		●	●	●	●			●	●	●					●	●					●	●	●	●		●			●		●		●		●		●	●			
BODNANT GARDEN			●	●	●	●	●		●	●		●					●				●	●			●					●			●	●	●	●		●	●	●		
BUCKLAND ABBEY															●							●						●				●		●			●	●	●		●	
BUSCOT PARK			●	●	●	●	●		●			●			●	●						●		●	●								●					●				●
CASTLECOOLE																																										
CASTLE DROGO										●															●					●			●	●	●	●		●	●			
CASTLE WARD				●		●	●		●	●					●	●				●	●	●								●		●		●			●	●	●			
CHARLECOTE PARK	●				●				●	●		●												●	●		●			●		●					●	●				●
CHARTWELL					●				●	●					●		●	●				●			●					●			●	●			●	●	●			●
CHIRK CASTLE					●					●		●					●				●	●			●		●						●	●				●	●	●		
CLANDON PARK				●	●											●	●		●			●	●		●				●								●	●				
CLAREMONT LANDSCAPE GARDEN					●				●	●		●				●			●	●		●			●									●	●			●				
CLEVEDON COURT					●	●				●							●		●			●										●					●	●	●			
CLIVEDEN		●	●	●	●	●			●	●						●	●		●			●		●	●		●		●				●	●	●	●		●	●	●		

	ORANGERY	CONSERVATORY	BRIDGE	STATUARY	ORNAMENTS	FOUNTAIN POOL	FORMAL WATER	MOAT	NATURAL WATER	TERRACE	RAISED WALK	HAHA	MOUNT	ICE HOUSE	WALLED GARDEN	TEMPLE	GARDEN HOUSE	DOVECOTE	GROTTO	FOLLY	ROCK GARDEN	GREAT TREES	PLEACHING	AVENUE	HEDGES	MAZE	TOPIARY	KNOT GARDEN	PARTERRE	FORMAL BEDS	BORDERS	ROSES	ROSE GARDEN	RHODODENDRONS	WOODLAND GARDEN	HERBACEOUS BORDER	MIXED BORDER	NATURALISED BULBS	NOTABLE SHRUBS	BOG OR WATER PLANTS	HERB BEDS OR GARDEN	FRUIT AND VEGETABLES
CLUMBER PARK			●		●				●	●					●	●	●		●			●		●										●				●				
COTEHELE						●			●	●					●		●					●			●					●		●		●		●	●	●	●	●		
THE COURTS, HOLT		●	●	●	●		●		●	●						●						●			●		●			●		●					●	●	●	●		●
CRAGSIDE			●						●	●											●	●												●								
CROFT CASTLE									●	●		●										●		●						●		●						●	●			
DERRYMORE																						●																●				
DORNEYWOOD						●				●												●			●							●		●			●	●				●
DUDMASTON					●				●	●				●			●				●	●										●		●			●	●	●			
DUNHAM MASSEY	●		●		●			●	●	●			●				●			●		●								●				●			●	●	●	●		
DUNSTER CASTLE		●	●			●			●	●							●					●													●			●	●	●		
DYRHAM PARK	●			●	●		●		●	●												●								●							●	●		●		
EAST RIDDLESDEN HALL									●						●															●		●					●	●				
EMMETTS ARBORETUM																						●												●				●	●			
ERDDIG					●	●	●		●	●			●		●		●	●					●	●	●					●		●			●			●				●
FARNBOROUGH HALL					●				●	●		●				●				●		●			●								●			●		●				
FELBRIGG HALL	●				●	●				●					●			●				●								●		●		●			●	●	●		●	●
FENTON HOUSE					●					●					●															●		●									
FLORENCE COURT			●						●			●			●							●												●				●	●	●		
GAWTHORPE HALL					●				●	●														●						●				●	●						
GIBSIDE CHAPEL																								●																	
GLENDURGAN			●			●			●	●					●							●				●	●					●		●	●		●	●	●	●		
GREAT CHALFIELD MANOR						●		●		●							●													●			●				●	●				
GREYS COURT			●		●	●				●		●			●							●								●		●					●	●				●
GUNBY HALL		●			●			●							●		●	●				●			●					●		●					●	●		●	●	●
HAM HOUSE	●			●	●					●					●		●						●	●	●			●		●			●				●	●	●			●
HANBURY HALL	●								●						●																		●					●				
HARDWICK HALL				●	●	●						●			●		●					●		●	●		●			●		●					●	●	●		●	
HATCHLANDS					●	●				●		●		●		●						●			●								●					●				
HIDCOTE MANOR GARDEN			●		●	●				●		●			●		●				●	●	●	●	●		●	●		●		●					●	●	●	●		●
HILLTOP																																●					●					●
HUGHENDEN MANOR				●	●					●		●																		●		●									
ICKWORTH			●		●					●	●	●				●						●			●												●	●				
KILLERTON			●		●					●		●		●			●				●	●		●					●					●	●	●		●	●			
KNIGHTSHAYES COURT				●	●	●			●	●							●				●	●			●		●		●			●		●	●		●	●	●			
KNOLE					●										●							●								●			●	●		●		●	●		●	

	ORANGERY	CONSERVATORY	BRIDGE	STATUARY	ORNAMENTS	FOUNTAIN POOL	FORMAL WATER	MOAT	NATURAL WATER	TERRACE	RAISED WALK	HAHA	MOUNT	ICE HOUSE	WALLED GARDEN	TEMPLE	GARDEN HOUSE	DOVECOTE	GROTTO	FOLLY	ROCK GARDEN	GREAT TREES	PLEACHING	AVENUE	HEDGES	MAZE	TOPIARY	KNOT GARDEN	PARTERRE	FORMAL BEDS	BORDERS	ROSES	ROSE GARDEN	RHODODENDRONS	WOODLAND GARDEN	HERBACEOUS BORDER	MIXED BORDER	NATURALISED BULBS	NOTABLE SHRUBS	BOG OR WATER PLANTS	HERB BEDS OR GARDEN	FRUIT AND VEGETABLES
LACOCK ABBEY					●	●	●		●	●		●			●							●										●						●				
LAMB HOUSE					●										●															●							●			●		●
LANHYDROCK					●				●	●							●					●		●	●		●			●			●	●	●	●		●	●	●		
LEITH HILL PLACE WOOD																						●												●	●			●				
LINDISFARNE CASTLE															●																						●					
LITTLE MORETON HALL			●					●					●												●			●									●				●	
LYME PARK	●		●		●	●			●	●							●			●					●		●		●	●			●	●	●	●	●	●	●	●		
LYTES CARY				●	●	●					●				●			●					●		●		●					●					●	●				
LYVEDEN NEW BIELD								●		●			●																													
MELFORD HALL					●	●				●	●	●					●					●		●	●		●			●		●					●	●	●		●	
MONTACUTE	●				●	●					●				●		●			●		●		●	●		●					●					●		●			
MORVILLE HALL					●	●	●			●												●										●					●	●	●			
MOSELEY OLD HALL																									●		●	●									●	●			●	
MOTTISFONT ABBEY			●	●	●	●			●	●				●	●		●					●	●	●	●		●	●		●			●			●	●	●	●			
MOUNT STEWART			●	●	●	●			●	●					●	●	●			●	●	●			●		●		●	●		●		●	●		●	●	●	●		
NOSTELL PRIORY		●	●						●						●		●					●										●		●				●		●		
NYMANS				●	●	●							●		●	●	●					●		●	●		●			●			●	●	●	●		●	●			
ORMESBY HALL					●							●													●		●			●			●			●		●				
OSTERLEY PARK		●							●	●				●		●						●		●								●		●				●	●			
OWLETTS															●		●								●					●		●					●	●				●
OXBURGH HALL								●		●		●			●										●				●			●				●		●	●			
PACKWOOD HOUSE					●	●	●			●	●		●		●		●								●		●			●						●	●	●				
PECKOVER HOUSE	●	●			●	●									●		●										●			●		●				●	●		●			●
PENRHYN CASTLE			●		●	●			●	●					●		●					●								●		●		●				●	●	●		
PETWORTH HOUSE			●	●	●				●			●				●				●		●												●	●			●	●			
PLAS NEWYDD					●				●	●		●										●			●		●					●		●	●		●	●	●			
PLAS-YN-RHIW									●																									●			●	●				
POLESDEN LACEY			●	●	●					●		●			●	●	●				●	●		●	●		●			●			●	●		●		●	●			
POWIS CASTLE	●			●	●	●			●	●							●					●			●		●					●		●	●			●	●	●		●
PRINCES RISBOROUGH MANOR HOUSE																														●		●										●
QUEBEC HOUSE															●								●							●		●										●
RIEVAULX TERRACE AND TEMPLES																●																										
ROWALLANE					●	●			●						●		●			●		●										●		●	●		●	●	●	●	●	
RUFFORD OLD HALL				●						●																						●		●		●	●					
ST JOHN'S JERUSALEM			●					●														●			●					●		●				●		●				●

	ORANGERY	CONSERVATORY	BRIDGE	STATUARY	ORNAMENTS	FOUNTAIN POOL	FORMAL WATER	MOAT	NATURAL WATER	TERRACE	RAISED WALK	HAHA	MOUNT	ICE HOUSE	WALLED GARDEN	TEMPLE	GARDEN HOUSE	DOVECOTE	GROTTO	FOLLY	ROCK GARDEN	GREAT TREES	PLEACHING	AVENUE	HEDGES	MAZE	TOPIARY	KNOT GARDEN	PARTERRE	FORMAL BEDS	BORDERS	ROSES	ROSE GARDEN	RHODODENDRONS	WOODLAND GARDEN	HERBACEOUS BORDER	MIXED BORDER	NATURALISED BULBS	NOTABLE SHRUBS	BOG OR WATER PLANTS	HERB BEDS OR GARDEN	FRUIT AND VEGETABLES
ST MICHAEL'S MOUNT										●											●				●					●									●			
SALTRAM	●			●	●	●						●				●						●		●			●					●		●			●	●	●			
SCOTNEY CASTLE GARDEN			●	●	●			●	●	●				●								●												●				●	●	●	●	
SHARPITOR		●		●						●														●	●					●							●	●	●			
SHEFFIELD PARK GARDEN			●						●								●					●		●										●	●			●	●	●		
SHUGBOROUGH			●		●	●			●	●						●	●			●		●					●			●			●	●			●	●	●			
SISSINGHURST CASTLE				●	●			●	●	●					●								●	●	●					●			●				●	●	●		●	
SIZERGH CASTLE			●						●	●							●				●	●		●						●		●				●		●	●	●		
SMALLHYTHE PLACE								● (Dry dock)																						●			●					●				
SNOWSHILL MANOR				●	●	●				●		●			●		●	●									●			●		●					●	●				
SPEKE HALL			●		●			●																			●			●				●			●	●				
SPRINGHILL												●			●		●					●										●		●			●	●	●		●	
STANDEN		●				●				●		●					●				●	●			●							●		●			●	●	●			
STOURHEAD			●	●	●	●			●	●		●							●	●		●												●	●		●	●	●	●		
SUDBURY HALL			●						●	●																				●												
TATTON PARK	●		●	●	●	●			●	●					●	●	●					●		●	●	●	●		●	●			●	●	●		●	●	●	●		
TINTINHULL HOUSE				●	●	●				●					●		●								●		●					●					●		●			●
TREASURER'S HOUSE					●	●									●							●								●												
TRELISSICK			●									●										●										●		●	●		●	●	●			
TRENGWAINTON									●	●		●			●						●	●												●	●			●	●	●		
TRERICE										●					●										●					●							●	●				
UPPARK					●					●		●	●				●					●											●				●	●	●			●
UPTON HOUSE			●		●		●			●					●	●					●	●			●					●			●			●		●	●			●
THE VYNE	●								●								●					●		●	●							●				●		●	●			
WADDESDON MANOR				●	●	●				●				●		●			●		●	●			●		●		●			●						●	●			
WAKEHURST PLACE			●	●	●				●						●		●					●			●					●				●	●	●	●	●	●	●		
WALLINGTON		●		●	●	●			●	●	●	●		●	●		●			●		●		●						●		●		●	●		●	●	●	●	●	●
THE WEIR									●	●							●				●	●																●				
WESTBURY COURT GARDEN			●	●	●		●		●	●							●					●			●		●	●				●					●				●	●
WEST GREEN HOUSE	●			●	●	●			●	●		●			●		●			●			●	●	●		●			●		●					●	●	●	●	●	●
WESTWOOD MANOR						●																			●		●															
WEST WYCOMBE PARK			●	●	●				●	●		●				●	●			●		●																●				
WIGHTWICK MANOR					●				●	●							●								●		●			●			●	●	●	●		●				
WIMPOLE HALL			●		●				●			●								●		●																●	●			
WINKWORTH ARBORETUM									●								●					●												●	●			●	●	●		

Plants raised at, or first grown in, or distributed from the Gardens now owned by the National Trust

★denotes those named since the Trust accepted the property

ANGLESEY ABBEY
Eranthis hiemalis, double green form

BENTHALL HALL
Chionodoxa luciliae (of gardens) (1877) [plate III]

BLICKLING HALL
Pear 'Blickling'

BODNANT
★ *Camellia williamsii* 'Citation' [plate XIII]
— 'Hiraethlyn'
Cercis siliquastrum 'Bodnant'
Embothrium coccineum lanceolatum 'Flamenco'
— 'Norquinco Valley'
★ *Enkianthus campanulatus* 'Hiraethlyn'
★ *Hamamelis mollis* 'Goldcrest'
Magnolia sprengeri 'Claret Cup'
★ *Menziesia* 'Ruby'
★ *Rhododendron albrechtii* 'Michael McLaren'
★ *R.* 'Aspansia'
★ *R.* 'Astarte'
★ *R.* 'Bartia'
R. 'Bluebird'
★ *R.* 'Camilla'
★ *R. campylogynum* 'Beryl Taylor'
R. 'Cardinal'
R. 'Charmaine'
R. 'Choremia'
R. 'Chrysomanicum'
R. 'Conroy' [plate I]
R. 'Coreta'
R. 'Dainty'
R. 'Dorinthia'
R. edgeworthii, Kingdon Ward Pink form 'Elizabeth'
★ *R.* 'Elross'
R. 'Ethel'
★ *R.* 'Fabia'

BODNANT (cont.)
R. 'Fabia Tangerine'
★ *R. fargesii* 'Budget Farthing'
★ *R.* 'Fascinator'
R. 'F. C. Puddle'
R. 'Gretia'
R. 'Hecla'
★ *R.* 'Kenneth'
R. 'Laura Aberconway'
R. 'Leda'
R. 'Matador'
R. 'May Morn'
★ *R. pachytrichum* 'Sesame'
R. 'Peace'
R. 'Portia'
★ *R.* 'Radiant Morn'
R. 'Royalty'
R. schlippenbachii, deep pink form
R. 'Seta'
R. 'Siren'
★ *R.* 'Snow River'
R. 'Sunrise'
★ *R.* 'Toreador'
R. 'Vanessa'
R. 'Vanessa Pastel' [plate IV]
R. 'Winsome'
R. 'Youthful Sin'
Sophora macrocarpa
Viburnum bodnantense 'Dawn'

CROFT CASTLE
Apple 'Croft Castle'
Helianthemum 'Mrs. Croft'
Pear 'Croft Castle'

FLORENCE COURT
Taxus baccata 'Fastigiata' (1780)

HARDWICK HALL
★ *Convallaria majalis* 'Hardwick Hall'

HIDCOTE
★ *Campanula latiloba* 'Hidcote Amethyst [plate VIII]

HIDCOTE (cont.)
Dianthus 'Hidcote' [plate XIV]
★ *Hebe* 'Hidcote'
Hypericum 'Hidcote' [plate IX]
Jasminum polyanthum
Lavandula angustifolia 'Hidcote'
— 'Hidcote Giant'
— 'Hidcote Pink'
Mahonia lomariifolia
★ *Penstemon* 'Hidcote Pink' [plate IX]
Rose 'Hidcote Gold'
— 'Lawrence Johnston'
★ *Symphytum* 'Hidcote Blue'
★ — 'Hidcote Pink'
★ *Verbena* 'Lawrence Johnston'

LYME PARK
Penstemon 'Rubicunda' (1906) [plate X]

MOUNT STEWART
Fuchsia 'Mount Stewart' [plate XV]
Rhododendron 'Thomas Bolas'
Rose 'Mount Stewart'

NYMANS
★ *Camellia* 'Leonard Messel'
— 'Maud Messel'
Desfontainea spinosa 'Harold Comber'
Eucryphia nymansensis 'Nymansay' [plate XV]
Forsythia suspensa atrocaulis 'Nymans Variety' [plate II]
★ *Magnolia* 'Anne Rosse'
★ — *loebneri* 'Leonard Messel' [plate II]
★ — 'Michael Rosse'
Rhododendron 'Anne Rosse'
R. cerasinum 'Hubert Mitchell'
R. 'James Comber'

NYMANS (cont.)
★ *R.* 'Leonard Messel'
R. 'Madonna'
R. pocophorum 'Cecil Nice'
Sorbus 'Leonard Messel'

PETWORTH
Rosa moyesii 'Fred Streeter'

POWIS CASTLE
★ *Anthemis tinctoria* 'Powis White'
★ *Artemisia* 'Powis Castle'
★ *Chrysanthemum maximum* 'Powis Castle'

OSTERLEY
Apple 'Osterley Pippin'

ROWALLANE
Chaenomeles 'Rowallane Seedling' [plate I]
★ *Chrysanthemum parthenium* 'Rowallane'
★ *Crocosmia masonorum* 'Rowallane' [plate XIV]
Hypericum 'Rowallane' [plate XII]
★ *Pieris formosa forrestii* 'Rowallane' [plate V]
Primula 'Rowallane Rose'
Viburnum plicatum 'Rowallane'

SHUGBOROUGH
Lathyrus nervosus (1744)

SISSINGHURST
Rosa gallica 'Sissinghurst Castle'
Verbena 'Sissinghurst Castle'

TRELISSICK
Rhododendron 'Trelissick Port Wine'
— 'Trelissick Salmon'

TRENGWAINTON
Eucryphia 'Penwith'
Rhododendron 'Bulldog'
R. 'Cherubim'
R. 'Cornish Cream'
R. 'Ding Dong'
R. 'Laerdal' [plate VII]
R. 'Lanyon'
R. 'Morvah'
R. 'Nanceglos'
R. 'Penalverne'
R. 'Penhale'

WAKEHURST PLACE
Camassia leichtlinii 'Eve Price'
Hedychium densiflorum
Magnolia campbellii 'Wakehurst'
Pieris formosa forrestii 'Wakehurst' [plate V]
Rhododendron arboreum 'Tony Schilling'
— *degronianum* 'Gerald Loder'
— *uvariifolium* 'Reginald Childs'
Viburnum tinus 'Eve Price'

SHARPITOR
* *Fuchsia magellanica* 'Sharpitor'

WINKWORTH ARBORETUM
Acer 'Madeline Spitta'

Plants associated with National Trust Gardens through their names:
Meconopsis sheldonii 'Slieve Donard' [plate VI]
Gentiana asclepiada 'Knightshayes' [plate XVI]
Apple 'Winston'
Rhododendron aberconwayi
— 'Marchioness of Londonderry'
Rose 'Dame Edith Helen'
— 'Marchioness of Londonderry'
Sorbus 'Wilfrid Fox'
Ranunculus acris 'Flore Pleno' found prior to 1596 by Sir Thomas Hesketh of Rufford.

Bibliography

Berrall, J. S. *The Garden* Thames & Hudson, London
Brown, A. E. and Taylor, C. C. *The Garden at Lyveden* Northamptonshire Archaeological Journal, Vol. 129 1972
Clarke, H. F. *The English Landscape Garden* Pleiades Books, London 1948
Cottage Gardener, The 1848–1861
Country Life London 1897 *et seq.*
Crowe, S. *Garden Design* Country Life, London 1958
Dutton, R. *The English Garden* Batsford Ltd, London 1950
Gardeners' Chronicle, The 1874 *et seq.*
Hadfield, M. *Landscape with Trees* Country Life, London 1967
— *Topiary and Ornamental Hedges* Black, London 1971
— *Gardening in Britain* Hutchinson, London 1960
Hix, John *The Glass House* Phaidon Press, London 1974
Hunt, J. D. and Willis, P. *The Genius of the Place* Paul Elek, London 1975
Hunt, Peter (ed.) *The Shell Gardens Book* Phoenix House, London 1964
Hussey, C. *English Gardens and Landscapes* Country Life, London 1967
Jones, B. *Follies and Grottoes* Constable & Co. Ltd., London 1953
Journal of Horticulture, The 1861–1915
Loudon, J. C. *A treatise on forming, improving and managing country residences* London 1806
— *An encyclopaedia of gardening* Longman, Rees, London 1827
Major, Joshua *The Theory and Practice of Landscape Gardening* London 1852
Mason, William *The English Garden* London 1772–9
Miller, Philip *The Gardener's Dictionary* 1731
Rackham, Oliver *Trees and woodland in the British Landscape*
Rohde, E. S. *The Story of the Garden* Medici Society, London 1933
Roper, Lanning *The Gardens of Anglesey Abbey* Faber, London 1964
Sandeman, P. E. *Treasure on Earth* Blackwood, London 1971
Sieveking, A. F. *The Praise of Gardens* Dent, London 1899
Stroud, D. *Capability Brown* Country Life, London 1950
— *Humphry Repton* Country Life, London 1962
Symons-Jeune, B. H. B. *Natural Rock Gardening* Country Life, London 1952
Temple, Sir W. *Upon the Gardens of Epicurus, Anthology* 1908
The National Trust Guide, compiled by Robin Fedden & Rosemary Joekes Cape, London 1973
Thacker, C. *Masters of the Grotto* Compton Press, Tisbury 1976
Thomas, W. B. *Gardens* Burke, London 1952
Thomson, J. *Poetical Works* 1908
Walpole, H. *Essay on Modern Gardening* Strawberry Hill 1785
Wedgwood, C. V. *Leith Hill Place*
Whately, T. *Observations on Modern Gardening* Dublin 1770
Woodbridge, K. *Henry Hoare's Paradise* The Art Bulletin of the College Art Association of America March 1965, reprinted by the National Trust
— *Landscape and Antiquity* Clarendon Press, Oxford 1970

Plant Index

Abelia × grandiflora (*A. chinensis* × *A. uniflora*) 119, 228
Abies alba (*A. pectinata*) 82;
— *bracteata* 248;
— *cilicica* 248;
— *concolor* 160, 191;
— *grandis* 82, 107;
— *koreana* 225;
— *magnifica* 248;
—*nephrolepsis* 248;
— *numidica* 248;
— *procera* (*A. nobilis*) 82
Abutilon × suntense (*A. ochsenii* × *A. vitifolium*) 229
Acacia longifolia 139;
— *dealbata* 139
'Acacia' (*Robinia pseudacacia*) 40, 48
'Acacia' Mophead (*Robinia pseudacacia* 'Inermis') 132;
Acanthus, Balkan (*Acanthus balcanicus*) 103;
— *mollis* 35
Acer campestre 129, 165;
— *capillipes* 205
— *carpinifolium* 203, 225;
— *davidii* 102;
— *griseum* 26, 89, 98, 105, 109, 139, 208 232;
— *henryi* 132;
— *negundo* 197;
— — 'Variegatum' 134;
— *nikoense* 105, 159;
— *opalus* 129;
— *palmatum* 'Dissectum' 116;
— — 'Ribesifolium' 208;
— — 'Senkaki' 160;
— *pennsylvanicum* 'Erythrocladum' 160;
— *platanoides* 129;
— — 'Cucullatum' 228
— *pseudoplatanus* 'Brilliantissimum' 177, 203;
— *rubrum* 129
Acidanthera (*Gladiolus calliantha*) 226
Aconitum napellus 'Carneum' 203
Acradenia frankliniae 160, 229
Actaea alba 108
Actinidia chinensis 123;
— *kolomikta* 110, 122
Adenocarpus decorticans 229
Adnophora tashiroi 203
Aesculus chinenis 98;
— *hippocastanum* 48;
— × *hybrida* (*A. flava* × *A. pavia*) 167;
— *indica* 129, 223;
— *parviflora* 189, 208
Aethionema grandiflorum 83
Agastache anisata 203
Alchemilla mollis 83
Allspice (*Calycanthus*) 122, 130
Aloe, American (*Agave americana*) 138;
— *aristata* 206
Alstroemeria aurantiaca 140
Alyssum saxatile 48
Amaranthus caudatus 38
Andromeda (*Pieris* species) 83
Anemone, Japanese (*Anemone × hybrida: A. hupehensis japonica* × *A. vitifolia*) 106;
— *narcissiflora* 109;
— *nemorosa* 'Allenii' 228;
— —'*Vestal*' 93, 228;
— *pavonina* 156
Angelica (*Angelica archangelica*) 166;
— Tree, Japanese (*Aralia elata*) 103, 155
Apple, Cider, 'Red Streak' 206;
—, Kangaroo (*Solanum aviculare*) 113;
—, 'Sunset' 168
Aquilegia alpina 48
Aquilegia hybrids 83
Aralia elata 160
Arauja sericofera 202
Arborvitae, Chinese (*Thuja orientalis*) 236;
—, Chinese, dwarf yellow (*Thuja orientalis* 'Nana Aurea') 113;
—, Western (*Thuja occidentalis*) 38, 212;
Arbutus × andrachnoides (*A. andrachne* × *A. unedo*) 107;
— *menziesii* 129, 177;
— *unedo* 40, 119
Arisaema andidissima 246
Arisarum proboscideum 103
Armeria caespitosa 83
Artemisia angustifolia 220
Artichoke, Globe (*Cynara scolymus*) 35
Arum creticum 156
'Arum' (*Zantedeschia aethiopica*) 74, 113, 130, 131
Arundinaria anceps 83, 196;
— *fastuosa* 131;
— *vagans* 83
Ash, Common (*Fraxinus excelsior*) 101;
—, Manna or Flowering (*Fraxinus ornus*) 48, 191, 256;
—, Weeping (*Fraxinus excelsior* 'Pendula') 139, 162, 179, 223;
—, Yellow-twigged (*Fraxinus excelsior* 'Jaspidea') 125
Astelia cockaynei 161, 246
Aster amellus 34;
— China (*Callistephus chinensis*) 77;
— × *frikartii* Mönch (*A. amellus* × *A. thomsonii*) 106, 216;
— *novi-belgii* 48;
— — 'Climax' 168
Asteranthera ovata 180
Astilbe rivularis 140
Athrotaxis selaginoides 212
Aucuba, spotted leafed (*Aucuba japonica* 'Variegata') 171, 194
Auricula (*Primula auricula*) 35, 80
Austrocedrus chilensis 190, 205, 255
Azalea 'Coccinea Speciosa' 159, 176;
— pontica (*Rhododendron luteum*) 74, 165, 221
Azaleodendron 'Fragrans' 105
Azara microphylla 122, 162; 'Variegata' 210
Azarole (*Crataegus azarolus*) 150

Ballota acetabulosa 245
Balm (*Melissa officinalis*) 110, 166
Bamboos, *see also Arundinaria* and *Phyllostachys* and *Sasa*
Banana, hardy (*Musa basjoo*) 210, 228
Banksia serrata 229
Baptisia australis 216
Bay, Bull (*Magnolia grandiflora*) 110;
—, Laurel or Sweet (*Laurus nobilis*) 38, 82, 122, 131, 178
Bean, Indian, Tree (*Catalpa bignonioides*) 170, 197, 256
Beech, American (*Fagus grandifolia*) 247;
—, Common (*Fagus sylvatica*) 69, 159;
—, Cut-leafed (Fern-leafed) (*Fagus sylvatica heterophylla*) 98, 171, 194;
—, Dawyck (*Fagus sylvatica* 'Fastigiata') 132, 180, 247;
—, Large-leafed (*Fagus sylvatica* 'Latifolia') 196;
—, Purple or Copper (*Fagus sylvatica* 'Purpurea') 75, 98, 158, 190, 195, 223;
—, Southern (*Nothofagus* species) 160;
—, Weeping Copper (*Fagus sylvatica* 'Purpurea Pendula') 98;
—, — (*Fagus sylvatica* 'Pendula') 98, 137, 138
Beloperone guttata 131
Berberidopsis corallina 189, 230, 246
Berberis darwinii 82;
— *hypokerina* 205;
— × *stenophylla* (*B. darwinii* × *B. empetrifolia*) 128;
— *thunbergii* 'Atropurpurea' 198;
— *wilsoniae* 89, 248;
Berchemia racemosa 195
Beschorneria yuccoides 131
Betula albo-sinensis septentrionalis 108, 198, 258;
— *ermanii* 108;
— *maximowiczii* 159;
— *medwediewii* 257;
— *papyrifera humilis* 129;
— *pendula* 'Dalecarlica' 129;
— *utilis prattii* 108
Big Tree (*Sequoiadendron giganteum*) 212
Bignonia, see *Campsis*
Billbergia nutans 194
Birch, Paper (*Betula papyrifera*) 98;
—, Weeping (*Betula pendula* 'Youngii') 211
Blechnum chilense 228;
— *penna-marina* 217, 221
Bluebell (*Endymion non-scriptus* or *Scilla nutans*) 113, 133, 168, 203, 221, 258
Bluebells, white at Derrymore 33
Blueberries (*Vaccinium* species)
Boenninghausenia albiflora 177
Bottle-Brush, Australian (*Callistemon citrinus*) 163
Bouncing Bet (*Saponaria officinalis*) 174, 232
Bowkeria gerardiana 177
Box, common (*Buxus sempervirens*) 36, 82, 268;
—, dwarf (*Buxus sempervirens* 'Suffruticosa') 34, 42, 173
Brier, Sweet (*Rosa rubiginosa*) 36, 39, 152, 171
Broom, Mt. Etna (*Genista aetnensis*) 105, 107, 216, 227;
—, fragrant yellow *Cytisus × spachianus* (*C. racemosus* or *Genista fragrans* of gardens) (*C. stenopetala* × *C. canariensis*) 195;
—, Spanish (*Spartium junceum*);
—, Moroccan (*Cytisus battandieri*) 250
Brunnera macrophylla 155
Buckthorn, Sea (*Hippophaë rhamnoides*) 152
Buddleia alternifolia 202;
— *auriculata* 122;
— *colvilei* 'Kewensis' 104, 119, 210;
— *crispa* 106, 107, 232
— *davidii* 82
Bupleurum falcatum 216
Buxus sempervirens 'Suffruticosa' 34

Cabbage Tree (*Cordyline australis*) 112, 177
Caesalpinia japonica 196
Calceolaria integrifolia 139;
— yellow (*C.* × *herbeohybrida*) 77
Callistemon citrinus 230;
— *linearis* 189;
— *pithyoides* 230
Callistephus hortensis 77
Calycanthus occidentalis 122
Camassia leichtlinii 'Eve Price' 246
Camellia japonica 75, 82, 164;

— — 'Holfordiana' 208;
— — 'Nobilissima' 118;
— 'Leonard Messel' 180;
— *reticulata* 'Captain Rawes' 107, 164, 195, 228;
— *sasanqua* 228;
— × *williamsii* 'Maud Messel' 189;
— — 'November Pink' 231
Campanula lactiflora 155;
— *latiloba* 155;
— — 'Hidcote Amethyst' 155
Campsis radicans 163
Candytuft, Perennial (*Iberis sempervirens*) 151
Canna indica 38;
— *iridiflora* 119, 164
Cannas 246
Cardamine raphanifolia 130
Cardiocrinum giganteum 83;
— — *yunnanense* 204
Carmichaelia platyclada 210
Carnation, Clove (*Dianthus caryophyllus*) 164
Carob (*Ceratonia siliqua*) 131
Carpenteria californica 104, 107, 177
Carya laciniosa 191
Caryopteris × *clandonensis* (*C. incana* × *C. mongolica*) 194, 217
Cassia corymbosa 177, 229
Castanea sativa 129
Castor Oil Plant (*Ricinus communis*) 35
Catmint (*Nepeta* × *faassenii*) 158, 191, 233
Cautleya 'Robusta' 164;
Cautleya species 246
Ceanothus arboreus 100;
— × *delilianus* (*C. caeruleus* × *C. americanus*) 175; 'Trewithen Blue' 139
Cedar, Blue (*Cedrus atlantica* 'Glauca') 98, 109, 161, 172, 190, 198, 235, 256;
—, Deodar (Indian) (*Cedrus deodara*) 84, 126, 129, 160, 190, 212, 227;
—, Golden (*Cedrus atlantica* 'Aurea') 98, 190
—, Incense (*Calocedrus decurrens*) 129, 159;
—, Japanese (*Cryptomeria japonica*) 227;
—, of Lebanon (*Cedrus libani*) 40, 95, 99, 118, 135, 140, 151, 158, 161, 172, 190, 197, 209, 226, 233;
—, Pencil (*Juniperus virginiana*) 48, 150
Celastus orbiculatus 123, 131
Celmisia species 205
Celtis australis 163
Centaurea atropurpurea 203;
— salonitana 203
Ceratostigma willmottiana 217
Cercidiphyllum japonicum 123, 198, 207
Cercis racemosa 180; — — siliquastrum 98
Cestrum 'Newellii' 229;
— *parqui* 164
Chaenomeles × *superba* 'Knaphill Scarlet' (*C. japonica* × *C. speciosa*) 127;
— 'Rowallane' 205
Chamaecyparis lawsoniana 'Erecta Viridis' 109;
— — 'President Roosevelt' 246;
— — 'Winston Churchill' 246;
— *obtusa* 'Nana Gracilis' 223;
— *pisifera* 'Squarrosa' 198, 208
Cherry, Autumn (*Prunus subhirtella* 'Autumnalis') 258;
—, Cornelian (*Cornus mas*) 37, 256;
—, —, variegated (*Cornus mas* 'Variegata') 103, 119;
—, Japanese 'Ukon' (*Prunus serrulata* 'Grandiflora') 198;
—, St. Lucie (*Prunus mahaleb*) 234
Chestnut, Horse (*Aesculus hippocastanum*) 40, 48, 95, 100, 197, 236;
—, Indian (*Aesculus indica*) 95;
—, Pink (*Aesculus* × *carnea*: *A. hippocastanum* × *A. pavia*) 223;
—, Sweet or Spanish (*Castanea sativa*) 44, 70, 129, 159, 172, 174, 196, 210, 222;
—, Variegated (*Castanea sativa* 'Albomarginata') 258
Chilean Fire Bush (*Embothrium coccineum*) 112, 115, 138;
— Lantern Tree (*Crinodendron hookeranum*) 115
Chionodoxa luciliae of gardens 103
Chives (*Allium schoenoprasum*) 166
Christ's Thorn (*Paliurus spina-christi*) 252
Christmas Rose (*Helleborus niger*) 35
Chrysanthemum haradjanii 246
Chusquea breviglumis 246;
— *culeou* 246
Cineraria (*Senecio cruentus*) 74
Cinnamomum camphora 210
Cissus striata 125
Cistus, Gum (*Cistus ladanifer*) 168
Cladrastis sinensis 205
Clarkia pulchella 77
Claytonia sibirica 96
Clematis armandii 89, 104, 116, 198;
— *cirrhosa balearica* 104
— *flammula* 173;
— *integrifolia* 127;
— × *jackmanii* (*C. lanuginosa* × *C. viticella*) 101, 134, 178, 202;
— *macropetala* 89;
— *montana* 'Rubens' 198;
— *rehderana* 161;
— *tangutica* 93;
— *viticella* 173;
— — 'Elegans Plena' 113;
— — 'Royal Velours' 128;
— 'William Kennett' 104
Cleyera japonica 159
Clianthus puniceus 138, 177
Coffee Tree, Kentucky (*Gymnocladus dioicus*) 225
Colchicum autumnale tenori 136;
— *speciosum* 83
Colletia armata 131
Colutea arborescens 36
Convallaria majalis 39, 152
Cordyline australis 77, 177, 210;
— *indivisa* 178
Coriaria terminalis xanthocarpa 217
Cornus capitata 138, 210, 228;
— *controversa* 180, 224;
— — 'Variegata' 210;
— *florida* 'Rubra' 180;
— *kousa* 82, 131, 138, 161, 165, 168, 180, 196, 210;
— *macrophylla* 127;
— *mas* 37;
— *nuttallii* 82, 115, 165, 197
Corokia cotoneaster 198
Correa alba 229
Cortaderia richardii 196;
— *selloana* 78;
Cotinus coggygria 'Foliis Purpureis' 205
Cotoneaster conspicuus 198;
— 'Cornubia' 175;
— *humifusus* 198;
— *microphyllus* 248;
— serotinus 131
Coventry Bells (*Campanula trachelium*) 168
Cow Parsley (*Anthriscus sylvestris*) 95
Cowslips at Clandon Park 33, 116
Crambe koktaibelica 203
Cranesbill, Mourning Widow (*Geranium phaeum*) 33
+ *Crataegomespilus* (*Crateagus* × *Mespilus*) 258
Crataegus crus-galli 48
Crataegus × *lavallei* (*C. crus-galli* × *C. stipulacea*) 171
Crinodendron patagua 104;
— *hookeranum* 177, 196, 208, 228
Crinum moorei 180;
— × *powellii* (*C. longiflorum* × *C. moorei*)
Crocus, Autumn, see *Colchicum* and *Crocus*;
— *nudiflorus* 103;
— *pulchellus* 103;
— *speciosus* 103;
— *tomasinianus* 103;
— *vernus* 103, 163;
— Yellow Dutch 34
Crown Imperial (*Fritillaria imperialis*) 35
Crucianella stylosa 215
Cruel Plant (*Arauja sericofera*) 202
Cryptomeria japonica 82, 118, 165, 212;
— — 'Spiralis' 180
Cuckoo Flower at Derrymore 33;
— — (*Cardamine pratense*) 177
Cucumber Tree (*Magnolia acuminata*) 247
Cunninghamia lanceolata 84, 118, 138
Cupid's Dart (*Catananche caerulea*) 174
× *Cupressocyparis leylandii* (*Cupressus macrocarpa* × *Chamaecyparis nootkatensis*) 162, 178
Cupressus cashmiriana 107, 177;
— *duclouxii* 205;
— *lusitanica* 'Glauca Pendula' 138;
— *sempervirens* 'Stricta' 157
currant, fruiting 35, 39
Curry Plant (*Artemisia angustifolia*) 220
Curtonus paniculatus 137
Cycads, *Cycas* 207
Cyclamen, Neapolitan (*Cyclamen hederifolium*) 104, 106, 128, 159, 207;
— *persicum* (Florist's) 74;
— *repandum* 159;
Cypress, Arizona (*Cupressus arizonica*) 212;
—, Bhutan (*Cupressus torulosa*) 246;
—, Italian (*Cupressus sempervirens* 'Stricta') 42, 73, 107, 180;
—, Lawson's (*Chamaecyparis lawsoniana*) 82, 201;
—, Leyland (× *Cupressocyparis leylandii*) 162;
—, Monterey (*Cupressus macrocarpa*) 82, 170;
—, Nootka (*Chamaecyparis nootkatensis*) 128, 195, 212;
—, pendulous Italian (*Cupressus sempervirens* 'Pendula') 127;
—, Swamp (*Taxodium distichum*) 48, 84, 98, 127, 163, 191, 212, 225
Cyrtanthus species 246
Cytisus battandieri 224, 250

Dacrydium franklinii 229
Dactylorrhiza elata 204
Daffodil, Citron Hoop-Petticoat (Narcissus *bulbocodium* 'Citrinus') 221;
—, Parkinson's Early Straw-coloured Bastard (*Narcissus pallidus praecox* of gardens) 158; —
—, Queen Anne's Double (*Narcissus eystettensis*) 97
Daffodils and other naturalised bulbs, *see* table of Garden Specialities
Dahlia 74, 77, 94, 172;
— *coccinea* 177
Daisy, Michaelmas (*Aster novi-belgii*) 48, 140, 172, 194
Daphne × *burkwoodii* (*D. caucasica* × *D. cneorum*) 198;
— *cneorum* 'Variegata' 104;
— *retusa* 189, 198
Daphniphyllum macropodum 210
Date-plum (*Diospyros lotus*) 38
Datura chlorantha 206;
— *sanguinea* 230;
— *suaveolens* 194
Davidia involucrata 126, 138, 156, 247
Day Lily (*Hemerocallis*) 38, 96, 115, 123, 174;
— —, Citron (*Hemerocallis citrina*) 127

Debregaesia longifolia 229
Decaisnea fargesii 225
Decumaria sinensis 246
Dendromecon rigidum 176, 230
Desfontainea spinosa 162, 205;
— — 'Harold Comber' 189
Deutzia × *elegantissima* (*D. purpurasceum* × *D. sieboldiana*) 'Rosealind' 172
Devil's Club (*Oplopanax horridus*) 225
Dianthus caryophyllus 48
Dianthus plumarius 48
Dicentra macrantha 246;
— *spectabilis* 151
Diospyros lotus 38
Dipelta floribunda 122
Dipladenia sanderi 226
Dipteronia sinensis 103
Distylium racemosum 225
Dock, Giant Water (*Rumex hydrolapathum*) 249
Dodonaea viscosa 'Purpurea' 229
Dogwood, white variegated (*Cornus alba* 'Elegantissima') 250
Dogwoods (*Cornus alba* and *C. sanguinea*) 99, 128, 223
Drimys lanceolata 231;
— *winteri* 122, 138, 196, 208;
— — *andina* 189
Dryopteris erythrosora 217;
— *pseudomas* 217;
— *wallichiana* 217

Eccremocarpus scaber 104, 202
Echeveria glauca 131
Eglantine (*Rosa rubiginosa*) 36, 152, 171, 173
Ehretia 159
Elaeagnus angustifolia 105;
— *argentea* 152;
— *macrophylla* 208
Elecampane (*Inula helenium*) 254
Elm, Camperdown (*Ulmus glabra* 'Camperdownii') 111;
— English (*Ulmus procera*) 110, 136, 264
Embothrium coccineum lanceolatum 109;
— 'Norquinco Valley' 109
Emmenopterys henryi 225
Enkianthus campanulatus
— *perulatus* 197;
— species 83
Ercilla volubilis 189, 247
Eremurus 203, 246
Erica canaliculata 177, 229;
— *carnea* 198
Erigeron mucronatus 203
Eriobotrya japonica 207
Escallonia 'Iveyi' 127;
— *macrantha* 82;
— *montevidensis* (*E. bifida*) 245
Eucalyptus coccifera 160;
— *globulus* 77, 177, 210;
— *gunnii* 195, 212, 247;
— *subcrenulata* 228
Eucalyptus viminalis 177
Eucomis punctata 210
Eucommia ulmoides 180
Eucryphia cordifolia 133, 180, 196, 208, 231;
— *glutinosa* 115, 133, 189, 195, 205;
— × *hillieri* (*E. lucida* × *E. moorei*) 'Penwith' 230;
— × *intermedia* (*E. glutinosa* × *E. lucida*) 137, 224;
— *lucida* 230;
— *milleganii* 245;
— *moorei* 180;
— × *nymansensis* (*E. cordifolia* × *E. glutinosa*) 'Nymansay' 133, 180, 203
Euonymus fortunei 'Coloratus' 137;
— — 'Variegata' 47, 123, 196;
— *japonicus* 'Ovatus Aureus' 210;
— *lucidus* (*E. fimbriatus* of gardens) 210, 245;
— *tingens* 160
Eupatorium micranthum 138
Euphorbia griffithii 'Fireglow' 108;
— *myrsinites* 113;
— *robbiae* 137
Euryops acraeus 205

Fagus englerana 197
Fascicularia bicolor 206, 246
× *Fatshedera lizei* (*Fatsia japonica* × *Hedera helix*) 158
Fatsia japonica 77, 158, 258
— — 'Variegata' 97
Feijoa sellowiana 131, 139, 174, 177, 210
Fennel (*Foeniculum vulgare*) 110
Ferns 80
Fern, Beech (*Gymnocarpium phegopteris*) 217;
—, Filmy (*Hymenophyllum tunbridgense*) 248;
—, Hardy Maidenhair (*Adiantum venustum*) 217;
—, Hart's Tongue (*Asplenium scolopendrium*) 130, 217;
—, Japanese Painted (*Athyrium goeringianum* 'Pictum') 217;
—, Lady (*Athyrium filix-femina*) 217;
—, Maidenhair (*Adiantum capillus-veneris*) 80, 172, 217;
—, Male (*Dryopteris filix-mas*) 217;
— Oak (*Gymnocarpium dryopteris*) 217;
—, Ostrich Plume (*Matteuccia struthiopteris*) 217;
— Polypody (*Polypodium vulgare*) 207, 217;
—, Royal (*Osmunda regalis*) 80, 162, 165, 209, 217, 221;
—, Soft Shield Fern (*Polystichum setiferum*) 130, 217;
—, Sword (*Polystichum acrostichoides*) 217;
—, Tree (*Dicksonia antarctica*) 115, 138, 226, 228
Fig (*Ficus carica*) 123, 157;
—, small-leafed (*Ficus pumila*) 226
Figwort, Cape (*Phygelius* species) 104
Filbert (*Corylus maxima*) 38
Fir, Californian Red (*Abies magnifica*) 128;
—, Caucasian (*Abies nordmanniana*) 128;
—, Cilician (*Abies cilicica*) 248;
—, Douglas (*Pseudotsuga taxifolia*) 82, 115, 128, 162, 178, 201;
—, European Silver (*Abies alba*) 82, 178;
—, Giant (*Abies grandis*) 128;
—, Grecian (*Abies cephalonica*) 128;
—, Noble (*Abies procera*) 128, 197, 223, 236;
—, — prostrate blue (*Abies procera* 'Glauca Prostrata') 217;
—, Spanish (*Abies pinsapo*) 128
Flame Flower, Scotch (*Tropaeolum speciosum*) 155, 196
Flax, New Zealand (*Phormium tenax*) 131, 178
Flower of the Snow (*Chionodoxa luciliae* of gardens) 103, 174
Forget-me-not, Chatham Island (*Myosotideum hortensis*) 177
Forsythia suspensa atrocaulis 'Nymans Variety' 190
Francoa sonchifolia 210
Fraxinus angustifolia 129;
— *oxycarpa* 129;
— *spaethii* 115
Fritillaria imperialis 35;
— *meleagris* 98
Fuchsia excorticata 177;
— *magellanica* 'Sharpitor' 210;
— '*Riccartonii*' 196

Galega orientalis 203
Gean or Common Cherry (*Prunus avium*) 129
Genista cinerea (of gardens) 115;
— *hispanica* 198
Gentian, Chinese (*Gentiana sino-ornata*) 211;
—, Willow (*Gentiana asclepiadea*) 194, 209, 217, 228
Gentiana acaulis (*G. excisa*) 107, 216;
— *sino-ornata* 89, 246
Geranium anemonefolium of gardens (*G. palmatum*) 229;
—, Armenian (*G. psilostemon*) 216, 249;
— *nodosum* 103
'Geranium' (*Pelargonium zonale* and *P. peltatum*) 48, 77, 235;
— *procurrens* 246
Germander, Wall (*Teucrium chamaedrys*) 166, 174
Gevuina avellana 178, 230
Gillenia trifoliata 164
Gladiolus 77;
— *calliantha* 226
Gleditsia triacanthos 48
Gloxinia (*Sinningia speciosa*) 74
Glycirrhiza glabra 35
Godetia 77
Golden Rod (*Solidago canadensis*) 48
Gooseberry 35, 39, 80
Gordonia chrysantha 229
Gourd 38
Grape, Dyer's (*Vitis vinifera* 'Purpurea') 127;
Grape, Teinturier (*Vitis vinifera* 'Purpurea') 127, 173; Fox, 252
Grapes 136
Grass, Pampas (*Cortaderia selloana*) 211
Grass, Pheasant Tail (*Stipa arundinacea*) 229
Grevillea rosmarinifolia 177, 205;
— *sulphurea* 177, 229
Griselinia littoralis 83, 195, 207
Guava, Chilean (*Myrtus ugni*) 229
Guinea Hen Flower (*Fritillaria meleagris*) 98
Gum, Cider (*Eucalyptus gunnii*) 212;
—, Sweet (*Liquidambar stryaciflua*) 48, 163, 195, 212, 234, 257
Gunnera manicata 84, 102, 196
Gymnocladus dioicus 225
Gypsophila paniculata 75

Haberlea rhodopensis 83
Hakea epiglottis 246;
— *sericea* 189
Hamamelis mollis 84
Handkerchief Tree (*Davidia*) 126, 138, 156, 205, 247
Hartia sinensis 245
Heath, Mediterranean (*Erica mediterranea*) 250;
—, Tree (*Erica arborea*) 195, 221
Heaven, Tree of (*Ailanthus altissima*) 170
Hebe albicans 231;
—, *speciosa* forms 231
Hedychium gardneranum 177
Hedychiums 246
Helenium autumnale 75
Helianthemum 'Mrs Croft' 128
Helianthus annuus 38
Hellebore, Corsican (*Helleborus corsicus*) 250
Helleborus niger 110
Heliotrope (*Heliotropium peruvianum*) 101, 161, 228, 250
Helwingia japonica 204
Hemerocallis flava 38, 152, 191;
— *fulva* 38
Hemlock, Eastern (*Tsuga canadensis*) 165, 212;
—, Western (*Tsuga heterophylla*) 84, 128, 212, 247
Heuchera americana 48
Hibiscus syriacus 38
Hickory (*Carya laciniosa*) 95;
— (*Carya ovata*) 221
Hippeastrum pratense 107
Hoheria glabrata
Hoheria sexstylosa 139, 228, 246
Holly, Common (*Ilex aquifolium*) 82;
—, 'Golden Milkmaid' (*Ilex aquifolium* 'Aurea Medio-picta') 98;
—, 'Golden Queen' (*Ilex aquifolium* 'Golden Queen') 255;
—, Hedgehog, Variegated (*Ilex aquifolium* 'Ferox Argentea') 47;
—, 'Lawsoniana' (*I.* × *altaclarensis* 'Lawsoniana': *I. aquifolium* × *I. perado*) 208;

—, Weeping (*Ilex aquifolium* 'Pendula') 152, 231;
—, —, Silver (*Ilex aquifolium* 'Argenteomarginata Pendula') 128
Hollyhock (*Althaea rosea*) 35
Holodiscus discolor 128
Honesty, Perennial (*Lunaria rediviva*) 194
Honeysuckle (*Lonicera*) 36
Hop, common (*Humulus lupulus*) 151
Horminum (*Salvia horminum*) 101
Hornbeam, Hop (*Ostrya carpinifolia*) 95, 196;
—, Pyramid (*Carpinus betulus* 'Pyramidalis') 196
Hosta fortunei 'Aurea' 247;
— — *hyacinthina* 171;
— *plantaginea* 106, 177, 228;
— *sieboldiana elegans* 107
Hyacinth, Summer (*Galtonia candicans*) 226
Hyacinths (*Hyacinthus orientalis*) 35, 94
Hydrangea anomala 202;
— *arborescens* 'Grandiflora' 175;
— *cinerea* 'Sterilis' 250;
—, *climbing* (*Hydrangea petiolaris*) 106;
— *heteromalla* 202;
— Hortensia (*Hydrangea macrophylla* 'Hortensia') 96, 228;
— *macrophylla* 75, 228;
— — 'Ayesha' 228;
— *paniculata* 'Floribunda' 97, 167;
— *petiolaris* 116, 174;
— *sargentiana* 106, 189, 204;
— *serrata* 228;
— *villosa* 174, 228, 250
Hymenophyllum tunbridgense 248
Hypericum calycinum 48;
— 'Hidcote';
— *kouytchense* 167;
— 'Rowallane' 189, 199, 205, 231;
— *uralum* 205
Hyssop (*Hyssopus officinalis*) 36, 194

Iberis sempervirens 198
Idesia polycarpa 258
Ilex aquifolium 82;
— — 'Ferox Argentea' 47;
— *glabra* 203;
— or Holm Oak (*Quercus ilex*) *see under* Oak, Holm:
— *yunnanensis* 203
Illicium anisatum 208
Impatiens roylei 251
Indian Poke (*Veratrum viride*) 103
— Shot (*Canna indica*) 38
Indigofera species 161, 208;
— *gerardiana* 202
Iris, Algerian (*Iris unguicularis*) 125;
— 'Aurea' 200;
—, Dalmation (*I. pallida dalmatica*) 174;
—, Florentine (*Iris albicans*) 174;
—, German (*Iris germanica*) 35, 200;
— *germanica* 166;
— 'Gracchus' 200;
— 'Iris King' 200;
—, Japanese (*I. ensata* or *kaempferi*) 115;
— *'Kochii' 200;*
— *laevigata* 'Rose Queen' 177;
— 'Lorelei' 200;
—, pale yellow Flag Iris (*Iris pseudacorus* 'Bastardii') 127
— *pallida* 35;
— 'Prosper Laugier' 200;
—, Siberian (*I. sibirica*) 174;
— *wattii* 210
Itea ilicifolia 224
Ivy, Boston, (*Parthenocissus tricuspidata*) 216

'Japonica' (*Chaenomeles speciosa*) 126
Jasmine, Sweet White (*Jasminum officinale*) 36, 217, 252;
—, Winter (*Jasminum nudiflorum*) 84, 189;
—, *yellow* (*Jasminum fruticans*) 36, 202
Jasminum primulinum (*J. mesnyi*) 119, 195;
— *polyanthum* 131, 195;
— × *stephanense* (*J. officinale* × *J. beesianum*) 163
Jovellana violacea 210
Judas Tree (*Cercis siliquastrum*) 38, 113, 125, 131, 163, 170, 191
Juglans nigra 48, 191
Juniper, Chinese (*Juniperus chinensis*) 104, 212, 249, 256;
—, common (*Juniperus communis*) 82;
—, Irish (*Juniperus communis* 'Hibernica') 220
Juniperus chinensis 'Japonica Aurea' 98;
— × *media* 'Pfitzerana' 98, 200;
— *recurva coxii* 89;
— *virginiana* 48, 150

Kalmia angustifolia 'Rubra' 130;
— *latifolia* 83, 130, 196, 209
Kalopanax pictus 133, 225
Kennedya rubicunda 230
Keteleeria davidiana 248
King Cup (*Caltha palustris*) 126, 177, 249; Greater, *Caltha polypetala* 140
Kirengeshoma palmata 108, 194, 204, 228
Kniphofia rooperi 228;
— *snowdenii* 177;
— *uvaria* 48
Koelreuteria paniculata 127, 158, 203

+ *Laburnocytisus adamii* (*Laburnum* × *Cytisus*) 156
Laburnum (*Laburnum anagyroides*) 38, 174;
— tunnel 109;
—, Weeping (*Laburnum alpinum* 'Pendulum') 101
Lactuca plumieri 105
Lady's Mantle (*Alchemilla mollis*) 156
Lagerstroemia indica 159
Lamb's Ears (*Stachys olympica*) 106
Lapageria rosea 196
Larch, Common or European (*Larix decidua*) 40, 48, 115, 139, 212;
—, Japanese (*Larix leptolepis*) 212
Lardizabala biternata 178
Larix decidua 48;
— *griffithii* 248
Lathyrus nervosus (*L. magellanicus* Aiton) 213
Laurel, Bay (*Laurus nobilis*) 38; 82, 122, 131, 178
—, Cherry or Common (*Prunus laurocerasus*) 42, 71, 82, 116, 158, 223;
—, Portuguese (*Prunus lusitanica*) 47, 100, 116;
—, 'Otto Luyken' (*Prunus laurocerasus* 'Otton Luyken') 137;
—, Spurge (*Daphne laureola*) 130
Laurelia serrata 180
Laurustinus (*Viburnum tinus*) 36, 130, 171
Lavandula dentata 89;
—, *see* Lavender
Lavatera maritima 216
Lavender, Cotton (*Santolina* species) 150, 191, 214;
—, Dutch (*Lavandula vera*, of gardens) 200, 220;
—, English (*Lavandula spica*, of gardens) 200
— 'Hidcote' (*Lavandula angustifolia* 'Hidcote') 157, 200, 214;
Lemon (*Citrus limonia*) 40, 130, 208
Lepachis pinnata 203
Lespedeza bicolor 107
Lewisia species 108
Leycesteria formosa 162
Libocedrus bidwillii formosana 245;
— *plumosa* 248
Ligularia veitchiana 151
Ligustrum chenaultii 208;
— *japonicum* 133;
— *lucidum* 'Tricolor' 210;
— *ovalifolium* 83;
— *vulgare* 83
Lilac, Dwarf Korean (*Syringa velutina*) 107;
—, Rouen (*Syringa* × *chinensis*: *S. persica* × *S. vulgaris*) 151;
— (*Syringa vulgaris*) 36, 173
Lilium giganteum (*Cardiocrinum giganteum*) 83;
— *martagon* 216;
— *pardalinum* 93, 215;
— *pyrenaicum* 216;
— *szovitzianum* 156
Lily, Arum (*Zantedeschia aethiopica*) 74, 113, 130, 131;
—, Belladonna (*Amaryllis belladonna*) 136;
—, Blue African (*Agapanthus* species) 206;
—, Citron Day (*Hemerocallis citrina*) 96;
—, Day, modern hybrids of *Hemerocallis*;
—, —, red (*Hemerocallis fulva*) 174;
—, —, yellow (*Hemerocallis flava*) 38, 152, 191;
—, Giant (*Cardiocrinum giganteum*) 177, 180;
—, Henry's Chinese (*Lilium henryi*) 127;
—, Jacobean (*Sprekelia formosissima*) 48;
—, Kaffir (*Schizostylis*) 164, 230;
—, Lent (*Narcissus pseudonarcissus*) 33, 138, 212, 216, 221, 248;
—, Madonna (*Lilium candidum*) 35, 115, 249;
—, Martagon or Turk's Cap (*Lilium martagon*) 103, 135;
—, Nankeen (*Lilium* × *testaceum*) 105;
—, Regal (*Lilium regale*) 226;
—, St Bernard's (*Anthericum liliago*) 174;
—, Tiger (*Lilium tigrinum*) 215
Lily-of-the-Valley (*Convallaria majalis*) 39, 152
Lime, Common (*Tilia europaea*) 191, 215, 264 *et seq.*;
—, Cut-leaf (*Tilia europaea* 'Laciniata') 179;
—, Red Twig (*Tilia platyphyllos*) 234, 264 *et seq.*;
—, Silver (*Tilia argentea*) 190, 235;
—, Small-leafed (*Tilia cordata*) 167, 264 *et seq.*;
—, Weeping Silver (*Tilia petiolaris*) 94, 126, 236
Linaria purpurea 233
Liquidambar formosana monticola 247;
— *styraciflua* 48, 98, 190
Liquorice (*Glycirrhiza glabra*) 35
Liriodendron tulipifera 48, 129
Lithospermum diffusum 229, 233
Lobelia cardinalis 48;
— *erinus* 77, 109;
— × *gerardii* (*L. fulgens* × *L. cardinalis*) 'Queen Victoria' 167;
— × *vedrariensis* (*L.* × *gerardii* qv.) 177
Lobster Claw (*Clianthus puniceus*) 110
Locust, False (*Robinia pseudacacia*) 40, 99, 234;
—, Honey (*Gleditsia triacanthos*) 48, 95, 99;
—, true (*Ceratonia siliqua*) 131
Lomatia ferruginea 229;
— *tinctoria* 190, 246
London Pride (*Saxifraga* × *umbrosa* of gardens) 151, 166
Lonicera etrusca 176;
— *splendida* 249;
— *tragophylla* 106, 115
Loosestrife, Purple (*Lythrum salicaria*) 123, 225, 249
Loquat (*Eriobotrya*

japonica) 83, 95, 138, 208
Lovage (*Ligusticum scoticum*) 110
Love-in-the-Mist (*Nigella damscena*) 35
Love-lies-bleeding (*Amaranthus caudatus*) 38
Lunaria rediviva 108
Lungwort (*Pulmonaria officinalis*) 110
Lyonothamnus floribundus aspleniifolius 161
Lysichitum americanum 83, 102

Machilus ichangensis 245
Madrona (*Arbutus menziesii*) 159
Magnolia acuminata 116, 158;
— 'Anne Rosse' 189;
— *campbellii* 89, 107, 158, 160, 164, 180, 203, 210, 229, 247;
— — 'Charles Raffill' 107;
— — *mollicomata* 89, 164, 180, 203, 229;
— — 'Wakehurst' 247;
— *cordata* 109;
— *cylindrica* 229;
— *delavayi* 110, 208;
— *denudata* 75, 108;
— *globosa* 190, 228;
— 'Goliath' (*M. grandiflora* 'Goliath') 107;
— *grandiflora* 75, 95, 123, 135, 175;
— *kobus* 160, 212, 224;
— *liliflora* 'Nigra' 208;
— × *loebneri* (*M. kobus* × *M. stellata*) 'Leonard Messel' 180;
— *macrophylla* 108;
— 'Michael Rosse' 180;
— *mollicomata, see M. campbellii mollicomata*;
— *nitida* 229;
— *obovata* 164, 165, 180, 221, 224;
— *rostrata* 230;
— *salicifolia* 180;
— *sargentiana robusta* 108, 231;
— *sieboldii* 180;
— *sinensis* 89, 126, 165;
— × *soulangiana* 164, 175, 221;
— — 'Alexandrina' 126;
— — 'Lennei' 164, 198;
— — 'Rustica Rubra' 126;
— *sprengeri* 'Claret Cup' 108;
— — *elongata* 109, 160;
— *stellata* and *M.s.* 'Rosea' 180, 196, 208;
— × *thompsoniana* (*M. tripetala* × *M. virginiana*) 162, 164, 229;
— *tripetala* 196, 197, 212, 224;
— × *veitchii* (*M. campbellii* × *M. denudata*) 108, 138, 164, 229;
— *virginiana* 164, 230;
— × *watsonii* (*M. obovata* × *M. sieboldii*) 108, 164, 177, 180, 204;
— *wilsonii* 126, 228, 250
Mahonia japonica 82;
— *lomariifolia* 110, 119, 156
Maidenhair Tree (*Ginkgo biloba*) 95, 96, 179, 194, 235
Mallow, Tree (*Hibiscus syriacus*) 38, 136, 174;
—, – (*Lavatera olbia* 'Rosea') 105
Malus 'Aldenhamensis' 168;
— *floribunda* 82;
— 'Gibbs' Golden Gage' 168;
— *hupehensis* 151;
— *sieboldii* 105;
— *trilobata* 258
Mandevillea suaveolens 131, 229
Manglietia hookeri 229
Maple, Coral Bark (*Acer palmatum* 'Senkaki') 160;
—, Coral-leafed Japanese (*Acer palmatum* 'Corallina') 221;
—, Field (*Acer campestre*) 150;
—, Japanese (*Acer palmatum* and *A. japonicum* forms) 126, 198, 217, 257;
—, Montpelier (*Acer monspessulanus*) 190;
—, Nikko (*Acer nikoense*) 127;
—, Norwegian (*Acer platanoides*) 191, 223;
—, Tatarian (*Acer tatarica*) 233
Marigold (*Calendula officinalis*) 35, 38, 167
Marrubium candidissimum 203
Marjoram (*Origanum vulgare*) 34
Masterwort (*Astrantia* species) 215
Maytenus boaria 247
Meadowsweet (*Filipendula ulmaria*) 195
Meconopsis betonicifolia 89, 204;
Meconopsis species 205, 246
Medicago arborea 206
Medlar (*Mespilus germanica*) 38, 130
Meehania urticifolia 247
Melaleuca hypericifolia 229
Melicytus ramiflorus 229
Meliosma cuneifolia 189;
— *veitchiorum* 180
Melon 38, 39
Mespilus, Snowy (*Amelanchier*) 212
Metasequoia glyptostroboides 89
Metrosideros florida 196
Michelia doltsopa 227, 229
Mignonette (*Reseda odorata*) 77
'Mimosa' (*Acacia dealbata*) 130, 131, 177
Mimulus aurantiacus 113;
— *cardinalis* 113
Mints (*Mentha* species) 110
Mitraria coccinea 113, 178, 229
Mock Orange (*Philadelphus*) 209, 224, 233
Monarda didyma 75
Monkey Puzzle (*Araucaria araucana*) 97, 248
Monstera deliciosa 194
Montbretia (*Crocosmia hybrids*) 164
Moon Trefoil (*Medicago arborea*) 206
Mourning Widow (*Geranium phaeum*) 33, 103, 166, 203
Mouse Plant (*Arisarum proboscideum*) 103
Mulberry, Black (*Morus nigra*) 39, 119, 130, 152, 158, 170;
—, White (*Morus alba*) 39, 234
Musa basjoo 210
Mutisia oligodon 178
Myosotideum hortensia 229
Myrtle, Common (*Myrtus communis*) 38, 40, 82, 168;
—, Tarentum (*Myrtus communis tarentina*) 168
Myrtus apiculata 178, 208;
—, *bullata* 230;
— *lechlerana* 230;
— *ugni* 229

Narcissus 'Barri Conspicuus' 212;
— 'Emperor' 212;
—, large flowered, naturalised 256;
—, older cultivars 207;
—, Pheasant Eye (*N. poeticus recurvus*) 93, 151, 195;
— *pumilis* 'Plenus' 246
— 'Sir Watkin' 212
'Nasturtium' (*Tropaeolum majus*) 48
Nepeta govaniana 203;
— *sibirica* 203
Nephrophyllidium crista-galli 205
Nerine bowdenii 83, 226;
— *flexuosa* 210
Nettle Tree (*Celtis australis*) 163
Nigella damascena 35
Nothofagus antarctica 178, 212;
— *betuloides* 161; 246;
— *cliffortioides* 246;
— *cunninghamii* 205;
— *dombeyi* 109, 161; 258;
— *obliqua* 203;
— *procera* 129, 258
Nutmeg Bush, *Calycanthus fertilis*
Nymphaea 'Escarboucle' 212

Oak, Algerian (*Quercus canariensis*) 95, 124, 168
—, American Red (*Quercus coccinea* and *Q. rubra*) 75, 98, 99, 198;
—, Cork (*Quercus suber*) 48, 125, 130, 159, 178, 191, 208;
—, English or common (*Quercus robur*) 126, 178;
—, Fastigiate (*Quercus robur* 'Fastigiata') 110, 162
—, Holm (*Quercus ilex*) 38, 40, 96, 115, 121, 154, 177, 178, 226, 253;
—, Hungarian (*Quercus frainetto*) 95;
—, Kermes (*Quercus coccifera*) 155, 216;
—, Lucombe (*Quercus* × *hispanica* 'Lucombeana': *Q. cerris* × *Q. suber*) 130, 160;
—, Pin (*Quercus palustris*) 191;
—, Turkey (*Quercus cerris*) 106;
—, Variegated (*Quercus robur* 'Variegata') 82;
—, Willow-leafed (*Quercus phellos*) 138
Olearia macrodonta 232;
— *semidentata* 112, 229;
— *virgata* 224
Olive (*Olea europaea*) 39, 131, 210
Oplopanax horridus 225
Orange 40, 194, 208
Oranges, Mandarin and Seville 226
Orchid, Madeira (*Dactylorrhiza foliosa*) 177; *D. elata* 204
Orchids, Autumn Ladies' Tresses (*Spiranthes spiralis*) 33, 104, 221, 232
Osmanthus delavayi 180, 198, 217, 221;
— *yunnanensis* 208, 247
Osmunda cinnamomea 247;
— *regalis* 162
Ostrya carpinifolia 160
Ourisia coccinea 161
Oxalis purpurata bowiei 246
Oxydendrum arboreum 208

Paeonia lobata 'Sunbeam' 204;
— *mlokosewitschii* 163;
— *officinalis* 35;
— *suffruticosa* 'Joseph Rock' 156
Pagoda Tree (*Sophora japonica*) 214
Paliurus spina-christi 150
Palm, Chusan (*Chamaerops excelsa*) 119, 131, 194, 208, 210;
—, European Dwarf (*Chamaerops humilis*) 119, 131
Pampas Grass (*Cortaderia selloana*) 78; *see also* 196, 211, 236
Papaver rupifragum 178
Parrotia persica 82, 105, 180, 197, 200
Parrot's Bill (*Clianthus puniceus*) 110
Passion Flower (*Passiflora caerulea*) 48, 168
Paulownia tomentosa 190, 195
Pea, Lord Anson's Blue (*Lathyrus nervosus* (*L. magellanicus* Aiton)) 213;
—, Perennial (*Lathyrus latifolius*) 251
Pear, 'Blickling' 104;
—, Silver Weeping or Willow leafed (*Pyrus salicifolia* 'Pendula') 161, 200
Peltiphyllum peltatum 126
Penstemon 'Garnet' 168;
— *gloxinioides* (of gardens) 'Rubicunda' 80
Pentapterygium serpens 229
Peony 'Madame Louis Henri' 156;
—, old double red (*Paeonia officinalis* 'Rubra Plena') 35;
— 'Souvenir de Maxime Cornu' 178;
—, Tree (*Paeonia suffruticosa*) 103, 115, 131, 135, 152, 156, 161, 233;
—, Tree (× *lemoinei*) (*P. suffruticosa* × *P. lutea*) 'L'Espérance'

Periwinkle (*Vinca*) 39, 174;
— , Lesser (*Vinca minor*) 110
Persea ichangensis 245
Philadelphus coronarius 36;
— 'Belle Etoile' 156;
— *delavayi* 177;
— *microphyllus* 173
Philesia magellanica (*P. buxifolia*) 180, 204, 231
Phillyrea latifolia 38, 82, 158, 220, 234;
— , variegated 47
Phlomis fruticosa 38, 233
Phlox drummondii 77;
— *paniculata* 75
Phormium tenax 210
Photinia davidsoniae 208;
— × *fraseri* (*P. glabra* × *P. serrulata*) 'Birmingham' 178;
— *serrulata* 119, 157, 207, 247;
— *villosa* 197
Phygelius aequalis 104
Phyllocladus species 178
Phyllodoce empetriformis 133
Picconia excelsa 177
Picea abies 'Clanbrasiliana' 233;
— — 'Gregoryana' 198;
— — 'Nana Compacta' 128, 180;
— *brewerana* 225;
— *glauca albertiana* 'Conica' 113;
— *likiangensis* 225, 248;
— *orientalis* 225;
— *sitchensis* 82;
— *smithiana* 138, 208, 225
Pieris formosa 207;
— , Forrest's (*Pieris formosa forrestii*) 107, 199, 246
Pine, Austrian (*Pinus nigra*) 195, 236;
— , Bhutan (*Pinus wallichiana*) 217, 256;
— , Bishop (*Pinus muricata*) 248;
— , Chinese Lace-Bark (*Pinus bungeana*) 190;
— , Crimean (*Pinus nigra caramanica*) 236;
— , Himalayan (*Pinus wallichiana*) 110;
— , Knobcone (*Pinus attenuata*) 248;
— , Macedonian (*Pinus peuce*) 223, 236;
— , Maritime (*Pinus pinaster*) 38, 195, 211, 227;
— , Mexican (*Pinus ayacahuite*) 161, 248;
— , Monterey (*Pinus radiata*) 82, 178, 212, 221;
— , Mountain (*Pinus mugo*) 128, 217;
— , Scots (*Pinus sylvestris*) 73, 82, 136, 137, 139, 165, 220, 234, 248;
— , Stone (*Pinus pinea*) 38, 42, 73;
— , Swiss Arolla (*Pinus cembra*) 128, 167, 217, 236;
— , Umbrella (*Sciadopitys verticillata*) 212
Pinus cembra 191, 225;
— *densiflora* 'Umbraculifera' 155;
— *montezumae* 212;
— *parviflora* 201, 217, 223;
— *patula* 207;
— *pinaster* 38, 195, 211, 227
— *pinea* 38, 42, 73
— *pumila* 225;
— *sylvestris* 73, 82, 136, 137, 139, 165, 220, 234, 248
— — 'Moseri' 155
Pink (*Dianthus plumarius*) 39, 80
Pipe-Tree or Lilac (*Syringa vulgaris*) 173
Pittosporum bicolor 246;
— *colensoi* 246;
— *crassifolium* 178;
— *eugenioides* 177;
— *patulum* 247;
— Purple Leafed (*P. tenuifolium* 'Purpureum') 113;
— *tenuifolium* 83, 208, 232;
— — 'Silver Queen' 207, 208;
— *tobira* 177
Plane, London (*Platanus* × *hispanica*) 48, 95, 174, 191;
— , Oriental (*Platanus orientalis*) 106, 153, 170, 191
Platanus × *hispanica* 48
Platycerium alcicorne 196;
Pleione 161
Podocarpus andinus 201;
— *salignus* 229
Poinsettia (*Euphorbia pulcherrima*) 83
Poker, Red Hot (*Kniphofia*) 48, 172
Polyanthus at Sissinghurst Castle 215
Polygonum affine 217, 248;
— *baldschuanicum* 232;
— *equisetiforme* 216;
— *milettii* 220;
— 'Reynoutria' (*P. cupsidatum* 'Compactum' of gardens') 127;
— *vacciniifolium* 217, 246, 248
Pomegranate (*Punica granatum*) 123, 202, 252
Poplar, Grey (*Populus canescens*) 99, 190;
— , Lombardy (*Populus nigra* 'Italica') 73, 82, 94, 122, 191, 264
Poppy, Blue (*Meconopsis betonicifolia*) 89, 108, 216;
— , Californian (*Romneya coulteri*) 139;
— , Oriental (*Papaver orientale*) 48, 215
Populus lasiocarpa 203, 258;
— *maximowiczii* 205
Potato (*Solanum tuberosum*) 38
Potentilla cuneata 248;
— *fruticosa* 198;
— — 'Red Ace' 173;
— , Vilmorin's (*Potentilla fruticosa* 'Vilmoriniana') 127;
Pretty Maids (*Saxifraga granulata* 'Plena') 177
Primrose, Evening (*Oenothera biennis*) 251
Primula florindae 89, 93, 167, 230;
— *forrestii* 108;
— *japonica* 84, 196;
— — 'Postford White' 161;
— × *pruhoniciana* (*P. juliae* × *P. vulgaris* etc.) 126;
— 'Rowallane Rose' 205;
— 'Wanda', *see P. pruhoniciana*
Privet, Common (*Ligustrum vulgare*) 36, 83, 251, 268;
— cream variegated (*Ligustrum ovalifolium* 'Argenteum') 107;
— , large-leafed (*Ligustrum lucidum*) 235;
— , Oval-leaf (*Ligustrum ovalifolium*) 83
Prunus sargentii 129, 205;
— *serrula tibetica* 109, 197;
— *tenella* 221;
— × *yedoensis* 89
Pseudopanax arboreus 245;
— *crassifolius* 247
Pseudowintera colorata 205
Psoralea pinnata 177
Pterocarya fraxinifolia 163, 225
Pumpkin 38
Puya alpestris 119
Pyracantha 36, 40
Pyrus ussuriensis 258;
— *nivalis* 200

Quercus canariensis 98, 129, 191;
— *coccifera* 155, 216;
— *coccinea* 75;
— *frainetto* 129, 191;
— *glauca* 247;
— *ilex* see Oak, Holm;
— *laurifolia* 258;
— *palustris* 191;
— *phillyreoides* 247
— *rubra* 75, 129, 191;
— × *schochiana* (*Q. palustris* × *Q. phellos*) 258;
— *suber* 48; *see also* Oak, Cork;
— *velutina* 'Rubrifolia' 258
Quince (*Cydonia oblonga*) 38, 130

Ranunculus 39, 80
Raspberry (*Rubus strigosus*) 35
Red Hot Poker (*Kniphofia uvaria*)
Red Ink Plant (*phytolacca americana*) 127
Redwood (*Sequoia sempervirens*) 82, 118, 129, 138, 158, 159, 165, 171, 201, 211;
— , Dawn (*Metasequoia glyptostroboides*) 130, 223, 225
Rehderodendron macrocarpum 165, 229
Reseda odorata 77
Rhaphithamnus cyanocarpus 229
Rhododendron aberconwayi 109, 111;
— 'Aladdin' 227;
— 'Albatross' 105;
— *albrechtii* 108, 111;
— 'Alison Johnstone' 165;
— 'Altaclarense' 74;
— *ambiguum* 132;
— 'Angelo' 212;
— 'Anne Rosse' 190;
— *arboreum* 74, 115, 159, 165, 189, 197, 208, 223, 228;
— — roseum 'Tony Schilling' 247;
— *argipeplum* 247;
— arizelum 230, 247;
— *augustinii* 108, 203, 223, 225;
— *auriculatum* 190, 203, 223, 225;
— 'Azor' 105, 225;
— *barbatum* 203;
— 'Beauty of Tremough' 228;
— 'Blue Tit' 167;
— 'Boddaertianum' 220;
— 'Bodnant Yellow' 108;
— 'Bo-peep' 111;
— 'Bow Bells' 227;
— *brachysiphon* 230;
— 'Britannia' 223;
— *bullatum see R. edgworthii*;
— 'Bulldog' 230;
— *bureavii* 197, 246;
— 'Bustard' 227;
— *calendulaceum* 74;
— *calophytum* 108;
— *calostrotum* 190;
— *campylocarpum* 197;
— *campylogynum* 190;
— *carneum* 230;
— *carolinianum* 111;
— *catawbiense* 74;
— *caucasicum* 74;
— *cerasinum* 'Hubert Mitchell' 190;
— 'Cherubim' 230;
— *ciliicalyx* 230;
— *cinnabarinum* 203, 223, 227;
— — *roylei* 227;
— *concatenans* 203;
— *concinnum* 227;
— 'Cornish Cream' 230;
— 'Cornish Cross' 161, 111;
— *'Countess of Haddington'* 230;
— *'Cowslip' 227;*
— *crassum* 178, 190, 198;
— *cubittii* 178, 230;
— 'Cynthia'
— *dalhousiae* 230;
— 'Damaris Logan' 167;
— 'David' 228;
— *davidsonianum* 109;
— *decorum* 190, 197, 203;
— *degronianum* 'Gerald Loder' 246;
— *delavayi* 159;
— 'Ding Dong' 230;
— *discolor* 105, 203;
— 'Earl of Athlone' 228;
— *edgworthii* 165;
— 'Elizabeth' (*R. forrestii repens* × *R. griersonianum*) 109, 228;
— *elliottii* 230;
— *eriogynum* 230;
— Fabia 'Tangerine' 109;
— *falconeri* 108, 165, 178, 230;
— *ferrugineum* 132, 225;
— *fortunei* 198;
— 'Fragantissimum' (*R. edgworthi* × *R. formosum*) 138, 198;
— 'Full House';
— 'Fusilier' 228;
— 'Glory of Penjerrick' 228;
— *grande* 230;
— 'Grandex' 178;
— *griersonianum* 230;
— 'Gwillt King' 228;
— *hypenanthum* 190;
— 'Impi' 223;
— *'Inamorata'* 105;
— *iteophyllum* 227;
— *johnstoneanum* 230;
— 'Kewense' 223;
— *lacteum* 247;
— 'Lady Alice Fitzwilliam' 160, 195, 198, 228;
— 'Lady Chamberlain' 227;

— 'Laerdal' 230;
— 'Lanyon' 230;
— *lepidostylum* 205, 225;
— *leucaspis* 227;
— *lindleyi* 160, 178, 230;
— *'Little Bert'* 228;
— Loderi 197, 223;
— *longisquamatum* 247;
— ludlowii 205;
— *luteum* 74, 167;
— *macabeanum* 178, 180, 230;
— *maddenii* 230;
— 'Madonna' 190;
— *magnificum* 230;
— *mallotum* 247;
— *manipurense* 230;
— 'Mary Swaythling' 227;
— 'May Day' 111, 228;
— *megacalyx* 230;
— *mollyanum* 198
—'Morvah' 230;
— 'Moser's Maroon' 225;
— 'Mrs A. T. de la Mare' 228;
— 'Mrs G. W. Leak' 228;
— 'Nanceglos' 230;
— *nipponicum* 231;
— Nobleanum 111;
— 'Norman Shaw' 128;
— *nuttallii* 176, 229;
— *ovatum* of gardens 225;
— *parryae* 230;
— *pemakoense* 205;
— 'Penjerrick' 161, 228;
— 'Pink Drift' 205;
— 'Pink Pearl' 197;
— *pocophorum* 'Cecil Nice' 190;
— 'Polar Bear' 111, 167, 198, 223;
— *polyandrum* 178, 228, 230;
— *polylepis* 159;
—, Pontic (*Rhododendron ponticum*) 105, 209, 213, 223;
— *ponticum* 71, 74, 82, 116;
— — 'Variegatum' 197;
— *praevernum* 198;
— *pseudochrysanthum* 246;
— *pseudoianthirum* 203;
— *rhabdotum* 176, 230;
— Richard Gill' 228;
— 'Romany Chai' 228;
— 'Romany Chal' 105;
— *roxieanum* 190;
— 'Russellianum' 74, 137, 228;
— 'St Breward' 111;
— 'St Probus' 228;
— *saluenense* 190;
— 'Sapphire' 205;
— *sargentianum* 205;
— 'Sarled' 205;
— *schlippenbachii* 108, 197;
— *serpyllifolium* 159;
— 'Shilsonii' (*R. barbatum* × *R. thomsonii*) 198, 223;
— 'Sigismund Rucker' 228;
— *sino-grande* 230;
— *souliei* 198;
— *stamineum* 247;
— 'Strategist';
— 'Susan' 167;
— *sutchuenense* 203, 227;
— *taggianum* 178, 230;
— 'Tally Ho' 228;
— *taronense;*
— *thomsonii* 132, 198, 227;
— 'Trelissick Port Wine' 228;
— 'Trelissick Salmon' 228;
— 'Trewithen Orange' 228;
— *tsangpoense* 190;
— 'Tyermanii' 230;
— *uvariifolium* 'Reginald Childs' 247;
— *valentinianum* 247
— 'Vanessa' 109;
— *vellereum* 190;
— *wardii* 227;
— 'White Wings' 230;
— *williamsianum* 109, 227;
— 'Winsome' 109;
— *yunnanense* 109, 159, 167, 207, 223;
— *zeylanicum* 247
Rhubarb (*Rheum rhaponticum*) 35;
— Chilean (*Gunnera manicata*) 102;
— Chinese, crimson (*Rheum palmatum* 'Atrosanguineum') 234
Rhus sylvestris 247;
— *verniciflua* 247
Ribes speciosum 122
Richea scoparia 246
Robinia pseudacacia 48; *see also* Locust, False
Rodgersia pinnata 'Superba' 204
Rosa alba 152, 172, 174, 252
— — Céleste 93 180, 215;
— — 'Maiden's Blush' 101;
— × *anemonoides* (*R. laevigata* × Tea Rose) 131;
— *arvensis* 173;
— *banksiae* 123, 128, 168, 202, 220;
— *bracteata* 104, 220;
— *brunonii* 119;
— — *'La Mortola' 128, 161;*
— *centifolia* 48, 252;
— *chinensis* 74;
— *cooperi* (of gardens) 106;
— *damascena* 252;
— *eglanteria, see R. rubiginosa;*
— *filipes* 'Kiftsgate' 128;
— × *fortuniana* (*R. banksiae* × *R. laevigata*) 162;
— *gallica* 'Officinalis' 171;
— *gigantea* 74, 176;
— *hugonis* 198;
— *laevigata* 106;
— *longicuspis* 160, 215;
— *moschata* 173;
— *moyesii* 172, 177, 203, 215;
— *multibracteata* 214;
— *multiflora* 180;
— *rubiginosa* 152;
— *rubrifolia* 155, 172;
— *rugosa* 137, 152, 189, 208;
— — 'Roseraïe de l'Hay' 101;
— *sino-wilsonii* 109;
— *soulieana* 250;
— *virginiana* 106, 234
Rose 'Alister Stella Gray' 191;
— 'Amadis' 152;
— 'American Pillar' 199;
—, Apothecary's (*Rosa gallica officinalis*) 252;
—, Autumn Damask (*Rosa damascena bifera*) 31, 106, 174;
— 'Betty Prior' 102;
— 'Blanc Double de Coubert' (*R. rugosa* form) 172;
— 'Blush Boursault' 170;
— 'Blush Noisette' 180;
—, Cabbage (*Rosa centifolia*) 48, 172;
— 'Camaieux' (*Gallica*) 215;
— 'Canary Bird' 198;
— 'Cardinal de Richelieu' 180, 215;
— 'Cécile Brunner' 163;
— 'Céline Forestier' 161, 172;
— 'Charles de Mills' 180, 215;
—, China hybrids 74;
—, — (*Rosa chinensis*) 74;
—, Christmas (*Helleborus niger*) 166;
— 'Cerise Bouquet' 152, 234;
— 'Climbing Devoniensis' 175;
— 'Climbing General MacArthur' 161;
— 'Climbing Lady Hillingdon' 107, 128, 174, 250;
— 'Climbing Pompon de Paris' 198;
— 'Cramoisi Supérieur Grimpante' 106;
—, Crimson China ('Slater's Crimson') 74;
—, 'Crimson Shower' 199;
— 'Cupid' 140;
—, Damask (*Rosa damascena*) 252;
— 'Dame Edith Helen' 179;
— 'Dorothy Perkins' 134, 199;
— D'Orsay 121;
— 'Duc de Guiche' (Gallica) 215;
— 'Duchess of Portland' 106, 172;
— 'Easlea's Golden Rambler' 107, 140;
— 'Ellen Terry' 218;
— 'Else Poulsen' 106;
— 'Etoile de Hollande' 200;
— 'Excelsa' 199;
— 'Fantin Latour' 215;
— 'Félicité et Perpétue' 220;
— 'Flora' 180;
— 'Frances E. Lester' 224;
— 'François Juranville' 199;
— 'Frensham' 102, 200;
— 'Frühlingsgold' 151, 214;
— gardens 81, 82, 102;
— 'Gardenia' 107;
— 'Gava' 130;
— 'Gloire de Dijon' 106, 140, 152, 202;
— 'Gloire de France' 215;
— 'Gloria Mundi' 106;
— 'Golden Wings' 173;
— 'Goldfinch' 152;
— 'Gruss an Aachen' 155, 168, 215;
— 'Guinée' 128;
— 'Hidcote Gold' 156;
— Highdown (*Rosa* 'Highdownensis') 250;
— 'Hippolyte' 215;
— 'Home Sweet Home' 200;
— 'Iceberg' 215, 236;
— Japanese Moss (*Rosa centifolia muscosa* 'Japonica') 106;
— Kiftsgate (*Rosa filipes* 'Kiftsgate') 123;
— 'Kirsten Poulsen' 106;
— 'Kronprinzessin Viktoria' 218;
— 'La Follette' 189;
— 'La Perle' 160;
— 'Lawrence Johnston' 140, 156;
— Lenten (*Helleborus orientalis*) 137;
— 'Lilac Charm' 173;
— 'Locarno' 106;
— 'Lorenzo Pahissa' 130;
— Macartney (*Rosa bracteata*) 126;
— 'Madame Alfred Carrière' 215;
— 'Madame Alice Garnier' 161;
— 'Madame Grégoire Staechelin' 104;
— 'Maiden's Blush' (*see R. alba*) 101, 180;
— 'Maréchal Niel' 127, 175;
— 'Mermaid' 199;
— 'Mount Stewart' 177;
— 'Mrs Anthony Waterer' 106;
— 'Mrs Inge Poulsen' 102;
— 'Mrs John Laing' 200;
—, Musk (*Rosa moschata* and *R. arvensis*) 36, 172, 173, 252;
— 'Nevada' 152, 158, 198;
— 'New Dawn' 162, 220;
— 'News' 173;
— 'Nuits de Young' 215;
— of Sharon (*Hypericum calycinum*) 48;
— 'Old Blush', China 172;
— 'Ophelia' 200;
— 'Paul Ricault' 152;
— 'Paul's Carmine Pillar' 106;
— 'Paul's Himalayan Rambler' 160;
— 'Paul's Lemon Pillar' 196;
— 'Paul's Single White' 106;
— 'Peace' 200;
— 'Perle d'Or' 163;
— 'Phyllis Bide' 104;
— 'Pink Parfait' 224;
— 'Polyantha Grandiflora' 160;
— Red of Lancaster (*Rosa gallica* 'Officinalis') 106, 174;
— 'Reine Marie Henriette' 140;
— 'Robert le Diable'
— Rock (*Cistus* species) 130, 233;
— 'Rosa Mundi' (*R. gallica* 'Versicolor') 180;

— 'Rose des Maures', *see* 'Sissinghurst Castle'
— 'Rose Gaujard' 200;
— 'Salmon Spray' 127;
— 'Sanders' White' 199;
— 'Sir Thomas Lipton' 106;
— 'Sissinghurst Castle' 215;
— 'Souvenir de la Malmaison' 162;
— — (climbing) 126;
— 'Souvenir de Madame Léonie Viennot' 161;
— 'Souvenir du Dr Jamain' 215;
— 'The Fairy' 224;
— 'William Allen Richardson' 106;
—, York and Lancaster (*R. damascena* 174) 'Versicolor');
—, Yorkist (*Rosa alba* 'Semi-plena') 152, 172, 174, 252;
— 'Zéphirine Drouhin' 126, 220, 224
Rosemary (*Rosmarinus officinalis*) 36, 37
Roses, Burnet (*R. spinosissima*) 93, 175, 215, 233
Rowan (*Sorbus aucuparia*) 39
Rubus spectabilis 128
Rudbeckia maxima 127
Rue (*Ruta graveolens* 'Jackman's Blue') 113, 191

Sage, Jerusalem (*Phlomis fruticosa*) 36, 233
St John's Wort (*Hypericum calycinum*) 200
Salvia coccinea 77;
— *confertiflora* 216;
— *fulgens* 177
Santolina chamaecyparissus 36
Sasa veitchii 247
Sassafras albida 189
Saxifraga cotyledon 35, 273
Saxifrage, Mossy (hybrids of *Saxifraga decipiens*) 151
Schima argentea 198, 230;
— *khasiana* 230
Schizandra grandiflora rubriflora 202;
— *spenanthera* 230
Schizophragma hydrangeoides 106;
— — 'Rosea' 156;
— *integrifolia* 174, 198
Scopolia carniolica 247;
— — *hladnikiana* 247
Seakale (*Crambe maritima*) 250
Sedge, Greater Tussock (*Carex paniculata*) 257
Self Heal (*Prunella vulgaris*) 110
Selinum tenuifolium 203
Senecio laxifolius of gardens (*S.* Dunedin Hybrid 'Sunshine') 123, 233
Senna, bladder (*Colutea arborescens*) 36
Sequoia sempervirens 'Prostrata' 229
Shallon (*Gaultheria shallon*) 128
Silk Vine (*Periploca graeca*) 103
Silver Bells (*Campanula*, white) 177
Smilacina racemosa 161
Smilax aspera 195, 220
Smoke Bush (*Cotinus coggygria*) 127, 200, 205
Snow in Summer (*Cerastium tomentosum*) 233
Snowberry (*Symphoricarpos albus*) 83
Snowdrop Tree (*Halesia tetraptera*) 130
Snowflake, Summer (*Leucojum aestivum*) 172
Soapwort (*Saponaria officinalis*) 174, 232
Solanum aviculare 229;
—, climbing (*Solanum crispum*) 107, 115, 177;
— *crispum* 'Glasnevin' 123, 176, 217;
— *jasminoides* 'Album' 228
Solidago canadensis 48
Sollya heterophylla 177
Solomon's Seal (*Polygonatum × multiflorum*) 167, 174
Sophora japonica 180, 196;
— *macrocarpa* 180;
— *tetraptera* 178
× *Sorbaronia* (*Sorbus × Aronia*) 258
Sorbus aucuparia 'Beissneri' 257;
— *hedlundii* 205;
— *latifolia* 129;
— 'Leonard Messel' 190;
— *meliosmifolia* 161;
— *sargentiana* 89;
— *scopulina* 220;
— *torminalis* 191
Sparrmania africana 206
Spikenard (*Nardostachys jatamansii*) 166
Spiraea nipponica tosaensis 173
Spiranthes spiralis 33, 104, 221, 232
Sprekelia formosissima 48
Spruce, Blue Colorado (*Picea pungens* 'Glauca') 128, 132, 198;
—, Colorado (*Abies concolor*) 103, 256;
—, dwarf Alberta White (*Picea glauca albertiana* 'Conica') 127;
—, Norway (*Picea abies*) 236;
—, Oriental (*Picea orientalis*) 104, 128, 197;
—, Serbian (*Picea omorika*) 212, 236;
—, Sitka (*Picea sitchensis*) 82;
—, Tiger-Tail (*Picea polita*) 128;
—, West Himalayan (*Picea smithiana*) 110, 227
Staphylea colchica 122
Stauntonia latifolia 162
Stewartia ovata 'Grandiflora' 190;
— *pseudocamellia* 197
— *pteropetiolata* 230, 245;
— *sinensis* 160, 247
Strawberry 33, 74
Strawberry Tree (*Arbutus unedo*) 119, 139, 195, 235
Styrax hemsleyana 109, 189, 198, 229;
— *japonica* 198, 205, 210, 229;
— *obassia* 196
Sumach, Stag's Horn (*Rhus typhina*) 99
Sunflower (*Helianthus annuus*) 38
Sweet Cicely (*Myrrhis odorata*) 110, 166
Sweet William (*Dianthus barbatus*) 35
Sycamore (*Acer pseudoplatanus*) 44, 70, 164;
— 'Prinz Handjery' (*Acer pseudoplatanus* 'Prinz Handjery') 228;
—, Variegated (*Acer pseudoplatanus variegatum*) 223
Symphoricarpos albus 83
Symplocos paniculata 159
'Syringa' or Mock Orange (*Philadelphus*) 209, 224, 233
Syringa emodi 'Aureovariegata' 210;
— × *josiflexa* (*S. josikaea* × *S. reflexa*) 'Bellicent' 151

Taiwania cryptomerioides 248
Tea Plant (*Camellia thea*) 246
Telopea truncata 246
Tetracentron sinense 180
Thalictrum delavayi 83
Thistle, Scots (*Onopordon acanthium*) 216
Thladiantha oliveri 104
Thorn, Cockspur (*Crataegus crus-galli*) 48, 99;
— (*Crataegus*) 136
Thrift (*Armeria maritima*) 34, 166
Thyme (*Thymus vulgaris*) 36
Thuja koraiensis 248;
Tibouchina semidecandra 'Grandiflora' 230
Tilia (*see also* Lime) *euchlora* 133;
— *oliveri* 129;
— *petiolaris* 98
Tomato 48
Tradescantia virginica 174
Tree of Heaven (*Ailanthus altissima*) 75, 125
Tricuspidaria lanceolata see *Crinodendron hookeranum*
Tropaeolum majus 48;
— *speciosum* 155
Trumpet Creeper (*Campsis radicans*) 125, 163
Tsuga mertensiana 128, 203, 225
Tulip 35, 39
Tulip Tree (*Liriodendron tulipifera*) 48, 98, 125, 132, 135, 138, 139, 159, 165, 221;
— —, Chinese (*Liriodendron Chinese*) 247
Tulipa sylvestris 93
Tupelo Tree (*Nyssa sylvatica*) 211

Vaccinium species 83, 230
Valerian (*Centranthus officinalis*) 174;
—, *dark-tinted* (*Centrathus ruber* 'Atrococcineus') 233
Varnish Tree (*Rhus verniciflua*) 247
Verbena × *hybrida* 77;
— 'Lawrence Johnston' 156;
— *rigida* 113
Veronica gentianoides 233
Vestia lycioides 178, 229
Viburnum erubescens 109;
— 'Fulbrook' 123;
— × *hillieri* (*V. erubescens* × *V. henryi*) 109;
— × *juddii* (*V. bitchiuense* × *V. carlesii*) 217;
— *plicatum* 'Mariesii' 112, 198;
— — 'Rowallane' 204, 205;
— *tinus*;
— — 'Eve Price'
Vinca difformis 100
Vine, Claret (*Vitis vinifera* 'Purpurea') 106, 234;
—, Coignet's (*Vitis coignetiae*) 127
Violet (*Viola odorata*) 38
Violet, African (*Saintpaulia ionantha*) 83;
—, Dog's Tooth' (*Erythronium* species) 160
Virginia Creeper (*Parthenocissus quinquefolia*) 40
Virgin's Bower (*Clematis flammula*) 36, 106, 173, 220
Vitis coignetiae 110, 189, 203, 217

Walnut, Black (*Juglans nigra*) 48, 95, 163, 208
Water-lilies (*Nymphaea*) 149, 233
Watsonias 131, 177
Weigela, Variegated (*Weigela florida* 'Variegated') 168
Wellingtonia (*Sequoiadendron giganteum*) 73, 82, 84, 128, 158, 159, 165, 171, 178, 195, 211;
—, Weeping (*Sequoiadendron giganteum* 'Pendulum') 108
Whitebeam (*Sorbus aria*) 157
Willow, Twisted Pekin (*Saix matsudana* 'Tortuosa') 131;
—, Weeping (*Salix babylonica*) 75;
—, White (*Salix alba*) 223, 234
Willows 162
Winter Sweet (*Chimonanthus praecox*) 123
Wistaria floribunda 139;
— — 'Alba' 107, 202;
— — 'Macrobotrys' (*W. multijuga*) 156;
— *sinensis* 123, 162;
— venusta 107, 177
Witch Hazel (*Hamamelis* species) 258
Woodbine (*Lonicera*) 39

Xanthoceras sorbifolium 127, 170

Yew, English (*Taxus baccata*) 42, 82, 219, 268;
—, Golden Dovaston (*Taxus baccata* 'Dovastonii Aurea') 217;
—, Golden English (*Taxus baccata* 'Aurea') 213
Yew hedges 39, 42, 268
Yew, Irish (*Taxus baccata* 'Fastigiata') 126, 134, 137, 164, 170, 202, 255
Yucca filamentosa 105, 175;
— *gloriosa* 38;
— *recurvifolia* 137, 172

Zanthoxylum ailanthoides 247
Zauschneria microphylla 161
Zenobia pulverulenta 133
Zinnia elegans 77

General Index

Numbers in italic refer to the main description of the garden.

Aberconway, Lord 87, 107
Acland, Cuthbert 89
Acland, Sir Richard, Bt 158
Acland, Sir Thomas, Bt 159
Acland, Sir Thomas Dyke- 231
Acorn Bank 33, *93*
Acorn Camps 22, 128, 169
Addison, Joseph 14, 63, 64, 71
Aesthetic movement 86
Albert, Prince 121, 195
Aldenham 167
alleys 39, 61, 102, 174, 189
American garden (plants) 70, 83, 130
Amory, Sir John and Lady Heathcoat 89, 160
amphitheatre 64, 69, 117
Anglesey Abbey 48, 84, 89, *93*, 265
Anne, Queen 46, 47
Anson, George, later Admiral Lord, 213
Anson, Thomas William 213
Antony House 47, 71, *95*, 267
arabesque 86
arboreta 84
arbours 32, 34, 173
arches, rose 81
architect, first recognised 34
architecture 15
Ardress 82
Arlington Court 33, 76, *96*, 266, 273
Arne, Dr Thomas 121
Arnold, Matthew 80
art-nouveau 86
Arundell, Sir John 231
Ascott 33, 47, 76, 77, 81, 82, *97*, 270, 273
Ash, Mr G. Baron 193
Ashdown House 43, *98*, 272
Ashridge Park 275
Astor, Viscount 120
Astor, William Waldorf 121
Attingham Park 48, 71, 99
avenues 44, 61, 71, 264
aviaries 45

Babylonians 31
Bacon, Sir Francis 39, 64, 72, 155, 172, 203
Badeslade, Thomas 133
balustrades 46
Banks, Sir Joseph 273
Barrington Court 36, 87, *100*
Barrington, Lord 154
Barry, Sir Charles 79, 121, 137
basket-shaped bed 80
Bateman's 87, *101*
Beaconsfield, Earl of 156, 235
Bean, W. J. 118
Bearsted, Lady 233
Bearsted, Viscount 233
Beckwith, George 176
bedding flowers 76
bedding, subtropical 77
bee-boles and hives 36, 99, 134
Belloc, Hilaire 136
Beningbrough Hall 47, 62, 82, 83, 267
Benthall Hall 83, *102*, 273
Benthall, Sir Paul 103
Berrall, Judith S. 191
Berrington Hall 33, 62, 70, *103*
Bevan, Miss K. 226
Biddulph Grange 66
Blackett, Sir Walter 66, 249
Blathwayt, John Povey 131
Blathwayt, William 131
Blickling Hall 22, 43, 44, 62, 76, 79, 87, *104*, 266, 269, 271
Blomfield, Sir Reginald 86, 132, 152, 192
Bodiam Castle 271
Bodnant Garden 22, 82, 87, *107*, 275
Bolitho, Lt Col Sir Edward 229
Bolitho, Major Simon 231
Boord, Sir Thomas and Lady 245
bowls (game), bowling green 36, 43, 169
Bowood 72
Bridgeman, Charles 61, 64, 117, 121, 256
Bristol, Earl of, 78, 157
Brompton Park 46
Brooklands Avenue, Cambridge 266
Brown, A. E. 169
Brown, Lancelot ("Capability") 25, 44, 64 *et seq*, 103, 113, 115, 124, 157, 196, 202, 210, 256, 265
Buckingham, Duke of 129
Buckland Abbey *109*
Bunyard, E. A. 176
Burges, William 79
Burghley House 70
Burlington, Lord 64
Burnett-Brown, Col and Mrs 163
Burne-Jones 111
Burney, Fanny 208
Bury, Lady Mairi 176
Bury, Lord 176
Busbridge Hall 153
Buscot Park 87, *110*, 265
Bythel, Miss A. P. 172

Cambridge, Duke of 82
Cambridge University Botanic Garden 155
Campbell, Robert 110
canals 32
Canning, George 121
Carew Pole, Sir John and Lady 95
Castlecoole 44
Castle Drogo 86, 87, *111*
Castle Howard 267
Castle Ward 44, 68, *112*, 266, 273
Cavendish family 151
Cawley, Lord 103
Chambers, Sir William 66
chapel 68
charitableness 18
Charlecote Park 32, 36, 39, 44, 62, 69, 79, *113*, 265, 271
Charles, I, King 40, 162
Charles II, King 39, 41, 44, 173
Charlotte, Princess 117
Charlotte, Queen 125, 208
Charnwood Forest 62
Chartwell 87, *114*
chase, hunting 62
Chatsworth 79, 151
Chaucer, 26, 32, 33
Cheere, John 113
Chelsea Physic Garden 273
Chichester, Miss Rosalie 96
China, Chinese 32, 66, 86
chinoiserie 66
Chippendale-style 66
Chirk Castle *114*
Churchill, Sir Winston and Lady 114, 126
Chute, John 234
Chute, Mr Wiggett 234
clairvoyée 62
Clandon Park 33, 65, 80, *115*, 272
Clare, Earl of 117
Claremont 64, 65, 69, 71, 72, *116*, 201, 272, 273, 275
classical architecture 64
Claude Gelée, of Lorraine 63
Claydon House 39, 62, 66
Clerk, Sir John of Penicuik 69
Clevedon Court 39, 66, *119*, 275
Clifden, Viscount 164
Clive, Lord 120
Cliveden 22, 39, 45, 47, 71, 74, 79, 86, 87, *120*, 265, 267, 269, 272, 275
Clumber Park 71, 72, *124*, 265, 267, 273
coal, used as gravel 47, 191
"Coke of Norfolk" 213
Colchester, Maynard 251
Comber, Harold 109, 180
Comber, James 180
Compton Castle 83
conservatories 76
Cook, Thomas 65
Coote, Sir Charles 73
Copeland, Mrs Ronald 227
coppice, coppicing 62
Cotehele 32, 80, *124*, 273
cottage garden 80
Country Life, founding of 87
Courts, The, Holt 88, *126*
Coutts, John 158, 275
Cowley, Abraham 46
Cowley, Mr 158
Cragside House, 72, 82, *127*
Croft Castle 44, 62, *128*, 265, 267
Croft, Lord 128
Cromwell, 231
Cross, the 33
Crowe, Dame Sylvia 227
Crusaders 32, 171
Cullen, Sir Rushout 233
Cyrus, King 13

dairy, Uppark 71, 232
Danbury Common 62
d'Arblay, Madame 208
d'Argenville, A. J. D. 46, 61, 117, 191
Dashwood, Sir Francis, Bt 254
Daubeney, Lord 100
de Bouillon, Godfrey 171
de l'Ecluse 168
de Rothschild, Baron Ferdinand 235
de Rothschild, Leopold 97
de Rothschild, Miss Alice 236
de Rothschild, Mr and Mrs Anthony 97
Derrymore 33, 73
design, garden, and rhododendrons 83
Destailleur, architect 235
Devonshire, Evelyn Duchess of 152
de Walden, Lord and Lady Howard 115
Dillistone, George 112
Disraeli, Earl of Beaconsfield 156
ditch as boundary 62
Dodoens, Rembert 37, 168
Dorneywood *129*
d'Orsay, Comte 121
dovecotes 36
Downshire, Lady 245
Drake, Sir Francis 109
Drewe, Mr Anthony 111
Dudmaston *129*, 273
Dunham Massey 35, 76
Dunster Castle 37, *130*
Dutch influence 37, 41, 45, 79, 167
Dyer, John 71
Dyer's Company, the 216
Dyrham Park 42, 45, 79, *131*

East Riddlesden Hall 43, *132*
Ebbott, Thomas 206
"ecological" planting 89
Edward VII, King 128
Egerton, Lady Louisa 151
Egerton, Lord, of Tatton 225
Egyptians 31
Elizabeth I, Queen 17, 34, 169
Elizabeth II, Queen
Elizabeth of Bohemia 98
Elizabeth, Queen (the Queen Mother) 94
Elizabethans 25
Elton, Sir Arthur, Bt 119
embroidery 34
Emes, William 133, 256
Emmetts 84, *132*
Enclosures, the 69, 70
Endsleigh 72
Erddig 44, 79, *133*
Evelyn, John 44, 46, 62 *et seq*, 82, 120, 149, 264, 273
evergreens 47, 61, 82

Fairhaven, Lord 89, 93
Faringdon, Lord 110
farming 96
Farnborough Hall 16, 70, *134*
Farrer, Reginald 159, 274, 275
fashion 16
Felbrigg Hall 43, 70, *136*
fences, early 32, 268
Fenton House 82
Fenwick, Mark 154
ferneries 80
Fetherston, John 192
Fetherstonhaugh, Sir Harry 232
Fiennes, Celia 162, 232
Fish, Margery 226
fish-ponds 33, 40
Fitzroy, Miss Yvonne 253
Fleischmann, Ruby 176
Fleming, J. 121
flint 272
floors, strewing 36
Florence Court 65, 74, *136*
flower improvements 47
follies 64
Folliott, General 165

Forbes & Tate, architects 100
forestry 62
formal gardens, see Chapters 1, 3, 4 and 6
Forrest, George 109
fountains 32, 33, 36, 39
Fox, Dr Wilfrid 257
Fox family, 139
Fox-Talbot, William Henry 163
frames, plant 47, 76
France, French 41, 44, 61, 74
Frederick, Prince of Wales 121
fruits, fruit trees 44, 69, 134, 252, 254, 269
fumigation 31

game-larder 71, 136, 232
Gardenesque, the 81
Gardens Committee and Fund 19 *et seq.*
Garth, Samuel 118
gatehouses 79
Gawthorpe Hall 71, 79, *137*
George III, King 125, 126
George V, King 94
George VI, King 94
Georgian period 61 *et seq.*
Gerard, John 37, 38, 173
Germany 74
Gibbs, Mr Vicary 167
Gibside Chapel 266
Gilbert family 227
Gilpin, William Sawrey 72, 124, 209, 224
Glendurgan 33, 42, 48, 84, *138*
Godwinsson, Harold (King) 104
Goff, Lady Cecilie 126
Goff, Major T. C. E. 126
Goff, Mis Moyra 127
Goldsmith, Oliver 19
Goldsmith's Company 161
Goodheart-Rendel, Mr H. 152
Gothick architecture 66
grafting 31
Grand Tour, the 62
grass seed 43
gravel 43
Great Chalfield Manor 79
Greece 62
greenhouses 46, 76, 79
Greville, the Hon. Mrs Ronald 199
Grey, Lord 231
Grey's Court 88, *139*
grilles 62
grottoes 66, 72, 80, 273
Guardian, The 27
Gubbay, Mrs Hannah 116
Gunby Hall 40, 87, *139*
Gunther, R. W. T. 173

Hadfield, Mr Miles 173, 201
Hadoke, Mrs Dorothy 130
haha 62, 69, 159, 227, 270
Ham House 16, 36, 44, 48, 62, 79, *149*, 269
Hampton Court 42, 47
Hanbury Hall 46, 86, *150*
Hanmer, Sir Thomas 40
Harcourt-Masters, C. 131
Hardwick, Earl of 256
Hardwick Hall 22, 34, 36, 62, 70, *150*, 265, 267, 268, 270
Hardy, Thomas 25
Hardy's Cottage 25
Hastings, Sir George 126
Hatchlands 87, *152*
Hatfield Forest 62, 68
Hatfield House 39, 42
Hawley, General 253
Hawkwood 265
heating 31, 167, 169, 208, 224
hedges 35, 39, 155, 268 *et seq.*
Helford River 84, 138
Henry I, King 33
Henry IV, King 217
Henry VIII, King 42, 66, 162, 206
herbaceous borders 87, 94, 164
herbals 37
herber (arbour) 32
herbs 93, 110, 151, 209, 216
Heveningham 72
Hidcote Manor 13, 22, 26, 88, *153*, 266, 270, 275
Hill, Abraham 43, 206
Hill, Christopher 206
Hill, Miss Octavia 19
Hill, Thomas 40, 173
Hilltop 25
Hoare, Henry 65, 116, 221
Hoare, Richard 221
Hoare, Richard Colt 75, 221
Holbech, William 135
Holford family, of Westonbirt 206
Holford, Sir George 88
Holland 34, 42, 44
Holles-Pelham, Thomas 117
Holroyd, John Baker 210
Hopetoun House 265
Hopkins, Mr Edrick 210
Horder, Mr P. Morley 233
Hornyold-Strickland, Lt Comdr T. 216
Hornyold-Strickland, Mr and the Hon. Mrs 216
hotbeds 40, 47
Howard, Lady Blanche 151
Hughenden Manor 79, *156*
Hull, Richard 165
Hunter, Sir Robert 19
Hussey, Christopher 100, 168, 209
Hussey, Edward 209
Hyde Parker, Dowager Lady 170

ice-house 84
Ickworth 78, 87, *157*
"improvers" 80
Indian-style architecture 71, 86, 112
Institute of District Nursing 21
iron work 76, 80
Italy, Italian influence 32, 33, 44, 45, 61, 167

Jacobean period 41 *et seq.*
Jago, Richard 135
James I of England, King, 38
James I of Scotland, King, 32
James, Henry 163
James, John 46, 61
Japan, gardens of 64, 86
Jardin Anglais 74
Jardin des Plantes 46
Jekyll, Gertrude 80, 87, 88, 100, 119, 155, 170, 195
Jellicoe, Mr Geoffrey 123, 174
Johnson, A. T. 109, 176
Johnston, Major Lawrence 88, 153
Jones, A. H. Brookholding 98
Jones, Gavin 274
Jones, John Elias 196
Joséphine, Empress 81

Keating, The Misses 199
Kent, William 64 *et seq.* 106, 117, 265
Kew, Royal Botanic Gardens 66, 267
Killerton 48, 62, 72, 74, 76, 83, 84, 86, 87, 89, *158*, 267, 271, 275
Kip, Johannes 45
Kipling, Rudyard 87, 101
kitchen gardens 41, 47, 69, 74, 76, 192
Knight, Richard Payne 72, 99, 124, 129, 209
Knightshayes Court 79, 82, 89, *160*
Knole 36, *162*
knot gardens 35
Knyff, Leonard 45
Koraku-en 13

Labouchere, Lady 129
labyrinth 42
Lacock Abbey 34, 40, 48, 62, 68, *163*, 271, 273
Lainé, M. 235
Lamb House *163*
Lamport Hall 274
Landscape Garden, English 68 *et seq.*
landscape, "landskip" 68
Lanhydrock 43, 44, 74, 76, 77, 79, 83, *164*, 265, 266, 267
Lauderdale, Duke and Duchess of 149
lawns 36, 43
Lawson William 161
Leasowes, The 64
Lees Court 122
Legh, Sir Piers 167
Leith Hill Place Woods 48, *165*
Le Nôtre 42, 46
Leonardslee 274
Levens Hall 41
Levey, Mr Kenneth 149
limestone 128, 272
Lindisfarne Castle 87
Lindsay, Norah 79, 105, 114, 154, 174
Lister, E. G. 79
Little Moreton Hall 35, 44, *165*, 271
Lloyd-Jones, Miss K. 233
Lochinch 83
Loder, Gerald 245
London, George 46, 197
London and Wise, nurserymen 46
Londonderry, Marchioness of 88, 176
Lothian, Lady 105
Loudon, J. C. 81, 97, 117, 118, 130, 167
Louis XIV, King 42
Lucy, Sir Thomas 113
Luttrell, Lt Col Walter, M. C. 130
Lutyens, Sir Edwin 87, 111
Lyle, Sir Ian 101
Lyme Park, Lyme Hall 36, 44, 77, 78, 79, 80, 87, *166*, 265
Lyte, Sir Henry 37, 168
Lytes Cary 37, 87, *168*, 270
Lyveden New Bield 33, *169*

Macartney, Lord 66, 220
Madresfield Court 266
Mall, The 43
Malmaison 81
Manchester, Greater, County Council 167
Maori Hut 80, 115
Maries, Charles 196
Martaban 173
Marvell, Andrew 41, 47
Mary Gardens 33
Mary, Queen 94
Mason, William 64, 72, 157, 176, 270
Maw, George 83, 103, 273
Mawe & Abercrombie 273
Mawson, T. H. 255
maze 42, 225
McLaren, the Hon. H. D. 107
Meade-Fetherston-haugh, Lady 232
meads, flowery 33
Meager, Leonard 166
medicinal plants 93, 110
Melford Hall 36, 62, *169*, 267
Meller, John 133
menageries 33, 179
Merrist Wood Agri-cultural College 116
Messel, Lt Col. L. C. R. 179
Messel, Mrs Maud 176, 179
mews 43
Miller, Philip 46, 61
Miller, Sanderson 68, 70, 135, 256
Milton, John 64
Mitchell, Alan 267
moats 32
Monasteries, Dissolution of 34
Montacute 22, 36, 37, 62, 79, 80, 100, *170*, 265, 266, 268, 269
Montgomery-Massingberd, Lady 139
Moore, Hugh Armytage 18, 89, 203
Moore, Rev. John 203
Moore, Thomas 62
Moors, the 32, 86
Morley, Earl of 88, 206
Morris, William 255
Morville Hall 34, *172*
Moseley Old Hall 36, 39, 42, 44, *173*
Mottisfont Abbey 31, 34, 68, 72, 82, *174*, 272
mounts 35, 41, 79
Mount Stewart 18, 72, 74, 87, 88, *176*, 266, 275
mowing, mowers, scythes 36, 76
Muir, Mrs Heather 154
Munstead House 87
Munstead Wood 87
music 15, 140
Mussenden Temple 77
Myddelton, Lt Col. Ririd 114
Myddelton, Lady Margaret 115

Napoleon, wars with 70
National Gardens Scheme 21
National Trust, The 18, 19 *et seq.*
naturalised plants 33, 83
Nesfield, W. A. 105
Newby 155
Newcastle, Duke of 117, 124
niches 45
Nicolson, Mr Nigel 216
Nicolson, Sir Harold and Lady 215
Nonsuch 66
Northumberland, Duke of
Nostell Priory 65, *179*, 265
Nymans Garden 22, 74, 77, 80, 83, *179*

obelisks 36
O'Neill, Lady, of the Maine 203
Onslow, Lord 116
orangeries 45, 46, 47, 68, 71, 79, 80
orchards 32, 33, 36
Orkney, Earl of 120
ornaments, garden 81, 95
Osterley Park 36, 48, 72, 84, *190*
Oxburgh Hall 32, 46, 78, *191*, 271
Oxnead 106

Packwood House 22, 36, 41, *192*
paille maille 43
painting 15
Palissade à l'Italienne 116, 156
Pall Mall 43
paradise or garden 13, 224
Paris Exhibition 1867 123
Parkinson, John 40
parks 62 *et seq.*
Parsons, Alfred 163, 255
parterres 42, 43, 46, 78, 79, 164
Paston-Bedingfeld, Sir Henry 46, 191
pavilions 64
Paxton, Sir Joseph 79, 224
Paycockes 87
Peckover House 47, 80, *193*
Penrhyn Castle 76, 79, *194*
Penrhyn, Lord and Lady 194

Pepys, Samuel 43
pergolas 81, 82
peristyle 80
perry 37
Peto, Harold A. 87, 110
Petworth House 47, 69, *196*, 271
pheasantries 40
Phelips, Mrs Ellen 171
Picturesque, the 72
pillars for roses 81
pipes, of elm trunks 45
plant-houses 40
Plas Newydd 70, 83, *198*
plasterwork 34
Plas-yn-Rhiw 82, *199*
poetry 15
Polesden Lacey 22, 70, 80, 82, *199*, 266, 267, 270, 274
pollards, pollarding 62
Pook's Hill 102
Pope, Alexander 47, 63 *et seq.*
Portugal, gardens 32
Potter, Beatrix 25
Poussin, Nicolas 63
Powis Castle 22, 41, 45, 66, 69, 80, 87, *201*, 270, 275
Pre-Raphaelite 86, 255
Price, Sir Henry 245
Price, Sir Uvedale 71, 72, 75, 99, 129, 209
Primrose League 157
Pulham & Sons 211, 236, 274

Quebec House 25
Queens' College bridge, replica 255
Queen's Institute of District Nursing 21
quincunx 44

rams, pumping 45
Rawnsley, Canon H. D. 19
Reiss, Mrs Phyllis 172, 226
Rendel, Lord 152
Repton, Humphry 64, 70 *et seq.*, 81, 95, 99, 107, 124, 131, 136, 198, 224, 232, 256, 265
Repton, John Adey 106
Restoration, The 39, 41
Revett, Nicholas 255
Rievaulx Terrace and Temples 70, 72
Robartes, John, and wife Lucy 164
Robinson, William 80, 86, 122, 133, 155, 158, 189, 274
Rochford, Earl of 45, 201
rockeries, rock gardens, rock work 41, 72, 80, 159, 204, 217, 272 *et seq.*
Rodney, Admiral 201
Roman campagna 63
Romans, techniques 31, 42, 46
Rome 62
Roper, Mr Lanning 209, 236
Rosa, Salvator 63
rose garden 79, 80, 213, 215
Rosse, Earl and Countess of 180
Rousham 64
Rowallane 18, 74, 83, 89, *203*, 268, 269, 275
Rowlandson, Thomas 150
Royal Horticultural Society, The 20, 213, 274
Royal Parks 150, 190
Royal National Rose Society 175
Ruffold Old Hall 82
Rule Britannia 121
Rupert, Prince 98
Russell, Mrs Gilbert 174
Russia 74
rustic woodwork, etc. 72, 79, 80

St John's Jerusalem 32, 34, 43, *205*, 271
St Michael's Mount *206*, 275
Sackville West, The Hon. V. 84, 171, 176, 214
Sales, John 22
salt extraction 224
salt, for weedkilling 47
Saltram 62, 66, 88, *206*, 265, 271
32, 72, *209*, 271, 275
sandstone 129, 197
Sandys, Francis 78
sarsen stone 98, 272
Savernake Forest 62
Saye and Sele, Lord 162
Sckell, Chevalier Charles 75
Scotney Castle Garden 32, 72, *209*, 271, 275
Scott, Sir George Gilbert 79
Scott, Sir Walter 61, 272
sculpture 15
Sezincote 71, 86, 274
shade 32
Shakespeare 113, 165
Sharpitor *209*, 266
Shaw, Bernard 25
Shaw, Richard Norman 127
Shaw's Corner 25
Sheffield, Earl of 210
Sheffield Park 19, 22, 68, 69, 70, 78, 82, 83, 84, 89, *210*, 266, 274, 275
Sheffield Place, *see* Sheffield Park
shell decoration 41, 72
shelter houses 37
Shenstone, William 63, 75, 116
Sheridan, Richard Brinsley 70, 200
ship masts 62
Shotover Park 66
Shrewsbury, Countess of 120, 151
Shrubland Park 79
Shugborough 66, 79, 182, *212*, 265
Shuttleworth, Janet 137
silk worms 38
Sissinghurst Castle 16, 34, 88, *214*, 270
Sizergh Castle 33, 80, *216*, 267, 269, 274
Slater Foundation, the 116
Smallhythe Place *217*
Snowshill Manor 18, *218*
Soames, Capt. Arthur Granville 89
societies, specialist flower 80
Society for the Protection of Ancient Buildings 170
Spain, gardens in 32
spars, used as gravel 47
Spectator, The 14, 71
Speke Hall 79, 219
Spenser, Edmund 31, 35, 64
Spitta, Mrs Madeline 257
Spode china ware 227
Springhill *219*
Spry, Constance 176, 214
Stagshaw 89
Standen 33, 80, 81, 86, *220*, 275
Stanley Smith Horticultural Foundation, the 149
statues 36, 39, 81, 95
Steele, Richard 63, 64
Stevens, Jan 113
stew-ponds 40
stone, rock 272 *et seq.*
Stonehenge 272
Stonehouse, Rev. Walter 39, 173
Stourhead 22, 48, 65, 70, 71, 72, 74, 75, 82, 89, *221*, 273, 275
Stowe 266
Strickland, Lord 217
Strode, William 100
Stuart period 41 *et seq.*
Sudbury Hall 44, 47, 72, *224*
Sumerians 31
summerhouses 68, 71, 72, 79, 272
sundials 41
Sutherland, Duke of 79, 121
Sutherland, John 73
swags for rose-pillars 81
Switzer, Stephen 131, 179
Symons-Jeune, B. H. B. 274

Talbot, Miss Matilda 163
Tallents, Sir Stephen and Lady 206
taste 16
Tatton Park 42, 71, 76, 79, 80, 86, *224*
Taylor, C. C. 169
Temple, Sir William 66
Temple Sowerby Manor, *see* Acorn Bank
temples 65, 71
tennis 36
Tennyson 149
terrace, raised 170
terraces 45, 70, 72
Terry, Ellen 217
Thackeray, W. M. 119
Theophrastus 19
Thomas Phillips Price Trust 267
Thomas, Sir William Beach 13
Tintinhull House 22, 88, *226*, 260
topiary 39, 42, 47, 79
Townsend, E. Loveden 110
trees, growing of 62, 70
trees, transplanting of 31
Trelissick 62, 74, 83, 88, *227*, 271
trellis, treillage 82
Trengwainton 22, 66, 74, 83, *229*
Trerice 44, *231*
Tresham, Sir Thomas 33, 169
Trevelyan, Mary, Lady 249
Tudor times 34
tufa (rock) 66, 80, 98
tulip mania 42
Turner, J. W. M. 196
Turner, William 37
Tusser, Thomas 37

Uppark 33, 44, 71, *231*
Upton House 22, 44, 47, 87, *232*, 273

Vanbrugh, Sir John 64, 116
variegated foliage 75, 97
vegetable gardens 39, 69, 213
Veitch, James, & Son 97, 133
Veitch, John 84, 159
Vereker, Mr and Mrs 210
Verney, Sir Ralph 39
Versailles 13
Victoria, Queen 94, 97, 121, 195
Victorian Age, the 86
vineyards 36, 37, 81, 130
Virgil 31
Vyne, The 43, *233*, 265

Waddesdon Manor 16, 76, 78, 80, 82, *235*, 273, 274
Wade, Mr Charles 218
Wakehurst, Lord 245
Wakehurst Place 36, 83, 87, *245*, 273, 275
walking in gardens 43
walled gardens 66, 69, 70, 79, 80, 169, 175, 195, 268
Wallington Hall 48, 66, 87, *249*, 267
wallpapers 66
walls, concave 40
Walpole, Horace 13, 149, 222
Ward, Bernard 112
Ward, F. Kingdom 109
Ware, Miss M. 226
Ware Park 39
Washington, George 25
Washington Old Hall 25
water in gardens 32, 43, 79, 135
water pump 232
Watt, Miss Adelaide 219
Watt, Richard 219
Wedgwood, Josiah 165
"weederwomen" 47
weedkillers 27, 47
Weir, The *250*, 273
Wells, H. G. 231
Westbury Court 34, 36, 44, 45, 48, 79, *251*
West Green House *252*, 267
Westminster, Duke of 121
Westonbirt Arboretum 88
Westwood Manor 79
West Wycombe Park 65, *254*, 272
Whateley, Thomas 73, 116
Wicken Fen 62
Wightwick Manor 86, *255*
wilderness 39, 44, 150, 162, 192
wild gardening 39
William III, King 45, 47
Williams, Dr Ralph Vaughan 165
Willmott, Miss Ellen 163
Wilson, E. H. 109
Wimpole Hall 68, 72, *256*
Winchester Centre, National Trust 175
Winde, William 120, 201
Windham, William 70, 136
Winkworth Arboretum 84, *257*, 275
Winn family 179
Wise, Henry 46
Wolfe, General 25
Wolryche-Whitmore, Alice Mary 130
Wolryche-Whitmore, Captain 129
Wolverhampton Centre, National Trust 173
woodland gardens 83
Worcester, battle of 42, 173
Wordsworth, William 75
wort yard 32
Wotton, Henry 39
Wrey, Florence 136
Wyatt, James 198
Wyatt, Sir Digby 105

Xenophon 13

Yorke, Mr Philip 133
Young, Arthur 105

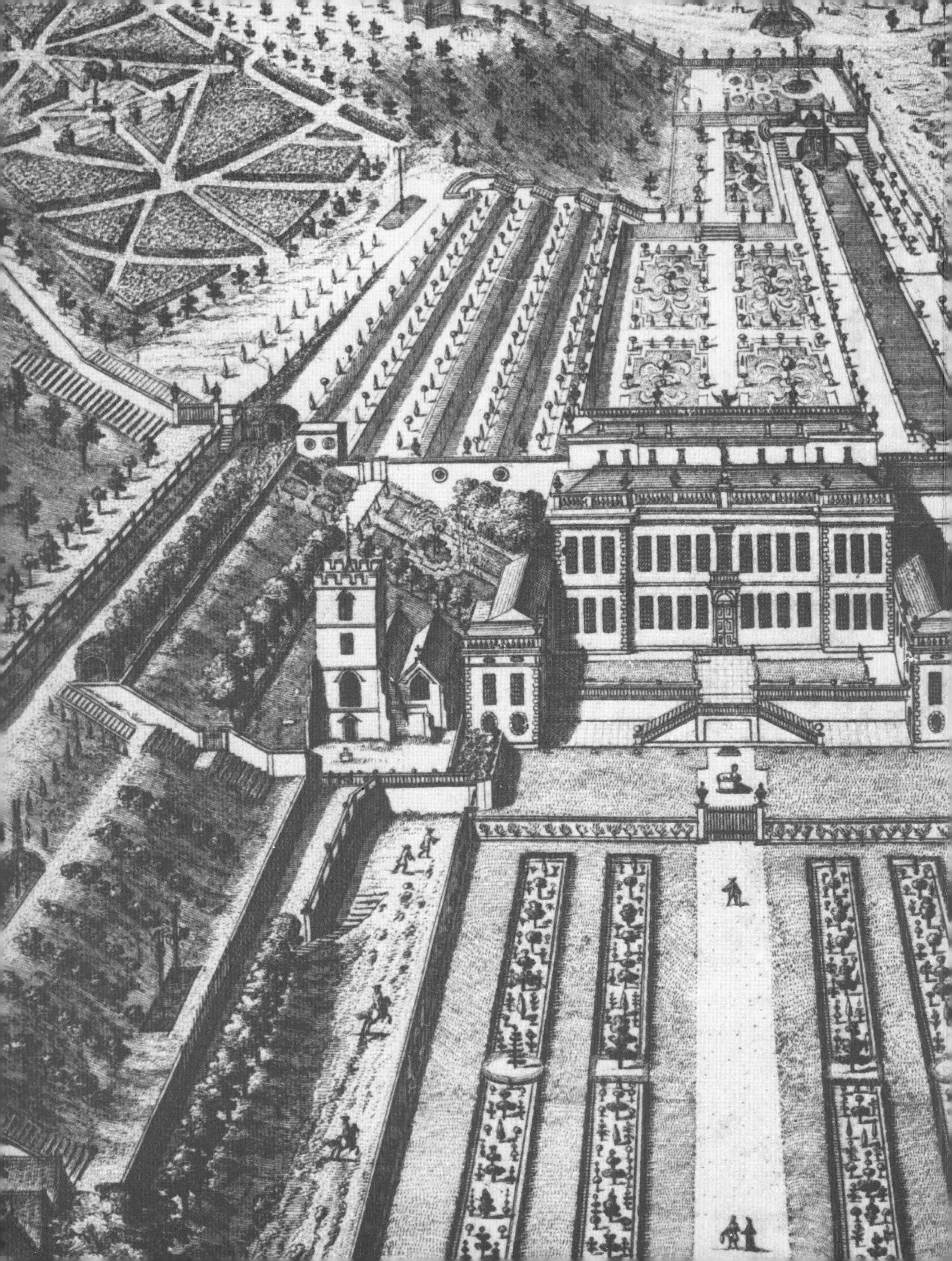